ROMANS
TO REVELATION

TEACHER
GENESIS TO REVELATION SERIES
VOLUME 4

ABINGDON PRESS
Nashville

ISBN 0-687-07248-4

Manufactured in the United States of America

This book is printed on acid-free paper.

99 00 01 02 03 04 05 06—10 9 8 7 6 5 4 3

GENESIS TO REVELATION SERIES
VOLUME 4
Table of Contents

How to Teach Genesis to Revelation. 5

How to Lead a Discussion 7

Romans 9

1 and 2 Corinthians, Galatians, Ephesians 73

Philippians, Colossians, 1 and 2 Thessalonians, 1 and 2 Timothy, Titus, Philemon 145

Hebrews; James; 1 and 2 Peter; 1, 2, 3 John; Jude 213

Revelation 285

HOW TO TEACH GENESIS TO REVELATION

Unique Features of This Bible Study

In Genesis to Revelation, you and your class will study the Bible in three steps. Each step provides a different level of understanding of the Scripture. We call these steps Dimension One, Dimension Two, and Dimension Three.

Dimension One concerns what the Bible actually says. You do not interpret the Scripture at this point; you merely take account of what it says. Your main goal for this dimension is to get the content of the passage clear in your mind. What does the Bible say?

Dimension One is in workbook form. The members of the class will write the answers to questions about the passage in the space provided in the student book. All the questions in Dimension One can be answered by reading the Bible itself. Be sure the class finishes Dimension One before going on to Dimensions Two and Three.

Dimension Two concerns information that will shed light on the Scripture under consideration. Dimension Two will answer such questions as

• What are the original meanings of some of the words used in the passage?
• What is the original background of the passage?
• Why was the passage most likely written?
• What are the relationships between the persons mentioned in the passage?
• What geographical and cultural factors affect the meaning of the passage?

The question for Dimension Two is, What information do we need in order to understand the meaning of the passage? In Dimension One the class members will discover what the Bible says. In Dimension Two they will discover what the Bible means.

Dimension Three focuses on interpreting the Scripture and applying it to life situations. The questions here are
• What is the meaning of the passage for my life?
• What response does the passage require of me as a Christian?
• What response does this passage require of us as a group?

Dimension Three questions have no easy answers. The task of applying the Scripture to life situations is up to you and the class.

Aside from the three-dimensional approach, another unique feature of this study is the organization of the series as a whole. Classes that choose to study the Genesis to Revelation Series will be able to study all the books of the Bible in their biblical order. This method will give the class continuity that is not present in most other Bible studies. The class will read and study virtually every verse of the Bible, from Genesis straight through to Revelation.

How many times have you stumbled over a biblical name or maybe even avoided discussing a person or place because you could not pronounce the word? While you are using the Genesis to Revelation Series, you may find a good Bible pronunciation guide helpful. These are available from any Christian bookstore. The *Harper's Bible Pronunciation Guide* (The Society of Biblical Literature, 1989, ISBN 0-06-068951-X) is one such guide.

An excellent additional resource is *Bible Teacher Kit* (Abingdon, 1994, ISBN 0-687-78006-3). It has Bible maps and a glossary of terms.

Weekly Preparation

Begin planning for each session early in the week. Read the passage that the lesson covers, and write the answers to Dimension One questions in the student book. Then read Dimensions Two and Three in the student book. Make a note of any questions or comments you have. Finally, study the material in the teacher book carefully. Decide how you want to organize your class session.

Organizing the Class Session

Since Genesis to Revelation involves three steps in studying the Scripture, you will want to organize your class sessions around these three dimensions. Each lesson in the student book and this teacher book consists of three parts.

The first part of each lesson in the teacher book is the same as the Dimension One section in the student book, except that the teacher book includes the answers to Dimension One questions. These questions and answers are taken from the New International Version of the Bible.

You might use Dimension One in several ways:

1. Ask the group members to read the Scripture and to write the answers to all the Dimension One questions before coming to class. This method will require that the class covenant to spend the necessary amount of study time outside of class. When the class session begins, read through the Dimension One questions, asking for responses from the group members. If anyone needs help with any of the answers, look at the biblical reference together.

2. Or, if you have enough class time, you might spend the first part of the session working through the Dimension One questions together as a group. Locate the Scripture references, ask the questions one at a time, and invite the class members to find the answers and to read them aloud. Then allow enough time for them to write the answers in the student book.

3. Or, take some time at the beginning of the class session for group members to work individually. Have them read the Dimension One questions and the Scripture references and then write their answers to the questions in the spaces provided in the student book. Discuss together any questions or answers in Dimension One that do not

seem clear. This approach may take longer than the others, but it provides a good change of pace from time to time.

You do not have to organize your class sessions the same way every week. Ask the class members what they prefer. Experiment! You may find ways to study the Dimension One material other than the ones listed above.

The second part of each lesson in this teacher book corresponds to the second part of the student book lessons. The Dimension Two section of the student book provides background information to help the students understand the Scripture. Become familiar with the information in the student book.

Dimension Two of this teacher book contains additional information on the passage. The teacher book goes into more depth with some parts of the passage than the student book does. You will want to share this information with the group in whatever way seems appropriate. For example, if someone raises a question about a particular verse, share any additional background information from the teacher book.

You might raise a simple question such as, What words or phrases gave you trouble in understanding the passage? or, Having grasped the content of the passage, what questions remain in your mind? Encourage the group members to share confusing points, troublesome words or phrases, or lingering questions. Write these problems on a large sheet of paper or chalkboard. This list of concerns will form the outline for the second portion of the session.

These concerns may also stimulate some research on the part of the group members. If your study group is large enough, divide the class into three groups. Then divide the passage for the following week into three parts. Assign a portion of the passage to each group. Using Bible commentaries and Bible dictionaries, direct each group to discover as much as it can about this portion of the passage before the class meets again. Each group will then report its findings during the class session.

The third part of each lesson in this teacher book relates to Dimension Three in the student book. This section helps class members discover how to apply the Scripture to their own lives. Here you will find one or more interpretations of the passage—whether traditional, historical, or contemporary. Use these interpretations when appropriate to illumine the passage for the group members.

Dimension Three in the student book points out some of the issues in the passage that are relevant to our lives. For each of these issues, the student book raises questions to help the students assess the meaning of the Scripture for their lives. The information in Dimension Three of the teacher book is designed to help you lead the class in discussing these issues. Usually, you will find a more in-depth discussion of portions of the Scripture.

The discussion in the teacher book will give you a better perspective on the Scripture and its interpretation before you begin to assess its meaning for today. You will probably want to share this Dimension Three information with the class to open the discussion. For each life situation, the teacher book contains suggestions on facilitating the class discussion. You, as the teacher, are responsible for group discussions of Dimension Three issues.

Assembling Your Materials

You will need at least three items to prepare for and conduct each class session:
- A teacher book
- A student book
- A Bible—you may use any translation or several; the answers in this teacher book are taken from the New International Version.

One advantage of the Genesis to Revelation Series is that the study is self-contained. That is, all you need to teach this Bible study is provided for you in the student and teacher books. Occasionally, or perhaps on a regular basis, you might want to consult other sources for additional information.

HOW TO LEAD A DISCUSSION

The Teacher as Discussion Leader

As the teacher of this series or a part of this series, one of your main responsibilities during each class period will be to lead the class discussion. Some teachers are apprehensive about leading a discussion. In many ways, it is easier to lecture to the class. But remember that the class members will surely benefit more from the class sessions when they actively participate in a discussion of the material.

Leading a discussion is a skill that any teacher can master with practice. And keep in mind—especially if your class is not used to discussion—that the members of your group will also be learning through practice. The following are some pointers on how to lead interesting and thought-provoking discussions in the study group.

Preparing for a Discussion—Where Do I Start?

1. Focus on the subject that will be discussed and on the goal you want to achieve through that discussion.

2. Prepare by collecting information and data that you will need; jot down these ideas, facts, and questions so that you will have them when you need them.

3. Begin organizing your ideas; stop often to review your work. Keep in mind the climate within the group—attitudes, feelings, eagerness to participate and learn.

4. Consider possible alternative group procedures. Be prepared for the unexpected.

5. Having reached your goal, think through several ways to bring the discussion to a close.

As the teacher, do not feel that your responsibility is to give a full account or report of the assigned material. This practice promotes dependency. Instead, through stimulating questions and discussion, the participants will read the material—not because you tell them to but because they want to read and prepare.

How Do I Establish a Climate for Learning?

The teacher's readiness and preparation quickly establish a climate in which the group can proceed and its members learn and grow. The anxiety and fear of an unprepared teacher are contagious but so are the positive vibrations coming from a teacher who is prepared to move into a learning enterprise.

An attitude of shared ownership is also basic. Group members need to perceive themselves as part of the learning experience. Persons establish ownership by working on goals, sharing concerns, and accepting major responsibility for learning.

Here are several ways the teacher can foster a positive climate for learning and growth.

1. *Readiness.* A teacher who is always fully prepared can promote, in turn, the group's readiness to learn.

2. *Exploration.* When the teacher encourages group members to freely explore new ideas, persons will know they are in a group whose primary function is learning.

3. *Exposure.* A teacher who is open, honest, and willing to reveal himself or herself to the group will encourage students to discuss their feelings and opinions.

4. *Confidentiality.* A teacher can create a climate for learning when he or she respects the confidentiality of group members and encourages the group members to respect one another's confidentiality.

5. *Acceptance.* When a teacher shows a high degree of acceptance, students can likewise accept one another honestly.

How Can I Deal With Conflict?

What if conflict or strong disagreement arises in your group? What do you do? Think about the effective and ineffective ways you have dealt with conflict in the past.

Group conflict may come from one of several sources. One common source of conflict involves personality clashes. Any group is almost certain to contain at least two persons whose personalities clash. If you break your class into smaller groups for discussion, be sure these persons are in separate groups.

Another common source of group conflict is subject matter. The Bible can be a very controversial subject. Remember the difference between discussion or disagreement and conflict. As a teacher you will have to decide when to encourage discussion and when to discourage conflict that is destructive to the group process.

Group conflict may also come from a general atmosphere conducive to expression of ideas and opinions. Try to discourage persons in the group from being judgmental toward others and their ideas. Keep reminding the class that each person is entitled to his or her own opinions and that no one opinion is more valid than another.

How Much Should I Contribute to the Discussion?

Many teachers are unsure about how much they should contribute to the class discussions. Below are several pitfalls to avoid.

1. The teacher should remain neutral on a question until the group has had adequate time to discuss it. At the proper time in the discussion the teacher can offer his or her opinion. The teacher can direct the questions to the group at large, rechanneling those questions that come to him or her.

At times when the members need to grapple with a question or issue, the most untimely response a teacher can make is answering the question. Do not fall into the trap of doing the group members' work for them. Let them struggle with the question.

However, if the teacher has asked the group members to reveal thoughts and feelings, then group members have the right to expect the same of the teacher. A teacher has no right to ask others to reveal something he or she is unwilling to reveal. A teacher can reveal thoughts and feelings, but at the appropriate time.

The refusal to respond immediately to a question often takes self-discipline. The teacher has spent time thinking, reading, and preparing. Thus the teacher usually does have a point of view and waiting for others to respond calls for restraint.

2. Another pitfall is the teacher's making a speech or extended comments in expressing an opinion or summarizing what has been said. For example, in an attempt to persuade others, a teacher may speak, repeat, or strongly emphasize what someone says concerning a question.

3. Finally, the pitfall of believing the teacher must know "the answers" to the questions is always apparent. The teacher need not know all the answers. Many questions that should be raised are ultimate and unanswerable; other questions are open-ended; and still others have several answers.

BIBLE TEACHER KIT (Abingdon Press, 1994, ISBN 0-687-78006-3)

This essential tool kit for teachers of Bible study classes is full of resources to enhance the learning process. The three-ring binder contains 160 resource pages featuring

- background articles
- charts
- a timeline
- a glossary of biblical terms
- ten one-color maps of Bible lands then and now

Many of the resource pages include photocopying privileges, so you can distribute additional copies to members of the class or photocopy onto transparencies.

The kit also includes

- eight 20" x 32" full-color maps of Bible lands
- a full-color video of Bible lands

ROMANS
Table of Contents

1. Paul Introduces Himself 10

2. Paul's Purpose and Situation 15

3. The Weak and the Strong in Rome 20

4. Righteousness and Wrath 25

5. Religion Perverted 29

6. Faith and Abraham's Children 34

7. God's Peace and Adam's Realm 39

8. Set Free From Sin 44

9. Set Free From the Law 49

10. New Life in the Spirit 53

11. Unbelief and World Conversion 58

12. The Love Ethic as Response 63

13. A Tolerant Ethic in a New Era 67

About the Writer

Robert Jewett is Senior Scholar of New Testament Interpretation at Garrett-Evangelical Theological Seminary.

I am so eager to preach the gospel also to you who are at Rome (1:15).

1

Paul Introduces Himself

Romans 1:1-15

DIMENSION ONE:
WHAT DOES THE BIBLE SAY?

Answer these questions by reading Romans 1:1-15

1. Identify the three expressions of Paul's self-identity in verses 1 and 5.

   In verse 1, Paul refers to himself as "a servant of Christ Jesus" and "called to be an apostle and set apart for the gospel of God." In verse 5, Paul says he has "received grace and apostleship to call people from among all the Gentiles to the obedience that comes from faith."

2. Locate the description of the audience of the letter, the so-called "address" (1:7)

   Paul addresses his letter "To all in Rome who are loved by God and called to be saints."

3. Read the opening verses of the other Pauline letters (First and Second Corinthians, Galatians, Ephesians, Philippians, Colossians, First and Second Thessalonians, First and Second Timothy, Titus). Which openings contain a reference to the "gospel of God" promised through Scripture (1:1-2) or the creed concerning Jesus (1:3-4)?

   Of 1 Corinthians 1:1-3, 2 Corinthians 1:1-2, Galatians 1:1-5, Ephesians 1:1-2, Philippians 1:1-2, Colossians 1:1-2, 1 Thessalonians 1:1, 2 Thessalonians 1:1-2, 1 Timothy 1:1-2, 2 Timothy 1:1-2, and Titus 1:1-4, only Titus contains something similar to these references in Romans.

4. What does Paul mention as the content of his prayers in the "thanksgiving section"? (1:8-12)

   Paul reveals that he gives thanks for the faith of the Romans (1:8) and prays that he may visit them (1:10-11).

5. In the "narration section" (1:13-15) Paul explains both his motivation in visiting Rome and the reason he has not visited earlier. Identify both points.

   Paul's motivation is to "preach the gospel" (1:15) because he is "obligated" (1:15) to all the Gentiles. His earlier plans to visit Rome "have been prevented" (1:13).

DIMENSION TWO:
WHAT DOES THE BIBLE MEAN?

The Problem of Teaching Romans

Romans is one of the most difficult books in the New Testament to teach, for several reasons. It does not fit the model of the other Pauline letters, which makes Romans hard to understand. For example, when people interpret Romans on the model of the Corinthian letters, they look at Romans as offering theological advice to a congregation that knows and respects Paul. This interpretation is obviously difficult because Paul did not found the church at Rome. Sometimes people interpret Romans on the model of Paul's letter to the Galatians, which is a defense of the gospel. When Romans is viewed this way, it is seen as a polemical letter, defending the true faith. The consequence of this view is that a particular approach to Romans, shaped perhaps by the Protestant or perhaps by the Roman Catholic tradition, is assumed to be the standard by which all other forms of the faith are being criticized by the Book of Romans. The crucial thrust of Romans as a document of early Christian pluralism is lost when the letter is approached in this way.

Many students of Romans, aware of the unique quality of the letter, understand it to be something of a theological treatise. They view Romans as a statement of pure doctrine, unrelated to any congregational situation. Since Paul had not been to Rome before writing the letter, people holding this view assume that Paul is summarizing his general teachings in a way that he thinks might be useful to the congregation. When this approach is taken, the missionary goal that Paul reveals in writing the letter is overlooked.

The peculiar abstraction of Romans also presents a barrier to understanding. That is, Romans is a formal writing with a large number of theological terms. These terms were each understandable in their original setting, but we easily become bogged down in a line-by-line and word-for-word debate on Romans. The problem of abstraction will prove particularly difficult for people in your class who think more concretely, who enjoy pictures and parables, and who lack formal philosophical or theological training.

The approach I suggest is to place Romans in a vivid historical situation and to relate this situation to each section of the letter. The basic purpose of Romans was to gain support from the Roman house churches for Paul's mission to Spain. To achieve this purpose, Paul had to deal with the conflicts between the branches of the house churches in Rome. When these house churches are unified in purpose, free of conflict, and in harmony, then Paul can seek their support for organizing his proposed mission to a difficult portion of the Roman Empire, Spain. Only when this concrete situation is kept in mind will Paul's letter assume a liveliness that many class members are likely to understand. Otherwise, the letter may remain the possession of those few class members who are skilled in abstract thinking.

The Structure of the Passage

The questions in Dimension One aim to make class members aware of the structure of Paul's introduction. When they compare the letter opening in Romans with the openings of other Pauline letters, the differences are going to become apparent. A grasp of these differences will help class members understand the unique purpose of Romans. You may want to write an outline of a typical letter opening on a chalkboard or on a large piece of paper. Your outline might look like this:

Sender—"Paul, a servant of Christ Jesus"
Recipient—"to all in Rome who are loved by God"
Greeting—"grace and peace to you"

This basic letter opening sometimes has slight expansions, but in no other letter are the expansions as large as in Romans.

Verses 1-7 reveal that Paul is introducing himself with considerable care to demonstrate the orthodoxy of his gospel and the authenticity of his apostolic calling. You will note that the expansions in the letter opening are in sections 1 and 2. Themes of "apostle" and "gospel of God" announced in verse 1 are developed in reverse order before Paul gets to the address of the letter. Part of this expansion involves the citation of an early Christian creed in verses 3-4. Quite likely, this creed is a composite of the viewpoints of conservative and liberal Christians in Rome; and many commentators feel that the creed was actually being used in the Roman house churches.

Verses 8-12 make up the "thanksgiving" section in the introduction to Romans. In most instances the thanksgiving of a Pauline letter announces the major themes of the letter and reveals Paul's purpose in writing. Note that the thanksgiving proper is only in verse 8 but that the themes of prayer and of the relationship between the believers before God continues. The thing that Paul stresses in this section is that he had long prayed to be able to travel to Rome in order to preach the gospel there. This reveals the most important reason why Paul is addressing this letter to a church that he does not know: He wishes to visit them in order to preach the gospel and to involve them in fulfilling the missional thrust of their faith that has already been "reported all over the world."

The final section in this lesson is the narration in verses 13-15. These verses explain the background of Paul's intended visit to Rome, stressing that his plans had repeatedly been frustrated. Paul's desire to preach in Rome is related in verse 14 to his feeling of obligation to preach the gospel to all persons everywhere. In verse 15 the narration ends on the theme of Paul's eagerness to preach the gospel to the Christians in Rome.

The unique structure and content of this introduction, thanksgiving, and narration serve to lead the congregation into Paul's letter and more importantly into the project for which he hopes to gain their cooperation, the mission to Spain. The content of this introduction is matched to some degree by the conclusion of the letter in Romans 15 and 16. Although we will not be dealing with these chapters until the next lesson, a knowledge of their content is essential for understanding Romans 1:1-15.

In Romans 15, Paul explicitly mentions the plan to carry his mission to Spain (15:24, 28). He also discusses some of the factors that have hindered his earlier arrival in Rome, including the difficulties in connection with the Jerusalem offering. Paul's great skill as a writer is shown as he lightly introduces these themes in Romans 1 and lays out his formal argument before returning to the precise details in Romans 15, details that might have alienated the congregation without the proper background.

Romans 1:1. The word *servant* in verse 1 is often translated "slave," which is sometimes felt to be far too humble for the high apostolic office that Paul claims in verses 1-5. Actually, the term *slave* had a formal bureaucratic meaning for the Roman audience. The Roman bureaucracy that was rapidly developing at the time Paul wrote this letter was made up of highly trained and highly paid slaves of Caesar. These persons were preferred in the imperial offices because they were loyal to the emperor alone, hoping for their freedom after some years of loyal service. Many of the slaves serving in the imperial bureaucracy became fabulously rich because of their handling of imperial finances. Also, during the time Paul wrote, the expression "slave of Caesar" was often used for imperial ambassadors or representatives of various kinds. Such persons carried the majesty and power of the emperor with them as they represented him in foreign courts.

The connotation that is most likely for 1:1 is, "Paul, an *ambassador* of Christ Jesus." In this way he was introduced to the Roman congregation with a term that had an official sound. Paul introduces himself as a representative of Christ, the one who advocates his gospel and promotes the cause of his Kingdom. The term *apostle* simply means a messenger or a person sent to deliver a specific message and/or to perform a specific mission. The term was often used in secular settings for a representative sent off on an errand by someone else. In this instance Paul qualifies the term *apostle* by the expression *called*, referring to his election to missionary activity at the time of his conversion.

Romans 1:3-4. The early Christian creed cited in verses 3 and 4 begins after the word *Son.* A literal translation is as follows:

> Born from David's seed according to the flesh, appointed Son of God in power according to the spirit of holiness, through the resurrection of the dead.

This confession likely originated in Jewish-Christian circles, with a stress on the messianic line from David and the appointment as Son of God through the Resurrection. This early creed is very close to some of the creeds found in the Book of Acts, stressing the seed of David and the adoption of Jesus as the Son of God on the basis of the Resurrection.

Apparently the liberal Hellenistic Christians had edited this creed. They would have wished to down play the nationalistic component of David's seed and to stress the power of the Spirit. They inserted the lines "as to his human nature" and "through the Spirit" in order to affirm that the business of David's seed was only on a fleshly and therefore human level, whereas the appointment of Jesus as the Son of God was by direct divine intervention, according to the Spirit. This addition made the creed universal, opening it up to people who were not of Jewish background and who were not loyal to the messianic hope of Israel.

Paul probably made the final change to the creed, adding the words "of holiness" to the phrase "through the Spirit." This revised phrase counters the tendency of those persons in the early church who liked to think in dualistic terms, opposing "flesh" to "spirit." As we know from the Corinthian letters in particular, the liberals who were most conscious of being in the Spirit tended at times to believe that they were superior to "fleshly" rules such as the Ten Commandments. The problem of libertinism, of believing that one is above the law, is countered at a number of other points in Romans, which indicates that this was something of a problem in the Roman house churches. By emphasizing holiness, Paul makes clear that the spirit of a new era is consistent with ethical responsibility.

Romans 1:5. In verse 5, Paul shifts from the first person singular to the first person plural: "*We* received grace and apostleship." Paul often speaks of himself in the first person plural, and in many instances he is referring to himself and his coworkers. Paul had a shared sense of missionary obligation. He wrote most of his letters in collaboration with his missionary colleagues. Since the Romans did not know Paul and his missionary team, it was inappropriate in this instance to mention them in the opening chapter. But it is worth observing that in Romans 16, Paul mentions greetings from Timothy and a number of other close colleagues.

Romans 1:6-7. You and the class members may notice a conspicuous omission in verse 7. Unlike the other letters addressed to Pauline congregations, this opening does not refer to a "church." This omission is perhaps due to the fact that only one of the five house churches mentioned in Romans 16 referred to itself as "church." Keep in mind that Romans was written at a time before a standard set of terms had come into use for early Christians. Each congregation probably called itself something different, especially in a place where the church was as decentralized as it was in Rome.

The suggestion in the student book is that Paul uses two typical names for church members in verses 6 and 7. He refers to one group as "called to belong to Jesus Christ," probably used for liberals and Gentile Christians. The title "called to be saints" probably is used for conservatives and Jewish Christians. Paul is being sensitive to the fact that not everyone has a consciousness of being in a "church." Therefore I think it is significant that the title of church membership that he places between the first and third titles is unique to Romans, namely, "all . . . who are loved by God." Paul wishes to stress that all Christians in Rome, whether conservative or liberal, whether Jewish Christian or Gentile Christian, are equal in God's love.

Romans 1:8-12. The stress on inclusivity is carried on in verse 8 where Paul gives thanks "for all of you" in his prayers. Sensitivity to congregational feelings is also shown in verses 11 and 12. In verse 11, Paul boldly states that he wishes to impart a "spiritual gift" or blessing, which might have been taken to imply that Paul did not feel that the congregation had spiritual power and fell short in some way. Paul immediately adds the tactful words in verse 12 to make clear that he expects to learn as much as he teaches when he comes to Rome.

Romans 1:13. In verse 13 where Paul describes the events behind his planned visit, he refers to the hindrances that have prevented his earlier arrival. Read 2 Corinthians 11:24-28 for an example of the kind of hindrances Paul had in mind. This section of the Corinthian correspondence was probably written not too long before Paul wrote Romans. By correlating the details of 2 Corinthians 8 and 9 with the indications of the problem in collecting the Jerusalem offering, we can see that the discord in Corinth set Paul's plan back for at least a year. Also, he was imprisoned more than once during this time. Acts 20:1-3 indicates other reasons for delays, namely, the hostility of Jewish zealots against Paul who were behind some of Paul's other imprisonments and troubles as well. His hope, as shown in Romans 15, had been to complete his work in the eastern mission field, deliver the offering, and arrive in Rome in order to get to Spain as quickly as possible. Paul's plans were delayed at least two and perhaps three years by the various forms of adversity that he experienced in his mission work.

Romans 1:14-15. In verse 14 "the wise and the foolish" probably relates to educational level. One might think of "the wise" as the highly educated and "the foolish" as working class people and slaves who did not have the benefit of higher education.

Paul stresses he is obligated to both sides of this stereotype. Paul makes it clear, therefore, that in the church, stereotypes like this are of no effect any longer. Paul implies in verse 15 that all these groups (Greeks and non-Greeks, wise and foolish) are represented in Rome and that his broad sense of responsibility is what leads him to include everyone.

DIMENSION THREE: WHAT DOES THE BIBLE MEAN TO ME?

In light of the problem of abstraction in dealing with Romans discussed earlier, I suggest that you spend a fair amount of time in the opening session dealing with the question of what the Roman church situation means to us today.

The Unique Circumstances of a Congregation

In connection with the unique history of the Roman house churches, marked by the adversity and conflict, reflect on the parallels with the experience of your local congregation. Tensions between conservatives and liberals may be relevant for your particular situation. The experience of serious disruption in the life of the congregation caused by external circumstances may be appropriate in case of fire, natural disasters, and so on. The competition among church leaders and groups loyal to particular leaders is also widely experienced in the modern church. In particular, we might consider the experience of churches where popular leaders come back after four or five years and start congregational work again in competition with existing pastors. The situation in Rome of having too many leaders of the congregation in competition for spaces might be similar to a situation of a denomination having too many ministerial members for the number of churches available. The conflicts caused by changes in liturgy, hymns, and location of worship services may parallel experiences your congregation has had in the past.

The point of thinking through these connections is to see the vivid parallels between modern church situations and the circumstances to which Romans was addressed. Only by making this imaginative leap can the abstract quality of the argument of Romans be overcome and the relevance of its argument perceived.

In connection with thinking about the unique circumstances of an individual congregation, it would be worth pointing out that Romans is addressed in a peculiar way to a peculiar congregation. In none of Paul's other letters does he address a congregation in just this manner. So each modern congregation also needs to be addressed by the gospel in unique and distinctive ways, reflecting their unique circumstances.

The task of a study of Romans, therefore, is to think through the connections between the ancient situation and the modern situation, to adapt Paul's argument to our different circumstances today for our particular congregation. No one interpretation of Romans is ever going to be universally relevant. Each congregation must discover the meaning of Romans for itself; each church school class must follow the same process of discovery.

Mutual Encouragement and Exhortation

We need tact and mutual respect when dealing with Romans. Part of this need is caused by the fact that the dogmatic tradition of past interpreters leads to preset formulas that tend to be argued in hostile manners by some persons. The abstraction of the argument of Romans leads certain people with an affinity to this kind of thinking to dominate others whose thought is more concrete and detailed. The elements of tact that are visible in the opening of Romans provide good models for both the teacher of Romans and the class members. In particular we need to live up to the principle of 1:12, involving mutual encouragement and exhortation, rather than the teacher laying down the truth for everyone else. Consistent with the content of this letter, you need to encourage mutuality, respect, and encouragement for the contributions of each member.

Inclusiveness

Paul's stress on inclusiveness also offers a significant resource for structuring a class on Romans. The diversity in theological outlook, background, and history of the members of a typical class need to be brought to the fore in order to show the parallels to the diversity of the Roman house churches. The formulas that Paul uses (for example, 1:14) might well be adapted to the situation in your class. The Greeks might be like those who speak a particular form of English, whereas the non-Greeks might be those for whom English is a second language. The wise might be those with university degrees, and the foolish might be those with a grammar school education. As we all know, some of the most intelligent persons in a class are often the ones with the least formal education. The diversity in educational level and cultural background in the class can be used to make plain the parallels between the Roman church situation and the situation in your local congregation.

The effort on Paul's part to include everyone, his frequent use of the word *all*, is a worthy model for your class. Paul's inclusiveness is particularly clear in the confession in verses 3-4. He does not take sides as to which version of the creed is most appropriate. He makes a small correction and simply cites the creed, thus making legitimate the viewpoint of both conservatives and liberals. Paul's effort is to unite, not to promote a single "right view." This strategy is appropriate for your class.

You need to honor the theological perspective and religious experience of each member in the class, to seek for common ground, and to encourage mutual respect even if one person continues to disagree. Romans is written to a series of house churches who are going to remain in disagreement. The whole question is whether they can be sufficiently united in the gospel to agree on a common mission. That is the agenda, not only of the Roman house churches, but for the modern church as well.

I glory in Christ Jesus in my service to God (15:17).

2

Paul's Purpose and Situation

Romans 15:14–16:2

DIMENSION ONE:
WHAT DOES THE BIBLE SAY?

Answer these questions by reading Romans 15:14–16:2

1. What are the references to the Spanish mission in this passage? (15:24, 28)

   Paul writes, "I plan to do so when I go to Spain."; and, "I will go to Spain and visit you on the way."

2. What details in our previous lesson on Romans 1:1-15 are similar to Romans 15:14, where Paul compliments the Romans for being "full of goodness, complete in knowledge and competent to instruct one another"?

   In 1:8, Paul refers to the Romans' faith as being "reported all over the world"; and in 1:12, he expresses the hope to "be mutually encouraged by each other's faith," which implies they are able to instruct others.

3. What is the geographic scope of Paul's previous mission? (15:19)

   The scope of Paul's earlier mission is from Jerusalem to Illyricum.

4. How long does Paul plan to spend in Rome? (15:24)

   Paul plans to stay in Rome "for a while."

5. Does Paul plan to deliver the Jerusalem offering before or after he arrives in Rome? (15:25, 28)

   Paul plans to visit Rome after delivering the offering.

6. What does Paul request that the Romans do for Phoebe? (16:2)

   Paul asks the Romans "to receive her in the Lord . . . and to give her any help she may need from you."

DIMENSION TWO:
WHAT DOES THE BIBLE MEAN?

Our motivation for moving to the end of Romans in this lesson is to come to terms with the historical situation behind this letter. The details concerning Paul's situation and his motivation for writing are found in the opening and closing sections, so this is where we must begin.

These sections of Romans are likely to be least understood and much less frequently read. Certainly, this material traditionally had not figured largely in the commentaries on Paul's letter to the Romans. But if we wish to overcome the dogmatic bias of our interpretive tradition—of viewing Romans as an abstract doctrinal treatise—it is essential that we take Paul's situation and motivation into account as we begin.

You need to understand the dramatic situation in which Paul's letter is actually placed. As we can see in 15:14–16:27, Paul is poised on the verge of several of his most daring and significant missionary enterprises. He is closing out the eastern mission field and is laying plans to complete the circuit of the Mediterranean world, moving toward Spain. Also, Paul is now ready to deliver the Gentile offering, which he hopes will unite the Gentile Christian and Jewish Christian wings of the church, thus preparing the way for the final mission.

Tragically, Paul did not end up in Rome as a free missionary but rather as a prisoner. The very process of carrying through this elaborate missionary scheme probably cost him his life. The political and personal aspects of Paul's situation at the time of writing this letter give the dramatic stage on which the letter should be interpreted.

Romans 15:14-19. If we want to understand Paul's self-image, the second half of Romans 15 is the best place to look. Far from describing himself as a theologian, an abstract thinker, or a writer, Paul presents himself as a missionary to the Gentiles. The language he uses has often appeared puzzling. He speaks of himself in 15:16 as "a minister of Christ Jesus to the Gentiles with the priestly duty of proclaiming the gospel of God." Nowhere else in the Pauline letters do we have this kind of priestly wording used in

Paul's self-description. This unusual description has led scholars to develop elaborate theories concerning Paul's understanding of himself.

The tendency of such theories, however, is to place Paul in the context of priestly institutions of established churches. This view overlooks the revolutionary, end-time horizon of his mission. It also leads to a misunderstanding of Paul's view of Christian ethics and of his view of the relation between Christians and Jews, if we conclude from this section that Paul advocates that a true Christian cult should replace a perverse Jewish cult.

The term *minister* in 15:16 is the same word used in 13:6 to describe governmental agents. This connotation of the word was widely used in the ancient world; it reflects the fact that priests and civil servants originally came from the same system and had interchangeable titles. We have something of that usage in modern language. In the terms of governmental officials in the British Commonwealth, the term *minister* is often used—Minister of Transportation, for example.

Minister therefore echoes the bureaucratic title that Paul used to describe himself in 1:1 as a "servant of Christ Jesus," meaning diplomat or agent of Jesus Christ. That this is the intended meaning of "minister of Christ Jesus" is further suggested by the phrase "to the Gentiles" that immediately follows it in 15:16. In the Roman world of the first century, this title would have sounded like the "Ambassador to the Parthians," or the like.

Paul understands himself here as the representative, the agent, of Jesus Christ to the Gentile world. Paul's task through the gospel is to restore the Gentile world to the holiness of the divine order, thereby completing the task of regenerating the world. For this reason he uses the phrase in verse 16, that "the Gentiles might become an offering acceptable to God, sanctified by the Holy Spirit." This language is reminiscent of the opening chapter of Romans, where Paul says, "for his name's sake, we received grace and apostleship to call people from among all the Gentiles to the obedience that comes from faith" (1:5).

A sweeping imperial vision is shown in the wording Paul uses to describe his vocation. Paul has the horizon of world mission in view; and he hopes for world conquest, not through force of arms, but through the power of the gospel. He understands himself in language that was directly parallel to that used by the Roman Empire. We can appropriately speak, therefore, of a fusion of the diplomatic, the bureaucratic, and the priestly viewpoints in this passage.

The crucial question for diplomacy, of course, is power. If the government one represents does not have sufficient power, then one's service is not likely to be effective. For this reason Paul is willing to say, in 15:17, "I glory in Christ Jesus in my service to God," which is elaborated in the following verses. The same Greek term is used here as in 3:27 for *boast*. Some translations, perhaps sensitive about the potential contradiction with Paul's rejection of arrogant "boasting" in 3:27, down play this with the less offensive term *glory in*.

Paul concentrates here on the power that is in the gospel allowing him to lead "the Gentiles to obey God" (15:18). This theme of power surfaces in the thesis of Romans (1:16), a passage that we will be studying in Lesson 4. That the gospel "is the power of God for the salvation of everyone who believes" is absolutely central for the argument of Romans. The means by which God will conquer the world, according to Paul, is not military or coercive force of any kind. The gospel changes people, leading them in a willing way under faith to work for the transformation of the world. When Paul returns to this theme in Romans 15, he draws together one of the most important emphases in his entire letter, the gospel as the power to transform the world.

In 15:18, Paul connects "word and deed." Unlike many modern theologians who tend to make the *word* of the gospel superior to *deeds*, Paul coordinates them. Ethics and theology are to be kept together. Both are inspired by the Spirit when properly carried out, and their integration is necessary for the gospel. The reference to "signs and miracles" in 15:19 refers to the miracles, healings, and spiritual transformations of early Christian missions. Unlike modern theologians and ministers, Paul does not separate the theological content of the gospel from "signs and miracles." Both reveal "the power of the Spirit" (15:19). Paul wants to make plain that this power, however, does not come from him personally. He is not a superman. The triumph of the gospel is due to what "Christ has accomplished through me" (15:18); Paul's success is entirely due to the "power of the Spirit" (15:19).

Romans 15:19-23. Paul has a clear geographical horizon for his mission, as is shown in the wording of 15:19. We may think it odd to view the trip from Jerusalem as going "around" to Illyricum (what we now call Yugo-Slavia) in a direction that obviously moves toward Rome and then on to Spain. We may also think it odd that Paul should refer to having "fully proclaimed the gospel," so that there was no more space for his activities in the East. We see here the peculiar world view of citizens of the Roman Empire whose conception of the world was shaped by the maps that were used by ancient travelers. Unlike our modern maps that give a projection with clear directions of north, south, east, and west, the maps of the Roman period were strip maps that showed the road network impressed into horizontal strips with directions given only on the basis of right or left. When one comes to a junction, one takes either the right turn or the left turn.

These maps showed the roads radiating out from Rome in every direction, and those that Paul had traveled in Asia Minor had the Mediterranean marked at the bottom of the strip map and the Black Sea marked at the top.

Paul's sense of the movement of the early Christian mission, therefore, was shaped by the Mediterranean and was moving in the direction of Rome and beyond. Paul had carried his mission as far west as Illyricum. From this point the strip maps showed ship connections across the Adriatic to the Roman road networks. Additional maps showed the Roman road connections on toward Spain, perceived in a real sense as the end of the world.

When we take this ancient world into account, we can see that Paul perceived his mission as one grand thrust from Jerusalem toward the end of the known world, namely Spain.

Paul was conscious of having "often been hindered" in arriving at Rome and completing the circle of his intended mission (15:22). Paul did not define the hindrance at this point but gave hints of his extensive missionary activities in 15:20-21. He gave other hints of the hindrances he had experienced in his greetings to missionary colleagues in 16:4 and 7. Two of the leaders Paul names, Priscilla and Aquila, had saved Paul's life on one occasion, risking their own lives in the process. And Andronicus and Junias were fellow prisoners with Paul.

When we reconstruct all the difficulties Paul had faced in the two-year period prior to writing Romans, the "hindrance" becomes clear. Paul was probably imprisoned at least two times and had a narrow escape from a third imprisonment. He had to deal with problems in the congregations at Colossae, Philippi, Laodicea, and Corinth. Many of these troubles required Paul to travel, to write letters, or to send missionary colleagues. He also had to face several postponements of the plans for collecting and sending the Jerusalem offering, which had to be completed before Paul would be free to pursue the circle path toward Spain.

Romans 15:24-33. What was there about the Spanish mission that required the tactful and elaborate preparation of a letter to the Romans and the sending of Phoebe? If indeed the entire letter was directly related to this project, why was it necessary? Could Paul not have completed the circle of the Mediterranean world by going straight to Spain? And why not begin a mission in Spain as he had in Thessalonica or Corinth? Why not simply arrive, start off preaching in a synagogue, get a foothold, take up work with a colleague like Priscilla and Aquila, and begin the kind of self-supporting mission that he had organized in the centers of the East?

Several factors could be suggested in answer to these questions. First, in the ancient world "all roads led to Rome." It would literally have been very difficult for Paul to travel from Corinth (where he was), or even from Jerusalem (where he planned to depart), and arrive in Spain without passing through Rome. The travel routes of the entire Roman Empire radiated out from Rome in all directions.

A second, more significant, factor was that Paul's usual missionary strategy was to begin by visiting and preaching in the local synagogue. Only after conflicts arose in that synagogue would he establish a new Christian house church in someone's home, if he could find a patron. Early

commentaries on Romans assumed that Jewish synagogues were established in Spain at the time Paul wrote Romans. But more recent studies indicate that Spain had neither large groups of Jewish settlers nor any synagogues during the first century. Jewish immigration to Rome did not begin until after the Jewish-Roman War of A.D. 66–70, more than a decade after Paul wrote Romans. Immigration was intensified after the Jewish revolt of A.D. 132–135. Doubtless early commentators on Romans had been led astray by outdated information on this issue, and the entire project of the Spanish mission and its strategy needs to be thought through again as a consequence.

The lack of a Jewish community in Spain would pose a serious barrier to Paul's mission. There would be no previous readiness to hear a message about an expected Messiah based on Jewish missionary preaching. Paul could not count on God-fearers or proselytes in the Spanish cities to create the cells of believing communities.

The lack of a Jewish community would also pose a significant economic problem to Paul. We know that the Jewish synagogues filled a social and economic as well as a religious function in the Greek and Roman cities. Travelers would use the small hostel attached to a typical synagogue when first arriving in a community. An easy network within the Jewish community in a city would thus be made available, and this would provide an avenue for employment opportunities. As a self-sustaining worker in the tent and leather business, Paul depended on such contacts to make his meager living. The problem of finding a "base of operations" would therefore be quite severe in Spain because of the lack of a Jewish population.

Another barrier to Christian mission in Spain related to the cultural environment: Spain had no Greek culture so far as recent studies have indicated. In fact, Latin, the official language of the western part of the Empire, was only used in the major urban centers. The rural population in most places continued to speak the obscure dialects of the original population before the Roman conquest. The linguistic barriers that Paul would face would therefore be quite severe. We know that he spoke Greek and Hebrew, but we have no indication that he had command of Latin. The Christian communities that had centered in the synagogues in Rome were also Greek speaking rather than Latin speaking, though several would have had resources for Latin within the congregation. Nevertheless, we do not know whether a tradition had already been established for proclaiming the gospel in Latin at the time Paul wrote. His missionary activity therefore would depend on translators.

An additional factor was that a series of Spanish revolts against Roman rule in the generation before Paul arrived led the imperial authorities to confiscate large amounts of private property. This property was placed in the hands of state authorities or of loyal citizens elsewhere in the Empire who could afford to pay for them. The populace was in many instances quite resistant to Roman rule. While resources from Rome would be absolutely crucial to getting a foothold in Spain, Paul could not put himself in a position of entering Spain as an agent of the Roman churches. This would have appeared far too imperialistic for the sensitive feelings of the Spaniards.

To mount an effective Spanish mission, therefore, required a wisely selected logistical base, the provision of formidable translation resources, and support from persons in Rome who were not identified in Spain as agents of the government. To provide these resources and to get the mission in Spain off on the right foot, Paul needed wise counsel and the cooperation of a wide range of resources within the Roman house churches, which at the time of his writing Romans were locked in conflict with one another. Paul desperately needed a peacemaker who could work out the arrangements for the Spanish mission before he arrived. This is where Phoebe comes into our story.

Romans 16:1-2. In question 6 of Dimension One, you find the request that Paul makes for Phoebe in Romans 16:2. This might provide a take-off point for discussing the details concerning this remarkable and largely unheralded woman. Phoebe was probably named after a Greek goddess, which indicates to us that she could not have been of Jewish background. She is introduced to the Romans as "our sister," which indicates membership in the early Christian community. The terms *sister* and *brother* were often used in the early church to show membership. The word *our* carries the nuance of her belonging to Paul as well as to all other Christians. *Our* has a legitimizing function. Phoebe is not an outsider to Rome, in a sense; she belongs to the whole Christian community as "our sister."

Paul goes on to identify Phoebe as a "servant [deaconess] of the church in Cenchrea." Our impression is that in the first generation of Christian leadership, each church had its own name for church leaders. Some called their leaders presbyters; others, bishops; others, deacons. Our impression, therefore, is that she is a leader of this particular congregation.

The most revealing title used for Phoebe, however, is the term translated in the student book as "patroness." It might be wise to ask class members to check the various translations they have at this point. Paul uses a technical term here that means the "protector" or the "patron," which had a clear legal and social connotation in the Greco-Roman world. Patrons and patronesses were upper-class figures who provided legal protection for their employees, slaves, friends, and dependents. The term that Paul uses here is associated with the Latin term *patrona,* which is closely related to the modern Italian term that is translated as "godfather" in popular American usage. We should think of Phoebe as a wealthy woman with a large estate who provides legal protection, employment, and leadership for the people around her.

Understanding Phoebe's social class helps us understand Paul's description of her activities in the Christian mission: "She has been a great help [patroness] to many people, including me" (16:2). This means that Phoebe had provided travel funds and support for a number of early Christian missionaries and that Paul was dependent on her as well. When he asks the Roman Christians to "receive her in the Lord in a way worthy of the saints," he is asking for them to roll out the red carpet for this prestigious and significant leader in the early Christian mission. And it is clear in the context that the help Phoebe requires is the task of her patronage.

Part of Phoebe's task would be to unify the Roman house churches by bringing Paul's letter to the churches, discussing its contents, and gaining assent to the plan to carry the mission to Spain. She would need to convince the house churches in Rome that Paul was a trustworthy partner for the Spanish mission. This task would be difficult, given Paul's involvement in so many controversial projects and conflicts. Conservative Jewish Christians would have known him as the radical Gentile missionary, the opponent of the Judaizer campaign. But the house churches close to the Roman government would be concerned over Paul's conflicts with provincial authorities, his several imprisonments and involvements at public disturbances. The potential damage that cooperation with a controversial troublemaker might cause for the images of their churches in Rome would cause them to be quite careful. Therefore, to gain their collective support for a project headed by Paul would not be easy.

Finally and most importantly, Phoebe's task would be to make the political contacts through Rome with potential supporters of a Pauline mission to Spain. This would involve providing a base of operations for Paul and his missionary colleagues, providing support for their travels and lodging, and providing translators capable of moving from Greek to Latin as well as to the Spanish dialects. Experienced advisors would be required in Rome to help find the right contacts in Spain and to use their influence to develop those contacts. Careful and wise preparation would have to be carried out ahead of time to make a Spanish mission feasible. A considerable amount of financial assistance would be required to replace the self-supporting missionary strategy that Paul had used, starting in the Jewish synagogues and other locations.

DIMENSION THREE: WHAT DOES THE BIBLE MEAN TO ME?

Mutual Sharing and Solidarity

The rationale for stewardship that Paul provides in Romans is quite striking in its contrast with some modern approaches. Paul emphasizes mutual sharing and solidarity. His premise is that you cannot give before you have received and that you receive out of a sense of mutual indebtedness. This seems quite different from the modern approach of encouraging people to contribute out of their guilt feelings. Also, Paul's sense that stewardship should provide a means of overcoming racial and cultural barriers is a provocative resource for the modern church. Discuss whether Paul's ideas have a significant bearing on the church today.

The Role of Women in the Church

The discovery of the crucial role of leadership by women in the Pauline mission movement is a striking one. Not only was Phoebe crucial for Paul's mission, a number of female missionary partners are recommended as reliable in 16:3-15, the material we shall study in our next lesson. One is struck by the role that could be played by an upper-class woman like Phoebe, whose business contacts and prestige would give her access to the wide range of Roman churches to achieve the delicate diplomatic task of unifying that church. Later developments in the Christian church also had a prominent role for women. One feature of such movements, however, is that in the second generation often the leadership role of women is crowded out by other considerations. At times of rapid expansion, however, women have played a very important role. The equality produced by the gospel calls forth the resources of both sexes in equal measure.

— 3 —

The Weak and the Strong in Rome

Romans 14:1–15:13; 16:3-27

DIMENSION ONE:
WHAT DOES THE BIBLE SAY?

Answer these questions by reading
Romans 14:1–15:13; 16:3-27

1. Who is in the outsider position and needs to be welcomed? (14:1)

   Paul writes that "him whose faith is weak" is to be welcomed.

2. Whom does Paul favor, the "weak" who consider "one day more sacred than another" and abstain "to the Lord" or the "strong" who do the opposite? (14:5-9)

   Paul's argument justifies each side as long as an individual member is "fully convinced in his own mind."

3. Since Paul's personal belief matches that of the "strong," who believe that "no food is unclean in itself" (14:14), what approach does he advocate for others? (14:15, 23)

   Paul urges the "strong" to avoid imposing their views on the "weak." He urges the "weak" to remain true to their principles.

4. What does the example of Christ support? (15:1-6)

   The example of Christ in these verses supports acceptance and tolerance and promotes "a spirit of unity."

5. How many times is the term *Gentiles* used in 15:8-12?

   Paul uses the term Gentiles *twice in verse 9 and once each in verses 10, 11, and 12.*

6. List the names of those whom Paul greets with a reference about either their experiences with him or their personal qualities. (16:3-15)

   1. Priscilla (16:3); 2. Aquila (16:3); 3. Epenetus (16:5); 4. Mary (16:6); 5. Andronicus (16:7); 6. Junias (16:7);
   7. Ampliatus (16:8); 8. Urbanus (16:9); 9. Stachys (16:9); 10. Apelles (16:10); 11. Tryphena (16:12); 12. Tryphosa (16:12a); 13. Persis (16:12b); 14. Rufus (16:13); 15. Rufus's mother (16:13).

7. List the names of those whom Paul greets without any personal references to indicate that he has met or worked with them. (16:3-15)

   1. The family of Aristobolus (16:10b); 2. Herodion (relative, probably means fellow Jew; 16:11); 3. the family of Narcissus (16:11b); 4. Asyncritus (16:14); 5. Phlegon (16:14); 6. Hermes (16:14); 7. Patrobas (16:14); 8. Hermas (16:14); 9. Philologus (16:15); 10. Julia (16:15); 11. Nereus (16:15); 12. Nereus's sister (16:15); 13. Olympas (16:15).

8. List the pairs of names that are linked together and/or give some other indication of being family members. (16:3-15)

   1. Priscilla and Aquila (16:3), a married couple; 2. Andronicus and Junias (16:7), probably a married couple; 3. Tryphena and Tryphosa (16:12), probably sisters, possibly twins; 4. Rufus and his mother (16:13); 5. Nereus and his sister (16:15).

9. List the persons sending greetings to Rome who are with Paul at the time of writing. (16:21-23)

   1. Timothy (16:21); 2. Lucius (16:21); 3. Jason (16:21); 4. Sosipater (16:21); 5. Tertius (16:22); 6. Gaius (16:23); 7. Erastus (16:23); 8. Quartus (16:23).

10. Estimate the proportion of women to men among the church leaders Paul mentions in 16:1-23.

    Ten out of thirty-seven (about twenty-seven percent) of the church leaders are women: Phoebe, Priscilla, Mary, Junias, Tryphena, Tryphosa, Persis, Rufus's mother, Julia, and Nereus's sister.

DIMENSION TWO:
WHAT DOES THE BIBLE MEAN?

The reason we are studying the material in Romans 14–16 in our third lesson is to complete the picture of the situation in Rome. Our effort to overcome theological abstraction in dealing with Romans means that a vivid picture of the situation in Rome must be kept in mind. The information concerning this situation is at the end of the letter, which requires a somewhat backward procedure for studying Romans.

The material in 14:1–15:13 is the culmination of the theological and ethical argument in Romans. These sections provide ethical guidelines for living in righteousness, thus developing the major theme of Romans 1:16-17. In these final chapters, we find evidence to identify who the weak and the strong were in Rome and also discover the direction of Paul's argument in response to their controversy. In 14:13-23, Paul develops guidelines for mutual upbuilding in the house churches. Righteousness is defined in these verses as the mutual acceptance and growth that unites rather than destroys the church.

In 15:1-6, Paul describes Christ as the model for the interaction between the groups in the church. In particular, edifying the "weak" is stressed in these verses, possibly because they are in a vulnerable position because the strong are in the majority.

Finally, Paul brings to a conclusion his formal argument in Romans (15:7-13). He begins with a summary in verse 7 of the tolerant argument concerning the weak and the strong; then Paul gives a series of Scripture quotations that bear on the question of the motivation and the horizon of the world mission. The emphasis on the Gentiles in this section was observed by the class members as they answered question 5 in Dimension One indicating the scope of Paul's argument in Romans in providing a rationale for world mission and unification. The promise given to Abraham, that in him all the nations would be blessed, is here brought to its fitting conclusion.

The Weak and the Strong

Traditional Bible commentaries present one of three views identifying the weak and the strong in these verses. The material I have written provides a fourth alternative, so clarifying the other options may help.

The traditional and most widely stated view is that the weak are the Jewish Christians, and the strong are Gentile Christians. Some details in the argument fit this view quite well. Some of the actions characteristic of the weak would be typical of Jewish Christians who remained true to the Torah.

Actions Characteristic of the "Weak"

14:2—"eats only vegetables"
14:5—"considers one day more sacred than another"

14:6—"regards one day as special"
14:14—believes something may be "unclean in itself"
14:21—refrains from "meat" and "wine"

In addition, Paul's strong identification of himself with the Gentile Christians in Romans 15:1 as well as in 14:14 would serve to confirm this traditional view. I can see some difficult barriers to holding this view, however.

First and foremost, we have no convincing evidence that conservative Jewish Christians were vegetarians, that they refrained from meat and wine. There is some evidence of fringe groups who tended toward asceticism, and it is understandable at certain times that Jewish groups in the Gentile world who did not have access to kosher butcher shops might temporarily refrain from meat. But that they would do so even on the great Jewish festival of the Passover is unthinkable. That they would refrain from wine at such a time is also difficult to believe.

This traditional view also labors under the burden that some of the Jewish Christians mentioned in Romans 16 had worked closely with Paul and in all probability shared his theology, which was closer to the strong than to the weak. Priscilla and Aquila can be mentioned here. It is likely also that a number of the persons that we identified in question 6 in Dimension One as closely related to Paul in his previous mission would have stood in this theological tradition as well and thought of themselves as strong.

An elaborate refinement of this traditional view is found in a book by Paul S. Minear, *The Obedience of Faith: The Purposes of Paul in the Epistle to the Romans* (SCM Press, 1971). Minear infers five groups from the evidence in Romans 14:1–16:27:

1. *"The 'weak in faith' who condemned the 'strong in faith' "* are viewed as consisting largely of converted Jews and a few Gentiles who had accepted the law when they became Christians.

2. *"The 'strong in faith' who scorned and despised the 'weak in faith' "* were uncircumcised Gentiles or Jews who relished the liberty that they had in Christ. They felt free from religious taboos because of their powerful experiences of conversion, and they despised persons who did not feel free to join in their celebration.

3. *"The doubters"* are viewed by Minear as persons coming from groups 1 and 2 who were unsure of their position and tended to waver between the extremes. Minear finds a reference to them in 14:23.

4. *"The 'weak in faith' who did not condemn 'the strong' "* are identified with those in the congregation who accepted Paul's argument and remained true to their Jewish-Christian convictions.

5. *"The 'strong in faith' who did not despise the 'weak' "* are identified as Paul's disciples who come primarily from the Gentile Christian background, though some Jews were included. These last two groups accepted Paul's argument and were intolerant toward other people.

The difficulty of this analysis is that it is poorly coordinated with the evidence concerning the five house churches in Rome that is found in Romans 16. In fact, as far as evidence of group life is concerned, only groups 1 and 2 are actually evident in Romans. Groups 4 and 5 are purely hypothetical because Minear simply assumes that some people among the so-called "weak" and "strong" accepted Paul's argument. Group 3 is not a proper group at all, since it consists of persons from other groups who are doubting their convictions. As a consequence, no other scholars have accepted Minear's elaborate proposal.

The third approach to the Roman house church situation is to assume that no clear identification is possible because of the peculiar quality of Paul's argument. Scholars who view Romans as a doctrinal treatise and stress the generality and general application of the argument sometimes tend in this direction. One scholar who takes this point of view, for example, argues that Paul is intentionally vague and self-contradictory in the details that he gives concerning the weak in Romans 14. This scholar says that Paul's purpose is to make an argument so general that it will fit a wide range of church situations. This presupposes that Romans is not really directed to a specific church situation but is a more general epistle aimed at providing guidance for a wide range of churches in the ancient as well as in the modern world.

The difficulty with this approach is that peculiar circumstances in the Roman house churches after the edict of Claudius are not taken into account. The evidence from Romans 14:1–15:7 that Gentile Christians are now in charge and that Jewish Christians are having a difficult time finding a place would fit the circumstances of a return after the time of exile was over. Nor does this approach take any account of Romans 16. Most scholars who follow this approach believe that Romans 16, in fact, was not directed to Rome at all but was a note sent to some other churches or to another church in particular, Ephesus. We will discuss later, briefly, the problem of the authenticity of Romans 16.

The viewpoint presented in this lesson is worked out in detail in my book *Christian Tolerance: Paul's Message to the Modern Church* (Westminster Press, 1982). I suggest that Paul defines the weak and strong in consciously broad categories, thus encompassing a range of congregational options within the extremes.

> The catchwords "weak" and "strong" that Paul employs . . . are highly misleading in their modern connotation, implying that the distinction had to do with weakness or strength of convictions and will power. Actually, as the research on this issue has made plain, the terms had probably been imposed by the "strong" who identified their superiority in terms of spiritual courage to defy traditional scruples. Rather than supposing that the "strong" comprised a single group, we may appropriately think of this term as roughly equivalent with "liberal" in the modern political sense, depicting a fairly wide range of ideological, racial, and temperamental differences. Similarly the "weak" should be thought of as roughly equivalent with "conservative," consisting of various groups of Jewish and Gentile Christians favoring a scrupulous attitude toward the Jewish law and certain liturgical and ascetic practices (pages 29–30).

I link this identification of the weak and the strong with the circumstances of the two years prior to Paul's writing the letter in which the Jewish Christians were allowed to return and conflicts over leadership developed between liberals and conservatives, old and new Christians, charismatics and traditionalists. I argue that "the controversies undoubtedly crossed racial lines because there were Jewish Christians who inclined toward the Pauline view of freedom from the law and others who were loyal to the more conservative pattern of Peter and the Jerusalem mother church." The Gentile side probably included some of a conservative stripe, likely associated with the two house churches within the Roman bureaucracies, those belonging to Aristobulus (16:10) and to Narcissus (16:11). I feel the Letter to the Romans must be placed within this tangled situation.

Romans 14:1-4. Romans 14:1 indicates that the strong who are in the majority position have accepted the weak only on the premise that they could successfully convince them to change their minds. The "disputable matters" are defined in subsequent verses as relating to food laws, the cultic calendar, and theology. In 14:3 the distinctive strategy to enforce conformity used by both sides is described. Apparently, the strong, or the liberals, are "look[ing] down on" those who are not able to join them at their level of freedom. The weak, or conservatives, are "condemn[ing]" those who do not live up to their high moral standards. The likelihood that these are the distinctive strategies to enforce conformity being used in Rome is strengthened by the fact that Paul uses precisely the same language in 14:10. In 14:1, however, *judgment* is used in a more inclusive sense to describe the behavior of both sides.

The question "Who are you to judge someone else's servant?" clearly alludes to the behavior of both the conservatives and the liberals. Both are acting toward their competitors as if they were the lord of the other. The "master" in verse 4 is clearly God.

Romans 14:5-6. In 14:5, Paul refers to "consider[ing] one day more sacred than another," which is a reference to feast days, fast days, and the sabbath. The conservatives spoke of a day being more sacred than another in that they saw the day as designated by God for a specific kind of activity. The persons who consider "every day alike" are obviously the liberals who have abandoned the cultic calendar of Judaism as well as, perhaps, the special feast days of the Greco-Roman world. In verses 5-6, Paul subtly equalizes the claims of both the conservatives and the liberals. The argument is that as long as each side acts in response to the Lord, their behavior must be supported and applauded by the others.

Romans 14:15-16. In these verses Paul deals with liberals causing conservatives to violate their standards by acting in ways that they really feel are inappropriate. In verse 16, Paul deals with the discrediting of freedom when it is used to cause the downfall of others. That which is "good" for the liberal is the freedom that she or he has in Christ.

Romans 14:22-23. The literal translation of verse 22 is as follows:

> Keep the faith that you have in accordance with yourself in the presence of God. Blessed is the one who does not judge himself by what he approved.

This verse is addressed primarily to those who are in danger of abandoning their convictions. Belief is defined here as an internal standard that each person must follow. Shakespeare stated the essential theme of this verse in the words, "To thine own self be true." Paul does not issue a command for privacy but rather for integrity. In this sense, 14:23 should be understood to mean that any act that does not proceed from your own belief violates your integrity and therefore is a sin. This standard needs to be followed by both liberals and conservatives in Rome.

Romans 15:1. I would render 15:1 differently from the NIV:

> We the powerful are obligated to bear the weaknesses of the powerless and not to please ourselves.

The NIV refers to "the failings of the weak." This phrase seems to imply that the conservatives have an ethical flaw or a lack of will power. I believe that a proper translation suggests that those who are liberal should bear with those who are conservative. On the basis of Paul's previous argument, he would not wish to place either side in a negative light.

Romans 15:5-13. In 15:5-6 and 15:13, Paul draws together his argument with powerful benedictions, expressing his desires for the congregation and the burden of his previous argument. The first benediction summarizes mainly the material from Romans 14:1–15:4. The second draws together the argument of the entire letter. The hope that is lifted up here is for the unification of the world through the gospel. The centrality of the Gentile mission for the entire Letter of Romans is magnificently caught by the series of scriptural quotations (15:9-12) that lead up to the final benediction.

Romans 16:3-16. Phoebe's activities require the support of the leaders of the Roman house churches, which is why Paul moves immediately from recommending her to greeting all the church leaders in Rome. The work that your class has done answering questions 6, 7, and 8 in Dimension One brings forth the material necessary for this discussion. Paul greets fifteen persons with whom he had worked earlier, only a few of whom appear to be actually attached to house churches. Since Paul knows them intimately, he probably can expect their cooperation in the Spanish mission. Some of these people are Christians of long standing. Adronicus and Junias are Jewish Christians who, according to 16:7, became leaders prior to Paul's conversion. So they had been Christians at least since A.D. 34. Their reputation and activities go back more than twenty years in the rapidly developing early church.

The thirteen leaders whose names Paul knows by hearsay are also needed to provide support for the Spanish mission. The resources of each of the five house churches would be required to make this mission successful. In particular, Paul would need the advice and counsel of those churches. The other three house churches mentioned would be just as significant a resource for the Spanish mission. But since the Roman administrators in the houses of Aristobulus and Narcissus would be involved in the imperial correspondence, they would be equally adept at Latin and at Greek and in an excellent position to provide translation resources and to make recommendations for traveling companions who would be able to understand what was happening in Spain.

Paul has no difficulty in working with Phoebe who, given the class structure of the Greco-Roman world, would clearly have been perceived as the senior partner in any collaborative mission with a person of Paul's social standing. The fact that ten of the thirty-seven persons that Paul greets in 16:1-23 are women indicates the openness to resources from females that marked the first generation of the Christian mission.

Romans 16:17-27. The textual history of Romans 16 is quite tangled and probably should not be raised unless someone asks about it. Here are the essential details in case the question is raised. The major problem is that the Greek manuscripts we have of Romans place the final benediction of 16:25-27 at a number of locations. Some of the other benedictions and greetings are also located at different spots, which has led text critics to the conclusion that at least three forms of Romans circulated in the ancient world:

1. A fourteen-chapter letter that ended with the benediction of 16:25-27 placed at the end of Chapter 14;
2. A fifteen-chapter letter with the benediction of 15:33 concluding the letter; and
3. A sixteen-chapter letter with the benediction in its current location.

Given the fact that one of our manuscripts deletes the word *Rome* from the opening chapter of the letter, it seems clear that some versions of this letter circulated as general epistles. Many scholars have inferred from this that Romans was written by Paul in at least two forms, a fifteen-chapter letter addressed to Rome and a sixteen-chapter letter with a final note and greetings directed to Ephesus where many of the people mentioned here were known to have resided. Research has made this theory less likely, however; and one problem in supporting this last theory is how Paul could have mentioned so many names without personal greetings if this were sent to an area where Paul had worked as long as he had in Ephesus. So current scholarly opinion tends to conclude that Paul sent Romans as a sixteen-chapter letter to Rome.

The material in 16:17-20 is highly controversial and disputed. In the event that members of your class have an interest in this material, here are some of the pros and cons. The suggestion that these verses were inserted by the early church that edited the Pauline letters rests on several observations. These verses break the flow of the argument and are completely out of the mood of the friendly greetings surrounding them. Romans 16:16 and 16:21 would be smoothly connected if these verses were eliminated. The mood of mutual cooperation and tolerance that this chapter conveys, particularly when one considers that Paul is treating as equals the members of all five house churches, is seriously disrupted by this warning against heretics.

The language inside these verses is also quite different from that used elsewhere in Romans and in the other authentic Pauline letters. The recommendation that persons who "cause divisions and put obstacles in your way that are contrary to the teaching you have learned" should be avoided flatly contradicts the argument of 14:1–15:13. Nowhere else in the Pauline letters does Paul make doctrinal conformity the crucial indication of legitimacy as in these verses. The vicious personal attack of 16:18 is also unparalleled in the authentic Pauline letters. This verse is reminiscent, however, of the way the Pastoral Epistles deal with their opponents. Verse 19 is also unusual for Paul in that obedience is used here without reference to the term *faith* with which it is connected at every other point in Romans. Here pure obedience to whatever Paul says is defined as the line dividing good from evil. This view is vastly different from the one in Romans 12:1-3.

Finally, the hope expressed in verse 20 that God will crush heretics in the form of Satan "under your feet" is far from the spirit of the cooperative letter that Paul has written. This wording encourages Christians to believe that their opponents are satanic and ought to be destroyed. These words, of course, were enacted with great effectiveness during the time of the Inquisition.

Many commentators, however, believe that these words are an authentic part of Paul's letter, establishing the limits beyond which tolerance should not go. Whatever position you or the members of your class come to, it is important to keep in mind that 16:17-20 is part of the canonical letter.

There are times in the Christian tradition when the application of these verses has become necessary. The key question that needs to be discussed, therefore, is which side of Paul's argument in Romans is more appropriate for the local church and the circumstances that you are facing. Is it the open-minded cooperation and the tolerance of diverse viewpoints in Romans 1–15 and the friendly greeting of the rest of Romans 16? Or is it, because of peculiar circumstances, the hard line of Romans 16:17-20? What is appropriate for the Christian ethic has to do with circumstances and the moment. One cannot decide which approach ought to be used in every situation.

DIMENSION THREE: WHAT DOES THE BIBLE MEAN TO ME?

Conservatives and Liberals

We are struck by the parallels between the ancient situation in Rome and that of modern congregations. The tensions between rich and poor churches is not only an embarrassment to the church but also in all probability a hindrance to its mission as well. The Letter to the Romans encourages us to think of the task of cooperation as an essential ingredient to mission. In Paul's circumstances, mounting the mission to Spain was not possible without the resources of all the house churches. There may well be circumstances in the modern world and certainly in local congregations where something similar could be said.

Making a Conscious Effort to Accept

Paul is seeking to enlist all the potential leaders in one cooperative effort. The tensions between those leaders, which we can only partially reconstruct, sound very much like the tensions between leaders in modern churches as well.

Pluralism

The pluralism manifest in the five house churches in Rome has many modern parallels. The church does not always require the same structure and leadership pattern, if the model of Romans is to be trusted. These relatively small house churches, perhaps comparable to church school classes or prayer cells in modern churches, became the vital centers of growth and spiritual development. The Letter to the Romans has a promise and hope that such can become the case today as well.

I am not ashamed of the gospel, because it is the power of God for the salvation of everyone who believes (1:16).

4

Righteousness and Wrath

Romans 1:16–2:16

DIMENSION ONE:
WHAT DOES THE BIBLE SAY?

Answer these questions by reading
Romans 1:16–2:16

1. In the thesis statement of 1:16-17, what does Paul identify as the "power of God," and where is the "righteousness from God" revealed?

   Both the "power of God" and the "righteousness from God" are linked to the gospel.

2. Where have God's invisible attributes been seen? (1:20)

   They are seen in "what has been made."

3. What are the consequences of refusing to acknowledge and glorify God? (1:21-22)

   Those who refuse to honor God become futile in their thinking, and their "foolish hearts [are] darkened."

4. How many times does Paul repeat that God "gave over" the wicked to the consequences of their deeds? (1:24-28)

   Paul says three times that God "gave them over" to the consequences of their sin, in 1:24, 26, and 28.

5. Does Paul describe "shameful lusts" as the cause or the consequence of divine wrath? (1:26-27)

   The phrase "God gave them over to . . ." indicates that shameful lusts are the consequence of divine wrath, not its cause.

6. How many forms of evil does Paul list? (1:29-31)

   Paul lists twenty-one forms of evil, starting with "wickedness" in verse 29 and ending with "ruthless" in verse 31.

7. On the basis of the wording of 2:5-10, is *wrath* in this section a present experience or a future expectation?

   The idea of "storing up wrath" in verse 5 implies a future "day of God's wrath." The future tense of the verbs "will give" (2:6), "will give" (2:7), and "there will be" (2:8, 9) indicates that it is the future wrath that Paul has in mind here.

8. How many times is the expression "first for the Jew, then for the Gentile" repeated in 1:16–2:11?

   Paul repeats this phrase three times, in 1:16; 2:9, 10.

9. Who is "righteous in God's sight"? (2:13)

   "Those who obey the law" are righteous before God.

10. What does Paul say about the Gentiles who do not have the law? (2:14-15)

   The Gentiles who do not have the law yet follow it do so by listening to their conscience and thoughts.

DIMENSION TWO:
WHAT DOES THE BIBLE MEAN?

Romans 1:16–2:16 begins the abstract, formal argument of the letter. Teaching this material presents a series of challenges. It is quite important that you devise a plan for your discussion of this material that avoids getting bogged down in tiny details but that nevertheless remains true enough to the flow of the argument that Paul's point is understood.

Keeping in mind that Paul is making a case throughout this letter for the unification of Jews and Gentiles, for the mission of the gospel, and for its world-transforming power may help you in dealing with this highly abstract argument.

Romans 1:17. English provides two different words for what in the original text of Romans was a single family of terms.

We speak of *righteousness* and *justification*, both of which have different forms and rather different connotations in English. The difficulty is particularly seen in 1:17. For instance, the King James Version translates this verse, "For therein is the righteousness of God revealed from faith to faith. . . . The just shall live by faith." The problem is that the word *just* comes from exactly the same stem as the term *righteousness*.

When this translation problem is not understood, as is often the case, "justification by faith alone" gets entirely separated from the "righteousness of God." That is, God's activity in transforming humans is understood basically as the gift of forgiveness that allows us to be "justified" even though we have violated the law. But being justified is different from being righteous. In fact, Paul wishes to speak of humans in this entire letter as being *rightwised*, that is, "to make right, to set one right, and to achieve a transformation in which humans come to reflect the righteousness of God."

Your class members may have difficulty defining *righteousness* and connecting it with their previous understanding of *justification*. A simple set of alternatives can be suggested here. An old-fashioned view is that *righteousness* is the standard for what is right for God as well as for humans. When this interpretation of righteousness becomes central, it leads to a moralistic understanding of what human salvation means. It can end up in a new form of the law, a major problem for Romans. That is, people can be led to think that if they simply conform to the high standards of the Christian faith, they are justified.

Another approach was shaped, in particular, by Martin Luther. In this tradition, *justification* or *rightwising* is understood to be the gift of freedom from condemnation. The difficulty with this interpretation, whether in its moralistic or abstract theological form, is that the parallel Paul wishes to create in Romans 1:17 between the righteousness of God and the "rightwising" of humans is lost sight of.

The viewpoint I am following in this course is that the "righteousness from God" in Romans refers to God's capacity to impose righteousness on the world. God has a claim on the creation that it reflect divine righteousness. Thus when Paul speaks of the "righteousness from God" as being "revealed," he is operating out of the Jewish tradition of God standing triumphant at the end of history, having vanquished or transformed all foes. This view lets us see the close parallel between the righteousness of God and the righteousness given to humans. When humans are caught up in the divine plan and made to conform to the divine will, they enter into a relationship with God that has righteousness as its major component. They achieve the goal for which they were created.

When communities are caught up in the righteousness from God, they become agents of the divine will over the whole created order. Thus the biblical idea that the fall of humankind led to the fall of the creation, to the distortion of ecology, to the destruction of the planet itself, is all caught up in Paul's notion in Romans. Paul hopes to offer a concept of the gospel that trusts the will of God to regain control over the whole world. In this way a basis is provided for a world mission that not only transforms persons but also ultimately transforms the principalities and powers and regains and restores the lost world itself. So, when Paul refers to "the righteousness from God," he is close to the Old Testament idea that the "glory of God" is manifest when God wins a victory over enemies.

One of the difficult issues in 1:19-32 is that of "natural revelation." The argument in these verses is that all humans have the capacity to recognize God by seeing what God has created. Many commentaries that were shaped by the neo-orthodox tradition of the 1920s through 1950s were highly sensitive on the issue of natural revelation. Some of these commentators tried to down play Paul's argument at this point.

Current scholars see that Paul in fact makes use of a widespread tradition of natural revelation that was typical of the Greco-Roman world as a whole and also of some Jewish theologians. Paul's argument in these verses reminds me of an idea that was widely shared in Greco-Roman culture, namely that an original stage of human existence and history allowed humans to see God's nature clearly and visibly. The second stage, the fall of the human race, came with the deterioration of humans and the rise of corrupt priests at temples that confused the divine image with nature itself.

The whole question of how God is visible in nature is a vital one for the Greco-Roman world and for Paul. A widespread assumption among serious religious thinkers in a place like Rome was that true worship should be a matter of contemplating the heavens and the earth and therefore cultivating a knowledge of what God was like. These ideas were picked up by the late Jewish thinkers so that quite likely Paul operated out of a double tradition as he wrote these words. For example, in the Apocrypha, the Wisdom of Solomon 13:5 suggests that "from the greatness and beauty of created things / comes a corresponding perception of their Creator." The idea here is precisely that which Paul argues, namely that God's attributes are visible in the created things.

Nowhere else in the Greco-Roman world or in Judaism do we have so strong an emphasis as here on the conscious repudiation of the knowledge of God on the part of humans. Paul's emphasis on suppressing the truth about God as the essence of sin and his contention that humans tend to confuse themselves with the divine sets Paul off from his contemporaries. The radical side of his idea of natural revelation that is consciously perverted by humans can best be explained on the basis of Paul's theology of the cross.

Paul discovered in the Christ event the depth of human perversion and twistedness, the tendency of humans to reject the truth and to deny its validity for their lives, even to the point of killing the Christ when they had him in their grasp.

Romans 1:29-32. As the student book makes plain, the problem of the human race, according to 1:19-32, is far more than a matter of breaking the law. It is more serious than breaking religious principles. It is instead the tendency to rebel and to repress the truth about the distinction between creatures and their Creator. Therefore, when you teach this material, be on the alert to avoid drifting into petty moralism. The moral features that Paul discusses in this passage are the consequences and results of basic human sin rather than its form. In fact, most of what is preached against as sin in Christian tradition, material such as Romans 1:26-31, is the result of something much more basic.

When we understand Paul's argument that humans have the knowledge of God but refuse to allow God to be God, falling into twistedness and darkness of mind, the parallel in the Hebrew Scriptures becomes particularly plain. The student book refers to the garden of Eden story, which is highly relevant for this passage.

In addition, you may wish to throw light on 1:23 by referring to the golden calf episode in Exodus 32. In that story humans felt uncomfortable with the absent and invisible God and set about to create an image that would provide them the fertility and prosperity they hoped to gain. Exodus 32 shows that idolatry, the making of "images made to look like mortal man and birds and animals and reptiles" (Romans 1:23), is rooted in the human yearning to achieve goals by manipulating God. Therefore I find it significant that Paul follows the logic of Exodus 32 in Romans.

After the Hebrews had created the golden calf, they danced about it and fell into a sexual orgy that was so destructive and noisy that it brought Moses back from the distant mountain. Similarly, in the argument here in Romans, sexual perversion, the free expression of the human will to dominate and to destroy, is the consequence of creating finite images for God and making God into nothing more than a projection of human desires.

The issue of twistedness, particularly the distortion of human sexual relations that one sees in 1:24-27, is likely to be of particular interest to some members of your class because of recent debates over the issue of homosexuality. One fundamental observation is needed to keep this kind of discussion in context. Paul is describing what he perceives as the consequence of human confusion between the divine and the finite. And he is operating out of a widespread tradition in his own Hebrew culture that sexual perversions are fundamentally a violation of the will of the Creator.

Given the limitations of our current understanding of homosexuality and the feelings that it can evoke in the church today, you would do well to steer away from this topic unless well-informed resources are at hand to help throw light on it. It is certainly not crucial for an understanding of Paul's argument to come to an agreement on what the current status of homosexuality ought to be in the church. No matter what decision is made on that, it seems to me that Paul's basic argument still remains true, namely that when humans confuse themselves with God and try to suppress the truth about themselves, they fall into various forms of twistedness.

Romans 2:6-7, 13-16. One of the most difficult puzzles about Romans 2:6-7 is that it appears to contradict the basic teaching of Romans, namely that humans are "rightwised" by faith alone. Particularly when one takes the thesis of Romans into account (1:16-17), the statement that God will "give to each person according to what he has done" (2:6) is quite puzzling. This puzzle is deepened with 2:13, which states that "it is those who obey the law who will be declared righteous" (will be "rightwised").

Many commentaries on Romans deal with these seeming contradictions by evading the clear force of what Paul says. One approach is to suggest that these verses deal merely with a theoretical possibility. If it is true that all persons sin, then we cannot say that we will be justified according to our works. These commentaries say that Paul, for the sake of a theoretical argument, develops here a purely theoretical option. This argument is hard to sustain in light of the direct references to the Roman audience in 2:5, 7-8. We do not get the impression from these lines that Paul is dealing with something that was not present in Rome.

A second evasive approach is to suggest that Paul is dealing only with Christian believers in this passage. In this way Paul can be seen as condemning non-Christians but suggesting that those who really have been transformed by the gospel have been rendered capable of producing works and therefore achieving salvation. But that Paul is dealing strictly with a Christian audience in these verses is flatly contradicted by 2:9-10 in which the phrase "first for the Jew, then for the Gentile" is repeated.

Perhaps Paul meant to leave open some loopholes in his earlier argument. And perhaps the statement about the righteous Gentile in Romans 2 makes it possible for Christians to recognize persons outside the Christian faith and even outside the Judeo-Christian tradition whose lives nevertheless have a degree of authenticity and goodness that seems difficult to dispute.

Romans 2:11. Recent studies in Romans have made us more aware of the crucial significance of Paul's argument that God shows no favoritism (2:11). This element is essential in the issue we have just discussed, namely whether God will accept those who have never heard the Christian gospel or the Jewish faith, those who have never heard or perceived the Jewish law but nevertheless perform it (2:13-16). An investigation by Professor Jouette M. Bassler of Georgetown University (*Divine Impartiality: Paul and a Theological Axiom*; Scholars' Press, 1982) shows the unusual way in which Paul has developed this traditional Jewish concept.

Of particular interest in Professor Bassler's study is the realization that the social consequence of God's impartial treatment of Jews and Gentiles is "that no distinction is to be made within the community itself." She also writes that God's impartial acceptance of the two groups expands to include mutual acceptance between the two groups. At this point her study is closely linked to the approach I take in this course on Romans. My aim is to show that at crucial points in Paul's argument, even points that sound abstract to the modern reader, Paul was addressing tensions within the Roman house churches. Paul's argument about the impartiality of God stands as a hedge against the competitive spirit among those house churches who believed that each had the total truth and that the other side was wrong.

God is not the possession of the weak or of the strong. We could also say that God is not the possession of the United Methodists or the Southern Baptists or the Roman Catholics or the Greek Orthodox. God is absolutely impartial. God treats persons of all races and nations and religions with a fair standard of performance. Until the Roman house churches understood this, they would not be able to overcome their tensions and cooperate in a mission to the world. And any gospel they would have for the world would be fatally flawed if it rested on the premise, often followed in the mission thrust of later Christianity, that one group has a corner on the truth and is therefore superior to others.

That kind of mission is nothing more than a vicious form of imperialism. And any such imperialism was bound to be rejected by the Spaniards who had already suffered so much from Roman imperialism that they would be unlikely to adopt another form.

DIMENSION THREE:
WHAT DOES THE BIBLE MEAN TO ME?

Romans 1:16-18—The Gospel and the Power of God

Given the difficulty of the material in this passage, it might help to think of widely experienced pieces of entertainment that might throw light on aspects of Paul's argument. The *Star Wars* films come to mind because of their emphasis on "the Force," which stands quite close to "the power of God" in Romans 1:16. Whereas Paul believes that the gospel is "the power of God for the salvation of everyone," the *Star Wars* films believe that light sabers and atomic torpedoes are the power of God for salvation. "The Force" in the *Star Wars* films is rather neutral and can be tapped particularly by the Jedi knights who are able to channel "the Force" in good or evil directions. Commoners do not have access to "the Force." This class-bound and elitist conception is in contrast to Paul's stress that the gospel is available to everyone who has faith.

Also, the contrast between the targeting of the gospel and the power of God is interesting. In the *Star Wars* films, as in so many other forms of current popular entertainment, the bad people need to be destroyed in order for the kingdom to come. These films therefore suggest that the average person does not require any form of transformation in order to be saved. Paul suggests, in contrast, that each person must be transformed. Evil does not simply emerge among those who have the black Nazi-style helmets of the *Star Wars* films. Evil affects everyone.

The film *Amadeus* embodies the key insight of Romans 1:18. The composer Salieri in the film is shown making a promise to God as a youth to serve God faithfully in his music in return for eternal popularity and the undying love of the world. Completely unconscious of the arrogant quality of this pact with God, Salieri becomes a famous court composer and is shocked when the genius of Mozart's music is discovered. While recognizing the inspired and even divine quality of Mozart's compositions, Salieri is appalled that God could pour his inspiration into such an unworthy vehicle.

In one dramatic scene, Salieri places the cross in his fireplace and declares war on God, saying, "From now on you and I are enemies. . . . I will destroy your creation." Salieri sets about to frustrate Mozart's career and even to cause his death. *Sin*, in the sense of rebellion—even hatred—against God, is displayed in these actions. But the film makes it plain that Salieri remains a moral agent. His moral rectitude and his feeling of being betrayed by life show themselves in hostility against the Creator.

In the end, the film also embodies Paul's key idea of forgiveness because Salieri finds an element of forgiveness and gives absolution to the other people in the asylum where he has been placed. This film opens up the profound dimension of sin as rebellion and suppression of the truth that Paul writes about in Romans.

Members of your class may suggest other recent materials they have read or seen that help embody key ideas in this passage. I strongly suggest that the abstraction of this argument needs to be captured by vivid expressions in popular imaginations so the power and force of Paul's argument can be fully understood.

You, then, who teach others, do you not teach yourself? You who preach against stealing, do you steal? (2:21).

5

Religion Perverted

Romans 2:17–3:20

DIMENSION ONE:
WHAT DOES THE BIBLE SAY?

Answer these questions by reading
Romans 2:17–3:20

1. How many claims of religious superiority does Paul list, and what are they? (2:17-20)

   Paul makes ten claims in these verses: (1) relying on the law (2:17); (2) bragging on one's relationship to God (2:17); (3) knowing the will of God (2:18); (4) approving what is superior (2:18); (5) being instructed in the law (2:18); acting as (6) a guide for the blind (2:19); (7) a light for those in darkness (2:19); (8) an instructor of the foolish (2:20); (9) a teacher of children (2:20); and (10) having the embodiment of knowledge and truth in the law (2:20).

2. How many rhetorical questions does Paul ask in 2:21-23?

   Paul asks five questions—two in verse 21, two in verse 22, and one in verse 23.

3. How is Paul's quotation of Isaiah 52:5 different from the original? (2:24; Isaiah 52:5)

   That God's name is blasphemed in Isaiah 52:5 is due to the Exile, in which "my people have been taken away for nothing." In Romans 2:24, Paul says God's name is blasphemed because Israel sins.

4. What does Paul argue about the value of circumcision? (2:25-26)

   Paul claims circumcision has value only if one actually observes the law. Otherwise, the circumcised Jews are no better than uncircumcised Gentiles.

5. How does Paul define the "real Jew"? (2:28-29)

   The "real Jew" has the "inward" circumcision of the heart, "by the Spirit, not by the written code."

6. How many rhetorical questions does Paul ask in 3:1-9?

   The New International Version has ten rhetorical questions asked by Paul.

7. What word that is not in Psalm 14:1-3 and 53:1-3 does Paul use in quoting these psalms? (3:10-12)

   Paul uses the word righteous *in quoting these psalms.*

8. Who does Paul say will be held accountable to God? (3:19)

   Paul writes that "the whole world [will be] held accountable to God."

DIMENSION TWO:
WHAT DOES THE BIBLE MEAN?

The material in this lesson is full of dangers as well as of promise. In a culture with a record of some anti-Semitism, it is particularly dangerous to discuss Paul's effort to show that Jews as well as Gentiles are involved in sin. Paul's conversation partners here included Jewish Christians in Rome rather than Jews who have never received the gospel. We therefore need to assume that this argument is within the Christian community, not between Christians and unconverted Jews.

Paul hoped to lead the house churches in Rome to a more realistic assessment of their situation. If you are convinced that you have earned grace, that you are in a superior position, you will never be able to understand the pure gift of grace. Only those who are empty can be filled. Only those who acknowledge their need can be helped. Therefore this material has a tremendous relevance for the Christian faith. But its dangers when used in preaching against other religions must constantly be kept in mind.

This lesson begins in the middle of the section of Paul's argument that deals with impartial judgment according to deeds. That section runs from Romans 2:1 to 2:29. Our lesson begins with the second half, beginning with verse 17, the material that deals specifically with the claims of the religious elite. Paul concentrates in these verses on the "Jews," by which he has in mind primarily the Jewish Christians who are struggling against Gentile Christians in Rome. Paul's contention throughout this entire section is that all persons, Jews as well as Gentiles, are involved in sin and that all persons, whether Jews or Gentiles, will be treated impartially and fairly by God. There are no exemptions. The severity of the argument here is designed to uncover the worst perversion of all, the perversion of religion into a system of superiority.

Romans 2:17-23. One of the remarkable features of 2:17-20 is that Paul does not finish the sentence. This incomplete sentence is somewhat disguised in the NIV and other modern translations where a dash appears at the end of verse 20. The impression is given that the sentence continues in verse 21. In fact, verse 21 in the Greek begins a new sentence; and modern scholars believe that Paul left the long sentence of verses 17-20 unfinished on purpose. One of the studies on this problem suggests that Paul wishes to express here what is too horrible to express completely, namely the fullness of human arrogance and the final perversion of the great religious heritage of the Hebrew Scriptures. He leaves the sentence incomplete because it is impossible to complete. When a great religious heritage is perverted into a system of superiority claims, the heritage becomes its unspeakable opposite.

In Paul's effort to show a scandalous excess of religious pride, he does not wish to subvert the proper use of that same religion. He forms his argument with some rather elaborate plays on the sacred numbers of Judaism. As we see from answering question 1 in Dimension One, Paul lists ten claims in the incomplete sentence. This matches the Ten Commandments. In the next section, 2:21-23, Paul asks five questions, matching the five books of Moses.

Romans 2:25-29. Circumcision had been under dispute within Christian groups in the seven or eight years before Paul wrote Romans. The opening phase of this dispute is reflected in Acts 15:1 when Luke reports that "some men came down from Judea to Antioch and were teaching the brothers: 'Unless you are circumcised, according to the custom taught by Moses, you cannot be saved.' "

Paul had struggled over this issue in the Apostolic Conference (Galatians 2:1-10), and it may have been an issue also to some degree among the churches in Rome. Circumcision as the sign of the covenant and as the proof of one's membership in the "seed of Abraham" was one of the most important features in the claim of moral and religious superiority on the part of Jewish Christians. That circumcision was seen as necessary for salvation is clear in Acts 15:1. We have no indications from the Jewish community that they saw circumcision as necessary for salvation. As far as Jews were concerned, circumcision was simply a sign of membership in the community of the law. Faithfulness to this law insured that the person would continue in the realm of salvation as far as Jewish theology was concerned.

But in the Christian community circumcision was being used as a sign of superiority of one group over the other. This misuse is what Paul counters in these verses.

Paul says that obedience to the law is what makes circumcision significant. The "true Jew" in this sense is the one who has accepted the law of God and obeys it from the heart. The effect of this argument is to make circumcision subordinate to the larger purposes of the law of God. The heart of the argument is that the "true Jews" are the just persons of every race. Whoever does the will of God from the heart is a proper Jew. Thus the claims of being superior that groups in Rome were holding over one another are defused.

Finally, in 3;1-9, Paul lists ten rhetorical questions. This structuring of the argument in groups of fives and tens indicates the degree to which he wishes to appeal to those who are loyal to the Hebrew tradition. He bases his case on the same Scripture, the same tradition, that is being perverted by religious pride in Rome. The Scripture is not at fault; human sin is.

The Citation of Scripture

Consistent with his effort to rest his case on the Scripture and tradition that have been perverted in Rome, Paul cites a number of scriptural passages in the section we are studying this week. A word of warning might be stated here. Finding the exact equivalent of the translation of Paul's citations in our translation of the Old Testament is difficult. Paul's citations come from the Greek translation of the Hebrew that had slight variations from the Hebrew. In some instances it now appears to textual critics that the Greek tradition of the Septuagint (Greek translation of the Old Testament) Paul was citing may well have been in existence in Hebrew at the time Paul wrote. Some of the Hebrew Old Testament evolved after the time of Paul's writing, and in several instances we can find examples of the rabbis altering the Hebrew text in a direction away from that which was being favored by Christian use.

At any event, it is important to see that Paul has the free attitude toward the Hebrew Scriptures that was characteristic of the other scholars of his time. Sometimes he quotes exactly from the Septuagint. At other times he changes the Scriptures, sometimes quite drastically, in order to fit his current circumstances. This freedom in dealing with the Old Testament shows that although the authority of the Old Testament was being maintained in the first century, it was not viewed in a literal sense. Paul is an advocate of a kind of spiritual interpretation of Scripture. He interprets Scripture in light of Christ. Thus when he finds an Old Testament quotation that is useful for his argument, he sometimes alters it in order to make that connection clearer.

The answer to question 3 of Dimension One shows that Paul has changed the quotation from Isaiah in Romans 2:24. In this instance the Septuagint had already expanded the Hebrew text by adding the phrases "because of you" and "among the Gentiles." In addition to this, Paul has rather drastically altered the original sense of this passage. In Romans 3:4, Paul is much closer to the Septuagint text of Psalm 51:4. From the long series of citations in Romans 3:10-18, I would like to lift up two examples for your class members' attention. The first is 3:10, where Paul has inserted the term *righteous* in order to relate it more closely with his theme that "the righteous will live by faith" (1:17). In the second example, 3:13, Paul uses a fairly literal citation from Psalm 5:9.

The Question-and-Answer Style

Recent advances have been made in our understanding of how Paul's first readers would have perceived the so-called "diatribe" style of 2:17–3:8. Question 2 in Dimension One deals with the "rhetorical questions" that Paul asks at one point that are typical of this style. Previous researchers felt that this was a combative debating style and that the audience was hostile. This view has been overturned by Stanley Kent Stowers in *The Diatribe and Paul's Letter to the Romans* (Scholars' Press, 1981). This professor from Brown University showed that the diatribe was widely used in the public schools of the Greco-Roman world and that its function was to allow the pros and cons about a given subject matter to come to the fore. This style was not used in controversial settings. The audience in this case is perceived to be friendly.

This discovery is significant in view of the long tradition of an anti-Semitic interpretation of these chapters. The fact that Paul is dealing with Jews has often led scholars to think that Paul is criticizing Judaism. But Paul is not dealing with unbelieving Jews at all in this section. He is addressing a friendly audience of the Christian community, which in this instance is made up of Jewish Christians as well as Gentile Christians. They would not have perceived these questions as hostile. Stowers writes, "The dialogical element of the diatribe does grow out of the argument or represents what is typical, but it is directed toward a specific group with which the teacher has a certain relationship. . . . The style is designed for those who have already made the basic commitment" (page 180).

The Issue of Religious Superiority

The major thrust of this passage is that claims of religious superiority must be refuted, no matter what their origin. Whereas the material in our last lesson dealt more directly with Gentile-Christian believers, the material in today's lesson deals with Jewish-Christian believers. The major challenge in presenting this material is to avoid falling into an anti-Semitic interpretation. Many commentaries that you might consult see Paul as arguing against Jews or Judaism in this passage. From the time of the Reformation, indeed nearly from the time when Christianity became the established religion in the Roman Empire, this view has been the major stream of Christian interpre-

tation. The presumed superiority of Christianity over Judaism is seen to be the purpose of Paul's argument. Nothing could be further from the point. This kind of interpretation simply leaves intact the very form of religious superiority that Paul is trying to overcome in Rome.

A major point to be made here is that Paul's targets are Christians and that the argument is a friendly one. Indeed, as we said earlier, Paul goes out of his way in the course of Romans to defend the prerogatives of Jewish Christians. Paul does not wish to attack Jewish culture or the Jewish religion. He wishes rather to make a case for the Roman house churches that the misuse of the great religious heritage of the Hebrew Scriptures is leading to serious disruptions in the life of the community and to the expression of sinful attitudes and acts among the Christian groups. When Paul lists the boasts of the Jews in 2:17-20, he is trying to describe the kind of pride and arrogance that was surfacing in the Jewish-Christian churches in Rome, not to make a general case against the Judaism of his day. The *you* in this argument is clearly the Jewish Christian.

Therefore, when you teach this material, you need to think through ways to relate the Scripture to modern expressions of religious superiority. I think of the feelings of superiority among denominations in the United States, for example. Many denominational conflicts in American history also have witnessed the expression of strong arguments based on the false notion of religious superiority. People having different views of the inspiration of Scripture or different attitudes toward abortion or toward military service have argued that their religious perception or their interpretation of Scripture is superior. They argue that they are saved and others are damned.

Paul's argument is aimed at overcoming this kind of situation. The argument needs to be recast to make it understandable in the modern world, and this task is one of the most important imaginative chores for the Christian teacher of Romans today.

The Question of Libertinism

In Romans 3:8, Paul deals with a notion that reflects a situation in the early church and in the later history of Christianity. The idea that one might well do evil that good may come, a perverse misunderstanding of Paul's doctrine of salvation by grace alone, is more than a humorous and malicious misstatement. Paul had dealt with a number of instances in the history of early Christianity when this kind of statement was being lived out. In the Thessalonian church, for example, the sense of membership in the new era and the powerful sense of spiritual change led people to reject the traditional family ethic, to repudiate the heritage of daily labor, and to resist the leadership that Paul had left behind in Thessalonica.

Even more serious were the problems that Paul faced in Corinth. A group of radicals who accepted Paul's doctrine of freedom from the law and spiritual maturity from Christ concluded that all ethics related to the body were now irrelevant. They lived the life of the mind, in their view, free from bodily restraints. In First Corinthians, Paul confronted the excesses of this group. Some of these people preferred sexual union with temple prostitutes to sex within marriage. One person in particular lived in an incestuous relationship. Paul's reference to this in 1 Corinthians 5:1-2 shows that the congregation was actually proud that this person felt free enough in Christ to be able to overcome the repulsion that Greeks would have felt about such a relationship. Many other incidents of this type are found in the Corinthian letters.

Similar examples of lawless and irresponsible behavior have been seen in later Christian tradition. Many times they come from the same kind of feeling of radical freedom and radical change. When one is struck by the force of the gospel, one recognizes the shortcomings of one's former life. One is torn from old loyalties and set free from the moral system connected with one's previous religious heritage. The experience of unconditional acceptance by grace brings a great sense of freedom and exaltation. When the manifestation of the Spirit surfaces, often converted persons have the feeling that they have truly transcended their past and even transcended the world. That one should have to submit to moral limitations and return to an old-fashioned-sounding law seems inappropriate. Furthermore, the freedom of emotions and the high sense of enthusiasm that are often connected with conversion of this sort leads to incredibly warm feelings toward other people, a feeling that sometimes can lead to promiscuity.

Most members of your class will likely identify promiscuous behavior with people who have not been converted. But Paul is dealing here with something that is not at all atypical of people who have undergone a radical conversion experience. Without perhaps consciously living out the logic of Romans 3:8, these persons unconsciously act out this libertinism. This behavior is one of the attendant dangers of a radical kind of Christian faith. In fact, the presence and danger of libertinism is what has led many established church leaders to resist the revivalistic spirit and to question charismatic events in general. Discuss this problem in terms of the experiences of class members. This discussion will help bring the reality of Paul's argument, not only at this point but also in later chapters, into clear focus. Paul is making a case for the kind of transformation that will allow a new and more responsible form of behavior to emerge rather than libertinism.

Works of the Law

Read and discuss Romans 3:20 with the class members. This verse is foundational for the next section of the argument of Romans. Instead of *declared righteous*, use *rightwised*. It is important for the class members to see how this verse relates directly to the thesis of Romans in 1:17.

When Paul refers to "observing the law," he has in mind the kind of works that the Roman house churches were using to prove that each was superior to the others. When people do what the law requires for the wrong reasons, performing acts of mercy and keeping a religious community afloat for the purpose of proving their superiority to others, they fall under the condemnation of this verse.

Paul is dealing here with the most dangerous of Christian vices, self-righteousness. Self-righteousness is the root of Christian arrogance and often is the fundamental cause of conflicts among Christian groups. The problem is that persons and groups use their conformity to a certain standard to try to make themselves "righteous." The whole purpose of Paul's argument from 1:18 on is to prove that this cannot work, that this effort is a form of sinful pride, an effort on the part of creatures to make themselves into the Creator, to gain control of their destiny, and to dominate others.

Paul is forced to make a sweeping and hard case, climaxing in 3:20, because he was confronting the kind of conflicts that would later become characteristic of Christian groups, namely self-righteous groups on the right and left claiming their superiority over others, believing that others are damned or lost. The self-righteous were acting in such a way as to disallow leadership or contributions by others. Paul's hope is to lead the congregation to see that this terrible perversion of the Christian faith was based on the kind of lie to which Romans 1:25 referred. Whereas the Christian groups in Rome felt certain that they were elect and secure, that they were certainly saved, Paul offers a forceful medicine of reality therapy in this argument, ending in 3:20: "No one will be declared righteous [rightwised] in [God's] sight by observing the law."

The conclusion of the first phase of Paul's argument, 1:18–3:20, comes in the last two verses. Paul insists that every person loyal to the Hebrew Scriptures must accept the judgment in those Scriptures (3:19). Paul wants to establish a universal kind of accountability. His hope is to lead the Roman house churches to recognize that "no one will be declared righteous [*rightwised*] in [God's] sight by observing the law." The thesis that Paul has established in 1:17 comes here to its appropriate development. Until human beings give up the claim that they are righteous in and of themselves and that they are superior to others, they will not be in a position to understand that God's righteousness comes as a gift, that forgiveness is free, and that faith is the basis of a true life.

DIMENSION THREE: WHAT DOES THE BIBLE MEAN TO ME?

The Issue of Religious Superiority

The issue of religious and cultural superiority is going to make little sense unless it is connected with modern developments. You might think of squabbles among Christians in your local community. You might recollect recent national conventions by major denominations in which conflicts between conservatives and liberals surfaced in prominent ways. You might think of the splits between denominations or between factions in local churches. You might also think of tensions between the major world religions that have surfaced in the Middle East. An important task is to allow the class members' imaginations and their observation of current events to lead them to see that we are all involved in one way or another in the human tendency to make ourselves superior—especially with our religion.

The Issue of Libertinism

The question of thinking through experiences of libertinism is an important one at this stage if the next chapters of Romans are going to make sense. You might think of examples of persons whose powerful religious feelings lead them to believe that normal standards of behavior should be abandoned. Bombers or persons involved in crimes for political or religious advantage often perform acts that their religious heritage would not condone. But they do so in the belief that they are loyal to the higher cause, that they will be forgiven, and that grace will cover whatever they do. These actions are as typical in modern Shiite behavior as they have been at times in Christian tradition.

No One Has an Advantage Over Anybody

Paul seems to be presenting a paradox when he insists that the Jewish advantage of the law must be maintained while still insisting that all persons, both Jews and Gentiles, have sinned and that no one has an advantage over anybody else. Paul argues this way, not only because of the problems in Rome among the house churches but also because of his understanding of the cross event. That the religious elite of the first century worked with the political leaders to put Jesus to death was a clear indication for Paul of the underlying hostility against God. Paul is inclined to believe that this plight is a universal one. It extends beyond the religious elite of his tradition to every person on earth. So convinced is Paul about this basic revelation of human hostility that he is willing to allow elements of contradiction to enter his argument. He will not give up the other side of the paradox, however, that the Jewish law must be maintained and that the Hebrew Scriptures retain their authority for Christians.

The Issue of Universal Depravity

A major resource for your consideration of this issue might be the work of theologians such as Reinhold Niebuhr, whose great book *The Nature and Destiny of Man* deals with the doctrine of sin. Many other books in more recent times have suggested the psychological and moral significance of this argument. At a time when American culture is having difficulty coming to terms with its own sense of limits and has failed to recognize in any meaningful way the sins that it has committed in its recent history, we recognize the serious social dangers of a society that loses a sense of limits. A doctrine of universal sin helps persons and cultures recognize limits. Until we see the places we have gone wrong, we cannot recognize that we are not superior.

When serious thinkers look about the world, they are sometimes inclined to say that the only Christian doctrine that can be fully proved by objective experience and observation is the doctrine of universal sin. Whatever side the members of your class choose to take on this question, point out the relevance of the issue for the Roman house church situation. Paul can hardly make a case for the Christians in Rome being equal in grace until he can first make a case that they are equal in sin. For, so long as they feel superior and sinless as compared to their competitors, they are unable to grasp the fact that they are all recipients at the same table, sharers of the same unmerited grace. Paul's argument aims at that practical goal.

In this and many other instances keep the same openness with class members that is reflected in the question-and-answer technique Paul uses. Questions and answers allow members of the class to work out their beliefs. This and other teaching techniques will encourage them to come to their own conclusions, to use their own mental energies to evaluate and assess the flow of the argument. Allowing disagreements on crucial issues like this to remain unresolved can be an important step in the direction of recognizing the universality of grace and the pluralism of a genuine Christian community. Everyone does not have to agree with every aspect of Paul's argument in Romans.

It was not through law that Abraham and his offspring received the promise . . . but through the righteousness that comes by faith (4:13).

—6—

Faith and Abraham's Children

Romans 3:21–4:25

DIMENSION ONE:
WHAT DOES THE BIBLE SAY?

Answer these questions by reading Romans 3:21–4:25

1. Assuming that *justify, righteous,* and *righteousness* are translations of the same Greek term, mark and count the number of times these words are used in 3:21–4:25.

   These words are used eighteen times, with at least one instance in which the term is translated two different ways in the same sentence: (1) 3:21; (2) 3:22; (3) 3:24; (4) 3:26; (5) 3:28; (6) 3:30; (7) 4:2; (8): 4:3; (9 and 10) 4:5; (11) 4:6; (12) 4:9; (13 and 14) 4:11; (15) 4:13; (16) 4:22; (17) 4:24; (18) 4:25.

2. Since *faith* and *believe* are translations of the same Greek term, mark and count the number of times these terms are used in 3:21–4:25.

   These two words are used twenty-four times, including two instances in which the term is translated both ways in the same sentence: (1 and 2) 3:22; (3) 3:25; (4) 3:26; (5) 3:27; (6) 3:28; (7 and 8) 3:30; (9) 3:31; (10) 4:3; (11) 4:5; (12) 4:9; (13 and 14) 4:11; (15) 4:12; (16) 4:13; (17) 4:14; (18 and 19) 4:16; (20) 4:17; (21) 4:18; (22) 4:19; (23) 4:20; (24) 4:24.

3. What proportion of the human race does Paul say has sinned? (3:23)

   Paul says that "all [100 percent] have sinned."

4. Does Paul say God belongs more to the Jews or to the Gentiles? (3:29)

   Paul says that God is the God of the Jews and "of Gentiles too."

5. What two important words does Paul retain in quoting Genesis 15:6? (4:3; see also Genesis 15:6)

Paul uses the words believed *and* righteousness *in describing Abraham. The same words are used in Genesis 15:6.*

6. When does Paul say that Abraham received circumcision? (4:9-12)

   Abraham received circumcision after his "faith was credited to him as righteousness."

7. Who inherits the promise given to Abraham? (4:16)

   Everyone who has faith is an inheritor of Abraham's promise, according to Paul's argument.

8. Mark the verses where the theme of giving life to the dead is developed. (4:17-25)

   Paul develops the theme of bringing life from death in 4:17; 4:19; 4:24; and 4:25.

DIMENSION TWO:
WHAT DOES THE BIBLE MEAN?

Romans 3:21-28 is the "heart of Romans." In this section Paul makes his marvelous declaration of salvation by faith alone. Here he proclaims freedom from the principle of performance. The righteousness of God in this passage is perceived as God's victory over sin, as shown in the Christ event. This victory transforms humans by making them acceptable to God, despite their failures, despite their rebellion. The setting right of the human race, through the death of Christ, conveys to us the grace of God, which we can never earn. Our lives no longer depend on what we are able to perform, on our obedience to the law. Salvation is understood here as the faithful response of humans to the love of God, as shown in the Christ event.

"Justification by faith" is a matter of being set right by this unconditional love of God, of being restored to the original righteousness that humans were intended to have from the moment of their creation. To stand under this righteousness is to become righteous. "Justification by faith" is also understood by Paul as entering the sphere of divine righteousness, that is, submitting to the lordship of Christ. Thus salvation in this passage is more than feeling accepted. It is a matter of submitting to this righteousness in everyday affairs.

In this lesson we deal with the final two sections of the main proof that supports the thesis in Romans 1:16-17. In 3:21-31, Paul states the positive argument concerning humans being "rightwised" by faith in the one true God. In 4:1-25, Paul sets forth Abraham as the example of such faith and the forebearer of all faithful persons. The key term in these final two sections is "rightwising," often translated, as we have discovered, as "justification" or "justify." As the first question in Dimension One has indicated, these terms are used no less than eighteen times in 3:21–4:25. Going through these passages and marking these terms will help identify one of the main themes of the section and will review the confusion about how this term should be translated. This reading will also aid the members of your class in seeing the way the material in this section connects with earlier material, particularly with the thesis of 1:17.

The Argument in Romans 3:21–4:25

The abstract quality of Paul's thought in 3:21-31 often leads people to concentrate on individual sentences rather than on the flow of the argument. Perhaps this way of reading is inevitable, but as a teacher you should have a sense of the way the argument as a whole is flowing. In the first phase of the argument, Paul states the major thesis in 21-22a. Verses 22b-26 interpret this thesis, insisting that no distinction can be made between Jews and Gentiles because all have fallen short. Therefore "rightwising" can only be achieved as a gift. This gift is then proved by the citation of a series of traditional confessional statements regarding the significance of Christ and his redeeming act of life and death.

In 3:27-31 the doctrine is discussed with questions and answers. If we can be justified only by faith, then our capacity to boast in our accomplishments under the law is eliminated. Paul restates the reason that this is so by putting forth the idea of "rightwising" by faith alone (3:27).

A second topic concerning the priority of Jews and Gentiles is taken up in 3:29-30, where the oneness of God is related to the doctrine of the justification of Jews and Gentiles by faith alone. In verse 31 a third brief dialogue is begun concerning the status of the law. Several points are stated here that are not fully developed until later chapters of Romans, principally Romans 7.

In Romans 4:1-8, Abraham is shown to be the forebearer of the faithful because he was accepted on the basis of his faith rather than on the basis of his accomplishments. In this section the primary and secondary texts are developed that dominate the rest of this chapter. The primary text is Genesis 15:6. The secondary text is Psalm 32:1-2, which indicates that the blessing comes only to sinners, to those who have not worked to accomplish the law.

Romans 4:9-12 makes the point that Abraham's justification occurred prior to the gift of the law and his own circumcision. Paul makes use here of the rabbinic tradition inferred from the Book of Genesis that circumcision occurred several years after Abraham's promise. Faith precedes the law, and circumcision is seen merely as a confirmation of being "rightwised" by faith.

Romans 4:13-25 shows Abraham's promise as having been fulfilled only according to faith. First, Paul makes the point that the promise given to him was not bound by law. Verse 15 suggests that since law provides the basis of measuring guilt, it produces wrath instead of life. Paul goes on in verses 17-22 to show that Abraham, as the ancestor of faithful Gentiles, responded to God and set his faith in the promise given by the one who "gives life to the dead." Since their heir could not have been provided by human means alone, Abraham had to trust in the Creator who brings something out of nothing.

Finally, in 4:23-25, Paul relates the entire argument to the present status of faithful Christians. The promise of being a child of Abraham comes to all faithful persons. The faith of Christians in the resurrected Jesus is therefore the proper fulfillment of the faith in God who gives life to the dead.

Defining Faith

As your class members will have observed in answering the second question in Dimension One, *faith* is really a crucial term in this passage, being used twenty-four times. It will come as something of a surprise, however, to the members of your class to discover that the Greek term is translated sometimes as "belief" and other times as "faith." The reason for this is that the word *faith* cannot be used as a verb in English. We can speak of *belief* and *believing*, but we do not ordinarily speak of *faith* and *faithing*. The awkwardness of using an expression like "having faith" has led the English translation tradition to separate *faith* from *belief*. The difficulty is that *belief* implies objective dogmas held by the mind. Very often the word *faith* has something of the same content, but in actuality its original significance is that of loyal response to a covenant partner. The analogy of being faithful to one's marriage vows brings us much closer to the biblical content that is needed for this term.

A prominent commentator on Romans defines *faith* this way: "Faith is basically human receptivity, as actively as it may express itself in obedience." Receptivity refers to the human response to God's word, which fits very closely into the context of Romans, where the power of the gospel is the guiding theme.

Suggest to the members of your class that they brainstorm on the current meanings of *faith* and *belief*. Discussing these alternatives in an open way will help bring the problem to consciousness and provide resources for the members of your class to distinguish between Paul's view and that of later Christian tradition.

For the sake of understanding what Paul is driving at in Romans, I think we need to abandon the translation of this term as "belief." Paul is not referring to a set of abstract ideas but rather to a relationship. It is the belief side of the Christian faith that was in dispute in Rome and that was leading the house churches to their vicious struggle against one another. Paul is hoping to unify them by offering an approach to faith that is relational. It is a matter of each person setting his or her trust in the Lord, thus submitting to the righteousness of God. I think that the most adequate expression of faith as used in Romans is "loyal response to God's word."

Romans 3:24-25. A number of scholars agree today that the material in these verses did not all originate with Paul. The content of these verses is unparalleled in the Pauline writings. While Paul speaks often, as we have discovered, about grace and "rightwising," he does not otherwise use language such as that found in these verses. The grammatical awkwardness of these verses and the stylistic differences from the rest of Paul's writings have led scholars to suggest that Paul is citing material from early Christian hymns and confessions. The cited material is interspersed with Pauline interpretation.

You might want to underline in your Bible the material that scholars feel is quoted. In that way you can easily identify the material that Paul apparently added. In verse 25, the words "God presented him as a sacrifice of atonement, through faith in his blood" should be underlined. Also, the words "because in his forbearance he had left the sins committed beforehand unpunished" should be underlined. Some scholars would also add a line from verse 24 to this list of underlined material: "through the redemption that came by Christ Jesus." Although Paul uses the term *redemption* in several other places in his writings, it is certainly not used very often; and this may be an indication that he is citing an early hymn or confession at this point as well.

Many commentaries debate the proper interpretation of these terms and in many instances prefer one over the other. Radical Lutheran theology, for example, sees the language of "rightwising" by faith that Paul integrates into this passage as simply unequal with the atonement thinking of faith in Christ's blood. Conservative commentators feel more strongly about some of these terms than others, and liberal commentators often redefine terms to make them more palatable.I think it is highly significant, however, that Paul cites these various theories, uses these terms with respect, and is able to integrate them with his own language concerning "rightwising" and faith. A quick look at your text of 3:24-26 shows the degree to which Pauline language has encircled, infused, and incorporated these other materials.

Paul gives no hint of argument here.In contrast to many commentators that feel Paul was "correcting" the more primitive Atonement theories that he cites, it appears to me from the fusion he has created that he has tried to incorporate, authenticate, and validate the theories that were in debate in the house churches in Rome. Paul is making a case in Romans for the coexistence of conservative and liberal branches of early Christianity.

Keep in mind what Paul was trying to accomplish as you present this material to your class members. Be sure to honor the differences in taste and theological perception of the members of your class, some of whom will find more meaning in some of these terms than in others. Perhaps a similar analogy can be found in your preferred hymnal, which probably incorporates hymns from a variety of perspectives into the same collection, thereby honoring a variety of theological attitudes and traditions.

Romans 4:16-25. One of the most striking features of 4:16-25 is the correlation between faith and resurrection. Paul sees the faith of Abraham as faith in God, who can create something out of nothing. Abraham believed that God was capable of creating a son even though Abraham and his wife were far past the age when this was physically possible. God as the Creator is affirmed in the fragment of confessional material that Paul uses in 4:17. The rough transition in verse 17, expressed by the dash in the middle of the verse in the NIV, indicates the use of liturgical or confessional material.

"Calls things that are not as though they were" (4:17) sounds very much like the Creation theology of Hellenistic Judaism and early Christianity in which God is the one who creates out of nothing. The interest in the question of what was there before Creation and the matter of God creating out of nothing was distinctively Greek. But Paul adapts it here to the Abraham story in a unique way. Abraham's faith is defined as faith in the God who raises the dead. This allows Paul to connect Creation theology with the Christ event, as he does in 4:24-25.

Paul also correlates salvation by faith alone with belief in the Christ event, in particular, belief in the death and resurrection of Christ. Salvation as experienced by early Christians was itself a new creation. It was experienced as the destruction of an old world and the creation of a whole new self. Under grace, persons were able to acknowledge that their former lives had indeed been nothing but that God had been able to create out of that nothing, out of that void of sin and depravity, a new life and a new future. Ernst Kaesemann, in his *Commentary on Romans* (Eerdmans, 1980), makes the clearest sense out of this point:

> As hardly anywhere else the full radicalness of Paul's doctrine of justification is brought out here. When the message of this justification is accepted, there is unavoidably linked with it a reduction to nothing which deeply shakes the righteous by associating them with the ungodly (page 123).

The key sentence in 4:25 connects the life, death, and resurrection of Christ and the transformation of humans into the new righteousness. Christ died "for our sins" in the sense that humans discovered their own hostility against

God in the death of Jesus. In that death we recognize the depth of human alienation and sin. But we recognize at the same time that we are forgiven at the very moment of Christ's death. He died for the sake of others, guiltlessly, dying in their place so that they might have communicated to them the surpassing grace of God. Since Christ was "raised to life for our justification [rightwising]," Paul is affirming that in the Resurrection the death of Christ was revealed. The theme of dying and rising with Christ, which will be developed in Romans 6, is first expressed here.

Under the power of the Christ event, we recognize that our former lives were null and void and that we have the possibility to share in his resurrection by receiving a new life based on grace rather than on our own accomplishments. For Abraham is indeed the forebearer of the faithful of all generations and all times.

DIMENSION THREE: WHAT DOES THE BIBLE MEAN TO ME?

Romans 3:21-31—Experience of Transformation

Since the material in this lesson, particularly 3:21-31, is so widely perceived to be the heart of Romans and therefore most directly related to salvation, class members may have a wide range of experiences to bring to bear on the passage. If you are able to, this would be a good opportunity to talk about their experience of transformation and conversion and their experiences of the lack of satisfaction in life gained from "observing the law."

Protestants and Roman Catholics on Justification

Christians have struggled for centuries to define what righteousness by faith means. Roman Catholics have consistently maintained that a radical doctrine of justification by faith undercuts the moral transformation required of Christians. Protestants have alleged that Roman Catholic insistence on moral transformation makes up "works righteousness," which is the opposite of genuine faith. A proper understanding of this passage, particularly Romans 3:21-31, would help show the common ground between Protestants and Roman Catholics at this point. It is interesting in this connection that the joint Lutheran-Roman Catholic consultation in 1983 issued an agreement on this point, namely that "salvation rests entirely upon God's merciful action in Christ." The long study released in the fall of 1983 attempts to lay aside the misunderstandings and allegations that have divided Protestants from Roman Catholics on this point for so long.

One aspect of Paul's argument has a particular bearing on this struggle, namely the issue in 3:27 concerning *boasting*. The term relates to the universal human tendency to compete with others and to claim superior status. The problem with the medieval use of indulgences and the system of penitence, Luther charged, was that it encour-

aged boasting. Boasting is the essence of sin, the reformers taught, because it expresses human rebellion against God. The fall of the human race had consisted in wanting to be like God, capable of boasting; and the essence of false religion, of works, was its boast: "I have performed better than you, therefore I am deserving of God's grace."

The leveling effect of Protestantism is directly related to this insight. If no human should boast of accomplishments, then no one has any claim to be any better than others. All persons are equal before God. Hence the class system is wrong, and every system of privilege should be dismantled. The logic of the radical doctrine of justification by faith inevitably runs toward radical equalization of human honor. Therefore the Protestant impulse is expressed in terms of liberation—of slaves, of industrial workers, of immigrants, of women, of the mentally and physically impaired, and so on and on.

What an irony, however, that this firm grasp of the danger of boasting should have been expressed in ways that led into new forms of boasting. Protestants have boasted that their theology was closer to Paul than that of Roman Catholics. Their boast included criticisms of Roman Catholics that, in effect, placed Roman Catholics with the Pharisees, outside the Christian faith itself.

Central to Paul's argument is the "principle of faith" that is stated in 3:28. Here is the formula that marked the most decisive attack on Roman Catholic theology during the Reformation. Some of the confessions of the Protestants included the expression "apart from works of the law," which became the basis of Protestant orthodoxy. The idea was that humans are acceptable to God solely on the basis of faith, not on the basis of whether they had performed works.

The good news in this verse lies at the heart of the Christian faith. This good news is that no matter how badly we have erred, no matter how far we have fallen from our calling to the disciplined life, no matter how unpopular we are, God loves and accepts us. Nothing we can ever accomplish on our own can provide us this acceptance. One of the thrilling aspects of current church history is that Protestants and Roman Catholics are united in affirming this central point.

The possibility of misunderstanding this gift, however, was there from the beginning; and it has caused suffering, death, and division. The word *faith* tended to be taken by Protestants and Roman Catholics alike as a set of beliefs rather than as a living relationship. Christians tended to infer that if you held a different set of beliefs, you could not gain salvation. For Protestants, "justification by faith" began to be understood as "justification by belief." And a new form of boasting arose: "I am better than you because I have the right beliefs." Roman Catholics, in contrast, held that this kind of radical belief was morally depraved. The boasting of one side came to be counterbalanced by the boasting of the other. In the process the unity of the church was shattered, and the peace of the world was mortally threatened. We see the battle still going on in Northern Ireland.

One of the features of Paul's argument in Romans 3:21-31 that has been overlooked thus far in the discussion between Protestants and Roman Catholics is that of the oneness of God. The relevance of this idea could hardly be grasped when Protestants and Roman Catholics were so confident that they possessed God in their formulas. I think the psychology of both sides has long led to an unthinking assumption that we have "the one God" on our side. We fight and torture our enemies in the name of that "one God."

Recent advances in our understanding of the Book of Romans make it clear how mistaken this view is. We know that Paul stressed the oneness of God to counter the exclusive claims of first-century liberals and conservatives, comparable to modern Protestants and Roman Catholics in some ways. Halvor Moxnes has made this clear in his study *Theology in Conflict: Studies in Paul's Understanding of God in Romans* (Brill, 1980). Paul's purpose in this section was to address "the problem of divisions between Jews and non-Jews within Christian communities. . . . In this con-text, 'God is one' served as an argument for the inclusion and co-existence of both Jews and non-Jews in the same community, on the basis of faith" (page 223). Moxnes points out that the argument in these verses concerning the oneness of God as God of the circumcised as well as of the uncircumcised constituted "a conscious effort to include" the less popular Jewish Christians in a hostile Gentile-Christian majority in Rome. The confession that "God is one" was originally meant to unify the Christian community.

When we apply this insight to the longstanding struggle between Protestants and Roman Catholics, we see how dangerous the doctrine of justification by faith was when combined with the belief that God takes sides, that God will oppose any whose definition is different from ours. This makes God into a human possession. It presumes that the God defined in our doctrines is the true and only God. God thus becomes the captive of our theological "work." And this is idolatry. To use Paul's language in this passage, it is a return to "boasting." To claim that God is on our side is this most terrible human mistake of identifying the one true God with our own little causes. In contrast, Paul contends, "God is one."

For just as through the disobedience of the one man the many were made sinners, so also through the obedience of the one man the many will be made righteous (5:19).

7

God's Peace and Adam's Realm

Romans 5

DIMENSION ONE:
WHAT DOES THE BIBLE SAY?

Answer these questions by reading Romans 5

1. Which comes first, justification or peace with God? (5:1)

   The gift of justification or righteousness by faith brings with it peace with God.

2. In contrast to the negative view of boasting in Romans 3:27, what are some proper objects of boasting or rejoicing? (5:2, 3, 11)

   Paul describes three things that believers can rejoice in: "the hope of the glory of God" (5:2), sufferings (5:3), and God (5:11).

3. How many times does Paul use the words *righteous, righteousness, justified,* and *justification* (all translated from the same Greek term) in 5:1-21?

   Paul uses these words nine times in Romans 5: (1) 5:1; (2) 5:7; (3) 5:9; (4) 5:16; (5) 5:17; (6) and (7) 5:18; (8) 5:19; (9) 5:21.

4. How is the love of God shown to humans? (5:5, 8)

   God's love is "poured out . . . into our hearts by the Holy Spirit" and shown in Christ's death for sinners.

5. Which experience is reserved for the future—being "reconciled," "saved," or "rightwised/justified"? (5:9-11)

   "Justified [rightwised] by his blood" is linked with a present tense verb and thus is portrayed as a current experience for believers. Being "reconciled" is linked with past and present tense verbs. Only being "saved" is in the future tense (verses 9 and 10), so being "saved" is an expectation still to come.

6. With whom does Paul say that death originated? (5:12-14)

   Paul says that death came into the world through the sin of Adam.

7. How many comparisons between Adam and Christ does Paul make in 5:15-21?

   Paul makes five distinct comparisons in these verses, each worked out in a different manner: (1) 5:15; (2) 5:16; (3) 5:17; (4) 5:18; (5) 5:19.

DIMENSION TWO:
WHAT DOES THE BIBLE MEAN?

The relation of Romans 5 to the rest of the argument of the letter has been clarified in recent decades. Earlier scholars under the impact of the Reformation point of view tended to place this chapter with the first four chapters under the general heading of "justification." One can see the reason for doing this in light of the opening and closing verses of Romans 5, both of which emphasize "rightwising."

A similar kind of division of Romans was popular in nineteenth-century German scholarship, which tended to place Romans 6–8 under the heading of a mystical-ethical doctrine of salvation, while placing 1–5 under the category of a forensic doctrine of salvation. Recent commentators, however, have placed Romans 5 and 6–8 as is done in this study. Within this framework, Romans 5:1-11 has an introductory role in the series of amplifications of Paul's basic argument that we find in Chapters 5–8. In particular, we see themes in 5:12-21, 6:1-23, and 8:1-39 introduced for the first time in 5:1-11. The restored relationship with God marked by peace provides the basis for future salvation despite all present sufferings. The paradoxical state of the new life is developed throughout Romans 5–8, in that the peaceful relationship with God and fellow humans is set in the context of a world in which the "principalities" and "powers" are very much present and effective. Christian realism is at the forefront of this passage.

The Artistic Structure of Romans 5:1-11

The role of this passage as a kind of hinge between the first and second sections of the formal argument of Romans is enhanced by the structure that Paul provides. The people in the Greco-Roman world were much more sensitive than we are to the way an argument is structured. They took particular delight in *chiastic* patterns in which the themes of an argument are crossed and reproduced in reverse order. We find a clear chiastic structure between the opening and closing verses of 5:1-11. In the first three verses the theme of "peace with God" is followed by the theme of rejoicing in hope and affliction. These themes reappear in reverse order in 5:11, which opens with rejoicing in God and closes on the theme of peace in the form of "reconciliation." The ancient audience of Romans would have felt at verse 11 a satisfying sense that the section has been rounded off and completed in an artful manner.

The "Eschatological Reservation"

At several points in Romans 5, we encounter what scholars of the last generation called the "eschatological reservation or proviso," an insistence that the final form of Christian fulfillment will take place only at the end of time. We find this proviso for the first time in 5:2 in which "the hope of the glory of God" is placed in the context of future hope rather than present experience. Even more clearly we see this in verses 9 and 10 where "rightwising" and reconciliation are contrasted with the future salvation. We see the same kind of contrast in 5:17 and 6:8.

Likely, Paul makes this distinction in order to insert a note of realism into early Christian enthusiasts. These persons believed that, with the dawn of the new era and the gift of the Spirit, they were already participating in the resurrected life. This belief implied that troubles would be completely eliminated and that evil had been overcome. Paul's contention in Chapters 5–8 is that the Christian life must be lived out against the threats of a still-fallen world. He does not wish to deny that regeneration has already occurred and that the new life is presently available. What the "reservation" implies, however, is that the fulfillment is yet to come. The Christian life makes no sense in the context of troubles and afflictions without the principle of hope. Any Christian who loses sight of this will remain terribly vulnerable in times of persecution and natural disaster. The peace that we have with God sustains us through persecution and trouble; it does not relieve us from them.

The Puzzle of Romans 5:12

This verse contains one of Paul's incomplete sentences, which mark particularly difficult and paradoxical parts of his argument. The incomplete quality of his sentence is somewhat disguised by the New International Version and other modern translations. They fail to provide a capital letter for the first word of verse 13, which would indicate that it is indeed a separate and independent sentence.

Verse 12 begins as the first half of an elaborate comparison, but the comparison is never completed. The first sections of this sentence present a thoroughly deterministic view of sin and death as caused by the first humans, Adam and Eve. But in light of the earlier argument in Romans, Paul is not content with this traditional and despairing determinism. Having argued so vigorously in 1:18–2:29 for free responsibility, Paul wishes to insist upon it here as well. Thus the final three words of verse 12 state the other half of the paradox: "because all sinned." It has been suggested that the paradox itself caused Paul's sentence to break off in midstream. At any event, the incompleteness of this sentence marks a significant issue within Pauline theology, an issue that class members may wish to discuss in some detail.

An important question is whether Paul advocates the traditional Christian doctrine of "original sin," which Augustine stated so eloquently much later in Christian history. Augustine's theory and the one accepted by Roman Catholic theology through most of Christian history is that the sin of the first humans was related to sexual desire. Original sin in this sense is carried forward by the sex act itself so that each person born from human sexuality carries the infection of human sin. This doctrine sustains the high value placed on the virgin birth and the immaculate conception of the virgin Mary in modern Roman Catholic dogma. It is also related to the ideal of a celibate priesthood.

Paul's writings give no hint that he interpreted sin as related to human sexuality. In fact, he had a more positive attitude toward the human body than much of Western Christianity has had. Therefore we should more appropriately describe Paul's view as that of "universal sin." He was convinced, in light of the Christ event, that all humans are involved in rebellion against God and that everyone stands in need of forgiveness. In 5:12-21 he develops the idea that Adam, as the first human, brought such sin into the world and became an effective power for subsequent world history. This view was widely shared in first-century Judaism. But Paul is unwilling to follow this determinist line through to the end. He wishes at the same time to maintain that each human is responsible for his or her own sin. Hence the addition of the paradoxical line in 5:12 concerning all humans sinning of their own free will.

The content of verse 12 gives you an opportunity to let class members voice various attitudes toward sin and the universality of evil. Some members will likely have a much stronger affinity for the final three words of 5:12 than for the preceding theme of the universality of sin after Adam. Either side of this paradox has strong Christian support. That sin is universally binding seems to be confirmed by observing the human scene. Yet if we take this idea alone, it can undercut individual responsibility for sin. Ethics and the law require individual accountability that the social causation theories of sin in their modern forms tend to undermine.

The strength of the voluntaristic view of sin is that it stresses human accountability. Its weakness is that it often is connected with an overly rosy appraisal of human perfectibility. And this view finds it difficult to account for the social poison that seems to influence the great bulk of persons in negative directions. Perhaps a serious discussion of this age-old problem in your class will increase appreciation for Paul's somewhat illogical and paradoxical solution. It is more than mere inconsistency. Paul, in light of the Christ event and loyal to his biblical tradition, wishes to affirm both the universality of sin and human accountability.

The Identity of "The One to Come"

Most commentators have assumed that the "one to come" in verse 14 refers to Christ and that Paul is preparing for the contrast between Adam and Christ in the next verses. This identification causes problems, however, because Paul does not really argue that Adam and Christ are similar. Those who hold this view are forced to build more contrast into this verse than Paul actually states.

Another approach may be suggested if members of your class raise this question, and that approach is to identify the "coming one" with Moses, who is also mentioned in verse 14. The contrast between Adam and Moses is basic to this sentence, and in a very real sense Adam prefigures Moses because both stood in Jewish theology in clear relationship to the law. The main point of verse 14 is that sin is intrinsically related to death, a point that Paul made with other argumentative means in Romans 1. In the Genesis story death was perceived to have come with Adam, but death also marks the rest of the history of Israel and the present time as well. Paul believes that this reign of death also pertains "over those who did not sin by breaking a command, as did Adam"; that is, persons who allow other forms of sin and rebellion are likewise under the power of death. From this wording we see that Paul is not advocating the idea that everyone exactly model his or her behavior after that of Adam. The element of free will, which we noted at the end of verse 12, manifests itself here as well.

The Image of Adam in Ancient Judaism

The members of your class may be interested in gaining a fuller picture of the way the figure of Adam was understood in the Judaism of Paul's time. A double interest surfaces in the literature of the intertestamental period and of early Judaism. On the one hand, Adam is the one who originated sin for the human race and caused death to reign. On the other hand, he is the one who had a true relationship with God, bearing God's image.

The idea of Adam as originating death, causing the corruption of human life, and beginning the era of sin that sweeps over all humankind is widely affirmed in the Jewish tradition. One writer speaks of Adam as the one on whom the commandment was placed; "but he transgressed it, and immediately you [God] appointed death for him and for his descendants" (4 Ezra 3:7). That humans were immortal before the Fall is also widely assumed. One writer says that "from a woman sin had its beginning / and because of her we all die" (Sirach 25:24). That the flood of evils afflicting humankind derives from Adam is also widely affirmed. Disease, mental anxiety, and murder and other moral sins are all seen as caused by the inaugurating sin of Adam.

Other writings of Judaism, however, affirm very strongly human responsibility for sin in a way that is quite similar to Paul. Second Baruch 54:15-16, 19 states the following: "For, although Adam sinned first and has brought death upon all who were not in his time, yet each of them who has been born from him has prepared for himself the coming torment. And further, each of them has chosen for himself the coming glory. . . . Adam is, therefore, not the cause, except only for himself, but each of us has become our own Adam."

The image of the exalted Adam also is quite widely shared in ancient Judaism so that there was substantial basis for understanding Christ as a kind of second Adam. The idea that Adam was the image of the humanity God intended in creation, a humanity that would be restored at the end of time, began to arise. When this occurred, of course, the role of Adam as the bringer of death and the originator of human sin tended to be downplayed. Several writers, in fact, suggested other explanations, blaming the Fall on Eve or Satan or the fallen angels. Sometimes Adam is shown as the first king, and in other instances the glory of Adam is emphasized. One writer refers to Adam as a creature "honorable, great, and glorious" (2 Enoch 30:11). I have found many affirmations of the idea that with the coming of the kingdom of God, true believers will regain the glory that Adam lost. Later rabbinic writers made a great deal of the glory of Adam and the wisdom that he showed. Prominent also was the idea of the gigantic body of Adam in which God created each subsequent person on earth.

Compared with these traditions, it is striking how sober and limited the role of Adam is in Romans 5. Paul uses Adam to contrast the world of sin with the world of salvation. Paul apparently wished to make plain that every person has to choose between Adam and Christ. To fall back into pride, arrogance, and self-will is to fall under the power of death once again. This choice had a direct bearing on the Roman house churches, which needed to understand the depth of sinfulness that was manifesting itself in their behavior. The promise of abundant grace and the "gift of righteousness" (5:17) needed to be cherished and lived out.

In a sense each Christian needs to recognize that the "old Adam" threatens to surface. The promise of the new life is heightened by its contrast to the old. As Robin Scroggs writes in *The Last Adam* (Fortress Press, 1966), "In order to speak of death Paul has to refer to Adam's sin; yet his major goal is to show that what lies ahead for the believer is the restoration of life, the life which had been God's intent for Adam. It is no accident that the section ends in verse 21 with an exultant affirmation of the gift of eternal life through Christ" (page 82).

DIMENSION THREE: WHAT DOES THE BIBLE MEAN TO ME?

The questions raised in the student book for this lesson point to personal experience in a large way. In order to make the abstract but powerful argument in Romans 5 understandable, it needs to be brought into relation to everyday experience. The critical judgment of the members of the class is also required at a number of points. In addition to this, two types of resources are suggested to bring out the meaning of this text.

The Relevance of African American Spirituals

The sense of experiencing faith in the midst of a world of affliction and suffering is supremely embodied in the traditional African American spirituals. The remarkable sense of rejoicing in our sufferings (5:3) is found in the well-known song "Nobody Knows the Trouble I See." This spiritual conveys the strong sense of identification with Jesus, who shares our troubles and bears our sins (5:8). Because of the certainty of the presence of God's love and the experience of it in the worship service (5:5), we have the possibility of rejoicing in the midst of suffering. The theme of this song is very close to the theme of Romans 5.

The significance of hope in the experience of suffering is also particularly prominent in the African American spirituals. Without such hope, affliction becomes impossible to bear. It destroys one's humanity.

The search for a firm relationship that will sustain one through suffering reflects the concern for "perseverance" and "character" referred to in Romans 5:4. The result of such a profound relationship with God as portrayed in the African American spirituals is peace:

I've got peace like a river,
I've got peace like a river,
I've got peace like a river in my soul.

This sense of life as a constant struggle, of the tension between a firm relationship with God and the current conditions of slavery and injustice, comes very close to the sense of the overlapping ages that we found in 5:12-21. The realm of Adam with its trouble and sin is consistently contrasted with the realm of Christ and the true homeland of believers. This sense of moving between two ages is particularly prominent in many of the spirituals. The unfriendly world of suffering leads the singers of the African American spirituals to be firmly convinced of their true homeland with Jesus.

A Separate Peace

Among the pieces of American literature that deal with the themes in Romans 5, I think particularly of John Knowles' novel *A Separate Peace* (Macmillan, 1959). This novel deals with the yearning to discover a private Eden where the evil of the world is overcome. The shock at the center of this novel is that evil rears its head even in the peaceful realm of "a separate peace."

The story tells of a group of students in a private Eastern school during the Second World War. The narrator, Gene, makes the discovery of the truth of Romans 5:12, so to speak, that all persons are involved in evil. When he is talking to his good friend Finny in the hospital room just before the operation that proves fatal, Gene tries to explain why he had jounced the limb to throw his friend out of the tree: "It was just some ignorance inside me, some crazy thing inside me, something blind, that's all it was" (page 174).

Whatever this thing was inside Gene, the novel reveals that he had desperately tried to conceal its incriminating presence. One of his friends penetrated this disguise: "You were always a lord of the manor, weren't you? A swell guy, except when the chips were down. You always were a savage underneath. I always knew that only I never admitted it" (page 128).

In the course of the novel, Gene comes to acknowledge this academic savagery within himself. And he uses this self-discovery to make sense out of the baffling world in which he lives. He uses it to explain the war: "Wars were not made by generations and their special stupidities, but . . . were made instead by something ignorant in the human heart" (page 183). When persons and nations find themselves pitted against evil in the world around them, they respond savagely and reach out to destroy and to cripple.

This point is worth reflecting on because Knowles here presents an explanation for war that is much closer to Paul's letter to the Romans than to the generally accepted view in our culture. Our assumption has typically been that war is caused by evil aggression on the part of enemies. Good persons and the good nation, though they may have minor flaws, are never pictured as the cause of the violent conflict. But Knowles has the audacity to shatter this stereotype, presenting savagery as an integral part of life. Gene, the most brilliant student in the class, is a savage underneath.

The novel *A Separate Peace* also deals with the sense of collective responsibility for sin that Paul describes with the Adam motif. Gene discovers that all relationships at Devon Academy are based on enmity, that a kind of savagery is carried out in the sports and even in the friendships in the school. This savagery is also connected in some way with the atmosphere of fear that pervaded Devon. Gene notes it as he revisits the campus at the beginning of the novel, recognizing this atmosphere more clearly now that he has escaped from it. He sees now that when he used to walk up the long white marble flight of stairs, "specters seemed to go up and down them with me" (page 3). This savagery is also connected in some way with the rules, with what Paul calls in 5:20 the law that came "so that the trespass might increase." The message in the Devon chapel services was that if you broke the rules, they would break you. The guilty obsession with the rules is expressed at many points in the novel.

In contrast to the other characters in the novel, Finny alone is perceived to be somehow free from the compulsion about the rules. His vibrant sense of life simply overcomes these petty boundaries. He skips class at the slightest pretext and breaks the dress code with such disarming innocence that he invariably gets away with it. This peculiar freedom from the law is also connected with the seeming sense in which Finny alone is free of the savagery that marks everyone else in the novel. His philosophy, for example, is that everyone wins in sports, that they are not a savage contest: "Finny never permitted himself to realize that when you won they lost. That would have destroyed the perfect beauty which was sport. Nothing bad ever happened in sports; they were the absolute good" (page 26).

Phineas (Finny) alone seems to escape the universal plight described in 5:12. "He possessed an extra vigor, a heightened confidence in himself, a serene capacity for affection which saved him" (page 184). The author pictures this young man as a person who retains his childhood innocence because of his self-confidence and affection. And this lack of savage rivalry is the essence of his inner peace. "Phineas was the essence of this careless peace" (page 16) that marks the summer session at Devon that is remembered in the novel.

The belief that someone, somewhere escapes the universal dilemma of savagery therefore lies at the center of the appeal of this novel. Yet John Knowles does not allow this optimistic picture to remain intact. He ends up close to Paul in Romans. Finny is shown toward the end of the novel as refusing to accept the reality of evil in himself or in his friends. He steadfastly refuses to accept the fact that Gene really had jounced the tree and that behind this action was, in Gene's words, "a primitive impulse to kill." When Gene reveals that he had done it, Finny responds with uncharacteristic vehemence: "I'll kill you if you don't shut up." Gene answers him, "You see! Kill me! Now you know what it is! I did it because I felt like that!" (page 59). When the investigation into the cause of the accident reveals beyond a shadow of a doubt that Gene, in fact, had done it, Finny must flee this recognition and tumbles down the marble stairs, in effect, ending his own life. The best the doctors can do cannot preserve him.

In a real sense the tragic ending of this novel rests in the refusal to recognize what Paul argues, that "death reigned from the time of Adam." To deny our limitations and to deny that there is savagery even in the best of us is to refuse to recognize our humanity. To believe this is to render oneself incapable of facing life in the real world. Sin becomes even more inevitable for those who deny it. There is no separate peace, no insulated refuge on this earth. The only peace that is available to us occurs in the midst of a fallen and broken world in which savagery remains.

But now that you have been set free from sin and have become slaves to God, the benefit you reap leads to holiness, and the result is eternal life (6:22).

— 8 —

Set Free From Sin

Romans 6

DIMENSION ONE:
WHAT DOES THE BIBLE SAY?

Answer these questions by reading Romans 6

1. What does Paul say about the idea of remaining in sin "so that grace may increase?" (6:1-2)

   Paul says, "By no means!"

2. With which does Paul connect baptism, with Jesus' life or with Jesus' death? (6:3-4)

   Paul connects baptism with Jesus' death.

3. What is the outcome of Christ's resurrection? (6:5)

   The outcome is that Christians "will . . . be united with him in his resurrection."

4. Is the sharing of Christ's resurrected life a present or a future prospect? (6:5, 8)

   Since Paul uses future tense verbs, "we will certainly also be united with him in his resurrection" and "we will also live with him," sharing Christ's resurrected life is solely a future prospect.

5. What is the result of being crucified with Christ? (6:6)

   The result of being crucified with Christ is the destruction of "the body of sin" so that "we should no longer be slaves to sin."

6. To what does Paul suggest that the "parts" of your body should be offered? (6:13, 19)

   Paul suggests that the "parts" of the body are capable of being "offer[ed]" to God as "instruments of righteousness."

7. What does Paul say about the possibility of being a "slave"? (6:16-18)

   Paul argues that everyone is a slave "to the one whom you obey," whether it be sin or obedience.

8. What was the "benefit" of being a slave to sin? (6:20-23)

   The "benefit" or "wages" of sin is death, according to 6:21 and 6:23.

9. How many times are the words *life, alive,* and *live* used in 6:1-23?

   Paul uses these terms a total of eleven times: (1) 6:2; (2) and (3) 6:4; (4) 6:8; (5), ((6), and (7) 6:10; (8) 6:11; (9) 6:13; (10) 6:22; (11) 6:23.

DIMENSION TWO:
WHAT DOES THE BIBLE MEAN?

In Romans 6, Paul continues to deal with the implications and objections of his doctrine of the righteousness of God. In 6:1 he takes up the issue that arose from the last verses of Chapter 5, that grace abounds more than the increase of sin. Verse 2 addresses this issue by pointing out the inconsistency of living in the realm of sin. Verses 3-7 explain this principle of inconsistency, showing that in baptism, believers have experienced the death of Christ and are set free to live in a new life with Christ. As your class members have discovered from answering question 9 in Dimension One, the theme of life runs through Romans 6, with a particular emphasis on living as agents of divine righteousness. The conclusion of the first section of the argument in verse 14 states the proper relation of grace to law by maintaining that sin cannot reign over those in Christ.

In Romans 6:15-23, Paul raises the rhetorical question that arose from the final verse of the preceding section. If believers are "not under law, but under grace," why then is there any necessity for moral urgency? Paul answers this question in the negative on the basis of the idea of the exchange of lordship, first stated in verse 16. Salvation here is understood as being redeemed from an old lord and made the slave of another. Romans 6:17-20 provides an expansion of this basic idea, contrasting the new lordship with the old. Romans 6:20-23 lifts up the consequences of the two lordships, the one leading to shame and death and the other leading to holiness and life.

Baptism With Christ

One of the major lines of interpretation of Romans 6 deals with the sacramental aspect of Paul's thought. Roman Catholic scholars were particularly interested in baptism as an experience of sacramental union in which saving grace is communicated and a new life is begun. Some scholars who are particularly oriented to the Greco-Roman religious scene have suggested that Paul was modeling his theology at this point on the mystery religions. In some of these Greco-Roman cults, initiates underwent a ceremony of dying and rising with the cult god or goddess. The result of such a ceremony was regeneration and the gift of divine power. Just as the god or goddess demonstrated divinity by triumphing over death, so the initiate was presumably given a form of immortality by going through the ceremony.

As can well be imagined, these suggestions for interpreting Romans 6 have raised a storm of protest and criticism. In particular some Protestant theologians and Bible scholars have been critical of the sacramental interpretation of Romans 6. One of the results of this discussion is the recognition that the Pauline language does not provide a precise analogy between the rite of going down into the water and coming back out in baptism on the one hand and the death and resurrection of Christ on the other. Jesus did not die by drowning. And there is no attempt in Paul's description of the baptismal experience in 6:3-4 to copy Jesus' crucifixion. Even more difficult, however, is that Paul refrains from completing the parallel of rising out of water and rising from the dead. Nowhere in this passage does the Christian gain, in this experience of baptism, present access to a resurrected state. Instead, in 6:4 Paul shifts into the metaphor of living a new life; and in verse 5 the participation in Christ's resurrection is separated from the baptismal event and postponed until the end of time.

So we cannot argue for a complete correspondence between the ritual of baptism and either the death and resurrection of Jesus on the one hand or an alleged death and resurrection of Christians on the other. One of the most striking aspects of Paul's use of the baptismal metaphor is what one writer has called the "element of temporal extension" in which the moment of baptism is seen to lead toward a life that is lived out toward the future triumph of righteousness with the return of Christ. The framework for Romans 6 is not so much the baptismal ceremony itself but rather the death of Christ and the return of Christ.

The Problem of Christ-Mysticism

The references in this passage to living with Christ and being identified with his life and death have led some scholars to suggest that a fundamentally mystical concept of the faith is being presented here. The references to the identification between the believer and Christ, according to this interpretation, do not come from baptismal experience but from the charismatic and mystical experiences in which the Spirit joins the believer with God.

One of the best-known studies along this line is Albert Schweitzer's *The Mysticism of Paul the Apostle* (Holt, 1931). He suggests that the center of Paul's theology is the idea of bodily union, not only with each other but also with Christ, a union that in a particular way "manifests the power of the death and resurrection, thereby achieving the status of resurrection before the general resurrection has occurred" (page 116, my translation from the German original). Schweitzer argues that Paul believed in a kind of double resurrection, that as Christ has a resurrected body, so the believers possess a resurrection body by virtue of their entrance into the messianic community in baptism. Phrases such as *in Christ, in the spirit,* and *Christ in us* should be interpreted on the basis of this bodily existence, capable of current resurrection, shared by the individual Christian in Christ. To sin after baptism is thus a fundamental violation of this new life, a sign that the power of the Resurrection has not yet taken effect.

This provocative hypothesis explains much about Pauline thought. But it does not do justice to Romans 6 in which Paul so clearly and explicitly reserves the believers' participation in the resurrection to the future (6:5, 8). In fact, in Paul's authentic letters he always sets the resurrection in the future. (See Philippians 3:10, 21.) In contrast, the so-called Deutero-Pauline epistles (those letters whose authorship has not positively been credited to Paul) indicate the possibility of current participation in the resurrected state (Colossians 2:12; Ephesians 5:14).

Much of Schweitzer's interpretation, however, remains valid even when corrections are made. You will perhaps observe in the commentaries that you consult how hostile a reception Schweitzer's book had and how much suspicion remains in scholarly circles against any idea of Pauline mysticism. The reason for this view is the long tradition of the Reformation, in which Martin Luther had difficulty with Christian mystics and enthusiasts.

We cannot deny that in Romans 6 substantial elements of mysticism are present. Paul does have a kind of personal relationship with Christ that is intense and real. This relationship is seen in Paul's intense prayer life and his expectation that the life of the believer should pattern itself after the life of Christ (6:10-11). But keep in mind that the kind of physical mysticism that is indisputably part of the Pauline tradition is also a kind of historical mysticism. Paul places the believer in the context between the death and resurrection of Christ, which is a past event, and the resurrection, which is a future event.

Those who wish to grasp the distinctive contours of Pauline mysticism, therefore, must take pains to separate it from traditional mysticism. Normally in a mystical theology, one is joined with the divine force so that a kind of union is achieved. This union sometimes involves even a loss of personal identity as the person is absorbed into the divine realm. A second distinctive feature of traditional mysticism is the loss of temporality. One has the sense in mystical experience of being set free from time, of being reunited with past or future figures and events. Time in such an experience seems to stand still or to be irrelevant. One has the sense of participating in divine time or in timelessness.

In both these regards Pauline mysticism is very different. Rather than a fusion between the believer and Christ, there is rather a kind of marriage, a relationship in which Christ remains Lord and in which the believer remains the servant. Romans 6 anchors the believer securely in this world between the poles of the death and resurrection of Christ in the past and the future resurrection and the triumph of righteousness at the end of time. The frequent shifts between present, past, and future verbs make this anchoring in time a distinctive and unusual feature of Pauline mysticism.

We also find little of the expected kind of inactive contemplation in Pauline mysticism. The result of baptism when properly understood is that Christians view themselves as "instruments of righteousness" (6:13) whose task is to yield their parts "in slavery to righteousness leading to holiness" (6:19). The ethical dimension of the Christian life is completely fused with Pauline mysticism in these verses.

The Idea of a "Change of Lordship"

An aspect of Romans 6:15-23 that may be a particular problem for your class members is the stress on being "slaves." We find this in verse 16 where Paul makes it clear that humans do not have a choice of being slaves; the only question is whom they serve. This point is a problem in a culture whose primary moral category is "freedom."

The assumption of American culture that there is such a thing as absolute freedom runs flatly counter to Romans 6. Paul's argument in 6:16 rests on foundations he laid down earlier in this letter, namely that human beings are natural idolaters. Humans cannot live without gods, without idols; so when humans refuse to recognize and worship the true God, they set about to create their own (1:23). Paul believes that humans are incapable of pure and absolute freedom. They wish to subordinate themselves to something, to serve something larger than themselves. They feel too puny to stand alone. When we think we are serving ourselves, in fact, we are serving some cultural image or idol, some image of what we believe we ought to be.

Salvation, therefore, appears to be a matter of exchanging lords, of shifting from an evil master to the proper and true master. Ernst Kaesemann has made popular the idea of salvation as "a change of lordship." He writes concerning Romans 6:16,

> It is presupposed here as elsewhere that a person belongs constitutively to a world and lies under lordship. With baptism a change of lordship has been effected. . . . The new [lord] sets those who are bound to him into freedom from powers and necessities. . . . We receive our freedom in allegiance to him and as a result of the right of lordship which God has graciously established over us. . . . He who belongs to the true cosmocrator [lord of the universe] strides erect through his sphere of power, breaks all the barriers and taboos arbitrarily set up there, and thus walks no less confidently through the sphere of the Torah, bearing witness thereby, in spite of appearances to the contrary, to God's peace on the earthly battlefield and to openness for brethren as the truth of the reign of God and as an announcement of the world of the resurrection (*Commentary on Romans*, page 179).

We can see from this formulation that Kaesemann does not wish to understand the lordship of Christ as resulting in a kind of Christian servility. We will follow this theme as it develops in Romans 8.

The Issue of Sanctification

When Paul mentions *holiness* (sanctification) in 6:19, he is stating an issue that is fundamental for this chapter. For centuries Protestants have tended to separate justification and sanctification. They viewed justification as the beginning of the Christian life and sanctification as verifying it. One result of this distinction is that sanctification is viewed as secondary, as a kind of add-on to the Christian life. A related problem is that justification was seen as the result of grace much more than sanctification was. The door was left open for sanctification to be seen as a human effort to conform oneself to the new law of God. Since this view so easily resulted in a new and devastating form of legalism, some Protestant thinkers downplayed sanctification and denied that it was possible or even feasible. Salvation was thus defined in Protestant orthodoxy as having the proper belief, while the issue of proper behavior was relegated to the secondary realm.

John Wesley made a major contribution at this point. While he sometimes followed the traditional separation between justification and sanctification, he insisted that sanctification was an expectation for all Christians. He wrote the following summary of the main points in "A Plain Account of Christian Perfection":

(1.) There is such a thing as perfection; for it is again and again mentioned in Scripture.

(2.) It is not so early as justification; for justified persons are to "go on unto perfection." . . .

(3.) It is not so late as death; for St. Paul speaks of living men that were perfect. . . .

(4.) It is not absolute. Absolute perfection belongs not to man, nor to angels, but to God alone.

(5.) It does not make a man infallible: None is infallible, while he remains in the body (*The Works of John Wesley;* Zondervan, n.d.; Vol. 11, pages 441–42).

Some features of Paul's argument in Romans 6 counter some of the negative tendencies of the traditional approach toward sanctification. One of them is that Paul understands sanctification as the natural result of the shift of lordship. Holiness is not understood as a merely human activity, the result of humans following high ideals. In 6:19, Paul referred to us offering our parts "in slavery to righteousness leading to holiness [sanctification]." Here the "rightwising" activity of God is understood to be united with the sanctifying activity of God, and both come to those who submit themselves to the gospel.

The union between justification and sanctification is even more firmly secured by our current understanding of justification as "rightwising," in which the righteous control of God over the entire world is in prospect. That humans could be "rightwised" without having their lives altered is inconceivable for Paul. This helps us understand the central thrust of Romans 6, that Christians cannot content themselves with a life under sin after they have been made part of the new era.

Sanctification for Paul is therefore not a human achievement. It is the gift that comes from a new relationship with God. Sanctification is closely related to the task of Christian believers to "offer the parts of your body to [God] as instruments of righteousness" (6:13). Paul would therefore find completely unnatural the currently popular division between evangelism and social action. For him, response to the gospel implies that one becomes a member of the realm of righteousness and promotes righteousness in everyday life as an automatic consequence. Sanctification must be united with justification if Romans 6 is to be properly understood.

The Problem of Interpreting Body in Romans 6

At two points in Romans 6 the term *body* is used in a peculiar way. In 6:6, Paul refers to the "body of sin" being rendered powerless, which could lead us to think that a kind of physical death was required of the physical body in order for sin actually to be overcome. The tradition of the "mortification of the flesh" has strong support in the wording of this verse. Paul's use at this point sounds very close to gnostic dualism, with its negative view of the body and its belief that salvation was strictly a matter of the mind. Also peculiar, though in a different way, is Paul's expression in 6:12 concerning not allowing sin to reign "in your mortal [dying] body." Why Paul stressed mortality in this particular verse needs an explanation.

Some scholars have held that the expression "body of sin" (6:6) referred to the mass of sins that one had committed in one's former life or was perhaps a figurative expression for the body of sinful desires. These interpretations try rather unsuccessfully to avoid the inference that this idea of the destruction of the sinful body would bring Paul close to gnosticism. The problem is not just that this reference implies that sin roots in the physical substance of the body but also that redemption would appear to take place by means of the destruction of the body.

That such ideas were current in the Pauline communities is shown by the reference in 1 Corinthians 13:3, "If I . . . surrender my body to the flames, but have not love, I gain nothing." These facts make it hard to avoid the conclusion that Paul in 6:6 has likely taken over a gnostic expression of some kind that was being used in the early church. But he corrects this understanding by inserting the decisive words *of sin.* These words not only serve to exclude the idea that the person who has transcended bodily existence was free to sin but also shift the blame of the human dilemma from the physical body to sin as a power in the old age. The expression "body of sin" is therefore likely the result of Paul's correction of the gnostic understanding of baptism as providing a destruction of the body.

Whereas a reference to the "dead body" would be quite appropriate in 6:12, expressing the idea that in baptism we die with Christ, I find it difficult to explain why Paul in fact uses the formula "mortal body" in this verse. One theory suggests that Paul was countering the libertinistic assumption that since the body was mortal, it was morally indifferent and could not affect the spiritual center of the person. This suggestion could be correlated with the observation that recent scholars have made, namely that Paul in Romans 6 refers to death with Christ in the past tense but to resurrection with Christ in the future (6:5, 8). That Paul is trying to correct the overly intense enthusiasm of some Christians at this point is widely assumed.

The use of the term *mortal* in 6:12 may well be part of an effort on Paul's part to correct an overly enthusiastic belief in the present possession of immortal life. By insisting on the continued presence of the mortal body, Paul seeks to avert the false conclusion that some people might have drawn from his references to having already died with Christ. He therefore guards against the danger of believing that death for the believer is a thing of the past.

DIMENSION THREE: WHAT DOES THE BIBLE MEAN TO ME?

Be Free

To grasp the shape of Paul's idea of change of lordship in Romans 6, some comparisons with current culture might help. Ask if some members of your class remember the lyrics of any popular songs that express the yearning to "be free." Write these lyrics on a chalkboard or on a large piece of paper and compare them with Paul's view. Since class members may prefer Paul to the composers of contemporary songs—especially while they are in the class setting—use care to make fair comparisons.

Yielding to Righteousness for Sanctification

When discussing Romans 6:19 in relation to John Wesley's view, it is interesting to recall that Wesley claimed that his views were entirely scriptural and had not essentially changed since early in his ministry. Albert C. Outler pointed out the originality of Wesley's view and said that

> Wesley asserted that his doctrine of "Christian perfection" had been the creative focus of his understanding of the Christian life from his first conversion to "serious" religion in 1725, and that it had continued as such without substantial alteration. He was as vitally concerned with the *"fullness of faith"* (i.e., sanctification) as with its beginnings (i.e., justification); as confident in the *goal* of the Christian life as of its *foundation*. He tried earnestly to maintain the parallelism between justification and sanctification—both by faith!—and between those good works appropriate to the reconciled sinner and to the mature Christian as well. This insistent correlation between the genesis of faith and its fullness marks off Wesley's most original contribution to Protestant theology (Albert C. Outler, ed., *John Wesley*; Oxford University Press, 1964; page 251).

The Old Age and the New Era

The idea of the Christian life poised between the old age and the new era has often been described as like standing between the invasion of Normandy by the Allies in June of 1944 and the climax of VE day, when victory in Europe was proclaimed. The beachhead of Jesus Christ's life signed the death warrant for the realm of sin and death, but fierce battles had to be fought before the terrain could be reconquered. Without the certain hope of a future triumph, those involved might not have had sufficient courage to continue.

We have been released from the law so that we serve in the new way of the Spirit, and not in the old way of the written code (7:6).

9

Set Free From the Law

Romans 7

DIMENSION ONE:
WHAT DOES THE BIBLE SAY?

Answer these questions by reading Romans 7

1. How many times is the word *law* used in this passage?

   Law *is used twenty-three times in this chapter: (1 and 2) 7:1; (3 and 4) 7:2; (5) 7:3; (6) 7:4; (7) 7:5; (8) 7:6; (9, 10, and 11) 7:7; (12) 7:8; (13) 7:9; (14) 7:12; (15) 7:14; (16) 7:16; (17) 7:21; (18) 7:22; (19, 20, and 21) 7:23; (22 and 23) 7:25.*

2. When is a woman considered free from the "law of marriage"? (7:1-3)

   A woman is free from the "law of marriage" when her husband dies.

3. What things are "aroused by the law," leading to death? (7:5)

   "The sinful passions" are aroused by the law and work toward our death.

4. Does Paul say that "law" or "sin" is responsible for leading people to break the commandments and to fall into death? (7:7-14)

   Paul argues that "sin" is responsible for death (7:9), whereas the "law is holy . . . [and] spiritual" (7:12, 14).

5. What causes Paul to do, as he confesses, "what I hate"? (7:15, 17, 20)

   Paul argues that "sin living in me" causes him to do what he does not really want to do.

6. What is Paul's attitude toward the law? (7:22, 25)

   Paul "delight[s] in" and is "a slave to God's law" in his "mind," while with his sinful nature he serves the law of sin.

DIMENSION TWO:
WHAT DOES THE BIBLE MEAN?

The argument in Romans 7 can be conveniently divided into three parts. Romans 7:1-6 describes life in Christ as freedom from the law. This section takes up the theme of the law that was announced in 6:14. The idea of a change of lordship or jurisdiction that we picked up in Romans 6 is stated in the form of this rhetorical question in 7:1. Romans 7:2-3 develops the analogy of secular marriage law to establish the point that jurisdiction does not continue after death has occurred. Verses 4-6 then apply this principle to Christians who had died to the law in experiencing this shift in lordship through Christ. Under Christ, a new relationship in the Spirit is established.

The second section, Romans 7:7-12, answers an objection concerning the law that arises out of Paul's statement in 7:5. His reference there to the sinful passions being aroused by the law could easily lead to the objection that law now falls into the moral status of sin. This false conclusion Paul denies in 7:7 and then goes on to explain with the idea of the law making humans conscious of sin. Romans 7:8-11 elaborates this idea, showing that sin merely found an "opportunity" in the law, leading to covetousness and death. This section is concluded by verse 12 reaffirming the point that the law is holy and good.

The third section, Romans 7:13-25, answers an objection that could arise from Paul's references to the deceit of the law in 7:11 and the goodness of the law in 7:12. The question in 7:13 deals with the effect of the law on humans. Paul's thesis is that sin invaded the law to produce death. This thesis is sustained by the argument in 7:14-23, showing how sin prevents a person from achieving the desired good. This is followed by the statements of 7:24-25 about the wretchedness of the human plight and the blessedness of the grace of God who saves humans from this plight

SET FREE FROM THE LAW

through Christ. The final half of verse 25 summarizes the argument.

Romans 7:1-6. Here Paul develops a comparison between marriage law and the situation of Christians standing between the two ages. The point of the comparison, as is easy to discern, is that once the husband dies, the woman is free from the marriage contract. Paul argues in the conclusion of this argument (7:4-6) that the law has jurisdiction only in the old age and that those who belong to the new are comparable to the woman whose husband has died. She is free and so are those who had formerly been held under bondage to the law. The reference to being controlled by "the sinful nature" in 7:5 refers to the status of persons in the old age, shaped by self-seeking and the kind of sinful self-will that is characteristic of Paul's use of the *sinful nature* in a context like this.

This question of freedom from the law as a mark of the new era plays a role in the conflict that has been discerned between the weak and the strong in Rome. In all probability, the conservatives were arguing that the Jewish law continues its jurisdiction in the new era. The thrust of Paul's argument at this point is clearly on the side favored by the strong, namely that with the dawn of the new era, the law no longer has jurisdiction. But it is interesting to observe that at the end of 7:6, Paul makes it clear that members in the new era continue to "serve," not in the old way, bound by the law, but in the new ethical situation of being bound to Christ. The crucial question for Paul is whom does one serve?

Romans 7:7-12. An interesting point is that the only commandment mentioned in 7:7-12 is the one concerning coveting. Paul follows a Hebrew tradition at this point that suggests that coveting was the beginning of all sin. The desire to assert oneself against God and the neighbor is revealed in coveting what the neighbor has and refusing to accept what in faith should have been viewed as the gift that God has given each person uniquely. This commandment stands close to the word *desire*, which is used in Paul's earlier argument in Romans, translated as "shameful lusts" (1:26).

Robin Scroggs has developed this theme of covetousness as the essence of sin in his book *Paul for a New Day* (Fortress Press, 1977). He connects covetousness to aggression and to Paul's basic idea that "sinful existence is *hostile* toward God." Scroggs suggests that

> covetousness is a primary expression of aggression—the attempt to possess, control, seize from another, and, metaphorically at least, to kill. To be obedient to the Torah in an attempt to justify oneself by works covertly expresses that primal hostility and aggression against God the Father. Aggression is the reaction against the authoritative, awesome Father, who says, "Thou shalt not . . . ," thus putting an end to freedom. The obvious act of rebellion is, of course, to defy the commandment (pages 12–13).

Scroggs goes on to suggest that a substantial element of rebellion and submissiveness is found in all obedience and that the sense of manipulating God by the law is closely associated with the idea of covetousness. Scroggs points out that Paul's expression "every kind of covetous desire" (7:8) points to this wide-ranging effort by humans to base their life on their own achievement under the law. Scroggs writes, "Life under law is a life of *total covetousness*. And covetousness is death" (page 11). Scroggs explains this connection by a theory of Oedipal energy in which the yearning to possess results in aggressive feelings toward parents. Submission to the law can become simply a form of this hostility. Whether this Freudian explanation is on track or not, Paul's own personal experience of persecuting the church suggests the serious effects of what Paul called our "shameful lusts."

Romans 7:13-24. A set of terms surfaces at the end of Romans 7 to explain how humans come under bondage to the law. An expression in this connection is 7:14, translated in the NIV as "I am unspiritual, sold as a slave to sin." The word *unspiritual* actually translates the word *fleshly*, a term that then connects directly with Paul's statement in 7:18 that "nothing good lives in me, that is, in my sinful nature (flesh)." Paul then moves to the cry of the captive, "Who will rescue me from this body of death?" (7:24). The two major lines of interpretation that have been used in the past to understand Paul's references to *sinful nature* (flesh) and *body* in Romans 7 are both in need of substantial revision. A brief description of these alternatives will help lift up the issues that need to be dealt with concerning Romans 7.

The idea of flesh and body as signs of human sensuality was widespread in earlier phases of Pauline research. This tradition was heavily influenced by the Greek heritage, which pitted the "lower nature" against the "higher nature" of the mind and spirit. This dualistic interpretation of Paul assumes that Paul had a negative view of the human body and in particular a negative view of human sexuality. This concept of flesh as sensuality surfaces in the medieval Roman Catholic idea of renunciation of the flesh as a means of holiness. It also surfaces in various forms of Puritanism and Protestant moralism in which the body is viewed as the source of temptations and evil.

The study of Paul's letters to the Corinthians is primarily what led scholars to revise or reject this traditional view. In 1 Corinthians 6:12-20, for example, Paul lays out a positive theory of sexual relations and contends that "the body is . . . for the Lord, and the Lord for the body" (1 Corinthians 6:13). His comment later in this section that "your body is a temple of the Holy Spirit" (1 Corinthians 6:19) would be impossible for anyone holding a dualistic viewpoint. Also, Paul's positive view of marriage in 1 Corinthians 7 as understood in recent research makes it clear that Paul rejected the dualism that was so characteristic of his society. Scholars who have attempted to understand Pauline theology on the basis of Jewish foundations have been particularly sensitive at this point. In contrast to the Greco-Roman world, the Jewish culture had a generally positive appraisal of the body and of the created order. To make Paul into an advocate of sin as sensuality is to bring his theology all too close to gnosticism.

A second and more widespread misinterpretation of Paul's concept of flesh and body concentrates on the issue of weakness. In this line, *flesh* symbolizes the inability of persons to achieve high ideals. This view was also popular in Puritan and post-Puritan thinkers. Whenever we are told that we know what is right but we do not have the will power to do what is right, we are following this line of interpretation from Romans 7. This view has expressed itself in two different theories about Paul. The first is the idea of the weakness of the Jews to obey the law. This idea was followed by Martin Luther and in general by the liberal theologians of more recent times who adhered to that tradition. This interpretation, as we have shown above, is a complete misinterpretation of first-century Judaism. And it imposes on Paul a kind of introspective conscience that was not characteristic of him.

A second way to apply this interpretation is to stress the weakness of Christians to obey the law of Christ. This interpretation leads to the conclusion that every Christian must recognize the impossibility of perfection in this life.

The major problem with this interpretation is that it runs so strongly counter to the argument that Paul has developed in Romans 6. Paul himself gives no indication that he found it impossible to live out the Christian ethic. He exhorts his fellow Christians not to let sin "reign in your mortal body. . . . But rather offer yourselves to God, as those who have been brought from death to life; and offer the parts of your body to him as instruments of righteousness. For sin shall not be your master" (6:12-14).

In addition to flying against the clear implications of Paul's argument in Romans, this interpretation also has some negative effects on the shaping of the Christian self-identity. It leads people to a sense of self-pity and an expectation of failure. The resultant stress on the lack of determination and will power tends to lead people back into a form of works-righteousness that is completely resistant to grace.

And as for those who succeed in fulfilling the Christian obligations, this interpretation lures them into an overly boastful attitude concerning their superiority over others. A self-image that fluctuates wildly between guilt feelings and insufferable superiority is one of the results of this misinterpretation of Romans 7.

The third alternative, which is advocated in this Bible study, suggests that Paul is showing the dilemma of the self-righteous person in Romans 7. He is describing his own experience as a persecutor of the church, zealously convinced that his own view is correct and therefore running pell-mell into opposition against God.

The dilemma of Romans 7 is seen to be explicitly laid out in Romans 10:1-4. In that latter section, Paul refers to Jews who "are zealous for God, but their zeal is not based on knowledge." Paul goes on to say, "Since they did not know the righteousness that comes from God and sought to establish their own, they did not submit to God's righteousness." These verses accurately describe Paul's own situation before his conversion. His life was not marked by a lack of zeal or a lack of righteousness, understood as conformity to the law. The basic flaw was the failure to recognize that God had revealed himself in a new and revolutionary way in Christ. The failure to submit to the righteousness of God means that something profoundly wrong lay at the heart of that piety that had marked Paul's earlier life. Rather than weakness of will or the lure of his sensual desires, Paul's problem was his zealous commitment itself. Only in the light of the cross event, as confirmed by the Resurrection, did Paul discover that his righteousness had a terrible internal flaw. The very good he sought to achieve, namely to obey God's will, turned against him; and he found himself an enemy of God.

This interpretation of Romans 7 potentially has wide relevance in understanding the circumstances of our current world. And it also allows us to understand the evidence within the Pauline letters in a straightforward way.

The consequence is that when Paul uses *flesh*, he is talking about the unconsciously self-centered, self-justifying tendency of humans. The person who is "unspiritual [fleshly], sold as a slave to sin" (7:14), is being held in bondage by this covetous orientation to the law. So long as the real motivation of the self is to gain justification, to prove superiority over others, this element of unconscious sin has corrupted the goodness of the law. Thus when Paul refers to deliverance from "this body of death" (7:24), he is describing the body dominated by the law of sin. The problem of humankind does not reside in our physical bodies but rather in the sinful distortion of human desires that turn even the goodness of religion into its very opposite.

Romans 7:25. Romans 7:25 alludes to the resolution of the problem described in Romans 7. This line picks up the themes that we have studied, particularly from Romans 3:21–4:25; 6. Paul is convinced that the grace of God as revealed in the Christ event finally exposes the self-righteousness of humans. In killing the Christ, the pious community was holding to its own righteousness. In zealously conforming to its law, religious persons found themselves opposing the righteousness of God. But Paul also discovered in the Christ event the possibility of forgiveness. When persons are struck by grace, their former efforts to gain status through conformity to the law drop aside as unnecessary. The illusion that humans can produce the perfect good by themselves drops away, and they begin to recognize themselves as they really are—finite creatures whose best glory always falls short of the glory of God. But they are also creatures loved by God, unconditionally. A new basis for self-esteem is thus offered and a new kind of work begins to emerge—work not aimed at boasting, but rather responding to the boundless grace of God.

The gospel thus provides a deliverance from the plight described in Romans 7. The argument in Romans 7 had a direct bearing on the Roman house churches that were responding to their threatening circumstances by discriminating against others and by trying to prove their superiority to others. Paul shows, through this argument in Romans 7, that such behavior is simply a sign of returning to the old age of bondage to the law. Any good that one achieves through such methods will turn out to be evil. Only by understanding our lives as based solely on grace do we have a possibility of overcoming the power of this covetousness in which *I* oppose the status that others have because *I* want the central status for myself and my group alone. Thus when Paul says at the end of the chapter that "in the sinful nature [flesh] [I am] a slave to the law of sin," he is describing the actual motivational structure of the house churches at Rome, locked in their battle with one another. Such battle is the flat repudiation of genuine faith.

DIMENSION THREE: WHAT DOES THE BIBLE MEAN TO ME?

Legalism

Since Americans are no longer shaped by the same kinds of legalism that marked an earlier generation or even the time of Paul, we need to consider whether Paul's argument has a direct bearing anymore. I believe that a good case can be made that the modern consumer society offers a similar appeal to "the flesh."

You might organize an experiment to test Paul's argument, making use of advertisements from television, magazines, or newspapers. In particular, I am thinking of the kind of advertisements that offer something beyond the product itself as a result of buying it. If one buys the "right" toothpaste or automobile, one wins the affection of the lovely or handsome partner. If one drinks the "right" beer, one gains fellowship and fulfillment. The motivation in these ads is to conform to the law in the sense of buying a particular product with the promise that fullness of life will be achieved.

Use the collection of ads to discuss the theme of covetousness, which is central for Romans 7. Some of the ads in some "upper class" magazines have this element of covetousness combined with high levels of hostility. One ad, for example, advertises an automobile that is so rare and expensive that your neighbors probably cannot buy one even if they want one. The caption on the ad is, "Demoralize Thy Neighbor." The idea of gaining a particular product that will lend prestige and permanent superiority is a characteristic new form of the law that, if Paul is right, leads to death rather than to life.

The theme of the flesh and sinful passions aroused by the law is illustrated by many of these ads. An advertisement can arouse the desire to gain a particular product so that by having it one will have achieved life. The "sinful passion" that leads buyers to follow the logic of such an ad is the yearning to gain something by one's own effort that secures life and renders one secure from vulnerability and criticism. But a disappointment pattern follows the law just as surely as is described in Romans 7. The good that one hopes to achieve fails to arrive. Thinking through the logic of the ad and the likelihood that one's love affair will really be guaranteed by the toothpaste or that one's marriage will be secured by the automobile allows one to gain a modern-day conception of Paul's basic point: "What I want to do I do not do, but what I hate I do."

Conflicts Between Children and Parents

The internal contradiction of a zealous attachment to the law that ends up in its opposite could be reconstructed from newspaper accounts of conflicts between children and parents. In a typical account that was published several years ago, a young man fell increasingly out of communication with his parents at the age of fifteen. His father was a salesman and active in the Little League and the Boy Scouts. The father became increasingly critical of the lifestyle his son was adopting. His son was attracted by the drug scene and often came home high.

The father and son came to blows several times as the father tried to force the young man to conform. He only wanted the best for this boy, but things continued to get worse. At one point the father placed a tap on the family telephone to check up on the boy—a ploy that backfired and increased the hostility. In one flare-up he told his son the following:

> I've tried everything I know to do. I've tried to reason with you, I have forbidden you to see kids who take drugs, I have asked you to stay home, I've taken you to family court, I've cried, I've told you I loved you, I've told you I'll do anything in my power to find you help. Your mother and I cannot talk to you anymore. So this is the way it's going to be. You're going to stay home Friday and Saturday nights if I have to lock you in your room.

After the young man wrecked the family car while driving under the influence of drugs, the fatal encounter took place in the ranch-style home in the suburban development. The boy demanded to know whether the father had reported his use of drugs. When no answer was forthcoming, the young man started after his father with a steak knife. The father pulled the trigger on the police revolver that he had in his belt. The bullet tore directly into the young man's heart, and he was dead.

The father had sought the good for his son, but it turned out to be evil. "I do not understand what I do. For what I want to do I do not do, but what I hate I do."

We know that in all things God works for the good of those who love him, who have been called according to his purpose (8:28).

— 10 —
New Life in the Spirit

Romans 8

DIMENSION ONE:
WHAT DOES THE BIBLE SAY?

Answer these questions by reading Romans 8

1. How many times are the words *Spirit* or *spirit* used in 8:1-27?

   The words Spirit *or* spirit *are used twenty-two times in these verses: (1) 8:2; (2) 8:4; (3 and 4) 8:5; (5) 8:6; (6, 7, and 8) 8:9; (9) 8:10; (10 and 11) 8:11; (12) 8:13; (13) 8:14; (14 and 15) 8:15; (16 and 17) 8:16; (18) 8:23; (19 and 20) 8:26; (21 and 22) 8:27.*

2. What are the marks of the "minds set on what . . . nature desires"? (8:5-8)

   Paul associates the "minds set on what . . . nature desires" with death (8:6), hostility to God (8:7), a refusal to submit to God's law (8:7), and an inability to please God (8:8).

3. What does Paul say about those who do not have the Spirit of Christ? (8:9)

   Paul says that if "anyone does not have the Spirit of Christ, he does not belong to Christ."

4. What does the Spirit communicate to believers who cry, "*Abba*, Father"? (8:15-17)

   The Spirit confirms that we are children of God and co-heirs with Christ.

5. What does Paul say the creation is expecting? (8:19-21)?

   Paul says the creation longs (a) "for the sons of God to be revealed" (8:19), (b) to "be liberated from its bondage to decay" (8:21), and (c) for "the glorious freedom of the children of God" (8:21).

6. How does Paul describe the Christian hope? (8:24-25)

   Paul writes that "we hope for what we do not yet have."

7. What is the role of the Spirit? (8:26-27)

   The Spirit "helps us in our weakness" and "intercedes for us."

8. List the verbs used in 8:29-30 to describe God's saving activity.

   These verbs describe God's saving activity: predestined, called, justified (rightwised), and glorified.

9. How many experiences and powers does Paul list in 8:35-39 that cannot "separate us from the love of God that is in Christ Jesus our Lord"? What are they?

   If one lists the final, cumulative item of "anything else" in 8:39, Paul lists seventeen experiences and powers in these verses: (1) trouble, (2) hardship, (3) persecution, (4) famine, (5) nakedness, (6) danger, (7) sword, (8) death, (9) life, (10) angels, (11) demons, (12) the present, (13) the future, (14) powers, (15) height, (16) depth, and (17) anything else in all creation.

DIMENSION TWO:
WHAT DOES THE BIBLE MEAN?

In Romans 8 we turn to some of the most relevant and accessible material in Paul's letter. You will perhaps find that for many members of your class this is the chapter of Romans they find most intriguing and most directly significant for daily life.

This chapter is divided into three large portions. Verses 1-17 deal with the cosmic struggle between the sinful nature (flesh) and spirit. In this section the work of the Spirit is integrated with the concept of salvation by portraying the Spirit as it conveys unconditional acceptance (therefore "rightwising") to believers. The second section, verses 18-30, deals with the hopeful suffering of the children of God. This section discusses the cosmic context of

Christian faith. The third section, verses 31-39, provides a conclusion for not only Romans 8 but also for all the material from Romans 5:1 onward. Its theme is that nothing can separate believers from the love of Christ.

We begin our consideration by studying the various approaches to the flesh/spirit tension in Romans 8. This material has been very influential in Western culture, primarily in a way that reflected some serious misunderstandings. The idea during the monastic period that true Christians should renounce the sinful nature rests on this passage. The ideas during the Puritan period of renouncing worldly honors and in the later Victorian period of renouncing sexual pleasure are both directly related to the idea of the minds set on the spirit versus the minds set on the sinful nature (flesh). These ideas also have had a direct impact in the most important American forms of entertainment, as will be discussed in the final section of this lesson.

Romans 8:1-17. In the first two questions in Dimension One, our attention is drawn not only to the centrality of the spirit but also to the marks of what Paul calls the "minds set on what . . . nature desires [the flesh]" (8:6-8). The elaborate description of the differences between the sinful nature (flesh) and spirit have been subject to a variety of interpretations throughout Christian history. The classic position developed by Eastern Orthodoxy was that Paul was a Platonic thinker and that this tension between flesh and spirit was between the sensual nature of humans and the pure realm of divine reality. This interpretation viewed evil as coming from the material realm and resulted in a grave suspicion of the body and of human sexuality. The spirit, on the other hand, was viewed as the realm of pure ideas, untouched by history or materiality. This approach to Paul is far too dualistic. It places flesh and body in too thoroughly negative a context and overlooks the central notion of sin that was laid down in Romans 6 and 7 as a foundation for what Paul is arguing in this passage.

The approach to the flesh/spirit dualism in Western Christianity was decisively shaped by Augustine. He offered a modified form of biblical Platonism. For him, flesh equals human nature in its conscious revolt against God. The lust of humans to gain life on their own accord is particularly associated by him with the sexual drive. But it is also rooted in human weakness. In contrast, spirit is understood as the divine will that sets moral limits to humans. This approach comes much closer to the Pauline view in Romans 8, but it still identifies flesh too closely with human sexuality. This approach also does not reflect very clearly the tension between the two ages reflected in this passage.

The view of the flesh/spirit dualism that emerged in the liberal theology of the nineteenth and twentieth centuries tended to view flesh as self-righteousness or human weakness. The inability of humans to perform the high ideals and to live up to the law was identified as the major problem of humankind. *Spirit* in this tradition tended to be viewed, not as the vital miracle-working action of God, but rather as the collection of high ideals toward which

humans should strive. The high ideals of the "brotherhood of man and the fatherhood of God" tended to be set against the fleshly side of humans, consisting of the reluctance to live up to expectations.

Breaking off from the liberal view, the perspective of the Christian existentialists was that flesh equals human dependency on self. Spirit in the interpretation that grew in the 1920s to 1960s was viewed as the manifestation of the Christ event whose subjective side was the knowledge that persons had of the Christ event, a knowledge that provided a new self-understanding. The existentialists tended to view the flesh versus the spirit dualism as a tension within the human psyche alone. The historical tension that is particularly evident toward the end of Romans 8 was completely lost from sight.

The most important steps in the direction of the view presented in this study were taken by two German scholars, Werner Georg Kuemmel and Ernst Kaesemann. Both scholars pointed out the cosmic dualism that is implicit in Paul's perspective. Both took account of the wording of Romans 8:7 concerning the sinful mind that is "hostile to God." That flesh acts independent of humans and is something of a power sphere was suggested by Kuemmel but finally and clearly developed by Kaesemann. In his more mature work Kaesemann identifies flesh with the old age and believes that people are thoroughly determined by the world to which they give their loyalty. Spirit, therefore, designates the new era and flesh the old. When Paul speaks of the sinful mind (flesh), he has in mind the world view around us and the powers that dominate our current society. They exercise an attraction for humans in particular directions, which, as Paul has shown in the earlier argument of Romans, are directly related to the social consequences of Adam's sin.

In the work that I have done on this problem (*Paul's Anthropological Terms*; Brill, 1971), a case was made that Paul's use of *flesh* arose directly out of the Judaizer crisis in the late A.D. 40s. *Flesh* came to designate the circumcised flesh of people who were advocating circumcision as necessary for salvation. It also came to be identified by Paul as the cosmic power of the old age, the age of self-justification and sin. We find this idea reflected in Romans 8. *Flesh* in Romans is characterized by the sinful desire to gain righteousness by works. Such a life leads to death because in depending on our own flesh to gain righteousness, we come into conflict with the righteousness revealed in the new era. The power of the flesh was broken by Christ who came in the flesh. Henceforth life may be achieved through obedience to the law by means of the spirit, and in this way the bondage to the flesh is superseded by life according to the spirit.

In Romans 8, Paul uses *spirit* as the apportioned spirit passed out to humans, as we can see in verse 15 as well as in verse 10. The Spirit is also identified with Christ and is perceived to be the mark of the new era, manifesting itself in charismatic forms as well as in transformed ethical behavior. Therefore the kind of dualism that Paul has in mind in Romans 8 is between the two ages, the new era of Christ and the old era of Adam. Paul's contention in this chapter is that these two ages are in opposition to each other and that, when Christians find themselves living "according to the sinful nature [flesh]," they are really falling back into the old age. Whether they intend it or not, the consequence is to come into opposition to God (8:7-8).

Liberation by Christ

A key term in Romans 8 is that we are "set . . . free from the law of sin and death" by Christ (8:2). This theme is dominant for the entire section, and it is developed in detail as Paul describes the work of Christ setting humans free from "the sinful nature." By sending Christ in "the likeness of sinful man," Paul suggests that God "condemned sin in sinful man" (8:3).

As we have seen from earlier chapters of Romans, Paul believes that the Christ event reveals the depth of human hostility against God. The function of Christ is to expose evil but also to relieve humans from it. That is why Paul urges that the consequence of salvation is to walk "according to the Spirit" (8:4). This verse develops the key theme of Romans 6, that those who belong to the new era become "slaves of righteousness." The means by which this transformation occurs, according to 8:3, is the sending of the Son in the "likeness of sinful man." By this Paul means that Christ was similar to us, yet not identical at the point of sharing the rebellion of humans, which is the essence of human sin. Christ shared our humanity but not our revolt. By exposing human self-righteousness and alienation, Christ set humans free from their bondage.

The death of Christ is understood in Romans 8, as elsewhere in Romans, to be the exposure of human sin, its condemnation, and its overcoming by pure grace. It results in a transformation of life so that the law is actually accomplished. What God wills for humans, namely that they accomplish the good, is made possible when the human rebellion is ended. Grace overcomes the hostility that had distorted the human race, a point that links Romans 1:18-32 with the striking words of Romans 8:7: "The sinful mind is hostile to God. It does not submit to God's law."

Romans 8:5-7. In 8:5-7, Paul describes the two realms of the sinful nature (flesh) and the spirit in constant opposition to each other. "The power sphere that attracts your loyalty determines your perspective" is the point set forth in 8:5. When Paul describes this outlook in terms of hostility and resistance to the law of God, he has in mind his own previous experience, as we saw in our interpretation of Romans 7 in the last lesson. Paul's persecution of the church for not conforming to his own standards and his resistance against Christ as a lawbreaker were revealed to him on the Damascus road as signs of an unacknowledged hostility against God. Here in Romans 8, Paul explains the kind of paralysis of the will that was described in Romans 7:19: "For what I do is not the good I want to do; no, the

evil I do not want to do—this I keep on doing." When Paul adds to this the idea that the sinful mind "does not submit to God's law," he has in mind the aggressive misuse of the law as a means of status formation. It is not that Paul or other Jews of his time were unable to obey the law. Far from it. The problem, as Paul discovered in his conversion, was that his perfect obedience to the law had unconsciously become a means of zealous rebellion against God.

Paul's point in this section is that the aggressive, competitive outlook of humans is determined by the old age. This outlook is built into human institutions and cultural systems. That is why Paul believes that "flesh" is more than simply a human individual characteristic. It has to do with what we would call today "the social world." This kind of behavior pattern, "the mind of the flesh," is pitted against a completely different outlook that Paul believes ought to be characteristic of the Christian community. The "mind of the spirit" is one that is capable of recognizing limitations. It is cooperative and therefore gives evidence of having overcome hostility and class differences.

Paul's idea of two mindsets and two power spheres in combat with each other had great relevance for the Roman house church situation. In a sense Paul is suggesting that the situation in Rome indicates that the "mind of the flesh" was still dominant there. What was needed in Rome were the features that Paul particularly identifies with the "mind of the spirit," "life and peace" (8:6). *Life* is understood to be an orientation toward realistic and mature relationships. It is full of thankfulness, but it is willing to accept death. Life in this sense is correlated later in the chapter with future hope and resilience in the face of opposition. The word *peace* in 8:6 has to do with overcoming barriers and hostility. It is a noncompetitive outlook. Peace involves harmony, not only with fellow humans but also with the world around us. Harmony was clearly a key issue for the Roman house churches. By contrast, the "mind of the flesh" is oriented, perhaps unconsciously, to competition and death. It is hostile, which results in separation between humans and God as well as between humans themselves.

Romans 8:12-17. The function of the Spirit to convey a sense of acceptance and self-identity is stressed in 8:12-17. That Christians are "led by the Spirit of God" (8:14) was widely assumed in the Roman house churches. But Paul connects this acceptance in a profound way to the main thesis of his letter, the triumph of divine righteousness and the conveyance of unconditional acceptance. To be given the Spirit according to 8:14 means to be confirmed as "sons of God." This idea is elaborated in terms of the strong feeling of acceptance and belongingness that is far from the "spirit that makes you a slave" in 8:15.

Paul goes on to connect this "spirit of sonship" with a term that the early church picked up from the historical Jesus. In a unique way, Jesus referred to God as "Abba," an intimate address to God, which might be translated "Papa" or "Daddy." Since this was a foreign word for Paul's Greek audience, he translates it here with *Father*. Jesus used this term for God to show the intimate sense of acceptance that he felt. Thus Paul suggests that when Christians find it possible to speak to God on terms as intimate as they would with a parent, the Spirit is conveying to them that they are "God's children."

Paul refers to our crying out this acclamation. The ecstatic element of early Christian worship and devotional life is in view here; and quite likely the term *Abba* was closely related to glossolalia, or speaking in tongues. This means that the experience of the Spirit does not make Christians divine. Rather, when properly understood, it conveys to us that we are unconditionally loved by the Abba. We are truly "God's children," beloved and accepted. As children, we are no longer outsiders; we are no longer slaves and subordinates. We are honored members of the household of God and inheritors of the promises.

Romans 8:18-30. The context for the struggle between the two ages, as Paul describes it in Romans 8, is far more than personal. It is cosmic. The struggle involves the whole creation, which is consistent with the thesis of Romans concerning the righteousness of God, because, as we saw earlier, *righteousness* has to do with God's righteous control over the whole created order.

Humans in relation to their environment are directly involved in what Paul has in mind. As we can see in 8:18-25, humans are intimately related to their environment. The world itself has suffered from human sin and arrogance. When referring to the creation being "subjected to frustration" (8:20), Paul probably had in mind the Hebrew conception that sin corrupts the world. Today we understand this idea in terms of the distortion of ecology, the destruction of war, the exploitation of nature by human greed and arrogance. Paul refers at this point to the theme that was characteristic of the Hebrew interpretation of the garden of Eden story. Human sin is seen to corrupt even the soil itself (Genesis 3:17-19).

That the creation therefore "waits in eager expectation for the sons of God to be revealed" (8:19) has to do with the expected transformation of humans in their relation to their environment. So long as humans remain bound by sin, the earth continues to suffer. Only when the human race is transformed will the ecology of this planet find its order once again. Paul refers in 8:21 to the hope of creation being "liberated from its bondage to decay" and obtaining "the glorious freedom of the children of God." This means that the creation itself will be restored to its original righteousness and beauty as humans are restored. In the meanwhile, as Paul describes it in 8:22, the whole creation along with us "is groaning as in the pains of childbirth."

The result of this cosmic view is that salvation for Paul requires an element of hope. This hope is defined by the thesis of Romans, the recovery of the righteousness of God, which involves God's control and restoration of the whole created order. The hope here is not for individual salvation alone but also for the salvation of the planet. The emphasis on hope makes it plain that Paul does not believe that

Christians living in the Spirit are already beyond their status as mortal human beings. Christians, as well as their environment, are still subject to the long legacy of the "mind of the flesh."

The distortion of human life, the erosion of the environment, and even the threat of death as a result of human sin are all implicit in this view. For Paul, the life of faith is lived between the ages. Death and disease are still a reality for Christians and for others. The hope that keeps us going is anchored in the triumph of divine righteousness at the end of time. Christians "wait for it patiently" (8:25) because they are certain that the triumph of Christ will come at the end of time. The daily struggle that Christians carry out is a struggle in behalf of this goal. Here we see what Paul had in mind in Romans 6 when he referred to believers becoming "instruments of righteousness" (6:13).

Romans 8:26-27. At two points in Romans 8, Paul uses language reminiscent of the ecstatic elements of Christian worship. The most explicit of these is 8:26-27, where the Spirit is described as helping humans in their weakness by "groans that words cannot express." Ernst Kaesemann in particular has made the case that Paul refers here in a positive way to early Christian glossolalia, the phenomenon of speaking in tongues. In the Pauline churches, speaking in tongues was understood to be inarticulate speech, the sighing and groaning of the creature at a level far too deep for human articulation. Kaesemann detects a polemical element, however, in the context in which Paul places this reference to speaking in tongues. Since it was understood to be heavenly speech in the Pauline churches and since enthusiasts in places like Corinth took great pride in their ability to speak in tongues, Kaesemann finds it striking that Paul places it here in the context of "weakness":

> Heavenly speech can be heard in worship as a work of the Spirit. But what enthusiasts regard as proof of their glorification [Paul] sees as a sign of a lack. Praying in tongues reveals, not the power and wealth of the Christian community, but its [weakness]. The Spirit . . . has to intervene if our prayers are to have a content which is pleasing to God. He does so in such a way that even in worship he brings us to that groaning of which the unredeemed creation is full and which speaks out of the longing of the assaulted for the redemption of the body (*Commentary on Romans*, page 241).

That Paul has in mind ecstatic dimensions of the Christian faith in either of these locations is debated. Some scholars wish to reduce to an absolute minimum any positive references in Paul's letters to ecstatic phenomena. But it seems quite likely in both these instances that Paul is incorporating the widespread use of glossolalia in early Christianity into his argument. Whether there is a polemical element in his use of these ideas in 8:26-27 is a problem, however, because Paul does not enter into polemic in Romans in general; and this particular context gives no indication of his rejection of any specific idea. That Paul is in tension with the "enthusiasts" is something that scholars like Ernst Kaesemann assume but have difficulty proving in detail. After all, Paul confesses in 1 Corinthians 14:18, "I thank God that I speak in tongues more than all of you." It is likely, therefore, that he would have considered himself a charismatic and that others in the early church would have perceived him in the same way. Glossolalia as an indication of human weakness, however, is a significant point in Paul's argument. Ecstatic cries are an ultimate expression of human vulnerability as well as a sign that people feel accepted at a deep level that is beyond speech. Therefore it is an integral aspect of Christian experience.

Romans 8:31-39. As we discovered in answering question 9 in Dimension One, Paul has an elaborate list of the cosmic powers in 8:35-39. In the first century, people believed that the world was dominated by forces and powers in the world around them. They had a personified idea of evil and economics and social forces. They believed that there were powers in the heavens—the "height"—and that there were powers below the surface of the earth—the "depth" (8:39). They were convinced that every human institution was something of the otherworldly power, capable of exercising an evil, superhuman control.

An investigation of this usage by Walter Wink (*Naming the Powers*; Fortress Press, 1984) suggests that the wide variety of terms used for these forces and the fact that so many of them appear to be historical or social powers or factors leads us to a single hypothesis concerning Paul's view. Wink suggests that Paul understood all human institutions as having an inner and an outer side. These institutions and forces have an external structure, but they also have an internal spirit or ethos. We know this to be the case of the institutions for which we work and of the governments that have been established by humans. Each has a different structure; but even those with the same structure have a different kind of spirit, shaped by the persons leading them and shaped by the peculiar history of each institution.

Wink suggests a simple formula for understanding the principalities (experiences) and powers: P = O + I. He means that "powers" equals the "outer plus inner" side. With this theory Wink is able to explain how experiences and powers sometimes become evil. They sometimes develop a concept of themselves as absolute. They may begin to call for absolute obedience from those who work in them or serve them. When the institutions of this world are actually revered as superhuman and ultimate, they can become demonic.

Paul's contention in 8:31-39 is that none of these institutions and forces is capable of separating humans from the love of Christ. Although the world remains fallen and these forces remain a reality, Christians have no need to lose heart. They have a basis for final confidence, a relational foundation for hope in the love of God that is demonstrated to us in that God "did not spare his own Son, but gave him up for us all" (8:32). The thrilling sequence at the end of Romans 8 affirms not only the triumphant power of God over all human institutions but also the basis of Christian realism and hope. These forces that are often distorted and cause uncounted evil, contributing to the groaning of the whole creation, do not have ultimate power. They are in the process of transformation. And as Christians become agents of righteousness, their task is to work for the transformation of these forces and institutions. The final transformation, of course, will not occur until the end of time. But in the meanwhile, Paul recommends an attitude that is the opposite of servility toward the principalities and powers of this world. Christians are not to be frightened of them, for they are incapable of separating believers from the love of God.

DIMENSION THREE: WHAT DOES THE BIBLE MEAN TO ME?

The Flesh/Spirit Dualism—The Modern Superhero

Among the areas of the modern world that have been influenced by a sometimes distorted grasp of the flesh/spirit in Romans 8 is the modern superhero. In the classic cowboy stories, the allegiance of the superhero to the higher realm was shown by the superhero resisting such temptations of "the flesh" as gambling, drinking alcohol, and sexual attraction. In more recent forms of the superheroic tales, such resistance is limited to remaining true to the righteous cause. The superhero or superheroine will not sell out when the crisis comes. The supervillains, on the other hand, are usually characterized as motivated by pride, arrogance, and other fleshly considerations.

The threat of evil in the modern superheroic fantasy is perceived to be caused by villains who are not really part of the democratic community. Thus redemption can occur when such villains are destroyed, restoring the community to a trouble-free situation. In contrast, Romans 8 suggests that the creation continues to groan under the weight of universal human sin even after the coming of Christ to redeem. In contrast to superheroic drama, Paul remains realistic about both the responsibility for and the duration of adversity. The key to redemption for him is the love of Christ that gives us courage in face of the distorted powers of the world, whereas superheroic stories offer a simplistic and illusory escape from threats.

For if their rejection is the reconciliation of the world, what will their acceptance be but life from the dead? (11:15).

11

Unbelief and World Conversion

Romans 9–11

DIMENSION ONE:
WHAT DOES THE BIBLE SAY?

Answer these questions by reading Romans 9—11

1. How many things does Paul list that belong to the people of Israel? What are they? (9:4-5)

   Paul lists eight privileges that belong to Israel. They are the sonship, "the divine glory," "the covenants," "the receiving of the law," "the temple worship," "the promises," "the patriarchs," and the Christ.

2. From whom did the people of Israel descend, from Isaac or from Esau? (9:6-13)

   In 9:7, 10 Paul argues that Israel descended from Isaac and Jacob, not Ishmael or Esau.

3. What does Paul give as the reason why God elects to have mercy on whom God wills? (9:16)

   The reason is to show that God's mercy does not depend on human "desire or effort."

4. Why did Israel not succeed in fulfilling the law? (9:30-32)

   According to 9:32, Israel did not succeed in fulfilling the law "because they pursued it not by faith but as if it were by works."

5. What is the word that is "near you . . . in your mouth and in your heart"? (10:8)

   Paul defines this word as "the word of faith we are proclaiming."

6. How does Paul say that faith comes? (10:17)

   Paul writes that "faith comes from hearing the message, and the message is heard through the word of Christ."

7. Why is Paul convinced that God "did not reject" Israel? (11:1-6)

   God has not rejected his people because "at the present time there is a remnant chosen by grace" (not by works).

8. Whom does Paul liken to the "wild olive shoot" grafted into the olive tree? (11:17-24)

   When Paul speaks of "you, though a wild olive shoot" (11:17) and contrasts this with "they were broken off" (11:20), identifying the latter as "the natural branches" of the tree (11:21), it is clear that the Gentiles are the wild olive shoot. (See also verse 13.)

9. What is the "mystery" that Paul reveals? (11:25-26a)

   The mystery that Paul reveals is that Israel will be hardened "in part until the full number of the Gentiles has come in. And so all Israel will be saved."

10. Who does Paul say has actually ever "known the mind of the Lord"? (11:33-36)

    Paul implies that only God really knows "the mind of the Lord."

DIMENSION TWO:
WHAT DOES THE BIBLE MEAN?

In Romans 9–11 we turn to material that has often been viewed as only loosely connected with the rest of Paul's letter to the Romans. Particularly to scholars oriented to the Reformation tradition, believing that the purpose of Romans was to teach the proper doctrine of justification by grace alone, the material in these chapters seems quite problematic. Among traditional interpreters, only the Calvinists have taken great pleasure in the content of these chapters and have tried to make a case that they connected closely with Romans. In the approach we are following in this course, an integral relationship between these chapters and the rest of the argument of Romans is presupposed. The proofs that confirm the basic thesis of Romans 1:16-17 are being continued in 9–11. These three chapters are an extended discussion of the plight of Israel as it throws light on the central thesis concerning the righteousness of God.

The three chapters are divided into ten well-organized units. The first is the introduction (9:1-5), describing the tragic riddle of Israel's unbelief. Paul then opens the formal argument with 9:6-18, discussing the fate of Israel and the righteousness of divine election. In this section Israel's destiny is seen to come through Isaac so that the true Israelites are "children of the promise" (9:8). The next section of the argument is 9:19-29, which answers an objection to Paul's argument. If Israel's destiny was the result of divine election, then how can God hold anybody else accountable for failing to perform? Paul deals with this by a series of scriptural proofs concerning the potter and the clay and Israel's uneven relationship with God in the past.

In 9:30–10:4, Paul answers the question about the righteousness of God by a doctrine of unenlightened zeal. Here he shows that Jewish zealotry had resulted in their rejecting the righteousness of God as it came to them in the Christ event. In the fifth section of the argument, 10:5-13, Paul argues that righteousness by faith alone is confirmed by Scripture. In this section he stresses the impartial quality of the righteousness of God, including Jews as well as Gentiles.

In 10:14-21, Paul describes the gospel that was freely preached to the whole world but rejected by some of Israel. Then in 11:1-10, Paul provides an answer as to whether indeed God had rejected Israel. Paul contends that a remnant of Jews has indeed been responsive to the grace of God and that God had in no sense repudiated Israel. In 11:11-24, Paul takes up the issue of the hidden purpose of Israel's rejection of the gospel. The gospel was thereby proclaimed to Gentiles so that the promise given to Israel (that Israel would be a blessing to the Gentile world) was indeed fulfilled. The word of God has not been empty.

In the ninth section of the argument, 11:25-32, Paul lays out the "mystery" of Israel's salvation. After the appropriate number of Gentiles has been brought into the church, Paul believes that "all Israel will be saved." The conclusion of the argument, 11:33-36, is a doxology concerning the mysterious mind of God. This ends with a suitable reference to the all-inclusive power and scope of the divine rule and glory (11:36).

Romans 9:1-5. The opening lines of Romans 9 convey the deep sense of personal anguish that Paul had experienced when his fellow Jews repudiated the gospel of Christ. The sincerity of his convictions on this point have apparently been called into question because he refers to his conscience bearing witness to the truth of this anguish. Paul feels so strongly about this that he wishes that he himself were cursed for the sake of his brothers if they could only be included in the Christian fellowship (9:3).

Furthermore, that Paul cannot abandon a Jewish role in the Christian faith is elaborated by his listing the eight privileges that belong to Israel. (See the answer to question 1 in Dimension One.) Here Paul picks up the rest of the theme that was left over from Romans 3:1-2. He had said at that point in answer to the question of what advantage does the Jew have, "Much in every way!" But in Romans 3, Paul only dealt with one of these advantages, the fact that Israel had been entrusted with the oracles of God. Here Paul lays out all the great contributions of Israel, contributions that were absolutely essential for a proper understanding of the gospel itself.

From this rather elaborate listing of Jewish contributions, we see that Paul does not wish to support an anti-Semitic view of the faith, an issue that was apparently raging in Rome at this time. The Jewish Christians were being discriminated against by the Gentile Christians; and Paul is making a case here that by rejecting Jews, Gentiles are rejecting their own religious heritage. Every one of the eight attributes of the Jewish tradition had played a role in the earlier argument of Romans. Paul cannot conceive of a Christianity apart from Judaism.

The great religious heritage shared by the Jewish people would all be null and void if the faithfulness of God were jeopardized. Paul undertakes to discuss this issue in Romans 9–11. Does the repudiation of the gospel by a part of the Jewish people prove that God's word is not indeed powerful? We have traced this theme throughout Paul's letter, showing its relevance from the moment of its initial statement in the thesis of 1:16-17 that the gospel "is the power of God for the salvation of everyone." If the gospel is not powerful enough even to convince God's own people, what hope is there for the salvation of the world? And if God cannot prevail and make his word stand, how can salvation be trusted? Thus Romans 9:6 states the fundamental issue to be dealt with in these three chapters, whether "God's word had failed."

After flatly denying that God's word failed, Paul supports his case on the premise that God's promise to Israel, given to Abraham, was that "through Isaac . . . your offspring will be reckoned" (9:7). This citation of an important principle of Jewish theology (Genesis 21:12) is interpreted in such a way that the true children of Isaac are understood to be "children of the promise," persons who have responded to God's word.

Romans 9:6-18. The problem that Paul faces in Romans 9–11 is a formidable one. Is it possible to believe that Israel was elected by God and yet that Israel had stumbled and was now being rejected? If the election of Israel had the power of God behind it, how could it be thwarted by human resistance? Paul deals with this issue in a forthright manner, interpreting the Isaac story in such a way that the election of God continues, "not by works but by him who calls" (9:12). Paul is building a case here that those who rest their reliance on their "works" are not truly the children of Isaac. Only those who see their life resting entirely on the mercy and the call of God are the true children of Israel. Paul at this point is elaborating the theme that we studied in 2:28-29, that the true Jew is the one who is circumcised in the heart. Similarly, Paul had argued in 4:12 that Abraham was the father of those who "walk in the footsteps of the faith that our father Abraham had before he was circumcised."

With this distinction, Paul is able to take seriously the problem of stumbling. That humans had repeatedly rejected the call of God and that Israel in particular had been unfaithful is proved by the Scripture quotations in 9:25-33. In the last of these citations (9:33), Paul correlates stumbling and the avoidance of stumbling with the possession of faith. Therefore God's promise to be faithful to Israel has not been broken. Those who have faith and act as children of the promise remain under the power of God. To them God has remained faithful (9:33).

Paul then goes on to explain this stumbling through a theory of unenlightened zeal that is closely related to his own conversion (10:1-4). We dealt with this theme in Romans 7. Here in 10:3, Paul explicitly correlates the theme of righteousness with the rejection of Christ on the part of zealous Jews. In rejecting Christ, they are seeking to "establish their own [righteousness, and] they did not submit to God's righteousness."

Romans 10:4. The underlying issue in the rejection by zealous Jews of the revelation of the righteousness of God in Christ was the law. The fact that Jesus was a lawbreaker and that he was executed in a way that revealed to popular perception that he was a lawless sinner made the center of the gospel an issue of disrepute among loyal Jews. The statement about the relation between Christ and the law in 10:4, however, is rather complicated and requires some sorting out.

I want to present three possibilities for the translation of the term that is rendered "end" in the New International Version. That Paul meant to say Christ was "the end of the law" has been most often supported by Lutheran scholars. This approach tends to make law and gospel into absolutely opposing realms. A representative of this view is Ernst Kaesemann, who writes, "The Mosaic Torah comes to an end with Christ" (*Commentary on Romans*, page 283). Others try to correlate this particular translation with the central theme of Pauline theology concerning freedom from the law and justification by grace alone. One tendency of those using this translation is to view Christianity as unalterably opposed to Judaism, to interpret Paul as opposed on principle to the law. Whether intended or not, it is clear that to call the Torah fundamentally into question is to undercut any basis of dialogue with Judaism.

The second view, one favored by Calvinist interpreters and many others, is that the word in 10:4 should be translated as "goal" or "fulfillment." The basic conviction in this translation is that Paul does not really believe Christ has abolished the law and that such statements as "apart from law" in 3:21 have been grossly exaggerated. The Calvinist

preference is to keep the realm of law intact so that there will be a viable basis for reconstructing the human community. Despite this element of theological bias, there appears to be little doubt that this translation fits the context better.

The third approach to the translation of Romans 10:4 is the least acceptable, though it is strongly advocated in some commentaries. The suggestion is that Paul intended the Greek word to mean *both* the end and the goal of the law. One scholar even goes so far as to suggest that Paul was "deliberately using the ambiguity in the word to cover up a subtle change in the direction of his thought on the matter. . . . Paul seems to be implying that, though the function of the law has been radically altered by the coming of Christ, it has not been altogether abolished." I see some major problems with this third alternative. First, Paul's wording of 10:4 gives no hint that he wished to insert an element of ambiguity. Second, I find a serious flaw in terms of method in this third interpretation, which can confuse the alternatives developed in the debate between current scholars with the original intention of Paul.

Several recent studies of 10:4 have lent weight to the second alternative described above, namelys that Paul intended to say that Christ is the *goal* of the law. A thorough investigation of the Greek word behind this translation suggests that originally it meant "apex, aim, or completion." The idea of goal or fulfillment is characteristic of Paul's use of this group of terms.

The consequence of this recent research is that 10:4 provides a much less polemical basis than usual for the relation between Jews and Christians. Paul's argument in 9:30–10:4 is that the ultimate purpose of the law was that all persons, Jews and Gentiles alike, might find righteousness. If Christ is the "goal of the law," the path of faith can be pursued without repudiating the Torah.

A crucial point here is that no one needs to become anti-Semitic to be a Christian. And Jews need not repudiate their legacy of the Torah if they become Christians. That Paul believes this is clearly indicated by his statement of the eight advantages the Jews have in 9:4-5. It is also strongly confirmed by the formulation Paul used to conclude 3:31: "Rather, we uphold the law." This verse has always given some scholars a terrible time because it seems so flatly to contradict what Paul wrote in 10:4. But when 10:4 is understood to say that Christ is the *goal* of the law, the contradiction disappears.

Romans 10:5-9. The references in Romans 10:5-9 to bringing Christ "up" or "down" may be puzzling to the members of your class. Several citations from the Old Testament are woven together here into an argument that bears directly on the question of gaining righteousness by law, the question that was crucial in Paul's understanding of the misguided zeal of 10:4. Paul acknowledged that the Jews had zeal for the law but that it was not "based on knowledge" (10:2). In trying to establish righteousness by conforming to "works," the zealots did not respond in the right way to the revelation of God's righteousness in the Christ event.

In 10:5-9, Paul argues that the person who is devoted to obeying the law is convicted of the error of that strategy by the law itself. Legalistic obedience that is motivated by the effort to bring the messianic era is defined here as wrong. Romans 10:5 states the basic principle that every person who lives by the law must obey it at every point. And then Deuteronomy 30:12 is cited—"Do not say in your heart, 'Who will ascend into heaven?' [that is, to bring Christ down]"—in order to show that the attempt to bring the Messiah through observing the law is explicitly forbidden by the law. The zealous Jews had assumed that if all Israel would obey the law just for one day, the Messiah would come and vindicate the righteous.

Paul shows that this kind of strategy of bringing in the Messiah is actually sinful now that the Messiah has already come. No longer does anyone need to "ascend into heaven" or "descend into the deep" to inaugurate and defend the messianic age. It has already come in Christ. What is required now, rather than frantic efforts to bring the Kingdom, is an appropriate response to the good news that the Kingdom has already come in Christ.

Paul's Attitude Toward Judaism

The issue of Romans 9–11 and particularly the question of Paul's expectation of the conversion of Jews to Christianity has been widely debated in scholarly circles. In order to provide some orientation for the members of your class, several of the major contributions to this important discussion need to be sketched.

J. Christian Beker deals with the issue of Jews and Gentiles within the context of his contention that Paul's theology was dominated by end-time thinking (*Paul the Apostle: The Triumph of God in Life and Thought*; Fortress Press, 1984). He defends Paul as the only New Testament writer who is passionately engaged with Jews as the people of promise. Although he recognizes that Paul had a different understanding of messianism than the Jewish community as a whole, he insisted that Paul was the New Testament writer who most consistently kept "his thought anchored in the Hebrew scriptures and in the destiny of Israel as God's people."

Beker suggests that Paul remained convinced of the priority of Israel, reflected in the repeated line in Romans, "first for the Jew, then for the Gentile" (1:16; 2:9, 10). Beker understands these statements within the context of the Roman community and the argument of the faithfulness of God to Israel. If the promises of God to Israel are annulled, then the inclusion of the Gentiles loses its foundation.

In relation to Romans 9–11, Beker insists that Israel is not expected to be absorbed by the church. When Paul refers to the "mystery" of Israel's salvation (11:25), he is talking about the mysterious dynamic of God's salvation history in which successive periods of Jewish and Gentile disobedience and conversion will finally result in the conversion and unification of the world.

Beker rejects the idea of Jewish conversion to Christianity and calls for a dialogue about the problems of under-

standing messianism in the modern world. He points out the distinctive feature of Christian messianism as an important issue to be discussed with Jews. From the Christian perspective, "the Messiah has come, but without his kingdom." That is, the fulfillment of the messianic promises is left to the future.

In both his books on Paul, E. P. Sanders has provided a bulwark against an anti-Semitic interpretation; but he does not approve of the rejection of a Jewish mission that marks the work of Beker. (See *Paul and Palestinian Judaism: A Comparison of Patterns of Religion*; Fortress Press, 1977; and *Paul, the Law, and the Jewish People*; Fortress Press, 1983.) Sander's basic contention is that Paul's critique of Judaism rests entirely on his Christian experience and thus has nothing to do with the actual shape of Jewish practice in the first century. Paul's only criticism of Judaism was that it did not accept Christ. Insisting on the same "entrance requirement" of faith in Christ, both for Jews and for Gentiles, Paul in effect established a kind of third race, the true Israel mentioned in Romans 2 and 4. Sanders, therefore, favors a straightforward reading of Romans 11:25-26, that, according to Paul, the only way to enter the ranks of the saved is by faith in Christ. Sanders goes on to argue that Paul denied two pillars common to all forms of Judaism, the election of Israel and faithfulness to the Mosaic law. I believe this is somewhat difficult to maintain because Paul explicitly affirms the election of Israel in Romans 3:1-2; 9:4-5, 11. Furthermore, Paul defends the legitimacy of the Torah as we have seen in 3:31 and 10:4.

In reviewing this research, I think it is important to keep in mind that in Romans, Paul defended the integrity of Jewish culture and of Jewish Christians. We have seen throughout Romans the interest in defending the "weak" against the "strong." And even though these are not flat identifications of Jewish Christians versus Gentile Christians, Paul's argument results in defending the minority in Rome, which in this instance contained the Jewish Christians. In Romans 14:1–15:13, Paul repudiates the idea of a monochromatic church in which cultural distinctions and theological tendencies need to be obliterated. While I think that Paul hoped for the conversion of Jews to Christianity in the sense of belief in Christ, he did not really insist on their abandonment of the law. In fact, he makes as strong a case as possible in Romans in defense of the law. But he wishes the law to be interpreted in light of Christ.

DIMENSION THREE: WHAT DOES THE BIBLE MEAN TO ME?

Unenlightened Zeal and the Conversion of the Jews

Probably the two most complicated issues to be discussed in relation to Romans 9–11 are "unenlightened zeal" and the question of the conversion of the Jews. While zealotism was a factor in Jewish rejection of Christianity according to 10:2-3, it has subsequently played a major role in Christian persecutions of the Jews. In the ferocity of the Nazi holocaust, a secular form of this same zealotism resulted in the deaths of millions of Jews, placing a permanent burden on the relations between Christians and Jews. Since the holocaust, with the rise of Islamic and Christian fundamentalism, unenlightened zeal is resulting in new forms of anti-Semitism. In this situation there is a need for sensitivity in interpreting Romans 9–11. It is time that Christians recognized that their traditional attempts to fulfill Paul's expectation in Romans 11:25-26 by trying to convert Jews often aimed, in fact, at cultural annihilation. Nothing in Romans provides warrant for the assumption that Jews will accept a Gentile gospel, abandoning their culture of the Torah. Such an assumption is itself a form of "unenlightened zeal," an effort to "establish the righteousness" of later Christian culture by absorbing others.

The issue of the salvation of the Jews thus calls Christians to rethink our entire approach to evangelism. In our Bible studies and mission boards, we need to create modern embodiments of Paul's hope of a generous and inclusive gospel that will counter zealous fanaticism, honor cultural and theological differences, and unite the fractured world. Just as in the case of the Roman house churches, the ones who need to stand first in line for such conversion are we Christians ourselves.

Love must be sincere. Hate what is evil; cling to what is good (12:9).

— 12 —

The Love Ethic as Response

Romans 12

DIMENSION ONE:
WHAT DOES THE BIBLE SAY?

Answer these questions by reading Romans 12

1. In view of what does Paul appeal to the Romans? (12:1)

   Paul appeals to the Romans "in view of God's mercy."

2. What does Paul urge the Romans to offer to God? (12:1)

   Paul urges the Romans to present their "bodies as living sacrifices, holy and pleasing to God."

3. How should the Roman Christians act toward the world? (12:2)

   Paul tells the Roman Christians not to conform to the world, but to be transformed by the renewal of their minds.

4. What points does Paul draw from the metaphor of the body? (12:4-8)

   "In Christ we who are many form one body" (12:5), and different gifts should be used by members "according to the grace given us" (12:6-8).

5. How many commands does Paul relate in developing the theme "Love must be sincere"? (12:9-20)

   When we count the imperative verbs in this passage, we find two in verse 9 (hate, cling), followed by ten commands in 12:10-13 that spell out aspects of Christian love (be devoted to one another, honor one another, never be lacking in zeal, keep your spiritual fervor, serve the Lord, rejoice in hope, be patient, be faithful, share, practice hospitality). The twelve commands in 12:14-20 deal more generally with relations to outsiders or members of other Christian house churches (bless, do not curse, rejoice, mourn, live in harmony, never be proud, do not be conceited, do not repay, do what is right, live at peace, never avenge, leave room for God's wrath). [Note that the command about avenging is supported by a citation from Proverbs 25:21-22 so that the commands in that citation (12:20) are not

counted as coming directly from Paul.] Finally, 12:21 has a double exhortation (do not be overcome, overcome). The grand total is therefore twenty-six. [Going through these commands will aid in comprehending the thought and structure of this passage.]

6. Check the Old Testament citation in Romans 12:19. Is the wording "It is mine to avenge; I will repay" closer to Leviticus 19:18 or to Deuteronomy 32:35?

   Romans 12:19 is cited more directly from Deuteronomy 32:35.

7. Romans 12:20 is an exact citation from Proverbs 25:21-22, except that one phrase is left out. What important theme in Romans would have been weakened if this phrase had been cited by Paul?

   The final clause in Proverbs 25:22, "and the LORD will reward you," is deleted by Paul. The central theme of Romans, salvation by grace alone, would be weakened by the inclusion of this clause promising a reward for good works.

8. Verse 21 is considered a summary of the preceding passage. In which verses of Romans 12 do you find the themes of good/evil and overcoming the world rather than being overcome by it?

   "Good/evil" are found in verses 2, 9, and 17. The theme of allowing the world to dominate your thought and behavior is stated in verse 2. It is implied in verses 14; 17; and, as Dimension Two will explain, also in 12:3.

DIMENSION TWO:
WHAT DOES THE BIBLE MEAN?

Structure

When you teach Romans 12, you may need to counter the tendency to see this material as unrelated to the earlier argument of Romans and also as a rather disorganized list of exhortations. The material is tightly organized and divided into three sections. (1) Romans 12:1-2 has a thematic statement that sets the tone for the whole ethical section of Romans that extends to 15:7. (2) Next we find a series of admonitions related to the proper exercise of Christian gifts within the church, Romans 12:3-8. (3) Finally, in 12:9-21, Paul gives us admonitions to express authentic love in the struggle between good and evil. Verses 9 and 21 serve as brackets for this passage, with the admonitions in verses 10-13 dealing primarily with life within a particular congregation and verses 14-20 dealing primarily with relations to persons outside one's particular Christian group. This section is concluded with verse 21 that not only refers to verse 9 but also sums up the themes of the entire chapter.

Romans 12:1-2. Romans 12:1-2 provides the earliest systematic basis for a Christian ethic. The important thing to explain is that the motivation for good behavior developed in these two verses comes from the entire first eleven chapters of Romans, as summarized by the expression "God's mercy." The tendency in the history of interpreting Romans has been to separate the theological section (Romans 1–11) from the ethical section (Romans 12–15). This way of viewing Romans reduces everyday behavior to a position of secondary importance and defines Christianity primarily as a set of beliefs. This view also misinterprets Paul's intent, as seen by the fact that he makes important ethical references in the so-called "dogmatic chapters" of Romans (See 2:21-23; 6:12-19; 7:5-23; 8:3-13.) and gives many theological details in the ethical chapters.

Given this tendency to separate ethics from its source, we need to interpret each admonition in the next chapters in light of the summary of 12:1-2. This summary requires us to think of the implications of justification by grace and the function of human gratitude, which contrast so strikingly with conformity to this world. Paul's appeal "in view of God's mercy" assumes that the Romans have experienced the reconciling love of God and are thereby capable of passing that love on to others.

Romans 12:3-8. The contrast in Romans 12:3 between "soberminded" and "superminded" (See the new translation of this verse in the student book.), conveyed in the elaborate play on the word *mind* (used four times in this sentence), would have been easily understood by educated people in the congregation. Greek philosophers had developed a negative evaluation of the superminded heroes like Achilles and Ajax, whose exploits and pride violated standards of decency. The Greeks had a positive attitude toward the soberminded heroes like Odysseus, who resisted pride and accepted limits. The well-known Delphic oracle is related to this contrast: "Know thyself . . . that thou art but mortal," which means knowing you are not a superhero and thus should follow sobermindedness.

Paul was tapping this Greek tradition (similar at some points to the Judaic heritage of pride going before the fall) because his experience had apparently shown him that persons who believe they are gods are impossible to live with. The tendency he is countering in Romans 12:3 is for early Christians to infer from their charismatic experiences that they are divine and thus that others should submit to their domination.

Paul develops in 12:3 the unique idea of an individual's "measure of faith," understood as a kind of measuring device by which ethical and theological judgments can be reached. Each Christian is given a unique experience of faith as the Spirit makes the gospel of divine love relevant to the condition of the heart. This measuring rod of faith must be kept by each Christian as the basis of a proper relationship with God and the world. But if one becomes "superminded" about one's measuring rod, the typical result is to coerce others to accept one's theology and ethical judgments.

A comparison between the body metaphor in 12:4-5 and 1 Corinthians 12:12-27 might help. Since First Corinthians was written several years before Romans, most commentators interpret the latter in light of the former. Actually, some important differences should be taken into account. Not only is the treatment much longer in First Corinthians, its focus is quite different. What begins as a metaphor in 1 Corinthians 12:12 ends up as a realistic identification of the church as the body of Christ in 12:27. This identification is avoided in Romans where Paul states that the church members who are many form one body in Christ. For some reason Paul does not use the idea of the church as the mystical body of Christ in Romans. Rather than stressing that individuals are part of Christ, he says in Romans 12:5 that "each member belongs to all the others." The most likely explanation of this shift in Romans is that Paul was guarding against "superminded" pretensions that certain gifted believers shared Christ's divinity and thus deserved the status of being the "body of Christ." The stress in Romans is clearly on the equality and interdependence of members with other members.

In dealing with Romans 12:9-21, decide whether to follow several recent commentators in viewing the individual admonitions as a random collection of traditional sayings. The student book tries to relate the admonitions to the prologue of 12:1-2 and to the brackets of 12:9 and 21, but you may find this unconvincing. The assumption behind the treatment in the student book is that Paul has selected, adapted, and carefully organized early Christian admonitions to fit the circumstances in the Roman congregation. If you accept this approach, lead a discussion of the relation of the sayings to that congregational situation; if not, then discuss the general significance of the individual sayings for early Christianity.

Some members of your class may be interested in an additional clarification of the different types of love in this passage. The student book identifies the reference in 12:9 as *agape,* the usual early Christian term for generous, self-giving love that demands nothing in return. The following verse uses the term *philadelphia* and should be translated literally, "having affection for one another with brotherly love." This term implies familial love that is reciprocal. Brothers and sisters share a love derived from common experiences, prolonged intimacy in one family, and common interests in the family's success and reputation. Unfortunately, both terms are translated with a single English word, *love*. Paul uses *agape* for the general admonition in 12:9, whose implications are spelled out in the next several chapters.

Paul resists the tendency to view generous, self-giving love as incompatible with ethical discrimination; if love is unearned and undiscriminating, how can it say no to anything? Paul rejects this approach by demanding that love be "sincere," as proved by its capacity to hate evil and to hold fast to the good. The emotional intensity of these verbs would be more properly conveyed by the literal translation "abhor" and "cleave" rather than "hate" and "cling." Paul obviously holds that the genuineness of *agape* can be measured by the intensity of the repulsion against whatever harms loved ones and of attachment to what preserves their lives. In 12:10, *philadelphia* is a more homey form of love that Paul feels would be suitable for the house churches in Rome, which in fact were treating one another as enemies rather than as brothers and sisters.

Romans 12:16 fits in smoothly with the need for harmony among Christian groups in Rome, but its translation is somewhat confusing and may raise questions in the mind of your class members. The commands "do not be proud" and "do not be conceited" seem to overlap. The same verbal element used four times in the word play of 12:3 appears here. It is visible as the term *mind* in the following literal translation of 12:16:

> Be of the same mind toward one another. Do not set your minds on exalted things but be drawn to lowly persons. Never be wise minded in yourselves.

This admonition is directed to the "superminded" (12:3) members of the congregation. Their attention is so fixed on "exalted" mysteries that they act in condescending ways toward unsophisticated members of the congregation. By requesting that they be "of the same mind toward one another," Paul aims to replace this dangerous sense of superiority with an admission of equality. The church cannot reflect "sincere love" (12:9) if it allows the intellectual and social distinctions of the fallen world to define the status of its members. This verse is important for Sunday school classes where gradations of intelligence and education are often barriers to real communication among equals.

To understand the background of Paul's discussion of vengeance in 12:19-20, we must realize that large segments of the Jewish community in the period prior to the Jewish-Roman war of A.D. 66–73 favored a vigilante strategy. Modeling their behavior on the heroic tales in the Old Testament, they believed that their vengeance against evildoers would achieve divine ends. In particular, these advocates of Jewish vigilantism felt that the Roman governing authorities should be opposed on principle and with force. And it was natural in this kind of environment that many persons who had suffered injustices at the hands of the

authorities felt called by the heroic myth to take the law into their own hands, to avenge themselves, and thus to avenge Israel.

In this context Paul's admonition "Do not take revenge, my friends, but leave room for God's wrath" (12:19) assumes significance. He was tapping the ancient tradition of never being a judge in one's own cause, a principle embodied in Jewish as well as in Greco-Roman law. This principle is crucial for modern jurisprudence as well. The trouble with the police or private citizens taking the law into their own hands is that the omniscience and impartiality of the heroic stories never seem to work out in reality. Zealotism is presumptuous, Paul implies here, for it refuses to give way to the prerogatives of divine justice. "Leave room for God's wrath, for it is written: 'It is mine to avenge, I will repay,' says the Lord."

The most significant question we have to face in regard to vengeance is what to do in the meanwhile. If we simply harbor our hatred and fail to express it, we sicken; or if we give way to our desire for vengeance and take the law into our own hands, we suffer disastrous consequences. So Paul's alternative is worth taking seriously.

In place of zealous vigilantism, Paul advises two things: an active concern for the life and well-being of one's adversary and submission to lawful governmental authority (Romans 13:1-7). At first glance these appear to be flatly contradictory, an issue we will take up in Lesson 13.

The concern for the good of one's enemies is dealt with first: Romans 12:20 specifies what was meant earlier in this chapter by the admonition "Do not repay anyone evil for evil" (12:17). Whereas the natural tendency is to respond to violence with violence, to meanness with reprisals, the actions of mercy aim to break the deadly cycle. The abiding guideline of the church is the commitment to "overcome evil with good," as the following verses (12:18-21) set forth.

The strategy Paul recommends seeks not only the well-being but also the transformation of persecutors and criminals. "Do not be overcome by evil, but overcome evil with good" (12:21). This is not to say that what one aims to achieve will actually be accomplished in every instance. Those commentators who accuse Paul of being an incurable optimist in these verses confuse, in my opinion, intentions with results. As Paul knew from personal experience, some adversaries react to being shamed by such unanticipated gestures of love by redoubling the intensity of their hatred. In the final analysis, what one aims to achieve is what is important: transformation, not vengeance.

DIMENSION THREE: WHAT DOES THE BIBLE MEAN TO ME?

Why Should I Do the Good?

The most important question in ethics is, "Why should I do the good?" Paul is much more careful to construct a consistent answer than most modern teachers or preachers. They tend to fall back into the language of conformity and earning acceptance through good works. One way to conduct a discussion of this matter would be to invite class members to share their reactions to moral appeals in the past and to compare them with the appeal in Romans. The contrast between the law and the gospel that we studied earlier in the course might be useful at this point. The most common ethical appeals today are based on new forms of the law. The point that needs to be made is that a healthier appeal would be based on the gospel of "God's mercy."

Vengeance

Romans 12 at several points touches on one of the most troubling aspects of current American culture, the super-heroic type of entertainment that makes vengeance popular. These stories began in the 1930s from a long tradition of fascination with vigilantism that has some similarities to the Jewish zealotism of Paul's time. We have long had an ideal of holy vengeance. Acting on the premise that God inspires and justifies the righteous to take vengeance in his behalf, we have celebrated many heroes who took the law into their own hands.

The vigilante ethos justifies direct violence so long as the evil is clear-cut, the vigilantes are disinterested, and their identity is kept secret. The appeal of this vigilante tradition has been that we could gain quick, public vengeance for terrible crimes that might otherwise go unpunished.

An example of this kind of story is *The Virginian*—Owen Wister's novel of 1902 that has the first main street duel in American literature. (This material about *The Virginian* is adapted from Robert Jewett and John Shelton Lawrence, *The American Monomyth*; Doubleday, 1977; pages 180–85.) The story is set in the context of the struggles in Wyoming between farmers and ranchers, specifically the range war in Johnson County in which lynching and systematic thievery practiced by both sides came to a climax in 1892. The ranchers imported a train load of Texas gunmen equipped with dynamite to put down the farmers who were home-steading land in the public domain that the ranchers had used without rent for years. The conflict came to a climax when federal troops finally intervened.

Wister took the ranchers' side of this struggle and created the Virginian, a tall, nameless cowboy who became the foreman of Sunk Creek Ranch. He was forced to track down a rustling gang, capturing two of its members, one of whom was formerly his best friend. True to the vigilante code, the Virginian renounced friendship and hung the thieves. The chief rustler, Trampas, escaped with a guile-less sidekick. When the trackers approached, Trampas shot his sidekick in the back so Trampas could escape on their only horse.

Several years later, Trampas rides past the Virginian and his fiancee, Molly the schoolteacher, who comments that it seems "wicked that this murderer" got off when others were hanged for rustling. "He was never even arrested," says the girl. "No, he helped elect the sheriff in that county," replies the Virginian.

In the dramatic climax of the novel, which became required reading for high school classes all over America, the rustler issues a formal challenge for a main street duel. The Virginian sought the counsel of the clergyman who had planned to perform his and Molly's wedding. The bishop was convinced that the rustlers had to be dealt with by vigilante tactics, that "they elected their men to office, and controlled juries; that they were a staring menace to Wyoming. His heart was with the Virginian. But there was his Gospel that he preached, and believed, and tried to live." He reminds the Virginian of the biblical injunction not to kill. The heroic cowboy responds, "Mighty plain to me, seh. Make it plain to Trampas, and there'll be no killin'."

As they parry about the contradictory demands of religion and law, the Virginian poses the key question: "How about instruments of providence, seh?" In other words, what about the biblical idea of providence taking the form of heroic vigilantes who rid the world of evildoers? The hero reluctantly departs for the duel that means the end of his hoped-for marriage as well as possibly of his life. The bishop finds he cannot repress the words, "God bless him! God bless him!"

The end of the story is so well known that your class members may know it without having read the novel or seen the film in which Gary Cooper played the title role. In an archetypal duel with Trampas, the bad guy draws and shoots first but is killed by the Virginian's bullet. The hero's friends marvel, "You were that cool! That quick!" which is an expression of the cool ethos of the vigilante tradition. The state of Wyoming is redeemed from the threat of crime because vengeance has occurred. Molly's New England conscience, which had resisted the vigilante tactic so strongly, finally relents; and she marries the Virginian. The novel ends with the hero and his family ensconced in prosperity and long life. The Virginian becomes a wealthy rancher and mine owner, passing the redemptive task on to the next generation.

This novel had hundreds of imitations; and shortly after its cinematic triumph in 1929, it was followed by the emergence of serialized stories featuring the supercowboy "The Lone Ranger," the supercop "Dick Tracy," and the super-heroes like "Superman" and "Captain America"—tales that embody the same kind of plot. *The Virginian* is one of the most formative tales in American culture, giving shape to the yearning for quick and effective public vengeance without using constitutional means. Here is vengeance without due process of law, yet done with dignity and heroic self-restraint. It allows us to see ourselves gaining vengeance against our enemies, but not exactly by our own doing. The public does not take the law into its own hands in this kind of story; heroes do it in our behalf. "Instruments of providence" take up the task of the "wrath of God" that Paul believed should never be shouldered by us in our own behalf.

Love does no harm to its neighbor. Therefore love is the fulfillment of the law (13:10).

13

A Tolerant Ethic in a New Era

Romans 13:1–15:7

DIMENSION ONE:
WHAT DOES THE BIBLE SAY?

Answer these questions by reading
Romans 13:1–15:7

1. Where does Paul say that governmental authority comes from? (13:1)

   Paul says that all governmental authority has been established by God.

2. How does Paul suggest that citizens respond to their fear of governmental authority? (13:3)

   Paul writes that by doing "what is right" you will receive the approval of the authorities.

3. The term *wrath* is used in 13:4-5. Can you recall where in Romans this idea is fully developed?

   "The wrath of God" is the topic of 1:18–2:16, with the term appearing in 1:18; 2:5; and 2:8. Wrath also is found in these verses: 3:5; 4:15; 5:9; 9:22; and 12:19.

4. What are the four forms of obligation to the Roman government Paul mentions? (13:7)

   Paul directs his readers to pay taxes, revenue, respect, and honor to the authorities to whom these are due.

5. What single obligation does Paul lift up for Christians that provides fulfillment of the law? (13:8, 10)

   Paul holds up love as the "fulfillment of the law."

6. On the basis of 13:11-12, when does Paul expect the return of Christ? (a) Very soon? (b) In another generation? (c) In the far distant future?

   Paul expects Christ to return very soon; "salvation is nearer now than when we first believed."

7. How many times is the relation of the believer to the Lord mentioned in 14:5-9?

   Paul describes the believer's relation to the Lord nine times—five times in 14:6, three times in 14:8, and once in 14:9.

8. What are the three aspects of the "kingdom of God"? (14:17)

   The kingdom of God is "righteousness, peace and joy in the Holy Spirit."

9. The summary in 15:7 calls for Christians to "accept one another." Where was this point made earlier in this lesson? (14:1, 3)

   This point was made in the introductory exhortation in the discussion of the "weak" and the "strong" (14:1). Also Paul affirms that "God has accepted him" (14:3).

DIMENSION TWO:
WHAT DOES THE BIBLE MEAN?

The material in Romans 13:1–15:7 provides guidelines for living in righteousness in relation to the problems the Roman house churches faced. This passage deals with the issue of the government in a way that has always been controversial in the United States. Since this section ends with an exhortation (15:7) that serves beautifully to summarize the theological and ethical argument of the entire letter, this is appropriate material for the end of our study.

The structure of the material is fairly easy to discern. Romans 13:1-7 deals with the issue of proper subjection to the government. Romans 13:8-10 sets forth the relation of love to law. Romans 13:11-14 describes and calls for moral alertness in the final days. Romans 14:1-23 provides guidelines for the weak and the strong and for mutual upbuilding in the congregation. Romans 15:1-6 provides an exhortation to follow Christ's example in accepting outsiders into the church. Finally, 15:7 draws the preceding argument together and opens the conclusion of the formal argument of the letter, which deals with world mission and unification.

In particular, draw class members' attention to the highly relevant rationale that Paul provides for tolerance within the Christian community. Given the fact that the question of mutual welcome between competitive branches of Christianity is such a problem in the modern period, this material has a practical relevance in showing the concrete bearing of Paul's argument on life today.

Romans 13:1-7. From the perspective of those committed to a modern democratic society, the argument in 13:1-7 is a problem. We experienced the impact of this in early American history. At the time of the American Revolution, the Tories, who were preaching against the revolution, argued on the basis of these verses for loyalty to King George III. In contrast, the preachers advocating rebellion took their texts from the Old Testament or other parts of the New Testament. This example could be duplicated many times in Western Christianity. In general, conservatives and defenders of the divine right of kings have appreciated these verses; reformers and democratic theorists have not. Taken out of context and interpreted from a literal perspective, these words have even provided support for vicious dictators. The "German Christians" in the 1930s and 1940s argued that Adolph Hitler was one "instituted" by God who did not "bear the sword for nothing" (13:2-4).

While the historical circumstances at the time of Paul's writings and the context in Romans 13 throw light on the situation, likely the members of your class will continue to be divided in their understanding of how these verses should be taken by the democratic society. The difference between our situation and that faced by Paul is substantial. The members of the Roman house churches, with minor exceptions, had no direct voice in governmental affairs. Even those who were involved in the bureaucracy had nothing like the kind of autonomy that we would expect in the modern world. No Christian voted that government into existence or selected its current emperor. The situation is vastly different in the modern world where, in our situation at least, the government is established by popular will and governmental authorities are routinely elected by popular vote. In a very real sense, we are the government in this society in a way that was inconceivable for the ancient world. This vast difference in circumstance needs to be taken into account as your class discusses Romans 13. Perhaps the wisdom of Ernst Kaesemann, the German scholar who struggled against Fascism and has written a major investigation of Romans 13:1-7, would be useful. Kaesemann writes,

> When a new situation is set up . . . by a democratic system, Paul's true concern, namely, that God be served in the political sphere as well, is not invalidated. But it does not tolerate holding fast to antiquated slogans, nor is it fostered by an outdated metaphysics. The old demand must be grasped in terms of the new reality and its problems, and

applied to these. Paul is confident that the charismatic community can do this (*Commentary on Romans*, page 359).

Several studies have thrown light on the historical circumstances that led to Paul's remarkably positive appraisal of government authority at the time of the mid-50s in the first century. Studies by Marcus Borg and Peter Stuhlmacher are particularly relevant. (See details in *Christian Tolerance*, by Robert Jewett; Westminster, 1982; pages 114–20.) Borg shows that the Jewish community in Rome had some "anti-Roman sentiments" that led it to agree with the Zealot resistance movement in Israel. Borg feels that Paul's major thrust in these verses, therefore, was that Christians should not extend their loyalty to Israel so far that it ended up in hostility against Rome. The message of Romans is that Christ has bridged the chasm between the nations. The Roman authority in this time, therefore, should be viewed as coming from the same God who was the God of the Israelite nation.

Borg goes on to suggest that the phrase "bear the sword" in 13:4 refers to the military and war-making ability of the Roman state rather than to its judicial punishment system. This point is rather a problem, however, because the Roman legions, which were entrusted with the defense of the frontier and military preparedness, also acted as police and judicial agents. Capital punishment in the Greco-Roman world was carried out by the military officers of the Roman legions.

Professor Stuhlmacher and his colleagues discovered a correlation between the wording about taxation in 13:6-7 and agitation in the Nero administration concerning overly high taxes. This agitation was to some degree public and may well have attracted the sympathy of the members of Roman house churches. In light of the troubles the churches had experienced with the edict of Claudius and the difficulty Jewish Christians were having in returning to Rome, Paul was suggesting that it would be unwise to get involved in potentially subversive tax resistance activities.

Another consideration in interpreting Romans 13:1-7 is that, during the period when Paul wrote, the Roman Empire had an exemplary form of law enforcement. The Nero administration was largely controlled by Seneca and Burrus, who were fair and efficient in their conduct of the law. At the time Paul was writing, the conspiracy laws had been abolished and the arbitrary death penalties for potential subversives that had marked the period before and after this time had been abandoned. Compared, in fact, with the lawlessness that Paul had experienced at the hands of zealots from the Jewish tradition, the Roman administration of law in the mid-50s looked as if it would be a positive ally of Christianity. This situation was drastically changed after A.D. 62 when Nero's administration became paranoid and the conspiracy laws were reenacted. Two years later, the first serious persecution of Christians at the hands of Roman authorities occurred after the fire of Rome. Nero was apparently directly involved in this vicious persecution, which set the precedent for a number of other persecutions for the next three hundred years.

Paul was not a fortuneteller, and he had no way of knowing that the Roman authorities that he placed such confidence in in the winter of 56–57 would turn so vicious a mere six years later. One of the questions that you might discuss with class members is whether they believe Paul might have formulated his argument differently after 62.

Romans 14:1-12. The underpinnings for Paul's argument in favor of mutual tolerance is the idea of the lordship of Christ. One sees this first in the theme of the "master" of servants in 14:4. It is developed in an elaborate way in verses 5-9, as the members of your class have discovered in answering question 7 in Dimension One. This theme was basic for early Christianity. The earliest Christian confession was that "Jesus is Lord." The idea of redemption as developed in Romans has as its premise that Christ has set people free from false lords and has now become their graceful Master. This theme is also strongly correlated with "righteousness," which prevails when the lordship of God is manifest. One finds this in early Christian hymns dealing with the bending of every knee to Christ in the Final Judgment. Paul uses precisely this line in his quotation in 14:11.

An important teaching of the lordship of Christ for early Christianity was that believers are truly subject to no one else. Even the power of the Roman government, as we saw in 13:1-7, is derivative. That authority is given by God. Therefore Christians are not to feel subservient to anyone. This teaching has a particular bearing on the competitive situation among the house churches in Rome because each group was acting like the lord of the other. In a very real sense, intolerance threatens the lordship of Christ. Or to place it in the framework of Jewish theology, refusing to recognize that it is "to his own master he stands or falls" (14:4) is a challenge to the sovereignty of God and thus a violation of the first and second commandments.

A proper grasp of the theme of lordship and its correlation with the first and second commandments allows one to see the basis for Paul's strenuous argument in favor of tolerance in Rome. The first commandment, that one should have no other gods before God, stresses as Paul does here that we should not play the role of lords to one another. To judge or despise one's competitors therefore violates the first commandment, representing the human effort to become God rather than to recognize and worship the one true God. This teaching is particularly difficult to grasp in a religious community where the basis of judging and despising is understood to be loyalty to God.

The second commandment, that one should refrain from worshiping graven images, guards the transcendent God from any idolatrous human definitions. In a sense, the competing house churches in Rome were each struggling for theological and ethical forms of graven images. They were making their definition of the truth final, demanding that others submit to it.

In light of Paul's argument in 14:1-12, we are able to see that tolerant pluralism can only be preserved when the tension between the first and second commandments is respected. Here is a summary of this argument from my book *Christian Tolerance: Paul's Message to the Modern Church*:

> Faith without tolerance violates the Second Commandment, making a graven image out of some finite definition of the transcendent. Tolerance without faith violates the First Commandment, refusing to choose the God who stands transcendent above all lesser realities. Zealous fanaticism thus violates the Second Commandment, while relativism and nihilism violate the First. Healthy tolerance is the social corollary of a faith that retains the discipline of both the First and the Second Commandment (page 69).

In Paul's view, the lordship of Christ, understood in the context of the first two commandments, provided a bulwark against the conflict among Christian groups that was jeopardizing the world mission and unification of the Christian community.

Defining Tolerance

I have used the term *tolerance* repeatedly to describe the thrust of Paul's argument in Romans 14:1–15:7. This modern term that came into use in Western civilization after the Reformation is not actually used in Paul's argument. When Paul speaks of "acceptance," he has a considerably more active and friendly attitude in mind than is usually conveyed by our modern term *tolerance*. Yet if the practical significance of Paul's argument is to be understood, we must relate it to the discussion of tolerance in our society.

Two broad types of tolerance have emerged over the last several centuries. "Formal tolerance" is based on closing one's eyes to the doctrinal issues or the personal convictions of persons who disagree with us. One finds this attitude in the Enlightenment and in the political arrangements for tolerance that fall under the definition of the separation of church and state. This kind of formal tolerance is advocated by John Locke, John Stuart Mill, and modern liberalism. Formal tolerance assumes that humans cannot know the final truth and that it is better for them to avoid conflicts on issues that cannot be settled. This tradition suggests that issues of conscience should be relegated to the private sphere and that government authorities so far as possible should avoid intervening in this sphere. The expression of erroneous ideas is to be tolerated by the state because it is too risky for the state to try to determine the complex theological and personal issues of life. The best the state can do is to preserve freedom of religion and conscience, allowing persons to do as they please so long as they do not injure others.

The form of tolerance that comes out of this tradition is very much "live and let live." It is expressed in what current-day sociologists call "civility." Our society, in fact, has some fairly elaborate rules of civility that used to include not discussing delicate and controversial issues, such as religion. In general, this rule still remains in our society. Americans refrain from discussing the intricate theological assumptions of one another's systems. We are willing to talk about the superficial aspects of someone else's religion but often avoid discussing the basics. We learn the polite smile and the shrug that allow us to hear offensive opinions without being particularly bothered or influenced by them. These rituals of civility let us live as a pluralistic society with a measure of tranquility.

Paul's concept is much closer to what some people have called "actual positive tolerance" or "intrinsic tolerance." This kind of tolerance is often found in mystical religious traditions both inside and outside the Christian heritage. This tradition recognizes that other persons whose convictions differ from ours have genuine encounters with the sacred. In this type of tolerance, the basis is the mysterious realm of divine truth that no system of dogmas can encompass. Persons who are grounded in this mystical truth are tolerant so long as they are able to distinguish between "truth as experienced reality" and "truth as rational correctness." That is, persons who approach tolerance this way can recognize the truth that other people have experienced; but they recognize that such truths cannot finally be defined in rational terms.

Unlike the mystics who promote "intrinsic tolerance," Paul believes in a publicly accessible revelation of the love of God in the Christ event. He sets forth in Romans the idea that no humans can justify themselves by conforming to their own principles. Therefore their lives must rest on God's gift to them. Since they are "accepted" unconditionally by God, they are given the power and the admonition to pass such acceptance on to others. Paul's concept of tolerance is "actual" and "positive." Paul's concept is also more strenuous and forthright about its assumptions than the philosophical tradition is often willing to believe. Paul offers in Romans a way of correlating tolerance with faith. Those who have faith in the "rightwising" activity of God in Christ recognize that God has treated them tolerantly. The love that has been poured into them is capable of being expressed to others because the barriers are destroyed and a new basis of community is achieved.

The horizons of Pauline tolerance, of course, are within the Christian community itself. Paul does not envision the kind of social tolerance that we enjoy in the modern world, though in a real sense the Roman Empire at this time was offering a kind of live-and-let-live opportunity. If we wish to extend Paul's theory of tolerance into the social ground today, we can only do so by analogy. But it should be acknowledged that the most difficult areas for tolerance are in fact within believing communities themselves.

The highest levels of hostility within the Jewish, Christian, and Islamic communities in recent years have been against internal dissenters. It seems to be much easier for Jews to live with Christians than for either to live with highly articulate and combative internal divisions. Therefore, Paul's argument for tolerance in Romans has a resource that extends far beyond the bounds of the Christian community itself. If Christian churches could find here a rationale for a new style of internal interaction, they would likely also gain the capacity to treat persons outside their community with new dignity and compassion. In a real sense Paul's hope of unifying the human race under Christ can only be accomplished when the Christian community itself begins to exhibit the kind of mutual acceptance that ultimately is intended for the whole created order.

Glory and Righteousness

At two points in our material for this week's lesson, Paul provides summary statements that draw the themes of his entire letter together. One of these is 14:17: "For the kingdom of God is not a matter of eating and drinking, but of righteousness, peace and joy in the Holy Spirit." We have repeatedly pointed to righteousness and "rightwising" as the central theme of Romans and have noted earlier how the motif of "peace" dominates the argument in Romans 5 and 15. That believers are given peace with God in the form of reconciling love, overcoming their hostility against God and other humans, is the central result of the gospel. This peace has a direct bearing on the Roman house church situation, and it is no accident that Paul identifies God as the "God of peace" in 15:33. Joy in the Holy Spirit is the human response to the gift of righteousness and peace, a response that Paul expects in the mission shortly to encompass the world. "Rejoice, O Gentiles, with his people" (15:10).

Closely associated with this great summary in 14:17 is the one in 15:7, which is developed in the student book at some length. To live for the glory of God in the context of the struggle in Rome would mean to give up claims to have the total truth and the insistence that everyone else agree. The tolerant welcome among the members of the house churches would reveal that God's glory rather than the glory of individual groups was now manifesting itself. One commentator describes the significance of this theme in the following words: "The work of Christ for Jews and Gentiles alike served the glory of God, in order that both, Jews and Gentiles, would be able to praise God, in the same congregation, with one accord and one voice."

The significance of this unique correlation between mutual tolerance and the glory of God is visible when you recognize how distinct Paul's view was in comparison with the rest of the biblical tradition. Many Jewish and Christian writers assumed that God's glory would only be manifest with the total victory of good over evil. One sees this, for example, in Psalm 79:6-10 where the psalmist asks God to pour out his wrath on

The nations
    that do not acknowledge you,
on the kingdoms
    that do not call on your name;
for they have devoured Jacob
    and destroyed his homeland.

The psalmist asks for God's direct intervention:

Help us, O God our Savior,
    for the glory of your name;
deliver us and forgive our sins. . . .
Before our eyes, make known among the nations
    that you avenge the outpoured blood of your servants.

Here the glory of God is manifest when God triumphs over foreign enemies. Those who have held Israel captive will be avenged. And when that vengeance takes place, Israel will be restored and God's name will be glorified. The more active form of this traditional approach to glory is found in Psalm 149:5-9:

Let the saints rejoice in this honor
    and sing for joy on their beds.
May the praise of God be in their mouths
    and a double-edged sword in their hands,
to inflict vengeance on the nations
    and punishment on the peoples,
to bind their kings with fetters,
    their nobles with shackles of iron,
to carry out the sentence written against them.
    This is the glory of all his saints.
Praise the LORD.

Here we see that the victory of one group over the other is understood to manifest the glory of God. To translate this into the Roman situation is to understand one reason why the house churches were so hostile to one another. They each apparently believed, as a broad stream of the biblical tradition did, that triumphing over the other would manifest God's glory. This belief is also the predominant idea of glory in the Islamic tradition and is widely popular in American religious and civic traditions. Probably nothing is more basic for our people than the idea that victory over evil enemies manifests the truth and glory of God. We may understand this today in more secular terms, but the ideas go right back to the Old Testament legacy.

The idea of victory over another is precisely what Paul has reversed in Romans. In place of the triumph of the weak over the strong or vice versa, Paul argues that the manifestation of God's glory comes through mutual respect and interaction. The theme of God's glory, therefore, places the issue of tolerance in a healthy context. To give glory to God is to place humans in their rightful spot as creatures whom it is dangerous to glorify. In this sense the "righteousness of God" which is the theme of Romans comes to its rightful expression only when "God's glory" in

its rightful sense is revealed. And this occurs, according to Paul, not when one group triumphs over the other, but when all groups submit to the lordship of Christ.

DIMENSION THREE: WHAT DOES THE BIBLE MEAN TO ME?

Subjection to the Government

Since Romans 13:1-7 was used in different ways by different people during the time of the American Revolution, it might be interesting to ask the members of your class how they might have placed themselves in relation to Romans 13 during that period. It could be that people would have answered the question differently in 1776 than they are inclined to answer it today. This discussion can help us realize that the appraisal of the relative justice of the government at any one time is crucial for one's understanding of Romans 13.

The Deeds of Darkness

The "deeds of darkness" that Paul mentions at the end of Romans 13 were related to forms of behavior that were highly popular in the Greco-Roman world. An average week of American television (news, drama, and comedy shows) would provide examples of each of these deeds. Bringing some of this material to mind in your lesson might well sharpen the distinction that Paul describes. You need to be careful, however, of falling into a biased assessment of popular entertainment.

Mutual Upbuilding

Romans 14 may help the members of your class distinguish between destructive and helpful criticism. The theme of "mutual edification" in 14:19 is important in this context. This theme implies that each person in the Christian community is responsible for urging others to remain true to their foundations and to grow on their own roots. This implies that the church needs to hold people accountable to their own standards. "Mutual edification" would imply that conservatives and liberals should each seek to encourage the growth of the other, each on the foundations of his or her own faith.

The Issue of Tolerance

In recent years a good deal of material has appeared in the newspapers that bears on the issue of tolerance. The conflicts between Protestants and Roman Catholics in Ireland would be a useful topic of discussion. An additional and quite terrible resource is the story of recent events in Bosnia, since the tradition of civility has been abandoned. Ask members of your class for other examples of places where a form of mutual welcome would be appropriate.

1 AND 2 CORINTHIANS, GALATIANS, EPHESIANS
Table of Contents

1. Unity in the Church 74

2. Personal Morality in the Church 80

3. Knowledge and Love in the Church 86

4. Worship in the Church (Part 1) 92

5. Worship in the Church (Part 2) / The Resurrection 97

6. Integrity Under the New Covenant 102

7. Ministry Under the New Covenant 108

8. Open-Hearted Sharing 114

9. Apostles: The False and the True 119

10. Paul and the True Gospel 125

11. Freedom in Christ and the Spirit 130

12. The Divine Plan 135

13. The Path to Unity 140

About the Writer

Dr. Edward P. Blair is professor emeritus of New Testament interpretation at Garrett-Evangelical Theological Seminary, Evanston, Illinois.

All things are yours, whether Paul or Apollos . . . or life or death or the present or the future . . . you are of Christ, and Christ is of God (3:21-23).

1

Unity in the Church

1 Corinthians 1–4; 16

EDITOR'S NOTE: This study of the letters to the Corinthians, Galatians, and Ephesians does not run straight through the letters from beginning to end. In order to bring greater clarity to the material, Dr. Blair has chosen to deal with material from the end of several of the letters out of sequence and earlier in the study.

DIMENSION ONE:
WHAT DOES THE BIBLE SAY?

Answer these questions by reading 1 Corinthians 16

1. Where is Paul at the time of writing this letter, and what are his future plans? (16:1-11)

   Paul is at Ephesus. He plans to journey to Corinth via Macedonia, leaving after Pentecost, and to remain in Corinth for a considerable time (perhaps over the winter). After arriving in Corinth, he will send a Corinthian delegation to Jerusalem with money for the church there and possibly go himself.

2. What does Paul desire the Corinthians to be and do until his arrival? (16:1-18)

   Paul tells them to take up an offering weekly for the Jerusalem Christians. They are to receive Timothy graciously, respect his authority, and send him back to Paul. They are to respect their own leaders, including the three-man delegation. They are to cultivate certain spiritual qualities: watchfulness, tenacity, courage, and love.

Answer these questions by reading 1 Corinthians 1:1–2:5

3. What does Paul say about himself and about the church at Corinth in the opening greeting? (1:1-2)

   Paul says that he is an apostle of Christ Jesus through divine appointment. He is joined in the writing of this letter by a

Christian brother, Sosthenes. Paul speaks of the church at Corinth as "the church of God," as "those sanctified in Christ Jesus," and "called to be holy." He indicates that the Corinthian church is part of a widespread Christian community.

4. What are the Corinthians quarreling about, and what is Paul's attitude toward their quarrel? (1:10-17)

   Rival groups in the church are claiming superiority for different leaders—Paul, Apollos, Cephas, Christ—and in their dissension are destroying the unity of the church. Paul is horrified that Christians should divide around different leaders and thus split up Christ.

5. Who are the advocates of the wisdom of the world? (1:18-20)

   The wise man, the scholar, and the philosopher of this age, according to Paul, are advocates of the wisdom of the world.

6. What is wrong with their attitudes and spirit? (1:18-23)

   Those who are advocates of the wisdom of the world arrogantly regard the preaching of the cross as "foolishness," demand "signs," and seek "wisdom." They do not believe the Christian preaching about Christ.

7. What is the result of their preoccupation with human wisdom? (1:21)

   Human wisdom does not bring them knowledge of God.

8. What attitude do the Christians have toward the preaching of a crucified Savior? (1:21, 29)

   They believe in Jesus Christ and humbly accept God's way of salvation.

9. What results have come to them from believing in such a Savior? (1:18, 21, 24, 30)

They have experienced God's power, salvation, wisdom, righteousness, holiness, and redemption.

10. Through what kind of words, concepts, and persons is the gospel properly proclaimed? (2:1-5)

The gospel is properly proclaimed in simple words. The gospel deals only with the crucified Jesus Christ and is announced by one who relies on the power (Spirit) of God, not on his or her own ability.

Answer these questions by reading 1 Corinthians 2:6–3:23

11. By what terms does Paul describe the condition of the Corinthians? (3:1-4)

Paul describes them as "worldly . . . infants in Christ, . . . mere men."

12. What three metaphors are used to explain who the Corinthians are in relation to God, Paul, and Apollos? (3:9, 16)

Paul uses the metaphors "God's field," "God's building," and "God's temple" to show who the Corinthians are.

13. What ideas in 1 Corinthians 1–3 are summarized in 3:18-23?

The following ideas are summarized in these verses: the foolishness and futility of the wisdom of this world; the inappropriateness of arrogant attachment to human leaders; God's desire to enrich believers through various persons, through the universe and its processes, and through Christ.

Answer these questions by reading 1 Corinthians 4

14. Why is it wrong to judge one another? (4:1-5; see also Matthew 7:1-5)

Judging the motives and stewardship of God's servants is the Lord's (Christ's) prerogative, not ours, and will be carried out when Christ comes again.

15. How do the attitudes of the Corinthians compare with the attitudes of the apostles? (4:8-13)

The Corinthians are boasting about the gifts they have received and are acting in their self-indulgence like kings. The apostles are humbly suffering for the sake of Christ and others—being "fools for Christ."

DIMENSION TWO: WHAT DOES THE BIBLE MEAN?

Background

Our First Corinthians is not the first letter Paul wrote to the church at Corinth, as 1 Corinthians 5:9 clearly shows. The letter mentioned there is lost. A letter between our First and Second Corinthians seems to be referred to in 2 Corinthians 2:1-4 and 7:8, 12. It too is lost. And our Second Corinthians may consist of two letters (see Lesson 6, Dimension 2).

Thus, Paul may have written five letters to that troubled church. Paul was determined that the Corinthian "infants in Christ" (1 Corinthians 3:1) should "become mature, attaining to the whole measure of the fullness of Christ" (Ephesians 4:13).

Paul's agony had a double source: his own situation in Ephesus, as well as the trouble in Corinth and possibly in other churches.

In 1 Corinthians 16:9 Paul speaks of his many adversaries at Ephesus and in 15:32 of having "fought wild beasts in Ephesus." The "beasts" probably were the silversmiths of Ephesus, whose business in silver shrines of Artemis was threatened by Paul's mission (Acts 19:23–20:1). As a Roman citizen (Acts 22:25-29), Paul would hardly have been subjected to an ordeal involving actual wild animals. The metaphor effectively indicates the ferocity of his opponents and probably serves to explain his utter despair and his brush with death there (2 Corinthians 1:8-10).

Possibly an imprisonment, nowhere specifically mentioned in our sources, occurred at Ephesus (note the "been in prison more frequently" of 2 Corinthians 11:23). Some scholars believe that Paul's prison epistles (Ephesians, Philippians, Colossians, and Philemon) were written at Ephesus, rather than at Rome. If so, the care of many churches lay on his heart when he was in Ephesus. His grief over the bickerings and downright immoralities of the Corinthian Christians, on top of everything else, must have made his cup of suffering almost undrinkable.

In the attempt to help the Corinthians with their problems—knowledge of which had come to him through "some from Chloe's household" (1 Corinthians 1:11), a letter from the Corinthians (7:1), and reports brought by a three-man Corinthian delegation (16:17-18)—Paul sent Timothy (via Macedonia) to assist them. (Whether Timothy ever got to Corinth we do not know.) Also Paul wrote our First Corinthians and probably sent it by the three-man delegation. As nearly as we can tell, he wrote this letter about A.D. 54.

Corinth

The divisions in the church at Corinth had deep roots in the political, economic, religious, and social life of Corinth.

The city, refounded by Julius Caesar in 44 B.C. and made the capital of the province of Achaia, in addition to its political importance was a bustling commercial center. Trans-shipping cargoes across the nearby isthmus, warehouse storage, banking, temple traffic (sale of artifacts and sacrificial meat, healing baths, religious prostitution), factories, shops, tourism, and business travel all contributed to the wealth of the city.

Corinth's religious life centered in worship of the old Greek gods and recently introduced exotic foreign deities imported from the East, along with the practice of astrology and magic.

As a Roman colony, not subject to taxation, Corinth's citizens enjoyed a large degree of independence. Cultural activities flourished. Philosophers and teachers, both native and foreign, offered their disciples learning and skills as keys to success in life. Professional people abounded. Slaves, though numerous, were often well educated and had legal rights. Upward mobility, regardless of national origin, was possible. Competition in business, religion, politics, and sports ran high, the latter whetted by the renowned biennial games held at nearby Isthmia. Corinth had a "do your own thing" culture, where unity and conformity were largely disdained.

The high individualism at Corinth naturally led to preferring different Christian leaders. All these leaders had somewhat different understandings of the gospel and the requirements of discipleship. Paul recognized the differing perspectives of the leaders, but he viewed them as God's way of enriching the Corinthians, not as threats to Christian unity.

What the different parties in the church stood for is not clear. The Paul group may have stood for salvation by faith alone (apart from merit through obedience to law) in Christ crucified and resurrected for our sins (1 Corinthians 2:2-5; Romans 4:25). The Apollos group may have delighted in that preacher's intellectualism and rhetoric and stressed human logic and eloquence as the essential requirement of Christian preaching. The Peter group may have been impressed with Peter's superior status as an apostle of Jesus and insisted with this great apostle that Jewish Christians must observe the requirements of the Jewish law. The Christ group may have rejected the exaltation of human leaders and favored life under the direct control of Christ and the Spirit (see 2 Corinthians 10:7).

Whether or not the church had four distinct groups with differing theologies, the whole church was clearly overemphasizing human knowledge and the freedom in the realm of conduct that knowledge brings. Arrogant human wisdom lay at the bottom of their divisions and of most of the problems Paul treats in First Corinthians.

In handling the problem of divisions Paul addresses two underlying misconceptions: about the basic nature of Christianity and about the proper function of Christian ministers.

1 Corinthians 1:12-17. Cephas and Peter are identical in meaning ("rock"), the former being Aramaic and the latter Greek. *Christ* is Greek for the Hebrew word *Messiah. Christ* rapidly became a part of the name of the new faith's Lord, "Jesus Christ."

These verses show that Paul believes Christianity is neither sectarian nor sacramentarian in character.

The Messiah and his people (Messiah's body) were regarded by Paul as an inseparable unity. To split up Messiah, whose function was the unification of humanity in the new citizenry of the kingdom of God, would defeat the whole purpose of God in the work of salvation.

In sacramentarian religion, leaders (priests) are water pipes through which divine grace and power are communicated to their followers. The special rites administered by them allow the divine grace and power to flow through the priests to the worshipers. Thus, the priests stand between the deity and the worshipers as mediators.

For Paul the leaders are signposts pointing to a reality beyond themselves: a personal relationship between the deity and the worshipers—a relationship effected not by rites and ceremonies directed by proper persons but by faith (trust) in God and in God's representative (Jesus) and by obedience to God's will. The leader is thus a preacher, a proclaimer of the good news, not an intermediary.

We can now understand Paul's subordination of baptism to the preaching of the gospel. That he valued baptism is evident from such passages as Romans 6:3-4 and Colossians 2:12. Probably all early Christians were baptized. But Paul seems to have held that unless baptism was preceded by preaching about God's deed in Jesus Christ, especially in his cross and resurrection, and by the response of believing acceptance on the part of the hearer, baptism would have no meaning. Paul's position is plain from the fact that he mostly left the work of baptizing to his assistants, as verses 14-16 here show.

1 Corinthians 1:18–2:5. You can treat this section effectively by contrasting on a chalkboard or a large sheet of paper what Paul says about the wisdom of the world and the wisdom of God. Line up the contrasts in parallel columns.

THE WISDOM OF THE WORLD	THE WISDOM OF GOD
1. *Is eloquently proclaimed —with "superior wisdom" (1:17; 2:1)*	*Is simply proclaimed—in down-to-earth language (2:1, 4)*
2. *Is held by high-born sophisticates—philosophers, scholars, wise men (1:20, 26)*	*Is held mostly by the low-born, the foolish, the weak, the despised (1:27-28)*
3. *Centers in human learning (implied)*	*Centers in God's saving activity in a person—* Jesus Christ and his cross (1:17-18; 2:2)

4. *Is validated by human logic and miracles—signs (1:22)*	*Is validated by believing (1:21)*
5. *Engenders arrogance (1:18-19; 29)*	*Engenders humility (1:29, 31)*
6. *Ends in futility*—no true knowledge of God (1:21)	*Ends in true wisdom, experience of God's saving, power, and transformation of life (1:21, 24, 30)*

Add any more contrasts you and class members may discover.

1 Corinthians 2:6-16. Paul next tries to describe the wisdom of God in some detail. You can look at this section through the following outline:

1. *The source of wisdom*—God (2:7);
2. *The nature of wisdom*—"secret and hidden" (2:7), yet understandable by the "mature" (adults, not infants [3:1]), though not by "the rulers of this age" who crucified Jesus (Pilate, the Jewish authorities, the demonic principles and powers mentioned in Romans 8:38; Galatians 4:3, 8-9; Colossians 2:15);
3. *The objective of wisdom*—the eternal enrichment and blessedness of humankind (2:7, 9, 12);
4. *The method of disclosing wisdom*—the Holy Spirit, who reveals the hidden purposes of God (2:10-12);
5. *The manner of communicating wisdom* (to those who are spiritually receptive)—"words taught by the Spirit," in spiritual language (2:13-15).

In some of the mystery religions of Paul's time people who were initiated by baptism and other rites were called "the mature." They were then "in the know" about the secret teachings and experiences of their new faith. Paul borrows their term for these persons and applies it to Christians who have come to understand "God's secret wisdom" (2:7).

"The rulers of this age" who crucified "the Lord of glory" (2:8) may be Pilate and the Jewish authorities; but, if so, Paul undoubtedly viewed them as instruments of the demonic powers whom Christ defeated through the cross (Colossians 2:15).

The New Testament often mentions the activity of the Holy Spirit in revealing to believers God's truth (2:10; also Luke 2:26; John 14:26; 16:13; Ephesians 3:4-6).

In 2:13-16 Paul speaks of two kinds of people: the unspiritual and the spiritual. The first are people who live according to what they naturally are, apart from any help outside themselves. The second accept God's Spirit and live out of his strength and help. The former live a "worldly" existence (1 Corinthians 3:1), whether they indulge their natural impulses (Galatians 5:16-24) or curb them in a moralistic pattern of life, as Paul did

(Philippians 3:2-6). The unspiritual (natural) person is thus one without the Holy Spirit and the spiritual person is one who possesses the Holy Spirit.

The latter is able to apprehend inwardly profound divine truths and can communicate these truths to others who possess the Spirit. "Words taught by the Spirit" (2:13) and possibly the last phrase of that verse (see footnote in NIV) speak of a spiritual language for this communication. This language cannot mean "tongues" of the type Paul speaks of later (12:10, 28; 13:1; 14), since he says that "tongues" are not given to all Spirit-filled Christians but only to some (12:30), and since here he is talking about a language of communication open to all who possess the Spirit.

1 Corinthians 3:5-23. The three metaphors (field, building, temple) used here to explain the relationship among God, the servants (Paul, Apollos, Cephas), and the Corinthians are skillfully developed. They serve to point up another misunderstanding on the part of the Corinthians. They have failed to see the proper role and function of Christian ministers.

These ministers are "servants" (3:5), not lords demanding homage from others. The real Lord, Jesus Christ, has given them their service. The Greek word behind *servant* here often means "waiter" —a lowly but useful form of service. Here their service is said to consist of gardening in God's field, of carpentering in God's building, and (in 4:1) of assisting Christ and serving as custodians (household administrators) of God's mysteries. All cooperate in God's work; they are not rivals encouraging partisanship.

Each leader has his own appointed task. Paul planted in God's field at Corinth. Apollos, coming after Paul at Corinth (Acts 18:27–19:1), watered what Paul planted. But the real credit goes to God, who gave the growth! Paul laid the foundation of the church there by preaching Jesus Christ. Apollos, Peter, and others built upon this foundation through their preaching and teaching. They used different materials for the superstructure. The value of each builder's work will be tested by Christ at the Day of Judgment. Some work will stand the fire test and some may not. But all workers will be saved, though some may barely escape the flimsy, flammable structure they erected and may even lose their pay. Paul assumes that all worked to the best of their knowledge and ability.

The structure (the temple), which enshrines God's Spirit, is here the church at Corinth, not the individual person so named later in the letter (6:19). All members are to preserve God's temple, not import into it beliefs and practices (sectarianism, sacramentarianism, worldly wisdom, Judaistic legalism) that will destroy it along with themselves.

This section ends with the affirmation that Paul, Apollos, and Cephas are part of God's magnificent plan for the enrichment of the church at Corinth, along with the enrichment that God intends should come through the world, life, death, present, future, Christ, and God. How tragic to cut oneself off by partisanship and exclusive attitudes from any portion of that lavish gift!

1 Corinthians 4:1-21. The Corinthians are to see their ministers as "servants of Christ" who are responsible to him and to God alone. To judge them (to put some down, to exalt others, and to pit them against one another) is insufferable arrogance (4:6-7). To do so is to assume a role that belongs to Christ at the coming Judgment. Even the servants, however clear their consciences, must leave judgment of their work to the Master whom they serve.

Paul, of course, did judge the so-called Christian preachers and teachers of Galatia, who were overturning his work there (Galatians 1:6-8; 5:1-12). By teaching salvation through Christ *plus* obedience to the Jewish law, instead of salvation through Christ by *faith alone,* Paul saw that they were destroying the Christian gospel and cutting the Galatians off from Christ (Galatians 5:2-4). Here a strong stand was required.

At Corinth all the leaders were building on Christ alone as the foundation (1 Corinthians 3:11-15). A false way of salvation was not involved—only different types of superstructure, such as different emphases and methods would produce. Here human judgments were inadequate and inappropriate. Only Christ could say whose service would prove more lasting and worthwhile.

In 4:6-13 Paul effectively deflates the arrogant self-esteem of the Corinthians by contrasting their attitudes with those of the suffering servants of Christ. The Corinthians are glorying like kings in the richness of the gifts they have received, indeed as if they were already enjoying in its fullness the salvation of the kingdom of God. Some were even saying that, since they had already been raised to new life in Christ, there would be no need for a future resurrection (15:12).

In 4:14-21 Paul offers practical suggestions for correcting their attitudes. Consider these and note the gem that appears in verse 20. The Corinthians are great talkers. Paul wants them to be great in power—the power of the Holy Spirit.

DIMENSION THREE: WHAT DOES THE BIBLE MEAN TO ME?

Few passages of the Bible are more significant for personal and church life than 1 Corinthians 1–4. Ask class members to share passages that seem particularly meaningful and explain why.

1 Corinthians 1:2—God's People

Paul says that the Corinthians are "sanctified in Christ Jesus" and "called to be holy." In 6:1 and 16:15 they are explicitly called "saints." In view of their unchristian attitudes and low morals, how can Paul describe them in this way?

Discuss the meaning of *saint* today, and ask whether Paul's use of the word differs from ours. Read these verses in other translations, such as *The Revised English Bible* and the *Good News Bible: The Bible in Today's English Version* (TEV). Actually the Greek word for *saint* means "set apart" or "dedicated" to God for a new kind of life and implies no particular degree of moral and spiritual achievement. "God's people" renders the idea well. They are, of course, a people who are going on toward God-likeness through their identification with Christ.

What attitude should we have toward those in our churches whom we often regard as unworthy of church membership?

1 Corinthians 1:13-17—The Meaning of Baptism

In these verses Paul seems to de-emphasize baptism or at least to subordinate it to the preaching and believing of the gospel message.

How important do the members of your class regard baptism to be? Ask them to share their experiences in and after baptism. Can a person be saved by participating in religious rites, such as baptism and the Lord's Supper? If more is necessary, what is that "more"? What are we to think of Quakers, who do not practice baptism and Holy Communion?

1 Corinthians 1:18–2:5—Human Wisdom

Paul disparages human wisdom and declares that it is futile in bringing knowledge of God. How seriously are we to take Paul? Was he against education? If he were here today, would he want to close our church colleges and universities? Can nothing be learned about God from the scientific and popular observation of nature? (See Romans 1:18-23.) How do study and reason relate to revelation and faith? Can a person be both a scientist or philosopher and a believing Christian?

1 Corinthians 2:6-16—Divine Wisdom

Paul claims that he and "spiritual" people know God and his purposes by means of the Holy Spirit who dwells within as "the mind of the Lord" (2:16). These people are not the high-born, the powerful, and the learned but the "foolish," the "weak," and the "lowly and despised."

Are there actually secrets that the spiritually minded know that are hidden from "unspiritual" persons? What has the Holy Spirit taught the members of your class that could qualify as Spirit-revealed truths? How can one know that these truths really come from the Holy Spirit?

Also, is there a Holy Spirit of "spiritual" language (excluding "tongues") by which God's wisdom must be communicated? Can you give examples of this sort of language? What about Paul's great words, such as *faith, grace, reconciliation, righteousness, redemption,* and the like? Must these words be kept today to convey Christian truth, or would others be more effective in our time and culture? What of the attempts to purge the Bible of its sexist terms?

1 Corinthians 3:5-23—Many-sided Christianity

Paul was sometimes tolerant of other Christian preachers and sometimes hostile, as we have seen. What groups or churches in contemporary Christianity might he accept and what ones might he reject, and why?

Some churches specialize in the personal gospel, some in the social gospel, some in ecclesiastical forms and ceremonies, and some in the fulfillment of prophecy (eschatology). Evaluate these varying emphases in the church today in the light of what Paul says in this section. What should our attitude be toward Christians who differ from us in theology and practice?

1 Corinthians 4:8-13—Servants of Jesus Christ

Paul describes Christian leaders as waiters, gardeners, carpenters, underlings, or assistants of Christ, household administrators, and finally as "a spectacle to the whole universe, to angels as well as to men" (4:9). The Greek word for "spectacle" is the word from which we get our English word *theater.* The word refers both to the place and to the show itself.

God has put the apostles at the end of the show in the arena as "men condemned to die," like wretches who must fight with gladiators or wild beasts to the shouts and jeers of the spectators. Note the words and phrases that characterize the lives of these suffering servants in these verses.

If the ministry were described in this way to college and high school students of today, how many would want to become ministers? What is the place of suffering in Christian service? What kinds of suffering do present-day servants of Christ endure? What is it to "fill up . . . what is still lacking in regard to Christ's afflictions" (Colossians 1:24)? Can we expect ministers today to suffer more than other Christians?

Do you not know that your body is a temple of the Holy Spirit? . . . You are not your own; you were bought at a price.
Therefore honor God with your body (6:19-20).

2

Personal Morality in the Church

1 Corinthians 5–7

DIMENSION ONE:
WHAT DOES THE BIBLE SAY?

Answer these questions by reading 1 Corinthians 5

1. What does Paul say about the nature and seriousness of the sin mentioned in 5:1?

   A man living with his father's wife, which is an immoral act, is repulsive not only to Paul but to pagans as well.

2. What is the attitude of the members of the church toward the sin? (5:2, 6)

   They are proud and boastful, rather than mournful.

3. What are Paul's directions for handling the problem? (5:2-5)

   When the church members are assembled, knowing that Paul's spirit is present with them, with the power of the Lord Jesus, they are to remove the man from membership and turn him over to Satan for the destruction of his sinful nature.

4. What does Paul hope to achieve by handling the matter in this way? (5:5)

   Paul hopes that the man's "spirit [may be] saved on the day of the Lord."

5. Why must the church purge itself of this sin? (5:6)

   The whole church will be affected by the sin, as yeast affects a batch of dough.

Answer these questions by reading 1 Corinthians 6

6. How should disputes between Christians be settled, and how does Paul motivate the Corinthians to handle them in this way? (6:2-6)

   Christians should find competent persons in the church to settle their disputes. Church members should be able to handle such trivial matters since they are destined to judge the world and angels.

7. Why are lawsuits among Christians wrong in principle? (6:7-8)

   Christians are called to suffer wrong, not to cause wrong.

8. What understanding of the kingdom of God does Paul give in 6:9-11? Who will be included in that Kingdom and who will not?

   The kingdom of God is for righteous, washed, sanctified, justified people, not for unrighteous, immoral people.

9. How does Paul qualify the statement, "Everything is permissible for me," and why does he think it must be qualified? (6:12-14)

   Paul qualifies the statement by balancing it with what is beneficial, by rejecting those things that may make a person a slave to them, and by distinguishing the spheres in which the principle applies. To act out the statement without qualification would result in the believer's destruction of the union he or she has with the Lord and the high destiny the Lord has for the believer.

10. Why should Christians not engage in prostitution, according to Paul? (6:15-20)

Sexual union with a prostitute creates a special bond: two persons are joined in a unique way, a way inconsistent with union with Christ. The body (the person) in exclusive union with the Lord has a high destiny, to be realized at the coming resurrection. This destiny must not be destroyed.

Answer these questions by reading 1 Corinthians 7

11. Why does Paul consider marriage and the marital relationship advisable? (7:2-9)

He knows the natural drive for sexual union and is afraid that attempted denial of it may lead to immoral relationships through lack of self-control.

12. What is Paul's view of celibacy? (7:1, 7-9, 25-35)

Celibacy is the best state when there is sufficient self-control. In this state one is freer from anxieties and can give more attention to pleasing the Lord, rather than a mate. Marriage will lead to worldly troubles.

13. What is Paul's view of divorce? (7:12-16, 39)

Marriage is meant to be permanent. On the authority of the Lord (Jesus) divorce by either husband or wife should not occur. In cases of mixed marriages (one partner a Christian and the other not) the marriage should be kept together, if at all possible.

14. Why does Paul want people (circumcised, uncircumcised, slaves, the free, the unmarried, the married) to remain as they were at the time of their conversion to Christ? (7:17-31)

Change of status is not important in the short time before the end of the age, but "keeping God's commands" is. Persons can please their master, the Lord, in the status where they were at the time of their call to discipleship; change may bring added troubles.

15. What counsel has Paul for persons who are unmarried or widowed? (7:8-9, 39-40)

If they can maintain control of themselves, they should remain unmarried. A woman whose husband is dead is free to remarry but only a Christian.

DIMENSION TWO: WHAT DOES THE BIBLE MEAN?

Paul turns from the problem of divisions in the church to problems in personal morality. These have to do with a case of incest (5:1-8); the relation of Christians within and without the church (5:9-13); lawsuits among church members (6:1-11); sexual freedom (6:12-20); and marriage (Chapter 7).

The boasting of church members over their "knowledge" and their consequent "freedom" has blown the little ship at Corinth into treacherous waters, where it is in danger of sinking. Paul believes that Christianity is supposed to lift the moral standards of the world, not debase them. What he has learned about the moral situation in the church at Corinth profoundly disturbs him.

The source of Paul's information about the moral problems of the Corinthians is not clear to us. But we can guess that it was either "some from Chloe's household" (1:11) or the three-man delegation (16:17).

In 7:1 we learn that the Corinthians had written to Paul about certain matters. These seem to be introduced by Paul with the formula "Now about" (7:1, 25; 8:1; 12:1; 16:1). Marriage is the first of these. His discussion of marriage on the heels of his treatment of the sexual laxity of some Corinthians indicates that the institution of marriage was being argued up and down with disastrous consequences for some of the church members. Clarification was badly needed.

1 Corinthians 5:1-5. At first it seems strange that Paul should begin the second section of his letter by discussing an individual case of sexual misconduct. One wonders why, in view of the personal and delicate nature of the case, Paul did not handle it privately in some way, perhaps by instructing the three-man delegation how to deal with it on their return to Corinth. Or he might have written a short letter to the offender, to be carried along with our First Corinthians.

Attention to the text of 1 Corinthians 5, however, makes it clear why Paul had to bring the matter out into the open. The whole church was involved, directly or indirectly. Members not only had not objected to the immoral conduct of the principal parties but actually had praised their conduct (5:2, 6). The church was guilty too. The entire membership needed to be rebuked and cleansed.

The nature of the sin is discussed in the student book. Additional background data may be helpful.

Strictly, Leviticus 18:6-8 forbids a sexual approach to one's own mother. In First Corinthians the relationship most likely involves a stepmother or perhaps a father's concubine, probably the former. Deuteronomy 27:20 seems to forbid intercourse with any woman who has belonged to one's father, which would cover the case Paul is discussing. The Jews stoned those persons guilty of incest. Roman law forbade union with a father's wife, even after his death. So Paul has a strong case against the Corinthian offender.

Separation of unrepentant sinners as a last resort appears in the Gospels (Matthew 18:15-17). The early church found it necessary to exclude heretical and factious people (1 Timothy 1:19-20; Titus 3:10; 2 John 7-11). (Note that in the passage from Second John the direction to exclude deceivers follows directly on the commandment to love—verses 5-6.) Paul ordered the cutting off of the food of the loafers in the church at Thessalonica (2 Thessalonians 3:10). Ananias and Sapphira were severed by death from the church and the God against whom they had sinned (Acts 5:1-10). Discipline of members was practiced throughout the early church.

Notice that the entire assembled church, plus Paul's spirit and "the power of our Lord Jesus," is to carry out the act of separation. The church's standard of sexual morality has been violated, and now the church must act to protect itself, under authority and power granted by Jesus himself (Matthew 18:15-18).

To "hand this man over to Satan, so that the sinful nature may be destroyed" calls for comment. By putting the man out of the church he will return to the world out of which he came (Ephesians 2:12), a world over which Satan rules (John 14:30; 2 Corinthians 4:4). There the destroying of the sinful nature, probably both the destruction of his sinful lusts (through sickness?) and the demise of his physical body, will occur. Perhaps Paul thinks he will repent in these sufferings. At least, he says that the punishment is meant to be redemptive at the last.

1 Corinthians 5:6-13. The purity of the church as a whole is Paul's next concern. The boasting must go and the root of the infection must be purged out, so that the church may become in actuality what it is ideally ("unleavened"). *Leaven* was a common metaphor for "evil." Get evil out of your midst, Paul is saying, so that you may be prepared to celebrate properly the coming Passover as a memorial of him who gave his life (as the Passover lamb) to deliver us from sin.

The injunction not to associate with persistent sinners in the church and not to eat with them seems superficially to conflict with Jesus' practice of associating and eating with tax collectors, sinners, and harlots (Matthew 11:18-19; Mark 2:15-17). But Jesus was seeking to bring the lost into the sheepfold (the new community he was raising up) through repentance and renewal of life. He did not intend that, once in, they should continue their evil ways and even act like wolves that destroy the flock. Jesus warned against false prophets who "come to you in sheep's clothing, but inwardly they are ferocious wolves" (Matthew 7:15). And he told a parable about a man who was excluded from a king's banquet because he was not clothed in a wedding garment of repentance and righteousness (Matthew 22:11-13; see Revelation 19:8). Jesus wanted followers who were dedicated to the elimination of evil from their lives and from the new community.

The statement "with such a man do not even eat" (5:11b) surely includes the church's common meal, at which the memorial bread and wine were taken (1 Corinthians 11:17-32). By partaking of that meal unrepentant sinners would bring judgment upon themselves (11:29).

1 Corinthians 6:1-11. Paul's statement that God's people will "judge the world" and "angels" is meant to inspire confidence in the church's ability to settle its disputes internally.

The participation of God's people in the Final Judgment of the world, referred to in Daniel 7:22, in several intertestamental books, and in the New Testament (Matthew 19:28; Luke 22:30; Revelation 20:4), was a fixed element of Jewish and Christian expectation.

For Paul and his contemporaries many angels were bad. In 2 Corinthians 12:7 Paul mentions "a messenger [literally 'angel'] of Satan"; and the Book of Jude, verse 6, refers to unfaithful angels who are being kept in chains "for judgment on the great Day."

Jude refers here to a story in the intertestamental Book of Enoch (First Enoch) about two hundred lustful angels, "the children of heaven," who came down to earth and married the daughters of men. From this union giants were born, who created great havoc on the earth. At God's command the good angel Raphael bound the leader of the fallen angels and cast him into a great, covered hole in the desert to await judgment at the last day. That Jude's reference is to this story from First Enoch is proved by the verbatim quotation that appears in Jude 14-15.

The strong New Testament emphasis on nonretaliation to evil (see student book on this passage) comes to its high point in 1 Peter 2:18-25; 3:13-17; and 4:12-16—passages to ponder deeply!

First Corinthians 6:9-11 makes it clear that practicing sinners of the kinds mentioned will not inherit the kingdom of God, but "washed," "sanctified," and "justified" sinners will. *Sanctified* means "set apart by God as members of his own people" and *justified* means "acquitted by God and put in right relationship with God."

1 Corinthians 6:12-20. The Greek text for this chapter has no quotation marks around the statement, "Everything is permissible for me." However, the context in which Paul qualifies the statement make it virtually certain that Paul is quoting something that the Corinthians, or possibly Paul himself, said but is being taken wrong. This phrase has become a slogan of libertine members of the church.

Paul himself had taught that Christians are not saved by law observance but by faith in Jesus Christ and that believers have been set free from all other masters. Such a teaching could easily become a pretext for libertinism, as Paul found out (Galatians 5:13-24).

Also, a philosophy we call *gnosticism* (from a Greek word meaning "knowledge") was growing up in the Greco-Roman world of that time and was having an influence on the Corinthians. This philosophy exalted knowledge of a secret sort, thought of matter as essentially evil, disparaged the human body, and declared the spirit as alone of importance. Gnosticism held that what one does in the body cannot affect what one is in the spirit.

Some Corinthian Christians may have believed that since their spirits had been saved and liberated through Christ, what they did with their bodies was not important.

They gloried in their spiritual liberation (1 Corinthians 4:8) and did not believe in the coming resurrection of the body (15:12). Thus, they could dabble in sexual pleasures of whatever sort with a clear conscience.

Two ethical consequences may result from such a view of matter and spirit. A person may indulge the body, as we have said, or one may deny bodily impulses as of no importance. Some Corinthians were sexual libertines and some disdained marriage and sexual union, as we shall see in Chapter 7.

The statement in verse 13, put in quotation marks by the translators of the New International Version, also appears to be an indication of the attitude of the libertine, gnostic Corinthians. Food and the stomach will both perish, since nothing material is eternal. Therefore, we are free to do what we like with the body without any harm to our spirits. Paul counters this by arguing that the body (by which he means the whole person) of the Christian is joined in an exclusive relationship with the Lord (Jesus Christ) and is destined to experience a resurrection like his. To form a union with a harlot—a *real* union of persons, not a casual act—is to sever the exclusive relationship with Christ and give up one's high destiny. So "flee from sexual immorality" and do not sin against yourself.

Furthermore, you individually are the temple of the Holy Spirit, who should have an undefiled dwelling place. And, finally, you belong to Christ, who bought you with a great price; you do not belong to yourself. "Therefore honor God with your body" (that is, through your whole person).

1 Corinthians 7:1-7. Paul now turns to the subject of marriage and begins with what appears to be another quotation from the Corinthians' letter. Though the NIV does not use quotation marks here, there are strong reasons for believing that the text should appear thus: "It is good for a man not to marry" (7:1b). The word *but* (in 7:2) indicates that Paul is moving immediately to a qualification of the statement, as he did in 6:12.

The declaration in 7:1b would thus represent the point of view of those at Corinth who deny the importance of the body and sexual relations—even regarding the latter as sinful—and not Paul's attitude. (See the footnotes to 7:1b in *The Revised English Bible* and in the *Good News Bible: The Bible in Today's English Version.*)

Paul does not despise marriage and sex and regard them as sinful (7:28, 36). As a Jew, brought up on the Old Testament, he knows that God has ordained marriage for humans (Genesis 1:27-28; 2:18-24). He is aware of the sexual drive and the proper fulfillment of it in marriage. Therefore, he says that sexual relations should continue in marriage, except for occasional suspensions for religious purposes (7:5). Proper sex in marriage, regularly carried on, will reduce the temptation to engage in illegitimate forms of sex.

1 Corinthians 7:8-9, 25-35. While sex and marriage are not to be despised, there may be reasons for forgoing them.

Single people can give full attention to pleasing the Lord, without the distractions and anxieties that marriage involves. And when one considers that human institutions and activities may soon cease through the passing away of the world (7:31) and that the end-time troubles ("crisis" —7:26) are already upon us, it may be wise to forgo marriage and be single, "as I am" (7:7-8).

Paul and the whole early church expected the world to end soon. (See Acts 1:6; Romans 13:11-14; 1 Thessalonians 5:1-11; James 5:8; 1 Peter 4:7; 1 John 2:18; Revelation 1:1; 22:7, 12, 20.) But the church's business was not to predict but to be busy (Luke 19:13-27; Acts 1:7-8; Ephesians 5:15; Colossians 4:5). God would take care of the time of the end (Mark 13:32; Acts 1:7).

Paul's counsel in 1 Corinthians 7 to "remain as you are," if you can remain chaste (7:9, 26-27) and if a special opportunity for change of status does not occur (7:21), now begins to make sense. He is advocating this "status quo" principle in all the churches (7:17). He is not against marriage as such, but only questioning its advisability in the time before the end.

1 Corinthians 7:10-16. Like Jesus, Paul is committed to the permanence of marriage (Mark 10:2-12; 1 Corinthians 7:10-11). The early church—indeed, the church in every age—found the absolute prohibition of divorce difficult to live by. Soon an exception appeared: "except for marital unfaithfulness" (Matthew 19:9; note the form of the question in 19:3 in contrast to the form in Mark 10:2). Even Paul realizes the difficulty of holding mixed marriages together but feels it important to try (7:12-16). He knows that God intended that two people should "become one flesh" (6:16) and remain that way.

In mixed marriages there is always the hope that the unbelieving partner will be converted by the believer (7:16). Patience is necessary. And it is not an unholy alliance in which the children are defiled by the nonchristian, as some may think; the holiness of the believer, in some sense, extends to the children and the unbeliever (7:14). Mixed marriages are essentially Christian marriages and must be held together, if at all possible.

1 Corinthians 7:36-38. The counsel concerning a man and "the virgin he is engaged to" is not entirely clear. Is the virgin a house-companion of the man, the two living in a "spiritual" relationship only? Such a practice existed later in the church, but we have no knowledge that it existed in the time of Paul. Most probably Paul is speaking about an engaged couple, who is uncertain whether they ought to enter into marriage because of the unsettling attitudes toward sex and marriage of church members at Corinth, Christian teachings about the end-time, and so on. Paul's advice again is that it depends on the degree of self-control in the relationship. If that is lacking, they should marry— "he is not sinning" (7:36b).

That Paul had a high view of marriage is evident from passages outside First Corinthians. He lived for a time with

Aquila and Priscilla and greatly admired them (Acts 18:2-3; Romans 16:3-4). Contrary to much modern opinion, he did not put women down but appreciated their service to the church (Romans 16:1-2, 6, 12, 13, 15). Paul said that "husbands ought to love their wives as their own bodies" and "as Christ loved the church" (Ephesians 5:28, 25). Though Paul was no feminist in the modern sense, like Jesus he was ahead of his time in his attitude toward women, marriage, and the home.

DIMENSION THREE: WHAT DOES THE BIBLE MEAN TO ME?

You should have no trouble starting a discussion about the subjects covered in 1 Corinthians 5–7. Valid conclusions concerning their meaning for our times will be harder to come by. Paul lived in a different world from ours and at least some of what he has to say is hardly applicable to our situation. But his basic theological insights and working principles command our respect, if not always our assent.

1 Corinthians 5:1-8
Subtraction as Well as Addition?

Excommunication is a harsh word and most Christians today want nothing to do with the word or the action it represents. But before we close our minds completely to what Paul demands here of the Corinthian church, we should ask ourselves some hard questions.

Are there some things that are right and some things that are wrong—period(!)? Is incest, for example, one of them? Society through the ages has not been tolerant regarding incest. Should the church remain silent and do nothing when a grave moral infraction of this kind is flaunted before the church and the world?

Should the church teach and seek to maintain among its members ethical standards that are higher than those of the society around it?

Is judgment contradictory to love, or does love require judgment and discipline? Was the early church wrong in separating unrepentant sinners (Matthew 18:15-17; 1 Timothy 1:19-20; Titus 3:10; 2 John 7-11) and teaching love and exclusion almost in the same breath (2 John 5-11)?

Should the church be maintained by subtraction as well as addition?

1 Corinthians 5:9-13—The Church and the World

Jesus associated with tax collectors, harlots, and the outcasts of society who did not keep Jewish laws. The Essenes, who lived in an elaborate monastery by the Dead Sea during Jesus' lifetime, avoided and hated sinners of this sort and ran away from the corrupt life of the city of Jerusalem. The Essenes have vanished. Christianity is still here. Do you think the attitude of each toward sinners had

anything to do with the longevity of each movement? If so, in what way?

How does one associate with sinners in the world without getting their "disease"?

How sharp a line should the church draw between itself and the world? Should it sponsor bingo and other games of chance? Should it rent pews to finance its budget, as is done is some places? Should it "showcase" actors, professional singers, and popular lecturers as drawing cards, without regard to their personal religious commitments?

1 Corinthians 6:1-11—Disputes Among Christians

To what extent, if at all, are Paul's pleas for the internal settlement of church disputes applicable in our time? Many judges in our secular courts are Christians, and Christian principles are built into many of our laws and their enforcement. In what kind of cases, if at all, should the church resort to the secular courts? Could the church do more than it is doing to keep its members from suing one another and airing "dirty linen" before the public? What are some things the church can do?

1 Corinthians 6:12-20—How Much Sexual Freedom?

Freedom is a badly misunderstood word and concept today. For many people freedom is an absolute right to do anything one wants. Some Christians, at least, have understood freedom in this way.

Ask members of the group to discuss Thomas Huxley's statement, "Man's worst difficulties begin when he is able to do what he pleases." What are the difficulties with this statement? How does Huxley's statement agree with anything you find in the passage from Paul?

To what kinds of slavery may the "I-do-as-I-please" philosophy lead?

What is Christian freedom according to Paul? See 1 Corinthians 10:23-34; Galatians 5:13-14. Compare and contrast this kind of freedom with modern secular views of freedom.

Many people today regard the sex act as a simple biological act with no spiritual implications whatsoever, not unlike eating or blowing one's nose. They therefore can justify prostitution and almost any form of sexual indulgence. What is the matter with this position from Paul's point of view, as expressed in this passage?

1 Corinthians 7:10-16—Divorce

Is it right to turn the teaching of Jesus and Paul on the subject of divorce into a law to be rigidly adhered to in modern church life? Justify your answer.

Matthew 19:9 offers an exception to the absolute prohibition of divorce one finds in Mark 10:2-12 and 1 Corinthians 7:10-11. Does this set a precedent for liberalizing the church's teaching about divorce? How far should this liberalizing go? One rabbi of the New Testament period thought divorce should be allowed if a wife so much as spoiled one's food!

When divorce does occur, as Paul admits it may (7:15), we are told that the Christian partner is not to remarry during the lifetime of the divorced partner (7:11, 39). Most churches do not follow this today. Consult your pastor or some church executive for an explanation of your church's practice.

When sin enters in and destroys a marriage and there is no possibility for various reasons of reconstituting that marriage, many Christian leaders believe that the most loving thing to do is to allow divorce and remarriage, even if a partner is living, provided that (1) the person has shown genuine repentance for previous sins; and (2) the person shows an honest intent to make the new marriage really Christian. They hold that this is more health-giving to all than to apply a law, even from the New Testament. Evaluate this position.

Knowledge puffs up, but love builds up (8:1).

— 3 —

Knowledge and Love in the Church

1 Corinthians 8:1–11:1

DIMENSION ONE:
WHAT DOES THE BIBLE SAY?

Answer these questions by reading 1 Corinthians 8

1. What seem to be the key words or topic addressed in the text of 1 Corinthians 8? What do they indicate about the views of the Corinthians? (8:1-5)

   "We all possess knowledge"; "knowledge"; "an idol is nothing at all in the world"; "there is no God but one"; "gods"; and "lords." These terms indicate that all the Corinthians profess to have knowledge and apparently are proud of their knowledge, especially their knowledge of the fact that idols have no real existence, since there is only one God.

2. Describe persons "who have this knowledge" (8:10) as Paul pictures them: their ideas, their attitudes, and their actions. (Chapter 8 as a whole)

   Persons of knowledge know with pride that there is only one God; that other gods and lords are not really such; that food that has been offered to gods who do not exist cannot possibly be affected by association with nonexistent beings; that they have a right to eat this food if they choose, even at table in an idol's temple, whether other Christians agree or not. Thus, these persons go boldly ahead.

3. Describe the "weak brother" (8:11): his ideas, attitudes, and actions. (8:7-13)

   This person is not sure that idols represent nothing real. He thinks that meat that has been offered to idols may be affected in some way by association with false gods. If he eats it, his conscience bothers him; and he feels defiled. When he sees another Christian eating it in an idol's temple, he sometimes eats it also and feels condemned afterward.

Answer these questions by reading 1 Corinthians 9

4. What evidence does Paul offer that he is a true apostle? (9:1-2)

   The fact that Paul has seen the Lord Jesus and the fact of the existence of the Corinthian church, fruit of his apostolic labor, are offered as evidence of Paul's apostleship.

5. What rights as an apostle does Paul cite? (9:3-6)

   Paul lists the right to food and drink, to be accompanied by a believing wife, and to refrain from working for a living.

6. List as many reasons as you can find why Paul has not made use of his rights as an apostle. (9:12, 15-27)

   Paul lists these reasons: to put no obstacle in the way of the gospel of Christ; to make the gospel free of charge, something that is not required of him; to win more people of various kinds to Christ; and to reach the goal of final salvation himself.

7. What "boast" does Paul have? (9:15-18)

   Paul's boast is that he is preaching the gospel free of charge, something not required of him.

8. To what groups of people has Paul become "a slave"? (9:19-22)

   Paul has made himself a slave "to everyone" —the Jews, those under the law, those outside the law, the weak, all men.

9. Why has Paul done this? (9:19-23)

   Paul can win more people by giving up his rights than by insisting that his rights be honored.

10. What must athletes do to win, and what is the prize Paul is striving for? (9:24-27; Philippians 3:10-14)

Athletes exercise self-control in all things, subdue their bodies (themselves), and strive hard to win. The prize is sharing with Christ in his resurrection from the dead, something to which God has called believers.

**Answer these questions by reading
1 Corinthians 10:1–11:1**

11. What blessings did the "forefathers" receive in the events connected with the Exodus from Egypt? (10:1-4)

They were led by the cloud; passed through the sea (a kind of Mosaic baptism); ate and drank "spiritual" food and water, being thereby sustained by the pre-existent Christ.

12. Why was God not pleased with most of the forefathers? (10:5-10)

They desired things that were evil: idolatry, with its idolatrous meals and pagan revelry; sexual immorality; putting God to the test; and grumbling.

13. What lessons should "we" (Christians) draw from their experience? (10:6-12)

We should learn not to desire evil.

14. What resources do Christians have to keep them from sinning and incurring God's displeasure, as the "fore-fathers" did? (10:11-13)

Christians have what is written in the Scriptures, a humble attitude, and God's help in temptations to keep them from sinning.

15. Why should the Corinthians have nothing to do with the worship of idols and the practice of idolatrous rites? (10:14-22)

Behind the worship of idols and pagan sacrifices are demons. By participating in this worship one enters into partnership with demons. This partnership will violate partnership with Christ and with fellow Christians. Christians belong exclusively to God, who is jealous about their loyalty.

16. What is the proper meaning of the cup and the bread for Christians? (10:16-17)

Through the cup and the bread believers participate together in the benefits of Christ's passion and form an exclusive unity with him and with one another.

17. What are the Corinthians to do about meat sold in the public markets? (10:25-26)

Since all food belongs to God and comes from God, the Corinthians may eat such food in good conscience.

18. What are they to do when unbelievers invite them to dinner? (10:27-29)

They should eat the food that is served without raising questions about its origin, unless they are specifically told that is was offered in pagan sacrifice and someone is present who would be offended. In that case, they should abstain.

19. What general principles should guide Christians in their relationship with other Christians and with unbelievers? (10:23–11:1)

Christians should seek to promote the good of others, not to exercise their selfish rights. They should have consideration both for hospitable unbelievers and "weak" Christians, so as not to give offense to either—or to anybody, if possible. Christians must do everything "for the glory of God." They are to imitate Paul, as he imitates Christ.

DIMENSION TWO:
WHAT DOES THE BIBLE MEAN?

We might title this section (8:1–11:1), "The Eating of Food Offered to Idols in the Light of Christian Principle." The principle is: knowledge and the rights that issue from it must be controlled by love.

Paul's discussion here falls into three parts: (1) the statement of the principle (Chapter 8); (2) the illustration of the principle (Chapter 9); and (3) the enforcement of the principle (10:1–11:1).

All over the Greco-Roman world huge temples, with elaborate sacrificial systems, were operating. When private sacrifices were presented (for blessings and good luck received or for inducement of a deity's help), certain portions of the food became the property of the priests; the rest was returned to the donor, for eating or for sale. When public sacrifices were offered by the state or city, huge amounts of food (principally meat) were left over. These leftovers were used in part by magistrates and the rest sold to shopkeepers. Since food had to be of the best quality to be presented as a sacrifice, it was in demand by the citizenry.

But was it right for Christians, who opposed idolatry, to eat that which had been associated with pagan worship?

Today we might ask, Should an organ or piano, known to have been used in a brothel, be bought by a church for use in its worship? What should one do with things belonging to the old life of sin when he or she has turned to the new life in Christ?

Hardy Christians might say, "There is nothing essentially wrong with the things that have been used in the old life. Let us now use them in the right way." Weaker Christians might well be afraid that those things would draw them back into the old life, and they would want to avoid or destroy them.

1 Corinthians 8. Paul's principle, stated in Chapter 8, is that knowledge (and the rights that issue from it) must be controlled by love.

Verses 1-3 subordinate prideful knowledge to Christian love. Prideful knowledge is partial knowledge swaggering as though it were full knowledge. It brings God's disfavor rather than God's favor. God's favor comes only through love for God.

Verses 4-6 admit that some knowledge is fundamentally important. Paul was not hostile to genuine knowledge—the sort that comes through divine revelation (2:6-16). That God is One; that idols represent only "so-called" deities; that this God is Father, Creator, and Redeemer; and that God has acted in creation and redemption through his Son Jesus Christ to raise up a people for God is essential knowledge, revealed by God. So the Corinthian stress on knowledge is not wholly wrong.

Verses 7-13 contradict the slogan of the gnostic Corinthians in 8:1. Actually, not all Christians at Corinth have a clear grasp of the being, nature, and activity of God. Many of them are "infants" (3:1). They must be brought to Christian maturity, not stunted by inconsiderate attitudes and actions of the "elite."

The "man who thinks he knows something," confident in his belief that "an idol is nothing at all in the world," sees nothing wrong in eating with his fellow guild members in an idol's temple and proceeds to put his knowledge into effect. But "weak" persons, not far out of idolatry, fear to go on Satan's (and the demons') territory and are scandalized or emboldened to do what they think they ought not. Sinning against their conscience, they fall back into the old life from which they came—a "brother, for whom Christ died" (8:11).

The right to eat meat in an idol's temple is not that important, Paul says. *People* are more important; the meat can go! Whether we eat or whether we do not makes little difference to God, but insensitivity to others does. Was it not Jesus who pronounced a woe on those who cause others to stumble (Matthew 18:5-7)? Often rights must give way to love.

1 Corinthians 9:1-14. Some of Paul's critics at Corinth apparently were claiming that he did not act like an apostle. He was too self-effacing in insisting that he support himself and in his general "servant" attitude. This attitude can only be explained, they may have said, because he knows that he is no true apostle and he hesitates to demand the rights of an apostle.

First Corinthians 8 would do little to change their opinion of Paul. Here once again, in his willingness to give up meat forever, they would see the same attitude manifested.

Sensing this, Paul hurries to defend his apostleship and to explain his attitudes and methods. His defense proceeds by using questions (note how many of them he uses in this chapter), a form of argumentation much in vogue by the popular philosophers of the time (the Cynics).

The negatives in the Greek in the opening questions require an affirmative answer and should be translated, "I'm free, am I not? I'm an apostle, am I not? I've seen Jesus our Lord, have I not?" "You are the result of my work in the Lord, are you not?" This form of putting questions strengthens their impact.

Paul is both free from the Jewish law and its ceremonialism and free as a Roman citizen. He is a true apostle because he has seen the Lord, as the other apostles had (15:5-10); and Paul was commissioned by the Lord (Acts 22:17-21; 26:15-18; Galatians 1:15-16), as they had been (Matthew 28:18-20; Acts 1:6-8). But the real authentication of his apostleship is its fruit: the Corinthian church.

The rights of an apostle that Paul has given up are the right to eat and drink what he pleases, to be married and accompanied by a wife, to refrain from working, and to receive support from his converts. This last right is the big one for him. He proceeds to show how really unusual the surrender of this right is.

Soldiers, husbandmen, shepherds, priests (Numbers 18:8) all receive support as they work. And the law of Moses specifically requires it.

In the reference to the ox, Paul treats the passage from Deuteronomy (25:4) as an allegory, taking it to mean that God was not really concerned for oxen but was really concerned about Christian preachers—a kind of interpretation used by the Alexandrian Jewish philosopher Philo and other interpreters of that time and later. The Corinthians would be familiar with this way of interpreting old texts and accept it readily.

The reference to the Lord's command (9:14) is one of Paul's rare citations of the words of Jesus and refers to Jesus' instructions to the apostles (Matthew 10:9-10; Luke 10:4-7). In Paul's mind the command of the Lord clinches the argument about his right to support from his converts.

1 Corinthians 9:15-23. Having proved that he has the right to be supported by his converts, Paul wants to be sure that he has not proved too much. The Corinthians may think that he at long last is going to claim his right. This he denies flatly.

Paul's ground for boasting is not that he is preaching the gospel. In preaching he is simply following a command that Jesus Christ has laid on him. He is Christ's slave and must do his Master's bidding. Preach he must, in discharge of his commission, and this without special reward, since he is a slave (see Luke 17:7-10). But Paul is not required to support himself and preach free of charge. From this work of supererogation (performance in excess of demand) he can expect a reward; for he has then something special and of his own to offer God.

Paul has said in verse 12 that he would go through anything "rather than hinder the gospel of Christ," the "hindrance" clearly being a financial demand on his converts from a mercenary preacher. Now he shows how much further than this he goes, in complete disregard of his rights, to carry the gospel to all people.

Some of Paul's critics today, echoing his first-century critics, have concluded from 9:19-23 that Paul was an insincere chameleon, an opportunist without clear moral principles. He could be anything to anybody to gain his ends. Certainly his claim to be a good Jew (2 Corinthians 11:22; Philippians 3:4-6) was false, as no good Jew would abandon his Jewish scruples and live virtually like a Gentile, as this passage suggests Paul did. But a careful examination of the passage and Paul's letters as a whole leads to a quite different conclusion.

Paul believed he had been sent by Christ to preach the gospel to all people. In obedience to this command he went where people (Jews, Gentiles, slaves, the weak) were: to synagogues, to marketplaces, to places of learning, to private homes. Like Jesus he identified himself with educated and uneducated, rich and poor, cultured and outcast. Paul ate with them and fraternized with them on their ground, while he announced the good news to them.

This was no violation of what Paul understood a good Jew to be: a person who was inwardly good, rather than outwardly correct (Romans 2:28-29). Here he walked arm-in-arm with Jesus (Matthew 23:23-26; Mark 7:14-23).

In addition, Paul believed that the whole Jewish law had come to its intended end in Jesus Christ and the salvation accomplished by him (Romans 10:4; Galatians 3:23-26). The Jewish law was no longer binding as law on him or any other Christian (Romans 6:14; Galatians 5:13). Paul's only obligation was to live under the law of love, which he here calls "Christ's law" (9:21). By so loving and living, the whole Jewish law was being fulfilled (Romans 13:8-10). Christians then are free from the law but slaves of righteousness (Romans 6:18). Living under the command to love, Paul's freedom consists not in rights but in the renunciation of rights for the sake of those to whom he has been sent.

1 Corinthians 9:24-27. In verse 23 Paul says that he wants to participate in the blessings the gospel brings, as well as win others to salvation. And so he comes to the last reason why he forgoes his rights. If he selfishly exercises them (instead of his legs!), he may lose out in the Christian race.

Though Paul preaches the gospel under commission by Christ, he is not exempt from the demands of that gospel. He does not have the rash assurance of some Christians that he is now "saved" and enjoying in full the benefits of the gospel (4:8). He is still in the race, as they too are, and the goal of final salvation is still ahead. You must run and I must run, Paul says, that we may win the prize.

To win will require self-control, pommeling oneself, and striving hard. We can even be disqualified in this contest, he says. Paul had little confidence in himself, though he had great confidence in the love and grace of God. We can win *by God's help*, he says in the next chapter (10:13), and receive not "a crown that will not last" but "a crown that will last forever."

The analogy of the race and the boxing match would make an impression on the Corinthians, for the great biennial games, held at nearby Isthmia, brought hundreds of athletes to Corinth. The Corinthian Christians and possibly Paul himself (he was at Corinth for eighteen months—Acts 18:11) had seen the fierce competition in track and in ring for a perishable wreath (a pine wreath). What would it take to win an imperishable one? (See also 2 Timothy 4:8 and 1 Peter 5:4.)

1 Corinthians 10:1-13. After stating the principle that knowledge and the rights that issue from it must be controlled by love (Chapter 8) and illustrating the principle by reference to his own attitudes and conduct (Chapter 9), Paul enforces the principle in Chapter 10. He appeals to history (10:1-13) and logic (10:14-22) and gives a summary of his conclusions in 10:23–11:1.

Paul is now in a position to drive home his message to the Corinthians. He has said that he has to exercise self-control if he is going to win the "crown that will last forever." Discipline, not freedom run wild, will bring him and them to the coveted prize. From his knowledge of the Old Testament he shows what happened to undisciplined people and says, in effect, "Don't let this happen to you!"

The lesson from history concerns the people of Israel at the time of the Exodus from Egypt. They, like the Corinthians, had high spiritual experiences and achievements.

They all were "under the cloud" (under God's hovering presence and guidance); they all "passed through the sea" (participated in a miracle of deliverance); they all were "baptized into Moses in the cloud and in the sea" (they passed through water above and around them, a kind of baptism into Moses); they all ate and drank "spiritual" food and water (God gave them heavenly bread [manna] and Christ's [the Messiah's] perpetually flowing water of life).

The Corinthians too had experienced all these blessings: God's presence and guidance, deliverance from sin, baptism into Jesus, and God's spiritual food and drink (the bread and wine of the Eucharist, Holy Communion). Paul suggests that the Christian experiences were foreshadowed in the experiences of Israel.

But for the forefathers these magnificent blessings and privileges led to self-indulgence, not to disciplined obedience; and most of "their bodies were scattered over the desert." Freedom can run into license, and license into God's displeasure and punishment. Without self-control and discipline one can fail to get into the Promised Land. High spiritual privilege is no guarantee of perpetual security.

To desire evil, to dabble in idolatry and idolatrous practices, to indulge in immorality, to try the Lord's patience by seeing how far one can go in one's freedom, to grumble or complain about God's ways and dealings—these will do to the Corinthians what they did to Israel.

In the time before the end (10:11) the Corinthians should heed the warnings of Scripture and be neither overconfident nor underconfident (10:12-13). The boastful are likely to fall and the fearful to think the struggle is too tough. But God can be relied on. He will provide a way of escape in every temptation.

Paul's interpretation of the Old Testament here is typological, not allegorical. The former assumes the reality of the historical events and sees them as foreshadowing future events. The latter often does not care whether the events ever happened—indeed, sometimes denies their reality—but finds in the record of them hidden, spiritual meanings. Paul allegorized in 1 Corinthians 9:9-10, when he said that the passage referred to preachers of the gospel, not to oxen. See also Paul's "allegory" in Galatians 4:21-31, where the historical facts are accepted as real but the spiritual meanings Paul draws out range far beyond the historical facts.

1 Corinthians 10:14-22. The Corinthians claim to be wise, so Paul gives them a chance to prove it: "I speak to sensible people; judge for yourselves what I say." He had insisted that there were wise people among them who could settle disputes within their group (6:1-6). Let them and all now weigh his final proposition.

Is it sensible to believe that one can go two ways at once, to "drink the cup of the Lord and the cup of demons," to "have a part in both the Lord's table and the table of demons" (10:21)? Paul's argument is that these two cups and these two tables represent two exclusive solidarities or communions: one centering in Jesus Christ and the other in demonic powers. To flirt with the demons, their idols, and their idolatrous practices is to provoke the Lord Jesus to jealousy. Can one pledged to him in loyalty get away with this?

Through the Christian cup and bread the benefits of Christ's death are appropriated and union with him and other Christians is established. A solidarity (sharing, communion) is found here like that of Israel when priests and worshipers partake of altar sacrifices and become one with God and one another. And they have another unity: that between worshipers and the demons who lurk behind the idols. Should Christians then enter idol temples and join in idolatrous feasts? God forbid that we should be guilty of this affront to our Lord!

The Old Testament taught Paul that behind idols were demons (Deuteronomy 32:17; Psalm 106:36-37). Jesus, Paul, and the whole early church believed in the existence of Satan and powers of evil and saw the beginning of the defeat of these evil powers in the ministry, death, and resurrection of Jesus. While there is only one God (1 Corinthians 8:6), God allows evil powers authority in this age (Galatians 4:3, 8-9; Ephesians 2:2), but their doom is sealed (Romans 16:20; Colossians 2:15). At the end Christ will destroy "all dominion, authority and power" and turn over the sovereignty to "God the Father" (1 Corinthians 15:24).

1 Corinthians 10:23–11:1. Paul's conclusions on the subject of knowledge and rights in regard to eating food offered to idols are summarized in the student book.

DIMENSION THREE: WHAT DOES THE BIBLE MEAN TO ME?

1 Corinthians 8:1-6—Theology and Love

Paul says that " 'Knowledge' puffs up, but love builds up." Then he proceeds to give the Corinthians a lesson in theology (8:4-6). How much theology does a person need anyhow? Would not it be enough if we loved God and all our fellow human beings? Is not experience more important than ideas?

In handling this problem you might discuss the relation between a road map and the territory a road map represents. Loving fellowship with God and with one another is the territory (the reality itself), while theology is the description (the road map) of that experience. To see Mount Rainier or some other beauty of nature for oneself is the goal of travel; but to find the way there and to help others find it, we need an accurate road map. Good theology provides this map. What damage has been done to Christianity through the centuries because of bad road maps?

1 Corinthians 8:7—The Old Life and the New

Most of the Corinthians had come out of a pagan background. They brought into the church ways of thinking and doing that had to be changed. What attitudes and practices in the church today reflect the pagan culture around us? Can you suggest problems in the church like the problem of eating meat that had been offered to idols? What solutions do you think Paul would suggest?

1 Corinthians 8:9-13—Individual Freedom and Social Responsibility

What cherished rights do each of us hold that we tend to want to practice and enjoy whether others like them or not? Where is the line between doing what I want and doing what others want me to do? How can there be any social change and progress if we always give in to other people's opinions and prejudices? Should we wait to do what we think is right until we have educated those around us to a new point of view? Explain your answer.

1 Corinthians 9:19-23—Adaptation and Compromise

To be "all things to all men" would be impossible without serious compromise at times. How far do you think a Christian should go in adapting one's lifestyle and conduct to those of one's associates? Some ministers have tried this and turned out to be "good Joes" and not much else! In what areas of life might one well adapt? Where not? Why?

1 Corinthians 10:14-22—Choose We Must!

Double-mindedness is the curse of our times. Many persons praise morality publicly but practice immorality privately. We put "In God We Trust" on our coins but really trust in our diplomacy or weapons. We want the pleasures that material things provide, while we praise the virtues of self-denial and altruism. We want our children to be strictly moral but apply looser standards to ourselves. We want to eat at "the Lord's table" and "the table of demons" at the same time. How can double-mindedness be overcome? How can we become whole, integrated persons?

Now you are the body of Christ, and each one of you is a part of it (12:27).

4

Worship in the Church (Part 1)

1 Corinthians 11:2–12:31

DIMENSION ONE:
WHAT DOES THE BIBLE SAY?

**Answer these questions by reading
1 Corinthians 11:2-16**

1. Is Paul in sympathy with the Corinthian practice of allowing women to participate actively in church worship services? (11:3-16)

   Paul does not challenge women's right to prophesy and pray in the services; he only directs them to cover their heads when they do it.

2. What is the order of authority (we might say, chain of command) in the universe, as Paul sees it? (11:3)

   Paul lists God, Christ, man, and woman, in this order.

**Answer these questions by reading
1 Corinthians 11:17-34**

3. What criticisms does Paul make of the way the Corinthians conduct themselves at "the Lord's Supper"? (11:18-22)

   Paul points out the "divisions" or "factions" at the supper: some plunge into their food without waiting for others, some get drunk, and some go hungry.

4. What similarities and what differences are there between Paul's account of the Last Supper and Mark's account? (11:23-26; Mark 14:22-25)

   Both have bread and cup (in that order), both have words of interpretation after each, both interpret the blood as connected with a covenant, and both have a closing reference to the future. Mark has details omitted by Paul: "while they were eating," "they all drank from it," "poured out for many," and more; and Mark's reference to the future has Jesus declaring

abstinence from wine until he drinks it again in the kingdom of God. Paul's account is shorter, twice adds the words "in remembrance of me," and makes the whole supper a memorial of Jesus' death until his coming again.

5. How should the Corinthians prepare themselves for eating the Lord's Supper? (11:28, 34)

   They should "examine" themselves; and, if they cannot wait until all the members can eat together, they should eat something at home before they come.

6. What consequences have followed and will follow the unworthy eating of the Lord's Supper? (11:27, 29-30)

   The unworthy eaters will be "guilty of sinning against the body and blood of the Lord" and judgment will come upon them. Many who have done this "are weak and sick, and a number of you have fallen asleep" (some have died).

**Answer these questions by reading
1 Corinthians 12:1-11**

7. What test does Paul suggest for determining whether a person has the Holy Spirit or some other spirit? (12:2-3)

   Whether a person says "Jesus be cursed" or "Jesus is Lord" will show what spirit is in the person.

8. Where do spiritual gifts come from? (12:4-6, 11)

   Spiritual gifts come from one source: the Holy Spirit, the Lord (Jesus Christ), and God.

9. What is the purpose of these gifts? (12:7)

   Each is given these gifts "for the common good."

10. What kinds of gifts are there? (12:8-10)

The message of wisdom and knowledge, faith, healing, miraculous powers, prophecy, the ability to distinguish between spirits, tongues, and the interpretation of tongues are the kinds of gifts.

**Answer these questions by reading
1 Corinthians 12:12-31**

11. What characteristics does the body of Christ possess, and how did it get that way? (12:12-13)

The body of Christ is a unit, comprised of many members of different origins (Jews, Greeks, slaves, free people). They were baptized by the Holy Spirit into Christ, and all received the Holy Spirit.

12. What parts of the human body does Paul refer to in his analogy? (12:15-24)

Paul refers to foot, hand, ear, eye, head, weaker parts, less honorable parts, presentable and unpresentable parts of the body. He also mentions hearing and smelling.

13. Why does Paul refer to all these parts of the body? (12:14-16)

He wants to show how all the parts work together in perfect harmony and how all, even the seemingly unimportant and unpresentable ones, are needed for the proper functioning of the body.

14. What differences are there in the two lists of kinds of gifts? (12:8-10, 28-30)

The first list deals with the kinds of gifts in abstraction; the second list identifies the offices and services of the persons who have these gifts. The first presents nine gifts; the second eight offices or services, with interpretation of tongues introduced in a question at the end. The second list seems to rank the persons and services in the order of their importance in the church.

15. Is one person supposed to have all these gifts, and is any one gift to be possessed by all? (12:29-30)

The rhetorical questions certainly expect the answer no to both questions. In 12:11 Paul says that the Holy Spirit "gives them to each one, just as he determines."

DIMENSION TWO:
WHAT DOES THE BIBLE MEAN?

The surge toward "freedom" in the Corinthian church affected not only the members' personal lives but also their corporate lives. Paul now attempts to stem its effects on the worship activities of the church. His treatment covers the following subjects: men and women in church worship services (11:2-16); the nature and proper conduct of the Lord's Supper (11:17-34); and the nature and function of spiritual gifts (12:1–14:40).

Only 11:2–13:31 will be considered in Lesson 4, the rest being reserved for Lesson 5.

For something like two centuries early Christians met in private homes for worship. The earliest Christian church known to us was found by archaeologists in 1932 at Dura-Europos on the west bank of the Euphrates River, in what is now southeastern Syria. About A.D. 250 a fairly large private house there was converted into a Christian church. It had a large room (with a rostrum at one end) that would accommodate about one hundred people and a nearby room with a baptistry. The walls of the room containing the baptistry were painted with scenes of Christ the Good Shepherd, the healing of the paralytic, the walking on the Sea of Galilee, the Samaritan woman at Jacob's well, and the visit of women to Jesus' tomb on Easter morning.

Church buildings thus grew out of home meeting places, probably out of the larger homes of the more affluent Christians. After the emperor Constantine made Christianity the dominant religion of the Roman Empire (early fourth century), large Christian churches were built all over the Empire.

Think, then, of some large home at Corinth as the meeting place of the church there. Luke mentions the house of Titius Justus at Corinth, which was next door to the Jewish synagogue (Acts 18:7), as opening its doors to Paul after he was ejected from the synagogue. This house may be where the women were expressing their new "freedom" by laying aside their veils.

1 Corinthians 11:2-16. The "teachings," mentioned in verse 2, are the teachings and practices of the church, passed along orally from evangelists and teachers to new converts before (and also for some time after) the rise of Christian literature. Paul refers to these traditions in 1 Corinthians 15:1, 3; 2 Thessalonians 2:15; 3:6; and possibly in 1 Corinthians 11:23 (see following).

The references to *head* in this passage are confusing. Sometimes the word means the sense of the fount or originating cause and connotes the idea of supremacy over (11:3). Sometimes the human physical head is clearly meant (11:7, 10). The second occurrence of head in both verses 4 and 5 may be taken either way. See the contrasting translations in *The Revised English Bible* and the *Good News Bible: The Bible in Today's English Version*, for example. Fortunately, the general thrust of Paul's argument is clear with either meaning.

Paul argues for male supremacy here by appealing to Genesis 2:18 and 2:21-23. He might have argued from Genesis 1:27, where both male and female are represented as made "in the image of God." Paul certainly knew this passage. He actually treated women in the light of this higher teaching and reflects this understanding of the position of women in Galatians 3:28. Maybe in the struggle to hold back the hell-bent "freedom" of all the Corinthians, and now the Corinthian women, he used whatever restraints he could muster. In another situation he might not have taken this tack at all.

1 Corinthians 11:17-22. Ideally, as Paul said in 10:17, the Corinthian Christians are "one body," because they are participants in one cup and one bread. But actually they are far from reaching this unity.

Similarly, he said that they are "washed," "sanctified," and "justified" (6:11), but actually some are little better than worldlings outside the church (6:9-10, 12-20). Sanctification (holiness) is not a static state but a relationship in which Christians move on toward perfection through the power of the Holy Spirit given to them at the point of beginning (6:11).

Paul is much harder on the Corinthians for their desecration of the Lord's Supper than he is for the "freedom" thrust of the women. Here he emphatically takes back his compliment of a few verses earlier (11:2). The issue now is not a social-conventional one. This conduct strikes at the heart of their new relationship to Christ and to one another.

Paul treats the "divisions" with irony here: only by dividing can one know "which of you have God's approval." Pride lies at the bottom of their differences, as in most church splits, then and now. Whether it is pride of social status (rich versus poor), of "knowledge" (wise versus foolish), of leadership ("I am of Paul," and so on), or of all these in some kind of combination, the unity the bread and the cup represents is deeply threatened, if not destroyed. And Paul is horrified.

1 Corinthians 11:23-26. A little background may help in understanding Paul's attitude toward the Lord's Supper here. The roots of the supper lay in Jesus' meals with his disciples and followers. These meals, which often included "tax collectors and sinners," brought severe censure on Jesus from strait-laced, law-abiding observers. The meals appear to have been regarded by Jesus as offering a foretaste of the coming banquet in the kingdom of God, in which all participants would be equal, without distinctions of any sort. Unity and fellowship as the new people of God was the essence of these meals.

Jesus' last meal with his disciples was at Passover time. Here the unity was marred by the presence of Judas, who left the supper to do his dastardly deed. Since it was both a Passover celebration and Jesus' last meal with his disciples, the meal had a distinctive character. The Passover meal focused on Israel's deliverance from bondage in Egypt, on the coming messianic deliverance (of which the first deliverance—from Egypt—was seen by Jews as a type), and on Jesus' impending death as the means by which the messianic deliverance would be accomplished.

Jesus evidently saw himself as the Passover lamb (through whose blood on the doorposts Israel had been saved—Exodus 12:21-27—and by whose blood the nation and all people would experience the greater deliverance). Jesus saw his blood as like that of the sacrificial victim that sealed the covenant at Mount Sinai (Exodus 24:3-8). By eating the bread (his broken body) and drinking the cup (his blood, which would seal the new covenant), the participants would share with Jesus in the banquet of the coming kingdom of God.

The Jerusalem Christians, in their daily breaking "bread in their homes" (Acts 2:46)—that is, in their regular meals—were blessed by the presence of the resurrected Jesus (Acts 1:3-4; 10:41), who evidently made the meals into joyful anticipations of the messianic banquet (Acts 2:46).

Paul seems to feel that, in view of the excesses that crept into these joyful meals (especially in the Greek world), he had to restore the commemorative element that had largely vanished from these meals. The meals look backward as well as forward, Paul says. Thus, he twice includes the words, "Do this in remembrance of me" (11:24, 25).

By telling the Corinthians to satisfy their impelling hunger at home and by placing the emphasis on one aspect of the meal—the symbolic breaking of the bread and drinking of the cup—Paul seems to have taken the first step toward a separation of the meal from the symbolic elements. As the hope of Christ's speedy return waned, the church dropped the meal and perpetuated only the elements as a solemn memorial of Christ's death.

It is unclear what Paul means by "I received from the Lord what I also passed on to you." Does he mean that what happened at the Last Supper was revealed directly to him by the resurrected Jesus (on the Damascus road or in some other vision or revelation [2 Corinthians 12:1-4])? Or does he mean that the Lord was the source of the tradition that had been handed down to him in the church or, possibly, the source of the meaning of the supper? At least Paul claims the authority of the Lord for what he tells the Corinthians about the supper.

Many scholars today believe that Mark's version of the Last Supper is closest to what happened at that occasion (Mark 14:22-25). This version seems to rest on a primitive Aramaic account. Paul's version may have come from the church in Damascus or Antioch, possibly an adaptation of the Aramaic account for churches in the Greek world. The accounts are similar, with Paul's stressing its memorial aspect. The promise of drinking of the fruit of the vine (at the banquet in the kingdom of God) is missing from Paul. Rather, the Last Supper proclaims the death of Christ until his coming.

1 Corinthians 11:27-34. Paul's requirement of self-examination before partaking of the Lord's Supper does not mean that he expects people to be perfect in order to participate, but it does require them to scrutinize their attitudes and conduct. No careless approach to the supper can be tolerated, for God stands as judge over the participants. If one by careless eating fails to recognize "the body" (the Lord's body, as distinguished from an ordinary piece of bread? or the church as the Lord's holy people? or both?), fearful consequences may result.

On the judgment of sickness and death, see the suggestion in the student book, pages 32-33.

1 Corinthians 12. Paul turns now to a subject about which the Corinthians seem to have asked him in their letter (7:1): spiritual gifts and spiritual persons. This subject was of special interest to them, as indicated by the length of Paul's treatment of it (Chapters 12–14) and his remark in the opening thanksgiving that "you do not lack any spiritual gift" (1:7).

Paul uses the word *power* (*dynamic*, from which we get *dynamite*) several times in First and Second Corinthians, often in crucial passages (for example, 1 Corinthians 1:18, 24; 2:4-5; 4:18-20). When the references to the Spirit or Holy Spirit (synonymous with God's power) in these letters are added, it is evident that Paul and the Corinthians, who had been converted and instructed by him, conceived of salvation in terms of power.

Paul meant the power to be disciplined and turned to loving ends (8:1; Chapter 13; 16:14). For the Corinthians power opened the door to the spectacular in speech, knowledge of mysteries, miracle-working faith, and dramatic acts of charity and self-sacrifice (13:1-3).

The discussion in Chapters 12–14 embraces several subjects: the proper test of the source of gifts (12:1-3); the character and purpose of the gifts (12:4-11); the relation of members with different gifts to one another in the body of Christ (the church—12:12-31); the "fruit of the Spirit" (Galatians 5:22)—love—by which all gifts are to be measured and controlled (Chapter 13); and the comparative worth of prophecy and tongues (Chapter 14).

1 Corinthians 12:1-3. Spirit-possession was a common phenomenon in the ancient world. With many gods, lords, and spirits everywhere (1 Corinthians 8:5) and their devotees vying for followers, it was important to have a test by which God's Spirit could be recognized.

The test given here (see student book) is, of course, of value only if speakers are sincere, if what they say expresses what they really believe and are. Sincerely to confess the lordship of Jesus is to put oneself under his authority and service. To curse Jesus means that one is serving some other master.

1 Corinthians 12:4-11. The key verse of this passage is verse 11. The gifts, though markedly different in nature and function, proceed from the same source (the Holy Spirit) and are distributed by the Spirit to individual members as he wills. Therefore, no one can boast of his or her gift or feel inferior because of the gift he or she has.

The Spirit here is tied closely to God and Jesus Christ. Paul refers to the three with great fluidity, as in Romans 8:9-11. Paul did not conceive of three separate and distinct personalities in affiliation but of one God in different manifestations and activities.

In the Hebrew concept of corporate personality, persons flow into one another: a man into his sons, who then are collectively called by his name (for example, Israel), all bearing the characteristics of their father, sharing in his achievements and mistakes (guilt), and representing one another in contacts outside the family. The individual is thus a sample of the whole family. Paul presents the Trinity against this background.

The gifts here are not classified, though they fall into loose categories: those connected with the mind (wisdom and knowledge, finding utterance in speech); those associated with the will (special mountain-moving faith [13:2], healings, miracles); and those associated with speech (prophecy, distinguishing God-inspired from demon-inspired speakers, tongues, interpretation of tongues).

All these gifts, distributed to individual persons, are meant for "the common good," the building up of the church (14:12).

1 Corinthians 12:12-31. To explain the unity in diversity of the church, Paul draws on the analogy of the human body, an analogy long used in the Hellenic world to explain social and cosmic unity.

Paul speaks first of the unity: "the body is a unit." The statement "so it is with Christ" (12:12) seems strange, as one would expect "so it is with the church" here. But for Paul Christ and the church are one reality. The church is Christ's body (12:27); and on occasion, Paul can speak of Christ as the "head of the body" (Colossians 1:18, 2:19). Again we find the Hebrew idea of corporate personality, which expressed itself in the concept of the oneness of the Messiah and his people.

The unity of diverse people (Jews, Greeks, slave, free) was the work of the Holy Spirit in baptism; and the possession of the Spirit, imparted at baptism and conversion, binds all members together in an indissoluble unity.

The long section on the different bodily members needs little comment. Verse 18 stresses God's sovereignty in creation and should silence jealous members, vying for dominance in the body. The weaker and less honored members of the body are of equal importance with the stronger and more honored. The body should have no discord, but be filled with mutual care and mutual rejoicing.

In verses 28 and 29 the possessors of the various gifts are listed, roughly in the order of their importance in the church. The order is very close to that of the list of gifts in verses 8-10.

Several types of service appear here: (1) ministry of the word in witnessing, preaching, teaching (the apostles, as Christ's personal representatives, were witnesses to the Resurrection [Acts 1:22; 10:40-41; 1 Corinthians 15:5-8]); (2) ministry to physical needs (miracle workers, healers); (3) ministry in administration (helpers, perhaps deacons; and administrators, perhaps bishops [overseers], as in

Philippians 1:1); (4) speakers in tongues (interpreters of tongues is suggested in 12:30).

No one has all the gifts and no one gift is possessed by all. All gifts are necessary, but not all are of the same rank: there are "higher gifts," as Paul points out in Chapter 14.

DIMENSION THREE: WHAT DOES THE BIBLE MEAN TO ME?

1 Corinthians 11:2-16—Social Subordination and Christian Theology

Paul believed that equality before God in redemption does not eliminate distinctions inherent in creation; and that women, therefore, should not try to break out of the position assigned them in creation.

Evaluate this position. Are there any distinctions inherent in creation that should be recognized and preserved by the present-day Christian church? If so, what are they? Was Paul simply wrong in including the subordination of women among these? What part did Paul's way of interpreting the Creation story in Genesis 2 play in the formulation of his view about the subordinate position of women? What view of this story should we take today, and how would a different view of it affect our conclusion about the status of women?

Many feminists hold that the Bible's and Christian theology's patriarchal attitudes toward women have badly distorted the proper course of Christianity and society down through the centuries. What illustrations of this can you offer?

What is valuable and what is of questionable value about the contemporary attempt to remove sexist language from Bible passages used in the church's lectionary?

1 Corinthians 11:17-34—The Lord's Supper in the Church

What advantages and disadvantages would come to the church today if the Lord's Supper were celebrated in its original context, namely, a churchwide meal?

Share together what the Lord's Supper has meant and does mean to you personally. Evaluate its contribution to the life of the church as a whole. What could make it more meaningful to you and to the church?

Is observance of the Lord's Supper essential to salvation? How does it compare in this respect with baptism?

Paul counsels self-examination before partaking of the Lord's Supper. What should be the nature of this self-examination? What consequences of unworthy participation would you foresee?

1 Corinthians 12:1-31—The Holy Spirit in the Church

The Holy Spirit was very important to Paul. Until about 1960, when the charismatic movement began, theology centered chiefly on Jesus Christ and only a minor place was given in preaching and Christian experience to the Holy Spirit. Today many ministers give the Holy Spirit a dominant place in their theology, preaching, and interpretation of Christian experience. What brought about this change, and what values and limitations do you see in it?

What has the Holy Spirit meant to you personally? How do you understand the gifts of the Spirit? What gift do you think the Holy Spirit has given you?

Now I know in part; then I shall know fully, even as I am fully known (1 Corinthians 13:12).

5

Worship in the Church (Part 2) / The Resurrection

1 Corinthians 13–15

DIMENSION ONE:
WHAT DOES THE BIBLE SAY?

Answer these questions by reading 1 Corinthians 13

1. With what subject does Chapter 12 end and with what subject does Chapter 14 begin? After reading Chapter 13, what can you say about the way it fits into its context? (1 Corinthians 12:27-31; 13; 14:1-5)

   Chapter 12 ends with a list of persons with various spiritual gifts, an admonition to desire "the greater gifts," and an introductory sentence to Chapter 13. Chapter 14 resumes discussion of spiritual gifts and shows what one of "the greater gifts" is—prophecy as contrasted with tongues. Chapter 13 thus fits its context only loosely.

2. What is the main idea of each paragraph in 1 Corinthians 13? (13:1-3, 4-7, 8-12, 13)

   The first paragraph deals with the necessity of love; the second with the characteristics of love; the third with the perpetuity (or permanence) of love; and the fourth with the superiority of love.

3. If you had only 1 Corinthians 13 by which to define *love,* how would you define it?

   Love is a spirit or attitude that directs all gifts and abilities of persons toward unselfish and constructive individual and social ends. Since love supports and rejoices in "the truth" and is eternal in nature, it is akin to God's Spirit and is an activity of that Spirit in human beings.

Answer these questions by reading 1 Corinthians 14

4. What does Paul mean by the gift of prophecy in 1 Corinthians 14? (14:3-4, 6, 22, 24, 31)

   Prophecy is the gift of rational, intelligible speech by which

church members are instructed, encouraged, and comforted and by which outsiders may be won to Christian faith.

5. What does Paul mean by the gift of tongues in 1 Corinthians 14? (14:2, 4, 14, 21-23, 28)

   The gift of tongues means speaking to oneself and to God about hidden truths in a language of prayer, which springs from the spirit, not the mind. This speech is chiefly for self-edification and is not understandable by others unless it is specifically interpreted for them. The speaking in tongues is of such a nature that outsiders who hear it may judge the speaker to be insane.

6. How do prophecy and tongues compare in value for oneself and for the church as a whole? (14:1-6, 12, 14, 18-24, 27-28, 31, 39)

   Paul regards prophecy as of infinitely more value than tongues; he even says that five words of prophecy are better than ten thousand words in a tongue (14:19). He does not oppose—in fact, he both engages in and encourages—private speaking in tongues as a way of building the self. But in congregational worship Paul wants both mind and spirit linked. Prophecy is to predominate, with limited supplementation from interpreted tongues.

7. What suggestions does Paul give for improving the worship services at Corinth? (14:14-16, 26-40)

   For improving the worship services Paul envisions spontaneous participation in a variety of activities (singing, praying, giving thanks, saying "Amen," teaching, revealing of hidden truth, speaking in tongues, and interpreting it). All members are allowed to prophesy. Only two or three are to be heard on a single occasion, though. Tongues are not mandated. If people wish to speak in tongues, only two or three should be allowed and then only if there is someone to interpret. Women are not to disturb the service with chatter or irrelevant questions. Self-control in the interest of decorum, good order, and edifying instruction is necessary.

8. Why does Paul discuss the subject of resurrection in this letter? (15:12)

   Someone apparently had reported to Paul that some church members at Corinth did not believe in resurrection of the dead.

9. How seriously does Paul take the attitude of those mentioned in 15:12? (15:1-2, 13-19, 29-34)

   Paul regards this disbelief as a serious threat to the life of the church. It nullifies the work of Christ, makes his ministry pointless and fraudulent, affronts the Christian dead, and leaves the disbelievers still in their sins.

10. How does Paul establish the reality of the resurrection of Jesus? (15:3-10)

    Paul declares that the resurrection of Jesus is official church teaching (tradition), not something of his private invention; that Jesus' death and resurrection occurred in fulfillment of the Scriptures; that Jesus appeared to many people after his death, including important church leaders; and that he appeared to Paul also and commissioned him to be an apostle.

11. What is the place and function of the Resurrection in the plan of God? (15:20-28)

    Through Adam all persons experienced death (of the total self). Christ ("the last Adam" [verse 45]) broke the power of death by his resurrection, and all can now be made alive. The resurrected Christ is "the firstfruits" of the new humanity that God is bringing into being, from the dead and the living. At Christ's coming he will gather together his own, destroy every opposing power and authority (including death), and finally subject himself and all things to the sovereignty of God.

12. What is the nature of the resurrection body, and why does Paul refer to the different kinds of flesh and bodies in the universe? (15:35-44)

    The resurrection body belongs to another order of being from this one. That God has many orders of being is evident from the cosmos itself: there are people, animals, birds, fish, and heavenly bodies of various sorts. The person (the self) will pass through death to a new kind of existence and be given a body appropriate to the new order of being.

13. What contrasts does Paul draw between the two Adams? (15:45-49)

    Adam had a natural body; "the last Adam" became "a life-giving spirit." Adam was an earthly being; "the last Adam" is a heavenly being, who intends that we should become like him.

14. What result will follow the future coming of Christ? (15:50-57)

    The Christian dead will be raised and, together with living Christians, will be transformed at the coming of Christ. Death, sin, and sin's base of operation (the law) will finally be defeated by the victorious Jesus Christ.

15. What consequence for daily living does faith in the Resurrection and the coming of Christ have? (15:58)

    Faith makes Christians firm and steady in their beliefs and labors in the Lord's work, since they know their efforts are not meaningless and wasted.

DIMENSION TWO: WHAT DOES THE BIBLE MEAN?

In 14:1 Paul resumes the thought expressed in 12:31, "Eagerly desire spiritual gifts." Structurally, Chapter 13 is a digression from the subject of spiritual gifts. But logically and theologically it is not.

Because of the rather loose structural relationship of Chapter 13 with its context, some scholars have argued that Paul did not write the essay or hymn about love, but that an editor of Paul's letters shortly after Paul's time inserted someone else's composition about love here.

Others have contended that Paul wrote it, but not originally for this letter. Either an editor, knowing it was Paul's, inserted it here; or Paul himself brought in a piece he had composed earlier because he thought it appropriate to this place.

The prevailing view is that it is Paul's composition, however it may have gotten into this letter.

What Paul means by *love* here and whose love it is that he has in mind has been much discussed. The definition of love is best derived from the passage itself. (See the answer to question 3 in Dimension One.) Both the context and verses 4-7 connect the love being described to persons who are in relationship with one another, but the spirit and attitudes described here are related (13:8-13) to a reality that is eternal and that only can be God. Love in persons, therefore, derives from the gift of God's Spirit to believers (Romans 5:5) and flows out from them to fellow believers and even to persecuting enemies (Romans 12:9-21).

1 Corinthians 13:1-3. Paul's use of the first person ("I") here, as if he is warning himself against valuing gifts above love, is a good approach psychologically to the off-center Corinthians, whom he has spanked enough already.

His reference to "the tongues . . . of angels" may indicate that the Corinthians thought their "tongues" were identical with the language of heaven, an understandable attitude for those who believed they possessed in fullness the benefits of the kingdom of God already (4:8). If one could speak the language of heaven, it would indicate to some people, at least, that the speaker was a person of great learning and piety.

Paul draws into his contrast with love the most prized values of the time: spiritual ecstasy ("tongues"), regarded as a sure sign of God-possession; all-knowledge, which only God could have; the ability to perform dramatic miracles; complete generosity toward others; and the surrender of life in martyrdom (for one's faith or for the state). All these are valueless (before God) without love, says Paul.

1 Corinthians 13:4-7. Paul sees the work of the Holy Spirit in the believer's life not so much in terms of the Holy Spirit's "gifts," as the Corinthians did, but in terms of the character the Holy Spirit creates. The person who has the Holy Spirit is altogether loving and seeks to act in a loving manner in every situation of life. So Paul describes here what love does and what it does not do. To say what love is would be to say what God and the Holy Spirit are—an impossibility for finite beings.

How love acts is described first in positives, then in negatives, and again in positives.

To be "patient" is to bear injustice without anger or despair. To be "kind" is to be gentle in the way one treats others.

The negatives say that love does not envy other people (and, in the Corinthians' case, other people's gifts), or brag about one's own achievements and abilities, or puff up one's ego, or act in a rude and tactless manner. Love does not pursue selfish interests, does not react in irritation and anger, does not compile a record of wrongful treatment, does not applaud wrongdoing (see Romans 1:32).

Rather, love applauds right doing (Greek: "the truth"). In sum, "there is nothing love cannot face; there is no limit to its faith, its hope, its endurance" (13:7, *The Revised English Bible*).

1 Corinthians 13:8-13. The gifts that the Corinthians so highly prize are of passing significance. Soon no one will need prophecy (preaching) and tongues, since the end of all things is near (7:29; Romans 13:11-12). Human knowledge, fragmentary and imperfect, will soon be superseded by full knowledge, as a child's knowledge gives way to adult understanding. The distorted images we see in a mirror will soon give way to face-to-face knowledge.

The perfect order lies just ahead, and in that order only three spiritual realities will have enduring significance: faith (trust in God), hope (openness to the future), and love (God's love for us, and our love for God and one another). Supreme above all is love "because God is love" (1 John 4:8).

1 Corinthians 14:1-25. In Chapter 14 Paul returns to the subject of spiritual gifts. Paul now contrasts two gifts of speaking: prophecy and tongues. The latter has eclipsed the former at Corinth to the detriment of the life and work of the church. In a long discussion Paul attempts to set their priorities straight.

The basic issue concerns the proper balance between the mind and the spirit (emotions) in worship. Prophecy comes from the mind of the speaker and addresses the minds of the hearers. Tongues come from the spirit, that is, from the nonrational side of personality, that side that is capable of ecstatic experiences by an individual or a group. Paul contrasts the mind and the spirit in 14:14-19, where he definitely tips the balance in favor of the mind.

Prophecy is intelligible communication between speaker and hearer. Its content and purpose is fairly clearly indicated in the chapter.

The content is the nature and will of God for the life of humankind. The Spirit of God reveals these to the prophets (2:10-15). Paul here describes the content as "revelation or knowledge or prophecy or word of instruction" (14:6). These are not four parallel subject matters. The latter two relate to the means of making the first two known. "Revelation" has to do with divine secrets made known through prophecy, and "knowledge" has to do with the exposition of Christian truth made known through teaching.

The purpose of prophecy is the "strengthening, encouragement and comfort" of the church (14:3-5, 12). Prophecy is principally for believers (14:22); however, if an outsider is present and hears it, the outsider may be convicted and converted (14:24-25).

"Speaking in tongues" appears in this chapter as nonrational communication with oneself and God (14:2, 28) and, without interpretation, as of no value to the church as a whole (14:7-11) and even as a hindrance to it (14:23). This speech is associated with prayer and a kind of prayer in which the mind is not active (14:14). It is audible utterance, apparently of an ecstatic kind, so that the uninitiated on hearing it would think the speaker insane (14:23). Speaking in tongues gives expression to private mystical experiences, secrets shared with God (14:2), something that is helpful privately but meaningless to the church, unless it is interpreted.

The nonrational character of tongues constitutes the problem for church worship. Such worship should involve both the mind and the spirit. Paul wants to pray, sing, and praise with both mind and spirit (14:15-17). When mind and spirit are joined, believers will be helped and unbelievers may be converted.

Paul does not dismiss tongues as valueless. He says that he himself speaks in tongues more than all the Corinthians (14:18) and that he wants all of them to speak in tongues (14:5). But there is a time and a place, and that time and place is not in the church's worship services, unless the tongues are interpreted. And then he wants only a limited amount of it (14:27).

In early Israel certain bands of prophets manifested ecstatic phenomena (1 Samuel 10:5-13; 19:18-24). In the mystery religions of Paul's time worshipers became frenzied and expressed their emotions in ecstatic speech. The popularity of such experiences and expressions in pagan religions probably served to dampen Paul's enthusiasm for "tongues."

Tongues were present in Christianity before Paul's mission, as Acts 2:1-13 and 10:44-48 show.

Luke seems to represent the tongues at Pentecost as many actual historical languages, spoken by Jesus' disciples and heard and understood by Jews from many foreign nations who were in Jerusalem at the time of the Feast (Acts 2:5-11). This speech Luke regards as a miracle wrought by the Holy Spirit (Acts 2:4, 12). He does not suggest that the tongues in the house of Cornelius at Caesarea (Acts 10:46) and those at Ephesus (Acts 19:6) were languages. Indeed, there would have been no need for them in those situations.

Luke's story of Pentecost gives some indication that the tongues there may actually have been like those at Corinth, but Luke represented them as languages. Since the foreigners were Jews, gathered in Jerusalem for the celebration of Pentecost, it is obvious that they all could understand one language (Aramaic, the language of Jewry at that time) and that most of them could understand Greek, the international language. Why then would the gospel have to be preached to them in many different languages?

Furthermore, the speaking of foreign languages does not ordinarily lead to the conclusion that the speakers are drunk (Acts 2:13, 15); but the unintelligible utterances of people under high emotion, such as existed at Corinth, might lead to that conclusion (1 Corinthians 14:23).

Possibly Luke or his sources reinterpreted the pentecostal tongues in order to make several theological points: (1) that the gospel is universal and was so from the beginning; (2) that the age of miracles, predicted by the prophets, had dawned, and (3) that the Holy Spirit had overcome the inability of divided humanity to communicate (because of the confusion of tongues at the tower of Babel; see Genesis 11:1-9). It is unlikely that there were two types of tongues-speaking in the earliest church: that at Corinth and in the house of Cornelius, and that at Pentecost.

1 Corinthians 14:26-40. (For Paul's suggestions concerning the improvement of the worship services at Corinth see the student book.)

Likely the church worship services at Corinth ended in the observance of the Lord's Supper and, therefore, 1 Corinthians 11:17-34 and Chapter 14 possibly refer to the same gathering. It is likely also that other elements, not mentioned in Chapter 14, were present in the church worship service, such as readings from the Law and the Prophets, confessions of faith, doxologies, and benedictions (at the beginning and end). Baptism was held on separate occasions, in running water, not at the common supper.

1 Corinthians 15:1-11. Paul's claim that Jesus' death and resurrection were "according to the Scriptures" has given rise to much discussion by modern scholars.

The phrase "according to the Scriptures" means in fulfillment of the Scriptures, which in turn means in accordance with God's purposes as expressed in the Scriptures. The Jews of Paul's day hotly denied this claim about Jesus (Acts 17:2-9).

Paul does not explain here how Jesus' death was "for our sins," though he attempts an explanation elsewhere (Romans 3:25; 2 Corinthians 5:21; Galatians 3:13). At this point he simply affirms it as part of what he had received from the church's traditional teaching (15:3).

Paul does not make clear what Old Testament passages he had in mind as fulfilled by the death and resurrection of Jesus. For the death the following have been suggested: Exodus 12:21-33; Deuteronomy 21:22; Psalms 69:9; 118:22; 143:2; Isaiah 52:13–53:12. For the Resurrection: 2 Kings 20:5; Psalm 16:10-11; Hosea 6:1-2; Jonah 1:17–2:10.

The Resurrection "on the third day" suggests only temporary residence in the place of the dead. According to Near Eastern custom, a person remaining longer than three days in a place was considered a permanent resident.

For Paul the most important evidence for Jesus' resurrection is his appearances to many witnesses, including himself. See for the appearance to Cephas (Peter): Luke 24:34; to the Twelve: Luke 24:36-51, John 20:19-29; to the five hundred: no other New Testament reference (unless Paul means the crowd at Pentecost); to James: no other New Testament reference; to all the apostles: at the Ascension, as in Acts 1:3-11, or in one-by-one appearances to others besides the Twelve (Romans 16:7); and to Paul: Acts 9:3-8, 22:6-11; 26:12-18; 1 Corinthians 9:1; Galatians 1:16.

The argument for the reality of Jesus' resurrection concludes with the statement that all the apostles have preached it (it is no private opinion of Paul's) and that this preaching brought into being the Christian church.

1 Corinthians 15:29-34. Paul's allusion to baptism "for the dead" as a practice going on (in the church and perhaps at Corinth?) is quite mysterious. A host of explanations has been offered by scholars.

Here are a few. (1) Out of respect and affection for dead Christians, people accept baptism and become converted. (2) Baptism is not meant literally but rather metaphorically. Works of penance for relief of the dead, sadness over them, or martyrdom accepted because of them are referred to as "baptism." (3) "The dead" are the bodies of those being baptized, which would perish without baptism. (4) Vicarious, substitute baptism in behalf of unbaptized dead persons is meant. These might be Christian believers who had died through illness, accident, or a plague before they could be baptized; or persons who had no opportunity to hear the gospel and be saved.

Jews made atonement for the dead by prayers and sacrifices so that even wicked dead might participate in the resurrection (2 Maccabees 12:39-45). There is evidence that some Christians of the second century and later practiced proxy baptism. The fourth view is the preferred one today. Paul does not say that he approves or disapproves of the practice but simply that it makes no sense if there is no resurrection of the dead.

On the meaning of "I fought wild beasts in Ephesus" (15:32), see Lesson 1, Dimension Two.

1 Corinthians 15:35-58. Paul's main point in this section is that God has an appropriate body (manner of being) for existence in the coming age. He argues from the analogy of the seed and the varieties of creatures and created orders. These created objects, with their differing splendors, surely indicate that God is capable of providing a body (form of being) appropriate to the new state of existence.

How Paul conceived the new body is uncertain. Three views are possible.

One view is that the present body will be restored. Some early Christians (for example, Tertullian around A.D. 200) insisted that no part of the present body will be lost, not even a hair, an eye, or a tooth; but the whole organism will arise at the resurrection.

The second view is that the resurrection body will be entirely new, with no connection to our present body. God will give us a body to replace this one—a spiritual body.

The third view is that the resurrection body will be at once the same body and a different body. A certain identity and individuality will persist through all our bodily changes in this life, and these make us distinctive as persons. This identity and individuality will persist in the resurrection body. Jesus was recognizable, as the person he had been, after the Resurrection, even though he was not limited spatially and temporally.

DIMENSION THREE: WHAT DOES THE BIBLE MEAN TO ME?

1 Corinthians 13—The Supremacy of Love

In Chapter 13 we are at the very heart of the Christian faith and life. If God is love and if God dwells in us as the power of love, then all that we do should be done in love (1 Corinthians 16:14).

Most of us think of love as an emotional response to a person or object we find desirable or appealing. That is not the biblical meaning of the word. Paul makes the point that God's love is precisely opposite to this. God manifested his love in Jesus Christ's death to save those Paul calls "weak," "sinners," and "enemies"—the kind of self-sacrifice no human being would make for the worthless and undeserving (Romans 5:6-11). Jesus demonstrated this kind of love by going to the aid of the outcasts of society (Mark 2:15-17), regardless of its cost to him personally.

You can begin a discussion of this kind of love by contrasting it with the various meanings of love in use today. Then call to mind people in Christian history and on the contemporary scene who have manifested this kind of love.

Ask class members to share experiences when they individually were moved to act in this way toward people whom they did not "like." What motivated them to act in this manner?

A striking fact about the teaching of Jesus is that he regarded love as a commandment: "Love the Lord your God . . ." and "Love your neighbor . . ." (Mark 12:28-31). Can love be commanded? Is it subject to the will? If so, love cannot simply be an emotional reaction to a desirable person or object.

Love acts and love responds.

Love has hands and feet. What would we be doing today in the church if we really took seriously the teaching contained in Matthew 25:31-46? What would we individually be doing if we took the passage to heart?

If I were the kind of person described in 1 Corinthians 13, what difference would it make in my personal, family, social, and business life? Write out a few ways; if appropriate, share them with the group.

1 Corinthians 14—Mind and Spirit in Worship

Around 1960 a Holy Spirit movement began sweeping the churches of America and the world. It has been called the "Charismatic Movement." This movement emphasized the gifts of the Spirit: prophecy, faith healing, teaching, distinguishing spirits, speaking in tongues, and the interpretation of tongues. Its worship is informal and spontaneous, its witnessing joyful, its zeal in outreach contagious, its social concern minimal but growing. Ask someone who has been in contact with this movement to share any personal knowledge and experiences with the group.

One of the aspects of the movement is its emphasis on tongues-speaking. Some of the leaders claim that the tongues spoken are often actual historical languages, by which the Holy Spirit reaches people of other linguistic backgrounds. Certain psychologists and linguists deny that the tongues are languages and regard them as the gibberish resulting from a state of ecstasy. They point out that independent interpretations of the tongues by those who claim to have the gift of interpretation often do not agree.

What have you learned from 1 Corinthians 14 that will help you understand and evaluate this movement? What elements of the early church's worship might we well incorporate into our own?

1 Corinthians 15—The Christian Hope

What problems have you had in believing in the resurrection of Jesus and in the possibility of the resurrection of dead people? What help with your problems has Paul given you in Chapter 15?

What do you think of Paul's view that, if they do not have faith in the Resurrection, people will turn away from moral standards to a life of fleshly indulgence (15:32)? To what extent is this true and not true?

What convictions about the nature of the next life do you have, and what led you to these views?

But thanks be to God, who always leads us in triumphal procession in Christ (2:14).

— 6 —

Integrity Under the New Covenant

2 Corinthians 1–3

DIMENSION ONE:
WHAT DOES THE BIBLE SAY?

**Answer these questions by reading
2 Corinthians 1:1–2:13**

1. What do the following passages tell us about Timothy: Acts 16:1-3; 18:1-5; 1 Corinthians 4:17; 16:10-11; Philippians 2:19-22?

    Timothy was a young, half-Jewish believer from Lystra, who was taken by Paul as a missionary companion. Timothy joined Paul and Silas in the evangelization of Corinth. Later he was sent from Ephesus by Paul to assist the Corinthians. He was Paul's closest and most trusted associate.

2. To what readers is Second Corinthians addressed? (1:1b)

    Second Corinthians is addressed to the church at Corinth and to all the Christians of Achaia.

3. For what does Paul give thanks? (1:3-11)

    Paul gives thanks for God's deliverance from and comfort in death-threatening trouble in Asia, through which experience he is able to comfort the Corinthians.

4. What is Paul's view of suffering? (1:3-7)

    The Christian in suffering shares in the sufferings of Christ; and in that suffering the Christian experiences the comfort of God and Christ, so that he or she can comfort others through the comfort he or she has received.

5. What does Paul say about the nature of his suffering in Asia (that is, in the Roman province of Asia)? (1:8-10)

    Paul's suffering in Asia apparently was a peril of so serious a nature that he thought he would die and one that caused him to rely not on himself but on God.

6. Against what criticism does Paul defend himself? (1:12-17)

    Paul defends himself against charges of insincerity and deceitfulness.

7. How does Paul's characterization of God, of Christ, and of himself refute this criticism? (1:18-22)

    Paul is the commissioned, God-owned, and Spirit-filled servant of a faithful and reliable God and Jesus Christ, God's Son. Paul could not, therefore, be deceitful and unreliable.

8. Why has Paul not come to Corinth as he had planned? (1:23–2:2)

    Paul has stayed away to spare the Corinthians "another painful visit."

9. What does Paul say about a letter he had written to the Corinthians? (2:3-4, 9; 7:8, 12)

    Paul says that he wrote out of deep emotion to declare his love for them; to avoid thereby a face-to-face, painful visit; and to test their obedience to his instructions concerning someone who had wronged him.

10. What is Paul's attitude and what should be the attitude of the Corinthians toward the person who caused Paul pain at Corinth? (2:5-11)

    This person has been punished enough. Paul has forgiven him. He should be forgiven by the Corinthians and comforted by them.

**Answer these questions by reading
2 Corinthians 2:14–3:18**

11. What opposite effects does the preaching of the gospel have on hearers? (2:14-16)

    Some people are being saved and put on their way to everlasting life; others are perishing and are progressing toward death.

12. What basic contrasts and results are there between the old covenant and the new? (3:3-6)

The old covenant was written with ink on "tablets of stone"; the new is written with the Spirit on "tablets of human hearts." The old "kills"; the new "gives life."

13. Why does the new covenant have more glory than the old? (3:7-11)

The new covenant has to do with the Holy Spirit's ministry, brings righteousness (rather than condemnation), and is permanent (rather than that which fades away).

14. Why did Moses wear a veil over his face? (3:13)

Moses wore a veil to keep the Israelites from seeing that the radience of the old covenant was fading from his face.

15. What is it that the Israelites of Paul's day fail to understand? (3:14-16)

The Israelites of Paul's day do not understand that the old covenant was destined to pass away at the coming of Christ (the Messiah) with the more glorious new covenant.

16. What results does turning to the Lord bring? (3:16-18)

Turning to the Lord brings understanding of the nature of the two covenants, freedom in the Spirit, and progressive transformation into the divine likeness.

DIMENSION TWO: WHAT DOES THE BIBLE MEAN?

Our Second Corinthians is not the second letter Paul wrote to that church. In 1 Corinthians 5:9 we learn that he had written a letter to them prior to our First Corinthians. That letter was not preserved. We shall call it Letter A.

Then came our First Corinthians, which we shall call Letter B.

Later a letter was written out of anguish and tears, mentioned in 2 Corinthians 2:3-4, 9; 7:8, 12. This letter is probably not our First Corinthians, and it was not preserved. We shall call it Letter C.

So our Second Corinthians is known as Letter D, unless, as many scholars have argued, this letter consists of two letters: (1) Chapters 1–9 and (2) Chapters 10–13. If this is so, Letter D would be 2 Corinthians 1–9; and Letter E would be 2 Corinthians 10–13. Thus, Paul may have written five letters altogether to the Corinthian church.

Evidently the Corinthians caused Paul much anguish. To bring the infants at Corinth (1 Corinthians 3:1) to Christian maturity was as difficult as child rearing is to any parent.

2 Corinthians 1:1-2. These verses tell us that Timothy is co-sending this letter with Paul. Paul, of course, was the actual author.

Timothy, as one of the founders of the church at Corinth (Acts 18:5) and as Paul's most trusted representative (Philippians 2:19-22), may have visited Corinth since the founding in an attempt to aid the Corinthians (1 Corinthians 4:17; 16:10-11), but without much success. Yet, for Paul to include him as author of this letter must mean that he was esteemed to some degree by the Corinthians.

The letter is addressed not only to the church at Corinth but also to all the Christians of Achaia (the Roman province comprising most of ancient Greece south of Macedonia). First Corinthians deals mostly with local issues, thus, the local address. Second Corinthians deals with the nature and authority of Paul's apostleship, which are being challenged widely and therefore are important for all the churches that stem from Paul's ministry.

2 Corinthians 1:3-7. Paul does not commend the Corinthians at the beginning of this letter, as he does in our First Corinthians, probably because of the church's continuous failings and the strained relationship he now feels with its members. He does, however, wish to follow his custom of thanking God at the outset for something concerning his readers and to establish some sort of rapport with them. This he does by speaking of God's comfort in his recent affliction and its spill-over benefits for the Corinthians.

That Paul should be suffering so deeply for the church and the Corinthians and should even be concerned to share with them the comfort he receives from God in his sufferings is a thought that should disarm the most vicious Corinthian opponents. And since Paul's sufferings are really Christ's sufferings (1:5), attacks on Paul are really aimed at Christ as well!

Added to this is Paul's recognition that the Corinthians are suffering too. Thus a fellowship of suffering exists: Christ's, Paul's, and the Corinthians' as well as a fellowship of comfort from "the God of all comfort" (1:3).

2 Corinthians 1:8-11. Having talked in general terms about his theology of suffering, Paul now speaks specifically about a recent horrible experience of suffering, out of which God mercifully delivered him. The life-threatening "hardships" in Asia (probably in Ephesus) cast him completely on God. Paul had no resources of his own to meet. it.

What the hardships were Paul does not say. They may have been a plot on his life or more probably an imprisonment that threatened "the sentence of death" (1:9). The riot of the silversmiths of Ephesus (Acts 19:23-41) can hardly be meant, unless there was a sequel to it not described by Luke. Whatever it was, it was a "sentence of death," which Paul was utterly unable to meet with his own resources but only by reliance on "God, who raises the dead." This deliverance assured Paul of God's future help, a help, however, that requires prayer as its precondition (1:11).

Paul's request for their prayers asks delicately for their sympathetic understanding of him and their participation in the fellowship of suffering. If the Corinthians pray for him, Paul knows that they hardly can judge him harshly and unjustly.

A more apt opening for a letter of reconciliation between somewhat estranged friends could hardly be devised than this one.

2 Corinthians 1:12–2:2. An obstacle to the Corinthians' good relationship with Paul is their mistrust of his sincerity. Some have accused him of hidden meanings and dubious purposes in the letters he had written to the Corinthians. According to 1 Corinthians 5:9-11, they had misunderstood what he had said about separation from sinful people; and he found it necessary to correct them. In 1 Corinthians 9:15 Paul seems afraid that they will take his comments about his right to support as a hidden appeal for that very thing. They see a discrepancy between what he says in his letters and what he actually is (2 Corinthians 10:10-11). In general, Paul knows that they do not trust him as they ought.

Here Paul affirms his complete openness and candor. Before God and the coming judgment of the Lord Jesus, he can say that his conscience is clear. He has acted not in worldly ways but in the God-kind of sincerity. He wants to be proud of them and they of him at the Day of Judgment.

Turning again from generality to specifics, Paul takes up a case of alleged deception: his change of plans for a double visit to Corinth. Instead of journeying to Corinth on his way to Macedonia and returning through Corinth on his way to Judea, he had crossed from Troas into Macedonia, without the Corinthian detour. Instead of going to Corinth, he apparently sent them a letter (Letter C, above) that pained and infuriated some of them (2:3-4, 9; 7:8, 12). This change of plans confirmed the suspicions of some that Paul was unreliable and devious.

Paul's answer is, first, that he cannot be a double-dealing, worldly man because he is a commissioned representative of a trustworthy God and a trustworthy Son of God, whose promises are reliable. Furthermore, this God has put his seal of ownership on Paul and his associates by giving them his Spirit as the first installment of their ultimate inheritance. Called (literally, "anointed"), sealed, and empowered by a faithful God, they cannot but be his faithful representatives.

Second, Paul answers that he changed his plans out of consideration for the Corinthians. His last visit there had pained them and him, and he saw no point in repeating the agony. The last visit was apparently a short one by ship from Ephesus, during which Paul was confronted, and perhaps slandered and insulted, by some Corinthian opponent (2:5-11; 7:12). Paul seems to have accomplished little and returned in frustration to Ephesus.

2 Corinthians 2:3-13. The letter Paul wrote from Ephesus (Letter C), now lost, was a mixture of loving entreaty and stern discipline. After it was dispatched, Paul regretted that he had sent it (7:8). The letter apparently dealt with the disciplining of the unnamed challenger. Paul's recommendations were carried out by the majority, probably in formal session (2:6). Some form of punishment was administered. Now Paul, perhaps on the advice of Titus who had just come from Corinth (7:6-7), counsels complete forgiveness and restoration of the offender. The letter had done its work (7:9-12). The church has repented and reaffirmed allegiance to its apostolic founder. Now love among all should prevail, lest Satan destroy the church through vengefulness and divisiveness.

Paul's brief comment about his experience in Troas, after leaving Ephesus, is introduced to show his abiding concern for the Corinthians. Even in the face of great opportunity of evangelizing in Troas, the saving of the Corinthian church was most important to him. His failure to come to Corinth as promised in no way indicates a lack of love and concern. He could do nothing else until he could find out how Titus had fared in Corinth in the attempt to bring about a reconciliation.

2 Corinthians 2:14-16a. At 2:14 Paul begins discussing the major theme of Second Corinthians: the nature of Christian apostleship. The criticisms he has faced up to this point (insincerity and deceitfulness in regard to his change of plans, domineering attitudes and insensitivity in the letter he wrote, and perhaps tarrying in Troas and Macedonia when he ought to have come to Corinth) are relatively minor compared to the central question: Is Paul a true apostle of Jesus Christ? His enemies at Corinth have raised serious doubts about his qualifications and actions.

Why Paul bursts out in praise so suddenly in verse 14 is not altogether clear. Had the mention of Macedonia in verse 13 brought to mind the good news given him there by Titus about the repentance, obedience, and renewed enthusiasm for Paul in the church at Corinth (7:5-13)? Does he suddenly see the barriers to the triumphal procession of the gospel through the world falling so that he must pause for a doxology? At several places in his letters, when some great vista of God's saving activity opens before his eyes, he breaks out in praise (Romans 7:25; 1 Corinthians 15:57; 2 Corinthians 9:15; and in a different form, Romans 11:33-36).

The true apostle's function is to spread the knowledge of God everywhere. Paul and his associates are doing this very thing. The Greek here is of uncertain meaning ("leads us in triumphal procession," New International Version; "leads us in triumph," Revised Standard Version; "leads us as captives in Christ's triumphal procession," *The Revised English Bible*). Paul may have in mind the victory processions of triumphant Roman generals, in which the spoils of conquest, humiliated captive leaders, and elaborate scenes of decisive battles were exhibited to the assembled multitudes. The apostles are not the triumphant generals but the suffering, humiliated, doomed captives, "a spectacle to the whole universe, to angels as well as to men" (1 Corinthians 4:9; see also 2 Corinthians 6:4-5). But God makes this spectacle a saving instrument for the whole universe. It is God's way!

The spreading abroad of the knowledge of God in this way has a double effect: to the believing, the suffering apostles are Christ's pleasing aroma, continuously savored, which results progressively in life; for the unbelieving, the aroma is "a deadly stench" (*Good News Bible: The Bible in Today's English Version*) that leads on to death. The apostles have an awesome task: that of forcing people to a decision for Christ or against him.

2 Corinthians 2:16b–3:6. Who is adequate for this awesome responsibility? Paul asks. His answer is that only we, who have been commissioned by God, who are accountable to God, and who sincerely speak God's message are competent for this task—not the many who are selfishly huckstering the gospel. Here for the first time in this letter self-appointed "false apostles" (11:13), claiming authority over the Corinthians in opposition to Paul, come into view.

We learn from what Paul says here that these "false apostles" brought with them letters of recommendation. Letters of this kind were widely used in the Hellenistic world of that time to help travelers secure accommodations and help of various sorts. Paul both used such letters (Acts 9:2; 22:5) and wrote them for others (the Letter to Philemon; Romans 16:1-2).

We do not know who had written the letters for the "false apostles." It may have been prominent Christians in the mother church at Jerusalem but possibly churches in the Hellenistic world where these "apostles" had been. The reference in verse 1 to letters "from you" suggests that churches wrote such letters.

Paul, in founding the church at Corinth, had brought no letters of this sort and felt no need of them, then or now. Nor should the Corinthians. Their conversion had demonstrated the authenticity of his mission. They were Paul's "letters of recommendation" for all to see, and what letters they were! The writing was on human hearts, done by "the Spirit of the living God," not with ink (on papyrus) or chiseled in stone. The in-the-heart writing fulfilled the prophets' predictions for the end-time (Jeremiah 31:33; Ezekiel 11:19; 36:26). Now, in the new age, *people* are better recommendations of authenticity than *letters*.

The mention of writing on "tablets of stone" and of writing in the heart introduces Paul's contrast between the old covenant and the new. God has appointed Paul and his associates as his servants and representatives in the new age of the Spirit. They are not self-appointed, like the hucksters; and their adequacy to fulfill this role is therefore entirely from God, who appointed them.

2 Corinthians 3:7-18. The contrast between the two covenants really begins in verse 3 but comes to focus in verses 7-18. Paul develops several aspects in his contrast.

1. The Names. Paul is the first writer we know of to use the term *old covenant* (3:14). The author of the Book of Hebrews refers to "the first covenant" (Hebrews 9:15). By the "old covenant" Paul means the declaration of God's will given to Moses at Mount Sinai and embodied in the laws of Moses. He does not mean what we mean by "the Old Testament."

By "a new covenant" (3:6) Paul means God's new declaration of his purposes as revealed in and worked out through Jesus Christ. Again Paul does not mean a collection of books. The term *new covenant* came into the vocabulary of Jesus and the early church from Jeremiah 31:31.

2. The Basic Nature. The old covenant was written (carved) on tablets of stone (3:3, 7). This covenant was thus of an external (to the person) nature. The new covenant is written "on tablets of human hearts" (3:3) by the Holy Spirit and is internal in nature.

3. The Actual Effect. The old covenant brings condemnation and death (3:6, 7, 9). As Paul explains in his Letter to the Romans, the law, though holy and good (Romans 7:12), is a condemning, not a saving, instrument and even incites to the doing of evil (Romans 7:7-12). (As we well know, when something is legally prohibited, people often perversely and daringly break the law.)

With the law written in the heart by the Holy Spirit, a person is "a new creation" (2 Corinthians 5:17). The person has "life" (3:6), "righteousness" (right relations with God and other people, 3:9), "freedom" (from bondage to sin and the law, 3:17), and progressive God-likeness (3:18).

4. The Degree of Splendor. The old covenant came with splendor, as indicated by the glory of God that shone on Moses' face. But Moses knew that the splendor was transient. He put a veil over his face so that the Israelites could not see that the splendor was fading.

The new covenant is "even more glorious" (3:8). Since it brings life, righteousness, freedom, and God-likeness through the activity of the Holy Spirit, God's purposes are fully realized through the new covenant, and it will remain a permanent covenant.

5. The Attitude of the Ministers. A spirit of timidity and concealment characterized Moses. He had something to hide: the fading glory and ultimate termination of the old covenant and the transient character of ministry under it.

The apostles under the new covenant are open and bold to declare the good news to all the world. They have nothing to hide. The new covenant is valid forever and surpassingly glorious.

6. The People of the Two Covenants. Paul hastens to say in 3:14 that not Moses but the people of Israel were responsible for their unbelief. "Their minds were made dull," he says; and he implies that this is the condition of Jews of his own time. Hardened, unbelieving Israel hears with veiled minds the Scriptures read in the synagogues and does not perceive that in Christ the old covenant and its ministry have come to an end. "Christ is the end of the law" (Romans 10:4), but the Jews refuse to see it and accept it.

The people of the new covenant have turned to Christ. They have no veil over their minds. They have come to an understanding of the purpose of God in Jesus Christ and the proper relationship of the two covenants, and they have experienced the work and gifts of the Spirit in their hearts. They are free children of God (Romans 8:14-17), beholding God's glory and being changed progressively into his image. (The "Lord" in 3:17-18 is God-in-Christ. For Paul, when one turns to God, one turns to Christ and vice versa, and this turning is the work of the Holy Spirit.)

DIMENSION THREE: WHAT DOES THE BIBLE MEAN TO ME?

Paul speaks powerfully to our spirits in Second Corinthians—the most personal of all his letters. Here is no plaster saint but rather a flesh-and-blood person who reveals his innermost struggles and convictions for all to see.

2 Corinthians 1:3-11—Christian Suffering

In several passages of his Corinthian letters we find lists of Paul's sufferings (1 Corinthians 4:9-13; 2 Corinthians 6:4-10; 11:23-29) and in other passages various sorts of references to them (1 Corinthians 2:2; 9:22; 15:30-32; 2 Corinthians 1:3-11; 2:1-4; 4:8-12, 16-17; 7:5; 11:7-9; 12:7-10). You may wish to examine these passages to get the full force of the character and extent of his sufferings.

In 2 Corinthians 1:3-11 we have Paul's theology of Christian suffering. It has four centers: God, Christ, Christian apostles, and Christian believers. What kind of God do we have, according to this passage, and what is God's purpose in our suffering? What is meant by the word *comfort* here? See how this word is translated in other versions. Examine also John 14:16; 16:7; 1 John 2:1 (the same Greek word is used in all three passages) in several translations. What is the common work of God, the Spirit, and Jesus? What can this work mean to you in your suffering?

What were the sufferings of Jesus Christ (2 Corinthians 1:5) like and what did they accomplish? See Romans 5:6-11; 1 Corinthians 1:17-18; 2:2; 15:3; Philippians 2:5-11; 3:10; 1 Peter 2:21-24; 3:18; 4:13.

What kinds of suffering did Jesus expect his apostles to experience? See Matthew 10:16-23; Mark 10:38-40; John 15:20. And why were they to suffer thus?

Paul says that in his sufferings he is completing "what is still lacking in regard to Christ's afflictions" (Colossians 1:24). Could he have meant that there was something lacking in the efficacy of Christ's sufferings that he and others could supply? Colossians 2:13-15 and many other passages stress the fullness and all-sufficiency of Christ's work. Could Paul have meant that the implementation of Christ's work (to get the gospel out to the nations), with the sweat, blood, and tears involved in this work, is what is lacking? Or did Paul believe that a God-appointed amount of suffering must be borne in the period before the end (Mark 13:19-20; Acts 14:22; 1 Thessalonians 3:3), that he could bear part of this suffering, and that thereby he perhaps could shorten the time before the coming of the Lord?

Paul believed that all Christians are called to suffer with Christ (Acts 14:22; 2 Corinthians 1:6-7; Philippians 1:29-30; 1 Thessalonians 2:14). What kinds of Christian suffering are we likely to experience today? What resources for help do we have available to us? What meaning should we see in these sufferings (Romans 5:3; 2 Corinthians 12:5-10; 1 Peter 4:1-2; 5:8-10)? What should our attitude be in the midst of these sufferings (Romans 5:3; 2 Corinthians 12:9; Colossians 1:24; James 1:2)? How can we be sure that our sufferings are really "Christian" sufferings and not the result of our own wrong attitudes or wrongdoings (1 Peter 2:20; 4:14-16)?

2 Corinthians 1:12-22 *God-like Holiness and Sincerity*

As we saw above, Paul was accused of insincerity and double-dealing. He begins his defense by describing his behavior "in the world" (that is, in everyday life) as marked by "holiness and sincerity that are from God."

Holiness results from God's separation of the believer from all that is evil (1 Thessalonians 5:23). Sincerity may be derived from two Greek words: one meaning "sunlight" and the other "to judge" and thus means that something or someone is able to pass the test of judgment by the sunlight. In the shadows something may look good, but not in the sunlight. Here for Paul the light is the light of God's Final Judgment, as the reference to "the day of the Lord Jesus" (1:14) shows.

Have our lives been separated by God from all that is evil so that they can stand judgment by the sunlight and the light of the Day of Judgment? Our conscience will tell us, Paul says here. For Paul the conscience is the faculty of self-evaluation (Romans 2:15; 9:1; 2 Corinthians 4:2; 5:11). Discuss the role of conscience in the regulation of personal conduct. Is conscience infallible? Can it be educated? Can it be dulled? What part will conscience play at the Day of Judgment (Romans 2:15-16)?

One of the great verses of this section is 1:20: "For no matter how many promises God has made, they are 'Yes' in Christ."

What promises did Paul have in mind? Read Galatians 3:6-29. Are there political and economic promises (land promises) in the Galatians passage? Did Jesus make such promises to his disciples? What promises did Christ fulfill? What promises will he fulfill in the future? What promises are you expecting God to carry out in your life, and why?

2 Corinthians 2:5-11 *Forgiveness and Reconciliation*

Paul wants the Corinthian offender forgiven and restored to the fellowship of the church. For Paul forgiveness is the only possible attitude a Christian can have "in the sight of Christ" (2:10), now or at his coming Judgment

(5:10). This calls to mind Jesus' strong emphasis on forgiveness as the prerequisite to God's forgiveness (Matthew 5:23-24; 6:12; 18:23-35). What are we to think of "Christians" who believe themselves forgiven by God and yet hold grudges against family members or neighbors and harbor hateful attitudes toward other races and nations?

2 Corinthians 2:14–3:18
People of the New Covenant

What qualities, what attitudes, and what activities characterize the people of the new covenant, according to this passage? How does this description fit you?

We do not lose heart (4:1).

7

Ministry Under the New Covenant

2 Corinthians 4:1–6:13

DIMENSION ONE:
WHAT DOES THE BIBLE SAY?

Answer these questions by reading
2 Corinthians 4:1–5:10

1. What charges is Paul defending himself against in 4:1-6?

   Paul is defending himself against charges that he uses secret, shameful ways; that he practices deception and tampers with God's word (falsifies the gospel); that his gospel is veiled (not understandable); and that he preaches himself (promotes his own interests).

2. How does Paul explain the unbelief of those who reject the gospel? (4:3-4)

   When the truth is proclaimed to them, they do not accept and believe it; and then "the god of this age" (Satan) blinds their minds.

3. What is the content of the apostles' gospel, and what is their way of presenting it? (4:1-6)

   The content of their gospel is that Jesus Christ is "the image of [exactly like] God," that he has glory (splendor), and is "Lord" (Master). Their way of presenting the gospel is by "setting forth the truth plainly" in preaching (public proclamation), addressed to the consciences of the hearers.

4. Why is it necessary and proper for Christ's apostles to suffer? (4:7-12)

   In suffering for Christ "all-surpassing [incomparable] power" of God is disclosed to others, the apostles endure the same death process that Jesus went through (4:10), and they experience his (resurrection) life in their bodies, so that others may live (4:11-12).

5. What supports the apostles in their suffering and causes them not to lose heart? (4:13-18)

   The apostles are supported by Scripture (Psalm 116:10), faith that the God who raised Jesus will raise them also and bring them into his presence, daily inner renewal, glimpses of the "eternal glory that far outweighs them all."

6. What final destiny do the apostles look forward to? (5:1-2)

   The apostles are looking forward to a new, divine, eternal, building-like (rather than tent-like) existence and to the spiritual body Christians will put on for living then.

7. What are the attitudes and activities of the apostles meanwhile? (5:2-9)

   The apostles groan in longing; they are always confident; they live by faith, not by sight; they make it their goal to be pleasing to the Lord.

8. What effect does the apostles' knowledge of the coming Judgment have on the character of their ministry? (5:9-10)

   They want to live a life pleasing to Christ, for they know that when he judges them, they will receive "good or bad" according to what they have done here.

Answer these questions by reading
2 Corinthians 5:11–6:13

9. What accusations against Paul and his colleagues does Paul refute in 5:12-13?

   Paul says that they are not commending themselves, nor are they out of their minds (insane or emotionally unbalanced).

10. What motivates the ministry of Paul and his associates? (5:14-15)

Christ's unselfish and redemptive love for all controls (compels) Paul and his associates.

11. What results does being "in Christ" have? (5:16-21)

The person who is "in Christ" has a new view of Christ, based on internal rather than external standards; this person is a new creation (or creature) in a new age, is reconciled to God, is given the ministry of reconciliation, and has God's righteousness (rightness).

12. What has God done in Christ for the world? (5:19)

God reconciled the world to himself through the forgiveness of sins and the preaching of reconciliation to that world.

13. What is the function of the apostles in view of what God has done? (5:19-20)

They are ambassadors for Christ through whom God makes his appeal to the world for reconciliation.

14. What are the Corinthians to do in view of what God has done? (5:20b–6:2)

The Corinthians are to be reconciled to God, to become righteous, and "not to receive God's grace in vain" (let it come to nothing) at this opportune time of salvation.

15. What are the marks of authenticity of true servants of God? (6:4-10)

True servants of God will have these marks of authenticity: endurance in severe sufferings, God-given qualities of character, the Holy Spirit (the power of God), and the offensive and defensive weapons righteousness supplies.

DIMENSION TWO: WHAT DOES THE BIBLE MEAN?

Second Corinthians is one of the most difficult of Paul's letters to outline. The subjects are not sharply marked off from one another, as they are in First Corinthians. Paul brings up the same themes over and over in Second Corinthians, weaving them into different contexts. He is both aggressive and defensive in the letter, often bringing these strands together in puzzling ways.

Chapter 4 does not mark a major break in thought. The subject continues to be the new covenant, the characteristics of which Paul has set forth at some length in 3:6-18. With Chapter 4 he begins (and to some extent resumes) discussion of the nature of his ministry under this covenant. Since 1:12 he has been discussing how a minister of

this sort of covenant would act: "in the holiness and sincerity that are from God. . . . not according to worldly wisdom but according to God's grace" (1:12). Second Corinthians 3:6-18 is thus a watershed passage, up to which we have been climbing since 1:12 and down from which we descend at 4:1 (in the sense of drawing implications).

The progress of thought from 4:1 to 6:10 may be outlined as follows:

1. The ministers are courageous and open (forthright) in proclaiming Jesus as God's glorious Messiah and Lord and themselves as servants (slaves) of both Jesus and the Corinthians (4:1-6).

2. The servants suffer and die in their ministry, as did their Lord, in order to reveal God's power and to bring life to the world (4:7-12).

3. The servants are supported in their ministry by their faith that God will raise them from death, as he did Jesus, and give them life in a new body in the coming, eternal age (4:13–5:5).

4. The servants, while they await their final destiny, walk by faith and live in a manner pleasing to God, so that they may realize that destiny (5:6-10).

5. The servants are God's reconciled and reconciling ambassadors, motivated by Christ's love and his redemptive activity in behalf of the world (5:11-19).

6. The Corinthians should respond by making their initial response to the gospel effective, in full assurance of the integrity and proper credentials of the ambassadors God has sent to them (5:20–6:10).

2 Corinthians 4:1-6. Probably Paul's opponents at Corinth had charged that his gospel was veiled (obscure, unclear). They might have found support for this charge in the fact that many who heard the gospel turned it aside without being convinced of its truth. His radical re-interpretation of the Old Testament in proving that the crucified Jesus was the Messiah, his view that the law had been fulfilled and annulled through the coming of the Messiah, and his view of the meaning of Jesus' death and resurrection in the purpose of God, to mention a few items, caused offense and were confusing to many. Even the church found some things in Paul's letters hard to understand (2 Peter 3:15b-16).

Paul here admits that his gospel is veiled to some. But he finds the blame not with himself and his gospel; the trouble lies with the hearers and Satan. Paul had submitted his gospel openly, not secretly, to the consciences of all for a verdict (4:2); and he holds that those who turn it down are themselves responsible for their decision. Thereupon, Satan, "the god of this age," blinded their minds. The text does not say that Satan blinded people so *that* they might not believe. When hearers turned away from the light, they became incapable, by the blinding activity of Satan, of distinguishing light from darkness; and they thus missed the glorious vision of the God-like Messiah. (For the blinding that follows unbelief see 2 Thessalonians 2:10-11.)

That Paul should speak of Satan as "the god of this age" is in line with Jesus' references to Satan as "the prince of this world" (John 12:31; 14:30; 16:11). While God is "King eternal" (1 Timothy 1:17), God allows Satan to operate in this age. But Satan's destruction began in the ministry and death of Jesus (Luke 10:17-19; 11:20; John 12:31; Colossians 2:15) and will be completely accomplished by Jesus and God at the end of this age (Romans 16:20; 1 Corinthians 15:24; Philippians 2:10; Revelation 12:7-10; 20:10). The New Testament message is that, while Satan has great power in this age, Satan can be resisted and overcome through faith in Jesus and trust in God (Mark 9:14-29; 1 Corinthians 10:13; Hebrews 4:14-16; 1 Peter 5:8-9).

What the apostles and believers have seen through responding to the gospel, and unbelievers have missed, is "the glory [the splendor] of Christ, who is the image of God." An *image* in the New Testament sense is a true representation of the original. Since Jesus Christ is God's Son (Romans 5:10; Galatians 4:4), he is an exact representation of the Father (Colossians 1:15-20; Hebrews 1:2-3). Paul would agree with the author of the Gospel of John that when we have seen Jesus we have seen the Father (14:9). Since no one has ever seen God (John 1:18), what a marvel it is to behold his exact likeness and to be progressively transformed into that same likeness (Romans 8:29; 2 Corinthians 3:18)!

2 Corinthians 4:7-12. Special privilege involves special responsibility. God's glory shines in the hearts of his servants so that they may illuminate others with the glory of God that shines in Jesus Christ. The apostles are to "preach . . . Jesus Christ as Lord" (4:5) and to "show . . . this all-surpassing power" of God in their sufferings (4:7).

The treasure, mentioned in verse 7, is "the light of the knowledge of the glory of God in the face of Christ" (4:6). Strangely, yet appropriately, this wondrous treasure is contained in fragile, expendable jars of clay. In Paul's time treasure was often buried in clay containers under the floor or in a wall of a house. The Essenes, who gave us the Dead Sea Scrolls, used clay jars for storing and hiding some of their valuable manuscripts. Gold and silver were carried in earthen vessels in Roman victory processions. The humble container served to accentuate the glory of the treasure within.

Paul seems to have been despised by some of the Corinthians because of his weak (perhaps emaciated and scarred) bodily appearance, unimpressive speech, humble manner, thorn in the flesh (perhaps a recurrent illness—see Lesson 9), and generally unsavory personal history (involvement in riots and imprisonments, and so on) (see 2 Corinthians 10:1, 10; 11:6, 23-29; 12:7). Paul evidently saw himself as a much battered jar of clay, but within him was an inestimable treasure. He had seen the glory of God in the face of Jesus Christ on the Damascus road and had been called to share what he had seen with people everywhere.

In this letter Paul turns the Corinthian argument against the authenticity of his apostleship upside down. He is indisputably an apostle precisely because of his weaknesses and sufferings. He is a servant of a suffering Christ. Paul's gospel is about one who in weakness and suffering died a shameful death upon a cross. But in that cross God's power was displayed for the salvation of humanity, and over that cross and the death it inflicted God's power was victorious. Paul states his position sharply in these words, "He [Christ] was crucified in weakness, yet he lives by God's power. Likewise, we are weak in him, yet by God's power we will live with him to serve you" (13:4).

The apostles thus are weak so that God's power can be revealed in them too and so that people can know that their strength is really God's and not their own. It is their privilege and glory to suffer with Christ, "always being given over to death for Jesus' sake" (4:11). The scars Paul received in Christ's service are brands signifying Christ's ownership of him (Galatians 6:17) and they thus validate his apostleship beyond the shadow of any doubt. Therefore, Paul will glory in his infirmities and weaknesses, for in them God's power "comes to its full strength" (12:9, *The New English Bible*).

2 Corinthians 4:13–5:5. "Therefore we do not lose heart," Paul says (4:16). His courage to be bold and to speak boldly is supported in part by the Scriptures, in particular by the faith of the psalmist who believed and spoke out (4:13). Paul's courage is also supported by his knowledge of the resurrection of Jesus and of the resurrection God will accomplish for those (including the Corinthians) who are identified with Jesus (4:14-15).

Though Paul knew that his physical self was rapidly decaying and heading toward death, he was gloriously aware that his spiritual self was being renewed daily. A marvelous light was shining in his heart and growing brighter every day, light that no amount of suffering could extinguish. Death offered no terror to him (1 Corinthians 15:54-57), for a transcendent life was at work in him (2 Corinthians 4:10).

It is noteworthy that Paul calls his horrible sufferings "our light and momentary troubles." The three catalogs of sufferings in this letter (4:8-12; 6:4-10; 11:23-29) stagger the imagination and add up to what Paul himself admits is a living death (4:10-12). But in comparison with the life in him and the "eternal glory that far outweighs them all" (4:17) lying ahead, his sufferings seem trivial. Paul has learned to keep his eyes fixed not on visible and transient things but on the invisible and eternal realities.

The incomparable glory ahead is set forth in a few bold strokes in 5:1-5 through the use of metaphors. Life here is a temporary, tent-like existence like Israel experienced during its wandering in the wilderness. Life there will be building-like in nature, like Israel knew in the Promised Land, yet God-made and eternal, not made by human hands and temporary. That Paul is speaking here of the new heavenly age, described in many Jewish writings of his time, is clearly evident.

That this new age will include a new type body seems to be indicated by the phrase "clothed with our heavenly dwelling" (5:2). Here the metaphor changes somewhat awkwardly to clothing. One cannot put on a new house but rather new clothing; and the new clothing is to cover our nakedness (5:3-4).

Exactly what the nakedness refers to is unclear. Is it the nakedness of death? Does Paul long for the coming of the Lord so that he will not have to die—and remain for a time in a bodiless intermediate state—but be immediately transformed into his spiritual body at Christ's coming (1 Corinthians 15:51-54)? Is it the nakedness of guilt and alienation, the result of inconsistency in Christian dedication and living, that will be distressingly revealed at the Day of Judgment (5:10)? The *nature* of the new age is Paul's concern at the moment, not *conditions* for entering it, as in 5:6-10. The new age and the new body belong together and both are the objects of longing here. And that the hope is not wistful but assured is attested by the Holy Spirit, whom God has given to believers as a down payment on their ultimate inheritance (5:5).

2 Corinthians 5:6-10. These verses describe the situation of the apostles and believers while they wait for the "glory that far outwighs them all" (4:17), that is, the new age and the new body. They are "at home in the body" (in their earthly tent-like dwelling) and away from their home with the Lord (in the heavenly, building-like habitation). Away from their heavenly home, they yearn for that home and walk by faith that they will come to it, though they cannot now see it.

But what is really important is not whether they are here or there; it is whether they are living in a manner pleasing to the Lord, who will one day judge their conduct in this tent-like existence.

The thought is similar to that in Romans 14:8: "If we live, we live to the Lord; and if we die, we die to the Lord. So, whether we live or die, we belong to the Lord." Identification with him and commitment and obedience to him are the crucial matters; God will take care of all else.

2 Corinthians 5:11-21. Paul has said that the apostles believe and speak (4:13). Now he comments in depth on the nature of their ministry in the world.

The apostles are God's reconciled and reconciling ambassadors, whose task is to make known to people everywhere that "God was reconciling the world to himself in Christ" (5:19) and to persuade them to "be reconciled to God" by accepting the One (the Messiah) through whom the reconciliation was made possible.

For the progress of thought through this section (5:11-19) see the student book. Here I want to comment on Paul's view of the work of Christ in reconciling the world to God.

Paul centers on four themes in 5:11-21: God, Christ, sin, and the new creation. Dominant here is God (5:11, 13, 18, 19, 20, 21). "All this is from God" (5:18) is the bedrock of the passage. God acted in Christ to reconcile the world unto himself (5:19). God made Christ to be sin (5:21). God forgives sins (5:19) and bestows his righteousness (5:21). God appeals through the apostles for the reconciliation of the world (5:18-20). The entire passage emphasizes reconciliation (salvation) as God's act.

Paul makes it clear elsewhere that salvation sprang from God's grace and love (Romans 3:24; 5:8; 8:39; Ephesians 2:4-5). Nowhere does Paul suggest that God has to be moved by humans or by Christ to be gracious to sinners. Grace and love are the very essence of God's being. God even loved us while we were sinners (Romans 5:6-10).

The instrument of God's work of reconciliation is Christ (the Messiah). Christ is mentioned here repeatedly (in every verse from 14 to 21) and always as an agent. The love of the agent is noted too. "Christ's love" (5:14), revealed in his dying that all might live (5:14-15), impels the apostles to preach the gospel. Paul elsewhere speaks of Christ's love (Romans 8:35; Galatians 2:20).

How Christ's death was effective, according to Paul, is not easily determined. In this passage Paul says that "one died for all" and in that act—apparently through faith-identification with him—"all died" (5:14). The result of dying with Christ was life with him, through participation in his resurrection (5:15). This passage teaches that Christ did for us what we could not do for ourselves and that he opened to us the benefits of what he was and did.

One of the most difficult verses in Paul's letters is 5:21: "For us" God made the sinless Christ (John 8:46; Hebrews 4:15; 1 Peter 1:19; 2:22; 1 John 3:5) "to be sin." Paul does not say here that Christ was a sin-offering, or that he took our human nature, or that he became a "sinner." Paul says that God made Christ "to be sin" !

How can a *person* become an *abstraction* like "sin"? We meet the same puzzle in Paul's statement in Galatians 3:13 about Christ's "becoming a curse for us." In both cases Paul surely is stretching language to define the indefinable. We can only grasp at his meaning.

Apparently, behind both statements lie Old Testament passages and conceptions. That Christ was made "to be sin" calls up Isaiah 53, where God lays on his innocent (righteous) servant "our transgressions" and "our iniquities" and where "we are healed" by his wounds.

To be made "sin," then, must mean that our sin is transferred in some way to Christ, that what ought to have happened to us by way of punishment happened to Christ, that in him God's righteousness is transferred to us (2 Corinthians 5:21b), and that we are set free.

Behind Galatians 3:10-13 lies Deuteronomy 27:26 and 21:23, where lawbreakers (including one hung on a tree) are said to be cursed. Jesus hung on a tree, "becoming a curse for us," in order that we might be "redeemed . . . from the curse of the law."

In both the above passages Jesus' act is vicarious, that is, he does for others what they cannot do for themselves, freeing them from sin and God's punishment for sin and putting them in right relationship with God (righteousness/justification and reconciliation).

Three views of the Atonement have been dominant in Christian history.

1. The so-called "Classic Idea" sees the Atonement as *God's* act in Christ, particularly in the cross and Resurrection, through which the demonic powers of the world were defeated and the people enslaved by these powers were rescued and reconciled with God. This view emphasized the fact that the Atonement is through and through God's doing and is cosmic in scale and purpose. This view was the major view in the church for something like the first thousand years.

2. The Objective (or Satisfaction) Theory views the Atonement as Christ's work, by which Christ satisfied God's justice through offering himself as a payment to God to free sinners from the punishment they should have received because of their sins. This theory holds that, if sin is to be regarded seriously, it cannot be simply forgiven. That would be laxity toward sin. It must be punished to satisfy God's justice. Christ stood in our place, took our punishment, and averted it from us. This theory, formulated by Anselm of Canterbury in the eleventh century, had great influence on subsequent conservative theology.

3. The Subjective (or Moral Influence) Theory was formulated by Abelard (1079–1142) in opposition to Anselm. This theory views the Atonement as a change wrought by Christ in our (human) attitude rather than in God's. God freely forgives and needs no satisfaction of his justice. We are estranged and need reconciliation with God. Christ, the great teacher and example, aroused love in people's hearts in response to God's love. We are saved by imitating Christ's spirit and life—by living in love and doing the deeds of love. Liberals of the nineteenth and twentieth centuries have held to this view of the Atonement.

Actually, all three theories have points of contact with Paul.

For the "Classic Idea" see Romans 3:25; 8:3; 1 Corinthians 15:24; 2 Corinthians 5:19; Colossians 2:15.

For the "Objective View" see 1 Corinthians 5:7; 2 Corinthians 5:21; Galatians 3:13; Ephesians 5:2.

For the "Subjective View" see 1 Corinthians 11:1; Ephesians 5:2 (where both the Objective and Subjective views appear together); Philippians 2:1-11.

Evidently, no one of the three views is adequate without the others. All contribute something to our understanding of this incomprehensible reality.

DIMENSION THREE:
WHAT DOES THE BIBLE MEAN TO ME?

Second Corinthians 4:1–6:10 is one of the richest sections in Paul's letters. Both its theology and its implications for day-to-day living are profound. You should encourage your class members to select passages for memorization, such as 4:2, 5, 6, 7, 8-9, 16-18; 5:1-5, 6-9, 14-15, 17, 18-19; 6:2b. Ask them to recite their passages at the next meeting. Memorized Scripture is an invaluable resource in the Christian life.

2 Corinthians 3:12; 4:1, 16; 5:6, 8—Christian Courage

Examine the contexts of the verses listed here and discover what it was that kept Paul from utter discouragement and despair. Do these kinds of supports help you in your troubles? Compare and contrast your sufferings with those of Paul and his associates. How do you account for the differences in the nature of Christian suffering today?

2 Corinthians 4:4—"The God of This Age"

Belief in Satan has increased markedly in recent decades, both on the part of intellectuals and in popular circles. Satan cults are flourishing in some parts of the world. Ask a member of the group to read the articles on "Satan" in *The Interpreter's Dictionary of the Bible (Volume R–Z)*, another standard Bible dictionary, or the brief treatment in the *Abingdon Bible Handbook* (pages 429–31) and report to the group on the biblical view of Satan. Discuss your reasons for belief or disbelief in Satan. What does the Bible teach about the overcoming of Satan in personal life?

2 Corinthians 4:6—The Face of Christ

Paul saw God's splendor in the face of Christ. You may have an artist or art student in your group who would like to investigate faces of Christ done by famous artists. To what degree have they caught God's splendor in their representation of Jesus? How would you paint Jesus' face, and why?

2 Corinthians 4:16-18—Daily Renewal

What elements in Paul's life contributed to his daily renewal? What use did he make of the Old Testament, as judged from what we have studied in First and Second Corinthians? What about his prayer life and teaching about prayer? Examine the following passages: Romans 1:9; 15:30; 2 Corinthians 1:11; 13:9; Ephesians 1:16; 6:18-19; Philippians 1:4; Colossians 1:9; 4:2-3; 1 Thessalonians 3:10; 5:17; 1 Timothy 2:1-2; 2 Timothy 1:3; Philemon 4. How does your prayer life compare with Paul's?

2 Corinthians 5:1-5—Our Heavenly Dwelling

It has been said that Christianity has always been too preoccupied with life after death and too little concerned about life here and how. To what extent, if any, do you think this criticism is justified? How does Paul relate the two in 4:7–5:10? Note especially 5:6-10. What was Paul's attitude toward growing old and dying? How does it compare with contemporary attitudes? What glimpses of the nature of the future life does 5:1-5 offer?

2 Corinthians 5:11-15—Persuading People

What were Paul's methods of persuasion as they appear in 4:1–6:10? Would these methods be successful in your Christian witnessing?

2 Corinthians 5:17—The New Creation

For Paul what was "the old" that had passed away and what was "the new" that had come into being? In group discussion talk about the old and the new in individual and family life that has resulted (and may still happen) from being "in Christ."

2 Corinthians 6:7—The Armor of God

Paul speaks of "weapons of righteousness in the right hand and in the left." These would involve offensive weapons (for the right hand) and defensive ones (for the left). Are any weapons suggested in verses 6 and 7? What weapons can be added from Ephesians 6:11-17?

Thanks be to God for his indescribable gift (9:15)!

—8—

Open-Hearted Sharing

2 Corinthians 6:14–9:15

DIMENSION ONE:
WHAT DOES THE BIBLE SAY?

Answer these questions by reading
2 Corinthians 6:14–7:1

1. What is the central idea that binds this section together? (6:14–7:1)

   The central idea in this section is that believers should not be "yoked together" (Greek: "misyoked") with unbelievers.

2. What, if any, logical connection do you see between this section (6:14–7:1) and 6:11-13, on the one hand, and 7:2-3, on the other?

   This section seems like an erratic boulder in the pathway of thought. The verses before and after deal with Paul's desire for open-hearted relationship with the Corinthians, and this section concerns believers' relations with unbelievers.

Answer these questions by reading
2 Corinthians 7:2-16

3. After reading this passage, what would you say Paul's mood was at the time of writing it? What words of his best describe this mood? (7:2-16)

   Paul's mood was one of relief from deep concern over the Corinthians, satisfaction over what Titus had accomplished, pride and confidence in the Corinthians, and joy over Titus's arrival and the good news he brought. Key words are comfort, confidence, pride, *and* joy.

4. What was the nature of Titus's news? (7:7b, 9, 11)

   Titus brought the news that the Corinthians are longing (to see Paul), mourning in repentance (over their bad treatment of him), eager to clear themselves with Paul, and zealous once more for him and his work.

5. What was the effect of Paul's letter on himself and on the Corinthians? (7:8-9)

   At first Paul regretted sending the letter, for they were hurt by it; but the letter's ultimate good effect on the Corinthians caused him to rejoice.

6. What was Paul's purpose in writing this letter? (7:12; 2:3-4, 9)

   Paul wrote this letter to avoid the pain both the Corinthians and he would experience by a face-to-face meeting, to let them know his love for them, to test the obedience (loyalty) of the Corinthians by whether they followed his instructions for disciplining the person who had insulted him at Corinth, and to reveal to the Corinthians the state of their devotion to him.

Answer these questions by reading
2 Corinthians 8:1–9:15

7. Why have the Macedonian churches given liberally to "this service to the saints" (at Jerusalem)? (8:1-5)

   The Macedonian churches donated liberally because they had given themselves to the Lord and to Paul and his associates and because the grace of God was at work in them.

8. Why should the church at Corinth give liberally to this project also? (8:6-15)

   This giving is an "act of grace"; they should "excel" in it, along with the other areas in which they excel; it will prove the sincerity of their love; it is their proper response to the Lord Jesus who gave so that the Corinthians might receive; they should complete out of their present abundance what they gladly began; and the recipients may give back to them in the future, if there is need.

9. Whom is Paul sending to take up the offering at Corinth? (8:6, 16-23)

   Paul is sending Titus and two unnamed (Christian) brothers.

10. Why is Paul sending these men to Corinth in advance of his arrival? (9:3-5)

Paul sends these men on ahead to make sure that his "boasting" to the Macedonian churches about the enthusiasm of the Corinthians for the offering does not turn out to be without substance and an embarrassment to him. Also, gathering the offering in advance will give the offering the character of a "gift" and not "one grudgingly given."

11. Why should the Corinthians give not only cheerfully but generously to this offering? (9:6-10)

A law of the harvest says that generous sowing brings an abundant crop. God will provide the Corinthians with abundance for their own needs and for sharing with others. By great generosity they will give thanks to God, meet the needs of the (Jerusalem) saints, and be blessed themselves. They should be generous because God has been generous.

12. What service to God will the Corinthians render by their generous giving? (9:11-13)

Since the offering is "through us" and is called a "service" (a technical term, meaning a priestly act of worship for the community), Paul suggests that he is acting as priest for the Gentile church in making a formal offering to God in Jerusalem.

13. In what way will the Corinthians themselves be enriched by their giving? (9:11, 14)

They will have the privilege of participating in a great thank-offering to God, help the needy, and be loved and prayed for.

14. In what way has God's and Christ's giving set the pattern for Christian giving? (8:1, 9; 9:8-10, 15)

God's and Christ's "grace" (graciousness) is the ground and pattern of all Christian motivation and activity. This grace, evident in what the Macedonians have done, also will be evident in the Corinthians' giving; and this grace is simply "indescribable."

DIMENSION TWO:
WHAT DOES THE BIBLE MEAN?

At 2 Corinthians 5:20 Paul begins his direct appeal to the Corinthians for reconciliation with God. Beginning at 6:11 he appeals for reconciliation with himself and his colleagues. In 6:11–7:16 we have both an appeal for reconciliation and an expression of thanksgiving for the degree of reconciliation already achieved through the letter he had written the Corinthians (7:8-12) and the successful visit of Titus to Corinth (7:5-7).

Chapters 8 and 9 follow logically. Since the Corinthians are now to some degree zealous for him and his cause, Paul makes bold to bring up the matter of the offering for the saints in Jerusalem he had projected a year before (8:10), but which the Corinthians had done little about—indeed, had lost enthusiasm for. As reconciled children of God and as reconciled followers of God's divinely ordained messengers, they must now have care for God's other children in Jerusalem who are in great need.

2 Corinthians 6:14–7:1. This passage fits awkwardly into its context, as reading 6:13 and 7:2 together easily shows. Scholars have wondered whether the passage was put here by Paul himself or whether the person who gathered Paul's letters near the end of the first century inserted it at this point from another letter of Paul's (possibly the one mentioned in 1 Corinthians 5:9) or from some other source.

A number of words and ideas in this passage are unfamiliar to us from Paul's other letters, even reminding scholars of expressions and concepts in the Dead Sea Scrolls. Other literary characteristics of the passage, however, are like Paul's. Possibly Paul adapted the passage from some unknown source and inserted it here himself. All known, ancient manuscripts contain the passage in this context.

If Paul put the passage here originally, it presents one problem that remains before complete reconciliation is possible. (See the student book for an explanation.)

Paul's argument here reflects the teaching and debating practices of his times. Commands and exhortations, as well as proofs drawn from the Scriptures, were the very stuff of Judaism. Skillful use of rhetorical questions to point up perspectives was widely used by Hellenistic moral philosophers and Jewish Wisdom teachers of the time. Paul used such questions frequently in his Letter to the Romans (Romans 2:3-4, 21-22, for example). This kind of argument would have been readily understood by the Corinthians.

2 Corinthians 7:3. The statement "you have such a place in our hearts that we would live or die with you" shows the extent to which Paul felt bound to his converts. He was no exploiter of people for what he could get out of them (7:2), but a "father" longing for the love and fellowship of his children (1 Corinthians 4:15; 2 Corinthians 6:13; Galatians 4:19). Nowhere is this better seen than in his First Letter to the Thessalonians, where he says, "Now we really live, since you are standing firm in the Lord" (3:8).

The statement in 2 Corinthians 7:3 may rest on a traditional formula of enduring friendship—by which people pledged their union in life or death—known to us from writings of the period. Paul seems to have Christianized the formula. In Christ Christians share death and life in an eternal bond, one that Paul would never loose.

2 Corinthians 7:5. The "conflicts on the outside" may be an allusion to the troubles Paul got into when he arrived in Philippi, the probable city where he and Titus met. In

Paul's Letter to the Philippians he warns the readers of "dogs," "men who do evil," "mutilators of the flesh" through circumcision (3:2-3), and those who engage in shameful "earthly" practices (3:18-19). We cannot tell whether they were Jews, Judaizers, or Jewish-Christian gnostics. But they were "enemies of the cross of Christ" (3:18). Paul may have become embroiled in this conflict when he arrived in Philippi.

The "fears within" may indicate the impact of this intense struggle on Paul's spirit, compounded by his concern for the safety of Titus and the uncertain loyalty of the Corinthians.

2 Corinthians 7:5-15. The New Testament does not give us much knowledge about Titus. He is only mentioned in 2 Corinthians 2:13; 7:6-15; 8:6, 16, 23; 12:18; Galatians 2:1, 3; 2 Timothy 4:10; and Titus 1:4. Titus was a Gentile Christian whom Paul seems to have taken to Jerusalem as an exhibit of Gentile Christianity. This occurred at the time of Paul's conference with the Christian leaders in Jerusalem about the relation of Gentile Christians to the Jewish law. Pressure was put on Paul by "false brothers" to have Titus circumcised. But Paul did not yield, and Titus was accepted as a Christian brother without this requirement (Galatians 2:3-4).

Titus was an important associate of Paul's, as judged by Paul's characterization of him as "my brother Titus" (2 Corinthians 2:13) and "my partner and fellow worker" (2 Corinthians 8:23). Probably only Timothy stood nearer to Paul than Titus (see Philippians 2:19-22).

Titus was a key instrument in the handling of delicate negotiations with the church at Corinth. Paul sent him from Ephesus, apparently after dispatching the painful letter (2 Corinthians 2:3-4, 9; 7:8, 12), to see whether the letter had been effective and to offer what assistance he could to the Corinthian church. Titus was to report to Paul at Troas, near ancient Troy on the west coast of Asia (Minor), but perhaps was unavoidably delayed (2 Corinthians 2:12-13). The two finally met in Macedonia (2 Corinthians 7:5), probably in Philippi, to which Titus had traveled along the great Roman road to the East, known as the Via Egnatia. The contact point may have been a private home in Philippi, possibly that of Lydia (Acts 16:14-15) or the "yokefellow" (Philippians 4:3), whoever the latter was (perhaps Epaphroditus; see Philippians 2:25).

Paul sent Titus back to Corinth (along with two companions) and probably with Letter D (see Lesson 6, Dimension Two) to complete the gathering of the offering for the Jerusalem church, on which Titus had made a beginning when he was there earlier (2 Corinthians 8:6, 16-17). Titus's fidelity and honesty in supervising the raising of the offering is pointed out by Paul in 2 Corinthians 12:18.

Paul calls Titus "my true son in our common faith" (Titus 1:4), an indication that he was one of Paul's converts. According to that letter (1:5), Titus was sent to Crete near the end of Paul's life to supervise the life and work of an undisciplined church in an unruly area—a task for which he was well prepared by his association with Paul. Whether Titus met Paul at Nicopolis (northwest of Corinth), as instructed in Titus 3:12, is not known.

Our last glimpse of Titus is on a mission to Dalmatia (the Balkans) (2 Timothy 4:10). He was Paul's "partner and fellow worker" par excellence (2 Corinthians 8:23)!

2 Corinthians 8 and 9. Paul's joyful satisfaction over Titus's report and the healing of the breach between the Corinthians and himself forms a natural springboard for his request to resume the collection for the poor saints in Jerusalem that had been begun at Corinth a year before (8:10). If the Corinthians are zealous for Paul and his cause (7:7, 12), they will of course support Paul in this "act of grace" (8:6).

Paul's discussion of the collection now covers two fairly long chapters (2 Corinthians 8 and 9). When the chapters are read consecutively, it seems that Chapter 9 repeats items that have been discussed in Chapter 8 (the reference to the Macedonians, to the sending of brothers as collectors, to the readiness of the Corinthians, and so on). Also, a fresh start seems to be made in 9:1, as if nothing has been said about the offering before. And some scholars find minor contradictions between the chapters. These scholars believe that two originally independent discussions of the collection, written a few weeks apart by Paul (one sent to Corinth and the other to the churches of Achaia), were joined by the editor of Paul's letters around the end of the first century and now appear as part of original Letter D.

In answer to these scholars it has been pointed out that Paul tended to repeat himself for emphasis, that the contradictions are more apparent than real, and that there may have been a short time break between the dictation of Chapters 8 and 9, so that Paul unconsciously started somewhat afresh and fell into repetitions. The arguments for two originally separate pieces are not conclusive. The chapters probably should be regarded as a continuous discussion of the collection and both chapters as originally a part of Letter D.

The chapters divide into three sections: (1) the enthusiasm and generosity of the Macedonian churches and the responsibility of the Corinthians (8:1-15); (2) the identity, the qualifications, and the function of the collectors Paul is sending to Corinth (8:16–9:5); (3) the reasons for cheerful and generous giving (9:6-15).

For a discussion of Paul's motives in taking the offering, see the student book.

2 Corinthians 8:1-15. Paul refers to two conditions in the churches of Macedonia: their "severe trial" and their "extreme poverty." For the severe trial at Philippi read Acts 16:16-40; Philippians 1:29-30. For that at Thessalonica read Acts 17:1-9; 1 Thessalonians 1:6; 2:14; 3:3-4. For Beroea see Acts 17:13.

The reason for the extreme poverty of these churches, in contrast to the relative abundance of the Corinthians (2 Corinthians 8:14), can only be surmised. The persecution by the Jews, who incited the local authorities against the Christians, was very intense in Macedonia, perhaps leading to severe economic repercussions (loss of business, jobs, and even forfeiture of peace bonds—Acts 17:9).

Only God's grace and the depth of their commitment to the Lord and to Paul, not any quality of character or abundance of resources, led the Macedonians to be so generous. Their spirit should be a challenge to the Corinthians: to excel in liberality as they excel in other ways (8:7).

Paul calls his remarks about the collection "advice" rather than "a command" (8:8, 10). He said in 1:24 that he was not trying to "lord it over your faith" but "we work with you." Some of the Corinthians regarded Paul as an autocrat (2 Corinthians 10:8), an attitude to which Paul evidently contributed by some of his remarks (1 Corinthians 4:18-21). Now he tries to change their—to him, distorted—image of his leadership.

Paul wants God's grace and "the grace of our Lord Jesus Christ," rather than his command, to be the motivating force in the Corinthians' giving.

"The grace of our Lord Jesus Christ," a phrase in common use in the church's liturgy and often in Paul's letters (Romans 16:20; 1 Corinthians 16:23; 2 Corinthians 13:14; Galatians 6:18; and other places), is expanded here into one of the most meaningful Christological statements in the New Testament. In luster it compares with the hymn-like affirmations in Philippians 2:5-11 and 1 Timothy 3:16.

All three passages presume that Christ existed in heaven with God and with divine prerogatives and that he surrendered these prerogatives when he took human form for our redemption—that he might make us what he himself was and is. This surrender of riches in order to enrich us is "grace" incomprehensible, "the mystery of godliness" (1 Timothy 3:16). Being thus enriched, how can we do otherwise than to manifest grace toward others? This idea is the essence of Paul's thought here.

Another motive for sharing with the poor in Jerusalem is the principle of *equality* (8:14), with which the Corinthians were familiar in Hellenistic thought and literature. It is basically the same as *koinonia*, the equal participation in material and spiritual benefits, such as is known to us from the early church's common life (Acts 2:44-45; 4:34-37) and in Israel's experience with the manna (Exodus 16:18). God means that all persons are to be cared for through the sharing of his benefits.

2 Corinthians 8:16–9:5. Paul speaks of Titus as being enthusiastic (earnest) (8:17). Throughout this part of Second Corinthians Paul has spoken several times of people as being *earnest* (7:11; 8:7, 8, 22). What does the word mean? Various modern translations use several English words for *earnest*: zealous, eager, concerned, keen, devoted, enthusiastic. The term is the opposite of *apathetic*, which the Corinthians had become as a result of their loss of faith in Paul, his message, and his program. *Earnest* is a fiery word, a "believe something" and "do something" word. *Earnest* describes the attitude of the Macedonians, Titus, one of the collec-

tors, and the repented Corinthians. And obviously *earnest* reflects the spirit of Paul!

Paul makes it plain to the Corinthians why a distinguished representative of the churches is to come with Titus to Corinth, along with another person Paul and his colleagues have chosen. They are to guarantee the integrity of the project. This "liberal gift" is "to honor the Lord" and an evidence of the "eagerness to help" of Paul's groups, not a scheme to enrich themselves (8:19-21). Paul wants the offering aboveboard in every respect.

In 9:1-5 Paul first appeals to the Corinthians' pride and seeks to protect his own. "I don't want you to look bad to the Macedonians, to whom I have bragged about your 'readiness' (eager good will) regarding this offering," he seems to be saying. And "I don't want to look bad to them either, when some of them come with me to Corinth." Even Christian egos need protection and affirmation!

Then, Paul wants the collection taken before his arrival. If the offering is an expression of "love" (8:8, 24), it must come as a "generous gift," not "one grudgingly given" under the pressure of his presence at Corinth. What kind of response would this kind of offering be to the God and the Christ who gave to enrich us?

2 Corinthians 9:6-15. If 2 Corinthians 10–13 belongs to Letter E, then this is the closing section of Letter D and the climax of this letter. The ending of Letter D, dropped by the editor of Paul's letters around the end of the first century, would have contained the usual concluding greetings and benediction.

Paul drives home his final appeal with the introductory words, "Remember this." And the point is that God wants both generous and cheerful giving. For support Paul introduces an agricultural metaphor and a reference to Scripture. The metaphor teaches that giving is getting, not losing; abundant seed produces abundant harvest. The Scripture (Proverbs 22:8a in the Greek Old Testament only) states that God blesses the cheerful giver. Giving under compulsion is not an act of love. Before God the quality of giving is more important than the quantity.

Paul wants the Corinthians to give daringly and to trust God that they can both give and have. Again Scripture (Psalm 112:9; Isaiah 55:10; and Hosea 10:12) comes to Paul's aid. The benevolent person will have abundance for himself or herself and increasing abundance with which to share (9:11). This person will help needy persons as required in the gospel of Christ, evoke their love and prayers, and participate in a great thank-offering to God—all in response to God's magnificent generosity (9:15).

DIMENSION THREE: WHAT DOES THE BIBLE MEAN TO ME?

Embedded in Paul's discussion of the collection for the saints in Jerusalem are basic principles of Christian giving. Some of them are listed here. They are presented in the order of the text, not in logical (or theological) order. See if you can discover other principles.

1. Christian giving is the result of God's grace (graciousness) at work in individual believers and in the church; it does not spring from natural human generosity or an excess of resources (8:1-3; 9:14).

2. Giving of one's substance must be preceded by the giving of oneself to God (8:5).

3. The "grace of giving" is as important as any other Christian gift or grace; we are to excel in it also (8:7).

4. Christian giving cannot be commanded; it arises out of loving response to God's grace and to that of the Lord Jesus Christ, who surrendered his riches in order to enrich us (8:8-9; 9:15).

5. Enthusiastic intentions regarding giving must be implemented by specific, practical action, according to the resources one has (8:10-12).

6. Christian giving is an aspect of *koinonia* (equal participation in material and spiritual benefits) and works for the good of both givers and receivers (8:13-15).

7. Christian giving involves responsible methods of collection and dispersal, such as God and human beings in general would approve (8:20-21).

8. Christian giving is glad giving, not giving that results from human pressure (9:5, 7).

9. Christian giving is daring giving, in the faith that God will care for one's needs and provide the means for generosity toward others (9:6-11).

10. Christian giving is an act of service to God and evokes praise of God (thanksgiving) on the part of those who are helped (9:11-13).

11. Christian giving is an act of obedience to the gospel of Christ, which one confesses (9:13).

12. Christian giving is a tangible manifestation of God's grace in (the hearts of) the givers and promotes deep affection and prayerful concern for the givers on the part of those who receive (9:14).

How would your personal giving and that of your church and the general church be affected if you took these principles seriously? Are there any with which you disagree? If so, why?

[The Lord] said to me, "My grace is sufficient for you, for my power is made perfect in weakness" (12:9).

— 9 —

Apostles: The False and the True

2 Corinthians 10–13

DIMENSION ONE:
WHAT DOES THE BIBLE SAY?

Answer these questions by reading 2 Corinthians 10

1. What charges does Paul refute in 10:1-6, and how?

   Paul responds here in exactly the opposite way to what is charged: he is "timid" and humbly entreats them by this letter. He also asserts that he may have to be "bold" (and can be!) when he is present. Paul declares that though he lives in the world, he does not fight with worldly but rather divine weapons by which to overcome every pretension to the knowledge of God.

2. How does Paul counter the claim and charge made in 10:7-11?

   Paul claims for himself whatever special relationship to Christ anyone else has. He admits that he may boast a little too much about his authority but claims it is for building the Corinthians up and not for tearing them down. Paul also asserts that his authority is binding whether he is present or absent.

3. What does Paul object to in the attitude and activity of his rivals at Corinth? (10:12-18)

   Paul objects to his rivals (1) commending themselves by comparing themselves with themselves; (2) attacking Paul for his attitude toward the Corinthians as his exclusive field and property; and (3) trying to reap the benefits of what he has done there.

**Answer these questions by reading
2 Corinthians 11:1-21a**

4. Why is Paul jealous of the rivals who have come to Corinth? (11:2-6)

   Paul sees himself as the father of a bride-to-be (the Corinthians). He has betrothed his daughter to Christ for marriage

and must keep her virginal until that time. The daughter is now in danger of being seduced by other lovers, who downgrade the father, disagree with what he stands for, and threaten to destroy the bride-elect's future.

5. What problems arose between Paul and the Corinthians because he insisted on supporting himself while in Corinth? (11:7-11)

   The Corinthians thought he did not love them as much as he loved other churches because he would not accept support from them as he did from those churches.

6. What estimate of Paul's rivals appears in 11:12-15?

   Paul calls them "false apostles," "deceitful workmen," disguised representatives of Satan.

7. In what ways have Paul's rivals ill-treated the Corinthians, and how have the Corinthians taken this treatment? (11:19-20)

   Paul's rivals have enslaved, exploited, taken advantage of, pushed themselves on (by pretense), and abused the Corinthians. The Corinthians have accepted this treatment without complaint, and even gladly.

**Answer these questions by reading
2 Corinthians 11:21b–12:13**

8. Why does Paul offer a catalog of his sufferings? (11:23-29)

   Paul offers this catalog to show that he is a better servant of Christ than his rivals.

9. How important as an apostolic credential does Paul think his experience of paradise was? (12:2-6)

   Paul does not boast about that experience or even understand it. The experience seems of relatively little importance to him. He boasts rather of his weaknesses.

10. What was the purpose of Paul's thorn in the flesh? (12:7-10)

The thorn in the flesh was to torment Paul and keep him from being conceited.

11. What signs of a true apostle did Paul exhibit at Corinth? (12:12-13)

Paul showed "signs, wonders and miracles."

Answer these questions by reading 2 Corinthians 12:14–13:14

12. What accusation does Paul refute in 12:14-18?

Paul and his friends have been accused of having hidden, selfish motives in raising the offering they are taking up. He and they really love the Corinthians and seek their best interests.

13. What does Paul fear he will find when he arrives in Corinth? (12:20-21)

Paul fears there will be strained relations between him and the Corinthians and the unpleasant wrangling resulting therefrom. He also fears that he will be reduced to humiliation and mourning over the lack of repentance of those who indulge in immoral practices.

14. What does Paul want the Corinthians to do before he arrives? (13:5-9)

Paul wants them to examine and test themselves with respect to their fidelity to their faith; to impress Paul and his associates favorably; to realize that Jesus Christ dwells within them; and to show improvement.

15. What is Paul's purpose in writing this letter? (13:10)

Paul is writing to encourage the Corinthians to make changes in their situation before he arrives so that he may be able to use his authority in constructive, rather than destructive (punitive), ways when he arrives.

DIMENSION TWO: WHAT DOES THE BIBLE MEAN?

Second Corinthians 10–13 probably originally belonged to a letter separate from and written later than 2 Corinthians 1–9 (see Lesson 6, page 32).

After the arrival of Titus with his favorable report (2 Corinthians 7) and the return of Titus with two brothers to implement the plan for the raising of the collection at Corinth (8:6, 16-24), Paul apparently remained for a while in the churches of Macedonia, perhaps at Thessalonica and Beroea. The plan was that when the time was ripe, perhaps on notice from Titus of the successful raising of the offering, Paul would proceed to Corinth and after a short stay there go on to Jerusalem with the offering.

But things did not go well for Titus and the brothers at Corinth. The rebellion against Paul, which Titus thought had subsided, intensified under the leadership of persons Paul calls "false apostles" and "super-apostles" (11:5, 13; 12:11). They seem to have come into the church at Corinth from the outside. These "false apostles" (see the discussion of their identity following in the section on 11:12-21a) maliciously attacked Paul and interrupted the collection of the funds for Jerusalem.

Information about their activity was carried by messenger or letter to Paul in Macedonia. Afraid of the total loss of the Corinthians to these "false apostles" and deeply concerned about the collapse there of the offering project, he wrote this rather bitter and often sarcastic letter (Letter E) in the hope that he could turn the situation around before his arrival (13:10). Paul dreaded the possibility of another painful confrontation with the Corinthians (12:20-21).

That Paul eventually was victorious is evident from the facts that the collection there was raised (Romans 15:26), that he spent three months at Corinth (Acts 20:3), that he departed from there for Jerusalem as planned (though by a different route, Acts 20:3), and that this letter was preserved by the church.

2 Corinthians 10:8-16. Paul believed that he had God-given authority over the Corinthians (10:8, 13-14; 11:10; 1 Corinthians 4:14-21). In fact, Paul believed that this authority extended over all the Gentile churches, for God had made him "a minister of Christ Jesus to the Gentiles with the priestly duty of proclaiming the gospel of God" (Romans 15:16). In this role Paul's function was to present the Gentiles as an offering acceptable to God (see also Romans 11:13; Galatians 2:9). The authority was conferred on him at the time of his conversion and call (Galatians 1:16) and was reaffirmed in the Temple in Jerusalem (Acts 22:17-21).

Paul believed that Corinth lay within the field of his proper jurisdiction (10:13-14). In the exercise of his commission he had laid claim to the territory—where no one else had worked before him—and fathered the church there. He makes much of the fact that he is the father of the Corinthians (1 Corinthians 4:14-15; 2 Corinthians 6:13; 11:2; 12:14).

The "false apostles," who had come to Corinth to destroy Paul's work and draw his children away from their father, were interlopers. They were interfering with God's plan for the Corinthians (their coming marriage to Christ at the Second Coming, 11:2-4) and indeed with God's purpose for the whole Gentile world. They were disguised servants of Satan (11:13-15), out to frustrate God's end-time purposes. No wonder Paul conceived of his struggle with them as a war and had faith that divine power would destroy "strongholds," "arguments," and "every pretension that sets itself up against the knowledge of God" (10:3-5).

Paul was aware that he asserted his authority somewhat too strongly in his letters (10:8-9) and sought to soften his approach (10:1; 13:5-9). He insisted, however, that his authority had integrity: what he was when absent he also was when present (10:11).

2 Corinthians 11:7-11. Paul's policy of not accepting support from his churches, except under unusual circumstances (see below), caused him much trouble with the Corinthians. He had explained his reasons for this policy in 1 Corinthians 9, after admitting that it was highly unusual in the light of general practice in Judaism and Christianity (see Lesson 3, Dimension Two).

Evidently Paul had not won the Corinthians to his point of view, or the matter would have been settled before the writing of the present letter (Letter E). Likely the "false apostles," who apparently came to Corinth after the Corinthians' receipt of our First Corinthians (Letter B), used Paul's practice on this matter as a way of undermining the Corinthians' confidence in him. The ironic thing about the situation was that Paul's unselfish policy, which ought to have helped the Corinthians give generously to the offering for the saints in Jerusalem, was actually inhibiting their giving to the offering.

Why were the Corinthians so upset with Paul on this point? First, it seemed to them a lack of trust and love (11:11). People feel closer to their friends if there is reciprocal giving. Paul had shared with them; they wanted to share with him.

Second, Paul did not consistently carry out this policy. He allowed the churches of Macedonia to send him gifts (11:8-9) but refused to accept them from the Corinthians. It may be that only the church at Philippi was excepted from his policy (Philippians 2:25; 4:15-16, 18), since his relationship with its members was particularly close and undisturbed by any questions about his personal integrity. This inconsistency may have contributed to the accusation of insincerity and duplicity Paul tried to refute in 2 Corinthians 1:12–2:2.

Third, self-support by manual work must have been regarded by the Corinthians as below the dignity of a teacher and preacher like Paul. Their philosophers and itinerant teachers were supported by students and benefactors.

Fourth, established missionary procedure in Christianity, based on the teaching and practice of Jesus and the first apostles (Matthew 10:9; Mark 6:8; Luke 8:3; 1 Corinthians 9:5-6; 1 Timothy 5:17-18), directed that "those who preach the gospel should receive their living from the gospel" (1 Corinthians 9:14). Paul's policy would seem to put him out of line with authentic Christian practice.

But Paul thought that his policy was not a denial of love but the very essence of love. Love means to seek "not your possessions but you" (12:14) and "children should not have to save up for their parents, but parents for their children"

(12:14). "Freely give" (Matthew 10:8), because of the grace (graciousness) of God and Christ, was also part of the gospel. Paul wanted so far as possible to clear himself of any charge of mercenary motives and to make visible and dramatic the gospel as "gift." And, as we have seen over and over in First and Second Corinthians, sacrifice and suffering—not personal advantage and privilege—should characterize the life and service of the messengers of a Christ who became poor in order to enrich others (8:9).

2 Corinthians 11:12-21a. The identity, the beliefs, and the practices of Paul's rivals at Corinth have long been debated. As yet there is no agreement among scholars, only different proposals.

Basic is the question whether there were two groups of rivals, one of whom Paul calls "super-apostles" (11:5; 12:11) and the other "false apostles" (11:13).

Some scholars have answered yes and have identified the "super-apostles" as important leaders of the Jerusalem church (perhaps Peter, James, and John), who sent out the "false apostles" as their representatives. Only the latter came to Corinth. The designation "super-apostles" would thus be a term of mild irony for these three apostles, like "reputed to be pillars" (Galatians 2:9). Paul did not attack this group but only its representatives.

Against this position is the hard fact that the contexts in which the two designations appear make a division into two distinct groups impossible. In 11:5 the "super-apostles" are clearly the interlopers at Corinth who are attempting to seduce the bride-to-be and who, Paul implies, are skilled in speaking, as he is not (11:6). The skill of Hellenistic rhetoric must be meant here, something in which the three "pillars" would hardly have exceeded Paul. In 11:13 and 12:11 the "false apostles" and the "super-apostles" are plainly the self-commending opponents of Paul, against whom his foolish "boasting" is directed. The two terms must refer to the same persons.

If the terms refer to the same individuals, who may they have been? Here are three suggestions.

1. They were Jews, probably Hellenistic Jews, who were sent out from Jerusalem with letters of recommendation (3:1) to Judaize the Gentile church and bring it under the authority of the Jerusalem church.

2. They were Jewish-Christian gnostics, like—if not identical with—those Paul opposed in First Corinthians (see Lesson 2).

3. They were Jewish-Christian missionaries of a charismatic type, probably with no direct connection with Jerusalem, who, by parading their visions and revelations, miraculous deeds, skilled speaking, and conformity to traditional missionary practice (living off the gospel), tried to discredit Paul and take over in some of his churches.

The weight of the evidence favors number 3. They were certainly Jews and proud of it, as Paul was, and like him Hellenized, but more philosophical and rhetorical in orientation and training and more mercenary and self-centered in motivation.

APOSTLES: THE FALSE AND THE TRUE

They thought Paul weak in appearance; unpolished in speech; authoritarian in letters; deficient in religious experience, knowledge, and intimacy of relationship with Christ; insincere and devious; lacking apostolic credentials (letters of recommendation); unfaithful to the missionary tradition of living off the gospel (even demeaning that tradition by manual work); and to be plotting a gigantic fraud on his churches (in the alleged offering for the saints in Jerusalem).

Paul refuses to dignify these rivals by using their names when he refers to them as "some," "anyone," "many," "such people," and the like—a way of belittling people in the Hellenistic world. He calls them "fools" (11:19) and labels them outright as "false apostles" and "deceitful workmen," disguised emissaries of Satan (11:13-15). Paul says that they are intruders into his apostolic territory (10:12-18); who boast of their credentials (3:1), their accomplishments (10:15-16; 11:12), and their relationship to Christ (10:7); who compare themselves with others by using human standards of judgment (5:12, 16; 10:12); who preach a false gospel and try to seduce Paul's converts from the true one (11:2-4); and who abuse and exploit Christians in their own selfish interest (in part, by taking money from them). Under their influence the church is deteriorating morally and spiritually (12:20-21). "Their end will be what their actions deserve," he says (11:15).

The struggle at Corinth was a hot one, with high stakes!

2 Corinthians 11:21b-33. Paul gives his "Fool's Speech" with obvious embarrassment. He is unaccustomed to bragging about himself and is against it on principle. He asks his readers to let him play the role of a fool since they "gladly put up with fools" —a slap at their acceptance of his rivals. "Since many are boasting in the way the world does, I too will boast," he says (11:18).

Apart from Paul's opening boast about his heredity, a worldly consideration, he boasts only of things God would approve of and that would be despised by his rivals, the disguised servants of Satan. His catalog of sufferings and defeats is like no worldling would draw up as a monument to his memory. These are the "marks of Jesus" on his body (Galatians 6:17), in modern terms, the stripes and medals on his uniform that mark him as a distinguished veteran in the "war" (10:3). If he must boast, he will boast of these.

"Been in prison more frequently" implies more than the one imprisonment mentioned up to this point in the Acts of the Apostles (that at Philippi—Acts 16:23-34). Paul may have been in prison in Ephesus also (2 Corinthians 1:8-10).

The "forty lashes minus one" agrees with Deuteronomy 25:1-3.

The beatings with rods were administered by Roman lictors, a severe form of punishment, by law not to be used on Roman citizens but often administered despite the law.

The stoning was at Lystra (Acts 14:19).

Acts tells us of no shipwrecks up to this point but helps us see by the one on his way to Rome how horrible an experience it was (Acts 27).

The danger from bandits must have been constant, particularly in the mountains of Cilicia, in spite of Roman attempts of policing the roads.

The "false brothers" may have been Judaizers who betrayed Paul to the authorities, a particularly bitter pill administered by "Christians."

His "concern for all the churches" is well illustrated by his agony over the Corinthians over about a five-year period.

Paul's humiliating escape from Damascus, like a criminal on the run, exhibited the weakness of his entire career. Through this kind of weakness God's mighty power and "the life of Jesus" are revealed, Paul says (4:7-11). It is strangely wonderful that, at the end of a catalog of sufferings like this, Paul can still praise God (11:31).

2 Corinthians 12:1-10. Paul's rivals, in supporting their claim to be apostles of Christ (11:13), had boasted not only of their superior credentials by virtue of their letters of commendation (3:1) but also of their "visions and revelations." Paul does not say directly that they glory in "visions and revelations," but the comment introducing this section ("I must go on boasting. Although there is nothing to be gained") and the remark at the end of it ("you drove me to it" [12:11]) indicate clearly that Paul would not have introduced his own visionary experience if he had not been pushed to it.

For Paul the marks of true apostleship are not how many or what kind of visionary experiences one has had, but whether one has been called and appointed by the Lord, has suffered for the Lord in carrying out his work in the world, has raised and built up the church in God, and is a person through whose weaknesses the mighty power of God is revealed (4:7-15). Here Paul had credentials aplenty! He seems not to want to be known as an ecstatic or visionary person. (Though he spoke in tongues, he laid no emphasis on this and preferred the rational over the emotional, at least in church worship [1 Corinthians 14:13-19].) Paul's way of describing his trip to Paradise reinforces this impression of his attitude.

Paul's oblique way of referring to himself ("I know a man in Christ"), his twice-mentioned ignorance of the manner of the journey (12:2-3), and his inability to disclose what he heard, reduce the experience to small importance—contrary to the kind of visions his rivals must have boasted of in great detail. He really does not want to talk about it at all but rather of his weaknesses (12:5). Yet, if his rivals insist that he must have such experiences to be an apostle, they should know that he has had them in abundance (12:6, 7). But Paul needs and wants no credit from "visions and revelations" (12:6).

To keep Paul from boasting of his special experiences and privileges, God gave him, through the instrumentality of Satan, "a thorn . . . in [the] flesh." (The passive voice ["was given"] was the customary Jewish way of avoiding mention of the divine name, as in the Beatitudes, where the blessings bestowed are God's [Matthew 5:3-11].)

That God uses Satan as an opposer or tester of people is taught in the Old Testament (Job 1:6-12; 2:1-7; Zechariah 3:1-5). Satan is under God's sovereign control and will soon be crushed (Romans 16:20). Meanwhile, Satan serves God's purposes (as in the crucifixion of Jesus—John 13:2). Here the thorn—though identified with Satan—results by God's grace in abundant power (12:9).

It is useless to speculate on the nature of Paul's thorn. Attempts to solve the problem fall into several categories: (1) some kind of spiritual weakness or temptation (sexual, a guilty conscience, agony over the unbelief of the Jews, depression); (2) a physical ailment (epilepsy, malaria, solar retinitis, a speech impediment, headaches); (3) persecuting enemies (hostile Jews and "false apostles" of Christ). If it was a physical ailment, it was of an intermittent nature, for Paul's travels and accompanying sufferings, as listed in 2 Corinthians 11, would require exceptional physical strength.

Prayer "three times" for the removal of the thorn may imply complete intercessory Christian prayer (compare Jesus in Gethsemane [Mark 14:32-41]); but the prayer was not answered in the way Paul asked. It was answered in God's way: through the infusion of strength by which to show to all that "the transcendent power" in jars of clay "is from God and not from us" (4:7).

Paul's rivals may have power, but it is only human, not divine, power, since they disdain weakness and boast "in the way the world does" (11:18).

DIMENSION THREE: WHAT DOES THE BIBLE MEAN TO ME?

2 Corinthians 10:3-5—The Christian's Weapons

A literal rendering of the Greek of 10:3 would be, "For though we walk in the flesh, we do not war according to the flesh" (American Standard Version). To "walk in the flesh" is to "live in the world" (New International Version) as a human being, a state ordained by God in creation. To live or to war *according* to the flesh (italics added) is to live and act according to sinful human standards, not divine ones. The Christian walks or lives "by [in, through] the Spirit" (Galatians 5:16); and thus, in battle against evil spiritual forces, the Christian uses divine, not human power.

To use a modern analogy, human power and strategy against superhuman evil powers is about as effective as ping-pong balls would be against armored tanks. Therefore, Paul fights with weapons that will do the job (5:6-7; Ephesians 6:17-18).

Often the church today tries to conquer the world by using worldly weapons: human wisdom and philosophy, popular forms of entertainment, secular money-making schemes, service-club types of recruitment, pressure tactics to effect social change, and the like.

Discuss the weapons used in your church. To what extent are they worldly? How effective are they against the church's real enemy? What weapons are you relying on in your personal spiritual war?

2 Corinthians 10:12—Offensive Comparisons

Ancient Hellenistic philosophers and teachers vied with one another, often through self-glorifying tactics, to attract paying students. Such tactics, as a way of attracting attention to oneself and "climbing the golden stairs" to prestige and money, are not altogether absent from modern education and church life.

Paul would have none of this self-glorification. He would not enter into comparison and competition with the rival apostles, who were comparing themselves with one another and with him. Paul had personal assets and knew it (Philippians 3:4-6). But after he met Christ, he counted these as "rubbish." What he had become was entirely by the grace of God (1 Corinthians 15:10). Paul could no longer boast of assets and credentials; he could boast only of the Lord (2 Corinthians 10:17). He believed that each Christian leader should work conscientiously and leave judgment of it to God (1 Corinthians 3:10-15; 4:3-4).

How would the church today be affected if Paul's attitude and actions were to prevail among its members and leadership? To what extent should the spirit of competition, so widespread in society today, operate in the church? What would happen to denominationalism if Paul's spirit should come alive in ministers and laity?

2 Corinthians 11:7-11—Selective Receiving

Paul would not accept gifts from the Corinthians but he did from the Philippians and perhaps others in Macedonia. Did the Corinthians have a just complaint about this policy? Might you have reacted as they did? To what extent is love promoted and manifested through giving and receiving? Would the church be better off if ministers received no salaries or gifts at all or took such only from certain churches, as Paul did?

2 Corinthians 12:1-5—Personal Witnessing

Paul seems to regard "visions and revelations" as he does speaking in tongues: both have value in private experience but little significance in corporate church life. He seems to feel that they are concerned with noncommunicable mysteries (1 Corinthians 14:2; 2 Corinthians 12:4) and even contribute to spiritual pride (1 Corinthians 13:1; 14:4, 20; 2 Corinthians 12:1, 5-6).

What should be the nature of personal witnessing in the church? To what extent should the speaker become vulnerable, as Paul did, by recounting his weaknesses? How can witnessing be saved from vagueness, due to the mysterious character of personal religious experience and the inadequacies of human language, and from the appearance, at least, of spiritual pride?

2 Corinthians 12:8-10—Intercessory Prayer

Paul's intercessory prayer did not bring him what he asked for: release from the thorn in the flesh. But it brought him something greater: God's abundant power, which he would not have experienced without the thorn.

Today some Christian preachers and teachers are promising physical healing to all who ask for it in prayer and faith. Some sick Christians are healed; and some, like Paul, are not. Is the fault with the pray-ers: that they do not have enough faith? Did Paul not have enough faith? Who could bring to God such a quantity as he? But is salvation by *works*—by presenting to God something worthy—enough to move God to act? Paul would deny this.

Faith is trusting God absolutely. Faith is knowing that God loves us, cares for us, and will do for us what we really need. Faith is leaving our future in God's hands. We tell God what we want, not what God must do. God may heal us now or heal us in the glory of the resurrection. Meanwhile, we are assured of God's grace and abundant power. Hallelujah!

— 10 —

Paul and the True Gospel

Galatians 1–2; 6:11-18

DIMENSION ONE:
WHAT DOES THE BIBLE SAY?

Answer these questions by reading Galatians (at one time, if possible); then reread Chapter 1

1. What are the main ideas Paul is seeking to impress on the Galatians? (1:1, 11-12; 2:16, 19, 21; 5:1)

   Paul wants them to know that he is a true apostle and servant of God (1:1); that his gospel of salvation by faith alone (that is, apart from observance of the Jewish law) is the one and only true gospel (1:11-12; 2:16, 19, 21); and that the Galatians should remain faithful to him and stand fast in the freedom this gospel gives them (5:1).

2. What differences do you find between the greeting in this letter and that in First Thessalonians? (1:1-5; 1 Thessalonians 1:1)

   The greeting in First Thessalonians is shorter, mentions by name Paul's companions, does not try to verify Paul's apostleship or define the nature of the gospel, and has no doxology.

3. Compare the spirit in which Paul opens Galatians with his spirit in the opening verses of First Thessalonians. (1:6-10; 1 Thessalonians 1:2-10)

   Paul expresses thanks for the conversion, fidelity, and witness of the Thessalonians but is aghast at the Galatians' desertion of God, himself, and the true gospel.

4. What does Paul tell us about his former life in Judaism? (1:13-14)

   Paul says he violently persecuted and tried to destroy the church. His extreme zeal for his ancestral traditions caused him to excel in Judaism.

5. What does Paul tell us about his conversion experience? (1:15-16)

   God in his grace set Paul apart before his birth and, by revealing Jesus to (in) him, called Paul to preach God's Son among the Gentiles.

6. How much contact did Paul have with the Jerusalem apostles in the first few years after his conversion? (1:17-24)

   Paul had little contact with them. Instead of consulting with the Jerusalem apostles after his conversion, he spent time in Arabia and Damascus. Only after three years did Paul spend fifteen days with Peter. Paul saw in addition only James, the Lord's brother.

Answer these question by reading Galatians 2

7. What was Paul's purpose in going to Jerusalem the first time and the second time? (1:18; 2:2)

   The first time Paul went to see Peter in private. The second time Paul went with others to consult with the Jerusalem apostles about the Gentiles, in order to gain their approval.

8. What part did Titus play in the second visit? (2:1-5)

   Titus, an uncircumcised Greek Christian, went with Paul and Barnabas to the consultation. Paul resisted the attempt of "false brothers" to force Titus's circumcision and that of Gentile Christians in general.

9. What groups of people were present at this second visit? (2:1, 4, 9)

   (1) Paul, Barnabas, and Titus; (2) "false brothers," who were in some way infiltrating spies; and (3) the persons "reputed to be pillars" (James, Peter, and John).

10. What agreement was reached between Paul and the Jerusalem apostles? (2:7-10)

They recognized that God had called Paul to preach his gospel to the Gentiles, just as Peter had been called to preach to the Jews. They laid no additional requirement (circumcision or law observance) on Paul. They divided the missionary enterprise into fields of operation (Paul and Barnabas for work among the Gentiles and James, Peter, and John for work among the Jews). They asked that Paul and Barnabas remember to help the poor.

11. Why did Paul square off against Peter at Antioch? (2:12-14)

Peter was eating with uncircumcised Gentile Christians until representatives from James arrived. Fearing their adverse opinion (and the circumcision party they represented) about what he was doing, Peter withdrew from this practice. Following Peter's lead, other Jewish Christians also withdrew from table fellowship with the Gentile Christians.

12. How had both Paul and Peter been justified? (2:15-16)

They had been justified through faith in Jesus Christ, not by works of the law.

13. What is the gist of Paul's rebuke of Peter? (2:17-20)

As Jews, Paul and Peter had no advantage over the Gentiles in becoming justified before God. Since salvation is by faith in Christ alone and not by obedience to the law, they had to take a position outside the law, along with the Gentiles, in order to be saved by faith in Christ.

Answer these questions by reading Galatians 6:11-18

14. Who is actually writing here, and why do you think he takes the pen in his hand at this point? (6:11)

Apparently Paul is writing here, wishing to personalize the letter, authenticate it as actually from him, and sum up and emphasize the message of the letter.

15. Why are the false teachers insisting that the Galatians be circumcised? (6:12-13)

They insist on circumcision "to make a good impression outwardly" (by getting a lot of Gentiles circumcised) and to escape persecution because of the cross of Christ.

16. What is Paul's attitude toward circumcision? (6:12-15)

Accepting circumcision somehow clears one of the likelihood of persecution because of the cross. It offers no sign that the law is really being kept but may indicate instead selfish motives. Circumcision counts for nothing with God, who wants instead "a new creation."

17. What are "the marks of Jesus" that Paul bears on his body? (6:17; 2 Corinthians 11:23-25)

The marks of Jesus are the scars that give evidence that one has suffered for Christ.

DIMENSION TWO: WHAT DOES THE BIBLE MEAN?

Exactly where the churches of Galatia were located is unknown. Scholars are divided between two possibilities:

1. They were located in upper central Asia Minor (modern Turkey), probably in the cities of Ancyra (modern Ankara, the capital of Turkey), Pessinus, and Tavium. Advocates of this view believe that Paul founded these churches on what Luke identifies as Paul's second missionary journey (Acts 16:6) and that he revisited them on his third journey (Acts 18:23).

2. They were located in south central Asia Minor in the cities of Antioch (in Pisidia), Iconium, Lystra, and Derbe. If they were located here, Paul founded them on his first journey (Acts 13:4–14:26) and revisited them on his second and third journeys (Acts 16:6; 18:23).

From where and when Paul wrote to the Galatians is equally uncertain. If these churches were located in South Galatia (at Antioch, Iconium, Lystra, and Derbe), Paul may have written the letter at the end of his first journey, perhaps from Antioch in Syria, about A.D. 48. Galatians would then be his earliest letter, written just before the Jerusalem Conference (Acts 15:1-21) of that same year.

If the churches were located in North Galatia (in Ancyra, Pessinus, and Tavium), the letter was probably written from Ephesus (Macedonia or Corinth are also possible) on what Luke represents as Paul's third journey. The date would be somewhere between A.D. 52 and 56.

During this period in Paul's ministry he wrote the Corinthian letters and the Letter to the Romans. Galatians bears a strong similarity in subject matter and theology to Second Corinthians (especially to Chapters 10–13) and to Romans, making it likely that Galatians was written during this time also.

On Paul's opponents in Galatia, see the student book.

Galatians 1:1-5. The student book lists the main elements of the greeting (1:1-5). The second element—that about God's redeeming grace in Christ crucified and risen—needs comment here.

For Paul the heart of the gospel was the saving effect of the cross and the resurrection of Jesus: not of the cross alone or of the Resurrection alone but of both together, as one saving event (Crucifixion-Resurrection). Jesus, as the Servant of the Lord, poured out his life, even unto death, and this sort of self-giving issued through the power of God in the glory of the resurrection life. Those who by faith identify with Jesus in crucifixion-resurrection share now and will share this same life in the presence of God (2 Corinthians 4:8-11, 14).

By striking this note at the beginning of his Letter to the Galatians, Paul challenges the teaching of his opponents in Galatia that obedience to Jewish law is necessary for salvation. In his crucifixion-resurrection, Christ dealt adequately with our sins and freed us from the demonic powers of this present evil age (1:4). Nothing more is needed, thank God (1:5)!

Galatians 1:6-9. Paul is astonished that the Galatians are deserting the gospel of God's grace (graciousness) in the crucifixion-resurrection of Christ and turning to a *different* gospel, not to another version of the true gospel.

This situation is not the same as that at Corinth, where other preachers built differing superstructures on the foundation Paul laid (Jesus Christ crucified-resurrected). There Paul left judgment to God and the testing of fire at the last day (1 Corinthians 3:10-15), for only individual versions of the *true* gospel were under consideration. Paul told the Corinthians to profit by the contributions of the various teachers (3:21-23).

Here a false teaching is involved—one that undermines the whole work of God in Christ and substitutes a different way of salvation: by "observing the law" (Galatians 2:16). This teaching contradicts what God had revealed to Paul at his conversion (1:15) and is simply a reversion to the legalistic, ineffective Judaism out of which Paul had come (1:13-14). No need to wait for God's verdict at the last day. God has already judged this kind of religion in the sending of his Son. So Paul can judge it now and does so in the strongest terms.

Paul's double curse here (1:8-9) and his blessing at the end of the letter (6:16) put the whole contents of the letter under divine sanction. Like Moses (Deuteronomy 27-28) and Jesus (Matthew 5:2-12; 23:13-36), who declared the awful consequences of obedience and disobedience to the will of God, Paul makes it known that life and death are at stake here.

Paul puts himself, his co-workers, and even an angel from heaven under the curse of God in the event of deviation from the true gospel. Placing himself under the curse removes the use of the curse from the realm of jealous self-interest.

Eternally condemned are words that denote something that has been removed from profane use and dedicated to the deity, either as a pleasing offering or as something offensive to be destroyed. Something to be destroyed as offensive to God is in Paul's mind here (also in 1 Corinthians 16:22).

Galatians 1:11-16a. "By revelation from Jesus Christ" could mean that Jesus was the revealer of something to Paul or that Jesus was what was revealed to him. Verse 16 makes the latter likely. In First Corinthians Paul claims to have seen Jesus (9:1; 15:8). The glorious appearance of Jesus to Paul could mean only that Jesus was not a dead heretic but the living Messiah and Lord, whom God had raised from the dead, as the first Christians claimed.

Since the appearance to Paul apparently was not visible and audible to other people as it was to him (Acts 9:7; 22:9), we can hardly conclude that it was of a wholly objective nature. The appearance must have had for Paul a partly subjective character and may be understood by us as a vision. The internal aspect is perhaps suggested by Paul's statement that God "was pleased to reveal his Son *in* me," (italics added) as the Greek text has it (Galatians 1:15-16). The internal character of the revelation appears in Galatians 2:20 ("Christ lives in me") and 4:6 ("God sent the Spirit of his Son into our hearts"). But the claim to having *seen* Jesus (1 Corinthians 9:1) implies something external as well. Thus, Paul may have regarded the appearance as external and internal. Whatever it was, it was for him and for all who experienced the same phenomenon compellingly real.

The reality of Jesus' appearances is confirmed by the lack of psychological preparation for it. Jesus appeared to the first apostles and others, not out of excited expectancy, but in the wake of bitter disillusionment over Jesus' crucifixion—or of hostility, in Paul's case. And the appearances were many and spaced over a considerable period of time (1 Corinthians 15:5-8). They were not the result of hysteria in a sort of chain reaction. And out of these appearances the church was constituted and impelled forward.

Galatians 1:16b-24. Here Paul stresses his independence of the Jerusalem apostles, evidently to counter the charge that he had received all that he knew about Jesus and the gospel from others with greater knowledge and authority. Elsewhere Paul admits that he did receive information from the church's tradition (1 Corinthians 15:3-7). But he insists here that his law-free gospel for the Gentiles is uniquely his own (Galatians 2:7-8).

Paul's time in Arabia and Damascus was occupied with preaching, not simply with meditating, in a ministry within the synagogues of those areas. He was trying to win Jews to faith in Jesus as Messiah and Savior.

The mission to the Gentiles was begun not by Paul but by Hellenistic Jewish Christians ("men from Cyprus and Cyrene") at Antioch in Syria (Acts 11:19-21). Paul was brought into this work by Barnabas (Acts 11:25-26) and apparently found here the kind of success in evangelism he had not experienced in the synagogues. The year at Antioch opened his eyes to the possibility of a full-scale Gentile ministry.

Galatians 2:1-10. A major problem in New Testament scholarship is whether Galatians 2:1-10 is Paul's account of the Jerusalem Conference that Luke reports in Acts 15:1-21, or whether Paul is referring to the visit to Jerusalem mentioned by Luke in Acts 11:27-30.

The majority view today is that Galatians 2:1-10 is indeed Paul's report of the Jerusalem Conference of Acts 15:1-21. The supporting arguments are too detailed to enter into here. Suffice it to say that the major issue (whether Gentiles need to be circumcised and otherwise obey the Jewish law in order to be members of the church) is the same, the participants are largely the same, and the place is the same.

On the issue of Gentile freedom from the law, Paul won the approval of the Jerusalem leaders, in spite of the hot opposition of legalistic Jewish Christians, whom Paul calls "false brothers" (Galatians 2:4). Titus was not compelled to be circumcised to be accepted as a Christian. It seems that the Jerusalem leaders had for some time agreed to the reception of Gentiles into the church without their acceptance of the yoke of the law (Acts 10; 11:22-24), but no formal agreement had been reached in the church and there was sharp opposition to this policy. The Conference upheld the liberal position.

According to Paul, a second issue was debated and settled. This issue involved the division of missionary territory into Gentile and Jewish areas and authoritative leadership in each. Paul was recognized as apostle to the uncircumcised and Peter, James, and John agreed to evangelize the circumcised.

Nothing was laid on Paul in the way of requirements (Galatians 2:6). The Jerusalem leaders asked him to remember the poor (in Jerusalem), which Paul said he was "eager to do" (2:10). The offering for the Jerusalem saints (Romans 15:25-27) fulfilled this request.

Galatians 2:11-14. Why Peter came to Antioch is not known. Did he flee there after his release from prison in Jerusalem (Acts 12:17), or was he eager to inspect the situation in the important church at Antioch, as Barnabas had done (Acts 11:22)?

The Jerusalem Conference had given Peter no guidelines for social and religious fellowship of Jews and Gentiles. Gentile Christians did not need to observe the Jewish law, but did Jewish Christians? Separation from ritually unclean Gentiles was an important element in the Jewish way of life. Was he (Peter) free to eat and associate with uncircumcised Gentiles when they had become Christians? His Christian instincts said yes—and he followed them, as did other Jewish Christians there, including Barnabas.

Why did Peter and the other Jewish Christians withdraw from table fellowship with the Gentile Christians on the arrival of emissaries from James?

James is a bit of an enigma. At the Jerusalem Conference he favored the exemption of the Gentiles from the yoke of the Jewish law (Acts 15:13-21; Galatians 2:6-9) and seems to have been generally conciliatory in contrast to the "false brothers." But after the Conference he appears to have turned in a legalistic direction, not far removed from the position of these "false brothers." When Paul came to Jerusalem on his last visit, James and his associates pressured Paul to give evidence of his own loyalty to the law and an assurance that he favored law observance by Jewish Christians in the Diaspora, "who live among the Gentiles."

Whether Jewish Christians were observing the law was a hot issue in Jerusalem at that time (Acts 21:17-26).

The explanation of James's change and the zeal of Jerusalem Jewish Christians for the law is undoubtedly the changing political atmosphere for the period. Jewish nationalism under the mounting influence of the Zealots was seeking to rid the country of Gentiles and Gentile defilement and was emphasizing strict loyalty to everything Jewish. Jewish Christians were looked on as collaborators with the enemy, Paul being the chief culprit. James must have sent the word out everywhere that, to avoid serious persecution by the rigid nationalists, the Jewish wing of the church would have to demonstrate its complete loyalty to the law. The message was given to Peter, Barnabas, and other Jewish Christians at Antioch, with the results recorded here. Peter, then, had real reasons for his fear (2:12).

Paul stayed by the Gentile Christians of Antioch and refused on principle to budge, since withdrawal of fellowship with the Gentiles would put pressure on them to Judaize. Later in Jerusalem, when no pressure on Gentiles was involved, he, as a Jewish Christian, could and did conform to the law (Acts 21:17-26), but not, of course, as a requirement for his personal salvation.

Galatians 2:15-21. This difficult section presents the issue to be argued in Chapters 3 and 4. Does anyone need to obey the Jewish law to be saved? Paul's position is no. Even Jews are not saved through the law but rather through faith in Christ crucified (2:15-16). They have to adopt common ground with the Gentiles as sinners and trust in God's gracious deed in the cross. The law has done its work in pointing out sin but has no power to save (2:19; 3:19-25). One can "live for God" only by faith-identification with the crucified and ever-living God.

DIMENSION THREE:
WHAT DOES THE BIBLE MEAN TO ME?

Galatians 1:6-9—Christian Certainty

Readers of Galatians are often taken aback by Paul's dogmatic certainty about his understanding of the gospel: certainty to the point where he can curse people who differ from him.

Paul also can appear tolerant of others with a different point of view, as in 1 Corinthians 3:5–4:7.

Discuss tolerance and intolerance in Christianity: the reasons for Paul's varying attitude; the attitude and practice of Jesus (Matthew 7:1-5 and Luke 11:37-44, for example); the attitude and actions of Martin Luther, John Wesley, and others; the attitude of fundamentalists and liberals in the church of our time; and your own feelings and practice in this matter. How flexible and inflexible should the Christian be?

Galatians 1:11-24—The Spirit of Independence

Allied to Paul's certainty was his spirit of independence. He was to some degree a loner, who kept away from the church's leadership (1:16c-24), was sometimes a bit contemptuous of the recognized apostles of Jesus (2:6, 9), had a showdown with Peter and Barnabas (2:11-14; Acts 15:36-40), and a veritable slugfest with the "super-apostles" (perhaps from Jerusalem) who came to Corinth (2 Corinthians 10–13).

Paul relied on inner guidance and visions (Acts 16:6-10; 18:9-10; Galatians 1:12), rather than on precedent and the advice of others.

Paul pioneered a new and radical theology, which included the practical annulment of the Jewish law and the establishment of a universal, democratic fellowship (including Gentiles, Jews, women, men, slaves, free, poor, and upper-class people in a relationship of equality).

What should be the attitude of the Christian toward human authorities, civil authorities, and religious authorities? When should they be consulted, obeyed, and defied? If Paul were a pastor or a layperson in a church today, what problems with fellow church members, the hierarchy, the church boards, and general church programs might he create?

Galatians 2:11-14—Thinking and Feeling Alike

Paul stressed the importance of unity in the church. He asked the Philippians to make him happy by "thinking and feeling alike" (Philippians 2:2, *The Revised English Bible*) and the Ephesians to be eager to "keep the unity of the Spirit through the bond of peace" (Ephesians 4:3). In his square-off with Peter and Barnabas at Antioch, the church there must have been in an unseemly uproar of dissension, with two great Christian leaders at the heart of it.

When is peace a healthy condition in a church? When is peace not a healthy condition in a church? What church disagreements have you witnessed and over what issues? What results came out of them? Are there ground rules that should be followed in such disagreements? Should there be peace at any price for the sake of the church's image before the world? To what extent should there be room for disagreement and diversity in the church?

It is for freedom that Christ has set us free. . . . But do not use your freedom to indulge the sinful nature (5:1, 13b).

—11—

Freedom in Christ and the Spirit

Galatians 3:1–6:10

DIMENSION ONE:
WHAT DOES THE BIBLE SAY?

Answer these questions by reading Galatians 3

1. What arguments from the Galatians' personal experience does Paul present to support his thesis that justification is by faith alone? (3:1-5)

   Paul uses two. (1) Their conversion (initial reception of the Spirit) came about through their faith-response to the preaching of the gospel, not by obedience to the law. (2) God's continuing supply of the Spirit to them and his working of miracles among them are the result of their response of faith to the gospel, not from obedience to the law.

2. How do Abraham's experience and expectation, as revealed in Scripture, support this thesis? (3:6-9)

   Scripture says that Abraham's righteousness was the result of his faith. Scripture also says that all who have faith are "children of Abraham" and will inherit the blessing promised through his descendants.

3. How does Scripture further prove the thesis? (3:10-14)

   Scripture shows that the law demands complete obedience and puts people who do not completely obey under a curse. Scripture indicates also that the way to righteousness and life is by faith. The object of this faith is Christ, who redeemed us from the law's curse and made it possible for all believers to inherit the blessing promised to Abraham and to receive the Spirit.

4. How does common legal practice confirm the thesis? (3:15-18)

   When once a will or covenant has been ratified, no one has the right to cancel it or add to it. God made a covenant with believing Abraham, giving promises to him and his seed (Christ), which the law, coming long afterward, cannot annul or change.

5. What was God's purpose in giving the law? (3:19-24)

   God gave the law, not that people should become righteous and be given life through the law, but that they should become transgressors through it, prisoners to sin and under the restraint of the law as a kind of custodian, until the coming of Christ and justification by faith in him.

6. What results have come about through faith in Christ Jesus? (3:25-29)

   We are released from the supervision of the law; we are free "sons of God," incorporated into the body of Christ with no human distinctions.

Answer these questions by reading Galatians 4

7. How does the law concerning inheritance support the thesis, and how are the Galatians violating the principle involved here? (4:1-11)

   An heir, while still a child, is virtually a slave and under guardians and trustees until the date fixed by the father for the receiving of the inheritance and autonomy. "We" (Jews and Gentiles) were in servitude to "the basic principles of the world." When the time appointed by God had fully come, God sent his Son to redeem us from servitude to the law and to make us full heirs. Though the Galatians have become mature heirs of God, they now want to return to childhood and servitude to "weak and miserable principles."

8. What appeal does Paul make on the basis of his personal relationship with the Galatians? (4:12-20)

   Paul recalls their first warm reception of him and his message and their generous spirit toward him. He wonders why they have turned away from him in favor of selfish intruders into his fatherly relationship with his children.

9. How does the law testify against itself as the way of salvation? (4:21-31)

Those who live under the law are slaves, children of Hagar the slave woman and her ("born in the ordinary way") son, Ishmael, while those who are free in Christ are children of the free woman Sarah and her promised ("born by the power of the Spirit") son, Isaac. The future inheritance is not for the slaves but for the "children . . . of the free woman."

Answer these questions by reading Galatians 5:1–6:10

10. What reasons does Paul give for his appeal to the Galatians not to become circumcised? (5:1-6)

To receive circumcision obligates one to keep the whole Jewish law, and this would comprise "a yoke of slavery." To seek justification through keeping the whole law is to make Christ unnecessary and indeed severs us from Christ and from grace. If we are in Christ and our faith in Christ is active in deeds of love, circumcision is irrelevant to the doing of God's will.

11. What have Paul's enemies in Galatia done to the Galatians and to Paul? (5:7-11)

They have obstructed the path on which the Galatians are running in the Christian race, in opposition to God who calls the Galatians on. The enemies accuse Paul of still preaching circumcision, an accusation he hotly denies.

12. What problem may result from the Galatians' freedom in Christ? (5:13, 16-17)

Freedom provides an opportunity for us to gratify the desires of the sinful nature.

13. What suggestions has Paul for dealing with a Christian caught in sin? (6:1-2)

Christian brothers and sisters are to restore the sinner in a spirit of gentleness, while remembering that they too may be tempted to sin. By carrying one another's burdens they will fulfill the law of Christ.

14. What warning against spiritual pride does Paul give? (6:3-5)

Spiritual people may look down on those who fall into sin, judge them harshly, and by comparison with them, inflate their own egos. They should not boast by comparing themselves with others but take account of their responsibility before God.

15. What is Paul trying to teach by the analogy of sowing and reaping? (6:7-10)

If we sow selfish attitudes and acts, we will reap the harvest of destruction; but if we sow spiritual attitudes and acts, we will reap the harvest of eternal life.

DIMENSION TWO: WHAT DOES THE BIBLE MEAN?

In Galatians 1 and 2 Paul has tried to establish the authenticity of his apostleship and his authority over the Gentile mission of the church. He shows that God called him to his task and gave him the content of his message to the Gentiles. Paul did not appoint himself or receive his gospel from human sources. The "pillars" in Jerusalem only approved what he was and what he was preaching.

Now Paul defends his gospel: that justification is by faith (trust) in Jesus Christ, crucified and resurrected, not by obeying the Jewish law. The argument here is intense and difficult.

Paul's argument rests basically on the experience of the Galatians, on the testimony of Scripture, and on common sense.

Galatians 3:15. Paul begins with a spirited attack on the false teachers of Galatia, the spell they have cast over the churches there, and the foolishness of the Galatians to allow themselves to be hypnotized by them. The Galatians are foolish for several reasons.

First, they have seen the crucified Jesus in dramatic portrayal through Paul's preaching, as if he had displayed painted pictures of the scene. Ancient lawyers sometimes held up in court paintings and other exhibits to impress the judge with the horror of a crime in order to obtain a conviction. The Galatians had no vague description of the cross.

Second, their new life in the Spirit had come about by their faith-response to the proclaimed gospel, not through acceptance of and obedience to the Jewish law. It is foolish to think one can bring to completion life in the Spirit through human endeavor to keep the Jewish law.

Third, going over to the law as the way of salvation ends one's life with Christ and negates all that has happened (see also 5:4).

Fourth, the miracles done among them by the continuous power of the Spirit, given by faith wholly apart from obeying the Jewish law, testify to the impotence and uselessness of trying to obey the law.

Galatians 3:6-14. Paul makes much of Abraham in his defense from Scripture, partly because his enemies in Galatia were saying that to be a true child of Abraham one would have to be circumcised as he and his household were (Genesis 17). These enemies must have argued that circumcision was the God-given sign and seal of the covenant with Abraham and his descendants and that, if the Galatians hoped to be included in this covenant, they would need to bear that sign and seal.

But Paul speaks of Abraham also because he sees in Abraham the basic principle of his gospel: Abraham "believed God, and it was credited to him as righteousness" (3:6). Along with his fellow Jews Paul believed in the great importance of Abraham in God's purpose of salvation for the Jews and all nations. But he differed from them on how this salvation was to be appropriated. They said it was by faith, like Abraham's, plus works (obedience to the terms of the covenant); Paul said it was by faith alone, like Abraham's.

Paul argues that Abraham's trust in God and God's promise, with its resulting righteousness, came before the requirement of circumcision (Genesis 15:6; 17:10-14) and 430 years before the Mosaic covenant (Galatians 3:17). Abraham's faith-righteousness, then, can have had nothing to do with obeying any law, but only with belief in God's promise. Therefore, anyone (including the Gentiles) who trusts in God and the promise of salvation is a child of Abraham and heir to that salvation.

In 3:10-14 Paul shows that to turn away from salvation by faith alone, as taught by a true understanding of Abraham, and to turn to salvation by obedience to the law brings two results: a curse (3:10) and no justification (righteousness) before God (3:11). Both consequences are proved by Scripture, according to Paul: the first from Deuteronomy 27:26 and the second from Habakkuk 2:4. And one cannot argue that doing the law and having faith are the same thing, for again Scripture (Leviticus 18:5) shows that the law-way of justification rests on *doing* rather than on *believing*. They are mutually exclusive ways of salvation.

If the Galatian Gentile Christians come under the law as a way of salvation, they then will come under a curse and not stand before God in justification (right relation). Jewish Christians, who once sought justification by law-observance, found deliverance from the curse only by faith in Christ (2:15-16; 3:13), who became a curse for them. If Gentiles want to share in God's salvation, the condition is faith in Christ alone (3:14).

How did Christ become "a curse for us" (3:13)? Scripture explains: by hanging on a tree (Deuteronomy 21:23), that is, for Paul, through the Crucifixion.

And what was the effect of Jesus hanging on a tree? He "redeemed us from the curse of the law." How the cross had this effect is not explained, but from other passages in Paul's letters we may find some help.

Paul assumes that, before Christ came, humans were enslaved by demonic powers ("the basic principles of the world," 4:1, 3, 8-9) who worked even through the Jewish law and its curse to effect human bondage. To deliver us from our terrible fate under the coming judgment of God, God sent his Son as a human being to come under the curse along with us. God's Son "redeemed" the doomed slaves so that they might be freed from sin, the bondage of the law, and the demonic powers, and become children of God (4:3-7).

How did Christ "redeem" cursed humanity? Did Christ become the object of the curse in our place and absorb God's penalty on sin? Was Jesus Christ a "sin offering," even a scapegoat, to remove the barrier between God and humanity? Since Christ "had no sin" (2 Corinthians 5:21), his death in our behalf had special merit before God; and all who identify with Christ share this standing (justification-right relationship) with God.

Galatians 3:19–4:7. Paul's statement that the law came 430 years after the promise made to Abraham (3:17), that nothing that came later could change what was promised, and that God's purpose of salvation was worked out through the fulfillment of that promise in Christ (3:16) naturally raises the question, Why then the law?

Paul flatly denies that the law is a saving instrument. The inheritance comes through the promise to Abraham and his "seed" (Christ) and not from Moses and the law (3:18). That seems to make the law pointless. Jews who believed that even Abraham practiced the Mosaic law intuitively or out of special revelation before it was actually given on Mount Sinai and who based their hope of salvation (eternal life) entirely on obedience to that law, found Paul's putting down the law in this way heresy of the rankest kind, even making him an enemy of the law and of Judaism.

For Paul the law's function clearly is negative and limited (3:19-25). For Jews it was positive and unlimited (eternal, having been practiced in heaven before Creation and to be practiced in the messianic age). That the law was given by "angels, by a mediator" (Moses), rather than by God directly, as in the promise to Abraham (3:19-20), further reduces the law's significance.

The law in Judaism had to do with the regulation and punishment of transgressions, the keeping of unruly life in check. But its regulations had no real effect in restraining sin. The law instead promoted sin by negative stimulation: a person wanting to do what the law forbids. Through knowledge of the law and through sin's demonic defiance of it, sin multiplied (Romans 7:5, 7-11). People under the law were "killed" by the law, not saved by it.

The law's only positive effects were to make sin recognizable and point to the need of a Savior (Galatians 3:22). The Savior, God's Son, came in human form and took part in the predicament of those under the law in order to deliver them from it (4:4-5). The Savior fulfilled the promise God made to Abraham by bringing those who believe in him into a universal family of Spirit-filled "sons of God," who are to be the heirs of all the richness God has planned for his children (3:26-29; 4:5-7).

Galatians 4:8-11. Up to this point Paul has been speaking mostly of the situation of Jews under the law and in Christ (note the *we* and the *us* in 3:13, 23-25; 4:3, 5). Now he addresses the Galatian Gentiles directly and shows that their former position under "no gods" was one of slavery like that of the Jews under the law.

For Paul the "weak and miserable principles" are the false gods, the demonic "rulers of this age" who, acting through human instruments, "crucified the Lord of glory" (1 Corinthians 2:8). They are the "powers and authorities" whom God exposed and triumphed over by the cross (Colossians 2:15). They are in part astral spirits, who control the heavenly bodies, the calendar and seasons, and the rules and rituals of sacred days and events (Galatians 4:10). They are the spirits of legalism, operating in Judaism under the law and dominating pagan religion.

In Christ we are liberated from them and are free.

Galatians 4:12-20. Paul now appeals to the Galatians on a personal level, noting their former warm mutual affection (4:12-15). The "illness" referred to here may be the thorn in the flesh mentioned in 2 Corinthians 12:7, though this is not certain. That the ailment was some sort of eye trouble, because of the reference to the Galatians' willingness to give Paul their eyes (4:15), rests on a literal interpretation of Paul's words here; whereas he may have been speaking only figuratively. Whatever the ailment was, the Galatians did not despise him because of it. Paul wants to revive their warm affection for him.

Galatians 4:21-31. Paul's clincher is an allegory in which he says that the Jews, with their center in the earthly Jerusalem, are children of the concubine and slave Hagar and are in slavery to the (old) covenant made at Mount Sinai, which she represents. The Christians (law-free Gentiles and Jews), with their motherland in the heavenly Jerusalem, are children of the true wife and free woman Sarah, who represents the new covenant (though not so called here).

Paul sees the present Jerusalem and all its institutions as Jerusalem "born in the ordinary way" and the heavenly Jerusalem as Jerusalem "born by the power of the Spirit" (4:29). These two cities are in conflict now, as their prototypes were before: the slave Jews are persecuting the free Christians. But the Jews will be disinherited and the Christians will be blessed as Abraham's true children.

For Paul to call the Jews of his time virtually "bastard Ishmaelites" must have been highly offensive to them and helps account for their desire to do away with him (Acts 25:2-3). Paul went to extreme lengths to try to halt the Galatian Christians' abandonment of the true gospel of justification by faith alone.

Galatians 5:1-12. One wonders why the Jewish-Christian teachers who had invaded the Galatian churches made such an impression on the Galatians. Was it their authority as representatives of Jerusalem Christianity and the venerable apostles there? Was it the persuasiveness of their arguments? Was it a lack of some sort in the Galatians' theology and Christian experience that drove them to look for new and better understandings? Had the enthusiasm of their first life in the Spirit waned and the life of the flesh begun to reassert itself? Was the freedom Pauline Christianity offered them too much to handle at their stage of Christian development? Perhaps all these were involved.

The Galatians apparently had taken their freedom seriously, perhaps too seriously. They had thrown off the bondage to those who are "not gods" (4:8). Their baptism into Christ had eliminated the racial, social, and sexual distinctions of their background (3:27-28). Paul had taught them that they were no longer under law but free in Christ and in grace. Apparently they were bickering (5:15). The "desires of the sinful nature" were strong (5:16-17). Paul's warning against "the acts of the sinful nature," listed in detail in 5:19-21, the instruction about dealing with people caught in sin (6:1-5), and the concluding appeal to the law of the harvest—destruction for sowing to the sinful nature and eternal life for sowing to the Spirit—all indicate that they were having trouble in their use of freedom.

The false teachers offered the Galatians a way to control their freedom: accept circumcision and the Jewish law. They must have said, "Come within God's covenant and, by doing his will as there expressed, the fence of the law will protect you from the defilements of Gentile life and the lusts of the flesh." In 5:2-12 Paul shows them in the strongest terms why they should not accept circumcision, submit themselves to the Jewish law, and surrender their freedom in Christ.

Galatians 5:13–6:10. Freedom is God's will for us and is the essence of what Christ has done for us (5:1, 13). We do not need to turn to the Jewish law in order to control it. Freedom need not be an opportunity for the indulgence of the sinful nature. There are two controls, which are basically one: love and the Spirit.

If we love our neighbors as ourselves, we both fulfill the law, which the false teachers so prize, and we serve, rather than exploit, our neighbor. Thereby peaceful, rather than hostile, social relationships will be promoted (5:13-15).

If the Galatians "live by the Spirit" (that is, let the Spirit control their lives), they will not "gratify the desires of the sinful nature." If the flesh is not controlled by the Spirit, the evil attitudes and actions listed in 5:19-21 will result. If, however, they live under the control of the Spirit, the noble attitudes and actions, called "the fruit of the Spirit," will characterize their living. As Christians the old life of sin and evil desire has been put to death (5:24), so that they may "live for God" (2:19; 5:25).

If the Spirit is to control a Christian's life and the principal fruit of the Spirit's presence is love, then Christians who have succumbed to temptation and committed sins (see 5:19-21) should be dealt with in love by their fellow Christians, not in arrogant self-righteousness. To help one another is to fulfill the entire law (5:14; also Mark 12:31; John 15:12). Love requires the supporting of Christian instructors who labor among the Galatians (6:6). Living in love (sowing to the Spirit) will bring the harvest of eternal life (6:8).

DIMENSION THREE:
WHAT DOES THE BIBLE MEAN TO ME?

Galatians 3:1-5—Coming to Maturity in Christ

Paul lamented that the Corinthians were still "infants" in need of milk and unable to take "solid food" (1 Corinthians 3:1-3). What was the cause of the Galatians' arrested development (3:1-5)? Does this cause operate in churches today? in your own life? What are Paul's suggestions for a cure? Do these apply to the church today and to you? Explain. What other causes, not mentioned by Paul here, exist? How may they be overcome?

Galatians 3:19–4:7—The Law and Human Sin

What is the function of law in human society? Why have laws been created? To what extent do they inhibit human sin and crime? To what extent do they promote sin and crime? How effective are moral codes (like the Ten Commandments and the Sermon on the Mount) in controlling conduct and promoting individual and social morality? Are those who are under law children and slaves, as Paul believed? Would a society without law be possible and desirable? Would the "law of Christ" be enough?

Galatians 5:1–6:10—Christian Freedom

Paul believed that freedom is what Christianity is all about: freedom from sin, freedom from bondage to the demonic powers, freedom from legalism, freedom from restrictive social structures, freedom to grow into the likeness of God.

But he did not believe that freedom gives one the right to do anything one pleases, as the Corinthians seemed to believe (1 Corinthians 6:12; 10:23). What might be the personal and social consequences of the attitude, "If it feels good, do it"?

What freedoms as a Christian do you think you have, and why? What restrictions have you placed on your freedom, and why?

He made known to us the mystery of his will according to his good pleasure, which he purposed in Christ,
to be put into effect when the times will have reached their fulfillment—to bring all things in heaven and on earth
together under one head, even Christ (1:9-10).

— 12 —

The Divine Plan

Ephesians 1–3

DIMENSION ONE:
WHAT DOES THE BIBLE SAY?

Answer these questions by reading Ephesians 1

1. For what is God praised in 1:3-6?

   God is praised because God blessed us in Christ with every spiritual blessing in the heavenly realms; God chose us before the creation of the world; and God predestined us in love to be "his sons through Jesus Christ."

2. For what is Christ praised in 1:7-12?

   Christ is praised for our redemption through his blood; the forgiveness of our sins; the unification of all things in the fullness of time; and our destiny and appointment to live for the praise of God's glory.

3. For what is the Holy Spirit praised in 1:13-14?

   The Holy Spirit is praised for our sealing as the guarantee of receiving our future inheritance.

4. Who is meant by *us*, *we*, and *you*? (1:3-14)

   In 1:3-10 us and we seem to be "all Christians." In 1:12-14 we seems to be "Jews" (who were the first to hope in Christ) and you seems to be "Gentiles."

5. How well does Paul know the readers of this letter? (1:15; see also 3:2)

   Paul does not know them well. He has "heard about your faith" and love and assumes they know of his administration of God's grace in behalf of the Gentiles.

6. For what about the readers does Paul give thanks? (1:15-16)

   Paul gives thanks for their faith in the Lord Jesus and their love for all the saints.

7. When Paul prays for the readers, what does he ask of God for them? (1:17-19)

   Paul asks for a spirit of wisdom and revelation in the knowledge of God (their eyes enlightened), so they may know the hope to which they have been called, the riches of their coming inheritance, and how great God's power at work in them really is.

8. What evidence of the greatness of God's power does Paul give? (1:20-23)

   Paul lists Christ's resurrection, exaltation, appointment to universal sovereignty, and headship of the church as evidence of God's power.

Answer these questions by reading Ephesians 2

9. Describe the condition in their former life of the persons designated as *you* and *we*. (2:1-3, 11-16)

   They (both you Gentiles and we Jews) were dead in trespasses and sins, were under the power of the "ruler of the kingdom of the air," and followed the pattern of life in this age with its sensual desires and passions (2:1-3).
   You (the Gentiles) were separated from Christ, Israel, the covenant-promises of God, and from God himself. We, the circumcised, called you "uncircumcised" and viewed you with hostile contempt stemming from our law of commandments and regulations (2:11-16).

10. How did the great change in *you* and *us* occur? (2:4-5, 8-9, 13, 17)

We were made alive with Christ through the mercy, love, and grace of God and through our response of faith, not through our works. Our reconciliation with one another and God was brought about "through the blood of Christ" and through his preaching of peace.

11. What privileges (present and future) are there for those who have been brought together by Christ? (2:6-7, 13-16, 18, 19-22)

We are now alive with Christ and sitting in the heavenly realms with him; in the coming ages God will show incomparable grace and kindness to us in Christ Jesus. The alien Gentiles have been brought into unity and peace with Jewish Christians; both are reconciled to God and to one another, have equal access to God, and together form a new temple where God dwells and is worshiped.

Answer these questions by reading Ephesians 3

12. What is the content of the "mystery of Christ" that was made known to Paul and the holy apostles and prophets? (3:6)

The Gentiles, as members of the church ("one body"), are heirs with Jewish Christians of the promises made in the gospel and to be realized in Christ Jesus.

13. What is Paul's role in relation to this mystery? (3:7-9)

God in his grace made Paul a servant of this gospel, and Paul is to preach to the Gentiles "the unsearchable riches of Christ," in order that all people may understand God's long-hidden purpose for the world.

14. What is the role of the church in relation to the mystery? (3:10)

The church's role is to declare to "the rulers and authorities" the manifold wisdom of God.

15. What does Paul ask God to grant to the readers of this epistle? (3:16-19)

Paul asks God to strengthen the inner selves of the readers through God's Spirit, that Christ may dwell in their hearts through faith, that they may be "rooted and established in love," that they may comprehend with the whole church the vast dimensions of God's plan and Christ's love, and that they may be "filled to the measure of all the fullness of God."

16. How great is God's power in the Christian? (3:20)

God is able to do far more than we ask or think possible.

DIMENSION TWO: WHAT DOES THE BIBLE MEAN?

Ephesians has been described as "doctrine set to music." Much of the book sings about God, Christ, human redemption, the church, God's ultimate victory over the demonic powers, and the final inheritance planned for God's children. Praise, prayer, and exhortation are strikingly intermingled in a composition more like a tape of an inspiring worship service than of a theological address.

Scholars have discovered that the author, whoever he was, caught up portions of the hymnody and the confessions in use in the church of his time and wove them, together with his own words of praise, into a summary of the church's worship experience.

Ephesians 1:1-2. Paul's authorship of Ephesians has been questioned by many scholars, while others have vigorously defended it. Actually, the value of the epistle for personal and church life hinges little, if at all, on the identity of the writer. You should therefore spend only a few moments on this question. But you will need some information if the matter is of interest.

Among the data that have been gathered against Paul's authorship of the epistle are the following:

1. The language and style of Ephesians differ somewhat from the language and style of the seven letters Paul certainly wrote (Romans, First and Second Corinthians, Galatians, First Thessalonians, Philippians, Philemon). For example, about ninety words appear in Ephesians but not in the above seven letters. Some important words of Paul are entirely absent from Ephesians. The long sentences and imposing liturgical style of Ephesians are unlike Paul.

2. Ephesians curiously overlaps Colossians in such a way as to suggest that some writer imitated the language and ideas of that epistle and shaped them for his own purposes.

3. The period of writing reflected in Ephesians seems later than Paul's. The Jewish-Gentile controversy is regarded as settled, something not fully achieved in Paul's lifetime. The veneration of the apostles and prophets (2:20; 3:5) seems unlike Paul's attitude toward them (Galatians 2).

4. Some of the theology is unlike Paul's, such as the highly developed doctrine of the church and of Christ's person and work and the absence of Paul's expectation of the return of Christ.

5. Ephesians is an example of the custom of New Testament times of ascribing a disciple's work to his master as a means of honoring him and perpetuating his teaching and authority in a later situation.

All these reasons are answered by those who believe in Paul's authorship:

1. Somewhat different language and style were required for a hymn of praise to God, Christ, and the church; and Paul was resourceful enough to produce it. Actually, the style of Ephesians is 90 to 95 percent like Paul's.

2. Ephesians and Colossians are alike because Paul wrote them both at about the same time, when the same ideas and words were throbbing in his brain, and sent them both by Tychicus (Ephesians 6:21; Colossians 4:7).

3. Paul recognized the foundational nature of the apostolic leadership in Jerusalem, as evidenced by his consulting Peter (Galatians 1:18) and other apostles (2:1-10), though he insisted on the validity of his own call and mission among the Gentiles.

4. The elements of the theology of Ephesians are to be found in Paul's genuine letters, such as the church as the "body" of Christ (1 Corinthians 12:27; Ephesians 1:23) and the Holy Spirit as God's seal and guarantee of the coming inheritance (2 Corinthians 1:22; 5:5; Ephesians 1:13-14). Ephesians looks forward to the judgment and triumph of Christ (4:30; 5:5, 27; 6:8), though the language may be somewhat different in other letters of Paul.

5. Point 5 above, while true enough, proves nothing about the authorship of Ephesians.

It is probably best to allow the traditional authorship to stand until better proof against it can be produced.

Ephesians 1:3-14. This blessing is poetry. Should it be printed in lines and stanzas, or is it poetic prose? Something like a refrain appears in verses 6, 12, and 14, possibly dividing the blessing into parts. But no clear poetic pattern can be established, and it is best to consider the section poetic prose.

God, the Father, is praised throughout—the God who acted in his Son, "the One he loves" (1:6), and in the Holy Spirit (1:13-14). While Paul presents no formal doctrine of the Trinity here, the materials for the later formulation of the Trinity are indeed here.

Ephesians 1:4-5. The words "he chose us" and "he predestined us" will raise questions about God's election. The *us* is, of course, the church; no individual predestination is suggested here. That God, before the foundation of the world, proposed the church to come into existence through Jesus Christ is the very heart of New Testament teaching. Paul believed that the church is a divine, not a human creation.

Holy suggests difference and separation. Christians are to be different from the secular, defiled people of the world among whom they live; and they are to be like God in character (5:1). *Blameless* suggests that, like the sacrifices of Israel, which were to be flawless (Exodus 29:1; Leviticus 22:19-25), God intends perfection as the standard for his children (Matthew 5:48).

Ephesians 1:9-10. The word *mystery* was widely used in Paul's day, both in Judaism and in Hellenism. Greek mystery cults offered people eternal life through rites of purification and through initiation into secret lore, which was never to be revealed to those outside the cult. In the Book of Daniel (Chapter 2) and in the Dead Sea Scrolls the word *mystery* occurs many times in the sense of a divine secret, hidden from ordinary people, which special God-enlightened wise persons and teachers alone can reveal and explain at the proper time. Paul regarded himself as such a person, appointed as God's interpreter "when the times will have reached their fulfillment" (Ephesians 1:10; 3:2-6).

In Judaism the divine secrets mostly concerned God's plan for the summation of history in the sending of the Messiah and the inauguration of the kingdom of God. Paul believed that he was appointed by God to make known an aspect of this plan: that God loves the Gentiles as much as the Jews and that God's salvation is open to the Gentiles on the basis of faith in the Messiah Jesus—without further requirement (Ephesians 2:8-9). Paul saw also that the incorporation of the Gentiles was part of a total plan for the unification of the universe, both in its earthly and heavenly dimensions. This secret purpose of God he now proclaims to the whole world.

Ephesians 1:13-14. That the Gentiles are really included has been certified by God in the Holy Spirit's sealing of them. The Holy Spirit both marks them as God's possession and constitutes the down payment of their future inheritance.

The word *guarantee* here really means earnest-money or down payment as assurance that the rest of a purchase price will be paid. This word was used in Hellenistic commercial documents: the sale of a cow and the hiring of dancing girls included an advance payment as a guarantee. So the Holy Spirit is the down payment of the full blessedness Christians are to receive in the kingdom of God.

Ephesians 1:15-23. Paul's prayer for his readers, like his praise to God (in the Greek text) consists of one long sentence. The prayer, like the praise, gushes forth like a mountain stream, gathering volume and force as it plunges along its way.

From the introduction to the prayer and the prayer itself, we can gain a partial insight into Paul's conception of what the church ought to be: (1) people who have faith in and are faithful to the Lord Jesus and who have love for and act in loving ways toward their fellow Christians (1:15); (2) people who are indwelt by the (Holy) Spirit and have the understanding and knowledge (experience) of God that the Spirit brings (1:17); (3) people who live in hope and have glimpses of their glorious future as the people of God (1:18); (4) people who possess inwardly the immeasurably great power of God—a power shown in Jesus' resurrection and exaltation to universal authority (1:19-21); (5) people who live in union with Christ, under his lordship, and derive their life and their witness from him (1:22-23).

In the Old Testament the word *head* suggests leadership and authority. For Paul to declare Christ the "head over everything" and of the church, "which is his body," would suggest to his readers Christ's authority, his life and power imparted to the church, and the functional unit of the two. Paul was not a pantheist who would declare the natural world essentially divine by creation. It is a creature, perverted through the Fall, that can be restored only through re-creation at the end of time (Romans 8:19-22).

The statement that Christ fills the church and everything (1:23) probably means that Christ, through his presence in the church as the Holy Spirit, equips it for its witnessing function in the world, until the whole creation is drawn together with Christ at its center.

Ephesians 2:1-3. Chapter 2 is built on the principle of contrast. The first characterization of the old life (the *you* being the Gentiles and the *we* being the Jews) has some interesting words and phrases.

Transgressions are false steps or sins, violations of the will of God, whether, as in Adam's case, before the giving of the Mosaic law (Romans 5:15) or after it (Romans 4:25), or the will of God as disclosed to Gentiles apart from the Mosaic law (Romans 1:18-23).

Sins are failures to hit the mark of God's purpose for us, to be what God wants us to be.

Lived means "walked." To the Jew *lived* or *walked* meant to follow a certain path. Early Christians were those who walked on "the way" (John 14:6; Acts 9:2; 19:9; 24:14).

The ways of this world is literally "the age of this world." Jewish teachers often spoke of "this age" and "the age to come," as Paul does in Ephesians 1:21. Paul's readers once lived for this age alone, without regard to the age to come.

The *ruler of the kingdom of the air* refers to the leader of the "powers and authorities" (Romans 8:38; 1 Corinthians 15:24; Colossians 2:15). Satan in Ephesians is called "the devil" (4:27; 6:11) and "the evil one" (6:16). The seat of his authority is "the heavenly realms" (6:12). Jews believed in several heavens, as did Paul (2 Corinthians 12:2), the lower ones being the residence of demonic powers (Revelation 12:7-9).

Objects of wrath parallels "those who are disobedient." God's wrath rests on "those who are disobedient" (Ephesians 5:6); thus, such people are "objects of wrath." *By nature* means simply that in and of themselves, without divine help, the readers were in that state, not that they were born with a corrupted nature.

Ephesians 2:4-10. The first description of the new life presented in these verses contains several key words and phrases.

Rich in mercy is one of the phrases in Ephesians emphasizing God's or Christ's "riches" (1:7, 18; 2:7; 3:8, 16). The God of Ephesians is lavish, not niggardly. *Mercy* is the New Testament term for the Old Testament's "loving-kindness" (King James Version) or "steadfast love" (Revised Standard Version) and means love beyond requirement or deserving.

Grace is God's undeserved favor or graciousness. It is love in action to help the helpless and undeserving, such as the sinful Gentiles (and Jews).

Saved and *salvation* are verb and noun of the same root. Their meaning is basically deliverance from all that threatens a person, a family, a nation, the human race, and the security, health, and well-being of such people. For Paul this deliverance begins in this age when one responds in faith to God's gracious gift of his Son as the means of rescue ("you have been saved," 2:5, 8), and one will be saved at the Last Judgment for participation in the age to come (Romans 5:9; 10:9-10; 2 Corinthians 5:10; Ephesians 2:7).

Faith is trust, a trust that involves the whole person: mind, will, and emotions. For Paul faith involves belief but it is not just a body of doctrine that one accepts. Trust is active, not static.

In the phrase *not by works, works* means meritorious human effort. For Paul, having faith is not our contribution to salvation. Even faith is the gift of God. Therefore, we cannot boast about our coming to salvation. We accept it in gratitude and freely act out our gratitude in a life of good works. Here "good works" are something God gives, not our meritorious achievement.

God's workmanship is translated in *The New Jerusalem Bible* "God's work of art," because the Greek word behind *workmanship* is *poiema*, from which we get the English word *poem*—a work of art. As God's work of art, his beautiful creation in Christ Jesus, we are to fulfill God's intention by doing deeds that express what we are.

Ephesians 2:11-22. These verses contain the second contrasting description of the old life and the new. Formerly there was separation and alienation between Gentiles and Jews, but now there is reconciliation and unity.

The means of reconciliation and unity is said to be "the blood of Christ." The reference here to "the blood" of Christ, rather than to his death on the cross, seems to point to his blood as somehow effective and to suggest that Paul had in mind a sacrificial meaning for Christ's death.

In the Old Testament blood has great significance: it cries out powerfully to God (Genesis 4:10); it seals covenants with God (Exodus 12:7, 13); it brings about cleansing from defilement and forgiveness (Leviticus 4:13-21; 16: 15-19; 17:11), essential for reconciliation with God.

That sacrificial imagery in Paul's mind here is clear from Ephesians 5:2. (For other interpretations of the death of Christ in Paul's letters, see Lesson 7).

The meaning of "the dividing wall of hostility" is not altogether clear. Many scholars have thought it a metaphorical reference to the low stone wall (about five feet high, with thirteen entrances through it) that surrounded the inner Temple area and divided it off from the Court of the Gentiles. Through those entrances none but Jews could go. A sign at each entrance in Greek or Latin read: "No Gentile is to enter the fence and barrier around the Temple. Anyone caught is answerable to himself for his ensuing death." If Paul has this wall in mind, as a symbol of Jewish-Gentile separation, he sees it as removed in Christ.

Paul may be thinking, however, not of this barrier but of the law itself and its interpretive elaborations by Jewish rabbis as a spiritual and ceremonial wall separating Jews from Gentiles. By annulling the Jewish law and inaugurating the new covenant, Christ removed the barrier between Jews and Gentiles and made possible their common access to God (Ephesians 2:18). The "holy temple in the Lord" (2:21) is the church as the dwelling place of God's Spirit.

Ephesians 3:14. "The Father" here is the cosmic Father: the Father of all families and clans, not just the Father of Christians. This point is indicated and supported by Ephesians 4:6. The heavenly families, mentioned here, apparently are the angelic families and powers, not families of the Christian dead in heaven. Jewish writings of the time refer to families of angels.

All these families bear, in some sense, God's name and therefore God's claim. God intends to bring the whole universe under his sovereignty (Jews, Gentiles, and the "principalities and powers"), so that there may be universal unity in the family of God.

DIMENSION THREE: WHAT DOES THE BIBLE MEAN TO ME?

Ephesians 1:4-5—God's Chosen People

The prophets pointed out that God chose the people of Israel not so much for special privilege as for special responsibility. Through their worship of God and obedience to God, they would reflect in their personal and communal life God's character and make God's character, deeds, and requirements known to the peoples of the world, so that all might worship God and become like God. This was a tough job, as the prophets saw.

Paul believed that the church has been called to this task, a responsibility not completed by Judaism. What privilege and what responsibility are involved today for this service for God, for individual members, and for the church as a whole?

Ephesians 1:15-23—Marks of the True Church

Paul's prayer reveals part of his understanding of what the church ought to be. Compare the major points in this prayer with characteristics of your local church. How can Paul's vision of the church be realized in the church where you worship?

Ephesians 2—The Old Life and the New

To what extent does Paul's description of the old and the new life fit your personal experience? What kind of change is required of people who have not gratified the cravings of their sinful nature or consciously followed "the ways of this world"?

By what human works do people today seek to be acceptable to God? Note Paul's attitude toward such human considerations (Philippians 3:4-11). Discuss works as a prerequisite to salvation and works as the consequence of spiritual transformation. Note especially 2:10. Why are grace and faith the way of salvation?

What barriers in yourself, your church, and your community do you think Christ could and should obliterate?

—13—

The Path to Unity

Ephesians 4–6

DIMENSION ONE:
WHAT DOES THE BIBLE SAY?

Answer these questions by reading Ephesians 4:1-16

1. What qualities of spirit contribute toward unity in the church? (4:2-3)

   Humbleness, gentleness, patience, loving forbearance, and eagerness for keeping the unity that the Spirit gives contribute toward unity in the church.

2. What unities already exist? (4:4-6)

   One body, one Spirit, one hope, one Lord, one faith, one baptism, one God and Father—these unities already exist.

3. What gifts has Christ bestowed on the church, and why were they given? (4:11-13)

   Christ's gifts were that some should be apostles, prophets, evangelists, pastors, and teachers. They were to build up the body of Christ until all members come to maturity of life in Christ.

Answer these questions by reading Ephesians 4:17–5:20

4. What attitudes and practices belong to the old nature? (4:17-22)

   Futility of thinking, darkened understanding, ignorance, hardness of heart, loss of all sensitivity, and greedy sensuality are the attitudes; and impurity and lust are the practices that belong to the old nature.

5. What is the new nature like? (4:23-24)?

   The new nature is a new attitude of mind and self and likeness to God in righteousness and holiness.

6. What specific antisocial attitudes and practices of the old life should be abandoned? (4:25-32)

   A Christian should put away falsehood, anger, stealing, unwholesome talk, bitterness, rage, brawling, slander, and malice.

7. What new attitudes and practices should take their place? (4:25-32)

   Christians should speak the truth, be angry without sinning, perform useful work, use helpful talk, show respect for the Holy Spirit, and use kind and compassionate attitudes toward others.

8. What attitudes and practices belong to the old darkness of pagan life? (5:3-18)

   Sexual immorality and other impurities, greed, obscenity, foolish talk, coarse joking, openness to deception, association with those who are disobedient, participation in secret and fruitless deeds of darkness, wasting opportunities, lack of understanding the will of the Lord, and drunkenness belong to the pagan way of life.

9. What attitudes and practices should characterize the "children of light"? (5:3-20)

   These attitudes and practices should describe the Christian: thanksgiving, ability to identify empty words, separation from disobedient people (in the church, 5:3); dedication to the good, the right, the true; effort to learn what is pleasing to the Lord; exposing fruitless deeds for what they are; silence concerning secret evil doings; moral alertness; using time to advantage; understanding the Lord's will; sobriety; full possession of the Holy Spirit; and joyful communal singing and thanksgiving.

10. To what relationship is the Christian husband-wife relationship compared? (5:21-33)

This relationship is compared to Christ and the church.

11. What is the standard for the husband's love of his wife? (5:25, 28-29, 33)

Christ's self-giving love of the church and the kind of love one has for oneself is the standard for a husband's love of his wife.

12. What reasons does Paul offer for children's obedience to their parents? (6:1-4)

Children and their parents share a common life "in the Lord," and in that life obedience to parents is proper. Such obedience accords with divine law and promise.

**Answer these questions by reading
Ephesians 6:10-20**

13. What is the posture of the Christian in the battle with the forces of evil? (6:11, 13, 14)

The Christian is to stand fast against the attacks of evil powers.

14. What aggressive attitudes and activities should the Christian warrior assume? (6:15, 17-20)

The footwear suggests active evangelization; the helmet suggests the victorious outcome of the warfare; the sword provided by the Spirit is the word of preaching; and the intercessory prayer for one another and for Paul is for the spread of the gospel through the proclaimed word.

DIMENSION TWO:
WHAT DOES THE BIBLE MEAN?

Chapters 1–3 deal with the church in the eternal purpose of God. They praise God, Christ, and the Spirit who have been working out in the rifted earthly and heavenly worlds a secret plan for the unification of all things in Christ. Prayer has been mingled with praise for the readers' full understanding of the plan and for their full participation in it.

What this participation means in detail is now spelled out. In Chapters 4–6 we see the church struggling to overcome the divisions by which it is plagued: functional (4:11-13), doctrinal (4:14), moral (4:25-32), domestic (5:21–6:4), and socioeconomic (6:5-9). "The devil's schemes" (6:11) are an ever-present threat to the church's future as the bride of Christ (5:25-27). Stern exhortations and warnings to help keep the church faithful to its high destiny are needed. Only the mighty power of God and God's whole armor, worn by every church member, can assure victory in this cosmic struggle (6:10-20).

Ephesians 4:4-6. Seven unities are presented here, falling into three groups: (1) one body, one Spirit, one hope; (2) one Lord, one faith, one baptism; (3) one God and Father of all. The unities begin with the church, in which the Holy Spirit dwells and guarantees the ultimate realization of its hope for the future (1:13-14; 2:22). They continue with the source of the church's life in the Lord, who is experienced by faith and baptism (1:7, 13; 2:4-8; 5:26). And they end with God, who is transcendent (over all) and immanent (through all and in all).

Ephesians 4:8-10. These verses seem to interrupt the flow of thought in a passage that reads smoothly from 4:7 to 4:11. The subject, beginning with 4:7, is the gracious gifts God the Father of all has bestowed on individual church members through Christ (the Messiah).

The concept of the Messiah's giving gifts calls to Paul's mind Psalm 68:18, which he interprets as referring to the Messiah rather than to God. In the psalm God ascends Zion for God's glorious enthronement with captives in his train. He receives gifts from his conquered subjects.

The transference to the Messiah of attributes and activities of God was common among Jewish interpreters of the Old Testament in Paul's time. And the change from receiving gifts to giving them may have arisen from the meaning of the Hebrew word for "to take" or "to receive," which in some Old Testament passages means "to take in order to give."

In the psalm the captives are God's human enemies, but for Paul they are the Messiah's supernatural enemies (the powers and authorities).

In Paul's interpretation of the psalm the Messiah's ascent implies a prior descent to the earth (in the Incarnation), followed by his resurrection and ascension to universal authority. After his triumph he gave gifts (the Holy Spirit and the Spirit's empowerments) to the members of the church.

Ephesians 4:11-16. The gifts here are types of service carried out by various people for the edification of the whole church.

Note the contrast here between children, who are easily deceived by false teachers and led into divisive cliques (4:14), and the mature person, who holds steady in the knowledge of the truth concerning the Son of God and contributes to the growth and unity of the whole body of Christ. In First Corinthians Paul regards the divisive cliques as a mark of childishness (3:1-4).

Ephesians 4:20-21. These verses assume that the church is a school in which the Messiah is learned. Christ's (the Messiah's) teaching was handed down in the church—at first orally and then in written form—for the instruction of converts. An early collection of Jesus' teachings (we call it today Q) was used as one of the sources of the Gospels of Matthew and Luke, and Matthew itself is a great compendium of sayings and deeds of Jesus intended for the guidance and edification of the church. The "teachers" mentioned in Ephesians 4:11 used material of this sort to instruct converts and to bring them to maturity in the faith.

The content of these teachers' instruction may be discerned somewhat from the context of these verses, as well as from the teaching of Jesus.

Gentile idolatry, resulting in licentious living, arises from futile, darkened, and ignorant minds. That there is "one God and Father of all, who is over all and through all and in all" (4:6) and that "an idol is nothing at all in the world" (1 Corinthians 8:4) was fundamental to Christian teachers, as it was to Jesus (Mark 12:29-30).

That this God is righteous and demands holiness of his worshipers (Ephesians 4:24) is stressed in 4:17–5:20 and in the Sermon on the Mount (Matthew 5–7). The old self and the old manner of life must be "put off" and a new self and manner of life must be "put on" (4:24). Both selves and ways of life are characterized in detail in 4:17–5:20.

Ephesians 4:30. The evil social attitudes and acts described in 4:25-32 are said in this verse to be painful to "the Holy Spirit of God," who has put his mark of ownership on the Christian as a guarantee of ultimate salvation at "the day of redemption."

That God grieves and suffers over our sins is an oft-repeated note in the Bible (Genesis 6:5-7; Isaiah 64:10; Jeremiah 2:4-13; Hosea 11:1-9; Luke 15:11-32). The God of the Bible is not an "unmoved mover," a deity who created the world and left it to its own devices, but a loving Father who is intimately concerned about the welfare of his children. It was this caring that caused God to send his Son into the world to deliver us from the consequences of our sins (4:32–5:2).

Here the grieving of the Holy Spirit is particularly connected with "unwholesome talk" (4:29) and "bitterness, rage and anger, brawling and slander" (4:31). In 5:4 "foolish talk" and "coarse joking" are forbidden as offensive to God, and in 5:18-20 the outflow of the Spirit's presence is the singing of psalms and hymns and the giving of thanks, making "music in your heart to the Lord." In Colossians 4:6 Paul writes, "Let your conversation be always full of grace, seasoned with salt."

Jesus emphasized the importance of what one says. Inner integrity, expressed in simple, sincere speech should characterize the life of a disciple (Matthew 5:33-37). And he warned that people will "give account on the day of judgment for every careless word they have spoken. For by your words you will be acquitted, and by your words you will be condemned" (Matthew 12:36).

What Christians do with their lips, as an expression of what is in their hearts, is important to God, these passages say.

Ephesians 5:1-2. Here Paul sets forth the ground and motive of all Christian ethics: the imitation of God and the love of Christ. The phrase *imitators of God* only appears at this place in the Bible. The Old Testament speaks of following God, or serving him, or walking in his ways (Numbers 32:11-12; Deuteronomy 28:9; Joshua 24:14-15) but not of imitating God.

The concept of imitating God was common in the Hellenistic world: in the mystery cults and even in the writings of the Hellenized Jewish philosopher Philo. Manual art was spoken of as an imitation of reality. Students were to imitate their teachers. Mimics (imitators) appeared on the stage in dramatic performances. Thus, Paul may have adopted a term here that would have special meaning for his readers.

But he put into the term his own meaning. Imitation of God becomes possible because God sent his Son into the world for all to see what he is like (4:32; 5:2) and what he wants of us (4:17–6:9). Therefore, in imitating Christ the Christian imitates God.

Imitating Christ's love for us involves the kind of self-sacrifice for others he made in offering up his life for us. The extent of this love is spelled out in 5:25-33 in the explanation of how husbands should love their wives.

Ephesians 5:8-20. In a striking passage Paul describes the "children of light." It is as though he opens the door on the early Christian fellowship and allows us to peer in.

First, we see what kind of people are there. They "are light in the Lord." In union with Christ they are what he is: *light.* Light is knowledge of what "pleases the Lord" (5:10), "what the Lord's will is" (5:17). These are wise people (5:15), not in philosophy and science, but in the art of living in a way pleasing to God. They are "good" (kind, benevolent), "right" (in right relations with God and their neighbors), and "true" (morally correct).

Second, we see what they are against. They do not participate in "the fruitless deeds of darkness, but rather expose them" (the worthlessness of such deeds), apparently by their conduct and their words. They do not dignify secret evil deeds by so much as discussing them, but instead they seek to dispel the darkness by turning it into light (5:12-13).

Third, we see that they are active in an evil world, "making the most of every opportunity." The implication is that evil people put precious time to wrong use; and Christians, by right living and witnessing, put it to proper use. The evil days may be seen by Paul as the perilous time before the end (Matthew 24:19-31; 2 Timothy 3:1-9). If so, Christians are to make the most of their opportunity in the remaining time before the end.

Fourth, we see what their fellowship gathering is like. It is not a debauch with alcohol, as a pagan drinking party is, but a gathering of people filled with the Spirit, joyful in singing "psalms, hymns and spiritual songs," making "music . . . to the Lord" with all their heart, and giving thanks to God.

One of the songs they sang may be quoted in 5:14. Scholars generally regard this poetic piece as from an early Christian hymn, possibly a hymn sung at baptismal services.

Ephesians 5:21–6:9. This domestic section reflects the ethical standards and practices of the Hellenistic world. Christians had to meet many problems in their everyday lives. Often teachings handed down from Jesus included no specific help on practical problems. The church naturally adopted the best elements in its culture and baptized them into Christ, as it were.

In that world male leadership was taken for granted. So was unquestioning obedience of children to parents. Fathers had absolute power of life and death over children. Slaves were common property, which could be treated and disposed of according to the whim of the owner.

Christianity did not and could not overturn basic structures. But it ennobled and transformed relationships within them. Onesimus was sent back to Philemon to continue his service to his master, but on a new level: he was to be regarded and treated as "a dear brother," to be received as Paul himself would be received (Philemon 16-17). Both master and slave were seen as under a common Master, who will judge both impartially (Ephesians 6:9).

Ephesians 5:21-33. Here Paul recognizes the dominance of the husband, in keeping with contemporary custom, but so transforms the relationship as to remove any sting from this dominance.

At the outset, he puts both husband and wife under the lordship of Christ and requires of them mutual subordination (5:21). In mutual subordination the husband cannot do as he pleases with his wife, such as divorce her for trivial reasons, as allowed by many in Judaism. Christ stands over both husband and wife as judge.

The wife's part is the kind of subordination appropriate to *mutual* subordination and appropriate to her position under Christ's lordship. Each partner is to recognize his or her assigned place, respect each other's position and function, and cooperate as the members of the human body do.

The comparison of the husband-and-wife relationship to that between Christ and the church elevates Christian marriage to the highest possible level. In the Christ-church relationship there is no autocratic dominance and submissive obedience but only the mutual cooperation that love expresses. The wife should take her place in this.

On his part the husband is utterly to love his wife. The degree of this love is the degree of Christ's love for the church. He "gave himself up for her" for no selfish reasons but only to benefit her and make her his spotless bride. As his bride she would inherit the riches laid up in "the kingdom of Christ and of God" (5:5). The marvel of Christ's sacrificial love simply overwhelmed Paul. Such love in marriage equals one's love for himself or herself (5:28-29)—nay, eclipses it by so much as God's love transcends human love.

The nobility and sanctity of human marriage is carried to its highest level here by the quotation of Genesis 2:24 in 5:31 and the application Paul makes of the passage. He sees in human marriage, as originally instituted, a prophecy of the new creation God brought into being in the church. There God promised that the Messiah would take a bride to be his own. This is the secret meaning (5:32) Paul finds in the passage. A higher view of human marriage could scarcely be imagined.

Ephesians 6:10-20. Paul's treatise about the church here reaches its final point. He has shown that the church was purposed by God before the creation of the world, brought into being by "the Beloved" (Jesus Christ), and sealed by the Holy Spirit as a guarantee of its final inheritance in "the kingdom of Christ and of God." The church was formed by the uniting of Jews and Gentiles into a dwelling place of the Holy Spirit, spearheaded and prayed for by a divinely appointed apostle (Paul), and continues to grow up into the full unity, maturity, and service God plans for it—in spite of the divisive and stunting factors it has to contend with inwardly.

But a major peril yet exists, Paul says. A mighty external foe is threatening the church's life and destiny: the devil, the rulers, the authorities, the powers of this dark world, and the spiritual forces of evil in the heavenly realms (6:11-12). To overcome this enemy the church will need to be equipped with "the full armor of God" and be empowered with God's great might.

Paul believed that a major blow on the kingdom of Satan had been struck by Jesus' death and resurrection (Colossians 1:13-14; 2:15) and that the church was the spearhead or outpost of the final kingdom of Christ and of God. To use one scholar's terms, Paul—like Jesus—believed that D-Day had occurred in Jesus' ministry, death, resurrection, and the formation of the new messianic community, and that V-Day would come soon at Jesus' return in glory to destroy completely Satan and his cohorts and to establish the final Kingdom (Romans 13:11-12; 1 Corinthians 7:29-31; 1 Thessalonians 1:10).

Meanwhile, the initial victory, won at the cross and Resurrection, needed to be proclaimed to the world by the expansion of the church through the transformation and inclusion of people of every race, class, and condition and—to use another of Paul's figures of speech—by the preparation of the bride-elect (the betrothed church) for the coming of the Bridegroom and her marriage to him and life with him in the heavenly kingdom (2 Corinthians 11:2; Ephesians 5:25-27).

The armor described in 6:14-17 is much the same as a Roman soldier would wear. The prisoner, Paul, was all too familiar with Roman equipment. With God's and the anointed king's armor and supplied with God's own mighty power, available always through prayer for oneself and others (6:18-20), the Christian warrior can be entirely invincible.

Ephesians 6:21-22. Tychicus, a native of the province of Asia, had accompanied Paul as a bearer of the collection for the church in Jerusalem (Acts 20:4) and is named in 2 Timothy 4:12 and Titus 3:12 as a messenger of Paul. He apparently was one of the bearers of the letter to the Colossians (Colossians 4:7). As a faithful minister and representative of Paul, he will tell the readers about Paul's situation and bring encouragement to them.

Paul ends the letter with no personal complaints and, as always, on a note of encouragement and with a benediction of divine peace and grace.

DIMENSION THREE: WHAT DOES THE BIBLE MEAN TO ME?

Ephesians 4:1-16—The Church as God's Unifier

Paul believes that God has called the church into being to serve as his means of unifying the cosmos. To carry out its work he says that it must have a certain spirit (4:2-3), a theology (4:4-6), a structure (4:7-11), and a task (4:12-16).

Apply Paul's teaching on each of these points to the church you know best. What is it that most often wrecks unity in a church, judging from this passage and your own experience in the church? Consider among other things the effect of self-centeredness and immaturity.

Ephesians 4:17-25—The Callous Life

The Ephesian church members were once ignorant and hard (callous) of heart. To what actual sins did this condition lead? Does it produce the same sins today? What other sins, not mentioned by Paul, does this condition produce as a threat to church and society today? How can ignorance and callousness be overcome, according to this passage?

Ephesians 5:1-20—Imitators of God

What is it about God that Christians are to imitate? How is this kind of imitation possible for human beings?

What is healthy language, according to Paul? Measure our speech, literature, movies, TV, and so on, by his perspective. What can the church do about the language situation?

Ephesians 5:21–6:9—Christian Home Life

How are self-love and love for one's spouse related in Paul's thought? What do you think of his comparison of the husband-wife relationship to that between Christ and the church?

Parent-child alienation has been about as serious a problem in our culture as the marital problem. Has Paul any help for us here?

Finally, though the slave-master problems of Paul's time do not exist today in our Western culture, owner-employee problems do. What in 6:5-9 might offer help with these?

PHILIPPIANS, COLOSSIANS, 1 AND 2 THESSALONIANS, 1 AND 2 TIMOTHY, TITUS, PHILEMON

1. Christ's Obedience and Christian Obedience 146

2. Christ's Resurrection and Christian Resurrection 151

3. Christian Faith and Christian Action 156

4. Relationships in the New Life 161

5. Comfort in Distress 166

6. The Coming of the Lord 171

7. Christian Life Between the Times 176

8. Christ for All 182

9. How to Behave in God's Household 187

10. Life in God's Household 192

11. Christian Endurance 197

12. The Life of Grace in the Church 202

13. Christian Refreshment 207

About the Writer

Dr. Van Bogard Dunn was Professor Emeritus and Dean Emeritus at The Methodist Theological School in Ohio, Delaware, Ohio, until his death in 1994.

— 1 —

Christ's Obedience and Christian Obedience

Philippians 1:1–3:1

DIMENSION ONE:
WHAT DOES THE BIBLE SAY?

Answer these questions by reading Philippians 1

1. Who sends the letter to whom? (1:1)

   "Paul and Timothy, servants of Christ Jesus," send the letter to "all the saints in Christ Jesus at Philippi, together with the overseers and deacons."

2. How do Paul and Timothy greet the Philippians? (1:2)

   Paul and Timothy greet them with grace and peace.

3. For what does Paul pray? (1:9)

   Paul prays that the Philippians' love "may abound more and more in knowledge and depth of insight."

4. What is Paul's situation as he writes the letter? (1:7, 12-14, 17)

   He is in prison, "in chains."

5. How does Paul interpret his situation? (1:12-14)

   He interprets his imprisonment as an opportunity to preach the gospel and to encourage others "to speak the word of God more courageously and fearlessly."

6. How do Paul's supporters interpret his situation? (1:16)

   They see Paul's situation as his opportunity to defend the gospel.

7. How do his foes interpret it? (1:17)

   They see Paul's imprisonment as an occasion to stir up trouble for him.

8. How does Paul expect his situation to turn out? (1:19-26)

   He knows that Christ will be exalted by his death or life, but Paul expects to be delivered from prison and to visit Philippi in person.

9. How does Paul expect the Philippians to act while he is absent? (1:27-30)

   He expects their manner of life to be "worthy of the gospel of Christ."

Answer these questions by reading Philippians 2:1–3:1

10. What behavior by the Philippians will complete Paul's joy? (2:1-4)

    "Being like-minded, having the same love, being one in spirit and purpose" will complete his joy.

11. What are the marks of this behavior? (2:6-8)

    The marks are not grasping for status, self-emptying, humility, and obedience.

12. Why is this behavior the norm for the Philippians? (2:9-11)

    This behavior is the norm because God has exalted the crucified Jesus as the Lord of all creation.

13. What action of Jesus is reproduced in the lives of his followers? (2:12-13)

    Obedience is the action.

14. What will make Paul proud "on the day of Christ"? (2:14-18)

    Their "hold[ing] out the word of life" will make Paul proud.

15. Whom does Paul plan to send to Philippi soon? Why? (2:19-24)

Paul plans to send Timothy in order to get direct news of the Philippians and for him to minister in Paul's stead.

16. Who came from Philippi to be with Paul and help him? (2:25-30)

Epaphroditus came to help Paul.

17. What do the Philippians hear about Epaphroditus's condition? (2:26-27a, 30)

Epaphroditus has been ill and almost died.

18. Why does Paul send Epaphroditus back to Philippi? (2:28)

Paul sends him so the Philippians may see that he is fully recovered.

19. What is Paul's basic feeling in this opening section of his letter? (1:4, 18; 2:2, 17-18)

Joy is Paul's basic feeling.

DIMENSION TWO: WHAT DOES THE BIBLE MEAN?

Philippians 1:1. One of the perplexing problems for the student of Philippians is the understanding of overseers (bishops) and deacons in 1:1. Scholars generally agree that these words in this context do not refer to officers of the church but rather to persons who performed particular functions necessary for the life of the congregation. Bishops were overseers of the corporate activities of the congregation. Deacons were responsible for certain supportive roles as the church cared for its needy members and organized itself for effective action. In this setting the bishops and deacons are first and foremost saints. Yet just as Paul and Timothy found their true status as servants, so service was the only reason for the existence of bishops and deacons.

Philippians 1:6, 10. For Paul, God's redemptive work begun in Christ awaited its consummation in the coming of the exalted Christ at the end of human history. Salvation, although a present experience for the faithful, was not complete and would not be complete until Christ came to judge and redeem the whole creation. Paul expected this final act in the drama of salvation, "the day of Christ Jesus," to come soon. But he made no temporal predictions, set no date, and in general exercised a great deal of restraint about the details of the event. His emphasis rather fell on the certainty of the event as the necessary fulfillment of God's saving purpose manifested in the life, death, and resurrection of Jesus Christ.

Philippians 1:7, 12-26. Paul's hope "in the day of Christ Jesus" is the context that gives meaning to his imprisonment (being "in chains"). Meaning is the decisive issue here, not geography. We cannot be sure where Paul was in prison when he wrote Philippians. Acts mentions two imprisonments, Caesarea and Rome. These are possibilities as well as any other city he visited, for Paul was always a controversial figure and could conceivably have been imprisoned at a number of places not mentioned in Acts. Some scholars argue for Ephesus on the grounds that the frequent messages from Paul to Philippi reported in the letter would have been more likely from the nearby Ephesus than from the distant Caesarea or Rome. Caesarea, Rome, Ephesus, some other city—all are possibilities that cannot be settled finally without more evidence than we possess.

But the meaning of Paul's imprisonment is set forth clearly by the apostle. His imprisonment is not accidental but rather is the result of his participation in "defending and confirming the gospel." For Paul the new age that will come fully "at the day of Christ Jesus" has already dawned in human history in the obedience of Jesus Christ unto death, "even death on a cross" (2:8). The enemies of Christ are Paul's enemies, and the suffering of Christ is Paul's suffering. Thus, Paul's imprisonment is the continuation in human history of the passion of Jesus Christ. Just as Jesus Christ confirmed the saving purpose of God in his life and death, so Paul confirms that saving purpose in his life and, if need be, in his death. Therefore, the outcome of Paul's imprisonment is essentially a matter of indifference. All that matters is that his whole being is a proclamation of Christ. Freed from anxiety about himself, about the church, and about the world, Paul can declare with amazing confidence, "For to me, to live is Christ and to die is gain" (1:21).

Philippians 1:19; 2:1. In the interim between the exaltation of Jesus Christ and "the day of Christ Jesus," Paul and all the saints are not left to carry on the struggle alone but are empowered by the Spirit of Christ. "Fellowship with the Spirit" is not limited to a special group within the church but is the common experience of all the saints. All who come to faith, who are set apart for God's service, who hold fast to the word of life, who suffer for Christ's sake are able to do so because they are helped by the Spirit of Christ. The Spirit of Christ is love in action. The Philippians have been loved into sainthood by Christ made present to them in the Spirit-powered preaching of Paul, and their continuing in love is the fruit of the Spirit in their lives.

Philippians 2:5-11. This passage is perhaps the best-known passage in the entire letter. Paul portrays Christ as the source and the substance of Christian conduct. Only in Christ, in the power of God's love, is Christian behavior a possibility. The reference to *attitude* in this context is not to a frame of mind but to the essential being of the whole person. "Your attitude should be" might be rendered "Have this true being." True being is not a private possession but a corporate possibility in a community of persons. This new possibility of personhood in community is not an ideal. It is a life lived.

Paul views Jesus' life as the center of human history. Since God's true being is self-giving for all of life, Jesus participated in God's true being, not by grasping after it as a status, but by losing himself in service. Jesus lived his unity with God by becoming one with all persons in humility, obedience, and death. Thus, Jesus is the source of personhood in community because in his life of self-giving love God's purpose for all persons is fully realized. In losing his life he found it not simply as a private possession but as the gracious gift of God for all humanity. (Compare this with Mark 8:31–9:1).

What Paul and all saints at Philippi experienced by faith in Christ Jesus is an anticipation of what all creation will acknowledge at "the day of Christ Jesus." Salvation, God's redemptive action in the cross of Christ Jesus, is not simply for the faithful individual nor merely for the faithful community but rather is universal in scope. The power in the cross of Jesus is nothing less than the power of God. Therefore the name or power of Jesus is absolutely superior to all other powers. In fact, it is the only real power. Nothing can resist that power, so when it is fully manifest at "the day of Christ Jesus," every knee will bow in submission to it. None are excluded, whether in heaven, on earth, or under the earth. The confession that is now made in the church by faith will finally be made by every tongue: "Jesus Christ is Lord."

Notice in this connection that Paul does not identify Jesus with God. Jesus is the agent of God and participates in the form of God as the revelation of God, but he is always subordinated to God in obedient service. All that Jesus does points beyond himself to God. His lordship is the exaltation of lowliness, the glory of humility, the fullness of emptiness, the life of death, the joy of suffering, the freedom of slavery. Therefore, at "the day of Christ Jesus" when every knee bows at the name of Jesus and every tongue confesses "that Jesus Christ is Lord," it is not for his glory but to the glory of God the Creator.

Philippians 2:12-13. The reference in this passage to "work out your salvation with fear and trembling" is often lifted out of context and interpreted to mean that salvation is a human achievement that is the result of anxious and fearful striving. Nothing could have been farther from Paul's mind. What he is saying here to the saints at Philippi is that their obedience of faith is God's work in them. They can confidently depend on God to continue to work for the perfection of their salvation in obedient service. The reference to "fear and trembling" is a warning that turning away from God's work to trust their own work will inevitably separate them from God and condemn them to anxious

self-seeking. Once again Paul is reminding the saints that a manner of life "worthy of the gospel" is a life created by the gospel, sustained by the gospel, and perfected by the gospel. In short, God is glorified by the saints who follow Jesus Christ on the way of absolute dependence on God. Just as Jesus Christ's lordship is to the glory of God the Creator, so their sainthood is to the glory of God the Creator.

Philippians 2:17-18; 3:1. Paul used the language of the Temple liturgy of Hebrew tradition to dramatize the possibility that his ministry to the saints at Philippi might cost his life. The imagery of a drink offering poured on the sacrifice and service of their faith is used here to remind the saints that their worship is a public act of allegiance to Christ that involves them as it involves Paul in suffering for Christ's sake. Suffering is not an end in itself nor is it motivated by a martyr complex. Instead, it is the consequence of public loyalty to Christ that challenges all other loyalties and exposes the saints to the same hostility that Jesus experienced. Moreover, loyalty to Christ is not simply a verbal transaction; it is obedience even unto death. Since Jesus Christ's lordship was revealed in human history in his life given for others, the confession of his lordship in human history is life given for others or, as Paul puts it here, a life poured out as an offering on the sacrifice of faith.

So the suffering of Paul and the saints is not a sign of their defeat or failure but rather the distinctive mark of their victory and success. But this victory and this success are hidden in their history under the sign of the cross and are theirs only in the sense of faith in Christ as the exalted Lord of death itself. For this reason Paul is glad and rejoices with all the saints. For this reason also he reminds them that "in a crooked and depraved generation," they should be glad and rejoice with him. Here Paul witnesses to the radical reversal of Christian faith that transforms the circumstances of despair into hope and finds in the terrible testing of suffering and death the ground for gladness and joy. Paul is not whistling in the dark but announcing his faith when he tells the Philippians to "rejoice in the Lord!"

DIMENSION THREE:
WHAT DOES THE BIBLE MEAN TO ME?

Philippians 1:1—Who Are We?

The student book encourages class members to consider the words *servant* and *saint* as clues to Christian self-understanding. One of the major barriers to a discussion of these words is their familiarity. Members of the class have heard them before and have some preconceived notions of what they mean.

Perhaps you can begin a discussion by asking each person to tell his or her perceptions of what these words mean. Test to see if a consensus of understanding is emerging in the group. This exercise will help class members experience the words anew and appropriate new insights as they come to voice in the discussion.

The exercise also may lead directly into a consideration of the meaning Paul had in mind as he referred to himself and Timothy as servants and to the members of the Philippian church as saints.

The distinctive Pauline meaning of the words arises from the fact that the apostle used them to describe relationships to Christ. Paul and Timothy were servants of Christ; the Philippian believers were saints in Christ. Guide class members into a period of reflection on the way our fundamental self-identity is usually a matter of relationships. We are children of our parents, husbands or wives of our spouses, employees of our company, citizens of our nation, members of our political party, and so on. Point out how relationships are usually specific and local. This opens the way to consider how personal identity is realized in communities of support and responsibility. Long before we are conscious of our identity we are told who we are; we are given names; we are accepted into a community.

How are the relationships implied in the words *servant* and *saint* created? How does Christian faith begin? Ask members of the class to report their Christian origins. Are there common points of emphasis running through a variety of experiences? Does the relationship to Christ create unity in diversity? Are the differences that divide the result of maintaining relationships with Christ or of neglecting those relationships?

As a conclusion to the issue of Christian identity, remind class members of the sacrament of baptism as a dramatic enactment of uniquely Christian relationships. How is baptism a symbol of God's action in Christ that creates servants of Christ and saints in Christ?

Philippians 1:27–2:18—What Must We Do?

When we know who we are, we will know what we must do. Ask class members to discuss whether this statement is borne out in their experience. Explore with them the connection between knowing who you are in your relationships to your family, to your work, to your neighborhood, and to your state and nation and knowing what you must do in these relationships.

At some point in the discussion you may need to clarify what it means to confess Jesus Christ as Lord. Paul seems to have an understanding of Jesus' lordship that includes all human relationships. If this is the case, then all our relationships become critical areas for our behaving in ways that reflect the fact that we are servants of Christ and saints in Christ. What might it mean for Christians to confess Jesus Christ as Lord in the home? at work? in the community? in all areas of political and economic life?

The discussion will probably reveal a wide range of opinions and perhaps some basic differences. One of the goals of this session might be to affirm these differences so that they will not become divisive but rather evidence of the unity of the group in its diversity. In order to do this,

you may want to have a member of the class read aloud Philippians 2:1-11. Ask class members to reflect on the relationship between "encouragement from being united with Christ, . . . comfort from his love, . . . fellowship with the Spirit, . . . tenderness and compassion" and "being like-minded, having the same love, being in one spirit and purpose." Do "being like-minded, having the same love, being in one spirit and purpose" mean uniformity of thought and action within the church? Or is it possible to allow differences of thought and action within the church and still have unity in the church? Are there limits? If so, who sets the limits and enforces them?

You may conclude that these issues cannot be resolved in any final way. Ask, then, how Paul's struggling with these same issues is relevant for us today. If he does not give us final answers to our pressing problems, why should we continue to study his life and thought? Again raise the subject of our relationship to Christ and explore the way Paul's letter to the Philippians is his witness to the lordship of Christ. Does Paul assume that his position is the last word and that his task is to make the Philippians agree with him? The answer, of course, is no. Paul begins not with Paul's ideas but with God's action in Christ. Ask class members to recall what God has done in Christ by reviewing Philippians 2:5-8. In light of this action, how is Paul relating in this letter to the saints at Philippi? Does he give up status? Is he humble? obedient? willing to die for others?

In drawing this section to a close, emphasize how Paul's relationship to Christ is the decisive factor in his relationships to others. Then discuss how our relationship to Christ is the controlling center of our thought and action.

Philippians 1:3-11; 2:14-18
What Is Our Hope?

Paul has a vision of salvation that is absolutely inclusive in scope. The universal sweep of his thought runs counter to much of the popular interpretation of salvation as merely the rescue of individuals from a world that is destined for destruction. The "day of Christ Jesus" in Paul's thought obviously has a dimension of judgment, but it is judgment always in the context of salvation and the redemption of the whole creation. One critical task of this lesson is to explore this issue with class members. Ask them to reflect on what it means to hope. What is distinctive about Christian hope? For what do we hope as Christians?

This exercise may suggest another line of approach as the group begins to identify those conditions in our personal and social life that are incompatible with our confession of Jesus Christ as Lord. In other words, the group will become acutely aware of the fact that we and our world are not fully saved but that we are being saved. Ask class members to identify personal conditions that are signs that God's work in us has not been completed. Explore evidence that the redemption of the world is incomplete.

A result of examining our personal and social life in this way could be a feeling of despair. Ask for an honest sharing of emotional reaction. Raise the issue of Paul's invincible confidence in the ultimate triumph of God's saving purpose in Jesus Christ. Discuss with class members the basis of this confidence. Remind them that Paul was not speculating about what God might do in the future but rather affirming that the future has already been assured by what God has done in the past and continues to do in the present.

The discussion may get sidetracked at this point because of interest in when Christ will come in glory to complete the work of salvation or what will happen when he comes. Remind class members that speculation of this kind has always been attractive, but that it has been fruitless at best and harmful at worst. Instead, focus attention on the cross as the revelation of God's love and on the Resurrection as the vindication of that love. Then help them experience anew the self-giving love of God as the power that assures the future of the church and the world. The logic here is quite simple: since Christ is the revelation of God's love, the "day of Christ" means nothing more and nothing less than the consummation of that love.

Show how Paul's concern for the future arose from his practical interest in present behavior. For Paul, although "the day of Christ" is always future, because Christ has already come, it is in a very real sense now. Therefore, Paul tells the Philippians to live now in this age as if the age of Christ's glory has already come. Faith in Christ is not merely words but also a life of obedient service, a life of love. We are called to live now as if the age to come had already come.

Close by discussing how God's love for us and our loving response are the ground of rejoicing in our past, present, and future.

Our citizenship is in heaven (3:20).

— 2 —

Christ's Resurrection and Christian Resurrection

Philippians 3:2–4:23

DIMENSION ONE:
WHAT DOES THE BIBLE SAY?

Answer these questions by reading Philippians 3:2-21

1. Paul warns the Philippians to watch out for whom? (3:2)

   He warns them to look out for the dogs, the men who do evil, and those who mutilate the flesh.

2. What are Paul's reasons for confidence in the flesh? (3:4-6)

   Paul gives these reasons for confidence in the flesh: he is circumcised, an Israelite, a Benjamite, a Hebrew, a Pharisee, a persecutor of the church, and under the law faultless.

3. What does Paul give up in order to gain Christ? (3:7-9)

   Paul gives up everything to gain Christ.

4. What are Paul's goals? (3:10-11)

   Paul's goals are to know Christ and the power of his resurrection, to share his sufferings and death, and to attain the resurrection from the dead.

5. What is the one thing Paul does? (3:13-14)

   Paul strains on "toward the goal to win the prize for which God has called me heavenward in Christ Jesus."

6. Paul tells the Philippians to follow the example of whom? (3:17)

   Paul tells them to follow his example.

7. What will the Lord Jesus Christ transform when he comes from heaven? (3:20-21)

   The Lord will transform our lowly bodies.

Answer these questions by reading Philippians 4

8. Whom does Paul mention in 4:2-3?

   Paul mentions Euodia and Syntyche, two women who are quarreling; a loyal yokefellow; Clement; and "the rest of my fellow workers."

9. Where are the names of Paul's fellow workers recorded? (4:3)

   The names of Paul's fellow workers are in "the book of life."

10. When does Paul tell the Philippians to rejoice? (4:4)

    He tells them to rejoice always.

11. What does Paul instruct the Philippians to do to relieve their anxiety? (4:6)

    Paul tells them, "by prayer and petition, with thanksgiving, present your requests to God."

12. How does Paul summarize his words to the Philippians? (4:9)

    His summary is "Whatever you have learned or received or heard from me, or seen in me—put it into practice."

13. What causes Paul to rejoice greatly in the Lord? (4:10)

    He rejoices greatly because the Philippians have renewed their concern for him.

14. What is Paul's secret for being well fed or hungry, living in plenty or in want? (4:12-13)

   Paul reports he "can do everything through him [God] who gives me strength."

15. Who helped Paul at the beginning of his ministry? (4:15)

   The Philippians helped Paul.

16. What is Paul's motive for accepting help from the Philippians? (4:17)

   Paul seeks not the gift but "what may be credited to your account."

17. Who will meet all the needs of the Philippians? (4:19)

   God will meet all their needs.

18. Whom does Paul refer to in his final greeting? (4:22)

   He makes special mention of Caesar's household.

DIMENSION TWO: WHAT DOES THE BIBLE MEAN?

Philippians 3:2-11. The persons whom Paul identifies as dogs, those who do evil, and mutilators of the flesh are probably Jews who had been converted to Christianity but who insisted that salvation still depended on circumcision and keeping the law of Moses. Paul condemns this position not only as a perversion of the gospel but also as a misunderstanding of Judaism. His opposition comes from the fact that he considers this interpretation to be a turning away from dependence on the power of God to trust in one's own strength for salvation. The "flesh" in this context does not mean physical existence but rather self-centeredness, the opposite of God-centeredness.

The "flesh" in Paul's experience is not the evil things that he has done but the best in his religious, cultural, racial, national, ethical, and liturgical heritage. He counts all this ("circumcised on the eighth day, of the people of Israel, of the tribe of Benjamin, a Hebrew of Hebrews; in regard to the law, a Pharisee; as for zeal, persecuting the church; as for legalistic righteousness, faultless") as rubbish because these noble achievements had separated him from God and from the human family. The only thing that now matters for Paul is that the risen Christ is the center of his life, assuring him of the love of God and enabling him to live out of that love in faith.

Paul does not mean that he despises his past or denies the value of his heritage. Rather he means that in Christ he is able to accept what he is as a gift and to use it in the service of the ministry to which the grace of God calls him.

Once the center of Paul's life is firmly fixed in Christ, he is free to use all his life witnessing to the lordship of Christ. Nothing can be allowed to challenge that center. Therefore, he writes, "But whatever was to my profit I now consider loss for the sake of Christ" (3:7).

To Paul, faith always refers to the gospel and is defined by the gospel. But faith is not simply believing or accepting statements as true. More fundamentally, faith is trusting the gospel action or the gospel person. Therefore, faith is essentially response to what God has done, is doing, and will do in Christ. Although faith occurs in persons, in human beings, it is not a human achievement but primarily a work of God. Paul affirms this in 3:8-11.

Resurrection is absolutely central to Paul's interpretation of the gospel. It is not to be confused with immortality of the soul. Briefly stated, the ancient and modern idea of immortality of the soul holds that the mortal body has an immortal soul that is released from the prison house of the body at death and then lives on forever. Resurrection from the dead holds that all persons, as finite creatures, are mortal. At death the whole person dies. God's love triumphs over death and raises the whole person from the dead. The continuity of the personal existence of human beings is broken by death but restored by resurrection. Resurrection, then, is not a logical conclusion from the observation of objective facts but a faithful response to the preaching of the gospel: Jesus Christ the crucified has been raised from the dead. Since God in Christ has broken the bonds of death, the grave no longer has power to hold the dead.

Philippians 3:12-16. The word that is rendered "perfect" in this passage might better be translated as "mature" or "complete." Paul uses the analogy of a race to describe the life of faith that he shares with all the saints. The basic point he makes here is that his life in Christ is never mature or complete until God is finished with him, until God has raised him up. Therefore, no matter how much he possesses in faith, the race is not finished, the prize is not his, until God gives him the victory in the resurrection from the dead. As he runs the race Paul and all who run with him are sustained by holding true to what they have already attained, "the righteousness that comes from God and is by faith" (verse 9). But holding true is possible because they are held by Christ who in the cross has made them his own.

Philippians 3:17-21. So, when Paul presents himself as an example to be imitated, he is really calling attention to the life of Christ that is his through faith. The race he runs is the example to be followed because it is the life of faith, always present yet always open to the future, always a death to self yet always a life to God, always a sharing in the cross yet always an anticipation of the resurrection. But some claim to be raised up already, free from discipline, mature. They are the libertines whom Paul denounces as enemies of the cross, whose god is the stomach and whose glory is their shame.

The point here is that those who claim to have already finished the race do so to indulge themselves and to deny the lordship of Christ. Paul, however, belongs to Christ as a humble or lowly servant. He and all the saints are called to continue in the race as servants of the Lord in the sure hope that as they are united to him in the cross, they will also be united to him in glory. Just as the resurrection of Christ is the vindication of the cross, so the resurrection of the saints is the vindication of the life of faith. Paul makes this assertion in his declaration of faith in 3:20-21.

Philippians 4:1-7. Paul's genius is expressed in the fact that he is able to join the most exalted discussion of righteousness and resurrection with the most mundane struggle with ordinary problems. Here we have an intimate glimpse of the saints at Philippi. We do not know what the issue was that had alienated Euodia and Syntyche. What we do know is that Paul took it seriously. His confidence in the ultimate triumph of the gospel does not result in acceptance of things as they are but rather motivates him to appeal to an unnamed "loyal yokefellow" to help the women become reconciled.

Paul assumes that the Spirit is at work in human lives and uses their resources to build up and unify the church. God in Christ is at work in them, "to will and to act according to his good purpose" (2:13); but God chooses to work through persons: Euodia, Syntyche, a "loyal yokefellow," Clement, and the rest of Paul's fellow workers.

Just as the Incarnation was a particular enfleshment of God in Jesus of Nazareth, so the body of Christ, the community of believers, is a particular enfleshment of the people of God in all the saints. Thus, we see in this passage Paul's doctrine of the church as it is controlled and informed by his doctrine of Christ. Christ and the church are realities that Paul understands as the work of God in human history. The church is constituted not by its membership roll but by God's "book of life." No matter what the church may seem to be, it always is the people of God, the saints.

Philippians 4:8-9. Once more the breadth of Paul's thought is illustrated as he reminds the saints that they can draw on the culture of the world about them as a guide for their life in Christ. Here he lists the conventional virtues of the civilized world as worthy of consideration as they shape their conduct with one another and the world: truth, nobility, righteousness, purity, loveliness, graciousness, excellence, worthiness. These were the recognized norms of behavior in Paul's world, and he assumed that these are the minimal standards of conduct in the church. Christian faith, instead of freeing one from the rigorous demands of ethical conduct, intensifies and extends those demands and puts one in touch with the power that changes them from impossible ideals into practical rules for action. The difference for Paul is that virtues that were formerly goals to be achieved by self-discipline are now gifts of the Spirit that are received in faith, by dying to self and living to God.

Therefore he urgently calls them to absolute dependence on God and not a program of works righteousness: "Whatever you have learned or received or heard from me, or seen in me—put it into practice" (4:9).

One of the central realities of biblical faith is peace. Paul uses it here to summarize the full meaning of salvation. In the Judaism of the first century, peace was primarily a hope for the future, focusing on the final consummation of God's saving purposes for all creation at the end of human history. Paul retains this future reference but makes a radical shift by claiming that the future has invaded the present in Christ.

Notice that the peace of God, while intensely personal, is not private or individual but public and communal. Those who receive God's grace through faith are put into a right relationship with God, with themselves, with their neighbors, and with the whole creation. Since the peace of God is always under attack by the enemies of God, it is always received in human history under the sign of the cross and awaits its full consummation as a hope beyond human history. Therefore, Paul's assurance to the saints, "the God of peace will be with you," is both a summons to be ministers of peace now and a promise of eternal peace in communion with God in the future.

Philippians 4:10-19. Again Paul is struggling with a basic challenge of Christian faith as he writes about the gifts the Philippians had sent to him earlier in Thessalonica and more recently in his imprisonment. The challenge is this: how to encourage the saints to give themselves in service without appearing to promote himself and without falling back into a form of self-righteousness. Paul meets the challenge by making it clear first of all that their gifts are not a condition for their relationship to God or to him but a consequence of that relationship. Since they are bound to God and to one another by the self-giving love of Christ, they live out of that relationship by giving themselves for one another and for Paul. Then he goes on to declare that self-giving, wherever and however it takes place, is not an achievement but a fruit of the gospel, a result of God's action in their lives. This is what Paul desires to see in the Philippians; and when it happens, his ministry is fulfilled because Christ has borne fruit in them.

Not only does Paul see their gifts for him as the "full payment" for his ministry, he also sees their gifts as evidence of the mind of Christ in them to the glory of God the Creator. Giving is an absolutely essential witness of Christian faith because it shows the world that God frees the church from anxiety by supplying every need of the saints "according to his glorious riches in Christ Jesus." Paul's tender affection for the Philippians is best understood as an expression of the fact that in their partnership with him in giving and receiving they had learned with him "the secret of being content in any and every situation, whether well fed or hungry, whether living in plenty or in want."

Philippians 4:21-23. These concluding verses, however conventional in form, are used by Paul to remind the Philippians once again of their unconventional identity in Christ. This self-understanding has controlled Paul's thought throughout the letter, and it is to this self-understanding that he appeals now as the basis for the unity, holiness, and universality of the church. Since they are saints in Christ Jesus, remembering who they are puts them in touch with Christ, who reconciles them to one another, sets them apart for their ministry, and subjects them to his universal reign. Thus the exchange of greetings at the close of the letter is the victory of Christ in the church over envy and rivalry, over self-righteousness and pride, over self-indulgence and destruction. It is a sign that grace is with them now and will be with them forever.

DIMENSION THREE:
WHAT DOES THE BIBLE MEAN TO ME?

Philippians 3:9—Righteousness

Ask class members to reread Philippians 3:2-11. Then discuss the difference between the two forms of righteousness contrasted in the passage: "righteousness of my own that comes from the law" and "righteousness that comes from God and is by faith." Keep in mind that righteousness as understood by Paul is primarily a matter of right relationship and only secondarily a matter of right action. Remind class members that Paul assumes that when we are in the right relationship to God, we will then behave in a manner worthy of that relationship. The following questions may help keep the discussion on track: How do we enjoy or receive a right relationship to God? What does Christ do to enable us to enter into and remain in a right relationship to God? How do we know that we are in a right relationship with God? The central thrust of Paul's argument is that we enjoy or receive a right relationship to God through Christ alone. For this reason he rejects the idea that we must do something ourselves to establish that relationship. Only in this light can we understand Paul's attack on those who insist that righteousness depends on keeping the law of Moses and Paul's complete rejection of his religious heritage and achievement. These things are destructive not in themselves but when they are depended on as the basis of a right relationship to God.

In order to make this argument relevant for class members, the discussion must identify those things in our lives that are destructive because we trust them instead of God. Here it is crucial to remember that the things Paul identifies are not wicked acts but the finest achievements of his religious, cultural, and moral heritage. Explore with class members the possibility that our national pride, our liturgical practice, our moral code, and our denominational structure could be examples of "confidence in the flesh."

Discussing these issues may become threatening and anxiety-producing for some or all class members. Do not avoid or deny the discussion for this reason, but fully recognize and affirm it as a sign that the conflict between the two forms of righteousness that engaged Paul and the saints at Philippi still engages us today. The conflict has no simple or final solution because it has to do with the fundamental relationship of Christian faith that must always be received anew in the changing circumstances and crises of human experience.

Paul does not seek to settle the conflict by proving that he is right and his foes are wrong but by pointing away from himself to Christ. Christ does not take sides with us in our disputes with one another. Rather he brings us all under the judgment of his love and offers us all the grace to live out of that love in faithful service. Ask class members to explore what it means to be judged by the love of Christ. Then lead them to a consideration of the way the love of Christ motivates us to ministry.

Philippians 3:10-11—Resurrection

Resurrection is perhaps one of the most difficult subjects for a Sunday school class to discuss. The biblical faith in resurrection from the dead is often confused with the idea of the immortality of the soul. Ask class members to state what they mean when they talk of resurrection from the dead. Then check to see whether the idea of the immortality of the soul has replaced the biblical faith in resurrection from the dead. Help them see that once you accept the idea of the immortality of the soul, there is really no need for faith in the resurrection.

Explore with class members how the death of Jesus and his resurrection are events that involve his whole being, not just some part of him. Then press class members to consider our death and resurrection in light of the death and resurrection of Jesus. This discussion will help them experience the difference between the idea of the immortality of the soul and the biblical faith in resurrection.

Another misunderstanding that hinders discussion of resurrection in the modern church is the identification of body with the physical aspects of existence. This is an oversimplification of the biblical position. Body in the biblical sense refers to the totality of individual existence, the whole person, the self. Therefore, when Paul refers to "the resurrection from the dead," he has in mind the release of the whole person from the bondage and destruction of death. He does not mean that the fleshly body of this earthly existence will be raised but rather that the self, the whole person, will be raised and given a new or spiritual body appropriate for the heavenly existence of the self.

Faith in the resurrection from the dead is quite different from stories about the miraculous return to life of those who have died. Rather it is the confidence that God who has given us a body for our life here on earth will give us a body for our life in heaven. Just as we have been whole persons in our lives this side of the grave, so we will be whole persons in our lives beyond the grave.

Ask class members to discuss what we mean when we say in the Apostles' Creed that we believe in "the resurrection of the body." It may help to have a member of the class prepared to report on Paul's discussion of resurrection in 1 Corinthians 15.

Remind class members that resurrection from the dead is meaningless unless it is connected to the cross of Christ. Since Paul and the earliest followers of Christ experienced his loving presence with them after his crucifixion and burial, they believed that he had been raised from the dead. This, then, becomes the decisive issue for class members to discuss. Lead them into an exploration of experiences of Christ's self-giving love in their lives and the lives of others. Help them see that these experiences are possible because Christ conquered death by giving himself for others in dependence on the love of God. The following questions may guide the discussion away from idle speculation into fruitful exploration of the issues: What is the most powerful reality in your life? Is this the most powerful reality in the universe? On what basis do you make these judgments? Does the answer you give make any difference in the way you live now and in the way you face the future? Why or why not?

Philippians 4:10-20—Giving

In a very real sense the letter Paul writes to the Philippians is enclosed in parentheses. The opening parenthesis is "Grace and peace to you from God our Father and the Lord Jesus Christ" (1:2). The closing parenthesis is "The grace of the Lord Jesus Christ be with your spirit" (4:23). This is not just a stylistic device but a clue to Paul's understanding of the life of faith. In addition, it offers the contemporary Christian a clue to understanding his or her life in Christ. The point is that our Christian life begins with grace and ends with grace. This is another way of saying that all that we are and all that we will become is the result of God's gift to us in Christ. What is the difference between this gracious self-understanding and other ways of understanding ourselves.? Is there a conflict between this way of understanding life and the common assumptions of our society? If so, what is the conflict? Ask class members to share with one another how they experience the conflict within themselves.

The discussion of God's grace will open the way to a consideration of the Christian life as basically response to God's initiative in Christ. One of the issues to be explored is why we often refuse to accept the gifts of God that are so freely offered. Be on guard against the tendency to focus on persons outside the group instead of those in the room. One way to do this is to ask class members to reflect on their efforts to be independent and to prove that they are self-sufficient. A result of this reflection may be the conclusion that God is powerless to give us what we do not admit we need.

If the discussion moves beyond the level of a polite exchange of ideas to a serious consideration of the way God's giving in Christ confronts our self-centeredness, then class members will be prepared to receive grace as judgment. Allow time to work through resistance to the idea that grace as judgment is a necessary part of our Christian life. Check with class members to see if they have had experiences of judgment that, although painful, were signs of God's love for them in Christ. Ask a class member to read aloud Paul's autobiographical statement in Philippians 3:2-11. Discuss this as an experience of judgment in Paul's life. How does Paul's experience help us identify similar experiences of judgment in our life? Is judgment the grace of God making us aware of need so that we can receive Christ?

Since all our life in Christ is grace, the gift of God's love, the distinctive characteristic of Christian existence is rejoicing in all circumstances. We are able to rejoice because our relationship to God in Christ does not depend on our situation in the world but solely on the fact that Christ's love has made us his own. God's grace is the beginning and the end of our living.

Help class members understand how rejoicing in the Lord is an occasion for listening to the Lord's direction that inspires giving in the Lord's service. Is this pattern discernible in our daily lives? Where do we most often fail to follow this pattern? How can we recognize these failures without becoming discouraged? How does remembering to whom we belong help us recover our joy and our sense of direction and our power to serve? You may want to bring this discussion to a close by reminding class members of Paul's statement, "our citizenship is in heaven." Help them understand how this is another way of declaring that God's self-giving love enables us to live on earth as instruments of that love.

So then, just as you received Christ Jesus as Lord, continue to live in him (2:6).

— 3 —

Christian Faith and Christian Action

Colossians 1–2

DIMENSION ONE:
WHAT DOES THE BIBLE SAY?

Answer these questions by reading Colossians 1

1. Who sends the letter to whom? (1:1-2)

   Paul and Timothy send the letter to "the holy and faithful brothers in Christ at Colosse."

2. What do Paul and Timothy thank God for? (1:3-5)

   They thank God for the Colossians' faith, love, and hope.

3. Who is the faithful minister from whom the Colossians learned the gospel? (1:7)

   The faithful minister is Epaphras.

4. What kind of life does Paul pray for the Colossians to lead? (1:10)

   He prays for them to "live a life worthy of the Lord."

5. What do Paul and the Colossians have in Christ? (1:13-14)

   They have redemption and the forgiveness of sins in Christ.

6. Who is the head of the church, and who is the body of Christ? (1:18)

   Christ is the head of the church; the church is the body of Christ.

7. Through whom does God reconcile all things to himself, and how does God make peace? (1:20)

   God reconciles all things to himself through Christ and makes peace by the blood of Christ's cross.

8. Of what is Paul a servant? (1:23b)

   Paul is a servant of the gospel.

9. In what does Paul rejoice? (1:24)

   Paul rejoices in his sufferings.

10. What is the purpose of Paul's servanthood (or ministry)? (1:25)

    The purpose of his ministry is "to present to you the word of God in its fullness."

11. Whom does Paul proclaim? (1:28)

    Paul proclaims Christ.

Answer these questions by reading Colossians 2

12. Whom does Paul include with the Colossians in his ministry? (2:1)

    He includes "those at Laodicea" and all who have not met him personally.

13. How is Paul with the Colossians? (2:5)

    He is with them in spirit.

14. What is "the circumcision done by Christ"? (2:11-12)

    Baptism is the circumcision done by Christ.

15. How does God cancel the written code that stood opposed to them "with its regulations"? (2:14)

    God sets it aside by "nailing it to the cross."

16. Who is to judge the Colossians "by what you eat or drink, or with regard to a religious festival, a New Moon celebration or a Sabbath day"? (2:16)

No one is to pass judgment on them concerning these matters.

17. Of what value are "human commands and teachings"? (2:20-23)

They are of no value.

DIMENSION TWO: WHAT DOES THE BIBLE MEAN?

Colossians 1:1-2. Paul understands himself and the church vocationally; that is, the decisive thing about apostles, saints, sisters, and brothers is that they have been called into a particular relationship and commissioned in that relationship for specific service. Although Paul and Epaphras perform functions that are different from the task assigned to the saints, they all are the creation of God in Christ. They all are responsible to confess the lordship of Christ in the exercise of their respective callings. All are called; all have the same status as servants; all confess the same Lord; all receive grace and peace from the same God.

Paul gives us little information about Colosse itself. Instead, he focuses attention on the relationships that distinguish the church from its surrounding geographical, cultural, sociological, and religious context. Paul emphasizes the fact that the church is different because by faith its members have been incorporated into a community that is defined no longer by human achievement but by the love of God in Christ. Therefore, the church at Colosse is also the church universal reaching to the ends of the earth, including Greek and barbarian, slave and free, Jew and Gentile. But it is all of this only to the eyes of faith. Paul is an apostle by faith. Timothy is a brother by faith. The Colossians are saints by faith. Paul's salutation is an act of faith on his part and required a faithful response on the part of his first-century readers. Colossians also requires a faithful response on the part of those who read it today.

Colossians 1:3-8. Paul's thanksgiving for the Colossians does not refer to anything that might set them off from other Christians but emphasizes those things they have in common with all believers: faith, love, and hope. They have received these things as gifts through the preaching and teaching of Epaphras. The gospel has produced in them the same fruits it has borne throughout the world. Paul is concerned to make this point here to establish the fact that the church that has been created at Colosse by Epaphras is no different from the churches that have been created by Paul in the cities he has visited. They are the same because they have been created by the same action of God in Christ, the gospel.

Paul and Epaphras are not competitors. They are fellow servants. Paul accepts Epaphras as an equal because they have both been instrumental in creating communities where the grace of God is heard and understood in truth. His purpose in praising Epaphras as a faithful minister is to contrast him with the false teachers at Colosse who are not proclaiming the truth and who are seeking to lead the saints away from the grace of God that they received in the beginning.

Colossians 1:9-14. We can neither identify the false teachers nor define their teaching precisely. It seems, however, that the false teachers were offering the Colossians additional spiritual blessings that they could obtain by secret rites and special visions. Moreover, the false teachers were insisting that "the dominion of darkness" (evil) still had to be appeased or overcome before the believers could enter "the kingdom of light" (good). Paul counters this by praying that the Colossians receive what is already offered them to Christ, knowledge of God's love that enables them to love and that increases as they love. What the Colossians need according to Paul's prayer is not secret rites and special visions but the endurance, patience, and joy that comes from hearing the gospel.

The love of God in Christ's death and resurrection has already been made public in the preaching of the gospel. In that love the Colossians have received redemption from the power of evil, the forgiveness of sins. Therefore, to live in the light does not depend on the deceitful promises of false teachers but on the word of truth proclaimed by faithful ministers like Epaphras. The false teachers are false, not because they disagree with Paul and Epaphras, but because they deny the lordship of Christ shown in the cross and resurrection of Jesus.

Colossians 1:15-20. Here we probably are reading a Christ hymn. Such hymns are found in Ephesians 2:14-16; Philippians 2:5-11; 1 Timothy 3:16; and 1 Peter 3:18-19, 22. They all contain the same basic pattern of Christ as the divine revealer who descends from the heavenly realm, carries out his saving work on earth, and ascends again to the higher sphere.

The hymn speaks of the life of Jesus, "his blood, shed on the cross." On the basis of that history, which is appropriated through faith in his Resurrection, the whole universe is understood. "His blood, shed on the cross" reveals the invisible Creator of all creation. "His blood, shed on the cross" is the life-giving power that brings all things into existence. "His blood, shed on the cross" establishes him as the source of all creation, the goal of all creation, and the unity of all creation. "His blood, shed on the cross" is the foundation of the church, Christ's body; and the mission of the church is to be the faithful sphere of Christ's lordship that ultimately includes everything. "His blood, shed on the cross" is the fullness of God, self-giving love, that reconciles all things to God and is manifest in human history by the forgiveness of sins.

In light of the mind-boggling affirmations made in this Christ hymn, the realm of redemption is expanded to include the whole creation. Redemption is always intensely personal but never exhausted by the merely personal because persons have their true being in community. Similarly, the community of faith, the church, is not the ultimate goal of redemption. Rather the church is a faithful sign in human history of the purpose of God to include the whole creation in the peace that Jesus Christ establishes by "his blood, shed on the cross." The work of creation begun in the self-giving love of Christ but destroyed by the sinful rebellion of the creation against the Creator is brought to completion by the victory of self-giving love over sin. That victory experienced now in the church through faith will be made manifest on "the day of Christ Jesus" when all things in heaven and on earth will be reconciled to God and enter into the realm of peace.

Colossians 1:21-23. In all this highly technical and profoundly theological discussion Paul never loses sight of his practical pastoral concern for the Colossians. In fact, it could be argued that Paul's relationship to the Colossian church, his diagnosis of the threatening danger of false teaching, and the remedy he recommends are the results of his faith commitments. In other words, the source of Christian behavior for the apostle and for the apostolic community is the gospel.

The gospel is basically what God has done in Christ to overcome the rebellion of the creation against the Creator. The most important thing for the Colossians to do in the present crisis is to remember "the word of truth" (1:5) as they learned it from Epaphras and as it is preached in the whole world. Colossians 1:21-22 is a summary of the gospel in action: "Once you were alienated from God and were enemies in your minds because of your evil behavior. But now he has reconciled you by Christ's physical body through death to present you holy in his sight, without blemish and free from accusation."

The phrase *your evil behavior* refers to all the misguided efforts of human beings, especially religious practices, to save themselves by their own efforts. Evil behavior includes idolatrous practices that give to the creation the glory that belongs only to the Creator. In Christ's self-giving love the whole creation is restored to its faithful relationship to God, not as an idea but in his body of flesh. Through faith in Jesus Christ's resurrection, his body, the church, now experiences the reconciling love of God that makes saints of sinners and assures them that at the "day of Christ Jesus" that love will present them to Christ "holy in his sight, without blemish and free from accusation." These adjectives are not moral achievements but the work of God in Christ, gifts of grace given by faith.

Therefore, the salvation that the Colossians received by faith can be enjoyed only by continuing in faith. The false teachers are to be resisted, not because they interpret Christ differently, but because they deny Christ by claiming that salvation is earned by acquiring a new wisdom or by practicing a new liturgy or by following a new morality. Paul reminds the Colossians that just as they began their Christian journey by trusting in the self-giving love of God in Christ, so they will persevere in their pilgrimage by trusting that love to sustain them along the way and to bring them at last to journey's end, the resurrection from the dead. The gospel is not trustworthy because it is certified by Epaphras and Paul. Rather they are authoritative teachers because they submit to the gospel and faithfully proclaim the word of truth as it is recognized throughout the whole creation.

Colossians 1:24–2:5. Boldly now Paul calls attention to his apostolic ministry as an example of what it means to "continue in your faith, established and firm, not moved from the hope held out in the gospel" (1:23). In brief, it means to live for others, not as a burden to be borne, but as a gift to be celebrated. Paul embodies the radical reversal of the gospel whereby suffering is the occasion for rejoicing because it is participation in the victory of Christ over sin and death. His ministry, as is the ministry of the whole church, is the extension of the passion of Christ to include the whole world. The apostolic succession as practiced by Paul is a chain reaction of love: Christ for Paul, Paul for the church, the church for the world. All this is possible because Christ is at work in Paul and in the church.

In this passage Paul uses the term *mystery* because in all likelihood it had been used by the false teachers to lure the Colossians away from "the word of truth" to accept a secret wisdom and understanding based on a revelation given only to those who were initiated into an elite inner circle of advanced knowledge. For Paul *mystery* is used paradoxically to refer to God's saving purpose, which includes Jews and Gentiles alike and is no longer hidden but made manifest to all the saints in the preaching of the gospel. The purpose of the revelation of the mystery of God's salvation in Christ is not to give a select group an advantage over others but to bring all persons to faith in Christ so that all persons will be perfect in Christ. Just as Paul the apostolic minister is bound to all the saints at Colosse and Laodicea, all who have not seen his face, by the love of Christ he labors for the apostolic community that they may be bound to one another in love. Everything that is necessary for the maturity of the saints has already been given in Christ: "the full riches of complete understanding, in order that they may know the mystery of God, namely, Christ, in whom are hidden all the treasures of wisdom and knowledge" (2:2-3).

Colossians 2:6-23. This entire passage is a tightly developed argument directed against the false teachers at Colosse. The section begins with an introduction in 2:6-7, which is a summary of the nature of Christian faith and the behavior that arises from it. Then in 2:8-15, Paul develops the argument that the false teachers are guilty of perverting the faith. In 2:16-23, he goes on to show that perversion of the faith results in the wrong kind of action.

Careful analysis of the structure of 2:6-7 is essential to understand the rest of the passage. Paul reminds the Colossians that their faith is a gift of Christ Jesus the Lord through the preaching of the gospel. What they have received is what all the saints receive, the self-giving love of God. Since they have received Christ Jesus the Lord, they now live in him, which means that they live in love. Love is the power that gives them life, and love is the power that enables that life to flourish and grow. The characteristic attitude of the saints who are created by love, sustained by love, and completed by love is thanksgiving.

False teaching is an empty deceit because it changes the nature of Christian faith from a gift of God into an achievement of a special group of enlightened people. This perversion of the faith is a rejection of Christ as the revelation of God and as the redeemer of the world. Again the central issues are the true nature of God ("all the fullness of the Deity" [2:9]) and the true purpose of salvation ("fullness in Christ" [2:10]). Paul insists in this passage that the life of Christ is the definitive revelation of God and the universal purpose of God for all creation. "All the fullness of the Deity" is "his blood, shed on the cross" and the "fullness in Christ" is a participation in "his blood, shed on the cross" through the faith created by the preaching of the gospel. Therefore, Paul warns the Colossians to avoid the false teachers who substitute philosophy according to human tradition for the revelation according to Christ.

The nature of the Christian faith as a gracious gift of God in Christ is dramatized in the public ritual of baptism. Paul here deliberately contrasts the open initiation of the saints into the church with the secret initiation of the elite into an exclusive society. The emphasis in baptism is on what God does in Christ. The central action is the establishment of a new relationship to God in the sense that the baptized no longer depend on themselves but on God. This new relationship is in Christ, that is, it is a dying with Christ to self and a rising with Christ to God. All the efforts to earn a place to stand in the presence of God, whether liturgical or ethical, have been canceled in the cross of Christ. What no person could ever earn, peace with God, is freely given by God in Christ. Thus, salvation is not the special achievement of the followers of false teachers but the free gift of God in Christ, proclaimed by the preachers of "the word of truth" and acted out in the drama of baptism.

Paul argues in 2:16-23 that since the false teachers misunderstand the true nature of Christian faith, they also misunderstand the way Christians should act. "Do not let anyone judge you," "Do not let anyone . . . disqualify you," expresses Paul's insistence that the saints stand in the presence of God, not on the basis of rules (concerning food and drink or religious observances or self-abasement or worship of angels or visions or any other works of the flesh), but solely by the grace of God given in Christ. All these practices are wrong because they arise from a self-righteous attitude that separates one from Christ, from Christ's body, and from God. They are to be countered or resisted, not by setting up another code of morality or another form of liturgy, but by holding fast to "the Head, from whom the whole body, supported and held together by its ligaments and sinews, grows as God causes it to grow" (2:19).

Paul goes on in 2:20-23 to remind the Colossians once again of what God does for them in baptism. Since in baptism they are dead to self-righteousness, it now makes no sense at all for them to practice the self-righteousness taught by the false teachers. All the prohibitions of the false teachers are wrong because they are based on "human commands and teachings" and not on "the word of truth." Their teachings are attractively seductive because they give the appearance of a higher righteousness by "their self-imposed worship, their false humility and their harsh treatment of the body"; but they are really a form of self-glorification. Instead of encouraging one to trust in God's righteousness, they encourage "sensual indulgence." "These are all destined to perish with use."

DIMENSION THREE: WHAT DOES THE BIBLE MEAN TO ME?

Colossians 1:7-8; 1:24–2:5
The Authority of Leaders

How do we understand authority in the church today? What guidelines in Colossians might help the church today know when leaders speak with authority? Lead class members in a discussion of experiences that have raised this issue for them. Why do they accept some leaders as authorities and reject others?

Another dimension of this problem is the role of each person in making judgments about truth. Leaders often are effective because they are successful in getting persons to let them make their judgments for them. Other leaders lead by enabling persons to make informed and independent choices for themselves. Evaluate Paul's leadership style. Does he make decisions for the Colossians? Or does he help them decide for themselves? How does he help them? Would Paul be a good model for modern church leaders?

Colossians 1:15-20
The Content of True Teaching

The debate about the content of true teaching often divides the church. The church is tempted to take one or the other of two equally untenable positions. The first position is relativism, which holds that the truth always escapes us; and therefore, one opinion is as legitimate as another. The second position is absolutism, which holds that the truth has been given in propositions that are eternally binding and normative. Both positions fail to do justice to the claim of the Christian faith that the truth is known only in relationship to Christ. Do class members sometimes resort to relativism to avoid stirring up trouble? Do they sometimes give in to absolutism because there must be clear and simple answers to perplexing problems? How is the truth made personal in Jesus Christ? How does trust in him give us an assurance that is not shaken by the fact that other persons in a personal relationship to Jesus Christ may think and act differently?

One critical issue to be raised in this context is what it means to have a personal relationship to Jesus Christ. Class members may be willing to tell of their experiences. If this happens, help them discover how different persons have different experiences. Then consider that our faith is not in our experience of Christ but in Christ. Therefore, we come to know the truth of Christ more fully the more we share with one another our richly varied experiences.

Colossians 2:16-23
The Source of Right Action

Paul's basic argument is that we cannot please God unless we are in a right relationship to God. Do class members agree with Paul on this point? Is this point true in our other basic relationships? Is it possible for husbands and wives (or friends or boss and employee) to please each other if their relationship is broken? How does this analogy shed light on our efforts to please God?

Remind class members that a right relationship to God is always, in Paul's thought, the gift of God received by faith. Since Christ is the gift of God that inspires faith, the source of right action is always Christ. We do not establish a right relationship to God by doing right. On the contrary, we do right because God in Christ has put us in a right relationship. Therefore, any action, whether liturgical or ethical, is wrong if it arises from an attempt to earn favor with God.

Ask class members to discuss how it is possible to do what seems to be right and then discover that it is wrong. Relate this to the subject of motivation. Then point out how difficult it is to know our own motives and how restrained we should be in making judgments about these matters.

Close the session by reminding class members that God's love in Christ has already established our relationship to God. Thus, we are enabled to live out of that relationship by faith so that our actions may be pleasing to God.

Whatever you do, whether in word or deed, do it all in the name of the Lord Jesus, giving thanks to God the Father through him (3:17).

4

Relationships in the New Life

Colossians 3–4

DIMENSION ONE:
WHAT DOES THE BIBLE SAY?

Answer these questions by reading Colossians 3

1. What does Paul tell the Colossians to set their hearts on? (3:1)

   He tells them to "set your hearts on things above."

2. Where is Christ? (3:1)

   Christ is "seated at the right hand of God."

3. Where is the life of the Colossians hidden? (3:3)

   Their life "is now hidden with Christ in God."

4. What have the Colossians put off, and what have they put on? (3:9-10)

   They have "taken off [the] old self with its practices and have put on the new self."

5. Who is all, and in all? (3:11)

   "Christ is all, and is in all."

6. How must the Colossians forgive one another? (3:13)

   They must forgive as the Lord has forgiven them.

7. What does Paul want to rule in their hearts? (3:15)

   Paul wants "the peace of Christ" to rule in their hearts.

8. Whom does Paul speak to in 3:18-22 and 4:1?

   He speaks to wives, husbands, children, fathers, slaves, and masters.

9. Whom do the Colossians work for, and who will reward them? (3:23-24a)

   The Colossians work for the Lord, who will reward them.

Answer these questions by reading Colossians 4

10. What does Paul ask that they pray for? (4:2-3)

    Paul asks that they pray that God may open for him "a door for our message."

11. Where is Paul? Why is he there? (4:3)

    Paul writes that he is in chains (prison) on account of "the mystery of Christ."

12. How are the Colossians to act toward outsiders? (4:5)

    They are to conduct themselves wisely toward outsiders.

13. Whom does Paul send to the Colossians? (4:7, 9)

    Paul sends Tychicus and Onesimus to the Colossians.

14. Who is with Paul in prison? (4:10)

    Aristarchus is with him in prison.

15. Who joins Aristarchus in sending greetings to the Colossians? (4:10-14)

    Mark, Justus, Epaphras, Luke, and Demas also send them greetings.

16. To whom does Paul ask the Colossians to send greetings at Laodicea? (4:15)

    He asks that they send greetings to "the brothers at Laodicea, and to Nympha and the church in her house."

17. What word does Paul send to Archippus? (4:17)

Paul tells him to "complete the work you have received in the Lord."

18. Who writes the closing greeting? (4:18)

Paul writes it in his own hand.

DIMENSION TWO: WHAT DOES THE BIBLE MEAN?

Colossians 3:1-4. "On things above" is probably a phrase that Paul has taken over from the false teachers. They used it to refer to a higher sphere of knowledge that they claimed was given to the elite inner circle of Christians through secret rites of initiation. Paul here turns the tables on the false teachers by using the phrase to affirm that the "things above" are not defined by the secrets of the select few but rather by the public revelation of God's saving purpose in the cross of Christ. "Things above" is the life of humble service to which all the saints are called in baptism. "Earthly things" is the life of self-centered privilege that the false teachers are tempting the Colossians to adopt. That which seems to be earthly, the cross of Christ, is actually heavenly. That which seems to be heavenly, false teaching, is actually earthly.

This radical reversal has been accomplished by the resurrection of Jesus Christ. His death, which from the point of view of world history is utter failure, is transformed by the Resurrection into complete victory. This victory is what Paul means when he says Christ is "seated at the right hand of God." "The right hand of God" is a conventional symbol for the power of God. In light of the Resurrection, the cross of Christ is the expression in human history of the invincible power of God.

Paul argues in this passage that the power of the Resurrection creates faith and raises the saints to life in Christ. But resurrection is only possible for those who die with Christ. So the power of the Resurrection is manifest in the saints as they die to self and take up the cross. The saints, then, participate in the power of the Resurrection, not by seeking their lives but by losing their lives in self-giving love. For Paul the victory of the saints over death is always in human history "hidden with Christ in God." The false teachers were offering the saints another victory based on their achievements, their superior wisdom, and their higher morality. They claimed that the Resurrection had freed them from the struggle and suffering of human history and given them a special status and privilege as divine beings.

To all this Paul says, "No!" For him the Resurrection puts the saints under the absolute lordship of Christ. Christ commands them to live a life of service in the world as they await the end of the world, in the confidence that God, who created all things in Christ, will redeem all things in Christ.

The saints witness to the power of the Resurrection, not by escaping into another world, but by living in this world as the agents of God's redeeming purpose revealed in Jesus Christ.

Colossians 3:5-11. As witnesses, the saints are called to live on earth as if they were already in heaven. They do this by conduct that points away from themselves to the ordering center of their lives: God revealed in Jesus Christ. The decisive mark of a saintly life is worship of God. The opposite of a saintly life is worship of self or idolatry. Paul does not understand idolatry narrowly as pagan worship but rather as selfish living. Since the saints have died to self and been raised to life in Christ, they "put to death" the old selfish ways: "sexual immorality, impurity, lust, evil desires and greed" (3:5).

Paul is probably drawing on a concept that he develops in Romans 7:7-8, namely, that all sins arise from the basic sin of covetousness. If this is the case, then Paul is arguing that when the self claims everything for its own satisfaction, the result is self-destruction. Self-centeredness breaks the relationship of the self to God and to others, so that the supporting interdependence of life is broken and life itself is ruined. Although Paul is probably referring to the Last Judgment in his reference to the coming wrath of God, this does not exclude a present experience of judgment that comes on all who claim for themselves what belongs to God alone.

Paul insists that Christian conduct cannot be compromised. A radical new center of life demands a radical break with the old way of living. He does not tell the Colossians to make a few minor adjustments but rather to put them to death. The logic of this directive is not exhausted by an analysis of the things he lists—"anger, rage, malice, slander, and filthy language from your lips"—but by considering how these things reveal that one does not belong to God but to the world, to the reign of "your earthly nature." Paul's thought here is reminiscent of the teaching of Jesus in Mark 7:14-15: "Listen to me, everyone, and understand this. Nothing outside a man can make him 'unclean' by going into him. Rather, it is what comes out of a man that makes him 'unclean.' " Human life is ruined by all acts that arise from serving any lord except the Lord Jesus Christ. In his service one knows the truth and speaks the truth, but in the service of other lords one knows the lie and speaks the lie.

The reference to taking off your old self and putting on the new self (3:9-10) must be set in the context of baptism, for the sacrament emphasizes that these actions are possible only in Christ. Without this emphasis on the grace of God, the recovery of the image of God becomes another form of works righteousness rather than the gift of God received by faith. As indicated in the student book, the image of God is what Jesus does as God's representative on earth. Christ is God's image, not for a select few who qualify for a special revelation, but for all humankind without distinction. All are included as sinners in the self-giving love of Christ, the forgiveness of sins. The ultimate source of human worth and dignity is not the achievement of culture or religion or class but Christ. Therefore, "Christ is all." The purpose of creation is not to separate humankind into hostile camps—"Greek or Jew, circumcised or uncircumcised, barbarian, Scythian, slave or free"—but to reconcile all in one body under Christ the Head. Therefore, Christ is "in all."

Colossians 3:12-17. The same logic that Paul follows to identify the distinctive marks of the old self he now follows to identify the marks of the new self. Just as the old self is self-seeking idolatry, so the new self is self-giving worship. He tells the Colossians to put on Christ, for Christ is the incarnation of "compassion, kindness, humility, gentleness and patience" (3:12). These qualities the Colossians know, not as the result of "hollow and deceptive philosophy" (2:8), but through the forgiveness of sins by the crucified Lord. What they know is what they are called on to practice. To put on Christ is to practice Christ: "Bear with each other and forgive whatever grievances you may have against one another. Forgive as the Lord forgave you" (3:13). Here again Paul sees no room for compromise. Since the saints have been forgiven, forgiveness of one another is no longer an option but an absolute necessity.

We can easily lose sight of the fact that Paul's purpose as he writes these paragraphs is not theoretical but practical. He is concerned about the false teaching that threatens to divide the church and to create confusion. His strategy is controlled by his theology, so he returns to basics—the revelation of God in Christ. The word that summarizes the fullness of God dwelling in Christ is *love.* Love here is not so much a human response as a divine action. Paul directs the Colossians to depend on that love, to "put on love," and thus to participate in the creative and redemptive power of God, "which binds them all together in perfect unity" (3:14).

Love is not an emotion or feeling but action for the welfare or peace of another. So to love is to give priority to the well-being of others, to live for others. What Paul fears is that the peace of Christ will be destroyed by the unloving words and deeds of the false teachers. They are to be resisted, not by clever arguments or by hostile attacks, but by responding to them in words and deeds that are devoted to their well-being. God's purpose for Paul and for the saints at Colosse is to give them peace. The Colossians and Paul participate in that purpose by loving one another, even the false teachers.

Peace, then, is not achieved by getting rid of the opposition or by winning an argument but by receiving the gift of God's love in Christ. The gift is not cheap, it is always the peace of Christ given "through his blood, shed on the cross" (1:20). To receive this gift is to take up the cross, to die to self by living for others. Yet through this incredible gift of God's love in Christ, God reconciles all things and brings all things together in one body. The only adequate response to such a gift is to be thankful.

Thanksgiving is the reflex action of those who depend on God's power and presence made manifest in the Lord Jesus Christ. Note the recurring direction to give thanks in 3:15-17: "be thankful," "with gratitude in your hearts to God," and "giving thanks to God the Father through him." The vehicle by which the power and presence of God are experienced by the Colossians is "the word of Christ," the gospel that they first heard from Epaphras and that they hear anew each time the church gathers for worship. Paul is confident that the gospel, "the word of truth," is more powerful than the "hollow and deceptive philosophy" of the false teachers. As "the word of Christ" is heard in the church, the church is built up by the truth and inspired by the truth to make a pleasing offering to God, to "sing psalms, hymns and spiritual songs with gratitude in [their] hearts to God." All that the saints are and all that they do is the result of the word of Christ dwelling in them. Their worship and their ministry are signs that God is at work in them. Therefore, they are not divided into quarreling factions by the lies of false teachers but rather are united in one harmonious body by the truth of faithful preachers of the gospel. It is as natural for the body of Christ to give thanks to God as it is for a physical body to breathe air.

Colossians 3:18–4:1. The household code presented to the Colossians in this passage can be misused in at least two ways. On the one hand, the rules can be lifted out of context and interpreted as absolutely binding on Christians at all times. On the other hand, they may be rejected out of hand as no longer having any value for contemporary Christians.

Paul recognized that the Colossians had to live within the social structures of the first century. For practically all of them the only social structure open to them as Christians was the family. In order for them to exist at all, a certain household order had to be maintained; and that required the acceptance of authority. In these verses Paul is simply urging the Colossians to support social stability by honoring the authorities who regulate their life.

Paul knew that the Spirit was at work transforming all of life, even the relationships within the established social order. The basic change occurred as persons were claimed by the spirit as the slaves of the Lord Jesus Christ. Thus, no matter what role one was assigned by society in the family, the decisive factor was not the role but the requirement to obey the Lord. The practical effect of this was to ascribe absolute authority to Christ alone and to make all other authorities subordinate to Christ. Also the absolute authority of Christ delivered those under authority (wives, children, slaves) from servility by giving them the highest dignity of serving the Lord in the performance of their societal duties. Thus, Paul in the form of the conventional morality of the first century affirms the unconventional faith that in Christ "God was pleased to have all his fullness dwell . . . and through him to reconcile to himself all things, whether things on earth or things in heaven, by making peace through his blood, shed on the cross" (1:19-20).

All that Paul has to say to the Colossians about their household responsibilities is colored by his conviction that "the day of Christ Jesus," the coming of Christ as the agent of judgment and redemption at the end of human history, is at hand. Therefore, Paul and the Colossians live in the hope that what God has begun in them in Christ, God will bring to completion in Christ. This confidence in God's ultimate victory includes the whole creation, which means God's saving purpose is not fulfilled until everything conforms to that purpose in self-giving love. This confidence does not lead to passive resignation but to active ministry so that now in the imperfections of human history the church may be a gracious sign of what awaits the whole creation at "the day of Christ Jesus." To live in hope is to accept one's specific role in the family as the opportunity to live now as if the end had already come. Faith in "the day of Christ Jesus," instead of taking the Christians out of the world, binds them to the world so that in their worldly service the world may know that they "have a Master in heaven."

Perhaps Paul is not spinning out a theory of family conduct but attacking the false teachers. Possibly one aspect of the false teaching was the claim that those who had gone through the secret rites of initiation and had attained the higher wisdom were delivered from the responsibilities of bodily existence in the family. If that was the case, then what we have here is a powerful counterattack by Paul based on his faith. For Paul, the public preaching of the gospel in word and sacrament set the Christian under the rule of Christ and empowered the Christian to witness to that rule in all family relationships.

Colossians 4:2-4. We see in these verses another expression of Paul's pastoral concern. The basic position of the false teachers was that salvation depended on human achievement instead of resting solely on the grace of God. Paul's direction to pray calls the Colossians to resist false teaching by clinging to the truth. Paul's reference to prayer in this context leads immediately to a statement about his imprisonment ("in chains"). Prayer for Paul is commitment to the rule of Christ that arouses the hostility of all other rulers and powers. Paul may be reminding the Colossians that just as Jesus' dependence on God in prayer led to the cross, so their dependence on God in prayer will lead them to share in Christ's suffering. Be that as it may, we cannot deny the fact that Paul does not ask them to pray for his release from prison but for his faithfulness in preaching the gospel.

Colossians 4:5-6. Paul assumes a positive stance toward the world in this passage. The saints are not called to abandon the world but to live in the world as witnesses to the Lord of the world. In relationship to the outsiders, to the world, they are to live the gospel and to speak the gospel. Here then is the beginning of an evangelistic strategy that rests on the assumption that just as the gospel is the fullness of God dwelling in Christ, so the spread of the gospel throughout the world is the rule of Christ embodied in the wise conduct and gracious speech of all who follow Christ.

Colossians 4:7-18. Contrary to surface appearance, Paul is not just stringing together a group of names as they come randomly to mind. Rather he is practicing his pastoral ministry as it expresses the new nature he has put on in Christ. The key to Paul's pastoral ministry is given in the word *receive* in 4:10. The Greek word used here has a rich meaning that is hardly expressed in the word *receive.* More correctly the word means "to offer hospitality, to provide shelter and food and drink." Probably included in this context is all that a modern traveler would expect to receive in a hotel plus the warmth and affection enjoyed in the intimate relationships of the family. The picture we have here is the church in any one place offering hospitality to persons from churches in other places as if they were all members of one extended family. This compassionate and efficient way of looking after the needs of Christian travelers was not just a cultural necessity because of the lack of public accommodation; it was also a responsibility that all the saints incurred by putting on the new nature in Christ. As God had received them in Christ, so in Christ they were called to receive one another.

In this connection the references to Onesimus and Archippus take on special meaning. As we learn from Paul's letter to Philemon, Onesimus was a runaway slave whom Paul was sending back to his master, Philemon. Paul dared to do this because he assumed that Philemon would respond hospitably according to his Christian duty rather than punitively according to his legal rights. The work that Archippus is urged to complete may be that of reconciliation between Onesimus and Philemon. That work is possible in a cruel and harsh world because the grace of God is with the church. "Here there is no Greek or Jew, circumcised or uncircumcised, barbarian, Scythian, slave or free, but Christ is all, and is in all" (3:11).

DIMENSION THREE:
WHAT DOES THE BIBLE MEAN TO ME?

Colossians 3:1-11—The Image of God

Paul uses the word *image* twice in Colossians, at 1:15 and at 3:10. In both instances he is influenced by Genesis 1:26-27 as he thinks in terms of God's image in creation. But it is important to keep in mind that Paul is not speculating about the beginning of life. Just as Genesis is a faithful affirmation about God's creative action in light of the Israelite experience of redemption at the Exodus, so Paul's understanding of Christ as the agent of creation arises from his experience of redemption in the cross of Christ.

How do we know anything about the beginning of life? Is it enough to say with Paul that all life begins with Christ? Does this mean that love is the source of life? Do we participate in creation by being agents of love? If so, how?

An important aspect of this discussion is the attitude of the Christian toward creation. The logic of biblical faith requires that we never exploit creation because it is the work of God's self-giving love. Is this a helpful way to view the creation today? What are the implications of this view for our stewardship of human and natural resources? What happens to creation when this view is ignored or contradicted? Is this sin? Why or why not?

Although the image of God is given to all humankind in creation, it is not automatic but may be lost or distorted. The Bible teaches that this happens when persons disobey God by living for self instead of living for others. Ask class members to reflect on the way selfishness blurs the image of God in us. Then discuss the cross as the love of God in Christ that enables one to die to self and live for others. Conclude by helping them explore what it means for us to live unselfishly in the world today.

Colossians 3:12-13—Forgiving One Another

Since Christian faith is not merely ideas about God but basically relationships to God, self, others, and the world, forgiveness must be explored in our relationships. Guide the discussion away from the duty to forgive by emphasizing how we experience forgiveness. Ask class members to tell of their experiences of forgiveness. A central concern in considering forgiveness should be the connection between receiving God's forgiveness and receiving forgiveness from others. Remind class members that God's forgiveness is revealed or made known in Jesus Christ. Does this suggest that God's forgiveness is made known today in our forgiveness of one another? What does this mean to us?

One critical issue to be considered in this regard is how our forgiveness of others relates to Christ's forgiveness of us. A common misunderstanding is that our forgiveness of one another is the condition for our receiving the forgiveness of Christ. This misunderstanding makes forgiveness an achievement of ours rather than a gift of God. One way to emphasize the danger of this misunderstanding is to discuss our need to be forgiven. Do we ever outgrow this need? Why or why not? Can we receive anything that we do not need? Is it possible that the only condition for receiving forgiveness is the acknowledgment of our need? Can we receive forgiveness without giving it to others? Explain your answers.

Colossians 3:18–4:1—Social Responsibility

Again the relational nature of Christian faith is the basic issue. Guide the discussion away from individual and private concerns to consider the corporate and public dimensions of Christian faith. Ask class members how Christian faith seems to involve one in ever-widening circles of concern: church, family, community, nation, world. What limit, if any, is there to God's love for the whole creation in Christ? If God's love is unlimited, does it follow that our responsibility has no limits? Explain your answer.

This discussion may be threatening to some class members. If this is the case, help them remember that Paul's raising of these issues with the Colossians produced conflict among the saints. The signs of tension and anxiety then as now are not to be suppressed or denied but welcomed as an indication that God is at work claiming us for ministry in the specific structures of our society. One way to deal positively with this matter is to move the discussion into a consideration of God's Spirit. In the biblical frame of reference Spirit is not a ghostly presence but the power of God at work in persons, calling them and equipping them for God's service in the world.

Ask a class member to read Jesus' address at Nazareth as recorded in Luke 4:16-21. Conclude the lesson by asking class members to reflect on life in the Spirit as life claimed and equipped for worldly ministry.

For what is our hope, our joy, or the crown in which we will glory in the presence of our Lord Jesus when he comes? Is it not you? Indeed, you are our glory and joy (2:19-20).

5

Comfort in Distress

1 Thessalonians 1–3

DIMENSION ONE:
WHAT DOES THE BIBLE SAY?

Answer these questions by reading
1 Thessalonians 1

1. Who sends the letter to whom? (1:1)

   Paul, Silas, and Timothy send the letter to "the church of the Thessalonians."

2. What does Paul remember about the Thessalonians? (1:3)

   He remembers their "work produced by faith, . . . labor prompted by love, and . . . endurance inspired by hope."

3. How did the gospel come to the Thessalonians? (1:5)

   The gospel comes to them in word, in power, in the Holy Spirit, and with deep conviction.

4. To whom do the Thessalonians become a model? (1:7)

   They become a model "to all the believers in Macedonia and Achaia."

Answer these questions by reading
1 Thessalonians 2

5. Where had Paul and his associates suffered and been insulted? (2:2)

   They were treated shamefully in Philippi.

6. Whom do Paul and his co-workers speak to please? (2:4)

   They speak to please God.

7. Why do Paul and those who serve with him as evangelists work day and night? (2:9)

   They worked day and night that they might not burden the Thessalonians.

8. What does Paul encourage, comfort, and urge the Thessalonians to do? (2:11-12)

   Paul encourages, comforts, and urges them "to live lives worthy of God."

9. Who has stopped Paul from coming to the Thessalonians? (2:18)

   Satan has stopped him.

10. What is Paul's "hope, . . . joy, or the crown in which we will glory" before the Lord Jesus at his coming? (2:19-20)

    The Thessalonians are his hope and joy and glory.

Answer these questions by reading
1 Thessalonians 3

11. Whom does Paul send from Athens to minister to their needs? (3:1-2)

    He sends Timothy.

12. What encourages Paul in his distress and persecution? (3:7)

    The faith of the Thessalonians encourages him in his distress and persecution.

13. Who may clear Paul's way to the Thessalonians? (3:11)

    God our Father and our Lord Jesus may clear his way.

14. Who strengthens the Thessalonians so they will be "blameless and holy in the presence of God"? When? (3:12-13)

The Lord strengthens them "when our Lord Jesus comes with all his holy ones."

DIMENSION TWO: WHAT DOES THE BIBLE MEAN?

1 Thessalonians 1:1. The student book points out that Paul uses the conventional form of a first-century letter to convey his message. Here he is clearly a man of his time, conforming to the norms and expectations of his society. But Paul is also a man who has been transformed by the reconciling love of God in Christ, so that he is always in tension with his social context. From the standpoint of what was customary in his world, Paul was a Jew who was separated from the Gentiles by insurmountable barriers of race, culture, and religion. But from the standpoint of the gospel, he was an agent of God's love, joined to the Gentiles by the irresistible power of grace in a universal community of peace.

1 Thessalonians 1:2-10. These verses are given extended treatment in the student book because they contain the heart of Paul's proclamation that is the basis for the rest of the letter. The focus of the proclamation is the action of God in Jesus Christ. The apostolic gospel is not the record of events in the past but the action of God whereby the history of Jesus is a present experience in the church. This dynamic use of God's saving action is made possible by the Holy Spirit; that is, God's present power enables Paul to preach Christ and inspires the Thessalonians to receive Christ. The Christ who is present in the Spirit is no fantasy but the Jesus who was crucified and raised from the dead.

Maybe in this earliest record of the faith and life of the church, Paul is addressing a problem that recurs again and again in church history. The problem is that some believers claim that the Spirit is their private possession because they have special spiritual gifts and unique spiritual knowledge. Paul counters this claim by insisting that the common experience of preaching and receiving the gospel is the supreme spiritual gift. The gospel is the only basis for authentic spiritual knowledge. All faithful preaching of the gospel is the work of the Holy Spirit, and all faithful response to the gospel is Spirit-inspired. According to Paul, every believer is in the Spirit and the Spirit is in every believer. The Spirit is the power of God by which the historical Jesus is present and available to the community of faith.

Faith, then, for Paul is sharing in the life of Jesus as God present in human history judging and redeeming all creation. Faith is a possibility because Jesus has been raised from the dead and in the power of the Spirit claims everything as Lord. Since the risen Lord is none other than the crucified Jesus, to confess him as Lord is to share in his suffering. Thus the power of the Spirit is manifest in the church in the faithful proclamation of the gospel and the steadfast endurance of affliction for the sake of the gospel.

Paul insists throughout this passage that the Holy Spirit, through the preaching and hearing of the gospel, creates a community that has clear and distinctive marks. The first mark is that it is a witnessing community from which the gospel, "the Lord's message," sounds forth. The second mark is that it is a fellowship in which what is proclaimed is practiced. As Paul says so pointedly of the Thessalonians, "your faith in God has become known everywhere. Therefore we do not need to say anything about it" (1:8). Here in precise language the apostle summarizes the evangelistic strategy that he lived consistently and challenged the church to pursue steadfastly.

The third mark of the spiritual church is the rejection of idols. This mark is nothing less than a declaration of war against every power that claims for itself what belongs exclusively to God. Participation in this warfare involves the believer in affliction, for it exposes those who confess Christ as Lord to the hostility of all other lords. The fourth mark is the service of God revealed in Jesus Christ. The service of God is the public acknowledgment of God's rule as the ultimate reality of human history and the final destiny of all creation.

The fifth mark of the community of faith is its confident hope that Christ, who has ascended into heaven, will come at the end of human history to complete the salvation that has already begun in the life of believers. Thus, the waiting of the community is not passive resignation to things as they are but active witnessing to the power of God as revealed in Jesus Christ. The expectation of a final conflict at the end of human history was a standard feature of Jewish literature of the first century. Paul uses this expectation to express his faith that in Christ the fulfillment of God's saving purpose has already begun and in Christ the beginning will be consummated. What was speculation about the end in Jewish literature in Paul is a vehicle for proclaiming his sure confidence that the God who has forgiven his sins in Jesus Christ is also the God who will complete the work of salvation in Jesus Christ.

Another standard feature of Jewish literature of the first century was judgment, or as Paul puts it, "the coming wrath." The assumption is that all will stand before God or God's agent at the Last Judgment, and all will be rewarded or punished according to their works. The disobedient will be cursed, and the obedient will be blessed. Again Paul uses conventional imagery to proclaim a distinctly Christian interpretation. The point is this: Just as the Christian has been forgiven of his or her sins by the love of God in Christ, so the love of God in Christ will deliver the believer from sin and death at the Last Judgment. The Christian stands now and at the end solely on the grace of God received by faith and witnessed to by preaching and hearing the gospel. The One who comes from heaven at the end is the One who has already come and who is present now to faith through the power of the Holy Spirit.

1 Thessalonians 2:1-12. The gospel Paul proclaims with such eloquence is also the gospel he lives with bold integrity. In these verses he subjects his ministry to the penetrating judgment of all that the Thessalonians know about his visit to them and all that they remember about his behavior with them. Where does he find the audacity to make the claims that pile up one after the other in these paragraphs? "Our visit to you was not a failure. . . . With the help of our God we dared to tell you his gospel in spite of strong opposition. . . . We are not trying to please men but God, who tests our hearts. . . . We were delighted to share with you not only the gospel of God but our lives. . . . We worked night and day in order not to be a burden to anyone. . . . You are witnesses, and so is God, of how holy, righteous and blameless we were among you who believed."

These audacious claims are not the self-congratulations of a self-righteous moralist but rather the confident witness of a faithful servant. They arise from Paul's faith that the God who called him into ministry also empowers him for ministry. Therefore, Paul's boldness arises not from self-confidence but from unshakable confidence in God. What the Thessalonians remember about Paul's visit and behavior is cataloged here so that they will be firmly established in their knowledge of God and their memory of God's grace. As is usually the case in the autobiographical sections of his letters, Paul is not calling attention to himself but rather focusing attention on his manner of life as the gracious result of Christ living in him.

Christ's life in Paul is Paul's faithful participation in Christ's death and resurrection. Paul dies with Christ to a manner of life pleasing to the world: error, uncleanness, guile, flattery, greed, human glory. He rises with Christ to a manner of life pleasing to God: courage, gentleness, self-giving, holy, righteous, blameless. All this is given concrete and specific expression in the fact that Paul does not demand of the Thessalonians the support and status that are rightfully his as an apostle. Rather, Paul renounces his rights in order to earn his living while preaching the gospel among them. Keep in mind that Paul is not giving a timeless precedent to be followed by all preachers of the gospel. Rather, Paul adopted this specific evangelistic strategy because of the unique demands of his situation.

The mode of life that is possible for Paul in Christ is also possible for all believers. Therefore, the claims that he makes for himself he makes for the church at Thessalonica. He exhorts and encourages and charges them "to live lives worthy of God" because God is powerfully present in them in the Holy Spirit. The community of faith does not have two standards of conduct: one more rigorous for the apostle and one less rigorous for his converts. On the contrary, both apostle and converts have their faithful existence in the self-giving love of Christ; and both come under the same mandate to live as obedient servants of Christ in the world. In Christ the true glory of God is revealed as humble service; and in Christ, Paul and the faithful community at Thessalonica enter into that true glory by emptying themselves in acts of self-giving love.

The pattern of life Paul reflects in his ministry and the pattern he holds up before the Thessalonians is Christ. But the pattern is not an ethical ideal remembered from the past; it is a living presence encountered wherever the Holy Spirit empowers faithful preaching of the gospel and inspires obedient hearing of the gospel. Thus, this entire section is Paul's testimony to the new creation that he and the Thessalonians share by dying and rising with Christ.

1 Thessalonians 2:13–3:13. Although it is true that Paul is not developing a systematic theological treatise in this letter, it is a mistake to conclude that he is simply jotting down his random thoughts. He intended this letter as careful instruction to the church, to be read by the Thessalonians in a congregational setting and to be shared with other congregations. Therefore, it is important to discover the unifying theme that binds the parts of this section into a coherent whole. The conflict that breaks out opposing God's saving action in Jesus Christ and the suffering that the church experiences as a result of the conflict seem to be the central issue here.

The word Paul uses to refer to this suffering is *persecuted/persecution.* Paul uses this word in 3:4 to refer to the suffering of the Thessalonians and in 3:7 to refer to his suffering. Again, *persecution* is a technical term that is taken from Jewish literature of the first century. There it is used to refer to the suffering of the faithful in the final conflict between good and evil that begins when God comes to establish justice and peace throughout all creation. Paul redefines *persecution* by stating that the suffering of Christ and Christ's followers indicates that the final victory of God has already entered the course of human history. The cross of Christ and the crosses borne by Christians because of their loyalty to Christ are no longer signs of defeat. Rather, they are witnesses to the final triumph of God over all enemies, even sin and death. Thus, a conventional symbol of suffering in Jewish literature becomes, in Paul's thought, a vehicle for proclaiming the power of God's love. That power is not manifest in the clash of armies but in the cross of Christ. Christians participate in that power and share in its victory by suffering with Christ.

With this background in mind, the logical progression of Paul's thought throughout this section becomes clear. In 2:13-16, he points out that in his preaching the Thessalonians were confronted not with a human word but with the word of God. The word of God does not refer to sacred writings but to the public proclamation of God's saving purpose, revealed and carried out in Jesus Christ. That purpose is being accomplished among the Thessalonians because the Holy Spirit is at work in them, enabling them to hear and obey the gospel, the word of God. The saving work of God stirred up opposition in Judea when it was revealed in Jesus and confessed among his followers. So now among the Gentiles the preaching and hearing of the word is opposed by the enemies of God.

The word of God draws opposition because of its universal offer of salvation without regard for racial, religious, social, or cultural distinctions. Those who seek to restrict salvation to their own group on the basis of human ethical and liturgical conditions are judged by the gospel. They must either die to their prejudices or get rid of the messengers who confront them with their resistance to God's purpose. The persecution of the church because of participating in God's saving work is not a sign of defeat. Rather, the church's persecution shows that sinful rebellion against God is revealed and judged by God. The wrath of God, contrary to what seems to be the case, does not come on the persecuted but on the persecutors. The fact that they are alienated from God and separated from God's people by self-righteous attitudes and cruel acts looks forward now to the judgment that awaits them at the end of history.

In 2:17-20, Paul applies this interpretation of *persecution* to his imprisonment. He is prevented from returning to Thessalonica, not by the accidents of history, but by the conflict that divides history into two realms of power: the reign of God and the reign of Satan. Since Paul has been called and commissioned by Christ to be God's messenger to the Gentiles, his whole life is under attack by the forces of evil, which seek to frustrate God's work. But the reign of Satan is itself an illusion and deceit; for in Christ, God has claimed the whole universe as God's realm of redemption.

In Christ's death and resurrection, God has shown that the power that determines the fate of the universe is not sinful rebellion but faithful obedience. The final victory of God over evil is not a far-off fantasy but a present reality in the life of the church, in the saints at Thessalonica who have been called into God's kingdom and glory. This harvest of his ministry comforts Paul in his imprisonment and inspires him to burst forth in a defiant affirmation of confidence in God's victory: "For what is our hope, our joy, or the crown in which we will glory in the presence of our Lord Jesus when he comes? Is it not you? Indeed, you are our glory and joy" (2:19).

However, as Paul indicates in 3:1-5, the final victory is only looked forward to in the faith of the church. The full consummation is not until Christ comes at the end. At any moment the church under attack may lose heart and fall away from its dependence on God. This possibility of backsliding creates Paul's fears for the Thessalonians and prompts him to send Timothy to establish them in the faith and to exhort them "that no one would be unsettled by these trials."

Paul sends a messenger of the gospel to them so that in hearing the gospel they will be sustained in the struggles against the enemies of God. Paul does not mislead the Thessalonians with a promise that everything will turn out all right. Instead, he reminds them that persecution for the sake of the gospel is what he told them to expect when he first preached in Thessalonica. His troubles and theirs are nothing more than the common lot of all believers.

Paul does not doubt the ultimate outcome of the struggle. That has already been settled in Christ. The only doubtful thing is whether the Thessalonians will remain faithful or be tempted in affliction to trust themselves or some other power. What troubles Paul is not the persecution but the possibility that in trying to escape persecution the church will become unfaithful and his labor will be in vain.

In 3:6-10, Paul reports that the effect of Timothy's return from Thessalonica has increased his ability to endure persecution. Timothy brings good news about the Thessalonians' relationship to God—their faith. Faith is the recurring theme in this paragraph. What Paul hears from Timothy is that the gospel is doing its work in the church of the Thessalonians. God is enabling the church to stand fast in persecution, to minister in love, to reach out to Paul in his distress. So Paul's anxiety gives way to thanksgiving; his affliction to joy; his frustration to determination. The ministry of Paul to the Thessalonians has now come full circle, as in the providence of God he gratefully receives their ministry to him.

As Paul moves to the climax of this section, his focus shifts in 3:11-12 from the faithful witness of the church in persecution to the assurance of the church's life in the future. The basis of that assurance is the absolute dependability of God to direct and empower the church now and forever. The God whose love is revealed in Christ Jesus is the God to whom Paul entrusts his future and to whom he commends the church. His prayer for himself and for his converts is not that they will be delivered from the struggle but that in the struggle they will increase and abound in love so that God's work of salvation will be completed in them. He wastes no time in idle speculation about the end because the end has already come in Christ Jesus. The one whom they await in hope is none other than the One whose love sustains them now and will finally establish their hearts unblamable in holiness before God.

DIMENSION THREE:
WHAT DOES THE BIBLE MEAN TO ME?

1 Thessalonians 1:6-7; 2:14-17; 3:1-7
The Persecution of the Church

Call attention to the issue of persecution as it arises naturally in the interpretation of the verses listed above. One way of considering the church as a community involved in suffering for the sake of the gospel is to ask a class member to read these verses aloud.

Give the other class members these instructions about how to respond to the reading of the verses: (1) Listen for any fresh meaning or emphasis as the Scripture is read. (2) Allow the words to create visual images so that you will see scenes of conflict and struggle as the text is heard. (3) Get in touch with the emotional reactions that the subject of persecution touches off so that your feeling level of interpretation will be tapped.

After a time of reflection, ask what fresh or surprising things the class members have heard as they listened to Paul's words about persecution. Resist the temptation to tell class members in advance what to hear. Allow them to do the hearing, and create an atmosphere of trust in which what they hear is honored and received.

Move quickly from considering ideas to try to visualize the action that is reported in the text. Have the class members report descriptively what they saw in their mind's eye as the Scripture was read. This task may be quite difficult as we are more familiar with abstractions than with visual images. But it will be worth the effort as class members become involved in a creative use of the imagination to reconstruct Paul's experience of affliction, not as an idea, but as an experience that believers of all times and places have in common.

The last step in the process will be to acknowledge the emotional impact of the Scripture on the hearers. Call the class members' attention to the emotional quality of such words as *suffering, persecution, joy, killed, wrath, torn away, intense longing, we could stand it no longer,* and *distress.* Remind them that Paul, Timothy, Silas, and the Thessalonians were real flesh-and-blood persons who experienced the same passions and the same temptations as we experience. These people become more helpful to us as we join them in the common human feelings of distress and hope and doubt and comfort and joy and boasting.

1 Thessalonians 3:6-8
The Comfort of the Church

This dimension of Paul's witness needs to be thoroughly explored by class members. If the emphasis of the lesson falls exclusively on persecution, some may be left with a feeling of despair. On the other hand, if comfort is interpreted as escape from the struggles of Christian faith, some may conclude that persecution must be avoided at all costs.

The following suggestions will help you guide the lesson between these pitfalls. Ask class members to tell of experiences that have led them to seek comfort. Which experiences are ours because of our common humanity? Which are ours because of our Christian commitment?

Ask how class members have received comfort in the Christian community. In all likelihood the responses will concentrate on personal relationships that have been comforting in times of distress. Ask them to describe persons who are able to give comfort. Is it necessary to receive comfort in order to give comfort?

The discussion of the personal nature of comfort may be concluded by asking class members to think about Jesus as a comforting presence. Remind them that Jesus did not seek to suffer but sought to comfort others and as a result was exposed to suffering on behalf of others. What attitudes and actions in the church keep us from being a community of comfort? Are these attitudes and actions related to our preoccupation with achieving success in the world? with our neglect of hearing and obeying the gospel? How is the gospel comforting?

May God himself, the God of peace, sanctify you through and through. May your whole spirit, soul and body be kept blameless at the coming of our Lord Jesus Christ (5:23).

— 6 —

The Coming of the Lord

1 Thessalonians 4–5

DIMENSION ONE: WHAT DOES THE BIBLE SAY?

Answer these questions by reading 1 Thessalonians 4

1. What have the Thessalonians learned from Paul? (4:1)

   They have learned "how to live in order to please God."

2. Who gives the Holy Spirit to the Thessalonians? (4:8)

   God gives them the Holy Spirit.

3. Whom does God teach them to love? (4:9)

   God teaches them "to love each other."

4. On whom are they to be dependent? (4:12)

   They are not to be dependent on anybody.

5. What does Paul believe about Jesus? (4:14)

   He believes "that Jesus died and rose again."

6. How will the Lord come from heaven? (4:16)

   He will come "with a loud command, with the voice of the archangel and with the trumpet call of God."

7. Who will rise first? (4:16)

   "The dead in Christ will rise first."

8. What will happen to those who are alive when the Lord comes from heaven? (4:17)

They will be caught up "in the clouds to meet the Lord."

Answer these questions by reading 1 Thessalonians 5

9. How will "the day of the Lord" come? (5:2)

   It will come "like a thief in the night."

10. Why won't the day of the Lord surprise the faithful? (5:4)

    It will not surprise the faithful, for they "are not in darkness."

11. What are the Thessalonians to do in preparation for the day of the Lord? (5:6)

    They are to "be alert and self-controlled."

12. What are they to put on? (5:8)

    They are to put on "faith and love as a breastplate, and the hope of salvation as a helmet."

13. What are the Thessalonians to do for one another? (5:11)

    The Thessalonians are to encourage and build up one another.

14. Whom does Paul beseech them to respect, hold in highest regard, and love? (5:12-13)

    He beseeches them to respect, hold in highest regard, and love those who work hard among them and are over them in the Lord.

15. With whom does Paul urge them to be patient? (5:14)

He urges them to be patient with everyone, including the idle, the timid, and the weak.

16. When are the Thessalonians to give thanks? (5:18)

They are to "give thanks in all circumstances."

17. How are they to greet all the brothers? (5:26)

They are to greet them "with a holy kiss."

DIMENSION TWO: WHAT DOES THE BIBLE MEAN?

1 Thessalonians 4:1-8. A key word in this section is *sanctified* (or *holy*, verse 3). It refers in this context to the action of God whereby the believers are made holy. Sanctification or holiness is God's will for all the church, the whole people of God. The point that Paul is making is that God not only establishes a right relationship in Christ but also nurtures that relationship, so that faithful persons are enabled to live faithfully. Just as the beginning of Christian existence is a dynamic relationship to God, so Christian existence is sustained and nurtured in a dynamic relationship to God.

Since Christian faith in its beginning and in its continuing growth is a relationship of trust in God's love revealed in Jesus Christ, all Paul's instructions to the Thessalonians are in Jesus Christ. This means that Paul is motivated and controlled by the self-giving love of God as he gives the Thessalonians instruction about how they ought "to live in order to please God." The method of Paul's teaching is Christ. Although he is introducing a specific problem— sexual morality—his strategy is to remind the Thessalonians of the gospel in the confidence that, when they remember the love of Christ, they will conform to that love in all their relationships. Therefore, sanctification is not a static condition but a process of growth in which the faithful become what they are by doing more and more what they have always done.

The background for Paul's specific teaching about sexual morality in the marital relationship is his understanding that in Christ, God claims the whole creation for holy obedience. This means that the husband does not exercise absolute control over his body or over the body of his wife. Rather, in the use of his body and his wife's body to express sexual love, he is controlled by the sovereign will of God. Both husband and wife belong to God. Therefore, their sexual relationships are not the occasion for "passionate lust" but for being "holy and honorable." Because of the social conventions of the time, the husband is singled out by Paul. But contrary to those conventions, the husband is told to keep in mind his marital and sexual responsibilities rather than his privileges. This not only applies to conduct within the marriage but also prohibits sexual relations with another man's wife. The position Paul develops consistently is that God's self-giving love in Christ has created a community where the sole norm for human behavior is that same self-giving love. Any self-centered sexual relationship is prohibited because it rejects God's call and is a decision to live in conformity to the spirit of the world rather than in obedience to the Spirit of God.

1 Thessalonians 4:9-12. Again Paul's understanding of Christian nurture as a dynamic process is clear in these verses. He is not simply being tactful as he states that the Thessalonians have no need for anyone to write them about loving one another. Rather, he is pursuing the logic of his basic position that Christian existence is primarily God's work and only secondarily human responsibility. Paul avoids the heresy of self-righteousness by reminding the Thessalonians that the source of their love for one another is not some inherent or acquired human virtue but the gift of God's love. Therefore, when he instructs them to love one another more and more, he is calling them to recover anew the center of their existence in the self-giving love of God and to live out of that center by giving themselves in acts of ministry.

Paul does not back away from giving specific advice about the disciplines that will help the Thessalonians love one another. They probably arise from his familiarity with their circumstances and should be read as counsel for a particular time and place rather than as timeless principles for Christian conduct. Controlling the specific teaching is the pattern of Christ's life that shapes and empowers Paul's ethical teaching. "To lead a quiet life, to mind your own business and to work with your hands" (4:11) is to die with Christ to a self-centered existence and to rise with Christ to a God-centered life for others. Paul tells the Thessalonians to follow this kind of gospel-ordered life because it is a life of dependence on God. Such a life sets the church free to serve God in the world. Just as Paul's understanding of the gospel is the result of his experience of God's love, so his understanding of evangelism is the embodiment of God's love in a loving community in order that the world may experience God's saving power.

1 Thessalonians 4:13-18. The distinctive feature of Paul's teaching about the last things is not the language of imagery that he draws from Jewish literature but the content that is determined by his faith in Jesus Christ. Faith in Jesus, who died and rose again, is the controlling center of Paul's teaching about the coming of the Lord, the resurrection of the dead in Christ, and the fate of those who are alive at his coming.

Jesus' death is the revelation in human history of God's love, and his resurrection is the experience of that love as the ultimate power of the universe. Thus, by faith, the Christian takes part in God's ultimate purpose—to bring all creation under the rule of love. What is experienced by the Christian now is only partial. Love is not acknowledged universally, nor is it practiced perfectly. Therefore, Christian faith in Jesus Christ's death and resurrection inevitably leads to the Christian hope that Christ will come to bring to full realization God's saving purpose for the whole creation.

For Paul and the Thessalonian church confessing Christ as Lord in a world where his lordship was contested by the forces of sin and death required that they live in hope that Christ would come soon to establish his lordship over the whole creation. However, hope in the coming of the Lord quickly created a crisis for the Thessalonians. Some believers died before the Lord's coming. Did this mean that they would not take part in the final victory of God over sin and death at the day of the Lord's coming? The survivors were not only stricken by sorrow over the loss of loved ones but also haunted by the possibility that these loved ones had hoped in vain.

Paul responds by going to the heart of the matter. Christian hope is not hope that one will be alive at the coming of the Lord but hope that the Lord who has come in love will return in love. The last word about those who die in Christ is not death but life, not judgment but grace, not hate but love. Therefore, those who die in the Lord are not separated from God's love by death. Rather, they are so securely united to God in love that death is no longer final destruction but sleep before the dawning of the day. Just as the resurrection of Christ is the sign of the victory of the cross, so it is the sign that the victory of Christ will be extended by the resurrection of the dead to include all God's people.

The authority for Paul's teaching on this matter is not speculation about the future but "the Lord's own word." Here he is not referring to the words of the historical Jesus as the ultimate sanction for Christian hope. That would be entirely contrary to Paul's understanding of the dynamic presence of the living Lord in the life of the church. Paul's authority is the gospel, the preaching of God's saving action in Jesus Christ whereby the church is confronted with God's call and empowered by God's Spirit to respond in obedient service. The Lord whom the church meets in the preaching of the gospel is the Lord who awaits the church at the end of human history and who sustains, empowers, and comforts the church through all the challenges and trials of its earthly pilgrimage. "The Lord's own word," the gospel, is the basis for Paul's assurance about the destiny of those who have fallen asleep and the fate of those who are still alive.

Paul is writing in this section to influence the thought and action of the survivors at Thessalonica. He wants them to have no doubt about their deceased brothers' and sisters' participation in God's final victory and no doubt about their own. Paul does this, not by admonishing or urging them, but by proclaiming to them the good news of the Lord's coming. The survivors have no reason to grieve over those who have fallen asleep and no reason to fear for their own welfare because God has claimed them and will claim them as God's own. This is what Paul means when he declares that "the dead in Christ will rise first. After that, we who are still alive and are left will be caught up together with them in the clouds to meet the Lord in the air" (4:16-17). His words proclaim the infinite power and presence of God that transcend history and give to history its ultimate meaning and purpose. The words have the potential to strengthen and encourage those who are frustrated by sorrow and discouraged by persecution because they point beyond themselves to the invincible power and the unfailing compassion of God.

The future of the church is assured by living out of the relationship of trust that God creates in Jesus Christ. Nothing in life or in death can destroy that relationship. In life and in death "we will be with the Lord forever." Since Paul and the Thessalonians share the riches of God's presence in the Lord Jesus Christ, they speak a common language and can encourage one another.

1 Thessalonians 5:1-11. In this section Paul addresses the tendency on the part of some believers to become preoccupied with predicting the time of the Lord's coming. This tendency was a critical problem at Thessalonica because the day of the Lord was delayed longer than they had expected. Paul begins by reminding the Thessalonians that they do not need to be informed on this subject because no one knows and no one can know. Since the day of the Lord will mark the end of human history, it cannot be charted as another event in human history. The day of the Lord is the unconditioned and unpredictable action of God that brings history to its perfection by conforming it to the will and purpose of the Creator.

For Paul the ultimate will and purpose of the Creator have already been established in creation through the cross and resurrection of Jesus. Therefore, the coming of the Lord at the end of history, although always known only to God as to time, is already anticipated in the faith of the church. "The day of the Lord will come like a thief in the night" on all who reject the lordship of Christ and live according to the standards of the world. For such the day of the Lord will mean destruction and pain and the reversal of all that they have assumed to be true, namely that peace and security can be achieved in the world on the basis of the world's values. They will be surprised to discover that their lives have been ruined by their idolatrous loyalties. They will not be able to escape from the judgment of the true and living God.

On the other hand, the faithful will experience no surprise at the day of the Lord; for the One who comes will be the One in whose service they have lived on earth. The dualism of light and darkness that Paul uses here to contrast the difference in quality between faith and unfaith is basically ethical. To be a child of the light is to live according to the day; to be a child of darkness is to live according to the night. What is revealed at the day of the Lord is that the night has been overcome by the day. Therefore, those who live by the night perish with the night; and those who live by the day are saved by the day.

Preparation for the coming of the Lord, then, has nothing to do with special revelations of times and seasons but rather is solely a matter of obeying the light in the daily routine of human existence. Paul's practical concerns prevail in these verses. He has no interest in speculation about the eternal punishment of the wicked or the eternal blessing of the righteous. Paul's interest focuses on reminding the Thessalonians of who they are and of what they must do. They are children of the day, which simply means that they have been created out of nothing by the incredible love of God in Christ Jesus. They must become what they are by living by the day, by keeping alert and self-controlled, which means that Christ has empowered them to live the life of love in the world. Now that the day of self-giving love, the day of wakefulness and self-control, has already dawned in human history, the worst thing that one can do is to fall back into the night of self-indulgence and to live as if the night of sleep and drunkenness still reigned.

"But, since we belong to the day" are the pivotal words in this text. They summarize the saving action of God that has changed everything for the church, and they indicate the firm foundation on which Christian conduct and Christian hope are built. The church belongs to the day, that is, to Christ because Christ has come and continues to come as the Lord of all creation. Self-control or self-restraint is possible because Christ constrains the church. The church is armed with faith and love because Christ reveals that God is trustworthy and invincible. The church is protected by hope because Christ's self-giving love provides all that the church needs now and forever.

What the church already experiences because of its ownership by Christ is a foretaste of what the church will receive fully at the day of the Lord. No matter what may happen in the future, nothing can prevent the promise of salvation in Christ from being fulfilled in Christ. The ground of this assurance is the fact that Jesus Christ's death for the church enables the church to live with Christ in this life and in the life to come. This clear and compelling proclamation of the gospel controls Paul's thought about the day of the Lord. He commends this gospel to the Thessalonians as they strive to remain faithful to their calling: "Therefore encourage one another and build each other up, just as in fact you are doing" (5:11).

1 Thessalonians 5:12-22. Paul's Christ-centered approach to pastoral care continues in these verses as he asks, admonishes, and urges the church about matters of order and discipline. Although not all have the same responsibilities for ordering the life of the community, all are accountable to the Lord for their relationships to one another. Leaders have their opportunity to lead "in the Lord," and it is "in the Lord" that members of the congregation are mandated to respect and esteem those in authority. In this context the phrase *in the Lord* refers to the self-giving love of God

as the power that creates the church as a corporate entity and the norm against which all corporate activities are evaluated. Officials of the church exercise authority only in so far as they are agents of Christ's love. They are to be respected and esteemed, not because they hold office, but because they labor and work for the good of the community.

By reading between the lines here we can find the real troubles that beset the church: conflict among the members, idleness, timidity, weakness, and impatience. Paul sizes up the situation as one in which the church is just as much at risk from impetuous reaction to those who cause trouble as it is from the troublemakers themselves. The mark of his genius is that he does not take sides. Rather, he brings all parties under the imperatives that arise from their common loyalty to Christ and their mutual responsibility to build up the body of Christ: be at peace, be patient, "be kind to each other and to everyone else."

But the power that binds them to one another does not come from concentrating on their human relationships. It comes rather from their relationship to God in Christ Jesus. The actions of their responsible community life are those that bind them to God as obedient servants: being joyful always, praying continually, giving thanks in all circumstances.

These actions are nothing more than the response that the Holy Spirit causes in the church. They supply the life of the church, for through them the power of God provides for all the ministries the church requires. So Paul warns the church not to quench the Spirit because the only life it has is life in the Spirit.

Among the most necessary ministries is prophesying, for the intelligent interpretation and application of the gospel under the guidance of the Spirit is the way the church is confronted with the claim of God on its life. But not everyone who claims to prophesy is speaking in the Spirit. So every utterance must be tested by "the word of the Lord," that is, by the received traditions about Jesus. Whatever agrees with that message is to be conserved as good; whatever does not agree with it is to be rejected as evil.

1 Thessalonians 5:23-28. In these concluding verses Paul practices what he has preached throughout the letter—unshakable confidence in the power of God to complete in Christ the work of salvation God has already begun in Christ in the church. Paul has said all that he knows to say in proclamation and exhortation. Now nothing more remains except to commend the saints at Thessalonica to the God whose love binds them all together and assures them that they will be kept holy and peaceful and sound and blameless until the coming of the Lord. Since everything depends on God, the most important thing Paul can do for the Thessalonians is to pray for them; and that is the most important thing they can do for him. Because they are at peace with God, they can greet one another with the kiss of peace. Thus, the grace of Jesus Christ is with them, not as an idea, but as life in a community of faith and love.

DIMENSION THREE:
WHAT DOES THE BIBLE MEAN TO ME?

1 Thessalonians 4:13-18—The Coming of the Lord

Ask class members to reflect on the death and resurrection of Jesus as the clue to understanding God's purpose for all creation. Consider the inclusiveness of Jesus' death. Jesus did not die for the godly but for the ungodly, not for the righteous but for the unrighteous, not for the holy but for the unholy, not for saints but for sinners. This line of thought may be expanded to include not only the church but all humanity in God's saving purpose and not only humanity but the whole created order as the object of redemption. Any purely personal or merely church-oriented understanding of Jesus' death is an inadequate interpretation of the love of God in Christ.

Reflection on the meaning of Jesus' death leads naturally into a discussion of his resurrection. The victory of Jesus Christ over sin and death is inclusive in that it is a sign that the love revealed in Jesus' cross is victorious over all the enemies of God and all threats to human existence. Is it possible to believe in the Resurrection as God's ultimate victory over evil and exclude any part of the human family and any part of creation from that victory?

This kind of reflection may open class members to a new appreciation of the breathtaking scope of the salvation Paul experienced in Jesus Christ. Paul, the devout Jew, could not be saved without the Gentiles, that is, without the whole human family. Can we as Christians experience the fullness of salvation in isolation from any of our brothers and sisters in the human family? It would seem, in the light of Paul's witness to the gospel, that any interpretation of the Resurrection that consigns a part of the human family or a part of creation to destruction is an inadequate understanding of God's victorious love.

But the facts of human experiences and the facts of the natural order contradict the faithful interpretation of the death and resurrection of Jesus. Pockets of sin remain in our personal and corporate life. The whole creation is distorted by our sinful rebellion against God. Death reigns, not simply as a natural end to life, but as God's judgment. So the salvation that the church experiences by faith and by faith announces to the world is incomplete and imperfect and awaits the fulfillment of the coming of the Lord at the end of human history. How can we continue to proclaim the love of God revealed in Jesus' death and resurrection without also proclaiming that love as the power that will bring all creation to fulfillment in obedience to God?

Ask class members to reflect on what this line of thought suggests about our attitude to criminals, to persons with disabilities, and to those whom we dismiss as our enemies. Have we neglected Paul's teaching about the coming of the Lord because it challenges our prejudices and our narrow preoccupation with our welfare?

1 Thessalonians 5:1-11
Preparation for the Lord's Coming

Paul expected the Lord to come soon, probably in Paul's lifetime; but he resisted all efforts to set a precise time for the coming. So that class members can see this same emphasis in Jesus' teaching, ask a member of the class to read aloud Mark 13:28-37. Paul shared the understanding of the end that is ascribed to Jesus in this passage. One problem this creates for us is how we can maintain the same urgency and eager expectation now that the coming of the Lord has been delayed almost two thousand years. What kind of problem is this for class members? How do they respond to the problem?

Some persons simply reject the whole notion of the Lord's coming as fantastic speculation that has no relevance for our modern life as Christians. This response impoverishes the church because it neglects a central aspect of Christian hope. Reflect on the possibility that Paul's sense of urgency and eager expectation do not come from the fact that he thought the Lord would come soon. Rather, Paul thought the Lord would come soon because he had experienced such a major re-orientation in his life that his whole manner of thinking and acting was dominated by that event. Has our Christian faith produced a similar radical re-orientation in our lives? If we cannot adopt Paul's timetable for the coming of the Lord, how can we recover his sense of urgency and eager expectation?

How does the church today prepare for the Lord's coming? Is the only adequate preparation for the Lord's coming a life that is lived as if he were already here? By faith it is possible for us to live with the Lord now. Does this mean that he is present in all our experiences? How do we practice the Lord's presence? Do we experience his presence as love? Is his love already the judgment of God on everything that is unloving? Is his love also the blessing of God on everything that is loving? Does the fact that we are judged and redeemed by love free us from all anxiety, so that we look forward to the coming of the Lord with rejoicing and thanksgiving? Paul tells us the conclusion of the matter is that the way of the Lord's coming is love, and we are prepared for his coming by receiving and practicing that love.

Now may the Lord of peace himself give you peace at all times and in every way. The Lord be with all of you (3:16).

— 7 —

Christian Life Between the Times

2 Thessalonians

DIMENSION ONE:
WHAT DOES THE BIBLE SAY?

**Answer these questions by reading
2 Thessalonians 1**

1. Of what does Paul boast? (1:4)

   He boasts of the perseverance and faith of the Thessalonian church in their persecutions and trials.

2. For what do the Thessalonians suffer? (1:5)

   They suffer for the kingdom of God.

3. To what end does Paul pray for the Thessalonians? (1:11)

   He prays that God will make them "worthy of his calling" and will "fulfill every good purpose of yours and every act prompted by your faith."

**Answer these questions by reading
2 Thessalonians 2**

4. Who must come before the Lord comes? (2:3)

   The man of lawlessness, the man doomed to destruction, must come first.

5. Who does the man of lawlessness proclaim himself to be? (2:4)

   He proclaims himself to be God.

6. Who will overthrow and destroy the lawless one? (2:8)

   The Lord Jesus will overthrow and destroy him.

7. How will the lawless one come? (2:9-10)

   He will come "in accordance with the work of Satan," displaying "all kinds of counterfeit miracles, signs and wonders, and in every sort of evil."

8. Why does Paul give thanks? (2:13)

   He gives thanks because God chose the Thessalonians "from the beginning . . . to be saved."

9. To what are the Thessalonians to hold? (2:15)

   They are to hold to the teachings that Paul passed on to them.

10. Who will encourage their hearts "and strengthen [them] in every good deed and word"? (2:16-17)

    Our Lord Jesus Christ and God our Father will comfort their hearts "and strengthen [them] in every good deed and word."

**Answer these questions by reading
2 Thessalonians 3**

11. For what does Paul request prayer? (3:1-2)

    He requests prayer "that the message of the Lord may spread rapidly and be honored" and that he and his associates "may be delivered from wicked and evil men."

12. Who is faithful? (3:3)

    "The Lord is faithful."

13. What will the Lord do? (3:3)

    He will strengthen the Thessalonians and protect them from evil.

14. In whom does Paul have confidence? (3:4)

    He has confidence in the Lord.

15. What does Paul tell the idle to do? (3:12)

    He tells them "to settle down and earn the bread they eat."

16. What are the Thessalonians to do to anyone who refuses to obey what Paul says in this letter? (3:14)

    They are not to "associate with him" or her.

DIMENSION TWO: WHAT DOES THE BIBLE MEAN?

2 Thessalonians 1:1-2. These opening verses of salutation and greeting reproduce the introductory verses of First Thessalonians almost word for word. Although nothing new needs to be added here in the way of commentary, the central place of grace and peace in Paul's thought can always be profitably reviewed. Two ideas to keep in mind are: (1) grace is the saving power of God revealed in Jesus Christ; (2) peace is the result of that power in the lives of those who believe. Wherever God's action is revealed, there is grace; and wherever a response of faith is elicited by that action, there is peace. Since the church presupposes the action of God and the response of faith, the church is in its very essence a community of grace and peace.

2 Thessalonians 1:3-4. For Paul thanksgiving is never a matter of making a list of the good things one is privileged to enjoy. Rather, thanksgiving is an acknowledgment of the goodness of God revealed in the existence of a community where "faith is growing more and more" and "the love every one . . . has for each other is increasing." In fact, as the content of these verses reveals, the circumstances of the Thessalonian church are the exact reverse of those good times we usually associate with thanksgiving. The saints are enduring persecution and trials because of their relationship to God. Yet, in that relationship they are empowered by God to remain steadfast and faithful.

God's goodness is shown in human history in God's self-giving love in Christ, which creates a community where that love is trusted and practiced. Paul's thanksgiving for the Thessalonians is his affirmation of the community where his faith in God grows more and more and his love for the sisters and brothers is increasing. Giving thanks in this context is not a formal exercise but an expression of those ties that bind the apostle to God in faithful dependence and to community in loving service. In this sense the apostle "ought always to thank God" for the saints at Thessalonica.

As the student book observes, the word *boast* is an important emphasis of Paul. He understands human exis-

tence as always taking place in a context of allegiance to some power outside the self. If one boasts of worldly achievements, boasting reveals bondage to the world. But if one boasts of God's grace and peace, boasting reveals allegiance to God. Our essential humanity finds expression in boasting. Boasting of anything that is not God's gift destroys our humanity because it is rebellion against God's rule. Boasting of God's grace and peace restores our humanity because it is obedience to God's rule.

Here Paul boasts of the Thessalonians "among God's churches" for their perseverance and faith in the persecutions that they endure. His boasting is his public pledge of allegiance to God and his open rejection of the worldly power of those who persecute and try the faithful. Boasting reveals to whom Paul belongs and in whose service he lives. Therefore, Paul's boasting is his enlistment with the persecuted, not as an act of hopeless resignation, but as a triumphant act of faith in the invincible power of God's self-giving love. Boasting is Paul's witness to the cross of Jesus Christ as the victory of God over sin and death that enables the church to grow in faith and to increase in love as it awaits the coming of the Lord in glory.

2 Thessalonians 1:5-12. Paul's development of the theme of judgment in these verses is not speculative but practical. The problem is that the trial and the persecution of the church, from the point of view of worldly standards, appear to be the punishment of God. The persecutors appear to be favored by God because they escape suffering. Paul is writing to assure the saints that they have not been abandoned by God in their distress. On the contrary, their distress is a sign that God is with them, using their suffering to prepare them through faith and love to receive the full disclosure of God's reign when the Lord comes.

Paul goes on in these verses to say that when the Lord does come, the present situation will be brought fully to light. Those who persecute the saints will be persecuted, and the saints will rest from all persecution. Although the details of the imagery are vividly drawn ("blazing fire," "everlasting destruction," and exclusion "from the presence of the Lord and from the majesty of his power"), attention is not focused on the details. Rather, Paul focuses on the claim that the final judgment is already taking place in persons' response to the preaching of the gospel. Those who reject the knowledge of God given in Christ Jesus and who do not obey his gospel in faith and love will discover that they have separated themselves from God when the Lord comes. Those who receive the revelation of God in Christ Jesus and who obey his gospel in faith and love will discover that they have joined themselves to God when the Lord comes. All this Paul proclaims because he has experienced the crucified and risen Jesus as the Lord who will come in glory to glorify or perfect the saints and to gather them to celebrate at his final victory.

Paul presents this material to encourage the saints to remain steadfast and faithful in their time of distress. In order to admonish, urge, and advise the saints concerning the eternal blessings of faithful living, Paul warns them of the terrible consequence of unfaithfulness. Since faith is always vulnerable to attack in the world and comes into existence as a decision to serve God rather than idols, it can only be maintained by living in dependence on the self-giving love of God. To depend on one's own strength or on worldly power is to forget God and to disobey the gospel. Therefore, Paul concludes this section by interceding with God on behalf of God's beleaguered people. Only God's self-giving love can empower them to confess their Lord when their lives are at risk. Only God's grace can enable them to love those who seek to kill them. Only God's faithfulness can keep them faithful and obedient when they are burdened by doubt and paralyzed by fear.

Paul's prayer for the saints expresses his firm conviction that Jesus' victory over sin and death will be consummated in the coming of the Lord and that the saints will be perfected or completed or sanctified through participation in that victory. His vision of the coming of the Lord is nothing more nor less than his abiding faith in God's self-giving love to accomplish God's saving purpose for all creation.

2 Thessalonians 2:1-12. For Paul assurance that the Lord will come is always a future hope based on his faithful experience of what happened in Jesus and continues to happen through the Spirit. Paul insists that these two aspects of Christian existence be held in tension. To neglect the now of Christian experience is to make Christian hope a matter of undisciplined speculation about the future. To neglect the not yet of Christian experience is to make Christian faith a matter of resignation to things as they are.

In these verses Paul attacks the false teaching that there is no *not yet* for the saints because the Lord has already come. He begins by disavowing this position and declaring that any letters that contain this idea and are ascribed to him are forgeries. Then he goes on to develop his teaching about what must happen before the Lord comes fully. He uses the conventional symbols of Jewish literature about the end, but he uses them to proclaim his unique understanding of the last things.

The first thing that must occur in order for the Lord to come fully is the complete disclosure of all the forces that oppose God's saving purpose. This disclosure is necessary so that the hostility to God that is now hidden in human history and often cloaks itself in the trappings of idolatrous religion will be brought into the open as rebellion against God.

Just as the leader of the community of obedience is Christ, so the leader of the community of rebellion is the man of lawlessness, the son of perdition. In fact, he is a parody of Christ. Christ humbles himself and claims everything for God. The man of lawlessness exalts himself and claims everything for himself. Christ is the mystery of God's saving purpose. The man of lawlessness is the mystery of destruction. Christ is filled with the power of God to perform signs and wonders. The man of lawlessness is filled

with the power of Satan to perform pretended signs and wonders. Christ speaks the truth that leads to salvation. The man of lawlessness speaks the lie that leads to destruction. According to Paul, some force or power now restrains the full expression of rebellion. But that will finally pass away, and the hidden opposition to God will be revealed at the day of the Lord. In other words, the idolatrous claims of the man of lawlessness and his followers will be uncovered by the faithful obedience of Christ and his followers.

Not only will the man of lawlessness and his followers be revealed, they will also be destroyed by the coming of the Lord. This is the second thing that must occur before the coming of the Lord is fully realized. This act is necessary because the self-giving love of God, which is now perceived by faith as the ultimate power of the universe, must be publicly demonstrated as the power that sustains and perfects the whole creation. The truth about God and God's saving purpose is the power that overcomes all false claims to power. Paul has this in mind as he writes: "And then the lawless one will be revealed, whom the Lord Jesus will overthrow with the breath of his mouth and destroy by the splendor of his coming" (2:8).

So the struggle between truth and falsehood is nothing more than the disclosure of the warfare now going on in the church. This warfare is between the rebellious messengers of deceit, whose hearers are perishing, and the faithful messengers of truth, whose hearers are being saved. The issues are drawn clearly by Paul, not to entertain the saints with fantasies about the future, but to help them see the awful consequences of believing what is false and refusing to love the truth. Lies about God, about Christ, and about the church are all rooted in self-seeking idolatry. These lies have the appearance of power because they are seductively attractive. But they have no real power. When the real power of self-giving love is revealed fully at the coming of the Lord, everything that has been built on the wicked deceit and strong delusion of self-seeking idolatry will be disclosed for what it is—nothing. But until that transpires in God's good time, the church is called to serve the truth in perseverance and faith in all its persecutions and trials. Any word that suggests that the struggle is over is misleading and destructive because it is itself a deceit.

2 Thessalonians 2:13–3:5. Although the struggle between deceit and truth rages in Thessalonica and the outcome seems to be in doubt, Paul does not lose heart. He is not controlled by appearances but by reality. Therefore, he breaks out in thanksgiving instead of falling into despair. His mood and his words are determined by the revelation of God's self-giving love in Jesus Christ. As a faithful apostle, Paul has no choice; he is bound to give thanks. What makes this remarkable is the fact that his thanksgiving is inspired by remembering the saints at Thessalonica, who are beset from without by persecution and trials and from within by false and deceitful teachings.

Paul expresses his thanks for the church as a profound affirmation of his faith. He offers it here in the midst of his instruction to the church so that his brothers and sisters may share with him the experience of God's saving love as a power infinitely greater than the cruelty and violence they receive at the hands of their persecutors. The saints are on the winning side. They know this not as an idea but as the life they have in Christ. They are the Lord's beloved, God's chosen. They are not alone in the world. Rather, the Spirit is at work in them making them holy and assuring them of salvation. Wicked deception and strong delusion have no power over the saints because they believe in the truth. All this they experienced at the beginning when Paul preached to them in person. All this they continue to experience as they hold fast to the gospel, the traditions about Jesus that Paul taught them in person and now sends them by letter. The persecutors and deceivers may seem to have the advantage. Since God is for the persecuted and believers in the truth, however, they have nothing to fear in this world or in the world to come.

Just as Paul has no doubt about the outcome of the struggle because it has already been won in Christ, so he has no illusions about the ability of other persons to meet the test. From the point of view of their own strength, the saints are doomed to defeat. Therefore, Paul commends them to God, knowing that the self-giving love of God in the Lord Jesus Christ is the only power that will keep them steadfast and faithful in their trials and persecutions. The only thing the saints need fear is that deceitful teachers will lead them to trust themselves rather than God. So long as they turn with Paul to God, they will find that God will encourage their hearts and "strengthen [them] in every good deed and word."

Paul does not write from a detached vantage point; he writes from the battlefield itself. Paul is vulnerable to all the testing that has befallen the saints at Thessalonica. His ministry is carried on in a world of unfaith where he is exposed to the hostility and attacks of wicked and evil people. He is no more capable of carrying out his apostolic mission on his own than the saints are capable of confessing Christ faithfully on their own. So the prayer he has offered on their behalf he now requests that they offer on his. Just as he prayed that they might be strengthened "in every good deed and word," so he asks that they pray for him, "that the message of the Lord may spread rapidly and be honored" (3:1).

The prayers of the church point beyond the church to God, the reality in whom the church exists. God is not neutral in the struggle. In Christ, God is for the saints and faithfully gives the saints strength and guards them from evil. Therefore, Paul is confident in the midst of persecution and trial that the saints will continue to hear and obey the gospel. The only thing he fears is that the crisis of the moment or the deception of false teaching will tempt them to trust something other than the self-giving love of God. Once again, then, Paul prays that Christ will keep their attention centered on the only power sufficient for their needs: "May the Lord direct your hearts into God's love and Christ's perseverance" (3:5).

2 Thessalonians 3:6-15. Paul seems to turn to an entirely different subject in these verses, but this is not the case at all. He deals with what he considers to be a threat from within the life of the church—idleness—in the same way as he deals with the threat from outside—persecution. His judgment that persecution and idleness are destructive is not arbitrary but the result of measuring conduct in light of the standard of God's self-giving love revealed in Jesus Christ. Those who persecute the church are doomed to destruction because they separate themselves from God's love. Likewise, those who live in idleness disobey the Lord by indulging themselves instead of serving the community as agents of God's love. Paul's strategy in response to these threats is controlled by the revelation of God's love in the cross of Jesus Christ. The church is called on in the face of persecution and trials to remain steadfast in the cross, the power that overcomes all evil. And the church is commanded in the challenge of idleness to persevere in the life of the cross, the power that edifies the community.

In these verses Paul is speaking only to the church and specifically to the discipline of the church. The action that he commands—have nothing to do with those living in idleness—is an extreme measure because idleness is an extreme danger. Paul is advocating withdrawal from a member of the community who openly violates his or her vows of responsibility for the community. The issue is of ultimate importance because those who have confessed Jesus as Lord are now living in the community as if they still belong to the world. The lordship of Christ in the church is at stake in how the church responds to the threat of idleness. This diagnosis of the situation prompts Paul to recommend extreme action.

The action Paul recommends is not punitive but corrective. Since it is done "in the name of the Lord Jesus Christ," that is, in the power of self-giving love, its intent is not the destruction but the reformation of the offending member. Nevertheless, it is drastic action because Paul considers idleness a form of self-serving that is totally incompatible with self-giving.

Perhaps idleness in Thessalonica was a particularly dangerous threat because those who practiced it claimed that they were practicing a higher form of righteousness. They may have believed that they were supposed to drop all their routine responsibilities in order to concentrate on preparing for the coming of the Lord through meditation and prayer. Paul argues that the best preparation for the coming of the Lord is the practice of the life of self-giving love revealed in Jesus and confirmed in Paul's apostolic ministry. Just as Jesus "did not consider equality with God something to be grasped, but made himself nothing, taking the very nature of a servant" (Philippians 2:6-7), so the apostle and all believers are called on to renounce self-centered privileges so that they may witness in the world to the rule of God's love in Christ.

But the centrality of love in the disciplines of the church does not lead Paul to relax the rigorous demands on the church. In fact, it intensifies those demands because the revelation of love in the cross of Jesus Christ is the standard that all accept when Jesus Christ is confessed as Lord. God's self-giving love does not offer cheap approval of unloving acts; rather, God's love reveals them as rebellion against God. As such, they are condemned. That condemnation is itself a sign of God's care for all who fall short of the norm of love.

But the God who judges in the cross also redeems in the cross. So God is not the enemy but the savior. Similarly, love in the church is not cheap approval of unloving behavior but disciplined rejection of all that falls short of the love of God. Discipline, however, is not motivated by hatred but by love. Even in its most extreme expressions loving discipline is not directed toward an enemy to be destroyed but toward a brother or sister to be saved.

2 Thessalonians 3:16-18. Paul's benediction expresses once again the theme he has developed throughout this letter. Peace, the total well-being of God's people, is God's purpose for them. Christ the Lord establishes peace by reconciling to God those who have been estranged from God. Peace, then, is the relationship of trust that is now a possibility because of the self-giving love of God in Christ. No longer is peace a long-delayed hope. Peace is a present reality for those who respond to God's action in faith. But peace is a present reality incomplete and under attack by persecution from without and idleness and deception from within. The church is sustained in persecution and disciplined in error by the abiding presence of the Lord. The Lord also gives grace to remain steadfast in faith and persistent in love.

Paul vouches for the truth of his message by adding his mark at the close of the letter so that all may know it comes from him instead of an impostor.

DIMENSION THREE: WHAT DOES THE BIBLE MEAN TO ME?

2 Thessalonians 1:2; 3:16—The Peace of God

One hindrance to discussing this issue is the assumption on the part of some that peace is a human endeavor that is only marginally relevant for Christians. If this attitude surfaces in the class session, try to get class members to explore what is meant by the peace of God. Point out that Paul viewed peace and salvation as interchangeable and that both refer primarily to what God does and only secondarily to what we do. Does this mean that God is the great peacemaker for the world? Does it also mean that to the extent that we reject peace, we also reject God's salvation? Explain your answers.

Another barrier to profitable discussion of the peace of God is to assume that God's peace is an inward feeling of contentment that has no bearing on political, social, and economic issues. The Hebrew word for peace is *shalom,* which includes the social as well as the personal dimensions of human existence. *Shalom* is an all-inclusive term that refers to all the components of personal and corporate well-being. How can one receive God's peace in isolation from a community of mutual responsibility? Does God intend peace for all people or for a select few? How can preoccupation with one's own peace or well-being constitute a threat to the peace or well-being of others? How does this question apply to nations as well as to individuals?

If class members come to some agreement about the central place of peacemaking in Christian experience, then explore various strategies for peace. Likely, one of the major items of concern will be the use of force. Some may accept force uncritically as needed to hold back evil and to secure peace. Others may reject the use of force equally uncritically as incompatible with the goal of peace. Try to lead the discussion away from these extreme positions to consider the circumstances in which force may enhance peace and the circumstances in which force is a threat to peace. What kind of force is permissible? Under what circumstances? What kind of force is not permissible? Under what circumstances? How can one be a responsible militarist? How can one be a responsible pacifist? Are the norms that Paul invokes in Thessalonians relevant as we struggle to decide these issues? Why or why not?

2 Thessalonians 3:6-15 Discipline in the Church

Resistance to Paul's recommendations concerning the discipline of those living in idleness will probably be outspoken. Encourage class members to explain why they feel so strongly on this subject. On chalkboard or a large piece of paper list the arguments against discipline in the church. Do the arguments concentrate on the misuse of discipline to achieve conformity in thought and action? Does the fact that discipline has a long history of abuse in the church justify the undisciplined approach to church life now current?

Direct attention to conduct within the church that threatens the life of the church. Consider behavior that seems to be incompatible with a life of self-giving love. Make a list of such conduct. Will such conduct eventually destroy the church if it is tolerated or ignored? Should the church make a disciplined effort to correct unloving behavior? Is the church more at risk today from the abuse of discipline or from the neglect of discipline?

The word *tolerance* may be used in the discussion. Be sure to discover just what is meant. Encourage class members to explain why they think tolerance is a help in the church. What limits, if any, does tolerance have? This may lead to the conclusion that just as discipline is not an absolute good, so tolerance is not absolute. What factors guide the church in deciding when to be tolerant of behavior and when to exercise discipline? List these factors and examine them as expressions of the self-giving love of God revealed in Christ. When is tolerance unloving?

One helpful aspect of the discussion may be to explore the responsibility for church discipline. We usually assume that discipline is the function of leaders or officials in the church, but Paul has a different view. He charges the whole congregation to accept full responsibility for discipline. He seems to do this because he understands the church organically and not institutionally. His argument is that Christ is the head of the body, and under the direction of Christ they all are responsible for one another. One part of that responsibility is mutual correction and edification. Is it possible that our loss of a sense of discipline in the church comes mostly from our forgetting that we are members of a body whose only head is Christ? Does this mean that all efforts to restore discipline in the church must be subordinated to recovering our relationship to Christ as members of his body?

Here is a trustworthy saying that deserves full acceptance: Christ Jesus came into the world to save sinners (1:15).

8

Christ for All

1 Timothy 1–2

DIMENSION ONE: WHAT DOES THE BIBLE SAY?

Answer these questions by reading 1 Timothy 1

1. Who writes the letter to whom? (1:1-2)

   Paul writes the letter to Timothy, "my true son in the faith."

2. Where did Paul leave Timothy? (1:3)

   Paul left Timothy in Ephesus.

3. What is the goal of Paul's command? (1:5)

   The goal of Paul's command is "love, which comes from a pure heart and a good conscience and a sincere faith."

4. For whom is law made? (1:9-10)

   Paul says that law is made "for lawbreakers and rebels, the ungodly and sinful, the unholy and irreligious . . . and for whatever else is contrary to the sound doctrine."

5. How had Paul acted? (1:13)

   He had "acted in ignorance and unbelief."

6. Why did Christ Jesus come into the world? (1:15)

   "Christ Jesus came into the world to save sinners."

7. Who is the worst sinner? (1:15-16)

   Paul is the worst sinner.

8. What was Paul shown? (1:16)

   He was shown mercy.

9. Who are among those who "have shipwrecked their faith"? (1:19b-20)

   Hymenaeus and Alexander are among them.

10. To whom has Paul handed them? Why? (1:20)

    He hands them over to Satan, "to be taught not to blaspheme."

Answer these questions by reading 1 Timothy 2

11. For whom should "requests, prayers, intercession and thanksgiving be made"? (2:1)

    They should be made "for everyone."

12. Whom does God our Savior want to be saved? (2:3-4)

    God our Savior wants "all men to be saved."

13. Who is the "one mediator between God and men"? (2:5)

    "The man Christ Jesus" is the "one mediator between God and men."

14. How are women to learn? (2:11)

    Women are to learn "in quietness and full submission."

15. Does Paul permit women to teach or to have authority over men? (2:12)

    He does not permit women to teach or to have authority over men.

DIMENSION TWO: WHAT DOES THE BIBLE MEAN?

1 Timothy 1:1-2. One of the distinctive marks of this salutation is the inclusion of mercy along with grace and peace.

Maybe mercy is included to emphasize the element of pity in God's relationship to human need. God is not the great unmoved observer of human distress but the loving Creator whose mercy is revealed in active response to all that hinders or cripples human well-being. Since God is our Savior and Christ Jesus our hope, we receive mercy or pity from God and Christ in every condition of need.

The relationship between Paul and Timothy that is described in this letter is well documented in Acts and other Pauline letters. One scholar summarizes their association as follows:

> Timothy, from Lystra in Lycaonia, was the son of a Gentile father and of a Jewish-Christian mother (Acts 16:1; according to [2 Timothy] 1:5, his mother's name was Eunice). Perhaps already won through the first mission of Paul in his hometown (Acts 14:6ff.), he was chosen by the Apostle on his second visit in Lystra as a missionary companion and was circumcised (Acts 16:3). Henceforth, he was a constant companion of Paul (Acts 17:14f; 18:5; 19:22; 20:4; I Thess. 1:1; II Thess. 1:1; II Cor. 1:1, 19; Phil. 1:1) and at intervals was sent by Paul to particular churches with special tasks (I Thess. 3:2, 6; I Cor. 4:17; 16:10; Phil. 2:19, 23). On the collection journey to Jerusalem he was in the company of Paul (Acts 20:4) and, according to Col. 1:1 and Phlm. 1, with him at the place of his imprisonment. . . . Phil. 2:20ff. shows the Apostle's great appreciation of the personality and the service of Timothy. What is historical in Hb. 13:23, the last place in the NT which mentions Timothy, lies in darkness (*Introduction to the New Testament,* by Werner Georg Kummel; Abingdon, 1965, 14th Revised Edition; page 260).

Thus, the specific historical relationship between Paul and Timothy is well documented; but this does not quite settle the matter for the interpreter. The letters that are addressed to the historical Timothy not only are directed to a specific person but also to a class of persons typified by him. Hence the letters reflect a historical situation more inclusive than the history of Timothy and raise issues and confront problems that reflect a later period in the church than that of Timothy's personal life. No doubt Timothy was Paul's personal companion, but he is more than that in these letters. Timothy is also the ideal minister, a representative type, who serves to extend the relationship between Paul and his companion to include a group of pastoral leaders at a much later time than Paul's and Timothy's lifetime. This kind of reflection leads scholars to name First and Second Timothy and Titus the Pastoral Epistles.

A similar line of thought is prompted by the picture of Paul we have in the Pastoral Epistles. This picture is grounded firmly in the historical Paul and has many points of contact with the Paul we meet in his other letters. But some elements in the picture of Paul in the Pastoral Epistles seem to move in the direction of portraying Paul as the ideal authoritative teacher whose instructions settle points of order and doctrine that are quite different from those dealt with by the historical Paul. Since the evidence is far from conclusive, it seems best in this particular study to leave the matter open and to assume that the Paul of the Pastoral Epistles is the historical Paul whose life and teaching have been idealized, so that the apostle's ministry includes a later period than his own and different problems from those addressed in his other letters.

1 Timothy 1:3-7. Paul assumes that the primary purpose of Timothy's ministry in Ephesus is to defend Paul's message from the corruption of false teachers. We do not know exactly what they were adding to Paul's message, for the references are vague and general and could mean any number of things. What is certain is that all these additions are the opposite of "God's work—which is by faith."

Here Paul is declaring that the gospel message always carries with it the discipline of a gospel life. The message that creates faith also empowers disciples who walk in the way of faith. The additions of false teachers are denounced because they destroy the integrity of the gospel life by encouraging controversies and meaningless talk that swerve from "love, which comes from a pure heart and a good conscience and a sincere faith" (1:5). The norm for distinguishing truth from error is eminently practical. Error produces the disintegration of a life of self-serving enslaved by vain discussion. Truth produces the integration of a life of self-giving liberated by faith.

1 Timothy 1:8-11. One reason that false teaching was so seductive is that it claimed to be based on the divine revelation in the law. These persons quoted the law (the Hebrew Scriptures) to support their claim that salvation in Christ was not effective unless accompanied by obedience to the ethical and liturgical requirements of the law. They were saying Paul's message of salvation by grace alone through faith was wrong and needed correction by authentic "teachers of the law." Paul denounces them as "not know[ing] what they are talking about or what they so confidently affirm" (1:7). What they were really saying was that the revelation in Christ must be corrected by their interpretation of the law. Paul says no; the revelation in Christ corrects the revelation in the law. Authentic teachers of the law know this.

In light of the gospel (Paul's message), the law has no saving power but is relevant only as a restraining power for the lawless and disobedient in a sinful and unfaithful world. So-called teachers of the law who claim otherwise, no matter how learned and eloquent, are advocating that which "is contrary to the sound doctrine."

1 Timothy 1:12-17. The decisive issue in distinguishing between sound doctrine and false is how one stands before God. False doctrine arises from the assumption that one stands before God on the basis of human achievement. Sound doctrine arises from the experience that one stands before God on the basis of divine grace. Paul appeals to his experience of grace as an example, not of his apostolic credentials, but of the salvation that he as a sinner shares with all sinners. His autobiographical references throughout this section focus attention on the divine initiative in his life: giving him strength, judging him faithful, appointing him to service. All this took place, not after he had reformed his life, but before any change whatsoever. In fact, the change from blasphemer, persecutor, insulter of Christ Jesus to an apostle of Christ Jesus is the work of Christ in his life—pure grace.

The key phrase in the entire passage is "I was shown mercy" (1:13, 16). This recurring theme picks up the reference to mercy in the salutation in 1:2 and may be the distinctive emphasis of sound doctrine. Paul received mercy because nothing in his life merited God's favor. This is especially true of Paul's religious life. His claim to know God on the basis of his rabbinic study and his efforts to please God on the basis of his Pharisaic rigor were of no avail. From the standpoint of the cross of Jesus Christ, "the glorious gospel of the blessed God," all that Paul once prided himself in knowing and doing is nothing but ignorance and unbelief. His ignorance and unbelief, however, are not the occasion for God's wrath to destroy his life. Instead, God's grace gives Paul the relationship to God that he could never earn and creates in Paul the faith and love that are humanly impossible. Sound doctrine reverses the common assumption that God rewards those who earn God's favor with the incredible assertion that God has mercy on those who deserve God's punishment.

Throughout these autobiographical references Paul has the community in mind. Just as God in Christ saved Paul from sin and death, so God in Christ intends to save sinners in general. Sound doctrine, however it is formulated and developed, is always an explanation of this simple yet profound statement: "Christ Jesus came into the world to save sinners." This general statement illuminates Paul's experience because it clarifies the fact that he experiences salvation as a sinner, and what Paul experiences is offered to all sinners. Paul's experience gives content to the general statement because it emphasizes that all are sinners, not simply in their moral and religious failure but also in their moral and religious success. Paul is an example, not of the ideal apostle, but of the salvation of sinners by a merciful God. His life embodies the gospel because it witnesses to God's perfect patience with those who deserve no patience. Since sound doctrine is reflection on "the glorious gospel of the blessed God," Paul's explanation of it in terms of his experience leads not to the exaltation of Paul but to the praise of God: "To the King eternal, immortal, invisible, the only God, be honor and glory for ever and ever. Amen" (1:17).

1 Timothy 1:18-20. Again the text focuses on Timothy's responsibility to maintain sound doctrine at Ephesus. Whatever other responsibilities he may have been given when he was selected for leadership in the church, the chief task that Timothy was designated to perform was to preserve the apostolic message that he received through Paul. Timothy was not called to succeed Paul as an apostle but to accept Paul's gospel as authoritative and to defend it against the controversies and meaningless talk of false teachers. Timothy's qualification for this task was the fact that the Spirit led prophets to set him aside for this purpose. His remembrance of that call will enable him to carry it out. Paul charges Timothy to "fight the good fight" against falsehood by living in dependence on the power of God in Christ that consecrated him for ministry and sustains him in ministry. The only defense of faith is faithful living, the integrity of a life lived in dependence on the self-giving love of God in Christ, "a good conscience."

Sound doctrine is primarily a matter of right relationships and only secondarily a matter of correct teaching. This may be the reason the content of Paul's gospel is always somewhat undefined and the substance of false teaching always vague and general. For Paul the truth is a person, the Lord Jesus Christ, and "holding on to faith and a good conscience" means trusting in that person and serving him in love. The test of correct teaching is how it enables one to receive grace, mercy, and peace as a sinner and how it empowers one to live gracefully, mercifully, and peacefully in the world.

False teaching is false because it destroys the integrity of the life of faith by leading persons to trust something other than the grace of God in Christ. False teaching is especially dangerous in the church because it creates a divided loyalty in the community and corrupts "a good conscience." When the relationship of trust and obedience to Christ as the source of salvation and the Lord of the church is broken, the result is shipwreck, utter disaster. Paul does not hesitate to name names. Hymenaeus and Alexander were persons who in seeking to save themselves destroyed themselves. Since they chose to live in dependence on what is not God (Satan), Paul gives them up to that power in the hope that the experience of sovereign falsehood will teach them to repent and turn once again to the truth.

It seems that Paul was not only instructing Timothy about his responsibility for maintaining sound doctrine, but he was also instructing church leaders in general. The substance of his charge is to insist that in the struggle against false teaching the only sure defense is a recovery of the gospel itself. In other words, the only security the church has in its fight against lies and deceit is the truth incarnate in Jesus Christ. The church does not possess the truth in the form of correct ideas about God. Rather, the truth revealed in the self-giving love of God in Christ possesses the church, calls it into existence, commissions it for service, and sustains it against all its foes. When church leaders remember how they received mercy when they deserved wrath, they will be inspired to "fight the good fight, holding on to faith and a good conscience." When they forget their origins in the gospel, they will reject conscience and make shipwreck of their faith.

1 Timothy 2:1-7. The mention of Hymenaeus and Alexander in the context of waging the good fight against false teaching seems to raise the question of the proper attitude of the church toward those who have been identified as enemies of the truth. For Paul the answer to this question was never in doubt. All persons, including false teachers, are to be included in the "requests, prayers, intercession and thanksgiving" of the church. They are to be included, not in order to persuade God to care for them, but in order for the church to witness to the fact of God's rule in human history. The prayers of the church proclaim the only God as the "King eternal, immortal, invisible." Under God's authority kings and all who are in high positions exist and receive strength and guidance for the performance of their duties. When the church publicly acknowledges its dependence on God, it also witnesses to the power that sustains the whole creation. In the assurance of this relationship, no matter how the church may be threatened from within or afflicted from without, it enjoys "peaceful and quiet lives in all godliness and holiness."

Including all persons in the ministry of the church is the absolute good for which the church has been created because it conforms to the saving purpose of God. God is not neutral in "the good fight," but God wants all persons "to be saved and to come to a knowledge of the truth." For the church to forget its enemies in prayer is absolutely impossible as long as it remembers that "Christ Jesus came into the world to save sinners." Since God desires the salvation of Hymenaeus and Alexander and kings and all who are in authority, the church prays for them as a sign of its faithful participation in God's victory over sin and death in the self-giving love of Christ. The love that the church receives from Christ is the love that the church offers the world in Christ.

False teaching is false because it is a rejection of the integrity of God's revelation in Christ Jesus. God is one in God's desire to save all. The unity of God's saving purpose is embodied in the obedience of Christ in giving himself for others. God shows no partiality. What is done in Christ is done for all: one God, one Christ, one salvation. The primary witness to the universal salvation of God our Savior is Christ himself. But that primary witness is followed by the timely witness of others: Paul, Timothy, the whole host of believers. The saving action of God in Christ was the purpose of Paul's ministry to the Gentiles. As he carried out that ministry in faith and truth, he was the model for all who are called to defend the gospel against false teachers. Paul's insistence that he is telling the truth is not intended to convince Timothy or the church but rather to contrast his faithfulness to the gospel with those false teachers who do not tell the truth, who are lying. Any effort to limit God's desire to save all persons by establishing exclusive ethical or liturgical conditions must be resisted, not on the grounds of human decision, but solely on the grounds of God's revelation of the universal scope of salvation in Christ's gift of himself for all.

1 Timothy 2:8-15. Paul's instructions about the conduct of public worship, the apparel of women, and the status and role of women in the church were motivated by his concern that the church conduct itself publicly in a manner that would support the evangelistic work of the church. He seems to be concerned that disorderly worship by the men and unconventional attire and conduct by the women will discredit the church with society at large and become a hindrance to God's desire to bring all persons to salvation and knowledge of the truth through the church.

The importance of these verses comes from the fact that they show the concrete form of faithful decision making. The object of faith is not Paul's teaching on this particular subject but the one God revealed in the one mediator Jesus Christ. Paul's response to that immortal, invisible God is, like all responses, conditioned by the historical and cultural circumstances of his life. Paul strove to obey God as a male participant in a male-dominated society. To the extent that his response is limited and distorted by those factors, it is inadequate. But to the extent that it is inspired and informed by God's self-giving love, it is faithful. Thus, it is possible to have a positive attitude toward Paul as a man of faith while being aware of his inability to transcend the historical cultural conditioning of his particular time.

We can apply this belief also to Paul's interpretation of the passages from Genesis 2 and 3 about Eve. He was following the accepted rabbinic understanding of these verses but seeking to appropriate them as God's word to the church on the subject of woman's role in public worship. The intent is admirable, but the result is something less than satisfactory. Faithful interpretation of Scripture, like faithful decision making, is always done in a context of historical and cultural limitations and must always be done anew in each generation. God does indeed speak through the biblical witness, but what is heard is always subject to interpretation in light of the changing historical and cultural conditioning of the hearer. We are not bound to hear what Paul heard, but we are challenged to listen for the voice of God in the biblical witness.

DIMENSION THREE:
WHAT DOES THE BIBLE MEAN TO ME?

1 Timothy 2:5-6—Christ Jesus as a Ransom for All

One way to begin a discussion of these verses is to focus on the word *all*. The revolutionary affirmation in the text is not that Christ Jesus gave himself as a ransom but that he gave himself as a ransom for *all*. Help class members understand the radical nature of this affirmation by raising the following questions: Does *all* include those whom we label as God's enemies? Are we included in *all* on the same terms as others? Are there any distinctions? any exclusions?

Consider ways in which we have avoided the inclusive nature of God's self-giving love. Ask class members to list ways the church has failed to give a clear witness to God's desire to save all persons. If racism, sexism, and ageism do not appear in the list, then press the issue so that the social relevance of Christ, a ransom for all, will become apparent. Is it possible for a racist, sexist, and ageist church to be an agent of Christ's ransoming love? Why or why not?

False teaching may express itself in the modern church, not as a perversion of classical Christian doctrine, but as a denial of the universal scope of salvation. Ask class members to identify examples of false teaching. Is the assumption that Christ is only for those who practice our morality false teaching? Is it false teaching to claim that Christ is a ransom only for those who confess our creeds and follow our liturgies? By raising these issues class members will come to appreciate more fully the revolutionary character of Paul's gospel and the nature of the opposition it provoked in Ephesus and everywhere it was preached.

1 Timothy 2:8-15
The Status and Role of Women in the Church

The discussion questions in the student book seek to establish a background for appreciating Paul's instruction as a missionary strategy, while recognizing it as unacceptable today. Another dimension of the whole matter is the great suffering that the misuse of this passage and similar biblical texts has caused among women. Explore with class members the authoritarian approach to Scripture. Ask if any class members are willing to accept what Paul teaches about women keeping silent, being barred from teaching and exercising authority because they were deceived and transgressed in Eden, and being saved through bearing children. Perhaps this discussion will open class members to reading the Scriptures as pointing to God's self-giving love as the final authority for faith and action. What is at stake here is not the reputation of Paul as an authoritative teacher but the Bible as an indispensable resource for Christian faith and action.

Discuss in what ways Paul's teachings on this subject are binding on the church. Then consider the ways in which his teachings are not binding. Are his teachings on this subject any different from his teachings on other subjects? Point out that the use of this text to subordinate women to men and to label them as transgressors because of their sex is a violation of Christ's lordship in the church. In fact, loyalty to the Christ who is proclaimed by Paul requires that the church reject this text as authoritative because it fails to meet the standard set by Christ Jesus, who gave himself as a ransom for all. Who has final authority in the church? How is Paul helpful in pointing to the answer to this question?

I am writing you these instructions so, if I am delayed, you will know how people ought to conduct themselves in God's household (3:14-15).

— 9 —

How to Behave in God's Household

1 Timothy 3–4

DIMENSION ONE: WHAT DOES THE BIBLE SAY?

Answer these questions by reading 1 Timothy 3

1. What kind of task is the office of overseer (bishop)? (3:1)

   The office of overseer is "a noble task."

2. What kind of person must an overseer be, and what must an overseer manage well? (3:2, 4)

   An overseer must be "above reproach, . . . temperate, self-controlled, respectable, hospitable, able to teach," and "must manage his own family well."

3. Who must think well of an overseer? (3:7)

   An overseer must be well thought of by outsiders.

4. What must deacons hold with a clear conscience? (3:9)

   "They must keep hold of the deep truths of the faith."

5. What must their wives be? (3:11)

   Their wives "are to be women worthy of respect, not malicious talkers but temperate and trustworthy in everything."

6. What do those who serve well as deacons gain? (3:13)

   They "gain an excellent standing and great assurance in their faith in Christ Jesus."

7. What does Paul hope to do? (3:14)

   He hopes to come to Timothy soon.

8. How does Paul describe the church? (3:15)

   The church is "God's household" and "the pillar and foundation of the truth."

Answer these questions by reading 1 Timothy 4

9. How will some abandon the faith? (4:1)

   They will abandon the faith by following "deceiving spirits and things taught by demons."

10. What is good? (4:4)

    "Everything God created is good."

11. What is Timothy to train himself in? (4:7b)

    He is to train himself to be godly.

12. For what does godliness hold promise? (4:8)

    Godliness "hold[s] promise for both the present life and the life to come."

13. Who is "the Savior of all men"? (4:10)

    The living God is "the Savior of all men."

14. For whom is Timothy urged to set an example? (4:12)

    He is urged to set an example for the believers.

15. What does Paul charge Timothy to devote himself to? (4:13)

    Paul charges Timothy to "devote [himself] to the public reading of Scripture, to preaching and to teaching."

16. Whom will Timothy save by watching his life and doctrine closely? (4:16)

He will save himself and his hearers.

DIMENSION TWO: WHAT DOES THE BIBLE MEAN?

1 Timothy 3:1-7. In these verses, as in so many of the New Testament passages that address the subject of church order, we see reflected the patriarchal family structure of the first-century world. The specific teaching in this section about the relationship of an overseer (bishop) to his wife and children and the assumption that only males will serve as overseers are evidence that the church is always set within the limitations of particular cultural patterns. Neither the office nor the requirements for holding the office as given by Paul should be made absolute and binding on the church for all time. What would seem to be essential is the recognition that the life of the church always requires some form of administrative leadership and that the persons chosen for that role should be mature in the faith, beyond reproach morally, and skilled in the techniques of management.

We must do more, however, than simply recognize the influence of a particular period of human history in these verses about the character of overseers. The text witnesses within the limitations of time and space to that which transcends time and space. Thus, the text is in tension with every culture and every society because it points beyond itself to God. The basic presupposition of the text is that God is at work in human history, creating a community of faith, providing for its nurture, and calling it to renewal when it fails to conform to God's purpose. The character of overseers is defined, not by the norms of Roman culture, but by the revelation of God's self-giving love in Jesus Christ.

The creative energy that provides overseers for the management of God's church is the gospel. The text declares that the gospel that calls persons to the office also empowers them for all that the office demands. The word *must*, which recurs at the point of every new emphasis in the text, is much more than a rhetorical device. It brings to voice the integrity of Christian existence as the total response of persons to the full revelation of God's saving power in Jesus Christ.

Although the specific function of overseers as developed in this passage is management or administration, the ultimate purpose of such service is evangelistic. The internal responsibility of the overseer is to promote gospel order among the members by embodying the gospel. The overseer's authority is not the authority of status but the authority of a servant, the authority of Christ who "did not come to be served, but to serve, and to give his life as a ransom for many" (Mark 10:45). The external role of the overseer is to represent the gospel to the world. Overseers must maintain good relations with outsiders, not as a public relations gimmick, but as an evangelistic strategy. If they discredit the church by incurring negative criticism in the world, they hinder the spread of the gospel and become allies of those evil forces that oppose God's work in the world.

1 Timothy 3:8-13. Deacons must meet the same high standards as overseers. The testing they must undergo is not an external examination given by others but an internal review of their lives in light of the revelation of God's love in Jesus Christ. To serve well as a deacon is to live a life of single-minded devotion to the duties that are necessary for the orderly and healthy management of God's church. Deacons are disqualified for service by any self-serving action (insincerity, addiction to wine, greed for gain) that reveals they are not serious about living for others in the household of faith.

Regardless of developments later in church history, at this stage there is no grounds for esteeming one office higher than another in the church. All functions arise from the needs of the church, and all offices are filled by persons whom the gospel has called and empowered for effective service.

Even in a time of male domination the action of God in Christ includes women among those chosen for service and qualifies them to perform essential tasks. Already, then, in the reference to their wives the text is in tension with the norms and values of the surrounding culture and opens the door for women to achieve full recognition in the ministry of the church. Finding the patriarchal structures of first-century society in the text is not surprising. What is surprising is to find an almost casual reference to their wives in the context of a discussion of overseers and deacons and a reference to the qualifications of their wives that are no different from those prescribed for overseers and deacons.

So once more we are confronted with the fact that the instructions for church order in First Timothy witness to the transcendent origin of the church in the revelation of God's self-giving love in Jesus Christ. The inclusiveness of that love calls every form of discrimination to judgment and releases a power in human history that moves relentlessly toward the establishment of a community of justice and equality for all.

1 Timothy 3:14-16. The instructions Paul gives concerning the character of overseers, deacons, and their wives apply to the whole church. These instructions are intended to carry forward in the time of Paul's enforced absence the nurture he began in Ephesus when he was present. However, the relationship that distinguishes the church, whether in Ephesus or any other locale, is not to Paul as the historical agent of God's saving purpose but to God in Christ as the ultimate source and destiny of salvation. Paul's specific instructions simply seek to make explicit what is already implicit in understanding the church as "God's household." The nature of God revealed in Christ is the norm that is binding on all the members of the church regardless of the function each is assigned. Since the truth is the saving power of God creating, sustaining, and perfecting the church, the church exists to serve the truth by living and speaking the truth in the world.

Neither the church in its entirety nor the church represented by its leaders determines the content of the truth. The content of the truth is determined by what God has done and is doing in Jesus Christ. The religion or faith of the community is what has been revealed to the church and has been transmitted faithfully by the church. As "the pillar and foundation of the truth" the church is always subordinate to the truth and accountable to the truth. This dynamic relationship to the truth marks the church as God's household and sets it off from the world. The truth is always experienced in the church as God's call to absolute obedience that is in conflict with all other loyalties and allegiances. "The living God" is the opposite of the false gods to which human beings turn in their efforts to save themselves. The confession of the truth in the church is a public decision to serve "the living God" by turning away from the myth of self-righteousness and turning to radical dependence on God's love in Jesus Christ.

This truth is great, not because it is the product of the speculative wisdom of human beings, but because it is the work of God's creative Spirit in Jesus Christ. Jesus Christ is the center of gravity in the text because in his flesh or person the nature of God is made manifest. God is not an idea but a life. That life is triumphant over death because it has been vindicated in the Resurrection as the invincible power of God. In his risen glory Jesus Christ is acknowledged in heaven by the angels and on earth by those who believe. God's work in the person of Jesus Christ is not a general idea but a personal encounter with the truth. The truth revealed in a person is presupposed by a community made up of persons who give absolute allegiance to the truth. This instruction enables the church of the living God to know how it ought to behave. The truth manifest in Jesus is the truth manifest in Paul and in Timothy, in overseers and deacons, in their wives, and in all members of God's household. Great indeed is the truth revealed to and confessed by persons in the household of God.

1 Timothy 4:1-5. Departure from the truth or the faith is a serious matter because it is a rupture of the personal relationship of allegiance between believers and the living God who is revealed in Jesus Christ. Those who follow false teachers are no longer obedient to the sovereign power of God but have given their loyalty to God's enemies: deceiving spirits and demons. This graphic language is used in the text to emphasize the fact that the truth revealed in Jesus Christ is always under attack in the world. Those who receive the truth are themselves involved in the struggle and sure to fail to meet the test unless they hold fast to the truth with a clear conscience. The struggle against deceit and lies is inevitable, but falling in the struggle can be

avoided if the church maintains its allegiance to God by remaining faithful to the truth revealed in Jesus Christ.

Faithfulness to the truth is itself under attack in Ephesus by those who teach that salvation depends on ascetic practices such as celibacy and abstinence from foods. These views are false because they give a higher authority to self-righteous disciplines than to the self-giving love of God revealed in Jesus Christ. Such teachings encourage rebellion against God by refusing to receive with thanksgiving (that is, in responsible dependence on God's grace) all that God has created. Faithfulness to God is not rejection of creation as evil but acceptance of all that God has made as essentially good. The truth revealed in Jesus Christ calls men and women to responsible relationships to one another as sexual beings and to disciplined enjoyment of all that God has created. Celibacy and abstinence instead of being the higher righteousness are in fact acts of disobedience that arise from ignoring God's word and neglecting the discipline of prayer.

1 Timothy 4:6-10. Just as Paul contrasts the truth revealed in Jesus Christ with the deceit and lies of false teachers, so here he contrasts the disciplines of "godless myths and old wives' tales" with the disciplines of godliness. The disciplines of celibacy and abstinence are wrong, not because they are evil in themselves, but because they manifest an idolatrous dependence on human achievement. By contrast, the disciplines of godliness are right, not because they are inherently good, but because they witness to faithful dependence on God's love revealed in Jesus Christ.

Regardless of what form ministry takes in God's household, its distinctive characteristic is always service. Timothy's role in reminding overseers, deacons, and their wives of their duties in the church is fulfilled only as he himself becomes the embodiment of "the truths of the faith and of the good teaching" that he has followed. His ministry is an opportunity for responding to the message of God's love by living for others in the community of faith. "Godless myths," celibacy, and abstinence from food and drink, are destructive of authentic ministry because they encourage self-centered preoccupation with saving one's life and hinder losing one's life in faithful service to God and neighbor.

Godliness or faithful obedience to God is the essential requirement of all good ministers. This requirement is not a condition for a relationship of trust in God but a consequence of living out of that relationship. If that relationship is neglected or broken, it is impossible to be a good minister of Jesus Christ.

Training to be godly is necessary because in this way those who minister witness to the fact that they belong to Jesus Christ. They receive the power to do Christ's work in the world by depending on him as the channel of God's saving love. Although the language of training to be godly seems to focus on human discipline, the fact that it is in godliness emphasizes God as the initiator, sustainer, and perfecter of the relationship of faith. Paul is not telling

Timothy to save himself but calling him to remember the action of God in Christ that commissions him for service and enables him to be a good minister.

Paul is urging Timothy to give training in godliness the highest priority in his life because, unlike athletic discipline, it is not limited in value to this present life but is also the foundation for hope in the life to come. Training in godliness is infinitely more important than bodily training because God alone saves the body from the destruction of death by conquering all the threats to human existence through the power of Christ's self-giving love. Good ministers toil and strive, not for worldly recognition or success, but because they belong to God and depend on God to complete the work of salvation begun in them by Jesus Christ.

The living God, whose saving work inspired Paul and Timothy and all who believe to toil and strive in hope, intends the salvation of all persons. Believers are the signs in human history of God's universal love. The church is not saved from the world but in the world so that God's ministry may be carried on in the world for the sake of the world.

1 Timothy 4:11-16. These verses summarize the instruction that has been given to Timothy in Chapters 1–4. Timothy's ministry in the church originates in and is empowered by the revelation of God's love in Jesus Christ. The authority to command and teach in God's household comes from the revealed truth. The importance of the minister's subordination to the truth of the gospel is not speculative but practical. Gospel authority is service, so that only the authority of service is exercised by ministers of the gospel. The content of the gospel is love, so that only those who teach love lovingly are teachers of the truth. Ministers of the gospel qualify as authoritative teachers of the truth, not by meeting external standards such as age, but by embodying the truth in what they say and do. Thus, ministerial integrity, like the integrity of all believers, is the response of a whole life to the unconditioned love of God in Jesus Christ. The love, faith, and purity of the gospel inspire the love, faith, and purity of believers regardless of what function they perform in God's household.

The gospel that inspires and empowers all who render service in the church operates as the Scriptures are faithfully heard and applied in the public gathering of the church. As an ordained or set-apart minister, Timothy is primarily a minister of the word. Paul's apostolic ministry is carried out in his absence as Timothy gives first priority to the public reading and public interpretation and application of Scripture. In this context the Scriptures are understood as the primary witness in the church to the living God. What is at stake here is godliness and the disciplines that promote godliness.

Timothy's ministry of the word is understood in these verses as a gift of the Spirit that he received through the prophetic speech of the church when the elders laid their hands on him. This language emphasizes the fact that God calls persons into ministry through the action of the community and empowers them to perform those duties that manage and nourish the community. The laying on of hands does not make ministers but recognizes that God has made ministers. The essential relationship of those who minister is not to those who ordain but to the living God who calls and empowers persons for ministry.

In these verses Paul reminds Timothy and through him all who minister in the church that only devoted attention to the disciplines of godliness will enable one to serve well in God's household. The imperatives in the text—"command and teach," "devote yourself," "do not neglect," "be diligent," "give yourself wholly to," "watch," and "persevere"—presuppose that Timothy has been claimed in the power of the gospel to do God's work in the church. In the power of the gospel he is equipped, not only to perform the duties of his office, but to live in such conformity to the truth as to secure salvation for himself and for those who hear his preaching and teaching.

DIMENSION THREE: WHAT DOES THE BIBLE MEAN TO ME?

1 Timothy 3:14-16
How to Behave in God's Household

Begin by pointing out the distinction between truth as a propositional statement and truth as encounter with a person. When truth is reduced to abstract propositions about what we know, we tend to give absolute value to our limited and incomplete knowledge. Thus, in equating truth with what we know, we deny the truth that is not only unknown but unknowable. On the other hand, truth as encounter with a person opens our lives to the mystery that surrounds and sustains the whole creation. The person Jesus is the truth because in him we experience God whom we can never know completely but in whom we live and move and have our being. Jesus reveals to us the mystery of God by loving us, being faithful to God, doing God's will, and enduring suffering for us.

The relationship between faith and action, belief and behavior, is radically different, depending on how the object of faith is perceived. If we perceive truth or the object of faith as propositional, we will tend to become rigid, dogmatic, judgmental, and self-righteous. If we perceive the object of faith as personal, we will tend to become flexible, open, accepting, and humble. How is the object of faith perceived in First Timothy? Is the truth propositional or personal? Does First Timothy encourage behavior that is rigid and closed or flexible and open?

If class members agree that the proper object of faith is personal, then it may be necessary to explore how faith in the person of Jesus requires a particular pattern of behavior. Faith in the person of Jesus means trust that God is like what Jesus did. Jesus' behavior becomes the revelation of truth, of God. How is it possible to believe in the God manifest in Jesus and refuse to love other persons? How is it possible to profess faith in Jesus while practicing disobedience to God's will? How is it possible to trust Jesus as the way to God and refuse to follow him in the way of suffering?

If faith is nothing more than assent to propositions about God, then it is possible to profess one thing and to practice something else. If faith is a personal encounter with a personal revelation of God, it is impossible to contradict what one believes with what one does. Does the fact of this contradiction in the life of the church and in our lives raise serious questions about our faith? How can this contradiction be removed? How does First Timothy speak to this problem?

1 Timothy 4:6-16
Qualifications of a Good Minister of Christ Jesus

Perhaps the most important qualification for ministry as laity or as clergy is given in the prepositional phrase "of Christ Jesus." What does this phrase mean? First, it means that the source or origin of ministry is not institutional but Christological. Ministry is not what society wants or what the church wants or what clergy want or what laity want. Ministry is what Christ wills. What does Christ will for the church and the world? Only those who are obedient to what Christ wills are qualified to be good ministers of Christ Jesus.

Second, "of Christ Jesus" means that ministers belong to Christ. Ministers are not the employees of the church or of society or of any institution. They belong solely to Christ and are accountable to Christ alone. What does it mean for ministers to belong to Christ? Is ministry a possibility for anyone who does not know to whom he or she belongs?

Third, "of Christ Jesus" means that the basic work of ministry is to represent Christ in the world. This representation requires that ministers proclaim Christ in their words and deeds. What they profess they must practice. Are ministers of Christ Jesus always ministers of the gospel regardless of their function and regardless of their status as clergy or laity?

Fourth, "of Christ Jesus" suggests that the only purpose of ministry is to help the world experience the love of God in Christ Jesus. This purpose is not carried out by professional competence or by any functional skill but by participating in the self-giving love of God in Christ. Does this mean that the way of the cross is the way of ministry? What is the way of the cross?

For we brought nothing into the world, and we can take nothing out of it. But if we have food and clothing, we will be content with that (6:7-8).

— 10 —

Life in God's Household

1 Timothy 5–6

DIMENSION ONE:
WHAT DOES THE BIBLE SAY?

Answer these questions by reading 1 Timothy 5

1. How is Timothy to treat older men, younger men, older women, and younger women? (5:1-2)

    He is to treat older men as fathers, younger men as brothers, older women as mothers, and younger women as sisters.

2. What happens to those who fail to provide for their relatives? (5:8)

    They deny the faith and are worse than unbelievers.

3. At what age are widows to be enrolled? (5:9)

    Widows are to be enrolled if they are "over sixty" years of age.

4. How many witnesses must testify to bring an accusation against an elder? (5:19)

    "Two or three witnesses" must testify to bring an accusation against an elder.

5. What is to be done to elders who sin? (5:20)

    They are to be rebuked publicly.

6. Why is Timothy urged to take a little wine? (5:23)

    He is urged to take a little wine for the sake of his stomach and because of his frequent illnesses.

7. How are good deeds described? (5:25)

    "Good deeds are obvious, . . . [they] cannot be hidden."

Answer these questions by reading 1 Timothy 6

8. How are those under the yoke of slavery to consider their masters? (6:1)

    They are to "consider their masters worthy of full respect."

9. In what is there great gain? (6:6)

    "Godliness with contentment is great gain."

10. What is a root of all kinds of evil? (6:10)

    "The love of money is a root of all kinds of evil."

11. What is the "man of God" to pursue? (6:11)

    He is to "pursue righteousness, godliness, faith, love, endurance and gentleness."

12. Before whom did Christ Jesus in his testimony make "the good confession"? (6:13)

    Christ Jesus "while testifying before Pontius Pilate made the good confession."

13. Who has seen the King of kings and Lord of lords? (6:15-16)

    No one has ever seen or can see the King of kings and Lord of lords.

14. Who "richly provides us with everything for our enjoyment"? (6:17)

    God "richly provides us with everything for our enjoyment."

15. How have some wandered from the faith? (6:20-21)

    Some have wandered by professing "godless chatter and the opposing ideas of what is falsely called knowledge."

DIMENSION TWO:
WHAT DOES THE BIBLE MEAN?

1 Timothy 5:1-2. The text approaches the relationship of ordained ministers to various groups within the church with stark realism. The warnings indicate that those with administrative responsibility were prone to forget that they were members of God's household and were tempted to use their power in ways that were destructive of the family. The directions, "do not rebuke," "exhort," "treat," gain their power from the fact that the gospel of Jesus Christ redefines the family, so that all who are united to God in faith are joined to one another in love.

1 Timothy 5:3-16. This section is especially interesting because it is an example of how the early church sought to solve a particularly difficult administrative problem. In verses 9 and 10, the requirements for those who are to be enrolled as "real widows" highlight some of the practical functions necessary for the daily life of God's household.

Real widows are known for their good deeds, such as bringing up children. This does not necessarily mean they have borne children, but they must be experienced in the care of children. Perhaps the widows were responsible for nurturing the orphans in the congregation. Those enrolled as real widows must have shown hospitality, the ability to receive and provide for Christian travelers in a hostile world where there were few commercial inns. The widows shared this responsibility with all Christians but were unusually well situated to fulfill it because of their availability as full-time workers in the church. Real widows must have washed the feet of the saints, for experience in this humble service revealed a disposition to perform the work of a servant in God's household. Real widows must have helped those in trouble. This probably refers to skill in caring for the special needs of the poor and the sick. The practical duties of real widows are summarized in the final generalization, "devot[ed] to all kinds of good deeds." This is not an empty abstraction but an affirmation of single-minded concentration of energy on living for others in the household of faith.

The fact that these requirements are developed in detail reveals that they were essential for the life of the church. The "real widows" selected to perform them were no less important than deacons, overseers, and elders. Therefore, they were to be honored in the double sense of respect for their functions and support for their physical needs.

Verse 16 is revealing because of the way women are singled out as the key to making certain that widows who have relatives are cared for by their families. The text seems to assume that accepting a widowed relative into a family would create a special burden for the woman of the house and could not be carried out gracefully without her whole-hearted approval. This was a serious problem in the ancient world because widows were either supported by their relatives or driven to prostitution. The text assumes that any believing woman would have been especially horrified by the prospect of her sister in Christ becoming a prostitute and therefore would have moved to do all in her power to provide for her widowed relatives in her household.

1 Timothy 5:17-25. The basic issue in this section is not the abstract matter of the role of ordained ministers in the life of the church but the practical consideration of the relationship between those ordained to manage, preach, and teach and those under whose supervision they serve. In fact, the unwavering focus throughout this letter is the way Christians ought to behave toward one another and toward the world. The primary consideration is not the office or the functions but the creation of a new community by the self-giving love of God in Christ Jesus. The text seeks to draw out the consequences of living in that community, not in terms of generalizations, but in terms of concrete responsibilities and duties. The reference to "in the sight of God and Christ Jesus and the elect angels" (5:21) acknowledges the fact that the new community of faith is more than the gathering of human beings. It is also the dwelling place of God and Christ Jesus and the elect angels. As such, the community is accountable to those transcendent realities for all that it does. What distinguishes the new community of faith from all other communities is not its organization, its leadership, or its membership. The new community of faith is known by its witness to the self-giving love of God in Christ Jesus through its organization, its leadership, and its membership.

The obligation to love must always be defined in light of the responsibilities and duties of concrete human interaction in a specific place at a particular time. Elders show that they are loving members of the community by ruling or managing well. Those whom they serve express their compassion for their ministers by respecting their work and by paying them wages adequate for their needs. Those who preach and teach are not idle chatterers but diligent interpreters of the gospel. They labor to find words to proclaim the message of salvation clearly and attractively. Their support is not a matter of option but a divine command sanctioned by the revelation of the Scriptures. The most mundane matters in God's household are occasions for the persons involved to manifest in their daily care for one another that their allegiance belongs to God.

Loyalty to God in a community of diverse members and various forms of ministry requires that those who make difficult decisions and who perform controversial tasks be protected from the criticism of the envious and the attacks of the disgruntled. Love for the ordained ministry is shown, not in pious platitudes, but in the careful distinction between warranted and unwarranted charges. This protection does not mean that ordained elders are above reproach but only that charges be made responsibly and supported by two or three persons. Love is more than a sentiment. Love is a commitment to see that persons in responsible positions are treated fairly and justly.

Since love creates God's household and mandates that all the members live together as a loving family, actions on the part of leaders or ordained ministers that fall short of the norm of love are serious threats to the life of the community. Occasional errors may be ignored, but persistent violations of the rules of the house must be dealt with publicly and forcefully. Such public discipline of offenders is the way the community expresses its love for its errant administrators. The purpose of public discipline of those who abuse their offices is not punitive but a reminder for the whole community that failure to love is an act of rebellion against God. Such an act is a fearful thing because it breaks the relationship of trust and unity and creates confusion, envy, and division. Discipline seeks to restore broken relationships and create order, good will, and harmony.

The discipline of love in God's household is carried out "in the sight of God and Christ Jesus and the elect angels." Since this is the case, those responsible for administering discipline are accountable to God and Christ and the elect angels for what they do. Ministers who abuse their office have no special consideration before God and must be disciplined without favor. Likewise, the discipline of love requires that they be rebuked without any show of partiality. Love in God's household is never self-indulgent or discriminatory. This love is always disciplined action on behalf of others even when that calls for the public rebuke and punishment of those guilty of the misuse of public trust. Failure to discipline is failure to love.

Verse 23 seems to break the flow of the argument as it introduces the subject of abstinence from wine. But this subject in this context has nothing to do with drinking wine for pleasure. It is raised here because of the medicinal value of wine. To be a drinker only of water in the ancient world was to refuse to avail oneself of a universally accepted medicine and thus to jeopardize one's health. Ministers in the household of God must not neglect their physical health. They cannot be effective agents of God's love if they become ill because they have refused to do all in their power to ward off disease. Therefore, they are urged to drink wine for the sake of their stomachs and their frequent ailments.

This whole section is brought to a climax with a ringing affirmation of the ultimate triumph of love in God's household. Unloving acts are often conspicuous in God's household because it is ruled by love. But some unloving acts are undetected and may appear to go unpunished. This situation is only temporary, for in the end every act must pass the test of love. Then whatever is unloving will be brought to light and judgment. Conversely, loving acts are usually recognized in God's household. But it may seem that some are passed over and ignored. This hiddenness is not permanent because, finally, love is known by God and blessed by divine approval. Although it is impossible for members of God's household to make final judgments about human behavior, in love they must make tentative distinctions between sins and good deeds in the confidence that God's love is the ultimate reality that judges and redeems all that they do.

1 Timothy 6:1-2. The ethical basis of all the exhortations in First Timothy is that the gospel claims and empowers persons to obey God in the concrete events of their lives. The gospel does not deliver them from their relationships but delivers them from self-centeredness so that in those relationships they may live for others. The gospel applies to all relationships, even to slavery, the most dehumanizing and demeaning institution of human history.

These verses do not endorse or sanction slavery. Instead, they call on Christian slaves to witness to the power of God and the gospel by obeying or honoring their masters. The "yoke of slavery" is the social relationship in which they are called to live for others, their masters, and thus spread the good news in a hostile or indifferent world. "Full respect" is to be given to their masters, whether they are Christian or not. But Paul recognizes that a special problem exists between Christian slaves and their Christian masters because of the gospel insistence that in Christ all are equal as members of God's household. The point of the text is that equality in Christ does not negate social responsibility but heightens it. Christian slaves are urged to repent and obey their Christian masters on the grounds that in so doing they are building up God's household by showing that the community is united in faith and love.

The text must be seen as a specific application of the gospel in a concrete historical situation and not as a timeless truth that has universal validity. In fact, close attention to the basic relationship of the text, God's self-giving love in Christ, confronts the reader with the gospel action, which at another time and another place demands that Christians oppose slavery "so that God's name and our teaching may not be slandered." God's love in Christ is always experienced in concrete social events and requires that believers respond by seeking to witness to that love by living for others in those events. Action that was ethically responsible in the first century is obviously ethically irresponsible in the twentieth. But what continues to be illuminating for the modern Christian is the faithful struggle of the text that calls the reader to become a responsible participant in that struggle today.

1 Timothy 6:3-5. These verses insist that an organic relationship exists between the content of the gospel and behavior. The gospel is always a way of life. Therefore, "these are the things" (verse 2) is used to summarize the entire message of God's action in Christ Jesus and the behavior that it demands and empowers in God's household. Since the message is essentially "the sound instruction of our Lord Jesus Christ and . . . godly teaching," it creates a community in which living for others is the standard for all action. But when "these . . . things" are neglected and replaced by a message that is self-centered, speculative, and controversial, the result is a community destroyed by "envy, strife, malicious talk, evil suspicions and constant friction." The characteristic attitude of those who teach false doctrine is self-centeredness. Since they begin by rejecting God's love, they end by living without love, serving themselves, and thinking "that godliness is a means to financial gain."

1 Timothy 6:6-10. The illusory gain of false teaching, greed, is now contrasted with the great gain in godliness with contentment, faith. "Great gain" is not something that is acquired but a relationship that is received as a gift. The key to human existence is not what is achieved by human effort but what is given by God's grace—life itself. Human life begins in absolute dependence on God ("we brought nothing into the world"), and it ends in absolute dependence on God ("we can take nothing out of it"). Therefore, between birth and death, life is sustained by God's grace ("food and clothing"), which is the only basis for being content. The desire to live on the basis of human achievement ("to get rich") destroys the relationship of trust in God ("fall into temptation and a trap"), creates hungers that can never be satisfied ("foolish and harmful desires"), and results in the loss of life itself ("ruin and destruction"). Greed ("the love of money") is the source of all that destroys contentment ("a root of all kinds of evil") because it breaks the basic relationship of faith in God that sustains life and promotes the anxious self-serving that undermines life. Those who turn from love of God to "love of money" exchange "godliness with contentment" for "foolish and harmful desires that plunge men into ruin and destruction."

1 Timothy 6:11-16. Just as the "love of money" ruins and destroys life, so the love of God redeems and fulfills life. Therefore, Timothy is urged to resist the temptation of greed by centering his life in the self-giving love of God revealed in Christ Jesus. The striving for riches is ultimately destructive because it fixes the center of life in that which perishes. The "good fight of the faith" is ultimately redemptive because it fixes the center of life in that which is eternal.

Human life is always a battleground of conflicting allegiances—God or the world. The "man of God" has been called in the world to a life of obedience to God. Baptism into God's household is a public act of allegiance by which the faithful enter into the "good fight of the faith." The fight is "good" because God "who gives life to everything" in Christ has overcome all that threatens life. By making the "good confession" in his testimony before Pontius Pilate, Christ Jesus has claimed all of life for God. The "good confession" of Christ Jesus is his life poured out for others in obedience to God. The appearing of the Lord Jesus Christ at the end of human history will bring to light his victory, now hidden in human history under the sign of the cross. Meanwhile, the church or God's household witnesses to that victory by living under the sign of the cross, which means to live for others in the world in obedience to God.

The reality that made the "good confession" of Christ Jesus possible is the reality that makes the "good confession" of all men and women of God possible, the glory of God. God's glory is God's eternal love revealed in Christ Jesus and in all the faithful. So the text concludes with praise to the glory of God. God's household is the community where "the blessed and only Ruler, the King of kings and Lord of lords, who alone is immortal and who lives in unapproachable light, whom no one has seen or can see" is honored and given "might forever" by those who with one voice say, "Amen."

1 Timothy 6:17-19. Paul recognizes that those most likely to deny God honor and eternal dominion are those who are rich, haughty, and dependent on their own acquired wealth. They are reminded in these verses that all they have is a gift of God's grace that can be enjoyed only by depending on God and doing good for others. Christians who are "rich in this present world" are charged "to be rich in good deeds" as evidence that they set their hopes on God's grace rather than on their wealth. The text is frankly realistic because it affirms that this worldly wealth is the initial arena for deciding other-worldly allegiance. The invisible God of the doxology of verses 15 and 16 is honored or dishonored in the visible use that the "rich in this present world" make of their wealth. When they use their wealth well, they lay "a firm foundation for the coming age" and demonstrate that they have taken hold of eternal life.

1 Timothy 6:20-21. What has been entrusted to Timothy and the whole household of God is grace. False teaching is destructive because it encourages the church to put its faith in human achievement instead of the gift of God in Christ. So the letter concludes with a reminder that grace alone is sufficient for those who "fight the good fight of the faith" (6:12).

DIMENSION THREE:
WHAT DOES THE BIBLE MEAN TO ME?

1 Timothy 5:17-25
The Remuneration and Discipline of Elders

Clearly the support of ordained ministers is a responsibility of the entire membership of the church. But the theological issues related to financial support of the clergy are hardly ever discussed. Why is it necessary to have ordained ministers who depend on the church for their sole support? Is this necessity the same for all churches and for all clergy? Should there be more flexibility to allow ordained ministers to support themselves and to serve part-time in the church?

The matter of wages raises the issue of accountability. Since the ordinary assumption of employer and employee is that those employed serve at the pleasure of those who employ, does the fact that clergy are paid for services by a congregation inhibit their freedom to lead and to serve as persons accountable to God? How can a congregation minimize this inhibiting factor? What role do the clergy play in this? Can the issue of wages for clergy be separated from the issue of fair and just remuneration for all persons who are employed

Perhaps the most pressing matter for discussion is the problem of wage differences among ordained ministers. Does the church simply reflect the values of the secular world in this regard? Is this the only alternative or the best? What would be the effect of a uniform salary base with a sliding scale to correct inequities? These matters are hardly ever given serious consideration by the laity, and thus, the status quo is allowed to continue unexamined. Since the laity are responsible for setting salaries, it appears that the laity should be much more involved in the discussion of the basic proposition for support of the clergy.

Likewise, the laity are seldom included in discussions of the discipline of clergy. This is probably the case because of the assumption that they lack the knowledge and the sensitivity to deal with difficult personal issues. This assumption is hardly defensible in light of the central role the laity play in deciding such issues in other realms of life. What are the disadvantages of including laity in the discipline of ordained ministers? What are the advantages of including them?

1 Timothy 6:12
The Warfare of Christian Existence

The warfare of Christian existence is not to be confused with the inescapable struggles of human existence. Christian warfare is the "good fight of the faith." This conflict arises, not from one's general human condition, but from one's specific commitment to Jesus Christ as Lord. Ask class members to identify particular struggles they have because of allegiance to Christ. Press them to discuss why Paul described these struggles as the "good fight of the faith."

"The good fight of the faith" is also different from the struggles of human existence because the victory has already been won. This may be a difficult idea to understand, but it is essential to do so. Otherwise, the experience of Christian warfare will be the occasion for despair and defeat. The point is that Jesus Christ in his death and resurrection has already defeated every foe of God and human life. All that is uncertain is whether we will participate in that victory. When we confess that Jesus Christ is Lord, we take our place in the struggle and witness to the fact of God's victory by living for others now. By loving we take hold of eternal life, for God is love.

Discuss the idea that the victory has already been won. Ask the group to tell of experiences that confirm this idea. Remind them that Easter is the church's victory celebration that makes "the good fight of the faith" possible.

I have fought the good fight, I have finished the race, I have kept the faith (4:7).

— 11 —

Christian Endurance

2 Timothy

DIMENSION ONE:
WHAT DOES THE BIBLE SAY?

Answer these questions by reading 2 Timothy 1

1. Whom does Paul serve? (1:3)

   He serves God.

2. What is Paul appointed? (1:11)

   He is appointed "a herald and an apostle and a teacher."

3. What is Timothy to guard? (1:14)

   He is to "guard the good deposit that was entrusted" to him.

4. Who is not ashamed of Paul's chains? (1:16)

   Onesiphorus is not ashamed of his chains.

Answer these questions by reading 2 Timothy 2

5. In what is Timothy to be strong? (2:1)

   He is to "be strong in the grace that is in Christ Jesus."

6. What do Hymenaeus and Philetus say? (2:17b-18)

   These persons hold "that the resurrection has already taken place."

7. What produces quarrels? (2:23)

   "Foolish and stupid arguments" produce quarrels.

8. To whom must "the Lord's servant " be kind? (2:24)

   The Lord's servant must be "kind to everyone."

Answer these questions by reading 2 Timothy 3

9. What comes in the last days? (3:1)

   "Terrible times" come in the last days.

10. Who rescued Paul from persecutions and sufferings? (3:11)

    The Lord rescued Paul from persecutions and sufferings.

11. Who will be persecuted? (3:12)

    "Everyone who wants to live a godly life in Christ Jesus will be persecuted."

Answer these questions by reading 2 Timothy 4

12. Who is to judge the living and the dead? (4:1)

    "Christ Jesus . . . will judge the living and the dead."

13. What is Timothy to preach? (4:2)

    He is to "preach the Word."

14. Who did "a great deal of harm" to Paul? (4:14)

    Alexander the metalworker did him great harm.

DIMENSION TWO:
WHAT DOES THE BIBLE MEAN?

2 Timothy 1:1-2. Paul's relationship to Timothy and to all the clergy who accept his apostolic authority is determined by "the promise of life that is in Christ Jesus." Union with

Christ Jesus is a present experience for all who respond to the gospel in faith. That union, although a present reality, is not complete. Therefore, life in Christ is both present and future, now and not yet, fulfillment and promise. In this salutation the emphasis falls on promise in order to correct at the beginning of this letter the false teaching of those who hold "that the resurrection has already taken place" (2:18). This emphasis is necessary in order to remind the church that God's saving work is still going on in human history and will not be consummated until the day of the Lord's appearing.

2 Timothy 1:3-7. Paul sees real danger that the faith he received from his ancestors and transmitted to others will not be passed on by those who come after him. The situation requires boldness and confidence on the part of those who are tempted to be timid and uncertain in the face of persecution. Paul seeks to fortify Timothy for his hour of testing by pointing out to him that his own ancestors, his grandmother Lois and his mother Eunice, persevered in the faith and passed it on to him. Now Paul reminds Timothy that it is his turn to do the same for those who come after him.

Faithful ministry is not automatic and is not guaranteed by ordination. The gift of God that Paul bestowed on Timothy by the laying on of his hands must be stirred up in the present crisis, or it will be lost. God has endowed Timothy with the gift that will enable him to meet a test: "a spirit of power, of love and of self-discipline" (1:7). Timothy and all the clergy are sure to fail if they rely on themselves, but in depending on God they will discover the inner strength to persevere, the deep devotion to endure, and the daily discipline to stand firm.

2 Timothy 1:8-14. Depending on God in bearing faithful witness to the gospel is possible because of what God has done in Christ Jesus. God has called and saved the ordained ministers of the church, not because of their qualifications, but because of God's self-giving love in Christ Jesus. Grace is the foundation of all ministry because God gives in the cross of Jesus Christ what no human could ever earn. The cross, rather than being a shameful defeat of God's purpose, is the vindication of God's love in human history. That love has conquered death by dying and, in the preaching of the gospel, offers life to all who die to self and live to God.

Paul and Timothy and all clergy are not ashamed of the gospel because in it they experience God's love for themselves and for all. Through God's love they are called to be faithful witnesses to that love. No matter what befalls them in their ministry, persecution or suffering or death, they live in the confidence that God who called them to ministry will sustain them in ministry until "that day."

The pattern for ministry is given in the gospel itself. It is a life for others. Just as Christ Jesus is "our Savior" because of his suffering for others, so his ministers in carrying out their witness to the Lord are not ashamed to be with him in suffering for others. They join "in suffering for the gospel, by the power of God," that is, in the Holy Spirit. Wherever the pattern of ministry given in the gospel is reproduced in the lives of ordained ministers, there the Holy Spirit is dwelling and working with them. No ministry is not a spiritual gift, and no spiritual gift is not ministry.

2 Timothy 1:15-18. How can the church distinguish between ministers who are spiritual and those who are not? In these verses Paul lays down a basic and practical test. Those ministers, like Phygelus and Hermogenes, who protect themselves from shame and suffering by turning away from their share in suffering are not spiritual. Those, like Onesiphorous, who expose themselves to shame and suffering by associating with persecuted and imprisoned preachers of the gospel, are spiritual. They join in suffering by reproducing in their lives the self-giving love of God revealed in Christ Jesus.

2 Timothy 2:1-7. Strength for ministry is given only in Christ Jesus. Grace, a gift of God in Christ Jesus, always is accompanied by responsibility. Paul reminds Timothy that grace is the claim of God's love that evokes absolute loyalty in the lives of those who receive that love. Timothy experienced grace, not as a general idea, but as a specific act of God proclaimed in the preaching of the gospel. The gospel is not Paul's private opinion but the message that many witnesses have transmitted. Grace, then, came to Timothy through faithful preachers; and Timothy is empowered by grace to guard what he received and pass it on to others. Therefore, to minister graciously is to pour out one's life for others, to "endure hardship with us like a good soldier of Christ Jesus."

The metaphor of "a good soldier" is particularly apt because it suggests that Timothy as an ordained minister is under orders. The military metaphor gives way to one from athletics that affirms that Timothy's ministry is subject to rigorous discipline. This athletic metaphor flows into one from agriculture that declares that ministry entails arduous labor. All these metaphors presuppose a commitment to live for others in obedience to the Lord. They all involve suffering, not for suffering's sake, but for the sake of the gospel. So what Paul teaches Timothy in these metaphors Timothy will come to understand only as he follows the Lord into dying to self and living for others.

2 Timothy 2:8-13. Ordained ministers can follow the Lord into suffering service because the Lord has lived the life of ministry on earth. The Lord's life is not a past event but a living presence because the One who died as a man, "descended from David," is raised up into glory. This gospel is the essence of Paul's preaching and the meaning of his suffering and imprisonment. Since Christ is raised from the dead, Paul's suffering on behalf of the gospel is good news that cannot be impeded by human opposition or defeated by any foe. By faith he lives and proclaims the

Resurrection and in his life reproduces the action of God that promises eternal life to all who respond in faith.

The life of faith that Paul shares with Timothy and the clergy and all Christians is a participation in the death and resurrection of the Lord, in his humiliation and in his glory. But what has been accomplished fully in the Lord is only imperfectly realized in his faithful people. Therefore, at any moment they may deny him and come under his judgment. This fearful prospect is clearly announced in verse 12 in order to call those who have failed to repentance. Nevertheless, the action of God in Christ cannot be revoked. The cross and Resurrection cannot be canceled out by human failure: "If we are faithless, / he will remain faithful, / for he cannot disown himself." The memory of Jesus Christ sustains all who struggle to remain faithful in times of persecutions and sufferings even when they fail to meet the test.

2 Timothy 2:14-19. The chief resource of ordained ministers is their responsibility to guard the truth and to transmit it faithfully. They can avoid "quarreling about words" and "godless chatter" by relying solely on "the word of truth," the self-giving love of God in Christ Jesus. Reliance on the gospel enables the clergy to stand approved before God solely on the basis of God's unmerited love. "Correctly handl[ing] the word of truth" is more than correct thought. It is basically living out of the relationship of faith made possible by the cross.

The life of ordained ministers, like the life of all Christians, is taking part in the gospel by dying to self and living to God. Since the Christian is always less than what God offers in Christ Jesus, the life of faith awaits the consummation of God's saving word on the day of the Lord. Those, like Hymenaeus and Philetus, who hold "that the resurrection has already taken place" deny the dynamic quality of Christian faith and encourage complacency and self-satisfaction in the church. They claim to have a superior knowledge, but in fact they are ignorant because they trust themselves rather than God. They are judged by God and cannot escape the fact that salvation does not depend on the certainty of human knowledge but on the certainty of God's knowledge. They are reminded of this by Paul in the hope that renewed memory will result in renewed faith.

2 Timothy 2:20-26. Life in the household of faith is always exposed to temptations and trials. Perfection is not possible since the work of salvation is a future hope based on present faith. So ordained ministers are called to prepare themselves to resist temptation by acknowledging their frailty and by seeking the company of all who turn to the Lord for strength. The unity of the church is built up, not by arrogant and self-confident clergy, but by those whose sense of need inspires them to "pursue righteousness, faith, love and peace." These qualities are the opposite of "foolish and stupid arguments" that breed quarrels because they are based on confident self-giving rather than anxious self-serving. Inasmuch as "righteousness, faith,

love and peace" are never fully realized, the teacher does not condemn those who succumb to temptation but rather is kindly, forbearing, and gentle with them. The basic attitude of the teacher is willingness to leave the result of one's labor to God in the knowledge that God alone leads persons to repentance and delivers them from bondage to evil.

2 Timothy 3:1-9. The period of history initiated by the death and resurrection of Christ Jesus is a time of severe testing for the servants of the Lord. Just as faithfulness to God involved Jesus in suffering, so his faithful people are involved in suffering. It is a time of sharp division between "lovers of themselves" (lovers of money and lovers of pleasure) and "lovers of God." False teachers are false because their lives are centered in self rather than in God. Their appearance is deceptive because they observe all the forms of religion while denying the substance of it. Their misplaced loyalty corrupts all that they are and do, so that they ruin themselves and others. They may seem to be powerful because they avoid suffering and shame by conforming to the world, but in reality they are impotent. Just as Jannes and Jambres, two opponents of Moses, were unable to hinder God's saving purpose, so godless men and women will achieve nothing in opposing the action of God in the church. God will judge and reveal their folly.

2 Timothy 3:10-16. On the other hand, those ordained ministers who guard the truth and who transmit it faithfully, although exposed to persecutions and sufferings, are safe in the care of the Lord. Paul's life illustrates this general truth. All that he is and does results in what the world considers shame and disgrace—"persecutions, sufferings." This is Paul's lot, not temporarily but permanently, as he makes his way from Antioch to Iconium to Lystra in the service of the Lord. Since Paul's life is centered in the Lord, he endures persecutions and is rescued from them all by the Lord, not in the sense of escape, but in the sense of victory over all that threatens his life.

Paul's sufferings and persecutions are not private. They are shared by "everyone who wants to live a godly life in Christ Jesus." Faithful ministers of the gospel are sustained by reality rather than appearance. It may seem that "evil men and impostors" are prospering because they avoid sufferings and persecutions. In fact, they are "deceiving and being deceived," going on from bad to worse as their love of self, love of money, and love of pleasure ruin their lives and corrupt their followers.

Timothy is encouraged by Paul to resist the deceit of false teaching by holding fast to what he has "learned and [has] become convinced of." The truth has been transmitted to him "from infancy" by faithful and reliable witnesses whose testimony is confirmed by the "holy Scriptures" of the people of God. The point in this context is that ordained ministers are equipped for their faithful witness to God's saving work by the "holy Scriptures" that were inspired by God's action in the past. The Scriptures are "useful for teaching, rebuking, correcting and training in righteousness" because they point beyond themselves to the living God who calls and equips the people of God for ministry in every age.

2 Timothy 4:1-5. Timothy is urged by Paul to understand that his ministry of the word is not subject to human evaluation, only to the judgment of God in Christ. Only his concern to please God and Christ will empower him to persevere in urgent, timely, consistent, and patient preaching and teaching. Timothy will please God, not by telling his hearers what they want to hear, but by correcting them in the truth of the gospel, rebuking them for falling away from the gospel, and encouraging them to return to the gospel. Such preaching and teaching will not be gladly received by the people because it will call them to become lovers of God rather than lovers of self. The truth will be offensive to them. They will seek teachers who will entertain them by leading them away from the truth into godless chatter and idle myths. Timothy as "the Lord's servant" will remain steady in the face of rejection of a fickle people by remembering that his suffering for the sake of the gospel is the work of God in which his ministry is fulfilled.

2 Timothy 4:6-8. Paul's ministry is coming to the fulfillment that he has just urged Timothy to pursue. He knows that his death is imminent, not as evidence of his failure, but as a sign that God's purposes are being consummated in his life. His life's blood poured out in faithful service is a sacrifice acceptable to God, for it is God's work in him. Paul's summation of his ministry, "I have fought the good fight, I have finished the race, I have kept the faith," is not bragging but the quiet confidence of one who has tested God's grace in the crucible of persecution and found it more than sufficient. Now he looks forward to his death and beyond death to his resurrection, the completion of salvation by the final triumph of God that God will freely award him "on that day." Paul's hope of ultimate victory over sin and death rests firmly on the invincible power of God revealed in Christ Jesus, power that guarantees him and "all who have longed for his appearing" eternal life.

2 Timothy 4:9-18. Paul's hope of eternal life, which includes all the faithful in God's final victory over sin and death, also binds him to the community of saints here on earth. He remains a vulnerable human being dependent on the ministry of his friends: Crescens, Titus, Mark, and Tychicus who are absent and Luke who is with him. Paul is especially sensitive to those who have hurt him because of their lack of loyalty: Demas who fled when he was in danger, Alexander who did him great harm, and all the unnamed who left him defenseless in his imprisonment. His disappointment at their failure is freely expressed and deeply felt.

But Paul does not lapse into self-pity. His death may be imminent, but he plans to stay on duty. So he asks Timothy to bring the cloak that he left with Carpus at Troas. In order that he may continue rightly to handle the word of truth, he also asks Timothy to bring the "scrolls, especially the parchments." Paul's indomitable spirit witnesses in his imprisonment to the fact that the Lord's grace was perfected in his weakness. Instead of his imprisonment hindering his ministry, it is transformed by the Lord into an occasion that "the message might be fully proclaimed and all the Gentiles might hear it." It is all the Lord's work. The Lord is faithful—for he cannot deny his saving work. Therefore "to him be glory for ever and ever. Amen."

2 Timothy 4:19-22. Paul knows that all his co-workers in the gospel face the same trials and tribulations that have befallen him. Therefore, as he greets them in closing he commits them to the Lord whose abiding presence with them is their only comfort and strength: "The Lord be with your spirit. Grace be with you."

DIMENSION THREE: WHAT DOES THE BIBLE MEAN TO ME?

2 Timothy 2:24-25—The Need for Kindness and Forbearance in Resisting Evil

Paul shows great passion and intensity in this letter as he mentions those whose teaching and behavior have hindered his ministry. But he also uses restraint, love, and self-control. Suggest here that Paul embodies the spirit of Jesus in dealing with those who have wronged him. Ask class members to reflect on instances in their experience when his Christlike spirit was lacking. How serious is this problem in the church today? Why is it so tempting to engage in reckless and destructive attacks on persons whom we identify as evil? When we give in to this temptation, are we overcome by evil? Explore how our zeal to defeat evil often leads us to become evil.

Paul's insistence that "the Lord's servant" must be "kind to everyone" may provoke a lively discussion. Guide the discussion to consider the basis for including one's foes in one's compassion. Remind class members that Paul became a Christian while he was an enemy of Christ by realizing that Christ included him in his love. Is it true that we are all included in the love of Christ precisely at the point of our need, our opposition to Christ? Does memory of his experience of grace help us act graciously and generously toward those who have wronged us? Look at the cross of Jesus Christ as the power that enables Christians to love their enemies.

Forbearing everyone means being patient and gentle with those who have failed. Explore forbearance as a willingness to sacrifice one's self-interest for the welfare of another. Does this mean that the impulse to get even or to punish must be subordinated to the responsibility to care for one another? Is forbearance indifference? How do you distinguish between them? Discuss forbearance as a positive strategy against the evil forces that threaten human existence.

2 Timothy 3:1-5—The Distinction Between the Form of Religion and the Power of Religion

One issue that is likely to surface is the place of liturgy in the life of the church. Point out that Paul is not attacking liturgy as a faithful response to God but empty forms that have the appearance of faith but no substance. Informal worship may be just as devoid of the power of religion as formal worship. The issue is how God is glorified or denied. When the church puts its trust in informality or in formality, it has lost its center and has the form of religion but denies the power.

Liturgy that glorifies God, regardless of its form, enables persons to respond to the power of God. The decisive issue is how that power is honored in the church. God's power is the self-giving love of Christ. Any religious act that is unloving is a denial of the power of God no matter how pious it may seem.

Ask class members to identify unloving actions in the church. Focus the discussion on your particular situation so that it will not become a condemnation of others. Close the discussion by relating the power of religion to the previous discussion of kindness and forbearance in dealing with evil.

For the grace of God that brings salvation has appeared to all men (2:11).

— 12 —

The Life of Grace in the Church

Titus

DIMENSION ONE:
WHAT DOES THE BIBLE SAY?

Answer these questions by reading Titus 1

1. What is Paul's responsibility as "a servant of God and an apostle of Jesus Christ"? (1:1)

   Paul's responsibility is "for the faith of God's elect and the knowledge of the truth."

2. To whom is the letter sent? (1:4)

   It is sent to Titus.

3. Where has Titus been left by Paul? Why? (1:5)

   Titus has been left in Crete to "straighten out what was left unfinished and appoint elders in every town."

4. What group is especially troublesome in Crete? (1:10)

   The circumcision group is especially troublesome in Crete.

5. How are the Cretans described? (1:12)

   They are described as "liars, evil brutes, lazy gluttons."

Answer these questions by reading Titus 2

6. What is Titus urged to teach? (2:1)

   He is urged to teach "what is in accord with sound doctrine."

7. Of what is Titus to be an example? (2:7)

   He is to be an example "of doing what is good."

8. To whom are slaves to be subject? (2:9)

   They are "to be subject to their masters."

9. What has appeared for the salvation of all? (2:11)

   "The grace of God that brings salvation has appeared to all men."

10. Who gave himself for us to redeem us? (2:13-14)

    "Our great God and Savior, Jesus Christ . . . gave himself for us to redeem us."

Answer these questions by reading Titus 3

11. To whom are the Cretans to be subject? (3:1)

    They are "to be subject to rulers and authorities."

12. Why are Christians saved? (3:5)

    They are saved because of God's mercy.

13. To what are believers in God to devote themselves? (3:8)

    Believers are "to devote themselves to doing what is good."

14. How many times is a divisive person to be warned? (3:10)

    Such a person is to be warned no more than two times.

15. Whom does Paul ask Titus to help on their way? (3:13)

    He asks Titus to help "Zenas the lawyer and Apollos on their way."

DIMENSION TWO:
WHAT DOES THE BIBLE MEAN?

Titus 1:1-4. One practical problem that Paul addresses in this letter is false teaching. Those who undermine the "faith of God's elect" and who substitute their speculations for revealed "knowledge of the truth" are liars. Paul combats them by insisting that God "does not lie"; that is, what God has promised God has fulfilled. Paul's ministry of preaching the word is an integral part of that fulfillment because God has entrusted the gospel to those faithful messengers who are commanded to guard and transmit the truth in the church. Since there is no church and no hope of eternal life if the gospel is not preached, an attack on the gospel and on those who preach it is an attack on God—an attack that calls into question God's faithfulness and power. These issues are raised in these opening verses of salutation, and they set the tone for all that follows in the body of the letter. This explains why the language is so intense and why Paul offers no possibility of tolerating the false teachers. Since these false teachers have denied the truth of the gospel, "they must be silenced" (1:11).

In Paul's gospel "knowledge of the truth" and "godliness" are inseparable. In other words, faith and works are integral parts of the message that God has commanded Paul to preach. "Godliness" is right living that is inspired by the message of truth. We have no hope of eternal life except as it is grounded in the word that creates a people who are identified by their relationship of obedience to God and their relationships of love and responsibility to other persons. "Godliness" is not a condition for God's action in the gospel, but since God's action is righteous, godliness is the inevitable consequence of God's action in the gospel. This joining of God's gracious initiative and the response of God's faithful people is the central theme of the letter.

Titus 1:5-8. The problem in Crete is not danger from without but corruption within. The church is threatened by ordained ministers who fail to realize the integrity of the gospel in their lives. The requirements for administrative leadership in the church laid down in these verses are intended as guidelines in the appointive process, but they also serve to call those who have erred to repentance. Ordained ministers are expected to be incarnations of the gospel in their private and public lives. Their conduct in the intimacy of their homes should witness to their obedience to God, not as an abstract ideal, but as the practical principle governing their relationships. If they are not ministers of peace in their homes, they are questionable servants of the grace of God.

Similarly, they must be beyond reproach in their public behavior. As God's stewards, ordained ministers are under control of the gospel. All forms of self-indulgence are repressed in the interest of promoting the welfare of the community by disciplined self-giving. Positively stated, administrative officers of the church who live by grace will be peacemakers in their homes and in their congregations.

Titus 1:9-16. Elders do not discover the gospel; they are taught the gospel. The "trustworthy message as it has been taught" is Paul's preaching. The first and foremost responsibility of elders who serve as bishops or overseers in the church is to hold firm to the gospel they have received. Holding firm will enable them to transmit the truth by teaching "sound doctrine" and thus confute the false teachers.

False teaching is seen in the behavior of the false teachers and in the confusion and unrest they create in the church. Their words have no power because their words are based on deceit rather than the truth. The basic deceit lies in the mistaken notion that salvation depends on the ritual or moral achievements of humankind. This fallacy is found in "the circumcision group." Adherents claim to follow a higher righteousness, but in reality they are disobedient and detestable. Instead of depending on God, they trust themselves. Since the center of their lives is self, they serve themselves and use others for selfish ends. They are aptly described as "always· liars, evil brutes, lazy gluttons." These harsh words of condemnation are intended to lead them to repent.

Repentance in this context involves coming to the realization that evil is not in disobeying the Jewish ritual laws but in disobeying God by living for themselves rather than for others. The circumcision party claims a higher knowledge of God. But all their claims are proved lies by the fact that they deny God's grace and use their position of responsibility for "dishonest gain." Instead of promoting peace in the church, "they are ruining whole households."

Titus 2:1-10. Against the background of the chaos and confusion wrought by false teaching in the church, Paul urges Titus to "teach what is in accord with sound doctrine." Just as a certain way of life arises from false teachings, so a certain way of life arises from "knowledge of the truth" (1:1). This way is not abstract or general but concrete and specific. This way of life requires different responsibilities and different actions from different people, but all are obliged to give themselves for others. The gospel is not a flight from the daily duties of human existence but a call to accept those duties as an opportunity for bringing credit upon "the word of God." God's word is credited, not by people skilled in winning arguments, but by people disciplined by the gospel to live according to the gospel in all their relationships.

Titus, as an authoritative teacher in the church, comes under the mandate of the gospel in the same way as all other members of the church. If he is to be an effective teacher of "what is in accord with sound doctrine," he must show himself "an example by doing what is good." This means that his teaching must be a disciplined life of love. Integrity in his teaching requires that his life embody what he teaches. This integrity is necessary so that the agreement between Titus's words and his deeds will silence his critics and leave them no reason to criticize his message or his life.

All this simply underscores the claim that the preaching of the gospel creates a community where "the word of God" is lived. This radical empowerment of the gospel transforms even the brutal institution of slavery into an opportunity for making attractive "the teaching about God our Savior." Christian slaves are called to live for their masters, not because their masters own them, but because the slaves belong to God in Christ. Since they are liberated by God from sin and death, they are freed from all self-seeking, so that they can "show that they can be fully trusted" to their earthly masters. The revolutionary power of the gospel rests in the fact that it frees men and women to live in their violent and imperfect world as if the power of God's self-giving love in Christ were accepted as the ruling power of the whole creation.

Titus 2:11-15. These verses are an eloquent and moving summary of the content of "sound doctrine." Without the transcendent inspiration of this passage the exhortations of verses 1 to 10 become an impossible burden. But when the two are joined, the nature and work of the church are securely grounded in the nature and work of God as revealed in Jesus Christ.

Although the entire passage is more liturgical than doctrinal, it has an inner logic that helps interpret its meaning. Referring to the appearance of the grace of God in verse 11 affirms the life and ministry of Jesus as the controlling center of Christian faith. The inclusiveness of the Incarnation is such that through it "salvation has appeared to all men." The grace of God, however, is not restricted to the past. It continues to operate in the life of the church by training the faithful to turn away from idolatry and self-centeredness ("ungodliness and worldly passions"). Here the preaching and teaching of the truth seem to be the means whereby God's grace revealed in the Incarnation continues to operate in the church. Preaching and teaching "sound doctrine," the gospel, enables the faithful to embody the truth by living "self-controlled, upright and godly lives in this present age." In this sense, through the preaching and teaching of the gospel, the church is the extension of the Incarnation in human history.

The work of the church is a sign that the church by faith already participates in the glory that will not be fully revealed until the appearing "of our great God and Savior, Jesus Christ." To await the blessed hope of eternal life is not to flee the world in flights of fantasy but rather "to live self-controlled, upright and godly lives in this present age." The life of hope is confirmed in the steadfast and disciplined love that the brothers and sisters give and receive in the church. Without hope we can give no consistent Christian witness. Without a consistent Christian witness hope degenerates into empty talk and deceit.

What, then, is the sure foundation of the church as it works and waits in the world? The answer is the person and work "of our great God and Savior, Jesus Christ." The ancient world was accustomed to emperors who claimed to be gods and saviors. The text here declares that Jesus Christ is the great God and Savior of all the universe because in him God's nature is revealed and God's work is accomplished.

This breathtaking claim is grounded not in human speculation but in the cross, in God's self-giving love. The church exists in working and waiting, in faith and hope, because God in Christ has redeemed it "from all wickedness" and purified it for God's holy work in the world. The redemption and purification of the church are not complete and will not be complete as long as human history continues. But the church looks confidently toward the consummation of God's salvation on the day of "the glorious appearing of our great God and Savior, Jesus Christ," because the One who comes is none other than the One "who gave himself for us."

Titus 3:1-8a. The first two verses of this passage grow out of Paul's understanding that "the grace of God that brings salvation has appeared to all men" (2:11). Since the action of God in Christ is not limited, those who obey the gospel are required not only to live at peace with their brothers and sisters but also with all classes of people in the world. This requirement entails submission and obedience to public rulers and authorities.

"Whatever is good" is the obligation Christians are called to accept as citizens. The requirements of self-control in speech and gentleness and courtesy in conduct, which are mandatory within the community of faith, are also the standards of behavior Christians are commanded to observe in their relationships with all persons. Christians show that they have been redeemed from all sin and purified as a people of God by living in the world as a colony of heaven. Instead of conforming to the standards of the world, they are a transforming and redeeming force in the world that brings credit to "the word of God" and makes "the teaching about God our Savior attractive."

All this inclusive public behavior is the consequence of "rebirth and renewal" wrought in the Christian by "the kindness and love of God our Savior." Christians remember that they were once slaves of "ungodliness and worldly passions." They were enemies of God, "foolish, disobedient, deceived and enslaved by all kinds of passions and pleasures. We lived in malice and envy, being hated and hating one another." They were alienated from God and separated from one another. They deserved God's anger and judgment, but God in Jesus Christ looked graciously on them. In "kindness and love" God saved them, not because they had done anything to merit God's favor, but simply because God had mercy on them.

The relevance of all this for Christian conduct in a non-Christian world is quite clear. Christians witness to their salvation by imitating God. This means that they show all persons, without regard for merit, the same "kindness and love" they have received from a merciful God.

The empowering center for Christian civic morality is, quite surprisingly, baptism. Baptism is a sacrament of God's grace. Baptism focuses attention on the action of God that cleanses the individual of the rebellion and iniquity that have separated the person from the community and alienated the person from God. This dramatic enactment of the gospel is accompanied by the Holy Spirit, the love of God poured out in the cross of Jesus Christ. This love renews broken relationships and sets the Christian in a new relationship. Thus, the Christian is justified, assured of the love of God in Christ, and enabled to live out of that relationship by faith. The future holds no fear because nothing can separate the heirs of God's household from God's love, not even death itself.

The startling dimension of this interpretation is that it applies the regeneration and renewal of inclusion in God's household to life in the world. Baptism and the outpouring of the Holy Spirit equip, empower, and claim God's people for ministry, not only in the church, but in the whole inhabited earth.

Titus 3:8b-11. The instructions Paul has given Titus are of the utmost importance for the life of his church. Therefore, Paul "wants" Titus "to stress" them. "These things" refer not only to the ethical exhortations in the letter but also to the theological presuppositions that are the source and norm of Christian behavior. The union of "sound doctrine" and "good deeds" essential to the integrity of the gospel is clearly shown in the expected result of Titus's ministry: "So that those who have trusted in God may be careful to devote themselves to doing what is good." Belief in God that does not produce acts of self-giving love in the church and in the world is empty talk and deception. On the other hand, the effort to do good deeds that is not controlled and empowered by belief in God soon degenerates into acts of self-serving arrogance, violence, envy, and malice. The union of "sound doctrine" and "good deeds," which is the distinctive mark of Paul's gospel, meets the practical test of promoting the welfare of persons in the church and in the world. "These things," belief in God and good deeds, are "excellent and profitable" because they enable Christians to be agents of God's peace in the church and in the world.

By contrast, the substance of false teaching destroys the integrity of the gospel. By focusing on "foolish controversies" and "genealogies" persons come to depend on their own superior knowledge and morality. They deny God and are preoccupied with "arguments and quarrels about the law." Since false teaching is powerless to produce good deeds in the church and in the world, it is "unprofitable and useless." Instead of promoting peace it creates rebellion, disobedience, and insubordination.

The trouble created by false teachers in Crete is no trivial matter to Paul. They are attacking God's saving work in Jesus Christ by seeking to replace faith in the gospel with faith in human achievement. Those who are "divisive," who promote and follow deception and empty talk, are to be admonished by Titus as a representative of Paul's authoritative gospel. If they persist in rejecting the truth for the lie after they have been warned once or twice, they are to be excommunicated.

In other words, when false teaching is seen in arrogance, quick temper, drunkenness, violence, and greed, the can-cerous threat to the entire body is so immediate and urgent that radical surgery is required. This extreme action is recommended only in those instances where the union of false teaching and detestable and disobedient action leave no doubt that the person involved has condemned himself or herself as "warped and sinful."

Titus 3:12-15. Paul's interest in the welfare of Titus and his urging that Titus come to see him and make provision for the mission of Zenas and Apollos are good deeds that are in accord with sound doctrine. The self-giving love of God in Christ creates a community of persons who are learning in the crises of urgent need to be fruitful in the gospel. By applying themselves to the disciplines of mutual ministry, they witness to the reality of God's grace in their lives. Thus, Christians live self-controlled, upright, and godly lives in the world as they await the hope of eternal life.

DIMENSION THREE: WHAT DOES THE BIBLE MEAN TO ME?

Titus 2:1-14—Relationships Among Christians in the Church

One basic idea for discussion is Paul's insistence that all Christians come under the same obligation to live for others. Lead class members into a discussion of ways in which the contemporary church seems to insist on a higher standard of morality for the clergy than for the laity. Ask them to list instances of this double standard. Then probe the reasons this has developed. Conclude by looking at the dangers of a double standard for clergy and laity in the church.

Another facet of this issue is how the self-giving love of God in Christ requires specific duties and responsibilities in concrete relationships. What might it mean for grandmothers and grandfathers to live for others in the church? Enlarge the discussion to include husbands and wives, fathers and mothers, children, singles, friends, and so on.

You may become aware of the frequent use of such words as *ought* and *should* in the discussion. These words express Christian imperatives. But they are often separated from Christian indicatives, statements about what God does in Christ to empower Christian response. Try to recover some of the Christian indicatives, affirmations of the gospel, that make self-giving love in the church possible.

Titus 3:1-8a—Relationships Between Christians and the World

Christians are obligated to show self-giving love, not only in the church but also in the world, for the simple reason that God's love in Christ is for the world. One important task of this discussion is to help class members see that the church and all Christians receive God's love, not because they are in the church, but because they are part of God's world. Focus on the fact that God has created all the world and intends the salvation of the whole world.

Look for ways to distinguish between the world and worldliness. The former refers to God's creation. The latter refers to creation in rebellion against God. What does God give the church that he has not given the world? Is the church distinguished from the world only by the fact that God's gifts are received and enjoyed in the church while they are rejected and ignored in the world?

One challenge for the church is the temptation either to conform to the world or to ignore it. What are some signs that the church conforms to the world? Help class members relate conformity to the world to false teaching. What are some signs that the church ignores the world? Look for a connection between ignoring the world and false teaching. Then raise the possibility of the church witnessing to God's self-giving love for the world by living responsibly in the world. How does this relate to baptism? Is baptism a public acknowledgment on the part of the church that the world is claimed by God's love? How are baptized persons empowered by God's love to live in the world as agents of that love? Pursue these questions in relationship to politics, economics, and community welfare. Help class members see that preaching and teaching sound doctrine always involve specific Christian behavior in the public domain.

I do wish, brother, that I may have some benefit from you in the Lord; refresh my heart in Christ (20).

— 13 —

Christian Refreshment

Philemon

DIMENSION ONE:
WHAT DOES THE BIBLE SAY?

Answer these questions by reading Philemon

1. To whom is the letter written? (1)

   The letter is written to Philemon.

2. Who else are included in the salutation? (2)

   "Apphia our sister, . . . Archippus our fellow soldier and . . . the church that meets in [their] home" are included in the salutation.

3. Why does Paul thank God always? (4-5)

   He thanks God always because he hears of their love and their faith.

4. What has Paul derived from Philemon's love? (7)

   Paul has derived "great joy and encouragement" from Philemon's love.

5. How does Paul identify himself? (9)

   He identifies himself as "an old man and now also a prisoner of Christ Jesus."

6. Whose father does Paul become in his imprisonment? (10)

   In his imprisonment Paul becomes the father of Onesimus.

7. Whom does Paul send back to Philemon? (10, 12)

   He sends Onesimus back to Philemon.

8. Does Paul want Philemon's goodness to be spontaneous or forced? (14)

   Paul wants Philemon's goodness to be spontaneous.

9. How is Philemon to receive Onesimus? (15-16)

   He is to receive him, not as a slave, but as "a dear brother."

10. Who will repay what Onesimus owes Philemon? (18-19)

    Paul writes that he will repay what Onesimus owes Philemon.

11. Of what is Paul confident? (21)

    He is confident of Philemon's obedience.

12. What does Paul ask Philemon to prepare for him? (22)

    Paul asks Philemon to "prepare a guest room for me."

13. Who is Paul's fellow prisoner? (23)

    Epaphras is his fellow prisoner.

14. Who are Paul's fellow workers? (24)

    Mark, Aristarchus, Demas, and Luke are his fellow workers.

DIMENSION TWO:
WHAT DOES THE BIBLE MEAN?

Philemon 1-3. This intimate letter from Paul to Philemon has been included in the New Testament because it sets the personal relationship between Paul and Philemon in the larger context of the nature and mission of the church. The general teaching concerning the Christian conduct of slaves and masters (see Colossians 3:22–4:1) is given concrete and specific implementation in the appeal of Paul to Philemon to receive Onesimus as "a dear brother." The letter also shows the integrity of the gospel as the action of God in Christ is understood in terms of the relationships created among the members of the community of faith.

The proclamation of "God our Father and the Lord Jesus Christ" is good news because it always transforms the hearers into prisoners, children, brothers, sisters, fellow workers, partners, and ambassadors. Just as the "church that meets in your home" is founded on grace and peace "from God our Father and the Lord Jesus Christ," so the grace and peace in Colosse includes the story of Paul, Timothy, Philemon, Apphia, Archippus, Onesimus, Epaphras, Mark, Aristarchus, Demas, and Luke.

This letter is properly interpreted when it is read as the tip of an iceberg that floats because it is supported by a vast underwater mass of complex and specific personal and social interrelationships. Those interrelationships are of no value unless they are interpreted against the background of all that God has done, is doing, and will do in the Lord Jesus Christ. God's story in this letter is the history of the human actors, and the history of the human actors is God's story.

Paul and his associates in the gospel have entered into a new world that is quite different from the world of their culture. One way to understand how radically different from the world of their culture is the world of the gospel is to pay close attention to the metaphors that define life in the church. In the world of their culture all persons have fathers who bind them into their respective families. In the world of the gospel all who have come to faith in Jesus Christ are children of God our Father who binds them into the universal household of God. In the world of their culture all persons are under the lordship of some earthly authority to whom they give their allegiance. In the world of the gospel all believers are subject to the authority of the Lord Jesus Christ to whom they give their absolute allegiance. The world of their culture has social distinctions that divide persons into masters and slaves and dictate the roles they are to play. In the world of the gospel all members under the fatherhood of God and lordship of Jesus Christ are equal as brothers and sisters and live under orders to serve one another. The basis of Paul's letter to Philemon is that the world of the gospel is the only real world and as such takes precedence over the world of cultural authority and class distinctions.

Life in the world of the gospel is not escape into fantasy. Rather, it is living in the world of culture by depending on the power and presence of "God our Father and the Lord Jesus Christ." For example, Paul as he writes to Philemon is a prisoner somewhere in the Roman Empire, probably in Rome. He is subject to the supreme authority of the culture. His destiny is in the hands of his captors. They control his physical actions.

But actually Paul is under the lordship and control of no human power. His lord is Jesus Christ. He is "a prisoner of Christ Jesus." This allegiance is the only real authority he recognizes. As a slave of Jesus Christ, Paul's imprisonment is transformed into an opportunity to serve his God.

Faith in this context is the decision to live in the world of culture as if the only real world were the gospel world of "God our Father and the Lord Jesus Christ."

Although Paul makes no explicit reference to the relationship of slave and master in these opening verses, by implication he has established the basis of his appeal to the master, Philemon, on behalf of the runaway slave, Onesimus. In the body of the letter Paul will make explicit what is here implicit. He will appeal to Philemon to decide to live in the world of master and slave as if the only real world were the gospel world of the family of God where all believers are beloved brothers and sisters in the Lord.

Philemon 4-7. Paul does not immediately raise the issue that will occupy his attention in the body of the letter. Instead, he recalls the action of God in the life of Philemon, which is the only reason a decision must be made about how a master should treat a runaway slave. From the point of view of the world of masters and slaves, a master's duty is to punish the criminal so the laws that insure a stable society will be maintained. But Philemon shares another point of view with Paul and all the saints because he has heard and obeyed the gospel. Here Paul is not flattering Philemon; he is glorifying God. God through Paul's preaching in Colosse brought Philemon to faith. Philemon is no longer defined by the circumstances of Colossian culture but by the reality of the fatherhood of God and the lordship of Jesus Christ. He is a new creation, and when Paul remembers that miracle of faith, he gives thanks to God always.

Philemon's faith, although intensely personal, is essentially communal. To live in the real world of the gospel is to become a transforming instrument of God's love in the world of culture. Philemon's love, since it springs from the self-giving love of God in Christ for all, includes all. Paul is counting on his reference to his memory to stir Philemon's memory so that he will recall how God came to him in the preaching of the gospel and accepted him as a child and beloved member of the family without condition.

The love of God shared in the gospel begets love shared in the community. Paul's evangelistic strategy is the creation of loving communities that live in the world of culture as if the only real world were the world of love and faith "in the Lord Jesus . . . and . . . all the saints." Love shared in the community promotes "a full understanding of every good thing we have in Christ." Paul's concern for Philemon's faith and love in the church is not a narrow ecclesiastical focus but a broad missionary commitment that includes the world of the flesh as the realm of God's saving love. The church that meets in Philemon's house in love and faith toward the Lord Jesus Christ is a sign of God's saving purpose for the world of culture. If the church turns its back on the world of master and slaves and their relationships, it has forgotten what it is and what it is required to do as the creation of God and as the slave of Jesus Christ.

Paul's joy and comfort are derived from the ministry of love that Philemon carries out in the church for the refreshment of the "hearts of the saints." In other words, what sustains Paul in the trials and tribulations of his imprisonment ("in chains") is the realization of the gospel in the work of faith and love in Philemon. The implication here is that the one thing Paul fears is that Philemon might fail to meet the test by refusing to receive Onesimus as "a dear brother" (16). Paul knows that if Philemon rejects Onesimus, he also rejects Paul and all the saints and the Lord Jesus Christ.

The refreshment or renewal of the church in its heart or essential being is hearing and obeying the gospel. The gospel is heard and obeyed when the world of culture, the world of masters and slaves, is transformed by the decision to live in that world as if the only real world were the world created by God and ruled by Jesus Christ. This is the issue that Paul will now address directly in his appeal to Philemon on behalf of Onesimus.

Philemon 8-14. Paul's authority as an apostle is not the authority of status or institutional office but the ministerial authority of the gospel. "In Christ" refers to the revelation of God's self-giving love in the cross and resurrection of Jesus. This invincible love is the norm of conduct in the church and the essence of "what you ought to do" for those who believe in Jesus Christ. Paul and Philemon stand in the same relationship of depending on God's love. Paul appeals to Philemon to act out of that love. Paul's sole authority for this passionate appeal is his role as an ambassador or representative of God's love. "What you ought to do" for Paul is exactly "what you ought to do" for all members of God's household, to act out of love, to live for others. Paul's imprisonment does not frustrate God's love but rather offers him an opportunity to live for Christ Jesus by doing the work of Christ Jesus as an agent of God's love.

As "an old man and now also a prisoner of Christ Jesus" what Paul ought to do is to live for others. In the first place, he must give priority to the welfare of Onesimus. His concern for Onesimus is rooted and grounded in his apostolic ministry, in his preaching of the gospel. In the gospel the runaway slave has been transformed into Paul's child. Onesimus is no longer a criminal, a fugitive from justice, but is now a member of the new world through the power of God's love. In that new world Paul is the father and Onesimus the child. In Paul's imprisonment, in circumstances that seem to deny the power of the gospel, the gospel has done its work. Paul and Onesimus are a new creation.

In the second place, to live for others requires that Paul have the same concern for Philemon, the master, as he has for Onesimus, the slave. In the play on the meaning of the name Onesimus ("Formerly he was useless to you, but now he has become useful both to you and to me"), Paul is not being clever. Rather, he is inviting Philemon to enter into the new creation of the gospel metaphor by accepting Onesimus, not as a runaway, but as a "dear brother." Philemon is invited to live now by faith as if the kingdom of God had already been established in the world of flesh.

Out of concern for Philemon, Paul sends Onesimus back to Colosse. In doing so Paul sends his very life, for Onesimus has become a part of him in the gospel. Paul sacrifices his self-interest, the service that Onesimus has rendered him during his imprisonment "for the gospel," so that Philemon of his own free will may "consent" to the status that Onesimus now has as "a dear brother" in Christ. The only way Philemon may experience how useful Onesimus has become in the household of faith is to receive him "as a beloved brother." Since Paul covets for Philemon the full riches of the transforming power of the gospel, he has no choice but to send Onesimus back and to wait for Philemon "to do what [he] ought to do."

Philemon 15-20. In all this complex relationship Paul discerns the purpose of God. Grace has brought Onesimus to Paul in prison. Grace has enabled Paul to father his child Onesimus. Grace has required Paul to send Onesimus back to Philemon. Now grace is at work in Philemon placing him under the command of Christ's love. Grace empowers him to act out of that love by recognizing that Onesimus is no longer a slave but now is more than a slave, "a dear brother."

The relationships of the world of masters and slaves are temporary, but the relationships of the gospel world are eternal, "for good." Paul has already received the grace of God in Onesimus. Now Philemon has an opportunity to receive that same grace but to receive it even more fully than Paul. Philemon is challenged to relate to Onesimus in the flesh as his master and in the Lord as his brother. In other words, since Philemon is Onesimus's master, the grace of God requires him to treat his slave as if his only real status were that of a brother in Christ. The grace of God is not limited to the relationships of the community of faith but claims the whole world for Christ and requires that believers live in the world as witnesses to the transforming power of Christ's love. "Both as a man and as a brother in the Lord" is Paul's recognition that the eternal relationships of the gospel must be honored in the temporal relationships of the world. Philemon is under orders, not from Paul but from the Lord, to treat his runaway slave as if he were "a dear brother."

Paul and Philemon are partners in ministry, but their partnership is not automatic. In order for it to be effective, both parties must conform to the gospel they are called to serve. Conforming to the gospel is basically living for others. Just as Paul and Philemon have been received into God's household, so they are called to receive their brothers and sisters. To fail to offer hospitality to "all the saints" is to renounce the partnership of ministry and to exclude oneself from the community. The solidarity of the church is such that to receive one is to receive all. Therefore, Paul, on the basis of the unity of the community, appeals to Philemon to receive Onesimus as he would receive Paul.

Paul's identification with Onesimus is such that he takes on himself the debt that the slave has incurred by running away from his master. Although Onesimus's identity as "a dear brother" takes priority over his identity as a slave, Paul recognizes that Onesimus has wronged Philemon and owes him restitution. The requirements of the world of masters and slaves are not canceled by the gospel. Rather, they are intensified so that Paul as an ambassador of the gospel takes on himself the responsibility of paying all that Onesimus owes Philemon. Paul is so committed to this action that he wants to make sure that no one misunderstands the seriousness of his commitment. He takes the pen from his secretary and signs his name to guarantee to all who read the letter that he is legally obligated to repay Philemon all that he has lost because of his runaway slave.

Paul's action in assuming Onesimus's debt to Philemon prompts him to remind Philemon of what he owes Paul. Philemon owes Paul in the gospel more than any person could ever repay: his "very self." This phrase probably refers to the fact that Philemon received his life as "a dear brother" in Christ through Paul's preaching of the gospel. All who have come to faith through the power of the gospel have a common identity as members of the household of God. Although Paul and Philemon and Onesimus have their respective obligations in the community of faith, under the fatherhood of God and the lordship of Jesus Christ, they are equal as beloved brothers. The only "benefit" that Paul expects from his brother Philemon is that he witness to the power of the gospel by receiving Onesimus as his equal, "as a dear brother."

Remember that Paul is writing from prison. His life is in danger. His heart, the very core of his being, is being tried by the trials and tribulations of captivity. What does he need in this crisis to refresh his heart, to restore and renew his strength? The only thing he needs is for Philemon "to do what [he] ought to do." Paul will be cheered and encouraged to persevere in his ministry when Philemon remembers who he is, a child of God in Christ, and receives Onesimus for what he is, "a dear brother" in Christ.

Philemon 21-22. Paul has done all that he can do. He has assumed full responsibility for interpreting the gospel to Philemon in the concrete situation of the return of his runaway slave. His appeal to Philemon on behalf of Onesimus has been motivated by God's self-giving love in Christ and has taken the form of that love as he has given himself for Philemon. Paul participates in the power of that love as he waits confidently for the triumph of the gospel in Philemon. He trusts the gospel to set Philemon free from the bondage of his culture so that he can live in the freedom of a slave of Christ. Paul does not presume to tell Philemon exactly what to do but rather sets Philemon under the command of Christ so that he can discover for himself what he is required to do. Since Paul trusts the grace of God to make a place for Onesimus in Philemon's house, Paul has no doubt that he will find a guest room prepared and waiting in Philemon's house should he be released from prison and make his way once again to Colosse.

Philemon 23-25. The letter ends as it began by setting the personal relationship between Paul and Philemon in the larger context of the church universal. The return of Onesimus to Philemon is not a private matter between master and slave but a corporate concern that involves the welfare of the entire community. This involvement is true because all are united under the sovereignty of Christ Jesus and all are empowered by his grace to live at peace in God's household as dear brothers and sisters. Therefore, the last word on the matter is not an appeal to Philemon but a blessing affirming what God offers all the brothers and sisters: "The grace of the Lord Jesus Christ be with your spirit."

DIMENSION THREE: WHAT DOES THE BIBLE MEAN TO ME?

Philemon 4-7
The Scope of Christian Refreshment

One startling thing about Paul in this letter is how vulnerable he shows himself to be. He does not pretend to be superhuman. Rather, he allows his need for "joy and encouragement" to become known as he makes his personal appeal to Philemon: "I do wish, brother, that I may have some benefit from you in the Lord; refresh my heart in Christ." Why does this revelation of Paul's dependence on others seem so startling to us? Explore the issue of the stereotypes that we tend to impose on biblical characters. How do we carry these stereotypes into our self-understanding and our understanding of others in the Christian community? Ask class members to identify these stereotypes by describing their mental images of an apostle, a preacher, a teacher, a saint.

This issue is crucial for growth in Christian community because recognizing need is the prior condition for receiving the ministry of others. Help class members identify personal needs and group needs. Is there any human need that is not a proper concern of the church? Which needs do we tend to ignore or suppress? Are there signs that some people have turned away from the church because their needs have been denied or ignored? How does Paul's attitude in this letter help us identify our need for refreshment and our need to give it to others?

Philemon 15-20
The Source of Christian Refreshment

How do we distinguish between a selfish preoccupation with personal and group needs for refreshment and a proper sense of personal and group dependence on God's love in Jesus Christ for restoration and renewal? Paul seems to be aware of his needs because he is engaged in a ministry of love that always demands more than he has to offer. Help class members see how Christian service is always a human impossibility. Ask them to reflect on how they often feel inadequate for particular forms of Christian service. Is refreshment of the heart, understood as restoration and renewal, an essential preparation for Christian ministry? How does one receive this rest? Ask class members to help you list specific experiences of restoration and renewal in ministry.

Perhaps class members will already sense that Christian refreshment is an experience of God's love in Jesus Christ. But it will probably help to explore this generalization in terms of specific instances. List persons whose lives of service are expressions of God's love. Be sure your list includes members of your church, individuals who refresh the hearts of others, as well as other, more well-known persons. What is characteristic of such persons? How are their attitudes and actions different from the attitudes and actions of our culture? What is the reason for the difference?

Review Paul's letter to Philemon as a document that reveals how the Christian community is a fellowship of refreshment. Conclude by pointing out that those who are effective in ministry are usually those who are able to receive ministry.

HEBREWS; JAMES; 1 AND 2 PETER; 1, 2, 3 JOHN; JUDE
Table of Contents

1. Jesus, God's Superior Messenger 214

2. Jesus, God's Superior High Priest 219

3. Jesus, Priest of a Better Covenant, Tent, and Sacrifice 224

4. Faith, the Superior Way to Do God's Will 229

5. The Demands of Enduring Faith 234

6. A Manual of Wise Instruction, Part 1 239

7. A Manual of Wise Instruction, Part 2 245

8. How to Live in a Hostile World 251

9. How to Handle the Crisis in the Church 257

10. The Basis of Christian Fellowship 263

11. Fellowship in the Family of God 268

12. Two Personal Letters From John 274

13. The Book of Jude 280

About the Writer

Dr. Keith Schoville, the writer of these teacher book lessons, is professor emeritus in the Department of Hebrew and Semitic Studies at the University of Wisconsin-Madison. He is the author of *Biblical Archaeology in Focus*, an introduction to archaeology, and numerous articles in dictionaries and journals on archaeology and the biblical world.

Dr. Schoville has excavated at Tel Dan in northern Israel, Tel Lachish in the south-central region of the country, and Tel Aroer in the southern region.

In these last days [God] has spoken to us by his Son (1:2).

— 1 —

Jesus, God's Superior Messenger

Hebrews 1:1–4:13

DIMENSION ONE:
WHAT DOES THE BIBLE SAY?

Answer these questions by reading Hebrews 1

1. List the characteristics that set God's Son above the prophets. (1:2-3)

   He is the heir of all things, the creator of the universe, the one who radiates God's glory and "the exact representation of his being." The Son also sustains all things by the power of his word. He made purification for sins, and he is seated at God's right hand.

2. How is the Son superior to the angels? (1:6-7, 14)

   The angels are to worship the Son. They are servants; the inferior worships the superior.

3. Why was the Son anointed above all his companions? (1:9)

   The Son was anointed above his companions because he "loved righteousness and hated wickedness."

Answer these questions by reading Hebrews 2

4. In 2:1, the reader is warned of the danger of drifting away. What is the reader warned of in 2:3a?

   The reader is warned not to "ignore such a great salvation."

5. Identify the three sources that testify to the "great salvation" provided in Christ. (2:3b-4)

   The great salvation was announced by the Lord (Jesus), "confirmed to us by those who heard him" (disciples and apostles), and testified to by God through signs, wonders and various miracles, and "gifts of the Holy Spirit."

6. Why was the Son, who is superior to the angels, made lower than the angels for a time? (2:9)

   The Son was made lower than the angels so that he could "taste death for everyone."

7. The writer of Hebrews emphasizes the human experience of the Lord (2:14-18). What specific human experiences of his are mentioned in this section?

   The specific human experiences of the Lord mentioned in the section are death (2:14), suffering, and temptation (2:18).

Answer these questions by reading Hebrews 3

8. Jesus and Moses are both described as faithful to God in 3:1-6. What phrases indicate Moses' relationship to God and the superior relationship of Christ to God? (3:5-6)

   Moses was faithful to God "as a servant"; Christ was faithful to God "as a son."

9. In 3:7-19, three dangers are listed: never entering God's rest, turning away from the living God, and the possibility of not sharing in Christ. What is the basic cause for these disasters? (3:12, 19)

   The basic cause for these disasters is unbelief.

10. What can be done to safeguard the believer from the danger of unbelief? (3:13)

    By encouraging one another daily, believers safeguard themselves against the danger of unbelief.

Answer these questions by reading Hebrews 4:1-13

11. In the previous section, failure to enter into God's rest was the result of unbelief. In 4:1-13, a different but equivalent word is used. What is that word? (4:11)

    In 4:11, disobedience *is the cause of failure to enter God's rest.*

12. Why is it impossible to hide unbelief from God? (4:12-13)

The penetrating word of God discerns "the thoughts and attitudes of the heart," and "nothing in all creation is hidden from God's sight."

DIMENSION TWO: WHAT DOES THE BIBLE MEAN?

Exploring Hebrews. Every teacher wants to communicate effectively. To enable class members to understand the message and the meaning of Hebrews, you must have a grasp of the basic information about the book. The following brief overview of Hebrews will provide direction toward your goal of helping class members benefit from their study of this fascinating book.

A Sermon, Not a Letter. The translators of the King James Version confidently entitled this book "The Epistle of Paul the Apostle to the Hebrews." Unlike the majority of the letters in the New Testament, however, Hebrews lacks the features we would expect in a letter. The text includes no introduction, indicating the sender and the recipient or recipients, and no greeting of grace, peace, and the like. The writer begins with a theological discussion that sets the stage for the major emphasis of the book, that Jesus Christ is God's final and complete revelation.

The writer's main arguments are followed by exhortations to the readers. In the last chapter the writer calls his communication "my word of exhortation" (13:22). Hebrews appears to be a written sermon to which has been added a brief closing such as we find in letters (13:22-25).

You will want to understand the major points in the sermon outline in order to follow the main thought of the writer.

Outline of Hebrews.
I. Jesus, the superior messenger (1:1–4:13)
   A. Superior to prophets (1:1-3a)
   B. Superior to angels (1:3b–2:18)
   C. Superior to Moses and Joshua (3:7–4:10)
   D. Exhortation (4:11-13)
II. Jesus, the superior high priest (4:14–10:18)
   A. A superior appointment (4:14–5:10)
   B. Exhortations (5:11–6:20)
   C. Seven superior aspects of his priesthood (7:1–10:18)
      1. An earlier order of priesthood (7:1-19)
      2. A priest by oath (7:20-22)
      3. A permanent priesthood (7:23-25)
      4. A sinless priest (7:26-28)
      5. Priest of a new covenant (8:1-13)
      6. Priest of a more perfect tent (9:1-28)
      7. Priest of a "once for all" sacrifice (10:1-18)

III. Exhortation: faith and endurance (10:19–12:29)
   A. Faith and endurance defined and illustrated (10:19–11:40)
   B. Exhortation to persevere (12:1-29)
IV. Concluding exhortations (13:1-25)

You will notice that our lesson divisions do not exactly follow the outline above. The lessons were arranged with space considerations in mind as well as the time available to study each lesson. This first lesson, however, does conform to the first section of the outline of the book.

The Origin of Hebrews. No one knows who wrote Hebrews, the place in which it was written, the date of writing, or who the intended first readers were. Even the original title, if one existed, is not known. The title, "The Letter to the Hebrews," seems to be based on the content of the book rather than being a formal title.

The writer was probably not the apostle Paul. He looks back on "those who heard" the Lord (2:3b-4), suggesting that he is a second-generation believer. Among other possible writers are Luke, Silas, Peter, Apollos, Barnabas, and Aquila and Priscilla. The Greek style of the book differs from that of Paul's letters. Hebrews approaches Luke and Acts in excellence of style. Detailed study of the ideas in Hebrews also confirms that Paul is unlikely to have written the book.

For whom was this document first intended? The content indicates that the first readers were Jewish Christians. The writer, however, makes no mention of circumcision, worship in the Jerusalem Temple, or ritual law, though he does refer to the Temple and ritual. Many converts from Judaism lived in the Diaspora, away from Palestine and in the Greek Roman world. Also, many God-fearing Gentiles who attended Jewish synagogues accepted Jesus as the Messiah. They had a general acquaintance with the Old Testament traditions that the writer assumes the readers know.

The first recipients of the letter were probably members of a mixed congregation of converted Jews and Gentiles. The document was likely sent to Alexandria, Rome, or Jerusalem. Rome is the best possibility. The writer exhorts the readers to stand fast in the face of persecution and suffering. Christians in Rome had experienced such hardships. Also, with the writer were "those from Italy" (13:24); and their greetings may have been sent "back home" to Rome.

Possible dates for the writing of Hebrews range from A.D. 65 to A.D. 95. The first reference to the work is that of Clement of Rome, about A.D. 96. Since the concerns of the book are with conditions in the period after the apostles, the date was probably close to the end of the century.

The Significance of Hebrews. Hebrews provides a powerful case for the uniqueness of Jesus Christ as God's final revelation for the salvation of people. From the time it was first written to the present, the work has provided instruction that makes specific what Jesus expressed in general terms in Matthew 5:17: "Do not think that I have come to abolish the Law or the Prophets; I have not come to abolish them but to fulfill them." To become familiar with Hebrews is to receive essential instruction in the faith once for all delivered to the saints. It is to receive the exhortations to constancy that every generation seems to need. The message of Hebrews is of timeless value.

Hebrews 1:1-3. This introduction reminds us of the Creation account in Genesis, where God speaks and the material universe comes into existence. The passage also reminds us of the first eighteen verses of the Gospel of John, where the creative Word of God is identified with Jesus. In John also, the testimony is that the Son was the active agent in creation; and he has made God known.

The idea of the Son having the same nature as God and radiating God's glory echoes the words of Jesus—"Anyone who has seen me has seen the Father" (John 14:9b)—and of Paul—"For God was pleased to have all his fullness dwell in him" (Colossians 1:19).

The writer introduces in the first three verses the two basic themes that will be expanded later: Jesus Christ is the superior revelation of God, and he has made purification of sins. This last idea will include both Jesus Christ's role as a fitting sacrifice for sin and as a supremely capable high priest.

Hebrews 1:4-14. The writer proves the superiority of the Son over angels by referring to Scripture. He assumes his readers are familiar with the passages he quotes. These quotations may pose a problem for modern readers who frequently are not as familiar with the Old Testament as believers were in the early church.

The sources for the quotations are discussed in the student book. The writer tends to quote from the Septuagint, the earliest Greek version of the Old Testament. The translation may not always agree exactly with our New International Version because the NIV was translated from the Hebrew text. Textual variations existed in Hebrew manuscripts even before the Septuagint was translated in the third century B.C. These variations were usually minor in extent and importance. They caused little concern to either Christians or Jews.

Sometimes the quotations in Hebrews are not exactly what we have in the Septuagint or the Hebrew. We can assume that the writer was quoting freely rather than exactly, or he was quoting from a manuscript that did not follow exactly the known Greek version.

"The name" (1:4) is more excellent than that of the angels in several respects.

1. It signals a more intimate relationship with God. The Son is the firstborn of God. None of the angels is as intimate with God.

2. At his birth the angels are called to worship him, recalling the angelic praise at the nativity of Jesus (Luke 2:13-14).

3. The Son is enthroned as a king forever. Angels are messengers for the heavenly king. They do not rule.

4. The Son is the source of salvation, as the writer will emphasize later in the letter. Angels, while servants of the king, are ministering spirits sent forth to do his will by serving the saved.

Hebrews 2:1-4. Therefore introduces the first of several exhortations in Hebrews. The writer fears that his readers may drift away from the revelation in Jesus that they have heard. Or they may neglect, that is, pay no attention to, what has been revealed—such a great salvation. Much of what is presented later in the book provides details of just how great that salvation is.

The previous message is the law of Moses. (See the student book.) Its promises were substantial and valid, as one would expect of a message delivered by angels. Anyone who drifted away from that message faced the consequences.

The superior message, the revelation in and by Jesus, was attested by more impressive evidence than was the law of Moses. Jesus delivered the message; the disciples who heard him speak confirmed it; and God bore witness to the validity of that message. God did this during the ministry of Jesus through signs, wonders, and miracles. These words echo those of Peter in his great sermon on Pentecost: "Jesus of Nazareth was a man accredited by God to you by miracles, wonders and signs, which God did among you through him, as you yourselves know—" (Acts 2:22).

God also bore witness to the validity of the message after the ascension of Jesus through the gifts of the Holy Spirit. Spiritual gifts are referred to in several places in the New Testament (Romans 12:3-8; 1 Corinthians 12; Ephesians 4:8-16).

Hebrews 2:5-13. Read the comments for this section in the student book. The idea of the superiority of the Son over angels is directly followed by the astounding evidence of the humanity of Jesus. While this happened historically, it has its ultimate effect in "the world to come" (2:5), when everything will be under subjection to Jesus Christ. He will be clothed again in heavenly glory, and many will share his glory (2:10, 13b). Jesus referred to these ideas in his prayer in the upper room (John 17:5).

The quotations in 2:12-13 are from Psalm 22:22 and Isaiah 8:17-18, yet our writer has treated them as the words of Jesus. As the fulfillment of God's revelation, Jesus is seen as speaking through the psalmist and the prophet. To hear the prophetic word is to hear the voice of Christ.

Hebrews 2:14-18. It may be more a judgment of our time than of Scripture, but the major difficulty you confront in discussing this section with class members may be the reference to the devil. We do not need to sidestep the issue of evil here represented by the devil. In a materialistic world the reality of spiritual forces is often denied, but this is to deny an essential part of our being; for we are more than matter.

The devil does not have the power of death in the sense of determining who dies and when. That power is retained by the Creator. (King Hezekiah is a case in point. God told him he would die but gave him an additional fifteen years of life on his tearful request [Isaiah 38:1-6].) The power of death here is the power of sin, the power to divert us from the true source of happiness in life—the fulfillment of God's will for our lives. The diversion is to some substitute that looks alluring but finally does not satisfy. Satisfying self is the substitute that draws people away from fulfilling God's will. Ultimately such bondage to self ends in death, "and after that . . . judgment" (9:27). Jesus suffered and died to save individuals from both bondage and judgment.

In 2:14, *destroy* can signify "to nullify; to render incompetent, inconsequential." The devil has been rendered impotent, but not to everyone. The devil is impotent to those who follow Jesus, the pioneer of their salvation.

Hebrews 3:1-6. Jesus is both an apostle (messenger) who brought God's superior revelation and the high priest who hears our confession. The confession here is connected with worship. An example of a confession that an Israelite was to make when he brought his offering to God before the priest is found in Deuteronomy 26:5-10. Essentially, the confession recounts God's deliverance and blessings.

The content of the Christian confession in mind here is also a recognition of God's deliverance from sin and blessings given to us in Jesus. Essentially this confession is praise to God.

The word *house* in this passage has no connection with a physical building. Verse 6 clarifies the meaning: "We are his house." This meaning of *house* is in line with, for example, Ephesians 2:19-22; for the church, the people of God, are his house.

Hebrews 3:7-19. Moses was faithful over God's people as a servant. Yet the generation over which he was faithful provoked the wrath of God by rebelling, by refusing to follow God's ways. The result was God's solemn oath: "They shall never enter my rest." As the student book indicates, the rest is the Promised Land.

Unbelief and disobedience are essentially the same. They lead people to turn away from the living God. The protection against the danger of unbelief is the daily encouragement of one another (3:13).

Hebrews 4:1-13. *Therefore* introduces an exhortation. This exhortation is based on the example of the Israelites under Moses who failed to enter into the Promised Land. A greater-than-Moses has brought good news to us, the writer indicates in 3:5-6. The promise of entering God's rest remains.

The writer's point is that, long after the Hebrews rebelled and failed to enter the Promised Land, God spoke of a rest again through David (4:7). The exhortation is that his readers have entered into that rest through faith (4:3). But a further aspect of that rest remains to be attained (4:11). The danger is that they will not reach that ultimate rest because of a lack of faith (4:1-2).

The sabbath rest of God began with the completion of Creation; however, according to Jesus, God was still at work (John 5:17). That work was completed in Jesus when on the cross he cried, "It is finished!" The rest of God in Christ is available for now and for eternity. Belief is the means of entrance now, and obedience is the manner by which we attain the future rest.

DIMENSION THREE: WHAT DOES THE BIBLE MEAN TO ME?

Hebrews 1—Pluralism and the Church

The problem of how to live as a Christian in a pluralistic society is not limited to our time. The Christians who first read Hebrews lived in a world in which a variety of religions and superstitions abounded. Christians were a minority group in the last half of the first century. Some of the Christians apparently were tempted to turn their backs on what they had confessed. Our writer wrote to those so tempted. He emphasized the superior and exclusive claims of Christ.

This emphasis is exactly the antidote for timid believers today. The hope of the Christian must be in Jesus Christ as the Lord. The testimony of the apostles is unswerving: "Salvation is found in no one else, for there is no other name under heaven given to men by which we must be saved" (Acts 4:12). The central teaching of the New Testament must be the foundation on which any church stands, or it cannot be the body of Christ.

At the same time, those who differ from us must be dealt with in a Christlike way. To confront error in an unchristian way is to alienate someone for whom the Lord died. Let our testimony be positive but not destructive.

Hebrews 2:1-4; 3:7– 4:13
Counteracting the Danger of Apostasy

Everyone ought to recognize that the danger of apostasy exists. The way is narrow, as Jesus taught. Those who find it have a climb to make. Perhaps the most helpful truth as we make our spiritual pilgrimage is to realize that we are not alone. Besides the help of Christ through the Holy Spirit, Hebrews tells us to "exhort one another every day" (3:13). The mutual support of Christians is essential to our lives. Be a friend and draw on the strength of your Christian friends. Jesus did.

Hebrews 2:9–3:6; 4:13
Developing a Personal Relationship With Christ

Drawing on our lesson material, we learn that we are encouraged to a personal relationship with Jesus Christ by God. For example, in 2:9, we are told that Jesus tasted death for us "by the grace of God." The atoning death of Jesus is for each of us personally. Further, the human experiences of Jesus indicate his concern for each of us personally. He is able (and interested) to help us when we are tempted.

Prayer is one means of personal access to God; but if you really want to communicate to God your personal love and loyalty, you can do so by being an obedient servant.

We have a great high priest who has gone through the heavens, Jesus the Son of God (4:14).

2

Jesus, God's Superior High Priest

Hebrews 4:14–7:28

DIMENSION ONE: WHAT DOES THE BIBLE SAY?

Answer these questions by reading Hebrews 4:14–5:14

1. Why should Christians expect to receive a sympathetic hearing at the throne of grace? (4:15)

   Our high priest, Jesus, sympathizes with us; for he "has been tempted in every way, just as we are."

2. What is the function of a high priest? (5:1)

   A high priest offers to God gifts and sacrifices on behalf of believers.

3. Of what benefit to other people was the obedient suffering of Jesus? (5:8-9)

   Through his suffering, Jesus became "the source of eternal salvation for all who obey him."

4. Why was the writer of Hebrews annoyed with those to whom he wrote? (5:11-14)

   The writer thought that his readers had failed to mature in their understanding of God's revealed word.

Answer these questions by reading Hebrews 6

5. The "elementary teachings about Christ" are mentioned in 6:1. What are included in these teachings? (6:1-2)

   The elementary teachings include repentance, faith, instruction on baptisms, "the laying on of hands, the resurrection of the dead, and eternal judgment."

6. To what spiritual blight does the writer compare cultivated land that bears thorns and thistles? (6:4-8)

   The writer compares such land to the sin of apostasy.

7. In what way does the faithful person show love for God? (6:10)

   The faithful person shows love for God in helping God's people.

8. What has been the basis of hope for believers from Abraham to the time when Hebrews was written? (6:13-18)

   The basis of hope for believers has been faith in God's promises.

Answer these questions by reading Hebrews 7

9. Why was the priesthood of Melchizedek considered endless? (7:3)

   No record of his birth or death exists, nor is there any record of a beginning or ending to his priesthood.

10. In verse 7, the words *lesser* and *greater* are used. To whom do they refer? (7:4-7)

    The lesser is Abraham; the greater is Melchizedek.

11. Why was the Levitical priesthood replaced by "the order of Melchizedek"? (7:11)

    Perfection (spiritual maturity) was not attainable through the Levitical priesthood.

12. The priesthood of the tribe of Levi was established under the law of Moses. How is the priesthood of the Lord justified? (7:12-17)

    The priesthood of the Lord is justified by a change in God's law. The evidence for the change is Christ's indestructible life.

13. What makes Jesus "the guarantee of a better covenant"? (7:20-22)

His priesthood was established on the oath of God.

14. List the ways in which Jesus, as permanent priest, is superior to the former priesthood. (7:26-27)

Jesus is "holy, blameless, pure, set apart from sinners, exalted above the heavens." None of these words were applicable to the other priests. They offered sacrifices often, for themselves and the people. Jesus offered himself as a sacrifice once for all people and for all time.

DIMENSION TWO: WHAT DOES THE BIBLE MEAN?

Having covered the superiority of Jesus as the revealer of God's will, beyond that of prophets, angels, and the major Israelite leaders, Moses and Joshua, the writer of Hebrews turns to his second emphasis: the function of Jesus as God's superior high priest. Jesus' priestly office is presented as superior to that of the line of Levitical high priests that began with Aaron, the brother of Moses.

The Levitical Priesthood. The basic information on the Levitical priesthood given below will help you and the class members understand more clearly the propositions of the writer of Hebrews. Comprehensive articles on the subject can be found in Bible dictionaries and encyclopedias.

The Israelite priesthood fell to the men of the tribe of Levi. Aaron and Moses were of that tribe. After the Exodus from Egypt and the subsequent establishment of the covenant between God and the Israelites at Mount Sinai, Aaron was appointed high priest (Exodus 28:1; Leviticus 8).

Aaron and his sons were to serve God in the Tent of Meeting. Priests always function in connection with sanctuaries, special facilities that are restricted for specific religious rituals. The Tent of Meeting was a portable sanctuary. As long as the Israelites lived in tents, migrating in the Peninsula of Sinai and in the desert, it was appropriate that God's sanctuary among them should also be a tent. It was a grand tent, as befitting God, in contrast to the simple tents of the people.

The instructions for building the Tent of Meeting (Tabernacle) and its furnishings are recorded in Exodus 25–27. The actual construction is detailed in Exodus 35–38, and the erection of the Tabernacle follows in Exodus 40. Without the Tabernacle, the people would not have needed a priesthood.

The priestly office was planned as an integral part of the Tabernacle. The tent represented the presence of God: "Have them make a sanctuary for me, and I will dwell among them" (Exodus 25:8). It is dangerous to live in the vicinity of God, who is utterly holy and who hates sin. Even when God met Moses on the mountain, the people encamped at the base were warned not to draw near and touch the mountain on penalty of death (Exodus 19:10-13). Yet God desired "a kingdom of priests and a holy nation" (Exodus 19:6).

How could this problem be solved? The answer was the Tabernacle and the priesthood. Aaron and his sons were set apart (consecrated) to serve as intermediaries between the holy God and the unholy people. In order to carry out this function, the priests attained a higher level of holiness than the common people. The priests wore special clothing. They were restricted in their nonpriestly activities so that they did not engage in anything that might make them ritually unclean. To do so would have made them unfit to serve in the Tabernacle and liable to die (Exodus 28:42-43).

Some of the restrictions for a priest are listed here: a priest with a physical defect could not serve, nor could a priest under the influence of alcohol. Priests were allowed to marry only a virgin of Israel, not a divorcée, prostitute, convert, nor, for the high priest, even a widow. A priest was not to touch the dead for fear of ritual defilement. The high priest could not have contact with the dead, even of his immediate family.

Despite all the restrictions on the lives of the priests, and especially of the high priest, their purity could not be completely established or maintained. On the Day of Atonement each year, the high priest had to make an offering for his sins as well as for the sins of the people. The people could bring their offerings to the door of the Tabernacle, but it was the priests who actually performed the sacrifices. The holiness within the sanctuary was too great to allow individual Israelites to come nearer than the outer door.

The holiness of the sanctuary increased from the outer door and courts toward the Holy Place within the tent and into the Most Holy Place. The Most Holy Place was separated from the Holy Place by a veil (a heavy curtain). This inner sanctum contained the ark of the covenant and represented God's presence. Priests entered daily into the Holy Place, but the Most Holy Place was entered only once a year, on the Day of Atonement, and only by the high priest after he had offered sacrifices for his sins and the people's sins. Thus the presence of the holy God in the midst of the people was maintained through the priestly functions.

The Tabernacle and the Temple. The system of the Tabernacle and the priesthood continued in Israel after the conquest of Canaan until the Temple in Jerusalem was built by King Solomon. The priests functioned in the permanent sanctuary as they had in the tent. That first Temple continued in use for over three hundred years, until it was destroyed by Nebuchadnezzar in his conquest of Jerusalem in 587 B.C.

The second Temple was built on the ruins of Solomon's Temple after the return of the Jews from the Babylonian Exile about 520 B.C. The plan of both temples was the same as that of the Tabernacle. The second Temple underwent a major reconstruction in the time of Herod the Great. It was this Temple Jesus taught at, cleansed of money changers, and wept over. The Temple was destroyed by the Romans in A.D. 70 as they crushed a revolt of the Jews. The priesthood of the Temple ceased to function after the destruction.

Hebrews 4:14-16. Just as the Levitical high priest passed through the outer sections of the Tabernacle and through the veil to reach the Most Holy Place, Jesus went "through the heavens" as he drew near to the true sanctuary—the actual abode of God, heaven itself. Christians can draw near with confidence to the "throne of grace." The equivalent in the earthly Tabernacle was the ark of the covenant in the Most Holy Place, a symbol of God's throne and presence.

The emphasis of this section is to "hold firmly to the faith we profess." Jesus is the subject of the "faith we profess" (Matthew 16:16).

Hebrews 5:1-10. Jesus and Aaron served similar priestly functions, acting on behalf of people in relation to God. The writer has pointed out that Jesus was tempted in every human way, yet without sin (4:15). Not so Aaron; he sinned when tempted. Jesus and Aaron do share one thing: they did not seek the priestly role. God called them both. In the case of Jesus, however, he was designated "high priest in the order of Melchizedek" (5:10).

Jesus not only experienced temptations like all individuals during the course of his life. He experienced excruciating suffering in those last hours of his life in Gethsemane (Luke 22:40-44), in his humiliating trials, and on Calvary. He "learned obedience" through these experiences. But did God answer his prayers and supplications?

The answer is clearly yes, and the answer was the provision of strength to fulfill God's will and purpose for his life. Jesus' words throw light on this subject in the incident when one of his disciples cut off the ear of the high priest's servant with a sword. Jesus ordered him to put the sword away, adding, "Do you think I cannot call on my Father, and he will at once put at my disposal more than twelve legions of angels? But how then would the Scriptures be fulfilled, that say it must happen in this way?" (Matthew 26:53-54).

Jesus fulfilled the will of God for his life. He was made perfect. He completed his life's purpose, and that purpose was that he would become "the source of eternal salvation for all who obey him."

Hebrews 5:11–6:8. Consult the student book for the comments on this section. Paul expressed similar thoughts in Philippians 3:13-15, pressing toward the goal of the heavenward call of God in Christ Jesus and calling on the mature to be like-minded. The mature are those who by exercising mental discipline have developed the ability to distinguish between the good and the less than good (5:14).

Being born into the kingdom of God does not assure maturity to the individual. Jesus provides the example for believers who want to develop into mature, well-rounded individuals. He increased in wisdom (Luke 2:52). Our spiritual sensitivities must be developed by exercising them. The inquisitive Jesus was discussing difficult questions with the religious leaders in the Temple when he was just twelve years old (Luke 2:46).

Constant discussions and bickering in churches and between Christian groups over the elemental doctrines of the faith indicate immaturity. The New Testament teaching taken at face value should be sufficient in respect to the first principles. All believers should seek to be united in matters of faith. Jesus prayed for the unity of believers. Friendly discussions of matters of opinion and nonessentials is acceptable. As Christians exercise their spiritual faculties, however, they should be able to go on beyond the elementary teachings (6:1-2).

The reason for our writer's emphasis on this matter is simply that immaturity opens believers to the danger of falling away (6:4-6). If the roots of faith are shallow, reaching only into the topsoil, the strong winds of adversity will uproot the weak. Apparently others in the early church were like Demas, Paul's traveling companion: "Because he loved this world," he forsook the apostle and the faith (2 Timothy 4:10).

One problem in the early history of the church was how to deal with the lapsed. The lapsed were those who, under persecution, complied with the Roman order to burn incense to the emperor. The church was faced with the problem of what to do with such people who had conformed with the civil law rather than face martyrdom. The viewpoint that finally won the day was that no human sin is beyond God's forgiveness. That forgiveness should be seen in the visible church as well as in the eternal church.

The apostates the writer of Hebrews has in mind, it appears, had fallen away from the Lord because they chose to remain immature rather than to grow in faith. Such were gullible enough to "abandon the faith and follow deceiving spirits and things taught by demons. Such teachings come through hypocritical liars, whose consciences have been seared" (1 Timothy 4:1-2). Falling from grace, they seem to have had their consciences seared, too, so that they could not be moved again by the gospel of love and grace in the way they once had been moved.

We have every reason, however, to pray for and encourage the unsaved. God is not willing that any be lost but that all should come to salvation. The story of the prodigal son is sufficient encouragement for us to continue in prayer for the lapsed of our time.

Hebrews 6:9-20. We ought to assume that most of the people in the church are honest, sincere, committed Christians who are attempting to live their lives to the praise of Christ's glory. That is really what our writer is doing in terms of his readers (6:9). We need not hunt for the negative, faithless person in the church. Jesus taught that the weeds should grow up with the wheat until the time of harvest (Matthew 13:24-30). And the harvest is God's.

The "better things" that belong to salvation for the sincere believer (6:9) are not specified. The writer was certainly not suggesting that persecutions would cease. Perhaps the idea here is that word of the Lord to his productive servant: "Well done, good and faithful servant" (Matthew 25:21).

The servant attitude fits well on the follower of Jesus. He said of himself, " The Son of Man did not come to be served, but to serve" (Matthew 20:28). The disciple, when mature, will be like the master. The people who first read the Letter to the Hebrews were not among the apostate, of this the writer was certain. They showed the marks of true discipleship. They loved one another (John 13:35). They looked after fellow Christians.

Believers who work for others in the name of the Lord can suffer burnout, the equivalent of being "lazy" (6:12). To guard against this possibility, the writer urges the readers to imitate the people of the past who attained the promises of God through faith and patience. Abraham is a prime example of one who patiently endured and who "received what was promised" (6:15).

Abraham had been promised a son, and the promise was affirmed by the oath of God (6:13-14). The fulfillment of the promise was in Isaac. God also promised Abraham that through his seed all the nations of the earth would be blessed (Genesis 22:18). This blessing is accomplished through faith in Jesus Christ. Those who believe the promises of God in Christ are children of Abraham by faith. He is the father of the faithful.

Those who trust in the promises of God in Jesus, as Abraham trusted in God's promises, have a strong encouragement. We are encouraged to hold on doggedly to our hope. Our hope is Jesus, who is stable and unswerving, as solid as an anchor. "Heaven and earth will pass away," he said, "but my words will never pass away" (Matthew 24:35). Jesus, our hope, is not something visible on earth. He has entered heaven on our behalf. His promise to his followers is "that you also may be where I am" (John 14:3).

Hebrews 7:1-28. The last verse of Chapter 6 ends the long exhortation that began in 5:11, right after a reference to Melchizedek. The writer turns the readers' attention back to the main topic: Jesus as a high priest in the order of Melchizedek. Then he presents the seven proofs of Jesus' superiority as a high priest. The first four are contained in Chapter 7.

The first of the proofs is a long argument presented in 7:1-19. The point is that the priesthood of Jesus in the order of Melchizedek is a higher order of priesthood than the Levitical priesthood.

Just before this (6:13-18) the readers were reminded of God's sworn promise to Abraham. Everyone who read the letter was aware of the primary place the patriarch Abraham held as a model in the biblical faith. The biblical information about Melchizedek is directly related to Abraham, so the arguments presented in Hebrews are weighty.

What does the writer indicate about the mysterious figure of Melchizedek?

1. Melchizedek is a historical shadow of Jesus as a high priest. He resembles the Son of God (7:3). Note these points of comparison:
   a. both are priests of the Most High God;
   b. the name *Melchizedek* anticipates the character of Jesus, who is righteous and the Prince of Peace (Isaiah 9:6);
   c. each is a priest forever, because there is no written record of the beginning and end of the priesthood.
2. In relation to Abraham, Melchizedek was greater because Abraham paid tithes to him and he blessed Abraham. (Symbolically, the forefather of the Levitical priests [Levi] also paid tithes to Melchizedek while Levi was yet unborn.)

The Levitical priesthood is shown to be imperfect (7:11-19), otherwise there would have been no necessity for the Son becoming a priest in the order of Melchizedek. The Levitical priesthood could not remove sin, so another priest was needed (7:11).

A new priesthood could only be established by a change of law. The Levitical priesthood was based on the law of Moses. The new priesthood is based on the power of an indestructible life, not on a written, legal requirement (7:16). The basis of the new priesthood is the statement of God in Psalm 110:4. This word of God was given in the psalm several centuries after the time of Moses. This change in the law allowed Jesus, who was from the tribe of Judah, to become a priest.

Second, Jesus was not only called and appointed by God (5:4-5), his appointment was confirmed by the solemn oath of God (7:20-21). None of the Levitical priests were confirmed by an oath. So Jesus is our guarantee of a better covenant (7:22).

Third, Jesus is an unchangeable priest because he lives forever (7:23-25). He is always available to intercede and save. The Levitical priests were replaced at their deaths. They were temporary and changeable.

Fourth, Jesus is a perfect priest (7:26-28). He offered himself once, a completely sufficient sacrifice for all people in all times. His perfection has brought him above the highest heavens. The Levitical priests were sinners, offering up animal sacrifices frequently for their own sins as well as for the sins of the people.

If you feel inadequate to deal with the ideas presented above, please do not let that keep you from the effort. Deal with the ideas as best you can, realizing that the more you read and think about Jesus as high priest, the more other passages in the Bible help enrich the concept. God will bless you with sufficient understanding to lead the class members to a more biblical understanding of what God was doing on our behalf in Jesus Christ. Please note that the last verse of Chapter 7 says it was God's initiative that provided such a superior high priest for us. Let us be thankful for God's love.

DIMENSION THREE: WHAT DOES THE BIBLE MEAN TO ME?

Hebrews 5:11–6:8
Spiritual Maturity and the Danger of Apostasy

The fact that you and the class members are studying the Genesis to Revelation Series of Bible studies indicates an interest in going on in your quest for spiritual maturity. Here are some points to ponder out of the advice the writer gives to those who read Hebrews.

He suggests that we can become slow of learning if all we do is hear. We also ought to teach. How can one become a teacher rather than simply a person constantly being taught? Continuing education is an essential part of being a Christian. We are called to be disciples of Christ, and *disciple* means "learner." Yet part of our learning should also be learning how to teach. What should be done on the individual level to develop teaching skills? What program or programs exist in your local church to assist the members in developing their teaching abilities?

On the other hand, does the text really demand that we all be teachers in a formal sense, that is, with a classroom full of students, books, and other equipment? What types of informal teaching might individual Christians do who would never feel comfortable standing before a class? Home Bible study groups are growing in popularity in many places. Could these groups be a good substitute for the formal teaching setting?

Finally, how useful is teaching as a tool for strengthening the faith and commitment of the individual teacher?

Hebrews 5:7-10—Prayer

Prayer is appropriate. If Jesus, the Son of God, depended on prayer in the midst of a crisis in his life, we ought to learn from his example.

Prayer can be an emotional experience. Let us develop a tender heart ourselves, and let us tolerate the tears of others.

We pray to One who has the power to save. With God, nothing shall be called impossible.

God's plan for your life, or for the life of the church in which you are involved, may mean that you must pass through the valley of the shadow of death. God's will for our lives must override our desires.

Be prepared for negative answers to prayer and what may seem to be unanswered prayers. All prayers are heard, and God's will is being worked out in the midst of it all.

3

Jesus, Priest of a Better Covenant, Tent, and Sacrifice

Hebrews 8:1–10:18

DIMENSION ONE:
WHAT DOES THE BIBLE SAY?

Answer these questions by reading Hebrews 8

1. Where is the high priest of Christians now located? (8:1b)

   The high priest of Christians is now seated "at the right hand of the throne of the Majesty in heaven."

2. Moses constructed the earthly Tabernacle after what pattern? (8:5)

   Moses constructed the earthly Tabernacle after the pattern of the heavenly sanctuary.

3. Why is the new covenant, under which Christ has his ministry, better than the old covenant? (8:6)

   The new covenant is better because "it is founded on better promises."

4. How can we be certain that the first covenant was not faultless? (8:7)

   If the first covenant had been faultless, God would not have found it necessary to establish a new covenant.

5. With what people did the Lord promise to establish the new covenant? (8:8)

   The Lord promised to "make a new covenant with the house of Israel and with the house of Judah."

6. What did the Lord promise to do for his people under the new covenant? (8:10)

   The Lord promised to put his laws in the minds and on the hearts of his people.

Answer these questions by reading Hebrews 9

7. What did the ark of the covenant contain? (9:4)

   The ark of the covenant "contained the gold jar of manna, Aaron's staff that had budded, and the stone tablets of the covenant."

8. What did the high priest always carry with him when he entered the second (inner) room? (9:6-7)

   The high priest always carried the blood of sacrifice when he entered the inner room.

9. How often did Christ enter into the "perfect tabernacle," and what did he take with him? (9:11-12)

   Christ entered only once into "the Most Holy Place" taking with him his own blood.

10. What is the blood of Christ able to do? (9:14)

    The blood of Christ is able to cleanse the conscience "from acts that lead to death, so that we may serve the living God!"

11. How did the old covenant make possible the forgiveness of sins? (9:22)

    The forgiveness of sins was made possible by the shedding of blood.

12. For whose benefit did Christ appear before God in heaven? (9:24)

   Christ appeared before God in heaven "for us."

13. For what purpose will Christ appear a second time? (9:28)

   Christ "will appear a second time . . . to bring salvation to those who are waiting for him."

Answer these questions by reading Hebrews 10:1-18

14. What did Christ desire to do when he came into the world? (10:7)

   Christ desired to do the will of God.

15. Under the new covenant, what two things did the Lord promise to do? (10:16-17)

   Under the new covenant God promised to "put my laws in their hearts, and . . . write them on their minds" and to remember "their sins and lawless acts . . . no more."

DIMENSION TWO: WHAT DOES THE BIBLE MEAN?

The entire Book of Hebrews focuses on the superiority of Christ over all who preceded him. We noted his superiority as the means of God's revelation (Lesson 1) and his superiority as a high priest (Lesson 2).

In this lesson we will focus on matters directly related to Christ's priesthood. These are the covenant that is connected to his priesthood, the tent (tabernacle/temple) in which he ministers, and the sacrifice that Christ presented to almighty God.

Hebrews 8:1-6. In 8:1, the writer draws on Psalm 110 for the idea of one "who sat down at the right hand of the throne of the Majesty in heaven." Verse 1 of the psalm reads:

The LORD says to my Lord:
   "Sit at my right hand
until I make your enemies
   a footstool for your feet."

"Majesty in heaven" is a substitute for God. This phrase is the same as "the Majesty in heaven" of Hebrews 1:3. Using a substitute expression, rather than pronouncing the name of God, was the usual way of referring to God in the period in which the New Testament was written. This practice grew out of the awe in which God was held and the fear of breaking the commandment not to take the Lord's name in vain. Our writer, apparently a devout Jewish Christian, found it natural to write in this fashion.

The idea of a throne or a temple in heaven was widespread in Jewish circles in New Testament times. The idea

had its roots in the Old Testament. There the Tabernacle first appears as a unique tent in the desert camp of Israel. The Tabernacle represents God's presence with the people. Such was the case until the Temple was built in Jerusalem. The Temple served a similar function as God's house. Solomon said of it: "I have indeed built a magnificent temple for you, a place for you to dwell forever" (1 Kings 8:13). He also prayed these words at the dedication of the Temple: "But will God really dwell on earth? The heavens, even the highest heaven, cannot contain you. How much less this temple I have built!" (1 Kings 8:27).

Jesus is called a minister in the (heavenly) sanctuary (8:2); that is, the Most Holy Place. The true tent is the entire sacred installation. As high priest, Jesus could serve as priest throughout the heavenly complex. Not all Israelite priests could enter all areas of the earthly sanctuary. Only the high priest had the authority and obligation to enter the Most Holy Place.

The writer envisions the heavenly sanctuary as a tent rather than a temple, for he uses the expression "set up," meaning "pitched," rather than the word *built.* This heavenly sanctuary existed before the earthly Tabernacle, which was built on the plan of the heavenly (8:5). The verse is a quotation of God's instructions to Moses on the matter in Exodus 25:40.

The thought of the writer progresses logically in these verses. Jesus is a superior high priest who serves a superior (heavenly) sanctuary, so his ministry is better than that of the earthly copy. It is as much better as the covenant he mediates is better. This better covenant is the main point of the section. The reference to the better covenant leads naturally into the discussion of it in the following verses.

Hebrews 8:7-13. Just as the heavenly tent surpasses in importance the earthly tent, so the new covenant surpasses the old. The new covenant has better promises than the old (8:6). But the main reason why a new covenant, or agreement, between God and humans is needed is that the old covenant is faulted.

As if someone among his readers had raised the question "How do you know the old covenant is not faultless?" the writer notes Jeremiah 31:31 in 8:8. Long after Moses, in the time of the prophet Jeremiah (about 600 B.C.), God revealed that the Mosaic covenant was not faultless. The fault was that God's people "did not remain faithful to my covenant" (8:9b). So the coming of a new covenant was revealed by God.

Jeremiah also prophesied an exile of God's people from Judah and Jerusalem to Babylonia. It was to last seventy years (Jeremiah 29:10). The fulfillment of this prophecy is noted in Ezra 1:1.

The fulfillment of Jeremiah's prophecy about the Exile helped the Jews look forward to the fulfillment of his prophecy about a new covenant. The Essenes, a community of devout Jews who lived at the northwest corner of the Dead Sea before and during the days of the early church, believed they had been chosen by God to be members of the new covenant. Jesus mentioned the establishment of the new covenant in his blood at the Last Supper, according to 1 Corinthians 11:25.

Notice that the covenant was faulted on the human side rather than on God's side. The people failed to keep their side of the bargain, even though they had promised to do so. They had said, "Everything the LORD has said we will do" (Exodus 24:3). When Paul discusses the law in Romans 3:3-4, he notes, "What if some did not have faith? Will their lack of faith nullify God's faithfulness? Not at all! Let God be true, and every man a liar." But this fault on the human side of the old covenant was the reason God planned to institute a new covenant "when the time had fully come." That occurred with the appearance of Jesus (Galatians 4:4-5).

Hebrews 8:10 indicates one of the ways in which the new covenant would be better than the old. Rather than being written on stone or scrolls, it would be written on the hearts of God's people. God's will would not be taught by specialized teachers under the new covenant. Here we must understand that God's Spirit would be at work in the hearts and minds of believers, as Joel prophesied (2:28-29).

Another blessing of the new covenant is God's promise to be merciful toward the iniquities of his people. God promises to remember their sins no more (8:12).

Hebrews 9:1-14. Christ is the mediator of this new covenant (8:6). Having established the superiority of that covenant, the writer now considers the superiority of the sacrifice of Christ under the new covenant. The writer does this by comparing that sacrifice with the pattern of sacrifices under the old covenant and in the earthly Tabernacle related to that covenant. Christ's sacrifice is related to the heavenly sanctuary, of course.

The writer assumes that the readers know in considerable detail about the earthly Tabernacle and the rituals connected with it. A brief discussion of the Tabernacle is provided in this section of the lesson in the student book. The biblical description of the Tabernacle's construction is found in Exodus 35–40. The Tabernacle consisted of two main parts, a rectangular enclosure and the tent proper, which was positioned within the enclosure. The enclosure was about 150 feet long and 75 feet wide, with an entrance at the east end. The enclosure was made of poles and connecting brackets of bronze that were covered with curtains. The enclosure was about 7 1/2 feet high.

The tent proper was situated toward the west end of the enclosure. It was 45 feet long by 15 feet wide, and it was 15 feet high. A heavy curtain (veil) separated the tent into two rooms. The eastern end was a room 30 by 15 feet, the Holy Place. An opening in the east end provided entry from the courtyard for designated priests. Within this room were a golden lamp stand and a golden table for twelve loaves of bread, representing the twelve tribes of Israel.

The inner room of the tent, the Most Holy Place, was entered only once a year by the high priest on the Day of Atonement. The room was a perfect cube of 15 feet. Within it stood a golden incense altar and a gold covered wooden chest called the ark. Within the ark were the tablets of stone engraved with the Ten Commandments, a golden jar of manna, and Aaron's staff. The lid of the ark, decorated with angelic symbols called *cherubim*, represented God's footstool. God's throne was in heaven. The Most Holy Place was in utter darkness except when the high priest entered on the Day of Atonement. (This assumption is based on the words of Solomon in 1 Kings 8:12.) The Day of Atonement falls near the autumnal equinox in late September. Sunrise on that day may have cast the sun's rays directly through the eastern door, through the opened veil, to illuminate the interior of the Most Holy Place for the high priestly ritual.

The Tabernacle was made of goat's hair cloth. Over this was a covering of red leather made of rams' skins. And over this was another covering of (goat?) skin. All the cloth of the panels of the entire complex was beautifully dyed, and the hardware consisted of bronze in the enclosure and silver and gold in the tent proper. The value of the materials increased the nearer to the Most Holy Place.

The outer court contained the altar of burnt offering and the large bronze water container called the *laver*. The water was used for the ceremonial washings of the priests and for washing the sacrifices. Many more people were permitted to enter the outer court than the tent. A number of priests would be on duty, and Israelite men who were ritually clean could enter this area. Here various offerings were sacrificed.

The sacrifices offered at the Tabernacle are discussed in Leviticus 1–7. *Burnt offerings* were entirely burned. They consisted of young bulls, rams, goats, doves, and pigeons. *Cereal offerings* were of grain, flour, or cakes baked without leaven. A portion was burned; the remainder was given to the priests. *Peace offerings* were of cattle, sheep, or goats. The fat was burned, and the remainder was eaten partly by the priests, partly by the worshipers. *Sin and trespass offerings* were similar to those mentioned above but for a specific sin or trespass. The fat was burned, while the remainder was in some cases burned outside the camp and in some cases eaten by the priests.

Animals (unblemished) were brought by the worshipers to the entrance of the enclosure. There, in the presence of the officiating priest, the worshipers laid their hands on them, signifying that the animals were substitutes for themselves. The animals were slain, and some of the blood was sprinkled or smeared on the altar and poured out at its base. Then the appropriate part or the whole was burned.

Two lambs were offered daily, one in the morning and one in the evening, as burnt offerings. This number was doubled on the sabbath. On the first day of each month, additional offerings were made. At the great pilgrimage festivals (Passover, Pentecost, and Tabernacles), great numbers of sacrifices were offered. Special offerings and procedures were followed on the Day of Atonement. Individuals might bring offerings for special occasions at other times.

Hebrews 9:6-7 speaks of the normal ritual pattern of the Israelite priests in the earthly Tabernacle. Verse 8 explains that the annual entrance of the high priest into the Most Holy Place was a sign that the way into the true, heavenly sanctuary was not yet opened to the worshiper, as it would be when opened by Christ (10:19-20). The ritualistic situation in the earthly sanctuary was incapable of actually cleansing the conscience of the worshiper (9:9-10). The focus of the system was on "food and drink and various ceremonial washings—external regulations." Apparently, with the sacrificial system associated with the Tabernacle, the worshipers were so isolated from the presence of God, whose forgiveness the worshipers were seeking, that their conscience was never completely at peace. The worshipers had no direct access to God.

This sanctuary and sacrificial system was only a dim copy of the heavenly sanctuary and thus was not nearly as effectual as the true sanctuary and sacrifice to be established at the "time of the new order." This expression must refer to the high priestly work of Christ and thus to the time in which the writer of Hebrews was living.

That this guess is correct is indicated by 9:11-14. The time of the new order, or correction, occurred "when Christ came as high priest of the good things that are already here." The "good things" would refer to the blessings that have come as the result of Christ's atoning death, burial, and resurrection. If the original text referred to "the good things that are to come" (see the footnote in the New International Version), the reference would be to the time when the promises of God in Christ would be fulfilled. That is the future hope of Christians.

Whichever version is accurate, the emphasis in 9:11-14 is on the superiority of Christ's ministry as high priest, on the better sacrifice he made, and on the superlative results. Christ's ministry actually accomplished what the inferior ministry and rituals only hinted at. The blood of Christ is the effective means for purifying the conscience. In every respect—in terms of the priestly ministry, in terms of the sanctuary and sacrifices, and in terms of the covenant—the heavenly realities are superior to the earthly copies.

Hebrews 9:15-28. Earlier in the lesson we noted the reference to the new, better covenant (8:6-13). The writer now returns to that subject. The blood of Christ not only makes possible the purifying of the conscience from "acts that lead to death, so that we may serve the living God" (9:14), it also establishes the new, better covenant.

We have seen that the earthly Tabernacle and priestly function were an imperfect picture of the better, heavenly arrangement. The heavenly is the original and superior sanctuary, priesthood, and sacrifice. The new covenant on which the heavenly arrangement is based has better promises. Now, we are shown that the new covenant is mediated and ratified by a superior mediator.

The background of these ideas is the historical establishment of the old covenant at Sinai. There Moses was the mediator between God (on the mountain) and the people (at the foot of the mountain). The old covenant was ratified by animal sacrifices and by the sprinkling of blood on the people, on the book of the covenant, on the Tabernacle (after it was built), and on all the ritual implements (9:18-21). The shedding of blood under the old covenant was for purifying the exterior of humans and of ritual things.

The new covenant was mediated by Christ and established by his blood. It redeems people from their transgressions under the old covenant. They are cleansed inwardly, in the conscience. The death of Christ put this new will, this new covenant, into effect. That his shed blood is more effective than that of sheep and goats is the focus of 9:23-28.

The pattern of the superiority of the heavenly reality to the inferior earthly copy continues. Christ has entered heaven, not just the Most Holy Place of an earthly sanctuary. He is in God's presence on our behalf, not on behalf of himself as well as others, as with the Levitical high priest.

Christ's sacrifice was so effective that it was offered only once and for all time. That sacrifice is in contrast to the annual sacrifice offered by the earthly high priest on the Day of Atonement. The purpose of Christ's sacrifice was to put away sin permanently for those who accept him.

Christ dealt with sin while he was here the first time suffering in the flesh. The next time Christ appears he will have no need to deal with sin (9:28). Christ bore the sins of many, of any who will respond to his invitation. When Christ returns, it will be to save those who are eagerly awaiting his arrival.

While Christ came to establish the new covenant at the "end of the ages," that expression does not mean at the end of the world. Rather the expression refers to the end of the era of the old covenant. Christ still has those on earth whose consciences have been purified by his blood and who are eagerly waiting for him. The "end of the ages" includes the span of the church's earthly existence until the Savior returns.

Hebrews 10:1-10. Earlier, our writer introduced the once-for-all nature of Christ's sacrifice. He expands on that idea in this section. Notice that the contrast here is between the ability of the sacrificial blood under the old system and that of Christ's blood under the new system to cleanse from sin.

Under the old system, there were "those who draw near" (10:1). These are called worshipers in 10:2b. Their consciences would have been free of a sense of sin had the sacrifices been effective. But they were not.

Then what of the sense of sin in Christians? Once we come to Christ in repentance, confessing our sins, dying to sin, and in baptism burying the old person dominated by sin, we rise to live a new life (Romans 6:4). Christians may sin and be aware of this after being initially cleansed by the blood of Christ, but they ought not to "live in it" (Romans 6:2). Prayer, confession, and communion at the

Lord's Table are means by which penitent Christians are cleansed. Any committed Christian who walks around bearing a burden of guilt for sin already forgiven is falling into a devilish trap. We are to accept God's assurances that in Christ we are free from that kind of perpetual burden. Christ's better sacrifice is final and effectual. We have been sanctified by Christ's sacrifice (10:10).

Hebrews 10:11-18. Whereas, in the earthly sanctuary the high priest fearfully entered the Most Holy Place standing, and remained standing as he carried out the prescribed ritual, Christ *sat down* at God's right hand. His sacrifice was once and for all. There was no need for him to exit from the presence of God in order to return again in the future with another sacrifice for sin (10:12).

Notice again how effective that sacrifice is for "those who are being made holy" (10:14). In fact, the final emphasis in this section is on the meaning of Christ's sacrifice for us (10:15). The Holy Spirit testifies to us, here through Scripture. The Scripture is Jeremiah 31:34. The testimony is that we are forgiven. When God forgives our sins, we have no more need of the Day of Atonement or any other kind of sacrifice to remove sin. No wonder the last words of Christ from the cross were, "It is finished" (John 19:30).

DIMENSION THREE: WHAT DOES THE BIBLE MEAN TO ME?

Hebrews 9:22-26
The Doctrine of the Blood Atonement of Jesus

The shed blood of Jesus is essential for the cleansing of our conscience before our Maker. Jesus died for me and he died for you. His blood was a substitute for yours and mine, and we have life because he gave up his. God accepted this selfless act as sufficient, and God raised Jesus from the dead. So we have a living Savior, a living Lord. This is only possible because Jesus is the Lamb of God who takes away the sins of the world.

The shed blood is an essential part of the Christian faith. It is, in fact, the ultimate evidence of the love of Jesus Christ. This evidence is essential for the faith of the individual and essential to the existence of any church of the living Lord.

Hebrews 9:14, 15, 28; 10:10, 14
Those Who Read Hebrews

To answer the question in the student book, see the section in this chapter on Hebrews 9:15-28, and draw on those ideas. We should recall that the word *gospel* means "good news." As Christians, we find very little good news if we are almost constantly reminded from the pulpit and from Christian publications that we are gross sinners under condemnation. We find the writer of Hebrews encouraging the readers in this way: "Do not throw away your confidence; it will be richly rewarded" (10:35).

Many New Testament passages teach the confidence Christians ought to have. For example, in 1 John 1:7 we read: "If we walk in the light, as he is in the light, we have fellowship with one another, and the blood of Jesus, his Son, purifies us from all sin." The "peace of God, which transcends all understanding" (Philippians 4:7), should keep the heart and mind of those in Christ; for he is our peace.

Faith is being sure of what we hope for and certain of what we do not see (11:1).

4

Faith, the Superior Way to Do God's Will

Hebrews 10:19–11:40

DIMENSION ONE:
WHAT DOES THE BIBLE SAY?

Answer these questions by reading Hebrews 10:19-39

1. In 10:19-25, five exhortations begin with the words *let us.* What five actions does the writer call for?

   The readers are urged to "draw near to God . . . in . . . faith" (10:22); to "hold unswervingly to the hope we profess" (10:23); to "spur one another on toward love and good deeds" (10:24); to "not give up meeting together" (10:25); and to "encourage one another . . . all the more as . . . the Day [approaches]" (10:25).

2. Who should fear falling "into the hands of the living God"? (10:29, 31)

   The person who should fear falling into the hands of the living God is the one who has been sanctified by the blood of the covenant and has then treated it as an unholy thing and trampled the Son of God under foot, thus insulting the Spirit of grace.

3. List the sufferings that early believers in Christ endured. (10:32-34)

   Early believers in Christ (Christians) (1) suffered public insult and persecution, (2) shared the similar persecutions of fellow believers, and (3) gave up property used to support fellow believers who were prisoners.

4. Who are the opposite of "those who believe and are saved"? (10:39)

The opposite are "those who shrink back and are destroyed."

Answer these questions by reading Hebrews 11

5. According to the writer of Hebrews, how can we understand the creation of the visible world out of things that cannot be seen? (11:3)

   We understand that the "universe was formed at God's command" by faith.

6. List the patriarchs given as examples of faith in 11:4-7.

   The examples of faithful patriarchs are Abel, Enoch, and Noah.

7. What did Abraham and Sarah have faith in? (11:8-13)

   Abraham and Sarah believed the promises of God.

8. What is the common feature of the faith of Abraham, Isaac, Jacob, and Joseph? (11:17-22)

   Each of these patriarchs trusted God for future blessings.

9. List the three things that Moses did by faith. (11:23-28)

   "By faith Moses . . . refused to be known as the son of Pharaoh's daughter," "by faith he left Egypt," and "by faith he kept the Passover."

10. Identify the two historical events that illustrate the faith of the Israelites. (11:29-30)

The faith of the Israelites is illustrated by the crossing of the Red Sea and by the conquest of Jericho.

11. The accomplishments of God's judges and prophets are listed in 11:32-38. How were these great deeds done?

The deeds of the judges and prophets were accomplished through faith.

12. The heroic figures of faith mentioned in Hebrews 11 did not receive in their time what was promised. Why not? (11:39-40)

God intended that they would share in "something better" with us, that they should be made perfect with us.

DIMENSION TWO: WHAT DOES THE BIBLE MEAN?

In our study of Hebrews we have reached the end of the writer's arguments that Jesus is superior to every aspect of the Israelite religion established under the law mediated through Moses. The previous presentation was intended to help his readers see that to fall back to the older way from which they had been freed would be to turn their backs on the better way, approved by God through Jesus Christ. Nothing remains for the writer to do but to exhort his readers to hold fast to what they have received through Christ. He will also add some final comments.

Hebrews 10:19-25. We have seen the word *therefore* introduce exhortations before in this book. Chapters 2, 3, 4, and 6 open with this word. *Therefore* is a conjunction, a word that joins what follows with what has gone before. The writer intends to say, "Therefore, brothers, . . . let us draw near." But he summarizes what he has presented before this point in two clauses that begin with *since*. We need to keep them in mind when we read, "let us draw near."

The first *since* clause reminds the readers of what they most need to hear: "We have confidence to enter" the presence of God. The first readers were tempted to give up Christ to return to the old covenant ways. They needed the confidence that, the writer assures them, he and they have. That confidence was based on the sacrificial blood of Jesus. Our writer already had pointed out that this sacrifice meant that God would remember their sins and misdeeds no more (10:17). Thanks to the sacrifice of Christ, Christians are cleansed and can confidently enter the presence of God.

The other *since* clause (10:21) draws attention to the high priestly presence of Jesus in heaven. He is at God's right hand. Christians have a friend in the house of God who has so loved them that he gave his life for them. He is seated on the right hand of the One who loved the world so much that he gave his only begotten Son in order that no one need perish. All can now have everlasting life. No wonder the writer encourages his readers to approach God confidently.

The condition of those who draw near is described next. One condition is that they have a "sincere heart." A sincere heart is a loyal heart. Such a heart does not question the truth that it is the shed blood of Christ, not works, that provides salvation. A sincere heart is a heart "sprinkled to cleanse [it] from a guilty conscience." Recall that the blood of Christ cleanses the conscience (10:1-4). The other condition is that they have their "bodies washed with pure water." Sacrifices were washed in the Tabernacle, but this is more likely a reference to Christian baptism, a symbol of cleansing from sin (Acts 22:16).

Besides the encouragement to draw near, the writer urges his readers to "hold unswervingly to the hope we profess." What is this hope? It is that God will bring to complete fulfillment soon the promises he made to Abraham. We will see at the close of Chapter 11 that all those who lived by faith did not "receive what had been promised. God had planned something better for us so that only together with us would they be made perfect" (11:39-40). The promises of God to Abraham are fulfilled in Christ. Paul expressed the idea this way to the church in Galatia: "If you belong to Christ, then you are Abraham's seed, and heirs according to the promise" (Galatians 3:29). The final consummation of the ages and the realization of those promises awaits the return of Christ; that is why it is yet a hope. Christians have great confidence in this hope, however, because they have a guarantee—the Holy Spirit (Ephesians 1:13-14).

Besides drawing near and holding fast, the writer urges his readers to "consider" (10:24). Instead of wondering about when the hope will finally be realized, the readers are pointed to constructive activities. *To consider* is to seriously think about something. The idea is to spend time encouraging one another, to care for one another. This kind of encouragement comes from providing an example. When Christians are showing loving concern for one another, they have no time to become discouraged and to grumble.

One of the best settings for stirring up support within the community of Christians is the assembly of believers. Not only are the problems and needs of individuals brought to the attention of the group in that setting, that setting also provides the mutual encouragement that comes from sharing what God is doing in the lives of believers. The day of the final fulfillment of the promises draws ever nearer. That, too, is encouraging. The promised victory in Christ draws nearer.

Hebrews 10:26-31. The opening lines of the exhortation (10:19-25) provide a powerful encouragement to faith. The other side of the coin is presented in these verses. If the readers fail to act confidently on their faith in the blood of Christ and his high priestly efforts on their behalf, grave danger lies near. The writer is concerned about the danger of deliberate sin, in contrast to unwitting sin.

The particular sin that the writer has in mind is specifically mentioned in 10:29. He draws a picture of a person who had at one time received the knowledge of the truth. Then that person spurned (trampled underfoot) the Son of God. That individual also profaned the very means by which salvation comes—the blood of Christ. To profane is to make common, to treat that which is sacred as unclean. The result of not only turning away from the Savior but also treating the Savior with contempt is to insult the Spirit of grace, the Holy Spirit.

God is patient, but God's patience can wear thin. Vengeance is the punishment inflicted on an enemy to retaliate for indignities done by the enemy. Here, to judge is to condemn as guilty and to punish. Anyone who would accept God's gracious gift of salvation only to later treat it with contempt faces a terrible consequence at the hand of God. When we deal with the God of the Bible, we are dealing with the living God. God is not a lifeless idol manufactured by human hands.

Hebrews 10:32-39. The writer has not charged his readers with the sin of apostasy. He has only reminded them of the danger in order to spur them on to greater endurance. In 10:19-25, he has used encouragement. In 10:26-31, he has used warning. In 10:32-39, he calls them to greater efforts in the faith by reminding them of their heroic lives in the past.

To receive the light is to come to a saving knowledge of the Lord Jesus Christ (2 Peter 1:3-4). Light expels darkness, permitting hidden truths to be seen. With the light of truth, one can distinguish God's will for one's life. The commitment of life to Christ brings peace with God but enmity with the world. The writer knew that his readers had suffered for their faith. The early days of Christianity were filled with open and sometimes violent persecution.

The sufferings experienced by the first readers of Hebrews fell into two categories. They personally suffered public abuse and affliction. This abuse could be physical abuse or the cutting remarks and disdain of their former friends or both.

The other category was the equally difficult struggle of seeing Christian brothers and sisters suffering and being unable to do anything about it but to endure. Paul, in Galatians 6:2, commanded: "Carry each other's burdens, and in this way you will fulfill the law of Christ." In Romans 12:15, he urged Christians to "mourn with those who mourn."

The first readers of Hebrews had endured such affliction. The writer commends them in 10:34. Confidence in their future under the promises of God is what sustained them. Their possessions in this world, used to support prisoners or taken from them by the pagan society that afflicted them, counted for nothing. They joyfully accepted such events in their lives. All this was temporary, but the treasures in heaven are abiding treasures.

The mention of prisoners reminds me of the difference between prison life then and now. Today, prisoners are given the necessities of life by the state. The survival of prisoners in the Roman world depended on food, blankets, and clothing provided by friends and families. That is why visiting those in prison was so vital and was commended by Jesus (Matthew 25:36).

Through all these activities—struggling with suffering, accepting insult and persecution, sharing the pain of others so treated, and suffering material loss for the sake of the Christian faith—the readers persevered in times past. They suffered while living in the will of God (10:36). The call is to continue to persevere. What is promised will come only to those who persevere.

For the proof of his point, the writer of Hebrews uses a quotation from Habakkuk 2:3-4. The need is to persevere to the end. The end will come in just a little while. "He who is coming" is the Christ. The "righteous one" is the faithful believer, the person who has in the past suffered ridicule and persecution for the faith and has persevered. But more recently that person has been tempted to give up. The point of the quotation in 10:38 is that such a person needs faith in order to live and to persevere until "he who is coming" comes. God will have no pleasure in the one who almost remains faithful to the end.

The writer hastens to reassure his readers that while he mentions these things to urge them on, he is not charging them with being unfaithful. They have what it takes to persevere—faith—and he recognizes their faith. But that faith can be deepened and strengthened, and to that end he now turns.

Hebrews 11:1-3. Encourage class members to memorize this powerful definition of faith (11:1).

The word translated *being sure* has the basic meaning of "that which stands under anything." So it can also be translated as "groundwork, title-deed, or substance." Faith is the foundation or basis for hope. One who has faith has a base on which to stand in the difficulties of life.

The other side of the coin of faith is certainty. Having a foundation of things hoped for is not enough. Hope can be an empty exercise, based on what is imagined rather than on reality. When hope is joined to confidence in the truth of God and God's promises—what we do not see—sustaining faith exists. This combination of having a hope based on the certainty of what we cannot see is faith.

Biblical faith is trust in the reality of God and the truth of God's revealed word. "The ancients" and people today receive divine approval through faith. As the readers are told in 11:6, "Anyone who comes to [God] must believe that he exists and that he rewards those who earnestly seek him." God, of course, is the great Unseen. "No one has ever seen God, but God the only son, who is at the Father's side, has made him known" (John 1:18).

The last idea in this section is that God created the universe by his command out of things not seen. The writer's exact meaning is not clear to us. Certainly he did not have our modern understanding of the nature of things—of unseen atoms, atomic particles, and energy. But it is amazing how well his expression of how the world came to be fits the scientific evidence that the material universe is made of unseen particles.

After defining faith, the writer of Hebrews presents to his readers illustrations of that definition based on the flow of biblical history. After mentioning the creation of the universe, which we understand by faith, he moves on to note faith before the Flood (11:4-7), the faith of the patriarchs (11:8-22), faith in the period of the Exodus and the conquest of Canaan (11:23-31), and the faith of later generations of biblical people (11:32-38). He then brings the saga of the faithful down to the rewarding of the faith of the past in the present. That present was the end of the first century A.D. (11:39-40).

Hebrews 11:4-7. The biblical people mentioned in this section who exhibited faith include Abel, the first victim of murder; Enoch, who walked with God; and Noah, who was considered righteous in his generation. The stories of these three are found in the first few chapters of Genesis.

The student book mentions that the Bible gives no direct statement to indicate why Abel's offering was accepted by God while Cain's was not. However, an expanded Jewish translation and paraphrase of Genesis does discuss the faith of Cain and Abel. In this book the explanation for Cain rising up and killing Abel is that they were arguing about why Abel's sacrifice was accepted and Cain's was not. Essentially, Abel argued that the world is created by the mercy of God and is governed according to the fruit of good works. Cain insisted that the world is not governed by good works. Then he went on to deny a judgment, a judge, and another (heavenly) world. Abel insisted otherwise, and Cain rose up in anger and killed him.

To the writer of Hebrews, the fact that God accepted Abel's gifts is evidence that Abel was righteous. First John 3:12b explains the first murder thus: "Why did he murder him? Because his [Cain's] own actions were evil and his brother's were righteous."

Enoch was the father of Methuselah. We are told in Genesis 5:24 that "Enoch walked with God; then he was no more, because God took him away." In a sense Enoch is mysterious like Melchizedek. The writer of the intertestamental Book of Jubilees (10:17) considered Enoch as more righteous than Noah. According to our text, "God took him away" means Enoch did not see death. The Septuagint (Greek) translation of the Old Testament says that Enoch was "pleasing to God."

Abel and Enoch are examples that establish the principle that "without faith it is impossible to please God" (11:6). God will reward those who believe that God exists and who seek God.

Noah's faith was established on the truth of God's testimony to him. He believed the Flood would come, even though it was unseen for a long time before it actually occurred. Noah's faith was expressed in a tangible form. He built an ark.

Hebrews 11:8-22. The faith of Abraham; his wife, Sarah; his son, Isaac; his grandson, Jacob; and his great-grandson, Joseph, is related to incidents in Genesis 12–50. The common thread that runs through all these incidents is the idea of a promise. A promise is a thing hoped for, something not seen. The faith of the patriarchs was a sense of assurance, a conviction of the reality of the promise.

Abraham obeyed the call of God to go to a land he had never seen but a land he trusted existed. Abraham saw that land and lived in it. Yet he did not see the fulfillment of God's promise that his descendants would possess the land of Canaan (Genesis 17:8). Isaac and Jacob, as Abraham, lived as wandering strangers in the land of promise. The contrast is between living in a tent as a sojourner and living in a city as a permanent inhabitant of the land. But in Hebrews 11:10, the writer spiritualizes the city. God builds this city.

Sarah's faith is not evident in Genesis 18:9-15. When she is informed that she (a woman past childbearing age) will have a son, she laughs. The writer of Hebrews assumes that she demonstrated her faith in God's promise by having intercourse with her husband and conceiving (Genesis 21:1-2).

Again, in Hebrews 11:13-16, the writer of Hebrews spiritualizes the promises to the patriarchs. The patriarchs are represented as desiring a heavenly city and country. This desire suggests prophetic insight on their part.

The theme of future, unrealized promises is continued with examples of Abraham and the offering of Isaac, the blessing of Jacob by Isaac, the blessing of Joseph's sons by Jacob, and the directions for his burial that Joseph gave to the Israelites. In each case something to be realized in the future required faith on the part of a patriarchal family member.

Hebrews 11:23-32. Moses provides another example of one who trusted in the promises of God. The example begins with his parents. The writer implies that they saw the potential of the child. Moses was "looking ahead to his reward" (11:26). He endured because, in his mind's eye, he saw "him who is invisible," that is, God. Moses believed the promise that the death angel would pass over the houses with blood on the doorway.

The faith of the Israelites crossing the sea and marching around Jericho also contains the element of a promise believed before they saw it realized. Rahab envisioned the future when the Israelites would conquer Jericho by God's help and acted on her belief. The assurance that these things would come to pass was faith for them.

Hebrews 11:32-38. The allusions to biblical characters and events in this section are so general that specific incidents are difficult to identify. For the writer of Hebrews, the point is that these kings, judges, prophets, and common people struggled against tremendous odds and suffered exceedingly. They were willing and able to do what they did because they had faith in things envisioned but unfulfilled. In other words, they trusted the promises of God.

Hebrews 11:39-40. To this point the writer has listed the faithful of the past as examples. Everyone on this list hoped for something that God promised. To some degree or other, each of them shared in the promises to Abraham. Those promises were yet unfulfilled when they died.

Now, the writer insists, the promises are being fulfilled in the very time in which he and his first readers are living. All the saints of the past are depending on the writer's generation to be faithful. If the readers become apostates, then the saints of God of the past will not be perfected. They will not see the promises fulfilled. God's intent is to bring to fruition God's promises of the ages in the time of the writer and the first readers of Hebrews. We are to understand that this fulfillment is in Jesus Christ as revealer of God's will and as high priest and sacrifice.

DIMENSION THREE: WHAT DOES THE BIBLE MEAN TO ME?

Hebrews 10:19-39—Christian Perseverance

For the church—the corporate body—and for the individual Christian, the sources of strength to live by faith are still the same as for the writer and first readers of Hebrews. These include looking to Jesus as an example and to the examples of the faithful in times past. The history of the church is filled with heroes and heroines of the faith. We should keep such stories of Christian men and women who suffered and triumphed by faith constantly before us.

But more than this, an effort should be made to arouse the awareness in the church and in the individual Christian of living examples of persevering faithful. In practically every church there are persons who trust in the promises of God in the midst of adversity and suffering. These persons should be recognized and publicized.

Hebrews 11:4-38 Biblical Heroes and Heroines of the Faith

The second discussion question in the student book is related to the first. Think first of the pioneers in the faith who helped establish your local congregation. Try to discover some of the problems they confronted and overcame by faith. Often, the present realities of the congregation are the result of envisioning things not seen, things hoped for, on the part of older brothers and sisters in the faith. Some of them are now gone from the scene, but their works follow after them.

Consider missionaries you may know or Christians who suffered for righteousness' sake during the Nazi domination of Europe.

One way of stimulating class members to think about significant people of faith is to ask, What Christian has been influential in your life?

Let us run with perseverance the race marked out for us (12:1).

— 5 —

The Demands of Enduring Faith

Hebrews 12–13

DIMENSION ONE:
WHAT DOES THE BIBLE SAY?

Answer these questions by reading Hebrews 12

1. The readers of Hebrews are called to take three positive steps in 12:1-2. List them below.

   They are called to throw off everything that hinders and sin, run with perseverance the race before them, and look to Jesus "the author and perfecter" of their faith.

2. The writer of Hebrews viewed the struggles of the Christian as the discipline of God. How should the discipline of God be understood by the Christian? (12:5-7)

   The discipline of God is evidence of God's love, proof that God is dealing with the believer as God's child.

3. For what two things ought we to strive as we run our race of life? (12:14)

   We are to "live in peace with all men" and strive for holiness before God.

4. Trouble that defiles many is the opposite of peace with all (12:14-15). What is the best guard against this cause of trouble? (12:15)

   The best guard against this cause of trouble (a "bitter root") is to obtain the grace of God.

5. Why were the Israelites and even Moses fearful at the place where they met God? (12:18-21)

   They were fearful because the sight was so terrifying.

6. Thanks to the new covenant that Jesus mediated, what will be the nature of the heavenly assembly of God's people? (12:22-24)

   They will join in joyful gathering with the angels.

7. Why will the earth and the heaven be shaken once more? (12:25-27)

   They will be shaken once more so that "what cannot be shaken may remain."

8. As a part of an unshakable kingdom, what two things are Christians urged to do? (12:28)

   They are urged to be thankful and to offer acceptable worship to God.

Answer these questions by reading Hebrews 13

9. How many admonitions are given to the readers of Hebrews in 13:1-5?

   Eight admonitions are given to the readers: (1) on brotherly love, (2) on hospitality, (3) on those in prison, (4) on the mistreated, (5) on marriage, (6) on the marriage bed, (7) on the love of money, and (8) on being content.

10. List the three things Christians should do in respect to their leaders. (13:7)

    Christians should remember their leaders, consider their lives, and imitate their faith.

11. Where did the sacrificial suffering of Jesus take place? (13:12)

    Jesus suffered outside the city gate.

12. Identify three sacrifices Christians are to offer to God. (13:15-16)

Christians are to offer God praise ("the fruit of lips"), to perform good deeds, and to share what they have with others.

13. The writer asked his readers specifically to pray for what? (13:18-19)

He asked them to pray that he might be "restored to you soon."

14. The writer included a prayer for his readers. What did he ask of God for them? (13:20-21)

He prayed that they would be equipped to do God's will and that God would work God's will in them through Jesus Christ.

DIMENSION TWO: WHAT DOES THE BIBLE MEAN?

In Lesson 4 we saw faith defined and then illustrated with a roll call of heroes and heroines of the faith. The intent of the writer was to set the stage to exhort his readers to endure. That exhortation makes up the first half of our lesson, Chapter 12.

Hebrews 12:1-2. As we noted in the preceding lesson, the saints of the Old Testament died without having seen the promises of God fulfilled. They were not made perfect apart from the writer of Hebrews and the first readers (11:40).

Those prophetic foreseers are now pictured by the writer of Hebrews as looking down on the arena of life in which Christians struggle. One can almost hear them cheering the struggling Christians on toward the goal.

The figures of speech used in 12:1-2 are taken from the athletic arena. Just as a runner in the games of the classical world removed the clothing that would hamper full exertion, so the writer urged the readers to lay aside anything that might hinder their speed and progress in the faith.

The Christian is also to lay aside "the sin that so easily entangles." This phrase is translated as "the sin which doth so easily beset us" in the King James Version. The Latin Vulgate translation has "the sin standing around us." The picture painted here is of sin, like a surrounding pack of dogs, hindering the forward motion of the runner.

Jesus is pictured as an example of faith as well as the One who brings the believer's faith to completion, if the believer's gaze is kept on Jesus. In keeping with the definition of faith in 11:1, Jesus was assured of what he hoped for and was convinced of the joy in the future after he endured the cross. He despised the shame. He died as a common criminal, but he took no thought of it for the sake of doing God's will. The main point of the example is that Jesus endured.

Hebrews 12:3-11. For Jesus, a part of the despicable situation at the cross was the hostility of the crowd. Even one of the criminals who was crucified at the same time railed against Jesus (Luke 23:39). Yet Jesus endured the cross, scorning the shame. The readers are asked to consider this example. Recalling what Jesus suffered becomes the antidote for curing fainthearted feelings or being tired in the faith.

Jesus struggled under the burden of the sin of others rather than under his own sin; for, as we have seen, he was sinless. Jesus shed his blood in his sacrificial death. While the readers of Hebrews had "stood [their] ground in a great contest in the face of suffering" (10:32), they had not resisted to the point of death, as Jesus did.

The suffering of Jesus was within the will of God for his life. God's children can expect suffering too, the writer next points out. He does so by noting that God addresses them as God's children.

The basis for the writer's understanding of Christians' relationship to God is the Scripture. To emphasize his point, he quotes Proverbs 3:11-12.

The emphasis, as with the example of Jesus, is on enduring a painful period. The suffering the readers experience is the discipline of God. The fact that they suffer for their faith is evidence that they are indeed the children of God. For God only disciplines God's actual children.

"Father of our spirits'" in 12:9b, is the equivalent of "God." God certainly is that, for "in him we live and move and have our being" (Acts 17:28).

The contrast between earthly fathers and the "Father of our spirits," however, is simply that we endure the discipline of earthly fathers and respect them. Even more we should endure and respect the discipline of God. By doing so we live. God's discipline is for our good, producing holiness, while our earthly fathers discipline for our good, but at their pleasure. The motivation for discipline differs.

The word *discipline* has a connection with the idea of being trained. A disciple is a learner. One undergoes the rigors of discipline in order to attain the benefits. The benefit of enduring God's discipline is "a harvest of righteousness and peace" (12:11). Nothing gives greater satisfaction than being right with God and our fellow humans.

Hebrews 12:12-17. This last *therefore* in Hebrews introduces the urging of the writer based on the first part of the chapter. The cloud of witnesses, the example of Jesus, and the assurance that the readers are God's legitimate children are the basis for encouragement. A part of the exhortation consists of specific steps to be taken by the readers.

Verses 12-13 picture the readers as tired and lame. They are urged to shake off these feelings. The "level paths" refer to religious paths. Walking in the narrow way will bring healing rather than injury.

Striving for "peace with all men" and for holiness are ways of making level paths for the feet. How could a believer miss "the grace of God" (12:15)? John Chrysostom, a powerful preacher and Patriarch of Constantinople from A.D. 398 to A.D. 404, explained this expression as similar to a group of travelers in which one lags behind and never makes it to the end of the long, difficult journey. The person who endures to the end shall be saved.

"Bitter root" is taken from Deuteronomy 29:18. There it reads "root . . . produces such bitter poison." The context indicates that idolatry and apostasy are the root. Potential apostasy was a major concern, too, of the writer of Hebrews. His point is that apostasy can cause a person to fail to attain the grace of God. It can also bear poisonous and bitter fruit by influencing many others, causing them to be defiled—that is, to fall away from the promise of God.

Not only must one guard against apostasy, one must guard against being immoral or godless. Esau is charged with acting without due reverence for the things of God. The birthright belonged to the eldest son by custom. Jacob purchased the birthright when Esau was very hungry. Later, when Esau wanted to inherit the blessing, he could not reverse the foolishness of his earlier actions (Genesis 27). This is the intended meaning of "he was rejected" (12:17).

The reader is warned by the example of Esau. Do not do something foolish that will forfeit your obtaining the grace of God. Walk carefully on the road of life.

Hebrews 12:18-24. The writer of Hebrews urged endurance in the race of life. He warned against the folly of apostasy and unthinking, godless actions. Now he brings his readers to compare appearing before God under the old covenant and under the new covenant.

Notice the similarity of the beginnings of verses 18 and 22. All the Israelites, even Moses, were absolutely terrified at Mount Sinai. "A mountain that can be touched" was a physical mountain. In contrast, the Mount Zion of 12:22 is a heavenly mountain. The earthly Mount Zion was a part of the earthly city of Jerusalem. It could be touched. But the earthly Jerusalem was a poor imitation of the heavenly Jerusalem, which could not be touched.

Earthly Mount Sinai was awesome when God's presence was there. The blazing fire, darkness, gloom, storm, trumpet sound, and sound of God's voice were elements of that experience. References to them are found in Deuteronomy 4:11 and Exodus 19:16-19; 20:18-20.

In contrast to earthly Sinai, the readers are reminded that they have come to a heavenly Mount Zion. Instead of hovering in fear at the foot of the mountain, they have entered a joyful gathering of angels. With the angels is the "church of the firstborn, whose names are written in heaven." *Firstborn* may refer to Jesus. In Colossians 1:15, he is referred to as "the firstborn over all creation." More likely, though, the writer of Hebrews has Christians in mind. James 1:18 refers to believers in this way: "He chose to give us birth through the word of truth, that we might be a kind of firstfruits of all he created."

Those "whose names are written in heaven" are those "whose names are in the book of life" (Philippians 4:3). Jesus told his disciples to "rejoice that your names are written in heaven" (Luke 10:20). Several references to the book of life appear in the Book of Revelation (3:5; 13:8; 17:8; 20:15; 21:27).

The readers need not fear in the presence of God because there is no sin there, only "the spirits of righteous men made perfect" (12:23). These include all the saints of old who looked forward to the time when the promises of God would be fulfilled in Christ. The reason they are made perfect is that Jesus is the mediator of the new covenant. The sprinkled blood of Jesus speaks graciously of forgiveness. Abel's blood cries out for vengeance. Both died unjustly.

Hebrews 12:25-29. The readers are warned not to refuse him who is speaking. The writer refers to the Israelites at Mount Sinai again. There the people wanted to be excused from speaking directly to God (Exodus 20:18-20). They asked Moses to talk with God on their behalf. "Him who speaks" must be God, as at Sinai. This time God speaks from heaven.

God's voice shook the earth at Sinai. Through the prophet Haggai, God promised to shake the earth again and with it, heaven (Haggai 2:6). Heaven and earth represent the entire universe. This second shaking is interpreted as a time when everything changeable will be removed. This probably refers to the faulted old covenant mentioned in 8:7-13. The old covenant is described there as aging and ready to disappear.

What cannot be shaken then remains. This is the kingdom of God (12:28). The writer urges the readers to be grateful, for they have received this unshakable kingdom.

Showing gratitude to God for receiving an unshakable kingdom is done by offering God acceptable worship. Recognizing God's real nature is what the writer is emphasizing. Acceptable worship is offered by those who respect and honor God as the Creator of the universe and the Source of salvation.

Perhaps nothing in human experience is as awesome as a consuming fire, such as a rampaging wildfire. Until the development of the atomic bomb, itself a consuming fire, a mighty fire was one of the most terrifying and destructive natural forces observed by humans. God's awesome power is likened to that.

Hebrews 13:1-6. Having completed his persuasive argument that the salvation offered through Jesus Christ is completely superior to all else, the writer of Hebrews closed with several exhortations. The first concerns general Christian responsibilities.

The admonitions in these verses relate to a Christian community or congregation, rather than to dealings of Christians with unbelievers. Brotherly love is to be a hallmark of the Christian. Jesus said, "All men will know that you are my disciples, if you love one another" (John 13:35). Paul called on the Roman Christians to "be devoted to one another in brotherly love" (Romans 12:10).

Love for other members of the family of God includes a genuine concern for fellow-believers whom we may not know personally. In an era before motels and hotels, showing hospitality to Christians who were passing through was widely practiced. The reference to "angels without knowing" is likely a reference to the hospitality that Abraham showed to some visitors who later were discovered to be angels (Genesis 18).

As strangers needed travel mercies, so those in prison needed the ministrations of the faithful. These prisoners were not common criminals justly imprisoned. These were brothers and sisters in the faith who were suffering for the faith (10:32-34). Such prisoners required food and clothing from outside the prison, since the necessities of life were not provided by the authorities.

Visiting those imprisoned for the faith was a form of identification with them. Christian support of the members who were suffering was the same as taking part in their suffering. "If one part suffers, every part suffers with it; if one part is honored, every part rejoices with it" (1 Corinthians 12:26).

Along with the loving deeds one ought to do, Christians must refrain from immoral and adulterous actions. Marriage is a sacred bond between a man and a woman. Adulterous relationships are exactly the opposite of genuine concern for one another, which is Christian love. And any adulterous thought or temptation can be squelched if the thinker will be genuinely concerned about the other person.

Sex and money have been the downfall of many. Sex alone can be a stumbling block. Money alone can cause an unwary person to fall away. Together the threat is doubled. The antidote for such sins is contentment. Contentment is the result of confidence in God's ability and willingness to provide for the needs of God's children.

To instill confidence in God's provision for the people, the writer quotes Deuteronomy 31:6. There Moses assures his people that God will not forsake them as they fight the Canaanites in the conquest of the Promised Land. Here the text is used to assure Christians that God will provide the necessities of life to them.

Hebrews 13:7-17. Verse 7 suggests that the leaders to be remembered had died for their faith or in the faith. Notice that the writer is not simply suggesting a line of action to the readers; he is commanding them to "remember. . . . consider. . . . imitate.''

Verse 8 sounds like a confession of faith. This saying has a double function. First, Jesus Christ is included in the group of leaders to be remembered, considered, and imitated. Second, no doubt Jesus Christ is the object of the faith of the leaders.

The Christian confesses an unchanging Christ who is able to save completely those who come to God by him (Hebrews 7:25). So the command is "do not be carried away." What might carry a believer away into apostasy are "all kinds of strange teachings." What these teachings are is not clearly indicated, but the reference to foods suggests the dietary restrictions practiced in the Judaism of the time.

These restrictions might have held some attraction for Jewish Christians who were suffering for their faith in Christ. We should keep in mind that it was to such believers, who were being tempted to return to the rules and rituals of the law of Moses, that this letter was written.

The heart and mind should be strengthened by grace rather than by rules concerning foods. Jesus taught that it is not what goes into the mouth that defiles a person but what comes out of the mouth (Mark 7:14-23). So the writer warns against teachings that do not focus on the grace of God in Christ Jesus.

Loyalty to Christ means adhering to the faith once for all delivered to the saints. That loyalty also means identifying with Christ's sacrifice. Christians find no value in adhering to the rituals of sacrifice of the Tabernacle or Temple. Christ's sacrifice was not in the sanctuary; it was outside the gate of the Temple and of the city. The blood of Christ's sacrifice can sanctify the people outside the city, that is outside the old system of rituals connected with the Temple.

To go forth to Christ outside the old sacrificial system is to share in the abuse that he endured (Hebrews 13:13). Jesus was misunderstood, falsely arrested, imprisoned, jeered at, spit on, beaten, whipped, and killed. An earthly city (Jerusalem) with its sanctuary and rituals is no permanent place for the followers of Christ. Our place is in heaven.

Jesus has gone to prepare for our arrival (John 14:2-3). In the meantime, Christians have a holy ministry to carry out. It involves praising God and doing good to others (Hebrews 13:15-16). Do not forget, the writer repeats, to pay heed to your present leaders (13:17).

Hebrews 13:18-19. This chapter begins by urging that brotherly love continue. The writer has shown a genuine concern for the readers. He has written frankly and fully, intending to help them endure in the faith. Now he asks them to show brotherly love toward him. Intercessory prayer is clear evidence of Christian love. The prayer he requests is that he may return to them.

Hebrews 13:20-21. This prayer is like the songs in our hymnal. Many were written by brothers and sisters in the faith who are long since dead. Yet each new generation of Christians sings their thoughts and words afresh. They speak to us and for us. The writer of Hebrews prays for us as well as his first readers.

Hebrews 13:22-25. Apart from speculating about some items in the content (see the student book), this postscript is of great value to us because it reflects the concern the writer had for his readers. He was not content to write to them only about religious and theological ideas; he included items about persons they knew. This sense of Christian belonging and fellowship is vital to the life of the church in all times and places.

DIMENSION THREE:
WHAT DOES THE BIBLE MEAN TO ME?

Hebrews 12:1-2—Running the Race of Life

As depressing as the idea of suicide is, it seems clear that individuals take their life when they feel desperately alone, confronted by some situation that is overwhelming and in which they have no hope of seeing a solution. Suicide is the ultimate example of focusing on oneself to the exclusion of others.

Suicide is a way of saying that one has no purpose or reason for running the race of life. We do not commit suicide because we have hope in someone or something that makes living worthwhile. For the Christian, one motivation of living is to attain the joy that is set before us in the Christian life, heaven itself. But most Christians find joy in this life in serving others. We are most motivated when we look beyond ourselves to find purpose and fulfillment in living. The church at its best is a community of like-minded persons who share the servant mentality and encourage one another to love and good works.

Hebrews 13:1-6—Love and Caring

More and more, the church and individual Christians are being challenged to respond to the needs of individuals and groups in our society and in the world. Perhaps you have contributed to feed the starving in a particular part of the world or to assist desperate farmers in a time of economic crisis or to work with the homeless in your city—the list can go on and on. Giving money is often the easiest way to respond to such needs, but personal involvement as a volunteer is more rewarding.

The needs in every place outstrip the responses. What programs does your church support locally? nationally? internationally?

Hebrews 13:18-22—Intercessory Prayer

We should think of prayer in terms of our personal practice; prayer in small groups—family, Bible study, and the like; and prayer when the congregation is assembled.

A personal prayer list can be useful. Update it regularly and pray at a particular time each day. I have found that meeting once a week, other than on Sunday, with a small group of believers for Bible study and prayer is a blessing to me personally as well as to those for whom we pray.

The small congregation that I am a part of has enriched the prayer period of the Sunday morning worship with brief prayers from the congregation and with prayer requests provided by individuals to the worship leader. In any size congregation the worship leader can mention specific needs and individuals for whom the congregation can pray. A slightly lengthened prayer period will benefit both the worshipers and those for whom intercessory prayers are raised. God will surely bless such Christian concern.

If any of you lacks wisdom, . . . ask God, who gives generously to all without finding fault, and it will be given to him (1:5).

— 6 —

A Manual of Wise Instruction, Part 1

James 1–2

DIMENSION ONE: WHAT DOES THE BIBLE SAY?

Answer these questions by reading James 1

1. What should happen when a Christian meets various trials? (1:2-3)

   The testing of a Christian's faith should produce perseverance.

2. Under what conditions will God answer a request for wisdom? (1:5-8)

   The request for wisdom must be made with belief and not doubt; for a "double-minded" person will not receive anything from God.

3. How does temptation develop into death? (1:14-15)

   Each person is tempted by personal desire. Then desire gives birth to sin, "and sin, when it is full-grown, gives birth to death."

4. What happens to the person who looks into the perfect law that gives freedom and perseveres? (1:25)

   The person who looks into the perfect law that gives freedom and perseveres does not forget (the law) but acts. That person will be blessed in doing.

5. James provides a concise definition of pure religion. What is it? (1:27)

   Religion that is pure and faultless is this: "to look after orphans and widows in their distress and to keep oneself from being polluted by the world."

Answer these questions by reading James 2

6. Why should a Christian show as much respect to a poor person as to a rich person? (2:5)

   A Christian should show as much respect to a poor person as to a rich person because God has "chosen those who are poor in the eyes of the world to be rich in faith and to inherit the kingdom he promised those who love him."

7. What is the royal law believers are expected to fulfill? (2:8)

   The royal law is, "Love your neighbor as yourself."

8. What example of dead faith does James give? (2:14-17)

   The example of dead faith is of a person who fails to clothe and feed another person who is hungry and cold, yet who says, "Go, I wish you well; keep warm and well fed."

9. What two Old Testament examples does James use to prove that faith is completed by deeds? (2:21-25)

   The two examples that prove that faith is completed by deeds are Abraham, when he was willing to offer his son Isaac on the altar, and Rahab, when she received the explorers and sent them out another way.

DIMENSION TWO: WHAT DOES THE BIBLE MEAN?

Among the books of the New Testament, James is in a class by itself. It is not like one of the Gospels, nor like Acts or Revelation. Nor does James have the characteristics of an epistle, except for the salutation (1:1). As a not-quite epistle, it fits better among the General Letters than it would among the letters of Paul. Hebrews does not read like a letter, either, except for the very end of that book. First and Second Peter do sound like letters, as do Second and Third John and Jude. James is a bit more like First John, which also lacks some of the characteristics we expect in a letter. Yet James is not exactly like any of these books.

What kind of work is James, then? We classify James as wisdom literature, something like the Book of Proverbs in the Old Testament. James is a collection of teachings to give specific instructions to Christians on practical matters. The Letter of James is like a manual of discipline for the individual Christian and for Christian groups. As a book of practical wisdom for living the Christian life in the midst of trials and temptations, James holds a unique position in the New Testament.

The Writer. The first word in the book is the name *James*. He calls himself "a servant of God and of the Lord Jesus Christ" (1:1). The only other information he gives about himself is that he is a teacher (3:1). Who could this James have been? Two apostles were named James—James the son of Zebedee and James the son of Alphaeus. But the first was executed around A.D. 44 (Acts 12:2), before the probable date when the letter was written. James the son of Alphaeus did not hold the important role in the early church that the writer of this book seems to have held.

The writer of the letter, then, must be James, the brother of Jesus (Galatians 1:19). The immediate family of Jesus seems not to have accepted him as the Messiah/Christ until near the end of his ministry. Mary, his mother, of course, appears never to have doubted his destiny. Following the Ascension, the brothers of Jesus, along with their mother, were in the upper room prior to the events on the day of Pentecost (Acts 1:12-14). Their presence indicates that they had accepted Jesus as the Christ.

James came to be known as the Righteous One or the Just. He became the most important leader in the Jerusalem church from about A.D. 40 until his death in A.D. 62 (Acts 12:17; 15:13; 21:18; Galatians 2:9). James was admired even by non-Christian Jews for his pious life, according to Josephus. (The works of Josephus, a Jewish historian, were all written after A.D. 70 and before A.D. 125.) According to Eusebius (A.D. 260–340), the first historian of the church, James was beaten to death with a club. But Josephus indicates that James, along with several others, was stoned to death at the instigation of the high priest. Another tradition has it that James was cast down from the pinnacle of the Temple. In whatever manner, James was probably martyred in an outbreak of the Jews following the death of the procurator Festus in A.D. 62.

The authorship of the letter was in dispute in the period after the apostles and before its acceptance as an authoritative work in the New Testament. Official approval came at the Council of Carthage in A.D. 397. Previously, Origen (A.D.. 185–254) had viewed the book as Scripture and James the Just as the writer. Eusebius cited it as Scripture, but he also noted that it was among the disputed books. Jerome (A.D. 340–420) included James in his translation of the Old and New Testaments into Latin (the Vulgate).

Modern scholars are divided on whom the writer was. The primary views on the problem, but without the supporting arguments, are listed here:

1. the letter was written by James, the brother of Jesus, before the Jerusalem Conference of Acts 15 (about A.D. 50);

2. much of the material was given orally or written by James before A.D. 50, then revised by another person between A.D. 55 and A.D. 65, or possibly A.D. 75 and A.D. 85;

3. the book was written by another person under the name of James, the brother of the Lord, between A.D. 75 and A.D. 125. This unnamed person might well have been a disciple of James the Righteous One and in a position to write in his name.

For the purposes of our study, it is not necessary to answer this question of authorship. We will assume that there is a connection of the letter to James, the brother of Jesus. The problem of authorship has no direct bearing on the validity of the Book of James as authoritative Scripture. Generations of Christians from early in the history of the church have turned to James for instruction in Christian living. We, too, can find instruction and inspiration in James for individuals and for the church in the midst of the trials and temptations of our day.

Place of Writing. Just as the question of authorship is unclear, so the place of writing remains an open question. If James the Just wrote it, then the Letter of James came from Jerusalem. If an unknown person wrote the book, suggested points of origin are Antioch in Syria, Caesarea in Palestine, Egypt, and Rome.

The Readers. In the salutation (1:1), the writer addresses "the twelve tribes scattered among the nations." Taken literally, this would refer to the tribes of Israel. But the tribal distinctions were essentially lost among the Jews at the time of the Babylonian Exile. In the Dispersion the tribes were blended. The letter could have been addressed to Jewish Christians only, or, more likely, to Christian congregations scattered across the Roman world. The congregations could include both Gentile Christians and Jewish Christians.

The reference to the twelve tribes is rooted in the understanding that the church is the spiritual Israel. Peter, at the home of Cornelius, perceived that "[God] accepts men from every nation who fear him and do what is right" (Acts 10:35). Paul taught that "it is not the natural children who are God's children, but it is the children of the promise who are regarded as Abraham's offspring" (Romans 9:8).

First Peter opens with a similar expression. The letter is addressed "to God's elect, strangers in the world." All believers in Christ are included in this expression.

Purpose of the Letter. The instruction in the letter is intended to strengthen the faith of the readers in the midst of the difficulties of life. We touched on this matter above, but a further word is in order.

Martin Luther's opinion of the Book of James is well-known. Compared to the Gospel of John, Romans, Galatians, and First Peter, Luther stated that James is a "right strawy epistle"; for he saw in it no real gospel character. Luther thought that James teaches against justification by faith because it emphasizes works. Luther was reacting to the medieval Roman Catholic emphasis on salvation by works. Luther knew from his experience that pious works and penance do not bring salvation, since salvation is by grace to everyone who believes. But, as we will see, James does not set faith against works; he joins them together.

Outline of James.

   I. Salutation (1:1)
  II. How to confront various trials (1:2-18)
     A. Be steadfast in trials (1:2-4)
     B. Pray for wisdom (1:5-8)
     C. Hold a balanced view of poverty and wealth (1:9-11)
     D. Recognize the real basis of temptation and the antidote (1:12-18)
  III. Listen carefully; act rightly (1:19-27)
  IV. Avoid the sin of snobbery (2:1-13)
  V. Show your faith by your deeds (2:14-26)
  VI. The tongue is dangerous—bridle it (3:1-12)
  VII. Instruction on the wise way to live (3:13–4:12)
     A. Show true wisdom—lead a humble life (3:13-18)
     B. Control your passions: submit to God and resist the devil (4:1-10)
     C. Do not judge your neighbor; leave that to God (4:11-12)
  VIII. Observations on the arrogant and the dishonest wealthy (4:13–5:6)
     A. Against arrogant boasting (4:13-17)
     B. Against ill-gotten gain (5:1-6)
  IX. Wise comments on various subjects (5:7-20)
     A. On waiting patiently for "the Lord's coming" (5:7-11)
     B. On avoiding oaths (5:12)
     C. On mutual prayer and confession (5:13-18)
     D. On bringing wanderers back (5:19-20)

James 1:1. The name *James* is the Greek form of the Hebrew *Jacob*. It has been a popular name through the centuries, taken from the patriarch Jacob, the grandson of Abraham.

James is "a servant [a slave] of God and of the Lord Jesus Christ." Paul used the same word of himself (Romans 1:1; Philippians 1:1; Titus 1:1). This designation is based on the concept that Christians are "bought at a price" and are not their own (1 Corinthians 6:20).

James is not a theological work. Jesus is only mentioned here and in 2:1, but clearly Jesus is the Messiah. He is to be served as God.

We have already noted the expression "the twelve tribes scattered among the nations" (the Dispersion). Jews still speak of the Diaspora, that is, those Jews living outside Israel. The expression "the twelve tribes" indicates the unity of God's people. James was saying that wherever Christians may be scattered in the world, they are a part of the one church.

James 1:2-27. In this section we can identify four main teachings about confronting trials. They are only loosely tied together with phrases and words, such as *lacking* in 1:4-5 and *ask* in 1:5-6. These teachings may have existed independently as oral sayings that were collected and arranged on the basis of these repeated words. This method of grouping sayings with similar words can assist memorization. The writer, a teacher, might have had the student in mind when arranging the material in his book.

James 1:2-4. This teaching is for congregations, primarily, and for individuals otherwise. James identifies with those to whom he writes and writes from his own experience.

Not every member of a congregation might undergo trials at the same time, but the church is the body of Christ. "If one part suffers, every part suffers with it" (1 Corinthians 12:26). In a world essentially hostile to people of the faith, various trials are certain to come. James tells us the way to meet these trials.

"Consider it pure joy." Do not consider confronting various trials as part tjoy and part misery. Regard it as complete joy. Persecution is no fun, and the early Christians were being oppressed (2:6). Apparently some of them had known sickness (5:13-16) and some poverty (5:1-6), neither of which brings pleasure. How then could James's first readers do what he suggests?

Jesus taught in the Sermon on the Mount: "Blessed [Happy] are those who are persecuted because of righteousness, / for theirs is the kingdom of heaven. Blessed are you when people insult you, persecute you and falsely say all kinds of evil against you because of me. Rejoice and be glad, because great is your reward in heaven, for in the same way they persecuted the prophets who were before you" (Matthew 5:10-12). First Peter 3:14 points out that "even if you should suffer for what is right, you are blessed." When James calls on Christians to consider difficulties a positive good, then, it is in line with biblical truth.

But the main reason for demanding that Christians count trials they meet as pure joy is that such trials are tests of one's faith. Meeting trials equals finding opportunities to develop steadfastness. Various trials have a bright side to them. They can be turned to our highest good. When our endurance is completely developed, we reach maturity in the faith and lack nothing that will separate us from eternal blessings with God.

James 1:5-8. A help in meeting temptations is to face them wisely. When James writes, "If any of you lacks wisdom," he assumes that some do lack wisdom. "The fear of the LORD is the beginning of knowledge, / but fools despise wisdom and discipline" (Proverbs 1:7). Knowledge consists of facts learned; wisdom guides in the use of knowledge. Jesus was realistic in instructing the Twelve when he sent them forth on a missionary journey: "I am sending you out like sheep among wolves. Therefore be as shrewd as snakes and as innocent as doves" (Matthew 10:16).

The main point of this section, however, is not wisdom but how to obtain wisdom. God is the source of wisdom. To obtain it, ask. Pray for it. Recall what Jesus said, "Ask and it will be given to you" (Matthew 7:7). God gives outright, with a single mind. It is the Father's good pleasure to give (Luke 12:32). But let the request be a prayer of faith. Doubting that God will grant the request destroys the purpose of prayer. Doubting while asking is the mark of a person unstable in the faith.

James 1:9-11. One of the constant temptations through the ages has been to count the rich as favored by God and the poor as sinners, suffering God's disfavor. Such a conclusion is not biblically valid.

The "brother in humble circumstances" (Christian) is poor, yet he is to "take pride in his high position" (1:9). To take pride here is to glory in the high position God has accorded him (2:5). Many poor persons were part of the early church. Paul wrote, "Brothers, think of what you were when you were called. Not many of you were wise by human standards; not many were influential; not many were of noble birth" (1 Corinthians 1:26).

The rich Christian, on the other hand, has nothing to take pride in except being humbled. Wealth can puff a person up with pride, yet a Christian is called to be humble (4:6). Further, wealth must be left behind. A rich Christian will exult in the fact that any pride held before coming to Christ has now been shattered. Selfishness is replaced by stewardship under God. Christians must hold a balanced view of poverty and wealth.

James 1:12-18. The wise instruction in this section begins with what sounds like a beatitude, as in Matthew 5:10. *Blessed* means "happy." The crown of life should make any Christian happy. The crown is the victory wreath, similar to those bestowed by the Greeks on winners of Olympic races. The thought echoes Revelation 2:10.

God is not the source of temptation. God is the source of "every good and perfect gift" (1:17). God is untouched by evil but knows its nature. God also knows people; God is well aware of our tendency toward evil. The source of temptation is a person's own desire. Desire is neither good nor evil, it is neutral. But desire lures and entices. Unchecked, the effect can be deadly. Desire can conceive and give birth to sin. Sin can fully develop into complete separation from God. That separation is death in the most profound sense.

Desire can be controlled. "No temptation has seized you except what is common to man. And God is faithful; he will not let you be tempted beyond what you can bear. But when you are tempted, he will also provide a way out so that you can stand up under it" (1 Corinthians 10:13). God has provided the antidote to temptation. We have been born again by God's word (1 Peter 1:23). As first fruits, we are to offer ourselves to God as a living sacrifice (Romans 12:1). The first fruits are always God's.

James 1:19-27. "Take note of this," introduces a new wise instruction. What the dear brothers are to know is what follows. Christians should be quick to listen to the word of God and to what is said by others. Everyone should also be slow to speak; that is, everyone should think before speaking. The quick reply often comes off the top of one's head and out of anger. So James warns everyone to be "slow to become angry."

James is writing to believers. Uncontrolled anger is unacceptable behavior for Christians. It does not accomplish good for God. To the contrary, uncontrolled anger will prove a stumbling block to those outside of Christ who see it in Christians. God will provide a way to overcome the temptation to get angry. James ranks anger as a part of "moral filth and the evil that is so prevalent." Anger will threaten the soul; "the word planted in you" has the power to save.

Just hearing the word is not enough; to hear and not to do is to fool ourselves. The illustration James uses to make his point is quite clear. The face one sees in the mirror may soon be forgotten, but one who has looked into the mirror of God's Word cannot forget that believers are sinners saved by grace. In Christ there is freedom from sin and liberty to love (Galatians 5:13). To look intently into the perfect law is to be moved to do and to be blessed in the process.

The coin of hearing and doing has two sides (1:26-27). One side is hearing. But that side is not enough. It brings forth only empty words from an unbridled tongue without appropriate deeds. The result is a worthless religion. Pure and faultless religion, according to James, also requires doing. The doing side of the coin involves visiting the weak and vulnerable in society and supplying their needs.

"To keep oneself from being polluted by the world" is a necessary part of pure religion as well. The world always exhibits a selfish or self-seeking attitude toward worldly goods. A Christian must constantly guard against adopting that view, else giving to the needy will cease.

James 2:1-13. This teaching would not have been included if showing favoritism were not a problem in the church. James is dead set against favoritism. An example of what was going on is given in 2:2-3.

Favoritism is not acceptable to those who trust in the saving grace of Jesus (2:9). He is "our glorious Lord Jesus Christ" (2:1); and all human glory, even that of a rich person, is as filthy rags in comparison. The ground is level at the foot of the cross. All are saved by grace through faith, as a gift of God; and none are worthy. There is neither Jew nor Gentile, bond nor free, male nor female in Christ; so snobbish distinctions among believers are unwarranted.

Further, favoritism dishonors those chosen of God "to be rich in faith and to inherit the kingdom he promised those who love him" (2:5). The rich tend to love riches. Jesus taught that we cannot love God and money (Matthew 6:24). The rich trust in wealth; the poor cannot do that. They trust in God.

Further, the love of money is the root of all kinds of evil (1 Timothy 6:10). That includes the evil of oppressing the poor (2:6). The rich slander "the noble name of him to whom you belong." This is the name of Jesus and is likely a reference to the baptismal formula (Acts 2:38; 8:16; 10:48).

Apparently the rich persons James has in mind in this passage are not rich Christians, as perhaps in 1:10-11. Rather, these are wealthy non-Christians from the community who have come to visit the meeting, either on someone's invitation or out of curiosity.

The correct Christian practice is to love others without showing favoritism. That love is the royal law of love that Jesus taught (Matthew 22:39). Just as breaking the Mosaic law made one guilty, so breaking the law of love by showing favoritism makes one guilty.

In 2:12-13, James concludes his teaching on the important matter of snobbery. His point is that Christians should speak and act with the Last Judgment in mind. God has graciously covered our sins by the blood of Jesus Christ, but we can hardly expect to be shown mercy for the sin of favoritism if we practice it. Christians are still required to do unto others as we would have them do unto us (Matthew 7:12). We are to be hearers *and* doers of the word.

James 2:14-26. The question in 2:4 introduces the core of the important instruction that this section contains. The instruction in these verses deals with faith and deeds and the relationship between the two.

The faith in mind here consists of the gospel facts and all that belief in them implies—repentance from sin, confession of Jesus as Lord and Savior, dying to self and rising to live a new life through Christian baptism, and living to the praise of God's glory. Faith alone cannot save. (The assumption is that the person with faith has the opportunity to live a life of faith.)

The person who has a warm feeling toward someone in need and has the resources to meet that need but fails to meet the need accomplishes nothing (2:15-16). So faith without deeds is without accomplishment. It is valueless—dead. A living faith is always shown by deeds.

To the person who might raise the question in 2:18, James provides three examples in response. The first example is of belief without deeds (demons). Two biblical examples follow. James states that Abraham was justified by deeds when he showed his willingness to offer Isaac on the altar (Genesis 22). Read carefully 2:22 and the conclusion of the example of Abraham in 2:24.

In 2:23, James quotes Genesis 15:6. Paul also used Abraham and this verse to establish that Abraham was justified by faith apart from deeds (Romans 4:1-12). Much has been made of the seeming contradiction between Paul and James on the matter of faith and deeds. But I can see no direct or indirect contradiction. Paul had in mind justification in connection with conversion and baptism; that is by faith. He also encouraged acts of Christian love, however, as does James. James, on the other hand, sees justification in terms of the Last Judgment. The deeds a believer does, or fails to do, determine the result of that judgment. Paul also held that the final judgment will be determined on the basis of the deeds of a believer (1 Corinthians 3:13-15; 2 Corinthians 5:10). This is in line with what Jesus taught on the Last Judgment (Matthew 25:31-46).

So a believer is justified by deeds and not by faith alone. Rahab (Joshua 2:1-21) is another example of this basic principle. She saved the lives of the spies Joshua sent to Jericho. She acted on her faith that God had given the land into the hands of the Israelites (Joshua 2:9). So Rahab is listed in the great roll call of the faithful in Hebrews (11:31).

James concludes his teaching on the relationship between faith and deeds with an observation. The body without the spirit is dead. It cannot fulfill a purpose or function. Just so, faith without deeds is without value. It is profitless.

DIMENSION THREE: WHAT DOES THE BIBLE MEAN TO ME?

James 1:13-15
Placing Desires Under the Lordship of Jesus

Essentially, the answer to the first question posed in the student book lies in the effort to bring every desire under the lordship of Jesus. Paul urged the Roman Christians to "put to death the misdeeds of the body" (Romans 8:13). We can assume that the deeds were stimulated by desires. Again, he told the Christians in Colosse: "Put to death, therefore, whatever belongs to your earthly nature: sexual immorality, impurity, lust, evil desires and greed, which is idolatry" (Colossians 3:5). Of himself, Paul also said, "I beat my body and make it my slave so that after I have preached to others, I myself will not be disqualified for the prize" (1 Corinthians 9:27).

If we consider any particular desire that may arise within us, we can always find a way to control it, often by turning our minds to other, more constructive thoughts. As Paul indicated, whatever is true, noble, right, pure, lovely, admirable, excellent, praiseworthy, think about these things (Philippians 4:8).

The church can assist its members to overcome desires by being aware of them. Support groups for particular problems can help. Frankly facing the problems that individual Christians confront in overcoming potentially harmful desires is important.

James 1:27
Pure and Faultless Religion

The second question in the student book is not to be isolated from the matter of faith and deeds. The problem in our society is to identify the equivalent of the widows and orphans of whom James speaks. The widows were vulnerable to those who coveted and stole widows' houses. This thievery was particularly bad in a culture in which almost every woman was under the protection of a father, husband, or male kin. The orphan, too, was vulnerable to exploitation and to suffering due to the lack of family support. Together widows and orphans made up the most vulnerable elements of society.

Who are the most vulnerable, the most disadvantaged in our society? Who are the vulnerable in your neighborhood? These are known of God. Do you know them? Does your church know them? Identifying and meeting the basic needs of such people will be the equivalent of caring for the widow and the orphan. These vulnerable people will include the homeless, the helpless, and the economically oppressed.

Helping individuals and groups that fall into these categories may require the cooperative efforts of many Christians. Most of us, however, can find those to whom we can minister personally. Let us act creatively to practice pure and faultless religion before God.

The wisdom that comes from heaven is first of all pure; then peace-loving, considerate, submissive, full of mercy and good fruit, impartial and sincere (3:17).

— 7 —

A Manual of Wise Instruction, Part 2

James 3–5

DIMENSION ONE:
WHAT DOES THE BIBLE SAY?

Answer these questions by reading James 3

1. Why does James discourage many of his readers from becoming teachers? (3:1)

   Teachers "will be judged more strictly."

2. What evidence does James provide to show that the tongue is "a restless evil, full of deadly poison"? (3:7-10)

   "All kinds of animals" can be tamed by humans but not the tongue. The tongue gives both blessings and curses.

3. How does James describe the wisdom that does not come from heaven? (3:15-16)

   The wisdom that is not from heaven "is earthly, unspiritual, of the devil." It is found "where you have envy and selfish ambition" and there is "disorder and every evil practice."

4. What are the characteristics of the wisdom that comes from heaven? (3:17)

   The wisdom from heaven is "pure; . . . peace-loving, considerate, submissive, full of mercy and good fruit, impartial and sincere."

Answer these questions by reading James 4

5. Why do people fight, quarrel, and kill? (4:1-2)

   People fight, quarrel, and kill because of their desires. They want and do not have, so they kill. They covet and cannot obtain, so they fight and quarrel.

6. What positive actions can believers take to show humility and receive God's grace? (4:6-8)

   To show humility and to receive God's grace, believers should submit themselves to God, resist the devil, and come near to God.

7. Who is capable of judging another Christian? (4:12)

   " There is only one Lawgiver and Judge, the one who is able to save and destroy."

8. To what statement does James refer when he says, "You boast and brag"? (4:13-16a)

   James refers to the statement "Today or tomorrow we will go to this or that city, spend a year there, carry on business and make money" as boasting.

Answer these questions by reading James 5

9. James foretold that the rich would suffer miseries (5:1-6). Why would this come upon them in the last days?

   James foretold that the rich would suffer miseries in the last days because they kept back by fraud the wages of the laborers and harvesters who mowed their fields.

10. James gives three examples of patient people in 5:7-11. Identify them.

    The three examples of patient people that James gives are the farmer waiting for the harvest, the prophets "who spoke in the name of the Lord," and Job.

11. Why is James against swearing by an oath? (5:12)

    James is against taking oaths because those who do might "be condemned."

12. What are James's recommendations for people who are in trouble, happy, or sick? (5:13-14)

James recommends that people who are in trouble should pray, that those who are happy should sing, and that the sick person should call for the elders of the church and let them pray over the sick person, anointing the sick person with oil "in the name of the Lord."

13. Who is a good example of a righteous man whose prayers were effective? (5:16b-18)

The prophet Elijah is a good example of a righteous man whose prayers were effective.

14. What is the proper thing to do when a Christian brother or sister wanders from the truth? (5:19-20)

The proper thing to do when a Christian brother or sister wanders from the truth is to bring that sinner back from the error of his or her way.

DIMENSION TWO: WHAT DOES THE BIBLE MEAN?

In Lesson 6, we studied the first four of James's wise instructions for Christians. The topics covered were confronting various trials, listening carefully and acting rightly, avoiding the sin of snobbery, and showing your faith by your deeds.

The subjects covered in this lesson are bridling the dangerous tongue, instructing on the wise way to live, observing the arrogant and the dishonest wealthy, and commenting wisely on various subjects. These subjects include waiting patiently for the coming of the Lord, avoiding oaths, praying mutual prayers and confession, and bringing wanderers back.

James 3:1-12. In a sense the subject in these verses was introduced when James admonished his readers to be quick to hear, slow to speak, and slow to anger. But the main focus of that section (1:19-27) was on being doers of the word and not just hearers. Here, the focus is on the importance of controlling the tongue.

Three segments make up this section. James 3:1-2a introduces the problem of proper speech. Then 3:2b-5a is a segment on the difficulty of controlling the tongue, and 3:5b-12 is a second supporting segment on the danger of a poisonous tongue.

James is writing to a congregation ("meeting" in 2:2) or a group of congregations. One of the spiritual gifts God gives the church is teachers (1 Corinthians 12:28; Ephesians 4:11). The calling to teach is a high calling. Jesus is the example to follow, for he was recognized as a teacher by the Jewish Sanhedrin (ruling council) (John 3:1-2). He was also called *rabbi* by his followers and by those who entered into discussions with him. As John 1:38 explains, *rabbi* means "teacher."

Apparently many of the believers in the congregation James wrote to thought themselves called to be teachers. James warns against taking on the responsibility of testifying to the faith publicly and instructing others in the faith. Teaching is a calling that is privileged, but the teacher is liable to more severe condemnation for errors than the lay person is.

James considers himself a teacher and is aware of the weight of responsibility. The wise instructions and advice that make up this letter prove that he was conscientious in carrying out his responsibilities.

A teacher, like everyone else, makes mistakes. The teacher has to be more accountable for errors than others, however, because what the teacher says directly affects the hearers (students). We all must answer to God for how careful and conscientious we were in our work. We all will "give account" for our words and either be justified by them or condemned (Matthew 12:36-37).

James may have the teacher in mind as he continues with the first supporting paragraph; but what he says fits every Christian, since we all speak (except for the person who is mute). The perfect (spiritually mature) person makes no mistakes in the content of what he or she says or the manner in which it is said.

None of us would claim that perfection. In striving for excellence, however, we attempt to make no mistakes. James indicates that the control (bridling) of the tongue is an essential part of becoming mature. In fact, control of the tongue is a major factor in controlling the whole body.

Why can James say this? Because, as a person thinks in his or her heart (mind), so is that person. Out of the heart "come evil thoughts, sexual immorality, theft, murder, adultery, greed, malice, deceit, lewdness, envy, slander, arrogance and folly" (Mark 7:21-22). Out of the abundance of the heart the mouth speaks (Luke 6:45). The Christian is to be transformed by the renewing of the mind (Romans 12:2), an ongoing process. The change will include controlling the tongue so that evil speech, slander, and foolishness do not gush forth.

We no longer live in the days when the horse was used for work more than pleasure. Yet most of the class members should be able to relate to the words *bridle* and *bits* and how these pieces of equipment function to control a horse. The point is, as a small thing like a bridle and bit can control the entire body of a horse, so by a bridled tongue a person attains self-control.

Small things do control large things. The pilot of a ship guides it with a small rudder. The pilot can even control the ship with the rudder when strong winds are blowing against the ship. Like a rudder or a bit and bridle, the tongue is a small part of the body. The tongue boasts of great things because it controls the whole body.

Forest and brush fires occurred in ancient times as well as modern times. James used a timeless saying to open the section: "What a great forest is set on fire by a small spark." A forest fire is awesome in its devastating power. It can destroy the one who set it, whether accidentally or on purpose, and it can destroy others. Just so, the tongue, when used maliciously, can destroy both the speaker and the object of the words spoken.

Evil speech is what James has in mind. James 3:6b-12 makes that clear. The tongue is a fire kindled from hellfire. That is, Satan is the source of acid, burning speech. It is "a world of evil." This whole verse (3:6) is difficult to translate.

The background of 3:7 is Genesis 1:28; 2:19; and 9:2. Humans are given the power to rule over animals. But who can tame the tongue? No one alone, but by God's grace the tongue can be controlled.

The tongue is a "restless evil" always moving like a snake on the go and venomous as a rattler. Psalm 140:3 may lie behind the words of James: "They make their tongues as sharp as a serpent's; / the poison of vipers is on their lips."

The tongue is an instrument of deception. We expect consistency in nature, as with a spring producing either fresh or salt water, or as in the other examples James provides. But the evil, uncontrolled tongue spews forth from the same source both blessings and curses.

We should be able to expect consistency in the speech that comes forth from the mouths of Christians. They should be slow to speak. They should refrain from speaking in anger. "Do not let any unwholesome talk come out of your mouths, but only what is helpful for building others up according to their needs, that it may benefit those who listen" (Ephesians 4:29).

James 3:13–4:12. This section of the letter does not appear to be directly connected with the teaching on the dangers of the tongue. Some persons, however, think that these verses appear here to make the point that pure speech comes from wisdom. I believe the main concern is on how to live a good life.

James 3:13-18. In 1:5, the person who lacked wisdom was encouraged to ask God for it in faith. Here, the attention is on those who think themselves wise and understanding (among the Christians in the congregation to whom James writes).

James will draw a sharp line between the wisdom from heaven and earthly wisdom. Here, as soon as he raises the question, he provides the test of the wisdom that is from heaven. The wise person lives a good life. That person shows evidence of wisdom and understanding.

The works the wise person performs are done "in the humility that comes from wisdom." Humble wisdom is the opposite of bitter jealousy and selfish ambition. Humble

wisdom is not weakness; it is gentleness. A Christian should be tough but gentle.

One of Jesus' Beatitudes speaks of the meek (Matthew 5:5). Paul exhorted Christian teachers not to be quarrelsome but to be kindly toward everyone, forbearing and correcting those in need of correction with gentleness (2 Timothy 2:24-25a). Peter urged defenders of the faith to speak gently and reverently (1 Peter 3:15b). These verses help us put the problem James is dealing with in perspective.

Earthly wisdom is looking at circumstances in an unspiritual way, even a demonic way (3:15). Paul stated flatly that "God made foolish the wisdom of the world" (1 Corinthians 1:20d). Bitter envy, selfish ambition, boasting, and lying are evidences of earthly wisdom. They do not bring the good life. They do not bring peace with God or other people. They result in "disorder and every evil practice."

Contrast the wisdom "from heaven" with earthly wisdom. The wisdom from heaven is pure. A Christian is cleansed by the blood of Jesus Christ and that person's mind is set on things that are above (Colossians 3:2). The peace of God that passes all understanding is available to the believer (Philippians 4:7) because of the reconciliation with God and people. Christians are to be open to reason, full of mercy because they know what it means to have received mercy from God, and full of good fruits. We are to follow in the footsteps of Jesus, and he went about doing good (Acts 10:38).

All these elements of the wisdom that is from heaven should be clearly evident in the life of the spiritual person. This wisdom, if any lack it, can be received by asking God for it (1:5). Instead of disorder, the result is peace.

James 4:1-10. Perhaps this section is logically connected with 3:13-18 because the wisdom from heaven results in peace while the wisdom of the world results in conflict. James may have had in mind the conflicts within a community of believers. He may have had in mind war in the world. Or, he may have been thinking of both. At any rate, his explanation of the cause of conflict is universally applicable.

Just as desire can lead to sin and death (1:14-15), so a person's desires can cause fights and quarrels. Paul wrote of the conflict between the law of sin and the law of the mind (Romans 7:23). Christ gives the victory, but there is a struggle.

In 4:2-3, James weaves the picture together so that we have no doubt about the cause of conflicts. Desire can even lead to murder. Coveting not only breaks the tenth commandment (Exodus 20:17), it also leads to savage efforts to obtain what is coveted.

The Christian has but to ask in order to receive all that is *needed* (Matthew 7:7-8). But God does not promise all that is *desired*. A parent does not give that which will harm his or her children just because they ask. Needs are not measured by desires.

James 4:4 opens with a strong statement. James actually says, "Adulterers and Adulteresses" in the original Greek.

This strange expression becomes clear in the light of the scriptural pattern of thinking. Spiritual infidelity is spoken of as adultery in Hosea 3:1, for example, and elsewhere among the Old Testament prophets. Jesus, too, spoke of "this adulterous and sinful generation" (Mark 8:38). Underlying these expressions are the metaphors of God as the husband of Israel and Christ as the husband of the church.

Those who can receive the wisdom from heaven by asking for it are committing spiritual adultery when they live by the wisdom of this world, when they are driven by their desires (James 4:4). Jesus taught essentially the same thing: "You cannot serve God and Money" (Matthew 6:24c).

The exact quotation in James 4:5 cannot be found in the Bible, nor has it been found in other known writings. The general thought occurs in Genesis 6:5-6 and Isaiah 63:8-16. The spirit God caused to live in us may be the human spirit, created in God's image. Or, the spirit may refer to the indwelling Holy Spirit given as a gift to those who come to God through Christ. We do not have to make a final decision on which of these views is correct, since both are. James may also be speaking of Scripture generally, summarizing the biblical view of God's concern for people.

The quotation in 4:6 is from Proverbs 3:34. The point of the quotation is to support the fact that God gives abundant grace to the humble. John wrote in his gospel, "From the fullness of his grace we have all received one blessing after another" (1:16). The gift of grace is a reflection of God's active yearning for believers to triumph over their desires. God wants every Christian to be God's friend, rather than to be a friend of the world. God desires peace for his children rather than wars and fightings.

Humility is an essential ingredient in the make-up of a sincere follower of Jesus. Jesus provides the example to follow: "Being found in appearance as a man, / he humbled himself / and became obedient to death—even death on a cross!" (Philippians 2:8). Humility is the opposite of the pride and vanity that characterize the wisdom of the world.

This section of James emphasizes the wise way to live. That way is clarified in 4:7-10. Two actions are required: submission to God, which is evidence of humility, and resistance to the devil, which provides the way of escape from the temptations that desire and passion arouse.

The world seeks self-exaltation. James calls on people to do things God's way. God is ready to meet the sincere seeker of grace more than halfway. God is like the father in the story of the prodigal son, gazing longingly down the road, awaiting some sign of his son's return, ready to run forth to meet him in glad embrace (Luke 15:20b).

God has also, by grace, made it possible for the erring person to be cleansed, the contaminated heart (mind) to be purified, and the double-minded person to find direction and stability. These blessings are possible thanks to the completed work of Jesus Christ.

Repentance, shown by sincere sorrow (4:9), is essential to receiving the gift of the Holy Spirit (salvation) through God's grace (Acts 2:38). Repentance, a complete reversal of the way one thinks and acts, is evidence of true humility before God. What the world seeks and grasps hungrily for through self-exaltation, God accomplishes for those who are humble before God. God exalts them.

James 4:11-12. The believer who lives wisely will refrain from condemning another Christian, for all are sinners saved by grace. Judgmental thinking about other believers followed by slander (harsh, critical) words judges rather than obeys the law. That is, that judgmental person has, in practice, rejected the royal law to love neighbor as self (2:8). Further, to judge a brother or sister in Christ is to place oneself in opposition to the one valid Judge. God alone is able to save and to destroy (Matthew 10:28). Since God will be my judge (and yours), who am I to condemn my brother or sister in Christ?

James 4:13–5:6. Two segments make up the wise instruction of this section. The first is against arrogant boasting (4:13-17) and the second against ill-gotten gain (5:1-6).

James does not object to good business planning. Jesus taught that planning is necessary, as in the parable of the shortsighted virgins who ran out of oil at the crucial moment (Matthew 25:1-13). The need for planning is understood, too, in the case of the man intending to build a tower and the king plotting a conquest (Luke 14:28-32). What James objects to is the arrogance of a Christian planning a venture without any thought of the One who controls history. Believers, above all others, should realize that "my times are in your hands" (Psalm 31:15).

To plan as in James 4:13 is to be arrogant. Such planners lack humility and a sense of living under the lordship of Christ. Their thinking and actions reflect a bad (inappropriate) way for Christians to think. Such people need to hear the word, to be taught, so that they know what is right to do. Ignorance does not justify arrogant attitudes. Even worse is the person who knows what to do and fails to do it. Knowing what to do and not doing it is a grievous error that misses the mark of God's will, and that is sin.

Does James address his remarks in 5:1-6 to rich Christians or to the rich outside the church? He seems to have in mind those outside the church, but echoes of what he says may apply to wealthy Christians.

The rich are often considered happy and carefree, in contrast to the poor who are burdened with labor in order to obtain the necessities of life. But the poor are a special concern of God's.

James calls on the rich to weep and wail. The reason why they should cry is in anticipation of the coming "last days" and the judgment of God (5:1-3). All the treasure the rich have laid up will prove to be worthless. In fact, what they have laid up will be evidence against them, evidence of their greed and coveting. What they trusted in will destroy them, consuming them like fire. This instruction reminds us of the story Jesus told of the rich man and Lazarus, the beggar (Luke 16:19-31).

The reason why the things treasured by the rich will condemn them is that they were acquired through fraud and injustice (5:4). The poor in particular suffered because of their fraud and injustices. The Bible has many teachings against paying wages late or legally bilking workers out of their just wages (Leviticus 19:13b; Deuteronomy 24:14-15; Job 7:1-32; Malachi 3:5; Matthew 20:8).

James 5:7-11. This teaching may be directly connected with the preceding warning to the rich. It could also stand as an independent instruction. Encouragement to patience is needed in the face of economic oppression, but it is also useful in other circumstances of life.

The first example of patience is that of the farmer. He plants and then must await both the early rains, which help the plants get off to a good start, and the late rains, which help the grain come to full development. The agricultural picture is that of the Middle East. Weather patterns there produce the early rains of the growing season after a long dry summer. The late rains fall before harvest the following spring.

James urges the readers to be patient for the harvest of souls with the coming of Christ. In anticipation they are to "stand firm." The coming of Christ will be soon and as certain as harvest time follows the rain. The coming of Christ was anticipated in the first generation of Christians, and it continues to be a living hope.

In 5:9, James admonishes his readers not to grumble. Grumbling is the result of impatience. Grumbling may be aimed at one another, blaming the stress of the times on a Christian brother or sister and generating disunity in the process.

Rather than grumbling and impatience, believers are called to suffering and patience (5:10). Suffering may result from the words and deeds of others, as in the case of oppression by the rich. Suffering may also come from one's own mistakes or foolish actions.

James also gives two other examples of suffering and patience. The prophets suffered for speaking "in the name of the Lord." Job remained steadfast despite the afflictions imposed on him at the hand of Satan.

James 5:12. Taking oaths seems to have been overdone in both Jewish and pagan society in the time of Jesus and the early church. What James says here echoes the words of Jesus in Matthew 5:34-37. An oath was taken by swearing by something or someone of higher position or authority than the oath taker. What James condemns is confirming the most mundane matters by an oath. Christians should always speak the truth; for the Christian, *yes* should mean "yes" and *no* should mean "no" without further emphasis.

That this is not an absolute prohibition against calling God to witness is shown by Paul (2 Corinthians 1:23; 11:31; Galatians 1:20; Philippians 1:8). Some serious occasions may call for an oath but never about trivial matters.

James 5:13-18. James presents his most positive teaching at the end of his letter. These verses and the last comment (5:19-20) represent that fellowship in the faith that is described as "the priesthood of all believers" (1 Peter 2:9).

Christians can do some things for themselves. If they are suffering, they can bring the matter before the throne of grace. Jesus taught the importance of persistence in prayer (Luke 11:5-10).

The redeemed of God have much to be grateful for, even in the midst of suffering and trouble. Let the cheerful sing praise, "speak to one another with psalms, hymns and spiritual songs. Sing and make music in your heart to the Lord, always giving thanks to God the Father for everything, in the name of our Lord Jesus Christ" (Ephesians 5:19-20). Such singing ministers grace to the hearers as well.

Is anyone sick? James gives a prescription that many churches do not follow. True, prayer for the sick is raised by members of the congregation corporately and individually. Here, the sick person is told to take the initiative. Call for the elders of the church. They should pray over that sick person and anoint that person with oil "in the name of the Lord." They are acting on behalf of the Great Physician.

Some persons will question anointing with oil. They may wonder of what value that can be, especially in light of the accomplishments of modern medicine. Yet, healing is more than diagnosis, prescriptions, and prognosis. The prayer of faith combined with the act of faith (anointing) will have its effect. The raising up of the sick from the sickbed is in the hands of God, in whose name the anointing and prayer are carried out.

Sometimes sin is the cause of sickness. Physical difficulties are often related to mental and spiritual causes. In these cases confession is therapeutic. Confession is to one another, to brothers and sisters within the household of faith. No one is without sin; "We all stumble in many ways" (3:2). So we all need to confess our sins to one another and to pray for one another. The healing we need may be physical, mental, emotional, or spiritual.

Prayer is the key to healing, following confession. Elijah is a good example of the truth expressed in 5:16b. (See his story in 1 Kings 17–18.)

James 5:19-20. James's final word of encouragement is indirectly related to the preceding instruction. A wanderer (backslider) has gone away from the caring, sharing fellowship of the church depicted in 5:13-18. This person has wandered from the truth of the gospel, which is the basis of the church.

Such wanderers are worthy of an effort to bring them back. Those who make that effort will experience the profound pleasure of knowing that the effort has saved a sinner (the wanderer) from eternal death (Revelation 21:8). A multitude of sins will be covered in the process (1 Peter 4:8). That is because the blood of Jesus Christ is able to cover all sin and to cleanse all from unrighteousness.

DIMENSION THREE:
WHAT DOES THE BIBLE MEAN TO ME?

James 3:1–4:17
Your Christian Experience

This discussion topic is not intended to damage persons but to stimulate self-evaluation. Class members may have experience dealing with one or more of the concerns listed in Question 1 in the student book. They may have come to grips with one or more of the concerns in their own life, or they may have suffered the effects of these concerns at the hands of others.

Seek to find in the context of each concern the positive instruction that will help with the problem. The scriptural solutions to the problems raised by these concerns should apply to the person or to a dominant problem in the life of a congregation. Solutions to such problems come as the result of an awareness that a problem exists, understanding the nature of the problem, determining through prayer and consultation the action to be taken, and by the grace of God acting positively.

James 5:13-18
Your Influence in the Life of Your Church

One hindrance to fellowship is the stress on individualism in our culture. The church is a community. Membership in it provides privileges and requires responsibilities. Christians are to share life. They are to "rejoice with those who rejoice; mourn with those who mourn" (Romans 12:15). In James we see that we are also to sing praises to God for the benefit of one another, to confess our sins to one another, and to pray for one another.

Explore the problem of retaining our individualism while we practice being a member of a community of the faithful. In what practical ways can we be more actively involved in the lives of fellow believers? What are some practical means by which we can allow Christian brothers and sisters to share more intimately in our lives?

Live such good lives among the pagans that . . . they may see your good
deeds and glorify God (2:12).

8

How to Live in a Hostile World

1 Peter

DIMENSION ONE:
WHAT DOES THE BIBLE SAY?

Answer these questions by reading 1 Peter

1. To whom is this letter addressed? (1:1)

   The letter is addressed to "God's elect, strangers in the world, scattered throughout Pontus, Galatia, Cappadocia, Asia and Bithynia."

2. What was the basis of the living hope in which the readers rejoiced? (1:3b)

   The basis of the living hope was "the resurrection of Jesus Christ from the dead."

3. What did the prophets predict about Christ? (1:10-11)

   The prophets predicted "the sufferings of Christ and the glories that would follow."

4. If someone claims God as Father, what effect should the claim have on that person's manner of life? (1:14-16)

   The person who claims God as Father should be holy in conduct, for God is holy.

5. What four expressions are used to describe all those who have received mercy? (2:9-10)

   Those who have received mercy are described as "a chosen people," "a royal priesthood," "a holy nation," and "a people belonging to God."

6. If we follow in the steps of Jesus, what specific things will we try to do? (2:21-23)

   If we follow the example of Jesus, we will try to commit no sin, to have no deceit in our mouths, to not retaliate when we are

insulted, to not threaten when we suffer, and to trust "him who judges justly" (God).

7. In relation to one another, how should wives and husbands act? (3:1, 7)

   Wives are to be submissive to their husbands, and husbands are to live considerately with their wives.

8. What characteristics should Christians show toward one another? (3:8)

   Christians should show harmony, sympathy, love of the brothers, compassion, and humility toward one another.

9. First Peter 4:7-11 lists a number of practices Christians should follow. Why should Christians practice these things? (4:11b)

   Christians should practice these things "so that in all things God may be praised through Jesus Christ."

10. Suffering as a Christian is acceptable, but Christians are warned not to suffer for certain things. What are they? (4:15)

    Christians should not suffer "as a murderer or thief or any other kind of criminal, or even as a meddler."

11. Identify the main theme in 1 Peter 5:1-6.

    The main theme of these verses is Christian humility.

12. First Peter 5:7-11 has two comforting promises for Christians. What are they?

    The first of the two promises is that God "cares for you" (5:7). The second promise is that after someone has suffered as a Christian, God will "restore you and make you strong, firm and steadfast" (5:10).

DIMENSION TWO:
WHAT DOES THE BIBLE MEAN?

The First Letter of Peter is a message of instruction and encouragement for believers who are under the stress of trials and persecution. Its content and tone of expression have strengthened Christians from the first through the twentieth centuries.

Writer, Date, and Place of Writing. The authorship of this letter is a matter of controversy. The opening verse of the letter indicates the apostle Peter is the writer. But several arguments against his authorship have been raised:

1. the excellence of the Greek could not be expected from the hand of a simple Galilean fisherman;

2. the intense persecutions mentioned in the letter did not take place until after the end of the first century A.D., long after Peter's death;

3. the expressions and ideas are too much like Paul's to come from Peter;

4. the letter does not reflect the personal acquaintance of Peter with Jesus that the Gospels indicate.

On the basis of these objections, the assumption is that the letter was written by a disciple of Peter in the apostle's name about A.D. 112.

Against this view and for Peter as the writer are the following points:

1. the Greek was from the hand of Silas, who wrote under Peter's direction (5:12);

2. the persecutions need not be considered late but in the time of Peter;

3. the influence of Paul is only apparent because the expressions were a common core used by both Peter and Paul;

4. that the letter lacks evidence of a close bond between Jesus and the writer is not valid and is overstated.

Our assumption is that Peter wrote this letter before his death as a martyr in Rome around A.D. 64. This view is based on early traditions in the church and the lack of compelling arguments to the contrary. Irenaeus (about A.D 185) was the first to quote First Peter by name. Eusebius (before A.D. 340) placed the letter among the acknowledged books of the New Testament.

The belief that Rome was the place of origin for the letter is based on the view that "Babylon" (5:13) is really a reference to Rome. Similar usage is found in the Book of Revelation (14:8; 17:5; 18:2).

The Readers. Peter wrote to Christians living in five provinces of Asia Minor (part of modern Turkey): Pontus, Galatia, Cappadocia, Asia, and Bithynia. These Christians lived in the region originally evangelized by Paul. The congregations likely consisted of Jewish and Gentile Christians.

The readers seem already to have faced some persecution. Peter writes to encourage them to stand fast in "the true grace of God" (5:12). They needed that because of "painful trial" that they were now facing (4:12). It was a time that tried their faith and their souls.

Outline of First Peter.
- I. Salutation (1:1-2)
- II. Appreciate your new life in Christ (1:3-12)
- III. Live a holy life before God (1:13–2:10)
  - A. Set your mind on Christ (1:13)
  - B. Individually, live as a child of God (1:14–2:3)
  - C. Collectively, live as God's own people (2:4-10)
- IV. On living a holy life before the world (2:11-25)
  - A. In relation to the general public (2:11-12)
  - B. In relation to legal authorities (2:13-17)
  - C. In relation to personal authority (2:18-20)
  - D. By following Christ's example (2:21-25)
- V. On living a holy life in the home and in the Christian community (3:1-12)
  - A. In the home (3:1-7)
  - B. In the Christian community (3:8-12)
- VI. How to suffer successfully (3:13–4:19)
  - A. Have a proper attitude toward suffering (3:13-22)
  - B. Live to the glory of God (4:1-11)
  - C. If you suffer, suffer according to God's will (4:12-19)
- VII. Maintain the Christian community by humility (5:1-11)
- VIII. Closing remarks (5:12-14)

1 Peter 1:1-2. The letter opens with Peter's name. Peter was an interesting member of the small group of special disciples that followed Jesus throughout his ministry. An enthusiastic and forceful man, some of Peter's character seems to be reflected in the forcefulness of this letter.

Peter's Hebrew name was Simon Bar (son of) Jonah (Matthew 16:17). Jesus gave him the nickname *Cephas,* an Aramaic word meaning "rock." The Greek form of *Cephas* is *Petros* with the same meaning; and Petros is the basis of the English name *Peter.*

Peter was married, and his wife apparently accompanied him on his missionary journeys. He was originally in business as a fisherman but left that at the call of Jesus. He had a mountaintop experience at the transfiguration of Jesus (Matthew 17:1-18). It was an unforgettable experience that he mentions in Second Peter (1:17-18).

Peter walked on water (Matthew 14:28-29), rebuked Jesus for suggesting Jesus' coming death (Matthew 16:21-23), and emphasized his allegiance to Jesus shortly before denying him (Mark 14:29, 66-72). Restored by Jesus, Peter went on to preach the first gospel sermon after the Ascension (Acts 2). Peter was instrumental in the conversion of the first Samaritans and Gentiles won to Christ. He traveled with the gospel among the Jews of the Dispersion (Galatians 2:9), while Paul went to the Gentiles. According to apparently authentic tradition, both Peter and Paul were martyred in Rome during the persecutions of Christians by Nero.

We discussed the Dispersion in Lesson 6. While the expression originated with the Jews, it was later applied to Christians. Later in this letter Peter addresses the readers as "aliens and strangers" (2:11).

Notice 1:2, which specifies the privileged position the readers hold. They are the elect, the chosen ones. (Peter anticipates with this word his teaching on the chosen ones that follows in 2:4-10.) God chose them and God "destined" them. The *Good News Bible* (*Today's English Version*) has "according to the purpose of God."

God chose them, destined them to be sanctified (to be made holy) by the Holy Spirit. A similar expression is found in 2 Thessalonians 2:13. They are destined as sanctified people to obey Jesus Christ and to be sprinkled "by his blood." At baptism, believers receive the sanctification of the Spirit (Titus 3:5); and in baptism they come into contact, symbolically, with the shed blood of Jesus, in that they are baptized into his death (Romans 6:3).

In other words, 1:2 acknowledges that the readers have been brought by God's providence into God's nation. Such believers receive grace and peace. Peter prays that these two benefits will be multiplied to them.

1 Peter 1:3-12. Peter proceeds from the theological to the practical in this letter. In this section he establishes the basis for the instruction that will follow. He will later challenge the believers to face courageously the difficulties ahead. They can triumph over every trial if they can catch a vision of what God has done for them in Christ Jesus. Peter, perhaps in his early sixties, has never lost the sense of wonder at what he has witnessed and experienced. He must bless God.

Peter wants the Christians to appreciate their new life in Christ. They have this new life by God's great mercy (1:3b). God was motivated by love and pity toward undeserving people (Titus 3:5).

"We"—Peter, his readers, all those who have accepted God's grace and mercy—are born again. Jesus told Nicodemus that unless one is born again that person cannot see the kingdom of God (John 3:3). Obedient believers are born again to a living hope. The resurrection of Jesus from the dead holds promise of the believer's resurrection (1 Corinthians 15:16-23). The living hope goes on beyond resurrection to include a heavenly inheritance, described in the timeless adjectives of 1 Peter 1:4. That inheritance is eternal life. The earthly shadow of this heavenly reality was the land of Canaan, ancient Israel's Promised Land.

The inheritance is kept in heaven; there those who will inherit are guarded by God's power (1:5). That guarding power is activated by the faith of the believer. The inheritance is salvation, anticipated now by faith, realized in "the last time."

Christians have a foretaste of salvation now, a guarantee. They are sealed with the Holy Spirit (Ephesians 1:13-14). They can rejoice in this guarantee while they face various trials. The trials will prove the genuineness of their faith. Their faith is more precious than gold because the end

result is the "inheritance that can never perish, spoil or fade." Even gold is perishable here on earth. The testing of faith will show the faith to be genuine. When the faithful are tested by fire and stand the test, they bring praise, glory, and honor to Christ now and at his appearing (Revelation 7:9-17).

Peter, who had seen Jesus, commends the faith of the readers who have not seen him. Even so, they love him. They find exquisite joy in Christ, and by faith they are in the process of obtaining salvation. Salvation in Christ has a past, present, and future aspect. In the present, "we live by faith, not by sight," as Paul said in 2 Corinthians 5:7. The full inheritance is only received at the appearing of Christ.

First Peter 1:10-12 indicates that Christians have an advantage over the pious of ages past. Christians walk by faith, and they have a much clearer picture of grace in Christ than even the prophets.

The prophets predicted the sufferings of Christ and "the glories that would follow" (1:11). That is the same pattern the readers must repeat—to suffer, then to attain glory.

The fact that the prophets were really serving the purposes of God for the time of the readers is stressed in 1:12. What the prophets foresaw has been preached to the readers. The good news (gospel) came through speakers under the inspiration of the Holy Spirit. The mysteries of God in Christ were so great that even the angels did not know them. (No wonder the angels sang with joy at the birth of the Messiah: the mystery was unfolding before them!)

The reason why Peter wrote this section is clear. These Christians have received what prophets and angels could not comprehend. This information would help the readers even more to appreciate their new life in Christ.

1 Peter 1:13–2:10. Peter has pointed out the incredibly great blessings of being chosen, destined, and sanctified by God's grace. Believers have every reason to be thankful for a living hope, a hope that in reality exceeds all that the human mind can imagine. Now Peter turns to call the readers to live a holy life before God.

1 Peter 1:13. The call to "prepare ["gird up," RSV] your minds" is related to girding up the loins. Oriental men wore robes. When in a hurry or preparing for activities that the robes would hamper, they would bind their clothing up around the waist with a rope (girdle). This girding up their clothes would free them for energetic activity.

Peter calls for preparing the mind for intense activity. (Paul called for similar actions in Romans 12:1-2.) A determined effort is required by a person to live a holy life and to obtain the grace that is coming.

Being prepared includes being self-controlled. Being self-controlled is facing realistically what the situation requires. It is counting the cost. The other activity that preparing the mind requires is setting one's hope on the promised future inheritance.

1 Peter 1:14–2:3. While Peter uses the plural (children, 1:14), what he calls for in Christian conduct must be done individually.

Peter calls Christians to be obedient. What are the specifics of obedience Peter has in mind? (1) Do not allow the "evil desires" of your former way of life to control you. (2) To the contrary, conduct yourself in a holy way. Be holy like the Holy One (1:15-16). (3) Live out your time here on earth with reverent respect for the Father to whom you pray. God is an impartial judge of the actions of each one of us.

At the same time, you can have confidence in God (1:21). You were ransomed from a hopeless life like that of your ancestors at an incredible price—the precious blood of Christ. This ransom was all God's work. The Christ was destined to shed his blood in death, be raised from the dead, and be given glory—all for your sake. God planned this saving act before the creation of the world. So you can have confidence in God. You can put your faith and hope in God (1:21).

To live as a child of God, love others earnestly with all your heart (1:22). You are able to do this because you have purified your souls by obedience to the truth. The first readers of Peter's letter would understand the truth as the gospel. A positive response to the gospel involves repentance from past sins, confession that Jesus is the Christ (therefore both Savior and Lord), and baptism into Christ. This response justifies a person before God and brings a person into the community of the redeemed, the church.

Purification of the soul is connected with baptism. At Paul's conversion, Ananias instructed him, "Get up, be baptized and wash your sins away, calling on his name" (Acts 22:16b). The cleansing is symbolized by the water but is actualized by sharing in the death, burial, and resurrection of Jesus (Romans 6:1-11). In relationship to Jesus' death we come into contact with the cleansing blood of his sacrifice. Purified, the baptized believer rises to walk in newness of life, no longer under the domination of sin or the condemnation of God.

Peter describes the believer's new relationship in Christ with family metaphors ("sincere love for your brothers," 1:22). We are conceived by imperishable seed, the word of God. This picture is similar to Jesus' parable of the sower (Matthew 13:18-23). In that parable the seed is the word of the Kingdom. When the living and abiding word of God has developed within us, we are born again. The good news that was preached has borne fruit (1:25b).

The new life that comes with the new birth is different from the futile ways of the old life. Living the new life in Christ requires action. "Rid yourselves of" malice (wickedness), deceit, hypocrisy, envy (jealousy), and all slander (insulting language). All these are the opposite of loving one another sincerely.

Besides the action of putting away the negative things mentioned in 2:1, Peter exhorts the readers to positive action in 2:2. "Crave pure spiritual milk" like newborn babies long for their mother's milk. The spiritual milk must be something taken into the mind of the believer that is the opposite of malice, deceit, and so on. This new thing must be the word of God. The King James Version uses the phrase "desire the sincere milk of the word." Rather than feeding on the deceit of the world, as they had in the past, the newborn children of God take into their mind God's word, so as to grow up to salvation. Salvation here is final salvation. No one will ever attain final salvation who does not first begin as a babe in Christ, then move on toward spiritual maturity. The first readers have already "tasted that the Lord is good" (2:3; Psalm 34:8).

1 Peter 2:4-10. To live as a Christian in a hostile world requires girding up the mind, purifying the soul, being born again, putting away malice and the like, and craving spiritual food. But God's children do not exist in isolation. The "family" metaphor used earlier now becomes a "spiritual house" metaphor. The spiritual house image is probably based on the Temple in Jerusalem. Believers are to "come to him, the living Stone" (2:4). That stone is Jesus Christ. Peter establishes that fact by the quotations that follow in 2:6 (Isaiah 28:16), 2:7 (Psalm 118:22), and 2:8 (Isaiah 8:14-15).

Jesus also quoted Psalm 118:22 in Matthew 21:42. He saw himself as the stone rejected by the builders. But God has made Jesus the head of the corner. Peter had referred to Jesus as the rejected stone, now head of the corner, before the Jewish leaders in Jerusalem years earlier (Acts 4:10-11).

Now the believers, who are also living stones, are instructed to be built into a spiritual house on the living foundation stone (2:5). They are also to be a holy priesthood in that living temple, presenting their bodies as living sacrifices to God (Romans 12:1).

Committed Christians belong to the family of God by the new birth. They have become a chosen people (Isaiah 43:20b), a royal priesthood, a holy nation (both from Exodus 19:6), a people belonging to God (Exodus 19:5), like Israel of old. The purpose of God's people is given in 2:9. Verse 10 is based on Hosea 1:9-10.

1 Peter 2:11-12. The readers are God's people in exile, aliens in a Gentile world. They are to refrain from indulging sinful desires. Peter agrees with James (3:13–4:10). These sinful desires war against the soul. God's people are to live a life that declares the wonderful deeds of God (1 Peter 2:9) through their own good deeds. The church is a letter from Christ, to be known and read by all persons (2 Corinthians 3:2-3).

1 Peter 2:13-17. To live a holy life before the world, submit to civil authorities. Do this for God's sake, for the sake of God's concern to redeem the lost and God's concern for the people. Show appropriate respect (honor) to all. But have a deep and abiding concern for the people of God—you and they are God's people—and show God profound respect.

1 Peter 2:18-20. Slavery was a fact of life for many of the early Christians. A slave, in order to live a life holy before the world, must be submissive to the master. This submission may require unjust suffering, but this suffering can be endured if one is "conscious of God."

1 Peter 2:21-25. Patience in suffering will win God's approval. To be patient is to follow in the footsteps of Jesus. God allowed Jesus to suffer on behalf of the believers, and they have benefited. Christian suffering for doing right will benefit others also.

1 Peter 3:1-12. Submission and consideration for others is a way of life for Christians. Slaves must submit to masters. Christ submitted to those who had authority to crucify him. The principle works in more intimate relationships as well.

1 Peter 3:1-7. Wives are to be submissive to their husbands, some of whom are not Christians. The lifestyle of a Christian wife can affect the faith of her husband. Submission involves doing right and can be done without fear of intimidation.

Husbands are to be considerate and understanding toward their wives. Do not use a greater physical strength to intimidate your wife, Peter writes. Honor her as one who is a joint heir of eternal life with you. Clearly, to fail to maintain this considerate treatment of your spouse will affect your spiritual life and your communication with God.

1 Peter 3:8-12. To live a holy life requires Christian unity. The unity of believers results from right attitudes, indicated in 3:8. Peter then quotes from Psalm 34:12-16 to remind the readers that God favors right conduct.

1 Peter 3:13-22. Ordinarily, no harm will come from doing good. But if suffering does come, set Christ in the heart. Through good behavior in Christ, an opportunity to give a reason for the Christian hope may arise.

Within God's purpose and will, suffering for doing right may come. Jesus so suffered on our behalf (3:17-18).

Verses 19-20 present one of the most difficult passages to understand that can be found in the New Testament. "Through whom" refers to the Spirit, the last word in 3:18. Christ went through the Spirit to proclaim a message of warning. Christ, who existed with God before the world began (John 1:1-5), through the spirit of inspiration moved Noah to warn his generation of the coming catastrophe. Noah's warning was a call to repentance.

This proclamation was to Noah's generation while they were alive. At the time that Peter wrote, they were "spirits in prison," awaiting the general resurrection and the final judgment. This Scripture cannot be used to hold out hope for those who reject Christ during their lifetime on earth. As Hebrews 9:27 makes clear, it is appointed for humans to die once, and after that comes judgment.

Although Noah's generation was destroyed, a few (eight persons) were saved through water; that is, they were saved by being in the ark on the water. The water bore it up. In a similar way, water, the water of baptism, now saves the few from "this corrupt generation" (Acts 2:40). Water might cleanse the skin; but in baptism, water is not what saves you. Water is a symbolic appeal to God: "Give me, I pray, a clear conscience. I know you have made it possible through the resurrection of Jesus Christ." Baptism apart from repentance and commitment to God in Christ is not Christian baptism.

1 Peter 4:1-11. Like Christ, live by the will of God rather than by human desires. It is enough, Peter wrote, that you formerly lived as the pagans live (1 Peter 4:3). But all will be judged, both those alive and those dead. The good news was preached to the dead while they were yet alive (4:6). God has had a witness in every generation (Romans 1:19-23).

Every generation of Christians has lived on the edge of the end of all things. In fact, the end of all things in this world for us comes the moment we die. Live to the glory of God now. Keep clear minded and self-controlled now. Pray now. Love now. Be hospitable now. Use your spiritual gift or gifts now. Do all these things now so that God will be glorified both now and "for ever and ever" (4:11).

1 Peter 4:12-19. Peter had experienced suffering. He advises his beloved readers not to be surprised when painful trials (persecutions) erupt. They are sojourners in an alien and hostile world.

Rather, be of good cheer when persecutions come, sharing in Christ's sufferings (the church is the body of Christ); you will also share in Christ's glory. Do not suffer as an evildoer. Suffer as a Christian, and praise God. Judgment is coming, beginning with the family of God, so do right. Do not worry about the Judgment. Trust your soul to God.

1 Peter 5:1-11. First Peter 5:1-4 is addressed to the leaders of the Christian community, "the elders." Peter, though an apostle, sees himself also as sharing the role of an elder. That role was as a shepherd of the flock of God, the people of the faith. Peter's emphasis here is on the proper attitude and actions. The appropriate attitude is one of humility.

Those subject to the elders should also be clothed with humility. Verse 6 seems to echo James 4:10. Humility now assures exaltation then, in God's tomorrow and by God's hand. Relax, God cares for you now. Let God bear your anxiety. "Do not be anxious about anything, but in everything, by prayer and petition, with thanksgiving, present your requests to God. And the peace of God, which transcends all understanding, will guard your hearts and your minds in Christ Jesus" (Philippians 4:6-7).

First Peter 5:8-9 is just as valid as the preceding verses. The devil is the personification of evil, waiting to swallow up the unwary and enticing Christians to forgo the suffering and to cave in to the desires. This advice is similar to that of James: "Resist the devil, and he will flee from you" (4:7b). You are not alone in resisting. You are not alone in suffering. Both will end, and you will receive the reward for faithfulness—to share in the eternal glory of Christ.

1 Peter 5:12-14. Silas was responsible for drafting the letter. He is probably the Silas of Acts 15:22-40. He, along with Timothy, was also involved in writing First and Second Thessalonians.

The last part of 5:12 gives the specific reason why Peter wrote. " The true grace of God" is the Christians' current situation of suffering. Rejoice in it (4:13). Stand fast in it.

Greetings from the church in Rome (Babylon) come with the letter. The Roman Christians, too, are chosen. Greetings also come from (John) Mark. We know Mark as the companion of Paul and Barnabas (Acts 15:37-40)

The warmth of the writer toward his readers is felt in the closing remarks. Peace refers to unity and harmony in the church. It is a fruit of the Holy Spirit (Galatians 5:22).

DIMENSION THREE:
WHAT DOES THE BIBLE MEAN TO ME?

1 Peter 2:5, 9—A Royal Priesthood

In Israel, priests represented the people in the ritual of the sanctuary. They mediated between God and the peo-ple. The high priest had a special role, as we have seen in the study of Hebrews. He entered into the Most Holy Place of the Tabernacle (Temple) to make atonement for the sins of the people. Christ has now become the believer's high priest. Immediate access to God is possible now through him.

All Christians are now able to offer spiritual sacrifices acceptable to God. All believers are now priests. In Romans 12:1, Paul explains that we are to present our bodies as a living sacrifice, and that is our reasonable or spiritual service. What he has in mind is a dedicated Christian life. The specific implications of that living sacrifice are given through the remainder of Romans 12.

Peter said that we (the royal priesthood) are also to declare the wonderful deeds of God, who called us out of darkness into his marvelous light. We are to be ready at any time to explain the hope that is within us (that you may declare [his] praises").

Another aspect of our priesthood is to offer sacrifices of praise (Hebrews 13:15). This praise is also called "the fruit of lips that confess [God's] name." Beyond that, the next verse encourages doing good to others and sharing what you have, "for with such sacrifices God is pleased" (Hebrews 13:6).

Be all the more eager to make your calling and election sure. For if you do these things, you will never fall (1:10).

— 9 —

How to Handle the Crisis in the Church

2 Peter

DIMENSION ONE:
WHAT DOES THE BIBLE SAY?

Answer these questions by reading 2 Peter

1. How does Peter describe his relationship to Jesus Christ? (1:1)

   Peter calls himself "a servant and apostle of Jesus Christ."

2. What can the believers in the great and precious promises of God expect to receive? (1:4)

   The believers can expect to "participate in the divine nature and escape the corruption in the world."

3. What one thing does Peter want to do for his readers? (1:12)

   The one thing Peter wants to do for his readers is to remind them of truths they already know.

4. What were the sources of the apostolic witness and the prophetic word? (1:16-21)

   The apostles were eyewitnesses of the majesty of Jesus (1:16), and the prophetic word came through the Holy Spirit (1:21).

5. What does Peter say that the false teachers will do? (2:1-3)

   The false teachers will bring in destructive heresies, deny the Lord, act in shameful ways, and exploit the readers with false stories.

6. In 2:4-10a, Peter uses three examples to show that God knows how to keep the unrighteous under punishment. List the three examples.

   The three examples are the angels that sinned, the people of the ancient world who died in the Flood, and the people of Sodom and Gomorrah.

7. The false teachers are seen as following in the footsteps of what biblical character? (2:12-16)

   The false teachers followed in the way of Balaam, the son of Beor.

8. Why do the false teachers fail to deliver on their promise of freedom for their followers? (2:19)

   The false teachers cannot give freedom to those who follow them because "they themselves are slaves of depravity."

9. Why do scoffers say, "Where is this 'coming' he promised?" (3:3-4)

   Scoffers say this because "everything goes on as it has since the beginning of creation."

10. Why does the Lord delay the Day of Judgment and destruction of ungodly people? (3:9)

   The Lord delays the Day of Judgment because God does not wish any to perish, "but everyone to come to repentance."

11. According to the promise of God, for what do Christians wait? (3:13)

   Christians are waiting for "a new heaven and a new earth, the home of righteousness."

12. Peter warns the readers to beware of two related things. What are they? (3:15-17)

   Peter warns them to beware of being "carried away by the error of lawless men and fall[ing] away from [their] secure position."

DIMENSION TWO: WHAT DOES THE BIBLE MEAN?

Writer and Date. After investigating the varying views on the authorship of this book, one remains perplexed. Every book in the New Testament is challenged by someone, but more scholars deny the genuineness of Second Peter than any other book in the canon.

I have attempted to present a concise, but fair, assessment of the major scholarly views below. Then I will indicate the position I have adopted for this lesson.

1. The letter is written as from the apostle Peter (1:1). The writer refers to the transfiguration of Jesus (1:17-18; Matthew 17:1-8; Mark 9:2-8; Luke 9:28-36). Peter was an eyewitness. The writer refers also to the words of Jesus about the coming death of Peter (John 21:18-19). A previous letter is referred to (2 Peter 3:1), doubtless to be understood as First Peter. The writer indicates a personal familiarity with the apostle Paul and accepts him as an inspired writer (3:15b-16). Based on this internal evidence, the traditional position is that Peter was the writer.

2. Second Peter was written by an unnamed follower of Peter sometime after the apostle's death. The writer's intent was to preserve the apostolic tradition. The language and imagery of the book is quite Greek in flavor. Peter, a Galilean fisherman, would be expected to write with a more Semitic flavor. Further, there is no new information about Jesus and the apostles in the letter that would not have been available to a follower of Peter.

The letter was written by this unnamed disciple about A.D. 90. Or, the letter was written between A.D. 125 and A.D. 150 by a member of the third generation from Peter. Reasons for dating the letter later than Peter are the following:

a. it draws heavily on the Letter of Jude, which was probably written about A.D. 90; and Second Peter is believed to be the borrower;

b. it mentions the death of the "fathers" the early church leaders (3:4b);

c. it refers to the letters of Paul as "Scriptures" (3:16), an expression used during the time of the apostles to refer only to the Old Testament books.

3. Origen, Eusebius, and Jerome refer to Second Peter; but they indicate that some people doubt that the letter was written by the apostle. Eusebius put it in the category of "disputed books." Second Peter was accepted into the canon by the council at Carthage (A.D. 397).

For our purposes we will view the letter as written by Peter shortly before his death, near A.D. 64. Despite differences between First and Second Peter that scholars have observed, the two books have significant similarities. Both letters emphasize Christ and his second coming as central doctrines; the importance of the story of the Flood and Noah; the importance of the prophetic word, the Old Testament, similar to Peter's use of prophecy in his Pente-cost sermon (Acts 2:14-36); and the necessity of Christian growth.

Place of Writing. Peter speaks of his approaching death (1:14). According to early Christian tradition, this took place in Rome about the same time Paul was killed, sometime between A.D. 64 and A.D. 67.

The Readers. Our writer mentions that this epistle is the second letter he has written to the readers (3:1). We can assume that it was written to the Christians in the five provinces of Asia Minor listed in 1 Peter 1:1.

The Form of the Letter. Second Peter is similar in form to a "testament." Testaments were a literary type begun by Jews in the intertestamental period. Christians also took up this literary form. Testaments in the New Testament include Jesus' farewell speech (John 13–17), Paul's farewell to the elders of Ephesus (Acts 20:17-35), and Second Timothy.

A testament is like a last will and testament to the church. It is written on the occasion of the approaching death of the writer. The content of testaments consists of admonitions and edifying words that point out the difficulties that will come. Peter leaves this work as a legacy to help remind his readers of important truths.

Outline of Second Peter.

I. Salutation (1:1-2)
II. Make your calling and election sure (1:3-11)
III. Keep the apostolic and prophetic word (1:12-21)
   A. The apostolic witness (1:12-18)
   B. The prophetic word (1:19-21)
IV. Beware of false teachers (2:1-22)
   A. False teachers will arise (2:1-3)
   B. They will be punished, but the righteous will be rescued (2:4-10a)
   C. The character and conduct of false teachers (2:10b-16)
   D. The folly of following them (2:17-22)
V. On the second coming of the Lord (3:1-18)
   A. Some will scoff at it (3:1-7)
   B. The answer for scoffers (3:8-10)
   C. How to await that day (3:11-18)

2 Peter 1:1-2. Simon (1:1) is the Hebrew form of Peter's first name as it appears also in Acts 15:14. Compared to the opening of First Peter, here the words *a servant* are added.

Rather than identifying the place to which the letter was sent, Peter addresses the recipients as "those who through the righteousness of our God and Savior Jesus Christ have received a faith as precious as ours." This phrase likely refers to Gentile Christians. The expression shows that the ground is level at the foot of the cross. "There is neither Jew nor Greek, slave nor free, male nor female" in Christ Jesus (Galatians 3:28).

The desire for grace and peace for the readers, found in First Peter, is repeated here (1:2). " Through the knowledge of God and of Jesus our Lord" is added. A deepening "knowledge of God and of Jesus our Lord" will result in multiplied grace and peace.

2 Peter 1:3-11. Verses 3-4 provide an introductory statement to the main statement that begins with verse 5. The main thought in this introduction is the gift God has given (granted) to people of faith (us). The gift mentioned here has several meanings. It is a complete package, providing all that is needed to live a godly life (1:3); it comes through knowledge of God, the One who called us through Jesus to share "his . . . glory and goodness" (1:3); it provides a protective shield, a means of escaping the life-destroying effects of evil desires (1:4; compare 1 Peter 4:1-6); and it provides the means for sharing God's essential nature (1:4).

God has made spiritual gifts and knowledge available to people of faith. Through what God has granted, they may escape worldly corruption. However, supplementary effort is required (1:5). They should do their utmost to add to what God has done for them. They need to confirm eagerly their calling and election (1:10).

Verses 5-7 list eight qualities Christians should have in their lives. Each quality promotes acquiring the next.

Faith is the foundation of the Christian life. Faith is assurance (Hebrews 11:1). Without faith it is impossible to please God (Hebrews 11:6). Faith includes believing in God and believing God. The basis of faith is accepting the testimony (knowledge) God has revealed about Christ (Romans 10:14-17).

Goodness is moral power, goodness of life, and strength of Christian character.

Knowledge is the knowledge "of God and of Jesus our Lord" mentioned in 1:2-3. " This is eternal life: that they know you, the only true God, and Jesus Christ, whom you have sent" (John 17:3). The Bible is the disciple's textbook. Contained within it is everything "useful for teaching, rebuking, correcting and training in righteousness, so that [God's servant] may be thoroughly equipped for every good work" (2 Timothy 3:16-17).

Self-control is promoted by knowledge of one's self. It involves the mind: Thoughts can be controlled. People can choose what they think about. Paul urged Christians to think about things true, noble, right, pure, lovely, admirable, excellent, and praiseworthy (Philippians 4:8). Self-control also involves the body: Christians can subdue passions and desires. "When you are tempted, [God] will also provide a way out" (1 Corinthians 10:13c). The body can be controlled and directed to alternative activities.

Perseverance is sometimes rendered "patience," sometimes "steadfastness." Perseverance is the ability to stand firm. Jesus, in foretelling persecution against his apostles, said, "By standing firm you will gain life" (Luke 21:19). The one "who stands firm to the end will be saved" (Matthew 24:13).

Godliness is a reverent attitude toward God. It includes devotion to God and imitating God's character. Practically, it means following in the footsteps of Jesus.

Brotherly kindness is love for the other members of the family of God. This quality of caring is also discussed in 1 Peter 1:22.

Love is a genuine concern for the good and welfare of another person. Christian love, like that exemplified in Christ, is not an emotional feeling. Such love is a deliberate attitude with related actions (Matthew 5:44).

The person who possesses an abundance of these qualities will actively apply the knowledge of the Lord to life situations. That person will be productive in the Christian life, full of love and good works. God saves people for a purpose, to be fruitful servants in the cause of righteousness.

On the other hand, the person who has saving faith but who does not add these characteristics to that faith is terribly handicapped (1:9). Shortsighted to the point of blindness and forgetful of the cleansing power of Jesus' blood, that person is destined for disaster. Faith without living a productive life is dead (James 2:26).

God in Christ chooses and calls us (1:3, 10). Whosoever will may come (Revelation 22:17). But the called must be zealous to confirm the call. This confirmation is done by adding to faith the qualities indicated in 1:5-7. Believers who diligently endeavor to confirm that call will be so engrossed in the effort and so engaged in the task that they will have no occasion to stumble. The end result will be a rich welcome into the eternal kingdom of God, into heaven itself. These are ample reasons to make one's calling and election sure.

2 Peter 1:12-15. Because of the importance of developing the Christian graces and thereby confirming their calling, Peter is determined to leave his readers a permanent reminder (1:12). His letter is that reminder.

The permanent reminder is not some new information that they have not previously received. Peter is confident that the readers know and are established in the truth. But Christians forget and need to be reminded ("refresh your memory," 1:13).

The time had come to leave this permanent reminder. Peter was still alive ("in the tent of this body"), but he knew that he was soon to die. Jesus had predicted Peter's death: "'When you are old you will stretch out your hands, and someone else will dress you and lead you where you do not want to go.' Jesus said this to indicate the kind of death by which Peter would glorify God" (John 21:18b-19). The passage may also suggest a further revelation from Christ to Peter shortly before he wrote this letter (2 Peter 1:14).

In the remainder of this section of his letter, the apostle emphasizes the apostolic witness and the prophetic word.

2 Peter 1:16-18. Peter, writing to former pagans who were steeped in the myths of Greek and Oriental culture, is emphatic that Christ is no myth. He reminds the readers that he and the other apostles had made known to them the details about the first coming of Jesus Christ. (Peter will discuss the second coming of Christ later in the letter.)

Jesus came in power. Peter was an eyewitness to his powerful works. Peter's mother-in-law was healed by Jesus' power (Matthew 8:14-15). Peter shared that marvelous power of Jesus over the natural elements; he walked on water (Matthew 14:28-29). In 2 Peter 1:16, the power Peter had in mind was that which he witnessed on the Mount of Transfiguration (Matthew 17:1-8).

Peter witnessed more than power on that mountain. He, James, and John also witnessed the majesty of Jesus Christ. "His face shone like the sun, and his clothes became as white as the light . . . then . . . Moses and Elijah [appeared], talking with Jesus" (Matthew 17:2b-3).

Moses and Elijah were great channels of revelation for God's will, and Peter was ready to classify the majestic Jesus into a similar category. Then he heard a voice from heaven that he would never forget: "This is my Son, whom I love; with him I am well pleased. Listen to him!" (Matthew 17:5). All this was in Peter's mind as he wrote, and his readers knew the story well.

The Transfiguration was a personal experience of Peter's and a historical occurrence on a rock-solid mountain. Jesus, in all his power, glory, and majesty was no myth. That is the apostolic witness to be remembered, to be kept.

2 Peter 1:19-21. Jesus verified the testimony of the prophets. When God bore witness to him on the mountain, what the prophets had said of the Messiah was made even more certain. Everything foretold about Jesus was true. That includes what was fulfilled during his life and ministry. It also includes that yet to be fulfilled—his second coming.

Christians, the readers of Peter's testimony, will do well to pay attention to the prophetic witness. The prophetic word is like a lamp in a distant window, guiding travelers through the dark toward their destination. You are not in danger of going astray when you follow the prophetic light. The day when Christ comes again will dawn. The morning star, the dayspring from on high, will completely illuminate Christians' hearts. That is, they will understand completely what now is partly hidden.

To keep the prophetic word requires understanding its source. The prophets spoke under the inspiration of the Holy Spirit (1:21). Likewise, the interpretation of Scripture must be by those inspired by the Holy Spirit (1:20). Peter is one of these. But false prophets are everywhere, and he warns the readers against them.

2 Peter 2:1-3. "There were also false prophets among the people, just as there will be false teachers among you," Peter writes. False prophets arose among God's people in Old Testament times (Deuteronomy 13:1-5; Jeremiah 6:13; 28:9; Ezekiel 13:9). Jesus warned against such false prophets (Matthew 7:15). Paul wrote to the Christians in Corinth, mentioning problems with false apostles and false brothers (2 Corinthians 11:13, 26).

Peter describes the false teachers:

1. they subtly bring in ideas of their own, private interpretations that are not of the Holy Spirit, that pose a threat to the unity and spiritual health of the church (2:1b);

2. they deny the Master who redeemed them, not by outright rejection but by cleverly twisting the truth about who he is, what he taught, and what he did (2:1b);

3. they entice others into sexual immorality, discrediting thereby the way of truth (2:2);

4. they are subtly covetous, using lies to exploit the gullible (2:3a).

The downfall of false teachers is certain. Their judgment is not far off. To underline this, Peter gives examples of deserved destruction on the ungodly in the next section. Similarities to passages in Jude are striking; you may want to compare Peter's examples with the comments in Lesson 13.

2 Peter 2:4-10a. Verses 4-8 contain a series of four *if* clauses. The *if*s are the equivalent of "as surely as." The result clause, introduced by then, begins in 2:9. Each *if* clause contains an example of deserved judgment:

1. When certain angels sinned, they were cast out of heaven into hell. The Greeks believed hell was a dark and dismal place where the wicked dead were cast. The angels went from realms of light to darkest night, there to await the final judgment (2:4; compare Jude 6).

2. The violence of the ancient world resulted in their destruction in the Flood. Only Noah, who was righteous in his generation, survived with his immediate family. They survived because God rescued them by means of the ark (2:5; compare 1 Peter 3:20).

3. Sodom and Gomorrah were the epitome of cities where people lived by sexual passions. Fire from heaven consumed them. Since the time of Abraham, Sodom and Gomorrah have been examples of judgment on godlessness (2:6).

4. On the other hand, God rescued "Lot, a righteous man." Here we have a view of Lot that is not included in the Old Testament account (Genesis 19). He is pictured here as deeply troubled by the lawless deeds of his neighbors, even though he had chosen to live among them (2 Peter 2:7-8).

If God did all this in the past, and God did, then God knows how to save the faithful ones while punishing the godless. God is particularly set against those who indulge their polluting passions and despise divine authority (2:9-10).

2 Peter 2:10b-16. Peter is devastating in his description of the false teachers, so-called Christians. He has mentioned that their condemnation is coming, their destruction draws near. Just as the ungodly mentioned in the previous verses were punished for their godlessness, so the false teachers will be punished. Here is the catalog of their godlessness:

1. The false teachers "slander celestial beings" (or things, 2:10b-11). Some translate *celestial beings* as "dignitaries," others as "glorious ones," others as "glories of the

unseen world." The act of slandering is the focus here. Instead of showing Christian humility, the false teachers exhibit arrogance and willfulness.

2. The false teachers act like brute animals and will be destroyed like beasts of prey (2:12b-13a).

3. The false teachers revel and entice others to join them in reveling (2:13b-14). They love to party, even in the daytime, looking for an opportunity to indulge in sinful lewdness. The false teachers entice others to share their pleasure, intending to take advantage of them to the profit of the false teachers.

4. These people are under God's curse. They started on the right way, then forsook it. Now they follow the pattern of Balaam (Numbers 22–24). He corrupted his prophetic calling for gain and turned God's people, Israel, into sinful ways. Ironically, a donkey, by God's power, spoke a prophetic word to Balaam to stop his irrational actions.

2 Peter 2:17-22. False teachers give a false impression to the naive (those "who are just escaping from those who live in error," 2:18). They are like dry wells to the thirsty and empty rain clouds to the dry land. They promise a freedom they cannot deliver because they are themselves slaves to corruption.

The false teachers and those foolish enough to follow them will end up worse off than they were before they accepted Jesus Christ as Lord and Savior. To turn their back to the sacred commandment (to love God and neighbor) in order to return to the defilements of the world is as sickening as to see the dog eat its vomit or the washed sow return to the mire.

2 Peter 3:1-18. Peter wanted to remind his readers to make their calling and election sure, to adhere to the apostolic and prophetic word, and to beware of false teachers. His last and major concern is the certainty of the second coming of Christ. Apparently this concern was due to the rejection of it by the false teachers.

2 Peter 3:1-7. Scoffers will appear "in the last days." Many mock the idea of the Second Coming in every generation (compare 1 Peter 1:3-7; 4:7, 13; and 5:4).

Scoffers are motivated by their own evil desires, not by the Spirit of God. Remove God, the heavenly hope, and the return of Christ and all that remains is to live for fulfilling your desires.

Scoffers deliberately ignore (forget) the power and certainty of the word of God. God created the earth and the heavens by God's word ("Let there be . . ." Genesis 1). From the heavens God poured forth water in the Flood to destroy that earth (Genesis 6–9). The present heavens and earth will be destroyed by fire, according to God's word. No direct statement in the Old Testament says that the earth will be destroyed by fire. In New Testament times, though, the idea that the world would end in a great blaze of fire was widespread.

The destruction of the heavens and earth by fire will take place in conjunction with the end of time. The end will mark the day of judgment and the destruction of the ungodly as well.

2 Peter 3:8-10. Peter makes it clear that the delay in the Second Coming and the attendant end of the world is due to two factors: God does not mark time the way people do and the grace of God. God is not willing that any shall perish but that all shall come to repentance. That day will come like a thief in the night, a quotation from Jesus (Matthew 24:36-44; Luke 12:35-40; and see Paul's expression in 1 Thessalonians 5:2). The day will come, unexpected and catastrophic.

2 Peter 3:11-18. In light of the catastrophic nature of the day of God, Christians should be waiting for that day (as Jesus taught, Matthew 24:36-44). They should be hastening its coming by living holy and godly lives. That day will hold no terror for the faithful of God's people, for they look for a new creation, a new world in which righteousness will be at home (Isaiah 65:17; Revelation 21:1).

In 1:10, Peter urges his readers to be eager to confirm their calling and election. Here, with a related meaning, he urges them to be eager to be holy and at peace, so they can be found that way when Christ comes. As they wait, "bear in mind that our Lord's patience means salvation," Peter advises. Judgment is delayed in order to allow others an opportunity to respond to the gospel.

Paul also urged godly living and preparation for Christ's return in his letters. Some ignorant and unstable people twisted his words, giving them false explanations. This false teaching will bring disaster on their heads (and on the heads of those who are gullible). They can twist his words because, like other Scriptures, some passages in his letters are hard to understand.

Peter closes the letter without the expected conclusion (as in 1 Peter 5:12-14). But he practically echoes his opening thoughts on "the grace and knowledge of our Lord and Savior Jesus Christ" (3:18). Peter saw Christ's glory on the mountaintop. Jesus Christ deserves that glory now and forever.

DIMENSION THREE: WHAT DOES THE BIBLE MEAN TO ME?

2 Peter 1:16-18
Jesus as a Historical Person

The contrast in 2 Peter 1:16-18 is between "cleverly invented stories" and an eyewitness account. The New Testament is written as a truthful record of historical people and events. The books are based on the testimony of eyewitnesses, as indicated, for example, in Luke 1:1-4. Indications of historical points are scattered throughout the accounts. We have no indication that anyone involved in the process of writing and transmitting the testimony was being devious. Every indication, both in the texts and in the traditions of the early church, is that the apostles and the early disciples were willing to suffer and die attesting to what they had seen and experienced.

The writers of the New Testament books were well aware of the nature of myths. Their world was engulfed in stories about pagan gods. Those stories were based on the imaginations of people rather than on historical events. The stories were connected to the rituals of pagan temples, in which sexually immoral activities were carried out in the name of the gods. Rather than elevating the human spirit, mythological religion pandered to human passions in the guise of the sacred.

Despite the views of some scholars, who think that they see myths in the New Testament, there is no myth in it. The New Testament writers knew myth and wrote history.

The validity of salvation in Jesus Christ rises or falls on the historical truth of the gospel. Paul stated it clearly in 1 Corinthians 15. If the gospel is not true history, then our faith is vain. Myths cannot save. Only the shed blood of Jesus Christ is able to take away the sins of the world, including yours and mine.

For the church, since it is made up of sinners saved by the blood of Jesus Christ through the grace of God, the historical validity of the faith is as important as it is to the individual Christian. Either the church is in truth Christ's body on earth, because Jesus was what the Gospels state, or it is nothing.

2 Peter 3—The Second Coming of Christ

A brief summary of the main points presented by Peter will help you and the class members think about the second question in the student book.

1. There is no question about the fact of the Second Coming from the point of view of the person of faith. Let scoffers come and go; the fact of the second coming of Christ remains a basic Christian doctrine.

2. The question of when Christ will come remains unanswered. God is long suffering; we are to be patient.

3. The events connected with Christ's second coming are only sketchily given. It is fruitless to speculate about further details.

4. Those who are patiently looking for Christ's coming need have no fear at his appearing. They are a new creation in Christ and await the creation of "a new heaven and a new earth" in which righteousness reigns.

5. Anticipation includes preparation through quality daily living. Holiness, godliness, and peace are three qualities of life Peter mentions.

If we walk in the light, as he is in the light, we have fellowship with one another (1:7).

— 10 —
The Basis of Christian Fellowship

1 John 1–2

DIMENSION ONE:
WHAT DOES THE BIBLE SAY?

Answer these questions by reading 1 John 1

1. With what physical senses had John experienced contact with the Word of life? (1:1)

   John had heard with his ears, seen with his eyes, and touched with his hands the Word of life.

2. What did John want the readers to share? (1:3)

   John wanted the readers to have fellowship with him and "with the Father and with his Son, Jesus Christ."

3. What benefits does walking in the light bring to the Christian? (1:7)

   The Christian who walks in the light will have fellowship with other Christians and will be purified from all sin through the blood of Jesus Christ.

Answer these questions by reading 1 John 2

4. How may Christians be sure that they know Christ? (2:3)

   If we obey his command, then we may be sure that we know him.

5. How can a person know that he or she is in the light? (2:9-10)

   The one who loves a brother (or sister) in Christ lives in the light, "and there is nothing in him to make him stumble"; but the one who hates a brother (or sister) is in the darkness.

6. For what three things did John commend the young men to whom he wrote? (2:14b)

   John commended them "because you are strong," because "the word of God lives in you," and because "you have overcome the evil one."

7. What is the evidence that the last hour has come? (2:18)

   The evidence that the last hour has come is that many antichrists have come.

8. How can an antichrist be identified? (2:22c)

   An antichrist is anyone who denies the Father and the Son.

9. What is promised to those who remain in the Son and in the Father? (2:24b-25)

   Those who remain in the Son and in the Father have the promise of eternal life.

10. How should those who remain in Christ act when he comes? (2:28)

    Those who remain in Jesus Christ should "be confident and unashamed before him at his coming."

DIMENSION TWO:
WHAT DOES THE BIBLE MEAN?

The Writer. The three letters attributed to John in the New Testament do not have the writer's name stated in them. Neither does the Gospel of John give the name of its writer.

The belief that John, the son of Zebedee and the companion of Jesus, is the writer appeared quite early in church history. Christian writers and works whose words seem to reflect expressions from First John, for instance, include Clement of Rome, who wrote about A.D. 96; Ignatius of Antioch, whose epistles are dated to about A.D. 110; and the

Didache, an early Christian manual written sometime between A.D. 90 and A.D. 120.

Irenaeus of Lyons (about A.D. 185) testified that both Polycarp and Papias, bishop of Hierapolis in Asia Minor in the early part of the second century, had known and heard the apostle John. Irenaeus quoted from First John and ascribed the quotation to John.

That First John and the Gospel are closely related is shown by phrases that are common to both. For example, "to make [y]our joy complete" (1 John 1:4; John 16:24); "walks [around] in the dark[ness]; [he] does not know where he is going" (1 John 2:11; John 12:35c); and Christ's title, "[his] One and Only [Son]" (1 John 4:9; John 1:14b, 18; 3:16). Many other words and phrases are common to First John and the Gospel: *abide, children of God, light, love, darkness, new commandment.*

Second John reflects the same concerns with love and truth that are expressed in First John. Second John appears to be addressed to a particular person (or church), but that person is not named. The writer identifies himself as "the elder." The writer of the third letter also identifies himself as "the elder." Third John is addressed to a particular person: Gaius. He is greeted with almost exactly the same expression as is used in the opening greeting in Second John. Concluding remarks in both Second and Third John are also strikingly similar.

Counter arguments to the early tradition of John as writer of these books have been offered. Some scholars have also argued against the internal support for the tradition. The majority of biblical scholars, however, accept that the writer of the Gospel and the letters is John, the beloved companion of Jesus, the son of Zebedee, and the brother of James.

Time and Place. The Gospel of John and the three letters probably were all written from the same place and in the same general period of time. According to early Christian tradition, John was the last of the original twelve disciples of Jesus to die. He lived in Ephesus in Asia Minor (western part of modern Turkey) during the later years of his life, carrying on a ministry to the church there and to the churches in the region. No one knows the date of John's death. The general assumption is that he died by A.D. 100. The letters and the Gospel would have been written, then, sometime between A.D. 90 and A.D. 100. The expression *dear children,* that appears scattered through the letters, suggests the writer was an elderly person, because it is used of young and old alike.

Persons Addressed. No particular person or group of persons is mentioned as the original recipients of First John. The letter is a general communication to all Christians. Perhaps it was originally intended for loyal believers in the region of Asia, the region in which the seven churches of the Book of Revelation were located. Because First John is a general communication to Christians wherever they might be found, the letter is of special significance to Christians today.

Purpose. The first four verses of First John provide an introduction to the remainder of the letter, and they contain the reason why John wrote. He wanted those who read to "have fellowship" with the Father and his Son Jesus Christ and with "us." The *us* must refer to the apostle and his supporters, the loyal Christians who received his testimony.

To have fellowship is to share. Fellowship implies certain things held in common. Connected with this are the ideas of oneness, unity, and community. John expected that the testimony he proclaimed would bring fellowship and that that fellowship would result in complete and lasting joy to himself, his associates, and the readers. This desire echoes that of Jesus for his disciples expressed in John's Gospel (15:11; 16:24; 17:13).

First John was also written to counter dangerous teachings that undercut the truth of the gospel and the basis of the fellowship John desired for Christians. The content of the letter indicates that these errors were threatening to lead unstable souls astray. The general label for the false teachings John opposed is *gnosticism.*

Gnostics taught that the world was made by an inferior power rather than by almighty God. The idea is rooted in views of the world developed by Greek philosophers. They held that the material world is by its nature evil, and the unseen, spiritual world is by nature good. Almighty God, who is spiritual and utterly holy, could not have created the sinful world. So some intermediate being must have created it.

Humans were viewed as both physical and spiritual. The spiritual (good) was trapped in the physical (evil). Salvation was spiritual and was made possible through special, secret knowledge. This secret knowledge was possessed only by special, gifted teachers and those who became their disciples.

Among the gnostic teachings was the denial of the humanity of Christ. They taught that he only appeared to be human, because to be human meant he was partly evil. In this view Jesus was a man born as other men. Because he was very righteous and wise, the Christ-spirit descended on Jesus at his baptism and left him before the Crucifixion. The human Jesus experienced death, burial, and resurrection; but the Christ did not.

One aspect of gnostic thought was a focus on mental enlightenment while permitting the body to be involved in immoral activities. John, by contrast, emphasized the demands of holiness that true faith and love place on the believer.

The gnostic element was active within the church. Their unscriptural teachings and practices threatened the survival of historic Christianity and the unity of believers. The problem became a crisis in the second century that resulted in the consolidation of the orthodox teaching of the church. The books accepted as orthodox and authoritative are our New Testament. The writings of John played an important role in overcoming this threat to the unity and survival of the church.

Form of the Letter. First John does not have the formal features of a New Testament letter such as we find in Paul's letters. No salutation indicates who the writer is and who the letter is intended for. No greeting of grace, peace, and the like is included. No conclusion appears like those in Second and Third John. Some people consider the book a sermon or a collection of notes on several sermons. Even though First John is technically not a letter, clearly it is a communication from an authoritative Christian leader to people he feels would heed his teaching, warnings, and encouragement.

Outline of First John. First John does not easily divide into a logical development of thought. Certain key words and ideas, however, surface again and again. The overall result is an emphatic statement of great truths of the faith. We will use the following outline as we consider the content of the letter:

I. Introduction. The testimony—foundation of fellowship (1:1-4)
II. The conditions of fellowship (1:5–2:29)
  A. Walk in the light (1:5-10)
  B. Walk in the footsteps of Jesus (2:1-6)
  C. Pass the test of brotherly love (2:7-11)
  D. Know God and keep God's commandments (2:12-17)
  E. Shun the antichrists; abide in Christ (2:18-29)
III. Fellowship—a family relationship (3:1–4:6)
  A. Children of God (3:1-3)
  B. Children of the devil (3:4-10)
  C. God's children love one another (3:11-18)
  D. God's children keep God's commandments and have confidence (3:19-24)
  E. God's children share God's Spirit (4:1-6)
IV. Facets of the fellowship (4:7–5:21)
  A. The love of God (4:7-21)
  B. Faith in Jesus, the Son of God (5:1-5)
  C. Trust in the testimony of God (5:6-12)
  D. The certainties of faith (5:13-21)

1 John 1:1-4. Verses 1-3 are complicated in construction. Note that verse 2 is an inserted remark. Having mentioned the "Word of life," John inserts this explanation before completing his main sentence. Verse 2 emphasizes that the testimony of John was based on his personal eyewitness of Jesus Christ.

We can summarize John's opening sentence this way: What we experienced with our senses concerning the Word of life, we proclaim also to you. We do this so that you may have fellowship with us and with the Father and with his Son Jesus Christ.

Expressions in 1:1 echo the opening verse of the Gospel of John (1:1). The subject in both instances is Christ. By using the word *we,* John associates himself with the disciples of Jesus, the "eyewitnesses and servants of the word" (Luke 1:2).

These men experienced the humanity of Jesus over a considerable period of time. They heard him speak and teach with their ears. They saw him with their eyes. They did more than just glance at the Christ—they observed him carefully. They personally touched him with their hands, even after the Resurrection (Luke 24:39). Jesus Christ was not a phantom. He was a living human being.

The Word of life can refer to Jesus or to the message of the gospel. Here it probably carries both meanings. The Christ was the Word. He was with God and was God. Both the Gospel of John and First John testify to the same truth about Christ.

John proclaimed the good news that through Christ individuals can be reconciled to God. Fellowship between people and God, both "the Father and . . . his Son, Jesus Christ" is possible. Fellowship between those who accept reconciliation is also possible.

When individuals are in Christ and Christ in them, they have reason for great happiness. The theme of joy fills the New Testament. Nothing made John happier than to hear that believers were following the truth (2 John 4; 3 John 3).

1 John 1:5–2:29. The testimony about Jesus Christ is the basis for the fellowship between believers and with God and Christ. But the fellowship is not without conditions. No one can maintain the fellowship who is indifferent to sin. In our outline we identify five conditions of fellowship.

1 John 1:5-10. John indicates that he heard the truth about God "from him." *Him* obviously refers to Jesus. The truth is that God is light. The opposite of light is darkness. Light and darkness cannot exist in the same place, so there is no darkness whatsoever in God.

Light and darkness have long been used as images of truth and error, good and evil, righteousness and sin. John used these expressions frequently in the Gospel and in the letters (John 1:5; 8:12; 12:35, 46; 1 John 2:8-9, 11). The Messiah was foreseen by Isaiah as "a great light" (9:2). In John's Gospel, Jesus is "the light [that] shines in the darkness" (1:5). He is the "true light that gives light to every man" (1:9).

God provides illumination to help a believer find the way along the path of life. Anyone who claims to share in the eternal life provided by God through Christ but walks in darkness (practices unrighteousness) is a liar.

John was likely thinking of the gnostic teachers here (1 John 1:6). They held that for the one who is enlightened by knowledge, one's moral conduct does not matter. To be saved, in the gnostic view, individuals needed mental illumination, not forgiveness. John calls sin SIN. One's walk, one's daily life, determines whether a person is walking in the light and in the fellowship.

The atoning blood of Jesus purifies in an ongoing process. Purifying requires the confession of sins. The person who will not or does not recognize sin and confess it cannot continue in fellowship with God, for the person makes God out to be a liar. God is light; that is, God is completely holy. Those who have fellowship with God must be holy too. God has made it possible for sinful individuals to be purified and made holy so that they can have fellowship with God.

Christians who walk in the light can see the way along which they are going, and they can constantly reaffirm, through confession and forgiveness, the fellowship they enjoy.

1 John 2:1-6. Sin hampers fellowship. Sin is rebellion against God's will. In 2:1, John indicates that another purpose of his letter is to help Christians deal with the problem of sin in their lives.

What John writes is in direct opposition to the gnostic view. Rather than seeing sin for what it is—evil—they saw it as a misfortune for which the individual was not really responsible. To gnostics, knowledge of God was the real issue of life; and this knowledge was obtained through mental activity apart from the physical part of life. What the mind knew was essential; what the body did was unimportant.

Christian doctrine sees the problem of sin as both in the mind and in the flesh. Jesus said, "The things that come out of the mouth come from the heart [mind], and these make a man unclean. For out of the heart come evil thoughts, murder, adultery, sexual immorality, theft, false testimony, slander" (Matthew 15:18-19). He also taught that as a person thinks, so is that person. Paul called on believers to "not conform any longer to the pattern of this world, but be transformed by the renewing of your mind. Then you will be able to test and approve what God's will is—his good, pleasing and perfect will" (Romans 12:2).

So the Christian must not make sin (rebellion against God's commandments) a way of life. A person may slip and fall into sin along the road of life, however, threatening the fellowship with God. If that happens, the fellowship is not broken; for the committed believer has an advocate (defense attorney) before God. That advocate is Jesus Christ. He is called "the Righteous One," reflecting the idea in Hebrews 4:14-16.

Jesus is also the atoning sacrifice for sins. That is, Jesus is the means by which all sins are forgiven. The just penalty of sin is death; and Hebrews 2:9 tells us that by the grace of God, Jesus tasted death for everyone.

One who is both a defense lawyer and the means by which our sins are forgiven is worth knowing. How can a person be assured of knowing Jesus Christ? A person can know Jesus Christ by keeping his commandments. Knowing and doing are identical, as far as John is concerned. This view is in line with the words of Jesus: "Why do you call me 'Lord, Lord' and do not do what I say?" (Luke 6:46).

To say "I know him" as the gnostics did, and then to ignore Christ's commandments is to be an out-and-out liar. To know Christ is to have fellowship with him. To obey him is to show love for God. Mature, complete love for God is shown by keeping God's word. Jesus is a perfect example of love for God and obedience to God's will. Walk in Jesus' footsteps; follow his example.

1 John 2:7-11. The "old command" is "love one another." Jesus taught that all the commandments are summed up in love for God and love for neighbor (Matthew 22:34-40). The "new command" is "As I have loved you, so you must love one another" (John 13:34b). Love is proven by sharing, as an expression of Christian fellowship. The darkness of sinfully hating and ignoring others who are in need is passing away. The light of the example of God's Son is shining. Jesus Christ gave his life for us out of love. Out of love we ought to share our life with others.

1 John 2:12-17. Those addressed by John in 2:12-14 include all groups of Christians in fellowship with God. Fellowship with God (knowing God) provides powerful benefits—forgiveness of sins, power to overcome the evil one, sustaining strength, and "the sword of the Spirit, which is the word of God" (Ephesians 6:17).

The testimony of the gospel is based on historical realities, not on the philosophical imaginings of would-be teachers like the gnostics. John commends those in whom the word of God abides. They will not be confused by the evil one, the devil.

All Christians who share in the benefits of fellowship with God are urged by John not to love the world. *World* does not refer to the natural creation; God considered that "very good" (Genesis 1:31). The word here refers to people who are governed by lusts, ambition, and jealousies. They are under the rule of the evil one (John 14:30) and in bondage to human desires. The world loves its own and hates God's own (John 15:19). The world is dominated by the three base motivations mentioned in 1 John 2:16. These motivations are not of God; they are of the evil one (5:19).

The world of selfish desires will pass away, but the person in fellowship with God, the Eternal One, will abide forever. That One has the eternal life John mentions in 1:2 and 2:25.

1 John 2:18-29. To continue in fellowship with God, God's Son, and God's people, believers need to be able to identify the antichrists and to remain in Christ. Since the last hour has arrived, these actions are essential.

Antichrist means one "against Christ, an opposer of Christ." One can oppose Christ by impersonating him, by teaching against him, or both. Jesus warned of those who would come in his name claiming to be Christ (Matthew 24:4-5). He also warned that many would be led astray in those last days.

In a real sense the last hour occurs for each of us in our lifetime. Since time is measured in this life but not after this life, we all live in the last hour as far as our earthly existence is concerned. The time between death and the resurrection is, in that sense, but the twinkling of an eye.

These antichrists, surprisingly, were once a part of the fellowship (2:19). So the antichrists were not ungodly pagans. They were false teachers, along with their followers, who had arisen in the midst of the faithful. We assume John was speaking of the gnostic teachers.

These persons had been identified as apostates by their teachings. The false teachings are mentioned in 2:22-23a. They denied that Jesus is the Messiah, the Christ, the Anointed One of God. To deny the Son and his role as Messiah is to deny the Father, for God bore testimony to Jesus that he was God's Son (Luke 3:21-22; John 5:30-47).

The gnostics claimed special knowledge of the truth, but they were really liars who denied the Son. Those believers to whom John wrote actually possessed the true testimony about Jesus (1 John 2:20-21). Further, they had the anointing of the Holy Spirit that Jesus promised the night before his crucifixion (John 15:26-27; 16:7-14).

All that the faithful believers were required to do was to remain in the truth that they had heard from the beginning (1 John 2:24). If they did this, then they would abide in Christ. The fellowship with God and Jesus Christ would remain unbroken throughout eternity.

To emphasize the fact that they had the truth and needed enlightenment from no one, especially from liars who did not have the truth, John repeated in 2:26-27 what he said in 2:18-25.

The last verses of our lesson (2:28-29) appeal to the readers to remain in Christ. His coming is certain. The Second Coming has been an essential doctrine of Christianity from the very beginning of the church. The call is to remain in the fellowship with God, Jesus Christ, and the faithful followers like John. Those who do can have confidence at his appearing.

Some persons will be ashamed at Christ's coming. The ashamed will be those who did not remain in Christ but who believed the lies of the antichrists. To follow such teachings is to live a life of unrighteousness. Those who do right not only maintain the fellowship but give living evidence that they are the children of God. To be "born of God" is a common expression in John's writings (John 1:13; 1 John 3:9; 4:7; 5:4, 18).

DIMENSION THREE:
WHAT DOES THE BIBLE MEAN TO ME?

1 John 2:6
Walk in the Footsteps of Jesus

A modern expression that is the equivalent of "to walk" is *lifestyle*. Our lifestyle is the expression of our beliefs about self, about others, about the world in which we live, and about spiritual realities. These ideas motivate us to do what we do in the ways that we do them.

For Christians who have believed the testimony of Scripture and the Christian witness of others, lifestyle ought to be determined by a sincere desire and effort to keep God's commandments. Jesus summed up the commandments with the word *love*. We are to love God with our total being and to love our neighbor as ourself.

Exactly what this means in terms of the lifestyle of each of us will be determined by how we understand what Jesus did and taught. We cannot follow in his footsteps unless we trace them. We will have to be learners (disciples) to know how he thought about himself, others, the world, and spiritual realities. What we will look for in the incidents of the life of Jesus are examples of how to relate to God, others, and the world.

Then we must apply our understanding of Jesus' walk to the circumstances of our life. This is a part of the adventure of living a Christian life. The process is ongoing, unique to each of us. We may help one another along the way, but we must be careful not to condemn one another because our walk is unique. As we walk, we should do so with thanks that we have our defense attorney in the courts of heaven to justify us before God when we slip and fall along the way.

1 John 2:16—Lust and Pride

We need to explore the meaning of *lust*. My dictionary indicates that the word was used in ancient times to mean "pleasure." By the time the Bible was translated into English, the word had developed the meaning we have today, "a strong desire to possess and enjoy," usually in a sexual sense.

Another way to gain a sense of the word in the context of 1 John 2:16 is to compare translations of the verse in several versions.

God created us with desires of the flesh that are not inherently evil. Without the sex drive, for example, there would be no human race. We are, however, to control and channel our natural desires. Paul stated it this way, "I beat my body and make it my slave so that after I have preached to others, I myself will not be disqualified for the prize" (1 Corinthians 9:27).

The renewing of our minds as Christians requires that we control what our eyes see. Jesus taught that if your eye causes you to sin, pluck it out and throw it away; it is better to enter eternal life with one eye than to be cast into the burning junk heap of eternity with both eyes (Matthew 18:9).

In the same chapter, Matthew recorded Jesus' words on humility (18:1-4). Humility is the opposite of pride. Whoever humbles himself or herself like a little child is the greatest in the kingdom of heaven. There is no place for overweening pride in the Christian. The Christian has been bought with a price and is not her or his own. Any praise goes to God.

Everyone who believes that Jesus is the Christ is born of God, and everyone who loves the father loves his child as well (5:1).

—11—

Fellowship in the Family of God

1 John 3–5

DIMENSION ONE:
WHAT DOES THE BIBLE SAY?

Answer these questions by reading 1 John 3

1. What two things can God's children be sure of when Christ appears? (3:2b)

   We know that when Christ appears "we shall be like him" and "we shall see him as he is."

2. How can the children of God be distinguished from "the children of the devil"? (3:7-10)

   The children of God do right. "Anyone who does not do what is right" and "anyone who does not love his brother" are "the children of the devil."

3. In what practical way can Christians show love "with actions and in truth"? (3:17-18)

   A Christian who has material possessions can provide for a "brother in need." That is loving "with actions and in truth," not "with words or tongue."

4. What are the two basic commands of God to Christians? (3:23)

   "This is his command: to believe in the name of his Son, Jesus Christ, and to love one another."

Answer these questions by reading 1 John 4

5. How can we determine who has the Spirit of God and who has the spirit of the antichrist? (4:2-3)

   Whomever has the Spirit of God "acknowledges that Jesus Christ has come in the flesh." Whomever "does not acknowledge Jesus is not from God" and has the spirit of the antichrist.

6. What two things did God do that show God's love for us? (4:9-10)

   God showed love for us by sending "his one and only Son into the world that we might live through him" and by sending "his Son as an atoning sacrifice for our sins."

7. Why is love a valid test of the love a person has for God? (4:20-21)

   "Anyone [who] says, 'I love God,' yet hates his brother, . . . is a liar." The person "who does not love his brother, whom he has seen, cannot love God, whom he has not seen."

Answer these questions by reading 1 John 5

8. What is the content of the faith that overcomes the world? (5:4-5)

   The faith that overcomes the world is the belief that "Jesus is the Son of God."

9. What three witnesses testify that God gave us eternal life in Jesus Christ? (5:6-8)

   "There are three that testify: the Spirit, the water and the blood; and the three are in agreement" (5:7-8).

10. John describes the two types of sin. What does he call these two types? (5:16-17)

    John calls the two types of sin the sin that does not lead to death and the sin that leads to death.

11. If "the whole world is under the control of the evil one," why is the one born of God not in the power of the evil one? (5:18-19)

    The one born of God is not in the power of the evil one because "the one who was born of God [Jesus] keeps him safe, and the evil one cannot harm him."

HEBREWS; JAMES; 1 AND 2 PETER; 1, 2, 3 JOHN; JUDE

12. Of what temptation in particular does John warn Christians at the end of his letter? (5:21)

John warns Christians to keep themselves from idols.

DIMENSION TWO: WHAT DOES THE BIBLE MEAN?

In our first lesson on First John, we discovered how the theme of fellowship ties the varied parts of the letter together in a loose way. The testimony of Jesus' apostles provides the basis for the fellowship. Although that much is clear from the opening verses of the letter, nothing in the letter gives any details on the testimony, except that Jesus was the Messiah (Christ) and that he came in the flesh. John assumes that his readers have the information about Jesus from the Gospel of John.

The Gospels do not give a complete history of Jesus, and each Gospel writer had a particular audience and purpose in mind as he wrote. While each is somewhat different from the other, together they give a fairly composite picture of the main events in the life and ministry of Jesus.

John's Gospel is quite distinct from the Synoptic Gospels—the collective name used for Matthew, Mark, and Luke. (They are called Synoptic because they are fairly similar to one another.) Luke indicates that his Gospel was written for Theophilus (friend of God) "that you may know the certainty of the things you have been taught" (Luke 1:4). Luke also indicates that many others had undertaken to compile a narrative of the things that had been accomplished in relationship to Jesus (Luke 1:1).

John wrote his account for a specific purpose as well. He stated it this way: "Jesus did many other miraculous signs in the presence of his disciples, which are not recorded in this book. But these are written that you may believe that Jesus is the Christ, the Son of God, and that by believing you may have life in his name" (John 20:30-31). So the readers of the letter had heard the testimony, believed, and received that life in his name that is described as "eternal life" in 1 John 1:2.

The conditions of the fellowship "with the Father and with his Son, Jesus Christ" (1 John 1:3) were presented in Lesson 10. To review briefly, they were (1) to walk in the light, (2) to walk in the footsteps of Jesus, (3) to pass the test of brotherly love, (4) to know God and keep God's commandments, and (5) to shun the antichrist and to remain in Christ. In this lesson we will read of the fellowship described in terms of a family relationship. Toward the close of the letter, John spotlights a number of facets of the fellowship.

1 John 3:1-3. The opening verse of this section is filled with the sense of amazement and appreciation that John experienced as he thought about the relationship to God that he and other believers have in Jesus. They are called children of God because it is true.

This idea is a continuation of an expansion on the thought in 2:29, "You know that everyone who does what is right has been born of him." The word *born* means "begotten" in this context. John 1:12-13 helps explain this idea: "Yet to all who received him, to those who believed in his name, he gave the right to become children of God— children born not of natural descent, nor of human decision or a husband's will, but born of God."

Paul calls Christians "sons of God" in Romans (8:14) and Galatians (3:26; 4:6-7) and "God's children" in Romans 8:16. Romans 8:14 is particularly helpful because it states that "those who are led by the Spirit of God are sons of God." This statement agrees with 1 John 3:1, where it is clear that the blessing of being God's children came at the initiative of God. And it agrees with John 1:12. To the one who receives Christ, that is, believes in his name, God gives power to become God's child. Later in First John the readers are told that "everyone who believes that Jesus is the Christ is born of God" (5:1).

In 1 Peter 1:3, God is praised because "in his great mercy he has given us new birth into a living hope through the resurrection of Jesus Christ from the dead." This new birth is "not of perishable seed, but of imperishable, through the living and enduring word of God" (1 Peter 1:23). Again in 1 Peter 2:2, believers are urged "like newborn babies, [to] crave pure spiritual milk." Two other New Testament writers use related expressions. Titus 3:5b uses the word renewal, the equivalent of "new birth"; and in James 1:18, we read that "he chose to give us birth through the word of truth."

All these expressions are evidence of God's great love. The initiative has been God's from the beginning, "for God so loved the world that he gave his one and only Son, that whoever believes in him should not perish but have eternal life" (John 3:16). God is not some uncaring deity so removed from the world that he has no concern for it, as some of the gnostics would have it.

That the world did not recognize Jesus, in fact rejected him, was discussed by Jesus in the upper room (John 15:18–16:4a). He clearly indicated to his disciples that the world would hate them as it hated him.

In 1 John 3:2-3, John clarifies what it means to be a child of God. It is, first, a present reality. But this family relationship also has tremendous potential for the future. The future will bring the fulfillment of all that God has prepared for those who love God. The future will be realized when Jesus Christ appears again (as in 2:28). A certain mystery is involved in this, but believers can have confidence that they will be like him when he appears. Jesus Christ is the first-born of God; believers are children of God by grace. The genetic relationship between the first-born and the lately born will be evident when he appears. "We shall be like him." Since purity is a characteristic of the family of God, those who hope in Christ will purify themselves (by the cleansing blood, 1:7).

1 John 3:4-10. The "everyone" of 3:4 is the opposite of the "everyone" in 3:3. The Greek verb used here indicates the "habit of sinning" and "practice of sinning." It is the opposite of doing right (2:29).

Sin is lawlessness. The gnostics thought themselves above the moral law. They considered themselves enlightened, but they turned freedom into license. They claimed superior fellowship with God and taught as though they had authority. The gnostics may have been those who said, "we have not sinned'" making God a liar (1 John 1:10). Lawlessness is disobedience to God's commandments, and that is sin. Perverting God's commandments is equivalent to disobeying them.

Jesus is the subject of 3:5. Second Corinthians 5:21, Hebrews 4:15, and 1 Peter 2:22 state clearly that Jesus was without sin. He came to take away sins. "He has appeared once for all at the end of the ages to do away with sin by the sacrifice of himself" (Hebrews 9:26b). Those who have received the testimony of the apostles have a relationship with Jesus that does not allow for living a life of sin. The family connection and the desire "to live in him" means that they "must walk as Jesus did" (2:6). The child of God practices doing right.

Devil is the English word for Greek *diabolos,* "accuser, slanderer." In the Greek version of the Old Testament, *diabolos* was used to translate the Hebrew *Satan.* In the New Testament, *devil* and *Satan* are essentially the same.

Jesus spoke of the devil as the enemy (Matthew 13:39), the evil one (Matthew 13:38), the ruler of this world (John 14:30), a murderer, a liar, and the father of lies (John 8:44). We do not have a complete picture of the devil from Scripture. His origins as a rebellious, fallen angel are hinted at but not detailed in the Bible. He is the personification of evil influences and activities in the world.

The devil has his offspring too (3:8, 10). They have their identifying characteristics. They practice sin, which is lawlessness. They do not practice righteousness. The children of the devil show their genetic relationship. The devil has sinned from the beginning. Sinning as a way of life is the major characteristic of those in his family.

The main mark by which the children of God can be distinguished from the children of the devil is their deeds. Children of God do right and practice family love. Children of the devil sin and do not show unselfish love for others.

1 John 3:11-18. Verse 11 reminds us of 2:7-11. Love between members of the family of God is not an option; it is essential. The tone of the relationships in the family is set by the nature of God—God is love (1 John 4:8).

From the very beginning family members were expected to love one another. In the first family, however, hatred, the opposite of love, lurked in the heart of Cain. He murdered his brother "because his [Cain's] own actions were evil and his brother's were righteous" (3:12). Cain can be identified as a child of the devil by his murderous deed.

As Jesus said, "By their fruit you will recognize them" (Matthew 7:16).

Cain's murder of Abel is another example of the way in which the world of sin and selfishness treats the children of God. A similar thought is expressed in 3:1c. The way of the world is death; it is passing away; it will die (2:17). In sharp contrast to the hatred and resulting murder that is the way of the world, the family of God has passed out of death into life (3:14). Eternal life is an essential part of the fellowship that John mentions at the beginning of the letter (1:2).

To love the other members of the family of God is to pass out of death into life. One who loves the world, of course, cannot love God (2:15) or the family of God. To fail to love the family is to remain in death, because the opposite of love is hate. Hate results in murder—actual murder or that which is committed in the heart (Matthew 15:19). The hater/murderer cannot possess an abiding eternal life. Revelation 21:8 makes this fact even clearer: "Murderers . . . their place will be in the fiery lake of burning sulfur. This is the second death."

It is not enough for John to draw this sharp contrast between love and hate in general terms. He provides clear and specific teaching on what the true nature of love is (3:16-18). Earlier, as we noted, he indicated that one of the conditions of sharing in the fellowship is to walk in the same way in which Jesus walked (2:6). Here he gives a specific example of what that requires. Jesus laid down his life for us. He suffered death on the cross on our behalf. We were desperately in need of forgiveness of sin; he satisfied that need. That deed of Jesus is a perfect definition of what the word *love* means.

Jesus acted selflessly, in sharp contrast to Cain who acted selfishly. Love is selfless action to meet the need of another member of the family of God. This love requires a willingness to lay down one's life for the other. Here one's life includes "the world's goods" that one has. That is easy to understand. A part of one's life is invested in obtaining the necessities of life.

To have material possessions, then to see a brother or sister in Christ in need, and to close up the heart to compassion is to act selfishly. That is the way the children of the devil act. The love of God abides in the hearts of God's children. True love is shown in deed and in truth, not in word or speech.

An example of two in the early church who spoke but did not do are Ananias and Sapphira (Acts 5:1-11). They apparently pledged to give all the proceeds from the sale of a property into the common treasury of the Jerusalem church. This treasury was used to provide for the necessities of widows (Acts 6:1) and perhaps for the needs of others. Ananias and Sapphira acted selfishly, however, withholding some funds rather than giving all, as they had said.

1 John 3:19-24. The phrase *this then* (3:19) refers to loving "with actions and in truth." The believer who normally shows that kind of love can know that he or she "belong[s] to the truth." To belong to the truth includes accepting the testimony about God and Christ and accepting the validity that sincere believers are children of God.

Belonging to "the truth" is not a matter of guessing that one is in God's grace. To love in actions and in truth is proof positive that this is so. Faith rests not on feelings but on historical facts and the promises of God. God's promises can reassure a person if and when one's heart may condemn that person.

Faithful followers of Christ may be conscience stricken at times, just because they know that "if we claim we have not sinned, we make him out to be a liar and his word has no place in our lives" (1:10). But even though the heart may condemn, God does not. "If we confess our sins, he is faithful and just and will forgive us our sins and purify us from all unrighteousness" (1:9).

In Hebrews 10:35, believers are encouraged: "So do not throw away your confidence; it will be richly rewarded." Paul assures Christians that "neither death nor life, neither angels nor demons, neither the present nor the future, nor any powers, neither height nor depth, nor anything else in all creation, will be able to separate us from the love of God that is in Christ Jesus our Lord" (Romans 8:38-39).

Believers ought to approach the throne of grace confidently (3:21-22). The writer of Hebrews urged, "Let us then approach the throne of grace with confidence, so that we may receive mercy and find grace to help us in our time of need" (4:16). Jesus taught his followers to approach God with the words *Our Father*. Being a part of the family of God makes that possible. What the Christian asks will also reflect the family connection.

Sincere believers can have confidence in the abiding relationship that has been established by receiving the testimony. They can know that they abide in God by keeping God's commandments. Those commandments are summarized in 3:23. Believers can also know that God abides in the person of faith. God has given the Holy Spirit to them for this purpose.

This section has close connections with the discourse of Jesus to his disciples in the upper room on the night before his crucifixion. John 13:34 and 15:12-17 contain the commandment to love one another. John 14:15-26; 15:26-27; and 16:7-13 deal with the promised coming of the Holy Spirit.

The Holy Spirit came in power on the day of Pentecost (Acts 2:1-4). As a result, Peter preached to those present. He closed his sermon urging them to repent and be baptized for the forgiveness of sins. They were then to receive the gift of the Holy Spirit (Acts 2:38). The Holy Spirit is the indwelling presence of God in the lives of God's children.

Another way of expressing God's presence in the lives of believers is "Christ in you" (Colossians 1:27). Paul also spoke of the body of a Christian as "a temple of the Holy Spirit" (1 Corinthians 6:19). At the same time, he could speak of being "in Christ" (2 Corinthians 5:17).

This mutual abiding is another way to express the idea of the fellowship that exists for those in the family of God. The indwelling presence of the Spirit blesses the believer with assurance.

1 John 4:1-6. The mention of the Spirit in 3:24 opens the way for John to warn about false teachers. The false prophets (teachers) have gone out into the world (from the church). They were the same as the antichrists mentioned in 2:18-20. They had gone out of the church, but they were apparently still teaching and preaching in the region.

John insists that God's children test the spirits. The way to discern between teachers who have the Spirit of God and those who have false spirits is simple. Those who confess that Jesus Christ was a fully human person have the Spirit of God. Those who do not confess the historical reality of Jesus as "a man attested to you by God with mighty works and wonders and signs which God did through him" (Acts 2:22) are not of God. Those who teach that the Christ-Spirit descended on an already existing man, like the gnostics teach, do not confess the historical Jesus. They are "the spirit of antichrist" (1 John 4:3).

John's readers are a part of the family of God (4:4). They have fellowship "with the Father and with his Son, Jesus Christ" (1:3). Jesus said, "In this world you will have trouble. But take heart! I have overcome the world" (John 16:33bcd). God's faithful children share in the family victory over the false teachers.

The false teachers are of the world. The source of their teaching is "he who is in the world" (1 John 4:4). Naturally the worldly minded would be drawn to them. But God's children share God's Spirit. They listen to "us'" the apostolic witness. They can discern between the two spirits.

1 John 4:7–5:21. John never tires of discussing the subject of love. Knowing the correct doctrine is one thing, but it is not enough. Correct doctrine without the inspiration and warmth of love can be very unattractive.

1 John 4:7-21. The source of the love that a Christian is to reflect in life is God. Love comes from God. And God is love. That God is love is shown by the evidence of his love for individuals (4:9-10). These verses reflect the truths found also in John 3:16.

A major facet of the fellowship, then, is love. Because God is love, God's children ought also to love. As John states later, "We love because he first loved us" (4:19).

First John 4:12 expresses the same idea in almost the identical words of John 1:18: "No one has ever seen God, but God the only Son, who is at the Father's side, has made him known." Jesus said, "Anyone who has seen me has seen the Father" (John 14:9b). The idea in our verse is probably this, however: God is invisible. You cannot expect to see the invisible God abiding in a person. The evidence of God abiding in a person is the presence of love in that person, since God's nature is love. When we love one another, love exists as God intended it to be.

John returns in 4:13 to the subject of the Holy Spirit, as in 3:24. By the power of the Holy Spirit within them, the apostles testified of what they had seen. They had not seen God, but they witnessed that God sent Jesus as the Savior of the world. The persons who accept and confess that testimony have the basis for a lasting relationship with God (4:14-15).

The family relationship of God's children to God is again highlighted in 4:16. The love of God is both an experience (*know*) and a matter of faith (*rely on*). A result of the perfection of love within a child of God is confidence. The Day of Judgment is not to be feared by Christians. You have no need to fear punishment when you possess the very nature of the Judge—love. Perfect love harbors no suspicion and no dread (1 Corinthians 13).

The perfection of God's love in believers is shown by their love for the other members of the family of God (1 John 4:19-21). We have no option on whether to love the other members of the family. Love for one another is commanded. From this we can see that love is not an emotion; it is an action. Love is not expressed by how one feels toward another; it is expressed in deed and in truth (3:18).

1 John 5:1-5. Faith and love have a vital relationship (5:1-5). The word *everyone* leaves no room for exceptions. Faith in Jesus as both the Christ and the Son of God (5:5) is the basis for being a part of the family of God. It is not enough to believe only that he is the Messiah foretold in the Old Testament. Nor is it enough to believe in his divine nature. Belief in both is necessary.

Jesus testified that he had overcome the world. Those who are a part of God's family have also overcome the world. The world is that selfish way of thinking and living that is the opposite of loving the children of God and meeting their needs. Christians are engaged in spiritual warfare against worldly ideas and practices. Properly outfitted (Ephesians 6:10-17), victory is certain. Faith is a shield that can quench all the flaming darts of the ruler of this world, the evil one.

1 John 5:6-12. The power to overcome the world comes by faith in Jesus, the Son of God. Three witnesses provide a basis for faith in Jesus Christ—the water (of his baptism, John 1:19-34), the blood (of his atonement, John 19:34), and the Spirit (of truth, John 15:26). The ministry of Jesus began with his baptism, which was marked by the coming of the Holy Spirit on him. At the cross, blood and water gushed forth when the spear was thrust into his side. "It is finished," Jesus said. The water and the blood testify to the humanity of Jesus, against the gnostic teachers. The Holy Spirit bore witness that Jesus was from God, for no one could do the things Jesus did unless God was with him.

God has testified through God's power in the life of Jesus. God has also provided the testimony of eyewitnesses like John. The one who believes also has the testimony within. The eternal life that God gives to the person of faith is a living testimony to the truth of the gospel. Their testimony is something akin to what Paul said of the Christians in Corinth: "You yourselves are our letter, written on our hearts, known and read by everybody" (2 Corinthians 3:2).

1 John 5:13-21. Verse 13 echoes the main ideas in 1:1-4. Those to whom John wrote had believed the apostolic testimony. That testimony was rooted in the witness of God. The apostolic testimony was the testimony of believers in God. It was the source of eternal life, the fellowship with God "the Father and with his Son, Jesus Christ" (1:3b).

John wants his readers to be confident of this fellowship. That confidence is expressed in an active prayer life. God's children, of course, will ask according to the will of God (Matthew 6:10). They will pray for one another. The prayer of a righteous person has great power in its effects. The prayer of faith will save the sick, and if that person has committed sins, they will be forgiven (James 5:13-16).

John mentions sin that is beyond the power of prayer but does not give a description by which such a sin can be identified. Perhaps this sin is the sin against the Holy Spirit about which Jesus taught (Mark 3:29). The human heart can harden. People can live in such a state of sin that they call evil good and good evil (Isaiah 5:20). Or, John may have in mind the apostate, as in Hebrews 6:4-6.

But John is confident that among his beloved readers are only those who are in the family of God, and they have overcome the world and the evil one. They do not practice sin (5: 18-19). John's confidence in God's children is based on the fact that they have received his testimony about God and Jesus Christ. He and they know the truth about Jesus. They understand and have no need of instruction from false prophets. John and his readers experience a fellowship with God and God's Son Jesus Christ that can only be described as eternal life (5:20).

An idol is any substitute for the true God. An idol can even be the false ideas about God that the gnostic teachers held. They worshiped a creation of their own imaginations rather than the true God whom the only Son made known. The closing thought of the aged apostle: Be on your guard against every false god.

DIMENSION THREE:
WHAT DOES THE BIBLE MEAN TO ME?

1 John 3:17-18
Help for Human Needs

The question posed in the student book is a difficult problem that each Christian has to resolve in good conscience before God. Here are some ideas to explore in thinking about the problem:

1. We have a primary responsibility to meet the needs of those God has placed in our immediate care. "If anyone does not provide for his relatives, and especially for his

immediate family, he has denied the faith and is worse than an unbeliever" (1 Timothy 5:8).

2. A distinction ought to be made between needs and desires. Living in an affluent society, Christians can easily convince themselves to spend all their resources for their or their family's desires, leaving nothing to meet the needs of others.

3. Paul gave instructions: "As we have opportunity, . . . [we are to] do good to all people, especially to those who belong to the family of believers" (Galatians 6:10).

4. Those who have an opportunity to work and are able to work ought to do so, "and not be dependent on anybody" (1 Thessalonians 4:11-12).

Response to First John

The following ideas in First John increased my joy in Christ and my appreciation of God:

1. we are in fact the children of God (3:1);
2. we shall be like Christ when he appears (3:2);
3. simply abiding: how important this idea was to John; how important abiding in God is to me;
4. I can overcome the world, every worldly tendency that threatens my ability to act in love (5:4);
5. John has given me an example of what, by God's grace, I can be as an elderly person.

This is love, that we walk in obedience to his commands (2 John 6).

—12—

Two Personal Letters From John

2 John and 3 John

DIMENSION ONE:
WHAT DOES THE BIBLE SAY?

Answer these questions by reading 2 John

1. How does the writer identify himself? (verse 1)

   The writer calls himself "the elder."

2. Identify the main word used by the writer in the salutation. (verses 1-3)

   The main word used in the salutation is truth.

3. Why was the author joyful about news he received concerning the "chosen lady and her children"? (verse 4)

   He was joyful because he found that some of them were following the truth, "just as the Father commanded us."

4. Above all else, what did the writer want the readers to do? (verses 5-6)

   He wanted the readers to "love one another," which is following Jesus' commands.

5. What is the identifying mark of a deceiver and the antichrist? (verse 7)

   The deceivers and antichrist "do not acknowledge Jesus Christ as coming in the flesh."

6. Why shouldn't a Christian receive into the house nor greet someone who does not continue in the teachings of Christ? (verses 10-11)

   To do so would be to share in "his wicked work."

7. Why is this letter so short? (verse 12)

   The elder hopes to talk to the chosen lady face to face.

Answer these questions by reading 3 John

8. How did the elder know that all was well with the soul of Gaius? (verses 2-3)

   The elder knew that it was well with the soul of Gaius because some of the brothers arrived and testified to the truth of his life.

9. In the elder's opinion, what is an especially worthy thing for a Christian to do? (verses 5-6)

   He thought that it was a loyal thing to render any service "for the brothers, even though they are strangers" and "to send them on their way" in God's service.

10. What specific things did Diotrephes do that the elder condemned? (verses 9-10)

    Diotrephes (1) liked to put himself first, (2) did not acknowledge the authority of the elder, (3) gossiped maliciously against the elder, (4) refused "to welcome the brothers," (5) stopped those who wanted to welcome them, and (6) put those who wanted to welcome the brothers out of the church.

11. Why did the elder commend Demetrius? (verse 12)

    The elder commended Demetrius because everyone, including the elder, spoke well of him.

12. Why is the elder's letter to Gaius so brief? (verses 13-14)

    The elder hoped to see him "face to face."

DIMENSION TWO:
WHAT DOES THE BIBLE MEAN?

Before we investigate the text of Second John and Third John, we will look at the relationship of the two letters to First John. Then we will note the similarities and differences between letters two and three.

The Writer. We discussed the authorship of First John in Lesson 10. There we concluded that the writer of the letter was likely the writer of the Gospel of John also. This opinion is held by many scholars who have investigated the letters in great detail.

The writer of the Gospel of John did not name himself, and neither did the writer of First John. From hints within the text of the Gospel, however, it seems evident that "the disciple whom he [Jesus] loved" (John 19:26) was the writer. He has been identified as John, the son of Zebedee.

First John contains many similarities to the Gospel of John. The vocabulary, the style, and several of the emphases are alike. That is why the apostle John is also believed to be the writer of First John.

The writer of Second John and Third John did not name himself either. He used the word *elder* in referring to himself. The question is, Does *the elder* refer to the apostle John or to some other person?

The word *elder* means an "older person." In Bible times the elders of a community were respected and honored for their wise counsel and leadership. So the word *elder* came to have an overtone of dignity and authority.

A council of elders guided each Israelite community. In Numbers 11:16, God instructs Moses, "Bring me seventy of Israel's elders who are known to you as leaders and officials among the people."

Israelite elders are also mentioned in Joshua 24:31. When Boaz arranged to marry Ruth, ten of the elders of Bethlehem were witnesses to the proceedings (Ruth 4).

In Jesus' time a great council of elders called the Sanhedrin controlled the religious affairs of the Jews in Jerusalem. Wherever Jewish synagogues were built, the elders of the communities had the chief seats of honor (Matthew 23:6 and Luke 11:43).It is likely that the "the synagogue rulers" in Acts 13:15 were a group of elders.

A similar pattern of leadership was used in the early church. The church in Jerusalem was first guided by the apostles and elders (Acts 11:30; 15:2, 4, 6, 22-23; 16:4; 21:18). Paul and Barnabas appointed elders in the churches that they established on their first missionary journey (Acts 14:23). Christian elders are mentioned in Paul's letters to Timothy and Titus. The title also appears in James and in First Peter. In Revelation 4:4, elders are pictured in heaven, seated around the throne of God.

Would John the apostle have called himself "the elder"? Quite likely. We know that in 1 Peter 5:1, the expression *fellow elder* is used of Peter. According to tradition, the apostle John was the last survivor of the apostles. He may have lived as late as the end of the first century A.D. The same tradition places him as a leader in the church in Ephesus during the latter part of his life, so he would have been an elder in both senses of the word—in age and in authority.

If the apostle John was not the elder and the writer of the letters attributed to him, then another John, a church leader (elder), might have written them. But the tradition appeared early that the letters and the Gospel were written by John in Ephesus when he was an old man. Irenaeus, who died about A.D. 200, reported that when he was just a boy he heard from the lips of Polycarp, bishop of Smyrna, about John in Ephesus. (Polycarp lived from about A.D. 69 to 155.)

First, Second, and Third John are similar in style and expression. They express different emphases because they were written for different purposes. Second and Third John are essentially First John applied to particular situations. This interweaving of expressions, style, and somewhat of content suggests that the same person wrote all three letters.

Date of Second John and Third John. First John seems to reflect expressions and ideas found in the Gospel of John. The Gospel was probably written toward the end of the first century A.D. Then followed the letters, but we do not know in what order they were written. They are arranged in the present order on the basis of length and relationship to the longest letter. In other words, the content of Second John is more closely related to First John than Third John, so Second John follows the longest letter.

Concerns of Second John. This letter is a brief, personal note "to the chosen lady and her children." The purpose of the letter is to encourage the readers to be ruled by love. Love is equivalent to following the commandments of God. The letter also has a warning to be careful not to assist deceivers by providing them with hospitality.

Outline of Second John.
 I. Salutation (1-3)
 II. Follow truth and love (4-6)
III. Beware false teachers (7-11)
IV. Conclusion (12-13)

2 John 1-3. We do not know where the writer was when he wrote, but we propose that it was Ephesus. The basis for that proposal is simply tradition.

We also do not know to what place the letter was sent. The letter is addressed "to the chosen lady and her children," but the writer gives no indication of where they were living. Some suggestions of the letter's first destination are Rome, Ephesus, or the Roman province of Asia.

Many interpreters understand *the chosen lady* to refer to an excellent lady of upper social rank and superior character who supported the church with her wealth and influence. The expression may, however, refer to a church rather than an individual. Or, it may refer to the church at large. That the letter was understood as a general letter to the churches is the reason why it is in the group called the General Letters (Hebrews, James, First and Second Peter, First, Second, and Third John, and Jude). But more likely than simply being addressed to the church at large is the view that it was addressed to the churches in a particular region.

That "the chosen lady" refers to a church or churches rather than a person also seems likely because of some statements within the letter. First, in verse 13, mention is made of a chosen sister. The children of the chosen sister, rather than the sister herself, send greetings. In verse 4, reference is made to "some of your children walking in the truth." That sounds like a church in which some members remain steadfast while others stray rather than a close-knit Middle Eastern family.

The use of female imagery to represent God's people Israel is well-known in the Bible, as in Jeremiah 31:21c, for example, where the nation is called "O Virgin Israel." In Revelation 18 and 19, both the church and its enemy (Babylon) are depicted as women.

The word *chosen* is used in the New Testament to refer to Christians. Paul asked, "Who will bring any charge against whose whom God has chosen?" (Romans 8:33). First Peter 1:2 uses the expression "chosen according to the foreknowledge of God the Father." The King James Version translates that phrase "elect according to the foreknowledge of God the Father." And in 2 Peter 1:10, believers are urged to "be all the more eager to make your calling and election sure."

For our study, then, we will assume that the letter was written to a church whose members were thought of as children by John. This assumption is in line with his frequent expression "dear children" in these letters, even when it is clear that he is writing to adults. Although written to a church, the letter was intended for circulation to other churches, because it was not addressed to a particular church in a particular place.

John loved "the church in the truth." The phrase may mean "truly" indicating in reality or in a genuine manner. The phrase can also be understood as "in the truth" of God revealed in Christ Jesus. John loved those to whom he wrote because they shared that truth. To love in the truth, then, is to love those who have heard and obeyed the truth. They are the members of the household of faith.

Not only John loved the church, "the chosen lady." All those who knew the truth loved her. Every sincere Christian loves the church because it is the body of Christ. To love the church is to follow in the footsteps of Jesus, who "loved the church and gave himself up for her" (Ephesians 5:25).

This truth that motivated John's love and the love of all others for the church lives in believers and will remain with them forever. In 1 John 2:14b, the word of God is described as that which "lives in you." Jesus taught, "If you remain in me and my words remain in you, ask whatever you wish, and it will be given you" (John 15:7). The enduring nature of the truth and those in the truth is emphasized in 1 John 2:17: "The world and its desires pass away, but the man who does the will of God lives forever."

John assures his readers that "grace, mercy and peace . . . will be with us," both readers and writer. He uses a form of the greeting found in most New Testament letters. Usually, only *grace* and *peace* are used. Sometimes one or both of the usual expressions are joined to *love* and/or *mercy*. Verse 3 is the only place in the writings of John where mercy is used. The word *grace* is used in the writings of John only here and in the beginning of the Gospel (John 1:14, 16, 17). *Peace* is found here, in 3 John 14b, and in the sections of the Gospel that deal with the Last Supper and the Resurrection (John 14:27; 16:33; 20:19, 21, and 26).

The source of grace, mercy, and peace is "God the Father and . . . Jesus Christ, the Father's Son." Grace is the free gift of salvation and God's favor, as in John 3:16. Mercy is God's willingness to forgive all sins and trespasses because the penalty of sin (death) has been paid by "Jesus Christ the Father's Son." Peace is the result of the mercy and grace of God and of Jesus Christ. When we are reconciled to God through Jesus Christ, "the peace of God, which transcends all understanding" (Philippians 4:7) is ours.

2 John 4-6. John was joyful because he found that some of the Christians to whom he was writing followed the truth. We do not know how he found this out. It may have been during a personal visit sometime in the past. We can assume that John visited churches as did Paul. It could be that he heard about their faithful Christian walk from a visitor from the congregation. Or he could have received a letter from them.

John was joyful because these "children" were following the truth. They were living life in an authentic way, living honestly before God and others. God had so commanded his children: "Whoever claims to live in him must walk as Jesus did. Dear friends, I am not writing you a new command but an old one, which you have had since the beginning. This old command is the message you have heard" (1 John 2:6-7).

That command is to love one another. Jesus said, "My command is this: Love each other as I have loved you. Greater love has no one than this, that one lay down his life for his friends. You are my friends if you do what I command" (John 15:12-14). First Peter 1:22 urges, "Love one another deeply, from the heart.'"

The joy of John must have been reduced somewhat because only "some of your children" were following the truth. In the context it seems evident that those who were not following the truth were not walking in love. The true measure of love is following Jesus' commandments. Although "commands" is in the plural (verse 6) rather than the singular form, they all can be covered by the word *love*. To follow Jesus' commands is to follow the way of love. Love was the message of Jesus from the beginning of his ministry, and it remains the core of true Christian teaching. "The man who says 'I know him,' but does not do what he commands is a liar, and the truth is not in him" (1 John 2:4).

2 John 7-11. Apparently some of the chosen lady's children were not following the truth. They were either among the deceivers or were deceived by them. The warning about these deceivers is identical to that in 1 John 2:18-27 and 4:1-6. The word deceivers denotes "wandering, roving."

Instead of following love, these deceivers have "gone out into the world." First John 4:1 also emphasizes that "many false prophets have gone out into the world."

First John 2:18-19 points out that "many antichrists have come. . . . They went out from us, but they did not really belong to us. For if they had belonged to us, they would have remained with us; but their going showed that none of them belonged to us."

The deceivers were in the company of the believers, but they went out into the world. They departed from the company of the faithful. The reason why they left the church is that they would not acknowledge the coming of Jesus Christ in the flesh.

The deceivers did not reject the second coming of Christ. They rejected the Incarnation, the humanity of Jesus. Again this is similar to 1 John 4:2. These heretical teachings were a part of gnosticism. Gnostics taught that the Christ did not actually come in the flesh; he only seemed to do so. The gnostic philosophy held that matter was evil and spirit good. The good Messiah, then, would never have stooped to taking on evil flesh; for flesh is matter. This view undercuts the atoning death of Jesus and makes the Resurrection unnecessary.

To the gnostics, salvation came through secret knowledge. The knowledge was available only to those who would seek it from special teachers who possessed it. Salvation was by knowledge rather than by faith through the grace of God. Such teaching undercut the historical foundations of the gospel. It transformed the gospel for all into the privilege of the few.

With antichrists like this, who had gone out of the congregation but who apparently still had contact with some of the congregation, more believers were in danger of being deceived by the deceivers. John therefore warns his readers: "Watch out that you do not lose what you have worked for" (verse 8). The idea is that they should not be gullible. They should watch so that they are not taken in by the false teaching of the deceivers.

Anyone who follows this new, deceptive teaching will lose the reward. That person will be going ahead, away from the doctrine of Christ. That person, desiring to be with God, will be without God. Instead of the full reward that the faithful follower of truth and love will receive, the person who follows the antichrist will lose all that the apostles of Jesus worked for and all that that individual hopes for.

The correct teaching is the way of love and truth. That way acknowledges the doctrine of Christ. He has come in the flesh. This doctrine is so true and so essential that hospitality must not be shown to anyone who comes to you without this truth.

The persons who might come to the church and be offered hospitality were wandering prophets and teachers. Congregations in the early days of the church met in homes, and Christian teachers who were passing through were housed and fed by the young congregations. The visitors would teach in return for their room and board.

From this letter we can see that in the latter part of the first Christian century some of these traveling teachers were deceivers. John warns his readers against such antichrists. To offer them hospitality would be to share in their wicked work.

2 John 12-13. The writer had used up approximately one sheet of papyrus, the paper of the day, for his letter. He chose not to write a longer letter. Instead, he hoped to visit his readers soon. And although he had considerable joy when he heard of the faithful who followed the truth (verse 4), there would be greater joy for visitor and visited when he could "talk with you face to face."

The last verse of the letter suggests that the greeting is from the church of which the writer was a part. The greeting is from the "children" of the chosen sister. Both they and the "children" of the receiving congregation are the chosen.

The Third Letter of John. We have discussed the date and authorship of Third John above. Second John and Third John have several similarities. For example, the openings of the letters use expressions that are alike. But Third John is written to an individual and is more personal than First John or Second John.

Gaius may have had a church in his house. While John expresses interest in Gaius as a friend, the main concern of the letter is that Christian visitors to the church be shown appropriate hospitality. Diotrephes is condemned for failing to do this. On the other hand, Demetrius is commended for doing good. This may imply that Demetrius is a model of a Christian host to visiting preachers and teachers.

Outline of Third John.
  I. Salutation (1-4)
 II. In praise of Gaius (5-8)
III. Warning against Diotrephes (9-10)
 IV. Commendation for Demetrius (11-12)
  V. Conclusion (13-14)

3 John 1-4. We do not know who Gaius was. Three of Paul's friends were named Gaius: Gaius of Corinth (1 Corinthians 1:14), Gaius of Macedonia (Acts 19:29), and Gaius of Derbe (Acts 20:4). The name seems to have been a popular one.

Just as in Second John, the one or ones receiving the letter are dear to the writer. John loves all who are followers of the truth.

John expresses a prayerful wish that Gaius will prosper in body as he has in spirit. To be in Christ is to be spiritually made whole. John had heard from visiting brothers that Gaius was flourishing spiritually. He was following the truth. And, as in 2 John 4, the writer could not have heard news that would make him happier. John had the heart of a Christian shepherd.

3 John 5-8. John uses the words *dear friend* rather than writing "Gaius." Gaius was a dear friend because he acted loyally toward visiting missionary-teachers, and that was exactly what John wanted Christians to do. Of course, as we have seen in Second John, those who were to be shown hospitality were loyal to Christ and not deceivers.

Gaius is commended because he was hospitable even though the visiting teachers were strangers. John knew about Gaius's loyalty to traveling Christian teachers because some of them had visited John. They had told (the church in Ephesus) of Gaius's helpful care when they visited him.

The writer commends Gaius for such service. Not only was it the right thing to do, but it was also good to "send them on their way." This means that Gaius was to provide the travelers with what they needed for the journey to their next stop. The idea appears also in Acts 15:3; Romans 15:24; 1 Corinthians 16:6, 11; 2 Corinthians 1:16; and Titus 3:13.

Christians should support those in God's service in this way. Christian workers should not have to seek support from nonbelievers. Those Christians who are hospitable toward brothers and sisters in Christ who are traveling in God's service are counted as "fellow workers" in the truth. The truth, of course, is the truth of the gospel message of salvation through Jesus Christ.

3 John 9-10. John had written a letter to a church, but we do not know what he wrote. Diotrephes was apparently a leader in that church. He did not accept the authority of John in the matter with which the letter dealt. In other words, Diotrephes sought to put himself first in authority over the church.

Besides failing to acknowledge the authority of John, Diotrephes refused to show hospitality to "the brothers." These may have been traveling teachers sent by John. To do this would have been another rejection of John's authority. Diotrephes also refused to permit other Christians in the church in which he was a leader to show hospitality to the visitors. Those who did show such hospitality Diotrephes excommunicated from the congregation. These were extremely highhanded actions.

John did not accuse Diotrephes of being a deceiver. The charge was not acknowledging proper authority.

Apparently Gaius was a member of the congregation over which Diotrephes put himself first, or Gaius knew the people and the circumstances. Since John wrote to Gaius and commended his hospitality, Gaius may have been one of those put out of the church by Diotrephes.

John hoped to visit the church. The *if* is particularly understandable in light of the tradition that he was elderly when he wrote the letter. On the proposed visit, he planned to address both issues—what Diotrephes was doing (in refusing hospitality to visiting missionary teachers) and what Diotrephes was saying against John. *Gossiping* is "chattering, talking nonsense." While these activities are not uplifting at any time, Diotrephes worsened them

by what he gossiped about. He slandered the faithful witnesses.

3 John 11-12. Again the writer addresses Gaius with the familiar expression of endearment, *dear friend.* He urges Gaius not to imitate the evil that is so evident in the deeds and words of Diotrephes. Rather, Gaius should imitate good.

Just as Diotrephes was an example of evil, John had an example of good ready at hand. We know nothing of Demetrius other than what John testifies about him in this letter. But Demetrius had the testimony of "everyone," including the writer, that he was good. Demetrius also had testimony from "the truth itself." This last testimony is probably the testimony of his life and witness, based on the saving truth that made him a Christian. In other words, his life was a true testimony to his goodness.

Gaius probably did not know Demetrius. He may have been the visiting missionary who carried the letter from John to Gaius. John urged Gaius to receive Demetrius. Diotrephes would not have done so. But Gaius had established a reputation as a faithful host to God's traveling servants. He had been a fellow worker in the truth with others in times past (verse 8), and now Gaius had the opportunity to host the good Demetrius in the face of the opposition and example of Diotrephes.

3 John 13-14. As in 2 John 12, the writer explains why the letter is not longer—he hopes to visit Gaius and to speak with him face to face. In light of the letter, one of the topics that would be discussed further probably was the case of Diotrephes.

"Peace to you" is patterned after the Hebrew *shalom,* which can serve as either a greeting or a farewell.

This letter to Gaius was written by a man who had a circle of supporters whom he called friends. They also sent their greetings to Gaius. They would have known the problem that the writer addressed in the letter. There were a group of disciples like Gaius in his community. They would have counted John and his friends as their friends. They likely were hospitable to traveling teachers and evangelists, as was Gaius.

DIMENSION THREE:
WHAT DOES THE BIBLE MEAN TO ME?

2 John 7-9—The Doctrine of Christ:
The Coming of Jesus in the Flesh

What we believe about Jesus may have two sources: (1) We may absorb the ideas and viewpoints of other, usually older, Christians. Then the ideas we absorb may be modified by our experiences. (2) We may go back to the historical source of our faith in Jesus—the Gospel accounts and the apostolic teaching concerning Jesus. As we mature, we need to lean less on our own understanding and more on the biblical testimony as the basis for what we believe.

That our Savior was fully human is an essential doctrine of the Christian faith. As we noted in Hebrews (2:17-18), because Jesus was tempted in every respect as we have been, he is able to help those who are tempted. His atoning death was a genuine suffering on our behalf. It was not an illusion perpetrated on unsuspecting humans by God.

We have "new birth into a living hope through the resurrection of Jesus Christ from the dead" (1 Peter 1:3b). If Jesus had not really come in the flesh, the Resurrection would not be a reality for us. John assured his readers that he had touched the human Jesus. Jesus was no phantom (1 John 1:1).

As the truth about Jesus is the basis for our individual salvation, so it is the basis for the existence of the church. The survival of the church depends on the testimony of the eyewitnesses to the gospel events being transmitted faithfully from one generation to the next. As the gnostics who denied the coming of Jesus Christ in the flesh have passed from the scene long ago, while those who acknowledge that truth survive generation after generation, so God has protected the truth of the gospel in his people.

3 John 5-7—Christian Hospitality

Hospitality practices vary from region to region. One tendency in modern American society that hinders easy hospitality is the sense that our homes must be show places when we have guests. Yet the greatest benefit that guests and hosts alike derive from hospitality is the personal contact, the fellowship of kindred souls. The experience of sharing food and faith will be remembered by our guests long after any details have faded from the memory. As Christians, we should learn to appreciate one another for what we are rather than what we have. Our homes are not hotels. Nor are they to be facades of economic status. They are to reflect our love for Christ and for one another as members of the family of God.

The local church should make every effort to encourage the members to be hospitable to visiting Christians. Often traveling choirs, youth groups, and visiting missionaries need hospitality. The church should never be guilty of putting guests up in hotels or motels.

But you dear friends, build yourselves up in your most holy faith, . . . keep yourselves in God's love (Jude 20-21).

— 13 —

The Book of Jude

DIMENSION ONE:
WHAT DOES THE BIBLE SAY?

Answer these questions by reading Jude.

1. How does Jude describe his relationship to Jesus and to James? (verse 1)

   Jude is "a servant of Jesus Christ and a brother of James."

2. What three words describe the people to whom Jude writes? (verse 1)

   They are called, loved, *and* kept.

3. What three blessings does Jude pray for his readers? (verse 2)

   He prays that they will have mercy, peace, and love.

4. What is the specific reason Jude writes to his Christian readers? (verse 3)

   He writes to appeal to them "to contend for the faith that was once for all entrusted to the saints."

5. What two actions are the godless persons guilty of? (verse 4)

   The godless persons are guilty of perverting the grace of God into immorality, and they are guilty of denying Christ.

6. In verses 5-7, Jude reminds his readers of God's judgment on three groups who were unbelieving and immoral. Who are these groups?

   The three groups are (1) those whom God saved out of Egypt, (2) the angels who kept not their own position, and (3) the people of Sodom and Gomorrah.

7. The men mentioned in verse 8 are guilty of three acts worthy of condemnation. List those acts.

   They "pollute their own bodies, reject authority and slander celestial beings."

8. What act have these men committed that even Michael the archangel would not commit? (verses 9-10)

   They have reviled "whatever they do not understand."

9. What examples from nature does Jude use to describe the men he condemns? (verses 12-13)

   He describes them as waterless clouds, fruitless trees, wild waves of the sea, and wandering stars.

10. According to Enoch, why is the Lord to execute judgment on the godless? (verses 14-16)

    The Lord is coming to judge the godless for their acts and for their harsh words "spoken against him."

11. Of what particular prediction of the apostles does Jude remind his readers? (verses 17-18)

    He reminds them that the apostles said, "In the last times there will be scoffers, who will follow their own ungodly desires."

12. What action words does Jude use to urge his readers on in the faith? (verses 20-21)

    He urges them to build themselves up, pray, keep themselves in the love of God, and wait for mercy.

13. What actions does Jude recommend toward weak Christians? (verses 22-23)

    He urges his readers to save some and to have mercy on some.

DIMENSION TWO:
WHAT DOES THE BIBLE MEAN?

Jude is the last of the General Letters and reflects the general characteristics of the works we have been studying. Jude shows a concern for the spiritual health of the early church. Whenever anything genuine appears, a substitute usually follows, claiming to be better than the original. Spiritually speaking, this describes the situation that brought forth this letter.

Ungodly men had joined the church. They were corrupting the morals of many in the church, and they were teaching false and unscriptural doctrines. Jude offers guidance for dealing with these godless men.

The Writer and the Date of Writing. The writer identifies himself as "Jude, a servant of Jesus Christ and a brother of James" (verse 1). Jesus had a brother named Jude (Judas) and another named James (Matthew 13:55). The brothers of Jesus did not accept him as the Messiah during his ministry (Matthew 13:57; Mark 6:4). Yet, after Jesus, death, burial, resurrection, and ascension, they are found among the disciples in the upper room, awaiting the promised coming of the Holy Spirit (Acts 1:14). Paul refers to James as "the Lord's brother" in Galatians 1:19. There can be little doubt that the writer of our book is identifying himself not only as the brother of James but also of Jesus.

The writer does not identify himself as the brother of Jesus, only of James. But long ago Clement of Alexandria (last decade of the second century A.D.) thought that, like James, Jude would not call himself the brother of Jesus. That might infer he was claiming too much authority.

Some scholars would attribute the letter to a later person, writing under the pseudonym of Jude. The reason for suspecting that the letter was written after the time of Jude the brother of Jesus is some expressions in the book that suggest a later date. He speaks of "the faith that was once for all entrusted to the saints" (verse 3) and asks his readers to "remember" the words of the apostles (verse 17). However, we do not know how much younger Jude was than Jesus. Jesus was Mary's first-born, and Jude could have been born fifteen to twenty years after Jesus. He could easily have been alive in the last quarter of the first century A.D.

No one knows precisely who wrote the book. The weight of tradition and the testimony of Scripture suggest that Jude the writer was the younger brother of Jesus.

We have no definite indication of the date the letter was written. In some respects the letter is quite similar to 2 Peter 2. The writer of Second Peter apparently drew on Jude as he wrote. The two books probably date to about the same time. But the dating for both is disputed, as is the identity of the writers of both books. Jude is dated as early as before the death of Peter, around A.D. 64 to A.D. 68, and as late as A.D. 125 to A.D. 150 by various scholars.

The church in general did not accept Jude as revelation from the apostolic era until after the time of Eusebius. He was a church historian in the time of Constantine and died about A.D. 339. Eusebius mentioned that not all the churches accepted the apostolic authorship of the book. Jude was recognized as an authentic book for the use of the church at the Council of Carthage in A.D. 397. Acceptance indicated that the book was widely known and used by many congregations long before the Council of Carthage.

The First Readers. The letter is addressed to "those who have been called." This reference is too general to identify them. From the many references to Old Testament history, Jude was either intended for Jewish Christians or for Gentile converts who were well acquainted with the biblical stories. Like some of the other General Letters, Jude was probably addressed to the church in general rather than to a specific congregation or individual. The book's teachings and warnings are certainly applicable to Christians of every time and place.

Outline of Jude.

I.   Salutation (1-2)
II. Purpose of the letter (3-4)
III. Judgment on the ungodly element in the church (5-16)
    A. Examples of punishment of unbelievers (5-13)
    B. Enoch prophesied judgment on the ungodly (14-16)
IV. Adhere to the true faith (17-23)
V.   Benediction (24-25)

Jude 1-2. As with the opening of the Letter of James, Jude calls himself a servant. This frequently used word in the New Testament is more accurately rendered "bond-servant" or "slave."

The people to whom Jude writes are "the called." This is a frequently used expression referring to Christians. The expression is used in 1 Peter 2:9: "him who called you out of darkness into his wonderful light." In 2 Thessalonians 2:13-14, Paul explains that God called the Christians in Thessalonica through the gospel to "be saved through the sanctifying work of the Spirit and through belief in the truth."

The idea of "kept by Jesus Christ" may seem peculiar at first glance. The phrase can also be translated as "kept for Jesus Christ." Christians have been "bought at a price" (1 Corinthians 6:20). Jesus will return to receive those who are his own, who have been kept for him by their love for him.

The words *called*, *loved*, and *kept* indicate the powerful forces at work in the believer's relationship to God. As Paul insisted, "neither death nor life, neither angels nor demons, neither the present nor the future, nor any powers, neither height nor depth, nor anything else in all creation, will be able to separate us from the love of God that is in Christ Jesus our Lord" (Romans 8:38-39).

Jude's desire is that those who read his letter will experience more and more of God's mercy, the peace that comes from reconciliation to God and other people, and love.

Jude 3-4. The writer states that he actually had intended to write "about the salvation we share." Because of the more immediate and pressing problem he addresses in his letter, we can only speculate what additional insights about the common salvation Jude might have shared with his first readers (and us).

As it is, Jude appealed to his readers to "contend for the faith," the faith once and for all time delivered to the saints. The faith is for all time, for all circumstances, for all purposes, and for all people. It is universal. That faith is no doubt the facts to be believed, the commands to be obeyed, and the promises to be received that make up the gospel.

The saints, of course, are all sincere Christians. The people of the faith, the church, are the living repository of the faith. The Bible cannot defend itself; only those who believe its truths will come to its defense.

The word *contend* refers to a vigorous verbal defense of the gospel. Paul charged Timothy to "fight the good fight of the faith. Take hold of the eternal life to which you were called when you made your good confession in the presence of many witnesses" (1 Timothy 6:12).

Jude's concern was for the influence in the church of some who had secretly gained admission. The Greek word used here has the idea of slipping in, as through a side door. These men appeared to have accepted the faith once for all delivered when they were converted, but they began to pervert the faith.

Jude states that these "godless men" were long ago designated for this condemnation. The word *condemnation* may refer to Jude's condemnation in the letter. More likely it is the idea that the wicked were known to God long ago and destined for condemnation.

What had these so-called Christians been doing that so endangered the church? They had perverted the grace of God into licentiousness. But more than this, these godless men were denying "Jesus Christ our only Sovereign and Lord." Jude had called himself a servant of Jesus Christ. He knew who his only Master was. As we have seen earlier in our study of these letters, God calls his people to be holy. Immoral activity is a direct denial of Christ's lordship over a person.

Jude 5-16. The heart of the letter of Jude is contained in this section. Jude has identified the problem and will attack it by reminding his readers of the way in which God has dealt with the ungodly in the past (verses 5-8). Then he vividly describes what these godless men do in the church and what will be their destiny (verses 9-13). Jude draws parallels between them and other perverters of the faith in the Old Testament. He also reminds his readers of the prophecy of Enoch, which he sees fulfilled in the ungodly of his time.

Jude 5-7. Jude tells his readers that they already know what he now stresses: The God who saves can also destroy. They know examples of that fact. He mentions three: the unbelieving Israelites who perished in the wilderness, the rebellious angels who came under judgment, and the destruction of Sodom and Gomorrah.

We are well aware of the reason why almost all that generation who left Egypt perished in the wilderness. The cause was unbelief, and this was stressed in our study of Hebrews (3:12-19). The events are recorded in Numbers 13 and 14.

We also know the story of the destruction of Sodom and Gomorrah (Genesis 19:1-28). This illustration fits well the concern of sexual immorality with which Jude charges the ungodly. The point of the illustration is the type of destruction that befell those notorious places. It was punishment by fire.

The fire is described as "eternal." Jesus used the expressions "the fire of hell" (Matthew 5:22c) and the "eternal fire prepared for the devil and his angels" (Matthew 25:41). In the Book of Revelation "the lake of fire" (20:14-15) is the place into which Death and Hades are cast, as well as anyone whose name is not found written in the book of life. This is likely the idea expressed by "eternal fire" in Jude.

What we find most puzzling is the reference in verse 6 to the angels who "did not keep their positions of authority." The first readers would have known exactly what Jude was talking about, but we have no such incident recorded in the Bible.

The story of the fallen angels is recorded in the Book of Enoch. This intertestamental book is a collection of stories and moral teachings that date from the second century B.C. to the beginning of the first century A.D. Jesus said, "I saw Satan fall like lightning from heaven" (Luke 10:18); and we have noted his reference to the "eternal fire prepared for the devil and his angels." So, even though we only have a nonbiblical reference (Enoch) to the revolt in heaven, evidently the story was well-known in pre-Christian Judaism and in the early church.

Jude's reason for mentioning the fallen angels was that their rebellion brought certain punishment. How horrible a contrast to go from being angels of light to bound prisoners of utter darkness! Jude intended to shock his readers into a realistic awareness of the danger of the godless in their midst.

Jude 8-11. Despite the general knowledge of examples of the sure punishment of God for ungodliness and immorality, these men "pollute their own bodies" through unholy sexual activity, "reject authority," and "slander celestial beings." All this is the result of their dreamings. They may have induced trances and claimed special revelations or inspiration, then claimed the right to be free from the demands of normal decency.

Jude addresses particularly the slandering of celestial beings. Exactly what the celestial beings are is unclear.

Slander basically means to cheapen. To slander is to address with abusive or shameful language. In contrast to the activities of godless humans (who are, remember, in the church), the archangel Michael, in a situation where he might have slandered the devil, refrained from doing so.

Again we have no biblical reference to this contention between Michael and Satan over the body of Moses. The story comes from another Jewish book of the intertestamental period called The Assumption of Moses.

These godless men act like "unreasoning animals." They slander what they do not understand and thereby set themselves up for judgment.

Woe is a familiar biblical expression. The English word comes from an old Anglo-Saxon expression meaning "pain, misery, affliction." The woe these ungodly ones can expect is like that of Cain (Genesis 4:3-16), Balaam (Numbers 22-24; 31:8), and those Israelites who died as the result of joining Korah's rebellion (Numbers 16). All these came to an evil end after rebelling against the authority of God or God's servant.

Jude 12-13. Here are a series of word pictures Jude has drawn from nature to describe the destructive character of the godless men in the church. "Blemishes at your love feasts" is more accurately translated "hidden rocks in your love feasts." These immoral church members were like reefs (rocks) hidden just beneath the surface of the sea, ready to bring the disaster of immoral conduct into the gathering of God's unsuspecting saints. They set a crass example, boldly carousing together, looking after themselves rather than having a sincere love of their brothers and sisters in Christ.

Waterless clouds give the promise of rain but produce no rain. Fruitless trees give the appearance of producing, but they have no mature fruit in the time of harvest. They are uprooted by the owner. They are twice dead—producing no new life and being uprooted. These men are like wandering stars, to be lost in space. Stars should remain fixed points of light. (This word picture likely refers to comets.)

Jude 14-16. Jude again calls attention to the Book of Enoch and quotes from it. (The "holy ones" are the heavenly host of angels around the Almighty.) He uses the quotation to show that this type of ungodliness was prophetically foretold long ago, and it has now appeared. Again, the words of Enoch point to the coming judgment on the ungodly.

The people who soil the church are grumblers and faultfinders. The words of Christians are to minister grace to the hearers (Ephesians 4:29). Christians are to be content (Hebrews 13:5). The ungodly follow their own desires; lust controls them. Christians are to control sinful desires (1 Peter 2:11). These men are boasters of self and flatterers of others, flattering for personal gain. Humility is required of Christians (James 4:10; 1 Peter

5:5b; and the example of Jesus, Philippians 2:8). Flattery was forbidden by Jesus. He insisted, "Simply let your 'Yes' be 'Yes,' and your 'No,' 'No'; anything beyond this comes from the evil one" (Matthew 5:37; James 5:12).

Jude 17-23. Not only does Jude provide examples of God's judgment on the godless from the Old Testament and from other traditions, he says Jesus' apostles also predicted that ungodly scoffers would appear "in the last times." We have no record of this prediction, other than this mention of it by Jude. Christians have been living in the last times since the ascension of Jesus and the days of the apostles.

The scoffers, those driven by fleshly rather than spiritual desires, are the ones who cause disunity among God's people. Worldly people are by definition devoid of the Spirit. The Spirit is a gift to the repentant, baptized believer (Acts 2:38). The unity of believers was a matter of prayer for Jesus (John 17:20-21). "There is one body and one Spirit—just as you were called to one hope when you were called—one Lord, one faith, one baptism; one God and Father of all, who is over all and through all and in all" (Ephesians 4:4-6).

Rather than be influenced by the divisive, ungodly element, Jude urges his readers actively to build up the protective walls of their faith. They can build themselves up through praying in the Holy Spirit, abiding in the love of God, and waiting (patiently and confidently) for the fulfillment of the promises that are in the Lord Jesus Christ.

Not only are the readers to look after their own faith, they are commanded to save whomever they can. Each group of those fellow Christians whose commitment is weak must be addressed in a different way. Doubters need to be convinced by the example and the testimony of the faithful. Those closer to the brink of hellfire must be snatched out. Others need mercy while letting them know that you fear for them. Let your disgust at their past, lustful deeds show; but showing a concern for them may save some.

Jude 24-25. Jude's benediction expresses great confidence in God's power to save. Even in the midst of a situation like that on which he has focused in the body of this letter, Jude assures his readers that God can save and save a person unblemished. That is possible because the blood of Jesus Christ, our Savior, cleanses the repentant and committed from all sin and unrighteousness. It is possible to be saved even in a polluted church and to enter the presence of God rejoicing.

The marvelous power of God to save to the uttermost those who come to him through Christ is evidence that to God is the "glory, majesty, power and authority." They are God's in the past, the present, and the future. The godless are but for a moment. They may trouble the church, but the Savior reigns forever.

DIMENSION THREE:
WHAT DOES THE BIBLE MEAN TO ME?

Jude 3—Contending for the Faith

To contend for the faith refers to a strenuous, verbal defense of what has been divinely revealed for Christians to believe. You may want to ask your pastor to provide some insights about what the essentials of the faith are.

Another source that you can consult is the entry on faith in a Bible dictionary. You cannot contend for the faith unless you can define it.

With a good understanding of the faith once for all delivered to the saints, help class members explore modern times and circumstances. How is our society different from the first century?

The point of Jude's letter, however, was to contend for the faith against that element in the church that followed godless desires. Grumblers, malcontents, boasters, those who cause divisions and the like were weakening the faith of weaker church members. How can dedicated, faithful Christians counteract such individuals or such tendencies?

Verses 20-23 likely provide the means by which to combat ungodliness and ungodly people in Christian circles. The call is to build up your faith, to pray in line with what the Holy Spirit lays on your heart (the concerns of the living God), to remain in the love of God by being conscious of that love (being aware of God's blessings and guidance), and to look for the return of the Lord Jesus Christ. An optimistic outlook is a powerful testimony of faith.

Contending for the faith means persuasively presenting your testimony to those who doubt (verse 22). Presenting your testimony is simply telling the doubters what great things God has done for you. The purpose is to save some, snatching them from the fire; so a genuine concern for them is essential.

Jude 16-19—Handling Our Sinful Desires

Perhaps the biggest conflict we have in developing into mature Christians is overcoming our tendency to consider self first and others last. Sinful desires can refer to lusts. The sexual drive is a normal part of being human, but it must be controlled lest it lead to ungodly thoughts, adultery, and perversions. The key to controlling ourselves is to "offer your bodies as living sacrifices" (Romans 12:1). That is, we are to willfully determine to serve God. Rather than be conformed to the norms of a society that is hardly Christian, we are to be transformed by the renewing of our minds. By setting our mind on things that are above, we can control our thoughts and our bodies. We can control what we allow to enter our minds through our senses.

The human sinful desires include other drives as well, for example, envy, coveting, anger, malice, and revenge. Ephesians 4:17–5:4 provides wise counsel on handling sinful desires like these. Humility, a genuine concern for the welfare of others, trust in the provisions of God to meet one's needs, and especially modeling one's life after that of the Master are powerful tools for transforming our base tendencies into godliness.

REVELATION
Table of Contents

1. In the Spirit on the Lord's Day 286

2. Seven Letters to Seven Churches 289

3. Worthy Is the Lamb 293

4. The Book of the Seven Seals 297

5. The Seven Trumpets 301

6. A Scroll Both Bitter and Sweet 305

7. The Woman Clothed With the Sun 310

8 Singing a New Song 315

9. Seven Bowls of Wrath 319

10. Babylon Is Fallen 323

11. The Sword of His Mouth 328

12. I Make All Things New 333

13. The Healing Stream 339

About the Writer

Dr. C. M. Kempton Hewitt is professor of New Testament in the Riley Chair of biblical interpretation at The Methodist Theological School in Ohio, Delaware, Ohio.

On the Lord's Day I was in the Spirit, and I heard behind me a loud voice like a trumpet (1:10).

— 1 —

In the Spirit on the Lord's Day

Revelation 1

DIMENSION ONE:
WHAT DOES THE BIBLE SAY?

Answer these questions by reading Revelation 1

1. To whom did God give the revelation? (1:1a)

   God gave the revelation to Jesus Christ.

2. Why was the revelation given? (1:1a)

   The revelation was given to show the servants of God "what must soon take place."

3. How did God make known this revelation given to Jesus Christ? (1:b)

   God sent an angel to God's servant John.

4. How is John described? (1:2)

   John testifies to "the word of God and the testimony of Jesus Christ."

5. What must those who are blessed do with John's account? (1:3)

   They must read it, hear it, and "take to heart what is written."

6. Who is John's message for? (1:4a, 11)

   John's message is for the seven churches in Asia: Ephesus, Smyrna, Pergamum, Thyatira, Sardis, Philadelphia, and Laodicea.

7. Who is described as the one "who is, and who was, and who is to come"? (1:4b, 8)

   John is describing the Lord God.

8. Who else is the message from? (1:4b-5a)

   The message also comes from the seven spirits who are before God's throne and from Jesus Christ.

9. How is Christ described? (1:5a)

   Christ is "the faithful witness, the firstborn from the dead, and the ruler of the kings of the earth."

10. How does John describe himself and his audience? (1:5b-6)

    John and his audience are loved by Jesus Christ, have been freed from their sins by the blood of Jesus Christ, and have been made a kingdom and priests to serve the God and Father of Jesus Christ.

11. What does John say about Jesus Christ being seen again by the world? (1:7)

    John says that "every eye" will see Christ when he returns.

12. Who is speaking in 1:8?

    "The Lord God" speaks in the first person ("I am") and is identified as the Beginning ("Alpha") and the End ("Omega") of all that is.

13. How does John describe himself with reference to the members of the seven churches? (1:9)

    John is their brother. He shares with them "the suffering and kingdom and patient endurance" that are theirs in Jesus.

14. Why was John on Patmos? (1:9)

    John was on Patmos "because of the word of God and the testimony of Jesus."

15. As John describes his experience of being in the Spirit on the Lord's day, what is he told to do? (1:11)

   John is told to write a book describing what he sees and to send the book to the seven churches of Asia.

16. What are the first things John sees in his vision? (1:12-13)

   As he turns to see the voice speaking to him, John sees seven golden lampstands and in the midst of the lampstands "someone 'like a son of man.' "

17. What are the symbolic items of Christ's description? (1:13-16)

   Christ is clothed with a long robe and a golden sash (girdle), his head and hair are white like wool or snow, his eyes are like fire and his feet like gleaming bronze, his voice is "like the sound of rushing waters," he holds seven stars in his right hand, a double-edged sword is coming from his mouth, his face is like the full strength of the shining sun.

18. What is John's response to this dazzling vision of Christ? (1:17)

   He falls down in fear "as though dead."

19. What two events in the life of Jesus are referred to by Christ in his first speech to John? (1:18b)

   Christ refers to his death on the cross and his resurrection from the dead.

20. As a result of these events, what does Christ possess? (1:18c)

   Christ has "the keys of death and Hades."

21. What does Christ command John to do? (1:19)

   John is to write what he sees.

22. What does Christ tell John that the seven golden lampstands (1:12-13) and the seven stars (1:16) are symbols for? (1:20)

   The seven lampstands are the seven churches; the seven stars are the angels of these seven churches.

DIMENSION TWO: WHAT DOES THE BIBLE MEAN?

Background. The opening statement places the Book of Revelation in a distinct category in the New Testament: "The revelation [or *apocalypse*] of Jesus Christ." *Apocalypse* comes from the Greek word *apokalypsis,* meaning "disclosure."

We need to be clear at the outset about the prophet John's understanding of his apocalyptic encounter. The revelation belongs to Jesus Christ, not to the prophet. God is the source of the revelation to Jesus Christ. In turn, Jesus Christ is the source of the prophet's experience of this revelation.

Many commentaries on Revelation suggest that the central factor in the book is a blueprint of the future entrusted as a revelation to John. This exact blueprint is then conveyed in the biblical text by means of mysterious codes and symbols. These commentaries suggest that all one has to do is crack the code to know exactly how current events are mirrored in Revelation's text.

This approach has done great harm to Revelation's interpretation. Worse, this approach is really contrary to the belief of Revelation's writer. John's theology teaches that Jesus, the exalted Christ, is the center of faith. Not history. Not the future. Not the evil powers being defeated by "the word of God and the testimony of Jesus Christ." But, especially, the prophet's experience is not the center of faith. In fact, John is very much an onlooker or observer of the action started by the "Lamb, who was slain" (5:12).

Revelation 1:1-3. John describes himself as "servant." But what he writes is often called *prophecy.* A great deal of scholarly debate continues about Revelation's proper category within the New Testament. Is Revelation an apocalypse only? Is it a prophecy with apocalyptic overtones? Or is Revelation a completely distinct writing with no parallels in or outside of Scripture?

Revelation is certainly apocalyptic. The heightened sense of conflict between the opposing forces of good and evil, the essential pessimism about the possibility of improvements in the here-and-now, the use of animal imagery, the heavy use of numerology and other veiled imagery—all these factors place Revelation clearly in the same class with classic and contemporary apocalyptic writing. But the real home of Revelation is prophecy as experienced in the early Christian church.

This book grows out of worship and is intended for the use of other Christian prophets ("the angels of the seven churches" [1:20]). John almost certainly implies the use of the prophecy in worship. His urgent exhortation to read aloud, listen carefully, understand, and keep the words of this book (1:3) tells us a great deal about John's understanding of prophecy. Above all, Revelation is to help the church grow in understanding and obedience. Prophecy tries to help the church understand today's message from the risen Christ, who is the Word of God and who still speaks. Prophecy does not dwell on previous proclamations of Scripture and their interpretations, nor is it interested in the neat categories of past, present, and future. Rather, prophecy tends to run all these together in the immediacy of the moment of the encounter with the living testimony of Jesus.

We are unused to this world of John's prophecy. This world is a strange and admittedly dangerous place in which to live, let alone visit. We like things more orderly, neat, and tidy. Revelation is orderly—but in its own way. For example, John alludes to biblical texts and images on almost every line of Revelation but uses only one direct quotation (15:3). Again, events of the "final end" of the world are spoken of in the narrative long before we would expect them if Revelation were an orderly, history-centered work. In some ways the creative approach of Revelation is more like the collage of a music video than a sequential, logical plan of history. This approach makes Revelation difficult for us to understand. But we only make Revelation more difficult if we try to force it into a mold that it does not fit.

Revelation 1:4-7. Revelation's rich theology about Jesus Christ is one of the most neglected and yet fruitful aspects of the Christian canon. Jesus Christ is described by many titles and actions in this passage:

Jesus Christ is
- "the faithful witness"
- "the firstborn from the dead"
- "the ruler of the kings of the earth"
Jesus Christ has
- loved us
- "freed us from our sins by his blood"
- made us to be "a kingdom and priests"

Revelation 1:8. *Alpha* is the first letter of the Greek alphabet, *Omega* the last. John chooses an interesting way of expressing himself when he writes that another revealed name of God is "First and Last." He then expands the name to include time: present, past, and future. If J. B. Phillips was right and our God is too small, reflect for a moment on Alpha and Omega as a proper name for God.

Revelation 1:9-20. The student book points out that audition (hearing as the primary experience) characterizes John's encounter with God. This focus on the sounds of religious experience reminds us that prophecy was probably purely oral in nature. True, John uses words in the text of Revelation to describe his experience; but even this betrays a certain oral character.

The Greek text of Revelation is the most difficult in the New Testament. The technical grammatical studies of the text are quite complex. Many scholars have despaired of understanding or even dealing with the nearly impossible Greek of Revelation. It is as if the experience of hearing and speaking "the testimony of Jesus" cannot be contained by written language.

DIMENSION THREE: WHAT DOES THE BIBLE MEAN TO ME?

When reading the first chapter of John's prophecy, we could easily concentrate on the fantastic elements of his strange experience. A careful reading of the text, however, shows that John tells little about himself. The main person in the text is Jesus Christ.

The description of such an unusual spiritual encounter raises the question of personal religious experience. The student book points out that the Book of Revelation is the source of great divisions of opinion. For some Christians, the kind of spirit-induced visions and auditory experiences described by John are not only sought after but considered essential for salvation. For others, the Book of Revelation is discredited because it is based on such an experience. This division of opinion is not simply a contemporary fact; Christians argued for centuries that Revelation ought not to be included in the Bible.

The spiritual challenge of Revelation is to allow its theological and religious value to penetrate our lives. One of the values we are taught by John is the centrality of Jesus Christ. The detail of belief about who Jesus Christ is and what he does for humankind is really quite extraordinary. The eye of the prophet is clearly fixed on Christ, not on the prophet's own mystical experience. Jesus Christ is in control of what is taking place in John's strange experience. Again and again this exaltation and empowering of Christ is affirmed.

In Revelation, John is especially fond of representing Jesus Christ as the great witness. John also writes about "the testimony of Jesus." John makes it clear that Jesus Christ is not only the firstborn from the dead but also the present, living voice of God in the church today.

We may have made Jesus Christ a historical, heavenly reality at the expense of finding ways of allowing Jesus Christ to speak in the present. Does Christ speak today? In whose voice do I hear him call? Is his testimony only in words? In whose actions do I see testimony to Christ?

Be faithful, even to the point of death, and I will give you the crown of life (2:10c).

2

Seven Letters to Seven Churches

Revelation 2–3

DIMENSION ONE: WHAT DOES THE BIBLE SAY?

Answer these questions by reading Revelation 2–3

1. Seven "mini-letters" are sent to seven churches in Asia. Identify the churches. (2:1, 8, 12, 18; 3:1, 7, 14)

   The seven churches are in Ephesus, Smyrna, Pergamum, Thyatira, Sardis, Philadelphia, and Laodicea.

2. In each case, to whom is the letter addressed? (2:1, 8, 12, 18; 3:1, 7, 14)

   Each letter is addressed "to the angel of the church."

3. Which of these seven churches receives no praise? (3:14-22)

   The church in the city of Laodicea is censured, never praised.

4. Which two churches receive only praise and no censure? (2:8-11; 3:7-13)

   The churches in Smyrna and in Philadelphia receive only praise and are not censured.

5. What are some reasons for churches being praised? (2:2, 9, 13, 19; 3:8)

   The churches are praised for perseverance, intolerance of evil persons, endurance in their afflictions and poverty, remaining true to the name of Christ, not denying faith in Christ, love, faith, service, and keeping the word of Christ.

6. Each church receives a promise on the basis of doing what? (2:7, 11, 17, 26; 3:5, 12, 21)

   Each letter ends with a call to overcome. Those who overcome will receive a gift from Christ.

7. What are some of the good things promised to those who overcome? (2:7, 11, 17, 26-28; 3:5, 12, 21)

   Those who overcome are promised to eat from the tree of life in paradise; survive the second death; receive the hidden manna; be given a new name on a white stone; be given power over the nations to rule; be given the morning star; be clad in white garments; not be blotted out of the book of life; be acknowledged before God and the angels; be made a pillar in the temple of God to dwell there forever; receive three names: God, the new Jerusalem, and Christ's own name; and receive the privilege of sitting on the throne of Christ with him.

8. Who provides the model of what it means to overcome? (3:21)

   Jesus Christ overcame and was thereby received by God to be seated with God on God's throne.

9. What exhortation closes all the mini-letters? (2:7, 11, 17, 29; 3:6, 13, 22)

   The closing words of each letter are "He who has an ear, let him hear what the Spirit says to the churches."

10. Who are some of the people censured? (2:2, 6, 9, 14-15, 20; 3:9, 17)

    Some of the people censured include those who call themselves apostles but are not (false apostles), the Nicolaitans, those who call themselves Jews but are not, those who hold the teaching of Balaam, Jezebel, and the rich in Laodicea.

11. What are some of the provocative images John uses to describe things Christ censures? (2:4; 3:2-4, 15, 17)

    John uses these images to describe the things Christ censures: forsaking one's first love, sleeping instead of remaining alert, soiling one's garments, being neither hot nor cold but lukewarm, and calling oneself rich and presuming to be self-sufficient.

12. The church at Laodicea is asked to do several things to be acceptable to Christ. What are these things? (3:18-19)

The Christians at Laodicea are called on to buy real gold from God in order to become rich, to wear white clothes to cover their nakedness, to put salve on their eyes so they can see, to be earnest, and to repent.

13. How is Christ described in the opening words of the seven letters? (2:1, 8, 12, 18; 3:1, 7, 14)

Christ is the one "who holds the seven stars in his right hand and walks among the seven golden lampstands." Christ is "the First and the Last, who died and came to life again." Christ has a "sharp, double-edged sword." Christ's "eyes are like blazing fire" and his feet "like burnished bronze." Christ "holds the seven spirits of God and the seven stars." Christ is the holy and true one. He "holds the key of David" and has the authority to open and shut. Christ is "the Amen, the faithful and true witness, the ruler of God's creation."

DIMENSION TWO: WHAT DOES THE BIBLE MEAN?

Seven Letters to Seven Churches: Background. Revelation 2 and 3 contain seven mini-letters to a collection of Christian churches in Asia Minor (present-day Turkey). The churches addressed in these letters formed some kind of logical network for John, but no one knows what the exact connection was. The cities are diverse and are clustered in a geographical area either on the western seacoast of Asia or in the watershed of coastal rivers linked with the Aegean Sea. At the time of Revelation they were not yet organized as a single Christian district as far as we know.

The reference in Revelation is the first knowledge we have, historically, of some of these churches (Smyrna, Pergamum, Thyatira, Sardis, and Philadelphia). Laodicea is mentioned in the Letter to the Colossians (2:1-3; 4:13, 15-16). Ephesus is one of the cities Paul visited (Acts 18:19–20:1) and is also associated in early Christian tradition with the apostle John. With such scant information available, we cannot correctly interpret the many oblique references made in these letters; but we have some clues.

While modern archaeological research is yet incomplete in some of these sites, much has already been learned. Many of these cities were enormously wealthy. Ephesus, for example, was a fabulous city at the height of the Roman Empire. Laodicea was a center of cloth and garment production and had a medical school. Pergamum was clearly the most impressive city of all, having been developed according to a master plan of great cunning. Sardis had been the center of Persian culture and political power in Asia Minor before the Romans and was a city of cultural and economic wealth. Philadelphia and Thyatira were modest cities, but both were prosperous and important in

their own way as centers of production and crafts. Smyrna was an important Roman post and a constant rival of Ephesus for importance, honor, and wealth. All these cities were diverse in population. Ephesus, Smyrna, Pergamum, Philadelphia, Thyatira, and Sardis were known centers of Roman cultic worship. Studies have also established that a significant Jewish population existed in these cities at the time Revelation was written.

These clues suggest four areas of potential conflict that may explain the tone of several of the letters.

1. Pagan worship and constant temptation to compromise Christian standards of conduct would have been everywhere. The life of some of these cities centered on the theater, the games, the cult of the Roman Empire, and the daily need to satisfy the whims of countless gods. The cults were doubtless so pervasive as to, for example, make even shopping for food a religious ordeal for the Christian. Nearly all the professions and trade guilds were based on the Roman gods. A person would have had difficulty surviving as a Christian in such a city.

2. As powerful and wealthy cities, many of these locations must have been dazzling. Surrounded by such riches, Christians would have been tempted to place the primary emphasis of their lives on accumulating a part of this wealth.

3. Both Christians and Jews suffered terribly under the Roman rule of the Hellenistic world. Many Roman citizens would have thought of Jews and Christians as being part of one and the same menace—those who refused to worship the gods.

At the time Revelation was written, Christians in all these cities were periodically in danger of losing their lives for confessing their faith and refusing to offer allegiance to Roman gods. The church in Smyrna, a few years after the writing of Revelation, produced the great martyr Polycarp. His story is the first recorded account of a Christian martyr outside the New Testament and one of the most thrilling accounts of Christian courage.

4. Sadly, another reality in many of these cities was the hostile conflict between the Christian church and the Jewish synagogue. References in some of the seven letters to Jews "who say they are Jews and are not" (2:9) may be explained by this hostility. Christians and Jews lived under periodic attacks of discrimination and abuse in these cities. Many Romans saw them as members of the same family. Indeed, some of the conflict between Christians and Jews had the earmarks of a family feud. This conflict often led to open hostility on both sides. Christians and Jews agreed, however, that the worship of pagan gods was wrong.

This survey of the seven cities, combined with the comments in the student book, will give you several points for discussing the seven letters. We can well speculate that the early Christians living in these cities were under tremendous pressure. One can imagine that sharply conflicting opinions arose about how Christians ought to respond to these pressures. ("Should we allow our son to be apprenticed to a goldsmith in a guild whose patron is a Roman god?") Tempers certainly flared, and opinions became entrenched. This period was a great test for the church.

As stands were taken and defended, we can see how one's enemies could become "wicked men" (2:2), "a synagogue of Satan" (2:9), those "who hold to the teaching of Balaam" (2:14), or "Jezebel" (2:20). If we could identify the exact nature of the disputes generating this name-calling, we might be surprised. In all likelihood the points were finely drawn. Perhaps these disputes were not at all unlike those issues that have divided the church recently. Many of the same issues were at stake, especially those concerning the degree of compromise allowable between Christian convictions and the dominant culture.

The Unity of the Church. To understand the larger scheme and this collection of mini-letters, we must look at two questions:

1. Why are these particular churches grouped together?

2. Why does John address the angel of each church rather than the church itself?

When Aleksandr Solzhenitsyn published his book *The Gulag Archipelago* (Harper & Row, 1973), the entire world was caught breathless by his searing insight into an evil system of torture and persecution within the Soviet Union. It was not simply his documented factual account of a bureaucracy of oppression that astounded us. Rather, his artistic conception of Soviet political prisons as an archipelago—a series of "islands" of mental and physical torture joined together in an identifiable mass of oppression—shocked us. He saw there a unity, a system of persecution.

Solzhenitsyn's description is really quite close to John's vision from Patmos. He sees the seven churches existing as an archipelago of spiritual concern. Like Solzhenitsyn, John's vision unites these churches and reveals to them a system of evil threatening their "crown of life" (2:10c) but not clearly perceived by them. The situation of these seven churches changes when the unity of their situation is perceived. An old trick of tyrants is to separate subjected peoples. If evil systems of oppression can be seen for what they are, much of their power is broken. Further, the unity of the church is seen in the risen Lord who "walks among the seven golden lampstands" (2:1) without ceasing.

I can find no other reason for addressing these particular seven churches. Certainly they were not yet organized under ecclesiastical government. Several cities neighboring these, which normally would have been included in a "region of churches," are not mentioned. Colosse, Troas, and Perga are examples. (Colosse was close to Laodicea; Troas and Perga figure prominently in Paul's missionary journeys.)

The second question is equally difficult: Why *angel* and not simply *church* in the first line of each mini-letter? If an archipelago of unity is created by the nurturing presence of the risen Christ, Christ must also have a means to intervene on behalf of these churches. Throughout Revelation angels carry out the will of God. Each church has its angel. Angels reprove as well as encourage. Angels destroy and angels build in Revelation. Angels are not present in these churches merely to condone and protect. They communicate the reality of the unseen world revealed in the vision portrayed by John. Angels make real the totality of Christ and his church.

Victorious Living. These letters portray a call to a life of victory. The churches are constantly reminded to remain faithful, to continue to resist evil, and to persist in endurance of the unendurable. Secular heroism is not what they are asked to follow. Rather, the courage and endurance called for are modeled on the life and example of the One who speaks "the words of him who is the First and the Last, who died and came to life again" (2:8).

Revelation makes great use of the life of Jesus of Nazareth as a living example. Constantly we find Jesus Christ in both the background and foreground of Revelation encouraging Christians who are experiencing exactly the same kind of rejection, torture, and death to which he was subject while on earth. Success under persecution, therefore, must have a longer perspective than earthly existence. The presence of angels reminds the hearers of Revelation that another dimension of existence transcends an earthly view. Death here is life "in the paradise of God" (2:7).

While this outlook on Christian existence may appear distant and strange to you, many people today can identify with it. The Book of Revelation has been brought to life again and again in those times and places where suffering for one's confession of Christ is a certainty. As you read this book, remember that somewhere today Christians are devouring Revelation's message with a hunger born of the immediacy of cruel oppression, torture, and hourly threat of death.

If Revelation seems abnormal to us, maybe what is abnormal is not the book but our easy circumstances. The irony of this condition is, of course, that Revelation seeks to demonstrate to all "who hear it and take to heart what is written in it" (1:3) that an unseen archipelago of evil threatens to destroy the testimony of Jesus Christ—even when the evil is not clearly evident.

DIMENSION THREE: WHAT DOES THE BIBLE MEAN TO ME?

The Challenge to the Seven Churches and Our Challenge

We may feel a lack of harmony with these mini-letters. They portray a lean, muscular form of Christianity that is distant from the variety practiced in many of the local churches we know best.

Is it possible to remain sharp and devoted to the call of Christ when persecution is almost unknown? Perhaps we are asking the wrong question, as many prophetic voices in our land are trying to teach us. They identify issues and concerns that are powerful and potentially dangerous for those who get involved.

We are not in such a different position from that of the time of Revelation. Difficult moral decisions face us every day. The consequences of these decisions may be of more import for the future of the world than in the time of John the prophet.

Perhaps the most helpful lesson of Revelation 2 and 3 for us is the recognition of Christ's presence in the church as we struggle with the gripping issues of our time. If so, then Christ's voice is still calling to us: Persist by patient endurance in seeking the good and in resisting evil.

The difficulty, of course, is in recognizing the good to be served and the evil to be engaged. The general tone of Revelation has a lesson for us: It is a labor worthy of the church to work and pray unceasingly to rip the mask from the face of evil.

Make a list of all the people in your community or state or region who, in living memory, have been arrested or charged because of actions motivated by religious beliefs. Include all religious groups, not just Christians. You may be amazed at the length of your list. Analyze the issues involved in the decisions these people made. Even better, interview them. At the end of this project you will have a better appreciation for the seven mini-letters of John.

Worthy is the Lamb who was slain, to receive power and wealth and wisdom and strength and honor and glory and praise! (5:12).

— 3 —

Worthy Is the Lamb

Revelation 4–5

DIMENSION ONE:
WHAT DOES THE BIBLE SAY?

Answer these questions by reading Revelation 4

1. What did John see and hear? (4:1)

   He saw an open door in heaven and heard a voice like a trumpet calling him to enter the door in heaven.

2. How did John get to heaven? (4:2)

   John was taken to heaven "in the Spirit."

3. How many thrones did John see? (4:2-4)

   John saw twenty-five thrones, one throne on which God was seated and twenty-four more thrones for the elders around the central throne of God.

4. How were the elders dressed? (4:4b)

   "They were dressed in white and had crowns of gold on their heads."

5. Who else is present at this throne scene? (4:5-7)

   The seven spirits of God and the four living creatures are also present.

6. What is the function of the twenty-four elders and the four living creatures? (4:8-11)

   They "give glory, honor and thanks" to God without ceasing.

7. What has God done to be worthy of such praise? (4:11)

   God is worthy because God created all things.

Answer these questions by reading Revelation 5

8. What did John see? (5:1-2, 6)

   John saw a scroll sealed seven times in God's right hand, a mighty angel shouting, and the Lamb of God.

9. Who is the mighty angel looking for? (5:2)

   The angel searches for someone worthy to open the seven seals on the scroll.

10. Can anyone open the seals? (5:3)

    Although several evidently try, both in heaven and on earth, all fail.

11. Who finally is found to open the seals? (5:5)

    Jesus Christ ("the Lion of the tribe of Judah, the Root of David") alone is worthy.

12. What does the Lamb do? (5:7)

    The Lamb takes the scroll from the right hand of God.

13. What happens when the Lamb takes the scroll? (5:8-9)

    The twenty-four elders and the four living creatures fall down in worship before the Lamb and begin to sing.

14. In the new song, what is it that makes the Lamb worthy to open the seals? (5:9-10)

    The Lamb has ransomed all humanity by his death and has created a new kingdom and priests to serve God and to rule the world.

15. How many angels respond in praise of the Lamb? (5:11)

"Many angels, numbering thousands upon thousands, and ten thousand times ten thousand" is the number of angels praising the Lamb—a countless number.

16. Do only the elders and angels sing praise? (5:13-14)

No, all creation, including all creatures, lift their voices to praise the Lamb and God who sits on the throne.

DIMENSION TWO:
WHAT DOES THE BIBLE MEAN?

The Book of Revelation often depends on spirits and angels of various lands. Some of the uses to which John puts these unseen beings in his book are quite unusual. We have already met "seven spirits" (3:1, 4:5) and seven angels (1:20). Revelation 4 and 5 describe the heavenly court of God and the Lamb, giving us a number of helpful insights about these beings.

In Revelation, God and Christ appear as elevated, sovereign figures. They rule and control the direction of the universe. They are concerned about the inhabitants of earth but do not deal with them directly. For example, Christ is present in the churches, but by means of his angels. In Revelation 1:20, the seven angels are symbolized by stars. In Revelation 4:5, the seven spirits are symbolized by blazing lamps. Stars and lamps are sources of light and are images for understanding or for revelation. These images make clear that Christ communicates his presence on earth through spirits and angels. *Seven* suggests the completeness of this activity.

Christ is everywhere present in his churches and elsewhere on earth. He is represented and his presence made real by means of seven spirits. The work of conversion and conviction rests in the hands of these spirits and the angels. But they do not work alone and unaided. Their means of communication is the prophets.

The Book of Revelation is the work of the risen and exalted Christ, who is worshiped with God in heaven. He has brought about this revelation by sending his Spirit to encounter the prophet John. What we see and hear in this book is "of the Spirit" and is itself a broad clue to the universal work of the seven spirits and angels at work in our midst. The source of revelation, in other words, is Jesus Christ. But this revealing Christ is also the *subject* of the Book of Revelation.

Revelation 4:4-8. We are now beginning to meet some of the many symbolic figures of Revelation. Some of these figures will have clear, precise meanings; others will not. Symbolism is complex as an art form. At times it has exact one-to-one meaning, while at other times symbolism works by means of being plastic and ambiguous. The images of the twenty-four elders and the living creatures in these verses are excellent examples of both kinds of symbolism.

The twenty-four elders are usually seen with the four living creatures and will appear again in Revelation 7:11; 14:3; and 19:4. The elders represent the redemption brought about through Christ, the Lamb who was slain. They are twenty-four because the twelve tribes of Israel made up the old covenant and twelve new tribes make up the church. Quite possibly, the new twelve are the twelve apostles of Revelation 21:14, the foundation of the new Jerusalem. We can be fairly certain about this conclusion, since John is so consciously aware of the "old-new" issue. Symbolically, then, John is saying that Christ has redeemed all history. Redemption cannot be complete unless the reality of Israel is taken into account.

The four living creatures are another matter. They have no precise equivalents in the concrete or historical reality of our existence. They are generally thought to represent creation's totality. These creatures are chosen as the strongest, swiftest, bravest, most intelligent representatives of Creation. (Christian tradition has also identified these figures as representative of the four evangelists—Matthew, Mark, Luke, and John.)

Revelation 4:11. God and Jesus Christ are called "worthy" by the massed worshipers. This verse reveals an important idea in John's theology. He believes that we can speak exactly the same way about God and about Christ because complete unity exists between them. This position is distinctive in the New Testament, characteristic only of the books associated with the name *John.* We will find later in Revelation that the key strategy of the evil forces will be to drive a wedge between God and Christ. John cleverly sees that once God and Christ are divided, the possibility of success in deceiving gullible earth dwellers is much greater.

Before the real action of the book begins, then, John is careful to make crystal clear the complete equality and unity of "the Lord God Almighty" and "the Lamb, who was slain."

Revelation 5:1-4. What is written on the scroll? The safest assumption seems to be that it contains the judgments that are about to take place. John's book is a crafted piece of biblical literature. If he had wanted to, he could easily have portrayed Jesus reading from the scroll as the judgments are pronounced. The fact is, John did not use this device, suggesting that what is written on the scroll is not at issue. Rather, the wax seals that keep the scroll from being revealed are the focus of attention.

The scroll comes from the hand of God. Perhaps we are to imagine that at some prior time God wrote on this scroll the divine design for history. Only the Lamb is able to initiate the events soon to break out. The scroll is perfectly sealed (seven seals); therefore only "perfection" can break the seals.

Revelation 5:5. While these names for Jesus ("the Lion of the tribe of Judah, the Root of David") might sound familiar, they appear nowhere else in the New Testament. Elsewhere, Jesus is "descended from Judah" (Hebrews 7:14) and the "root of Jesse" (Romans 15:12). Why does John use these names here and now? We have already seen that John finds fulfillment of promises to the twelve tribes of Israel in the redemption of Christ. These distinctive titles for Christ remind readers of Christianity's connection to Judaism. The Lamb is not only of the tribe of Judah, he is the Lion of Judah. Likewise, he is not only sprung from the root of Jesse (David's father), he is the root of Jesse and David.

These titles fix the Christ as the co-Creator of human history. Without this belief, we might assume that Jesus Christ is subordinate to the twists and turns of history. John pushes the recognition of Christ's predominance further back into history than other New Testament writers. For the prophet John, as for the author of John's Gospel, Christ existed before existence itself.

In a sense the whole of Revelation pivots on the fact that Christ "triumphed" and thus was worthy to open the seven seals. If he had not triumphed, the scroll would remain sealed.

We have already seen in the seven mini-letters a repetitive call to overcome. This call will be a constant theme in Revelation. At various times the evil forces of Satan will seek to overcome the faithful. On the other hand, the people of God will be encouraged to triumph. In Revelation 3:21, the example for the church at Laodicea is Christ's overcoming: "To him who overcomes, I will give the right to sit with me on my throne, just as I overcame and sat down with my Father on his throne."

But what has Christ done to overcome? The answer is hinted in the full title of Jesus: "the Lamb, who was slain" (5:6, 12). In death's exaltation Jesus overcame the powers of Satan. He has presented his victory to God who sits on the throne and is granted a place there with God. The fact that Jesus Christ is accepted there by the heavenly court as "worthy" means that God has judged his death victorious. For John the death of Christ is a glorious victory that must be confirmed by the heavenly court. Put another way, our salvation is based on a heavenly judgment, witnessed by countless hosts.

Revelation 5:8-10. The student book speaks of the rich liturgical heritage in Revelation. When John speaks about golden bowls of incense as the prayers of the saints, he adds immeasurably to our understanding of prayer. The use of incense as a symbol of prayer is common in the Old and New Testaments. A delightful twist is added by John. The language of the text suggests that the saints of earth, not yet present with Christ, are made present by their prayers. This idea makes prayer representational. Usually prayer is thought of as petition. But here John finds the absent saints present by anticipation through their prayers. John describes a remarkable insight—that Christians can "visit"

heaven by means of prayer. His account also implies that worship in the heavenly court would be incomplete without the prayers of the saints. How can this be?

In Revelation the heavenly court is influenced several times by the actions of the saints. John thus places great importance on what Christians do and say. His point is exactly this: In the confessions and moral actions of the faithful, the Lamb again and again conquers. His conquest of evil does not depend on the conquest of his people; but his conquest is also not complete until they, too, have triumphed. By the conquest, the Lamb created a new kingdom (5:10); and this kingdom must be filled. The kingdom is not a place; it is people.

A "new song" is being sung in heaven (5:9). The texts of the old songs are, "Holy, holy, holy / is the Lord God Almighty, / who was, and is, and is to come" (4:8); and "You are worthy, our Lord and God, / to receive glory and honor and power, / for you created all things, / and by your will they were created / and have their being" (4:11). Notice that the "old songs" are not out-of-date, old-fashioned, or null and void. Rather, they are completed.

The song to God in 4:11 speaks of creation. This creation includes the formation of a redeemed people. The redemption of Christ has created this kingdom of priests. With Christ's redemption comes the glimmer of the final victory for God's people. This victory has been established as the final outcome since before the foundations of the world.

DIMENSION THREE:
WHAT DOES THE BIBLE MEAN TO ME?

Revelation 4

Class members will be able to describe recent fantasy films and literature that include pictures of existence far more fantastic than this heavenly court scene. Or you may display newspaper or magazine pictures of creatures from these films and stories. The difference is, of course, that John's prophetic description is meant to challenge the suggestion that God is removed and indifferent. The remarkable aspect of Revelation 4 and 5 is the involvement of the Godhead with our human situation. The scene, as it is played out, sets in motion events that are intended to bring history to the conclusion intended by God from the beginning. This involvement is hardly indifference.

Again, to speak of God as *worthy* is distinctly odd. This word involves an evaluation of God. At first glance evaluating God might seem inappropriate. What right does the creation (us) have to judge whether God (the Creator) is worthy?

Revelation is very much concerned with the real world of pain, persecution, and suffering. John presents here an implicit recognition that whether it is right or not, the created order does question God's worthiness. The reader will do well to keep in mind the answer (4:11). Without it we might despair as we read on.

Revelation 5

The marvelous drama portrayed so vividly by the prophet makes us want to stand and cheer. We are often reminded by the events of the day that were we totally dependent on our human heroes, we would be in a sad condition. Revelation has a distinctive perception of Jesus Christ. He is seen on more than one occasion as a champion among the best heaven, hell, and earth can field. Jesus Christ alone survives the contest.

Perhaps we do not like Jesus to appear competitive. The inner core of truth, however, is that the creature will always try to pull down God, the Creator, from the divine place of honor. The only solution is for the co-Creator, Jesus Christ, to demonstrate that God is God and cannot be put down by angels, creatures of the nether realm, or human agents of evil.

You are worthy to take the scroll and to open its seals (5:9).

— 4 —

The Book of the Seven Seals

Revelation 6–7

DIMENSION ONE:
WHAT DOES THE BIBLE SAY?

Answer these questions by reading Revelation 6

1. What happens when the Lamb opens the first seal? (6:1-2)

   One of the four living creatures tells a white horse and its rider to "Come!"

2. What does the rider of the white horse do? (6:2)

   The rider goes out "as a conqueror bent on conquest."

3. What happens when the Lamb opens the second seal? (6:3-4a)

   A second living creature tells a red horse and its rider to "Come!"

4. What happens to the rider of the red horse? (6:4bc)

   God permits the rider "to take peace from the earth," causing violent conflict symbolized by a "large sword."

5. What happens when the Lamb opens the third seal? (6:5)

   A third living creature tells a black horse and its rider to "Come!"

6. What does the rider of the black horse do? (6:6)

   He weighs out grain at greatly inflated prices, symbolizing scarcity of food.

7. What happens when the Lamb opens the fourth seal? (6:7-8a)

   A fourth living creature tells a pale horse and its rider to "Come!"

8. What does the rider of the pale horse do? (6:8bc)

   He (Death) and Hades are "given power over a fourth of the earth to kill."

9. What did John see when the fifth seal was opened? (6:9-11)

   He saw the martyrs being comforted.

10. What happened when the sixth seal was opened? (6:12-17)

    There was an earthquake, and all the people hid from "the wrath of the Lamb."

Answer these questions by reading Revelation 7

11. What happens at the opening of Chapter 7? (7:1)

    An interlude is created by four angels holding the wind from all points of the compass, thus causing a great calm.

12. What takes place in the next scene? (7:2-3)

    A fifth angel brings a seal and, with the help of the other four angels, places a mark on the forehead of God's servants still on earth.

13. How many of God's servants are sealed, and how is the number determined? (7:4-8)

    Twelve thousand from each of the tribes of Israel are sealed, making a total of 144,000.

14. Where does the next scene take place? (7:9)

    The next scene takes us back to the heavenly court, standing before the throne of God and in front of the Lamb.

15. Who is present that we have not seen before? (7:9)

A multitude of human beings who have come from all parts and cultures of the globe are standing before the throne.

16. How did this group get to heaven? (7:13-14)

They "have come out of the great tribulation" to get to heaven.

17. What is given to this great multitude? (7:15-17)

They are granted satisfaction of all their needs, the task of serving God in the heavenly precincts, the Lamb for their shepherd, the springs of living water to drink, and consolation of all their sorrows.

DIMENSION TWO: WHAT DOES THE BIBLE MEAN?

The Structure of Revelation. With the opening of the seven seals, we confront the issue of the literary structure of Revelation. Since the time of the earliest theologians, this issue has been argued in and has even divided local churches.

The Book of Revelation is not nearly as complex as is the history of its interpretation. Those who have carefully studied the history of Revelation's interpretation have learned to concentrate on the value of Revelation's ideas rather than on its structure. The lives of many people have been severely damaged by means of misguided and compulsive dissection of Revelation. Much of this search was for the hidden "key" of Revelation that would unlock the secrets of the future of the nations.

Revelation 6 and 7 give an excellent example of the structural issues in Revelation. We begin with an orderly opening of the seals. But soon interruptions occur. The description of the martyrs at the foot of the heavenly altar (6:9-11) interrupts the opening of the fifth seal. The interlude created by the scene of the 144,000 being sealed (7:1-8) and the description of the multitude in white robes (7:9-17) break the pattern of the sixth (6:12-17) and seventh seals (8:1).

These events are just the beginning of "broken patterns." The seventh seal is described in Revelation 8 and 9. Within the action of the seventh seal, the seven trumpets appear.

Consistent with a pattern of interruptions, Revelation 10:1-11 concerns fresh subjects. Another clear break in Revelation's development occurs in 12:1, which announces the woman clothed with the sun. While all the seals have been broken and all the trumpets sounded by the time we come to 12:1, we find similar material again in Revelation 15:1–19:10. In these chapters we meet seven angels with seven bowls, all of which create more havoc and destruction, punctuated by scenes of heavenly worship.

This collapsing of time—past, present, and future—does not seem to bother John, nor should it bother us. God has saved his people in the past, saves them in the present, and will save them in the future. This central, evangelical message of salvation is bound to be overlooked if we begin to be preoccupied with where the great tribulation is located with reference to the millennium as it relates to the Last Judgment. In the end these efforts serve only to classify and divide people one from the other, an outcome contrary to the central message of Revelation. That central message is this: Christ is working out the creation of the one people of God, a priestly nation of all peoples of the world, who will join together with the entire created order in the joyful service of the praise of God.

Revelation 6:1-8. John prepared us well in Chapters 4 and 5 for this scene. When we left the heavenly court, the Lamb was holding the sealed scroll. He was surrounded by myriads of angels, the four living creatures, and the twenty-four elders. All these personalities will have distinct roles to play in the events that follow.

When John was spiritually transported to the open door of heaven, a voice invited him to "Come" (4:1). The action following the breaking of the first four seals will be initiated in the same way. Voices (this time like thunder, not like a trumpet) summon each of the four horses and its rider with the powerful, bold command "Come!"

The First Seal: The White Horse and Rider (6:1-2). This description is not completely parallel with the three that follow. The rider is armed with a bow, an instrument of war; but no specific destruction is described. The action this rider takes is general: He conquers. We learned in the previous chapter that *overcoming* is what Jesus as the Lamb has done. Because the Lamb opens the seals, it is unlikely that we are to take the rider of the white horse for Christ. Rather, this rider probably conquers for Christ. The image is military. A reader in the ancient Roman world would understand this figure to symbolize a victorious warrior.

The Second Seal: The Red Horse and Rider (6:3-4). We are not to think that these figures of destruction disturb God's role as Ruler of history. The second horse and rider are given temporary permission by God to keep the peacemaking efforts of nations from succeeding. The peace created by earthly leaders is seen as a frail peace in Revelation. Political peace is unreliable and can easily lead to war. This idea, also firmly entrenched in the Old Testament prophets, is presented with startling boldness here. The horse and rider do not need to incite war. Peace is broken when the hand of God is withheld. This rider's task is a chilling reminder that all peace comes from God, even the fragile peace of human design. We would be wrong to conclude that it is useless for human beings to try to "make peace." Rather, the witness here is to the Source of all peace.

The Third Seal: The Black Horse and Rider (6:5-6). The conditions of famine following the trail of the horse and rider are grotesque. A day's wage (one denarius) will buy only enough grain to permit a scant measure for a small family. We are not told what causes this scarcity, but events in our world today give us insight into the causes of hunger: political chaos and injustice, war, a breakdown in trade, hoarding, and drought. We are to use our imaginations, which is not difficult in an era when millions starve for all the above reasons in every part of the globe.

The Fourth Seal: The Pale Horse and Rider (6:7-8). The worst is saved until the last. This horse is pictured with a rider and one who follows him: Death and Hades. The color pale might better be translated "sickly green," the color of death. Why Death and Hades? Hades is the place of death. One could just as well say "double death" or "death with a vengeance." The death brought by this ghastly pair is caused by armed violence, famine, and plague (disease). Finally, even nature turns on humanity when animals maul and kill people.

The devices of narration are worth following carefully. John's account is peppered with "I heard" or "I looked." He weeps. He counts. He agonizes. He converses with the actors in his vision.

Revelation 6:9-11. *The Fifth Seal.* What causes this violence? Why has God permitted such destruction? Revelation lives and breathes in an atmosphere unlike the rest of the New Testament. In the Gospels, Jesus enters Jerusalem on a donkey, a sign of his peaceful kingdom. Here, he sends out warriors mounted on steeds of war. John and his churches lived in a violent world. Rome was constantly making war on the church. Under this seal, the fifth, we will see that those who have been killed by the sword of Rome cry for vengeance from God for the blood of the Christian martyrs (6:10).

This entire chapter is an example of realism. The world exists by violence. As tragic as this is, it is true. The violence of the world spills over to crush the lives of good people.

The Gospels and the Book of Revelation argue that injustice will not forever go unpunished. The Bible is clear, however, that justice must be left to God. The careful reader will observe that in Revelation the saints who suffer on earth conquer by their faithful witness, not by the sword. The irony of violence in Revelation is that the saints are nonviolent.

The saints who have been martyred for their witness to Christ dwell under God's altar. With this detail a new piece of equipment is added to the vision of the heavenly court. The altar of God is the place of prayer. The saints are there because their lives of sacrifice are a heavenly imitation of Christ's supreme sacrifice. Their blood cries out for the complete ingathering of all God's people to be with Christ.

This passage gives hope to those who in John's time must yet die a martyr's death. Christ has already said to those in Smyrna, "Be faithful, even to the point of death" (2:10c). This passage has continued to give great comfort to the millions of Christians who have lived in daily fear for their lives through the centuries. Revelation 6:9-11 is one of the few places in the Bible that provides a sustaining image for those who must die by reason of their Christian confession.

Revelation 6:12-17. *The Sixth Seal.* The dangers lurking behind the sixth seal would have been especially believable to John's readers. Some of the cities he was addressing had been destroyed by massive earthquakes, and the people of the geographical area lived in constant fear of them. The heavens were studied intensely, not only by navigators and scientists but also by religionists. Many of the cults that form the background to John's warnings about "Satan's so-called deep secrets" (2:24) were based on astrology. All these factors make John's writings quite believable. When stars fall from the sky like figs from a tree, when the moon turns blood red and the sun is eclipsed, then the entire basis for finding security in the universe will vanish.

Revelation 7:1-8. John's appreciation for the place of the twelve tribes in the restoration of God's people is taken directly from Ezekiel 48. The idea of sealing the forehead is also from Ezekiel (Chapter 9). In the Ezekiel story the seal is to protect the righteous from the approaching slaughter. The purpose in Revelation is unclear and seems simply to be a matter of identifying the "servants of our God." We are reminded of the promise to the Philadelphians: "I will write on him the name of my God" (Revelation 3:12c).

The tribe of Dan is missing from this list. This omission is due to an obscure tradition that the antichrist of Revelation was to come from the tribe of Dan. (The list in Ezekiel 48 begins with Dan.)

Revelation 7:9-17. This entire section anticipates the final victory of the Lamb and the restoration of heaven and earth. Gradually John builds a more and more complete picture of the heavenly precincts. At first we know only of the throne of God (4:2-3). Then we have an altar introduced (6:9). Now we learn of a temple (7:15). We need not be troubled that in the new Jerusalem there is no temple "because the Lord God Almighty and the Lamb are its temple" (21:22). John is speaking in artistic images. A further example of this ambiguity is that the Lamb is also a shepherd (7:17). These beautiful word pictures of theological truth should not be damaged by overly zealous scrutiny. Enjoy them for the access they provide us.

The worship of God's court has become more elaborate (7:12). The list of divine attributes is now quite long. Ascribed to God are praise, glory, wisdom, thanks, honor, power, and strength. By no accident does the prophet John include seven attributes in this list.

As we will learn, the saints who suffer tribulation on earth can conquer only by their testimony. A synonym for bearing witness is to praise God. A particular kind of biblical theology is implicit in the seemingly simple idea of the righteous conquering by their testimony. This understanding of "how life works" is often at the root of Jesus' teaching. This understanding of life can lead to a remarkable sense of relief and liberation. In fact, it is quite possible that this understanding is the basic purpose of John's prophecy.

The idea is that the key to living and acting correctly is to recognize the truth of creation. God is ruler of all that exists because all existence was caused by God, who sustains all that is and directs all that will be. Humans are a part of that creation.

When humans attempt to act powerfully, they usurp the place of God. This act is idolatry. To live in harmony with the rest of the created order and with God requires the human creature to ascribe all power and glory to God, by word and by deed. When this is done, all other power finds its rightful perspective. In this perspective all other power but God's is powerless. Therefore the best way to defeat the power of evil is to bear witness to the only power of consequence—that of God the Creator. When we witness to God's power, a true sense of power is shared with the human confessor. In this way the righteous conquer by testimony.

DIMENSION THREE: WHAT DOES THE BIBLE MEAN TO ME?

Suffering for Christ is a dangerous idea. We know from the biographical and clinical studies of some modern martyrs that death was the compulsive choice of the person, not the glorious result of a heroic life. Every movement has those persons who become attached to it who do not truly care for the cause or values of the movement but only seek a reasonable excuse for a meaningful death. At times it would seem that the world is filled with sick minds who are desperately seeking to find a cross upon which they might hang in public view. We must, therefore, be extremely cautious when speaking favorably about the glory of suffering for Christ.

Yet this misuse of Christian suffering must not allow us to neglect careful attention to the thousands of modern saints whose lives are well worthy of reflection and imitation. Encourage class members to list the names of persons who fit this description. You may want to do it by looking first at well-known, international figures such as Father Damien, Mother Teresa, and others; moving next to persons such as Martin Luther King, Jr.; then to those saints class members know personally. All these people live selflessly in seeking to witness to justice; to make life better for others; and to relieve the suffering of those who are ill, homeless, in prison, or outcast.

5

The Seven Trumpets

Revelation 8–9

DIMENSION ONE:
WHAT DOES THE BIBLE SAY?

Answer these questions by reading Revelation 8

1. What takes place when the seventh seal is opened? (8:1)

   "When he [the Lamb] opened the seventh seal, there was silence in heaven for about half an hour."

2. What happens immediately after the silence? (8:2)

   Seven trumpets are given to the seven angels.

3. What two objects does the other angel have? (8:3)

   The angel has a golden censer and is given incense to burn in the censer.

4. What rises and mingles with the smoke of the censer? (8:4)

   The prayers of the saints rise and mingle with the smoke of the censer.

5. What happens when the angel takes fire from the altar and throws it on the earth? (8:5)

   The fire creates a display of thunder, lightning, loud noises, and an earthquake.

6. What is the next series of seven to be introduced? (8:6)

   The seven angels who will blow seven trumpets are introduced next.

7. What happens following the blowing of the first trumpet? (8:7)

   Hail and fire, mixed with blood, fall on the earth, destroying one third of the plants of the earth.

8. What happens when the second trumpet is blown? (8:8-9)

   A great mountain of fire falls into the sea, destroying one third of the life in and on the sea.

9. What happens when the third trumpet is sounded? (8:10-11)

   A falling star named "Wormwood" turns one third of all fresh water bitter, causing human death.

10. What happens when the angel blows the fourth trumpet? (8:12)

    The sun, moon, and stars lose one third of their light, changing greatly the nature of day and night.

11. Does the action of trumpet blowing continue? (8:13)

    No. A brief interlude takes place in which an eagle announces that the next three trumpets will unleash more devastation for humans.

Answer these questions by reading Revelation 9

12. The sounding of the fifth trumpet sets in motion what event? (9:1-3)

    The Abyss is opened, allowing locusts with "power like that of scorpions" to emerge.

13. How are these creatures limited in their torture? (9:4-5a)

    They cannot harm the vegetation, nor those with the seal of God. They cannot kill, but they can torture. The torture can last only five months.

14. How is their terrible work described? (9:5b-6)

The locusts' torture is "like that of the sting of a scorpion." People seek to die but can only suffer.

15. How would you describe these creatures? (9:7-10)

They are fantastic creatures bearing no resemblance to any known reality. They look like horses with human faces, woman's hair, lion's teeth, "breastplates like breastplates of iron," and "tails and stings like scorpions."

16. Who is their king? (9:11)

Their king is an evil angel who up until now has been dwelling in the Abyss under lock and key. His name is Abaddon (Hebrew), or Apollyon (Greek).

17. How else are the last three trumpets described? (9:12)

They are called "woes."

18. What other group of numbers is introduced when the sixth trumpet is blown? (9:13-14)

A voice from the horns on God's altar calls to the sixth angel with the trumpet, commanding that the four destroying angels of the Euphrates be released.

19. What do these destroying angels do? (9:15)

They make war and kill one third of humankind.

20. What are the troops of these angels like? (9:16-19)

Hordes of the troops appear ("two hundred million"). Their appearance is fantastic, not unlike the "locusts" described in 9:7-10.

21. What is the effect of these woes or plagues on those who are not killed? (9:20-21)

Remarkably enough, the woes do not cause them to repent of their sins—idolatry, murder, sorcery, sexual immorality, and theft.

DIMENSION TWO:
WHAT DOES THE BIBLE MEAN?

Revelation 8:1-5. References to time are frequent in Revelation. Here silence is maintained "for about half an hour." Does this half hour symbolize a definite number of days, weeks, months, or even centuries? The same question may be asked of the "five months" (9:10). In both cases it is logical to assume that the prophet John did have some actual, temporal equivalent in mind. But what this time period might be is a mystery that died with the prophet. "Half an hour" probably means a short but discernible period.

The vision of John progressively fills out the picture of the heavenly precincts. The picture will continue to be drawn right to the end of the book, in Chapter 21, where we get the most elaborate picture of the new heaven and new earth joined as one in the new Jerusalem. Here we learn that the altar (8:3, 5) is something like the altar of burnt offering, associated with the Temple in Jerusalem. One of the most detailed descriptions of the Temple altar is found in Ezekiel 43:13-17. Historians have often depended on this description to reconstruct what the huge sacrificial altar may have been like. Ezekiel clearly describes "horns" on each of the corners of the altar (43:15). These were projections of the stonework. The four corners are important because they form a kind of divine lightning rod between earth and heaven. The blood of sacrifice was sprinkled on these corners (horns) to consecrate the entire altar prior to burning offerings. At the blowing of the sixth trumpet, a voice speaks from each of these corners of God's altar (Revelation 9:13).

Revelation 8:6-12. The destruction described at the blowing of the first four trumpets echoes the account of Creation in Genesis 1.

The destruction of vegetation of the first trumpet recalls the creation of the third day (Genesis 1:9-12) in which the land, the sea, and all vegetation were created. The destruction of the second and third trumpets (when sea and fresh water are contaminated) recalls the creation of the fifth day in which life associated with water was created (Genesis 1:20-22). Finally, the darkening of sun, moon, and stars announced by the fourth trumpet recalls the creation of the first day—day and night and the light to govern both (Genesis 1:3-5a).

The implication of this literary technique is that if God can create the world, God can also destroy it. Here the final destruction is hinted at by limiting it to "a third." But if creation is partially destroyed here, it is restored and made new at the conclusion of Revelation. God is never portrayed in the Bible as only a God of destruction.

Several details concerning the description of these various destructions require some explanation:

First Trumpet (8:7). Destruction by hail is an echo of the seventh plague brought upon Egypt through Moses (Exodus 9:22-26). The description in Exodus also mixes hail with fire. Perhaps this description is of a massive thunderstorm complete with lightning and hail.

Second Trumpet (8:8-9). The phrase "something like a huge mountain, all ablaze" is unclear and reminds us that John is reporting a vision. He is often at a loss to find adequate comparisons from his own experience. The description here probably means a monumental molten object that destroys the water of one third of the seas.

The precise point of "turned into blood" also is unclear. Maybe the color of the sea changed to red. Or perhaps the sea became "red hot." This heating of the water would explain why ships on the sea were destroyed, along with the sea life.

Third Trumpet (8:10-11). The great star falling from heaven is an evil angel, as in 9:1. "Wormwood" is the name of this angel. Revelation frequently makes destruction personal, and this is an example. Wormwood is mentioned elsewhere in the Bible (Proverbs 5:4; Jeremiah 9:15; Amos 5:7) and is a known plant in Palestine. Wormwood will turn water bitter, if not actually poisonous.

Fourth Trumpet (8:12). To be precise, it should be noted that the lights of day and night did not shine for one third of the normal time. It does not mean that they shone one-third less brightly.

Notice that the result of the seven bowls of wrath poured out in Revelation 16 is, in part, quite similar to the destruction of the first four trumpets.

Revelation 8:13. The narrative is interrupted at 8:13 to help the reader understand that the first four trumpets are of one kind of destruction and the next three will be of a quite different kind.

Eagles figure prominently in both Ezekiel and Revelation. Recall the four living creatures described in Revelation 4:6b-8, one of which is "like a flying eagle." Ezekiel 17 is an extensive prophetic parable about "a great eagle." (Your preparation for teaching this lesson would be enhanced by reading Ezekiel 17.)

The repetition of warning ("Woe! Woe! Woe") is not simply for emphasis. The next three trumpets are all called "woes" (9:12; 11:14). The prophet keeps count of the woes, possibly because of the break between the second and third woes in Revelation 10–11. (The first, second, and third woes are equivalent to the fifth, sixth, and seventh trumpets.)

Revelation 9:1-11. *The Fifth Trumpet.* The narrative depends on two ideas described more fully elsewhere in Revelation: (1) an angel opening the Abyss is more explicitly and graphically described in Revelation 20:1-3, and (2) the people of God who are not to be harmed have already been introduced in Revelation 7:1-8. This hole may be the same as hell and is conceived of as a place of chaotic evil that is contained by a lid over it under lock and key.

The description of the locusts (demonic beings) does not mean to suggest they look like any particular known animal. These creatures sting like scorpions; are as big as horses; have long, wavy hair and long, sharp teeth; and are frightfully noisy. The comparison with locusts may have any or all of these points: They move as on wings, they devour at an incredible rate, they move in swarms, and have many legs and/or wings. (The Middle Eastern species of locusts have six legs and four wings.) We need only recall numerous descriptions given by primitive people of their first experience of an airplane or train to realize how difficult and dangerous it is to make too much out of the details of the description.

The five months is a mystery (9:5, 10). It certainly means a period of considerable length. The visitation is not momentary. In this sense these demonic creatures are not like locusts, which come and go swiftly.

Revelation 9:13-19. *The Sixth Trumpet.* The language of 9:14 might easily be confused. Four angels have not been bound or restrained at the river Euphrates. Rather, as in the case of the four winds being personalized as four angels in Revelation 7:1, the four angels are restraining the cavalry. This is expressed in a kind of shorthand. Revelation 9:15 suggests that these two hundred million (ten thousand times ten thousand times two) cavalry troops are under the control of these four angels. The number is not meant to be taken literally but to convey the sense of an army larger than any before seen.

The command from the four corners of the altar is evidently what determines the number of angel-commanders, but the number could also be explained as representing the four points of the compass.

The "three plagues" (9:18) are a bit difficult to make out. There do not appear to be three different destructions described but, rather, one great machine of death. The three plagues probably refer to the "fire, smoke and sulfur that came out of their mouths."

John gives a fantastic description of the chaos and death created by marauding troops. The result is clear ("a third of mankind" is killed), but the means is not. Because the territory beyond the Euphrates held the dreaded enemies both of Israel and Rome, we are encouraged to conclude that this description is of especially frightening, bloodthirsty human troops. On the other hand, the description, especially of the horses (9:17-19), recalls and echoes that of the demonic locusts of the fifth trumpet (9:7-10).

Revelation 9:20-21. The sin of idolatry is on the mind of John and is described here in much greater detail than the other sins. This sin is also reflected in the seven "mini-letters" to the Asian churches (Chapters 2 and 3). We know from history and archaeology that the worship of many gods was a major preoccupation of the Roman world. The description given here of idolatry, however, has a genuine flavor of the Old Testament (Psalms 115:4-7; 135:15-17).

The word translated "sexual immorality" probably is meant to cover a range of sexual practices prohibited to Christians. This area of concern is related to idolatry, since many of the Roman cults were based on practices and beliefs of a sexual nature.

A wide range of practices are grouped under the sin of "magic arts." The Greek word used means "poison," in the sense of "magic potion." The use of magic is, therefore, virtually the same as idolatry.

DIMENSION THREE:
WHAT DOES THE BIBLE MEAN TO ME?

The student book suggests that you center your reflection and discussion on the portrayal of God's judgment in Revelation. Adopting the generalization that Revelation is distinctive in its view of God and of the judgment that God brings on the world is easy. Revelation is the only book of its kind in the New Testament. However, each of the Synoptic Gospels (Matthew, Mark, and Luke) contains at least one chapter called "the little apocalypse," a chapter that contains material similar (and even at times identical) to that in Revelation. (Read Matthew 24; Mark 13; and Luke 21.)

The God of Revelation is not vindictive or cruel. Rather, Revelation is different from other parts of the New Testament because it portrays, in detail, the nature of God's justice when it confronts unrepentant evil. In Revelation, God does freely grant grace to those who repent of evil. The truth of this good news is seen in the constant references to "the saints" who are redeemed by the blood of the Lamb. These two chapters of Revelation (8 and 9) have none of this grace to balance a sickening portrayal of the partial destruction of creation. If the class members' discussion leads to comments about the shock of finding God to be this kind of God, you may want to discuss this information.

Mature faith is required to accept a God of both grace and judgment. The current impression of God in our culture does not admit of much judgment by God of unrepentant sins. Of course, we must be careful how we ourselves charge others with sin. Such an activity is always dangerous and may end up with our charges of sin being the real sin. In Revelation 9:20-21, the prophet John bases the judgment he has just witnessed squarely on laws taken from the Ten Commandments. Therefore his judgment of sin is based solidly on the witness of Scripture. Further, he has been a witness to these things and is not basing his conclusions on hearsay or rumor.

The student book also suggests using the collective imagination of class members in re-creating inventions and events, both of human origin and of nature, that are like the partial destructions narrated in these two chapters. You may be amazed at how many of these you will discover. (The list may include the "El Niño" phenomenon, the phenomena of acid rain and destruction of the ozone layer, biological warfare, cluster bombs and napalm, and so on.)

Since the writing of Revelation, entire populations have been injured or maimed both by events in nature and at the hands of humans. At times this destruction has exceeded Revelation's "a third" of the population. Both political cruelty and famine caused by drought have, in our times, created conditions far worse than some of those described in these two chapters of Revelation. How are we to view these things? Are they the result of God's judgment? Or, are they more the evidence of exactly the same sins spoken of in Revelation 9:20-21—theft, immorality, murder, and idolatry?

The student book also raises the possibility of identifying "locked lids over hell." A good example might be nuclear instruments of war. Have we left the lid off an Abyss of pain and suffering by permitting our nation to arm itself with nuclear weapons? This issue seems a perfect one to illustrate the relevance of the concept as well as the description of the possible result.

6

A Scroll Both Bitter and Sweet

Revelation 10–11

DIMENSION ONE:
WHAT DOES THE BIBLE SAY?

Answer these questions by reading Revelation 10

1. How is the "mighty angel" of John's vision described? (10:1)

   The angel is "robed in a cloud," has a rainbow above his head, has a face glowing like the sun, and has legs "like fiery pillars."

2. What is the angel holding? (10:2a)

   He has an open scroll in his hand.

3. Where is the angel standing? (10:2b)

   He stands spanning earth and sea, with one foot on each place.

4. After John hears the seven thunders, he is told by another voice not to do what? (10:4).

   He is told not to write down what he has heard the thunders say.

5. What has the "mighty angel" come to do in John's presence? (10:5-6)

   The angel takes a vow that what he says is true. "There will be no more delay!"

6. What will happen, according to this angel, when the seventh trumpet is sounded? (10:7)

   "The mystery of God will be accomplished."

7. What is John instructed to do with the scroll? (10:9)

   He is told to take the scroll from the angel and to eat the scroll.

8. What happens when John eats the scroll? (10:10)

   John discovers that the scroll is sweet to eat but bitter to digest.

9. What is John told this action means? (10:11)

   John must again prophesy concerning many peoples and their leaders.

Answer these questions by reading Revelation 11

10. What is John told to do in this vision? (11:1)

    Using a measuring device, he is to measure "the temple of God."

11. How long will "the Gentiles" be permitted to "trample on the holy city" (Jerusalem)? (11:2)

    They will have "forty-two months" there.

12. Who is given "power . . . [to] prophesy" for 1,260 days in sackcloth? (11:3)

    "My two witnesses" are given the power to prophesy.

13. How else are these two witnesses described? (11:4, 10)

    They are also called (a) "the two olive trees," (b) "the two lampstands," and (c) the "two prophets."

14. What kinds of things are the witnesses given power to do? (11:5-6)

    They can defend themselves from harm by a consuming fire that issues from their mouth; they can cause rain to cease, creating droughts; and they can cause plagues of whatever kind they choose.

15. What happens when their testimony is finished? (11:7-8)

They are killed by the beast from the Abyss, and their bodies are cast into the streets of Jerusalem.

16. What happens to their bodies? (11:9-10)

For "three and a half days" they are exposed to the taunts of rejoicing and the observation of the people.

17. What happens later to the bodies of the two prophets? (11:11-12)

The prophets are raised from the dead by the breath of God and are called to heaven.

18. What follows this remarkable event? (11:13)

A great earthquake destroys a tenth of the city of Jerusalem and its people.

19. Are the people of earth affected by the blowing of the seventh trumpet? (11:15-19)

There is no immediate impact on earth; the scene concerns events in heaven.

20. What do the elders thank God for in their hymn of praise? (11:17-18)

They thank God (a) for taking power and beginning to reign, (b) for rewarding the prophets, and (c) for destroying those who destroy God's creation.

21. What new object in the heavenly precincts is introduced? (11:19)

John sees the ark of the covenant.

DIMENSION TWO: WHAT DOES THE BIBLE MEAN?

Revelation 10:2a, 8-11. The action of this chapter centers on the small, open scroll. This scroll appears first in the hand of a "mighty angel" and then is eaten by the prophet John. The entire scene is parallel with that of Revelation 5, in which another "mighty angel" introduces the sealed scroll.

While the little scroll scene of Chapter 10 occurs about midpoint in Revelation, it has the character of an initial vision in which the prophet receives his call and is charged with his task. Such a vision is seen in Ezekiel 2:8–3:3, where a similar event takes place. But there are significant, probably intentional, differences. Ezekiel is not sent to speak to foreign people but only to the house of Israel (Ezekiel 3:5).

The rebellious nature of his own people makes Ezekiel's task so bitter. In the case of John the bitterness is in the task of speaking his prophecy to "many peoples, nations, languages and kings" (10:11). One of these nations—Rome—is killing God's people, both Jews and Christians, by the thousands.

Conveying a message by means of making the prophet act it out is typical of the prophetic tradition. Such events are sometimes called sign-acts because the prophet symbolizes a message by acting out a scene. In this rather strange street theater, God is the divine playwright and director. The prophet is a one-person repertory company.

Jeremiah and Ezekiel were often called to act out signs of prophecy. Perhaps the best known is Jeremiah's construction and wearing of a yoke to symbolize the desire of the Lord that Judah submit to the will of Babylonia and its king, Nebuchadnezzar. (Read Jeremiah 27.)

Prophets are considered by most to be divine fools. In the ancient world the link between such bizarre behavior and holiness was more obvious than it is for us. An honored place in Scripture is kept for those who are willing to appear as fools in the course of being obedient to a divine mandate.

Revelation 10:3-7. The student book suggests that the "seven thunders" is a kind of polite and poetic way of speaking about God. This image for God's voice is frequent in Scripture (Deuteronomy 5:22; Psalm 29:3-9), sometimes quite literally suggesting that thunder is God speaking (John 12:28-29).

Verse 4 is potentially confusing. Since we have already seen a sealed scroll (5:1), the casual reader might assume that the angel is being commanded to seal up the open scroll. This is not the case. The order to "seal up" means "do not write," as the rest of the sentence makes the point. Scholars have puzzled for centuries over this order. I can find two logical reasons, in addition to those suggested in the student book, for the prophet not being permitted to write what God had spoken:

1. In contrast with reports of the Old Testament prophets, Revelation never portrays God as speaking directly with humans. On many occasions a voice or voices "from heaven" speak. But the words of these voices represent a general heavenly mandate. Because Revelation is seriously concerned about the contamination of idolatrous Roman cults (9:20), it is not surprising that John would be reluctant to describe a humanlike God who can be easily contained by a literal quotation. The God of Revelation must remain sovereign in every sense.

2. The bulk of Revelation 12, 13, and 14 likely is meant to convey by means of narrative action the content of the little scroll. Therefore, in the drama of this narrative, it is better to have the prophet wait and witness the content firsthand than to write it down now. This, of course, lends a kind of urgency and drama to the action.

We have no other example in Scripture of an angel swearing an oath. The Old Testament presents a great deal of vow- and oath-swearing; the New Testament tells of much less. Jesus prohibits swearing at all in Matthew 5:33-37, a passage without parallel in the other Gospels. If John knows of this prohibition, it does not seem to bother him here. The swearing is for effect and lends itself, with several other devices of this chapter, to creating a sense of the moment. Something serious is about to take place! Taking an oath and raising one's hand are virtually synonymous (Daniel 12:7).

The content of the oath is that there will be no more delay. What will not be delayed is further defined only as "the mystery of God" (10:7). While mysteries and secrets figure highly in Revelation, the use here is singular and quite unique. We are reminded that Jesus told his disciples that they had been entrusted with the secret (mystery) of the kingdom of God (Mark 4:10-12). The key word, both in Mark and in Revelation 10:7, is the Greek word *musterion*, often translated "secret" but here correctly translated by the New International Version as "mystery."

In the rest of the New Testament, Christ is God's mystery personified (Colossians 2:2). We could well capture the meaning here into a paraphrase: "The kingdom of Christ in all its fullness will not be delayed." This is the essence of the message given by the "mighty angel." This interpretation is strengthened when one recognizes that the term *delay* is a technical one in the Gospels and is always connected with the return of Christ in power. Christians are constantly warned not to grow lax during the delay of Christ's coming.

Notice, too, how this mystery is characterized. God has consistently announced through the ages that the mystery of God's kingdom will be fulfilled. The history of the prophets is the history of God's mystery of salvation. An exciting moment has come for the prophet John, for soon he will witness personally the drama of this mystery unfolding with the sights and sounds of heaven.

Revelation 10:8-11. Why does this story about the prophet's call come here, rather than earlier? In part the answer is clear only when Revelation 10 and 11 are viewed together. As we will see, the drama of the two martyred prophets in Revelation 11:1-13 is a kind of synopsis of prophet ministry from Moses until the time of John, the prophet of Patmos. This perspective from Revelation 11:1-13 causes us to pause to recognize the role of prophecy suggested by Revelation.

The fundamental role of the prophet is to give guidance to the people of God. Also, prophecy is most at home in oral discourse. The immediacy of speech in a particular situation with a particular people makes prophecy what it is. The oral nature of prophecy is why the concept of testimony and witness is so crucial to the thought of Revelation (11:3, 7). Testimony is confession with the tongue; martyrdom is confession with one's life. The prophet testifies because Jesus testified. Both bear witness to the truth of God. But Revelation goes even further. Testimony is possible for the prophet because it is participation in "the testimony of Jesus" (1:2).

We have seen consistently that John's remarkable auditory and visual experience is not for his private benefit or enjoyment. Prophecy is intended to help people understand God's will for the present. When the message is announced, however, it is often misunderstood. Even when the message is understood, it is usually rejected by the majority of those for whom it is intended. Again and again, from Moses to John, the prophets were rejected, beaten, punished, exiled, and ridiculed. The work of the prophet has a bitter core to it. No wonder prophets of the Old Testament consistently resisted their vocation!

Revelation's viewpoint is that just as Jesus remained faithful and triumphed by his testimony to the truth, so also the prophets can remain faithful and triumph if they, too, testify in a way consistent with the witness of Jesus Christ. The Greek word for "testimony" is *marturia*; the word for "martyr" is *martus*. This obvious, intimate connection makes the point of Revelation eloquently. The final testimony of Jesus was surrendering to a martyr's death. The final witness of the representative two prophets in Revelation 11:1-13 is martyrdom in the same city "where also their Lord was crucified" (11:8).

We have already seen the high honor given the masses of martyrs in Revelation (6:9-11). How does this help the Christians of the Asian churches who are suffering daily and expecting their own death? Indeed, how does it help today's Christians who are in the same circumstance? Revelation gives an answer. This answer is not limited to the hope that the day of final judgment will no longer be delayed—although this is certainly basic to the apocalyptic viewpoint of Revelation. Much of Revelation is concerned with how Christians "overcome"—are victorious in their persistence and faithfulness in the interim—before the final judgment of God. The answer to victorious survival is to live the life of "the testimony of Jesus" and his prophets of all ages.

Eating the scroll is an image for internalizing the good news of Christ and his kingdom. Taking in the good news is prior to speaking ("You must prophesy again" [10:11].).

What is it that is spoken? Above all, this is modeled in the many scenes of worship around God's throne. Christians survive by the praise of God in liturgy, music, prayer, and testimony. (The vision that generated the Book of Revelation came to John while he was in the Spirit on the Lord's day [1:10].)

No other New Testament book provides such a remarkable rationale for the necessity of well-ordered worship. Liturgy, in the eyes of Revelation, is necessary for Christian survival. Countless case studies in church history uphold this conviction. For instance, Sunday morning worship has kept alive the aspirations and courage of the black community in the United States and in South Africa. Only those Christians who have not lived under inhuman conditions might not understand this biblical principle.

There is more. Since the entire Book of Revelation is John's vision of the testimony of Jesus, we must not miss the forest for the trees. The circumstance of the first readers of Revelation was one of powerful, destructive political forces at work in the Roman Empire of the first century. We may be tempted to accept the categories of earthly powers in the attempt to understand our circumstances. Revelation will not let us do this. This vision invites hearers to engage other more powerful but unseen realities in assessing their circumstances.

The powerful images of Revelation are an invitation to Christians to use their imagination—sanctified by the concept of the "Sovereign Lord, holy and true" (6:10)—in rethinking their situation. Armed with this witness, that which may at first appear overwhelming may be seen for what it is: crippled, desperate, frightened, and powerless. This remarkable perspective is precisely the point of the interview between Pilate and Jesus:

> [Pilate] went back inside the palace, "Where do you come from?" he asked Jesus, but Jesus gave him no answer. "Do you refuse to speak to me?" Pilate said. "Don't you realize I have power either to free you or to crucify you?" Jesus answered, "You would have no power over me if it were not given to you from above." (John 19:9-11a)

Revelation 11:1-3. The temple of God mentioned is the Jerusalem Temple known to Jesus. This Temple had been trampled over (11:2) by the Roman legions of Titus in A.D. 70. The destruction and looting of the Temple was a traumatic event for Christians as well as for Jews.

For the Jewish Palestinian community this event accelerated the development of rabbinical forms, institutions, and practices. Judaism has not seen a return to a priestly cult and a system of sacrificial worship since A.D. 70.

For Christianity the devastation of Jerusalem and its Temple also created a crisis, since the "mother church" of Christianity was in Jerusalem and was associated with the Jewish-Christian pillars of the apostolic era. Western Christians may have a difficult time understanding this crisis feeling; but for Christians of the Pauline church, Christianity without a center in Jerusalem would have been difficult to conceive. This fact is reflected in various passages of the Synoptic Gospels, where the destruction of the Temple is viewed as evidence that the return of Christ in judgment cannot be far off (Mark 13:1-2, 14-22).

The reason for not including the Court of the Gentiles in this protection is difficult to explain. Certainly it must have something to do with excluding those who have not remained faithful to Jesus Christ. Ironically, the Court of the Gentiles is the only remaining part of the Temple precincts. The western wall of the Herodian Temple formed one of the boundaries of the Gentile court. This wall can be seen in Jerusalem today.

Revelation 11:4. Olive trees, as cultivated in Palestine, are noted for their strength, age, and dependability. Thus these trees are a frequent biblical image for blessings bestowed by God. Oil from the trees is essential to Palestin-ian life. A measure of their importance is the command given by God regarding holy war. While humans and beasts were to be put to death utterly, Israel was strictly prohibited from cutting down fruit trees (Deuteronomy 20:19-20). These trees would have been primarily olive trees.

The lampstands may represent the entire church as enlightened by the prophetic ministry of John and others like him. The connection may seem remote, but the idea is essential to understanding Revelation. In essence the affirmation suggests that without prophecy the church cannot be a light in the world.

Revelation 11:5-6. Is it credible that prophets could have such power? A careful reading of the Old Testament narrative history of Israel will confirm the claim made here. Quite literally, prophets caused nations to rise and fall. (We may also remember that Martin Luther King, Jr., created an entire epoch in American history with his prophetic leadership.) Of course, personal power was not at stake. Rather, the prophet's commission to speak the word of the Lord was at issue. The call and the message of the prophet create the power. Often prophets resist their commission, pointing to their frailty. (Moses pleaded his lack of eloquence [Exodus 4:10], Jeremiah his youth [Jeremiah 1:6], and Isaiah his sinfulness [Isaiah 6:5].) The message between the lines is easy to miss: John wants his oppressed and seemingly powerless listeners to see the depth of the power that lies in "the testimony of Jesus" (Revelation 1:2).

Revelation 11:7-13. Jerusalem was the site both of divine revelation and of the attempt to snuff out the source of that revelation, the prophets. In this sense Jesus is the great prophet. The Gospels are careful not to limit Jesus to a prophet's role because he is more than a prophet. Jesus is the fulfillment of the law and the prophets (Matthew 5:17). Still, he is a part of the prophetic tradition and suffers the prophet's normal fate: exile and death.

In this passage the connection between the two prophets and Jesus is so clear as to be unmistakable. The effect is to unite the guild of prophets with Jesus. Even the resurrection and ascension of the two prophets are modeled after Jesus (Acts 1:9). John will soon hear that "the testimony of Jesus is the spirit of prophecy" (Revelation 19:10d). In Chapter 11, we see how this is precisely the case: Prophets then and now, says John, destroy evil with their testimony; but they are also tormented, killed, and raised from the dead. We see in these prophets the life of Jesus, the great Prophet.

Revelation 11:17-18. This hymn of praise is weighted heavily with Revelation's faith. The basis of hope for a victorious outcome is, throughout the book, the absolute sovereignty of God. God has the power over creation and exists before time and space.

Two phrases need explaining because of the complexity of the poetry in 11:18:

• "The nations were angry; / and your wrath has come" pivots on a play on words in Greek. A paraphrase to make the meaning clear might be, "The pagan peoples were filled with wrath, but the moment has come for your wrath."

• "The time has come for judging the dead" is meant to be a positive hope for the faithful, since the resurrection of the dead is implied in the lines following. The logical connection is that the righteous will be vindicated at the general resurrection.

Notice that this magnificent hymn is a fitting poetic prayer such as might be found in liturgies for the Lord's Supper. The song begins with the word of thanksgiving appropriate to such prayers: "We give thanks to you, Lord God Almighty."

Revelation 11:19. This chapter begins with a vision of the earthly Temple in Jerusalem and ends with a vision of the heavenly temple. This vision is a subtle reminder that while the Temple in Jerusalem lies in ruins, inhabited by the pagan Roman legions, the temple of God is still intact. God is still in control of life, even though earthly realities may suggest otherwise.

The ark of the covenant in the Old Testament was the item that most clearly conveyed the sense of God's presence. In the Temple the ark resided in the Holy of Holies. At the time of Revelation's writing, the ark was no longer in the Jerusalem Temple. The reminder that the ark is still in the heavenly temple is a powerful metaphor for the claim that God has not abandoned the people of God. The description of power surrounding the ark leaves no doubt that God is present in power.

DIMENSION THREE: WHAT DOES THE BIBLE MEAN TO ME?

Revelation 10

The student book asks questions for discussion about the bittersweet nature of life's most important tasks and experiences. The biographies of those persons who have made significant contributions to the church and society invariably speak about experiences of conflict. These conflicts might be internal, but more often they tell of proposing changes that are stubbornly resisted by others. This resistance has been true in the history of the antislavery movement and in the women's liberation movement. All these movements have depended on countless women and men who sacrificed themselves for a cause essential to human welfare and dignity. Some end their experiences in bitterness, some in despair. Most recall something sweet about their involvement.

Not all social reform movements are of equal worth, but most fair-minded people admire the courage and commitment of those who care enough to try to change things for the better. Those who do get involved always find it is a bittersweet experience. This bittersweet experience can extend to the level of congregational life. Perhaps in your congregation as in many congregations, local church leaders face overwhelming challenges and decisions.

How are we to be faithful to this Scripture in these circumstances? Certainly one aspect concerns the recognition that the course of action that is purely "sweet as honey" may not be the best. John's experience suggests that "bitterness" (conflict, suffering, opposition, being misunderstood, and so on) is almost always a part of the most important actions taken in life.

Revelation 11

The subject of modern prophets is an important one to consider. Very likely, given past history, prophets are all around us today who, if listened to, could lead us to a better understanding of our circumstance, enlighten the factors on which we must base individual and group experiences, and give us the courage of our convictions. The fact is, of course, that we are also surrounded by false prophets. Most of us are reluctant to make judgments about these matters, as well we should be.

Often the true prophets have been branded false and killed or otherwise silenced. Martin Luther King, Jr., fit all the criteria as a modern prophet. At the height of his leadership, however, many Christians and others judged him to be unfit to listen to, let alone to follow.

The people of God must always face the agonizing problem of distinguishing between true and false prophets. In part our response to the claims of prophets must be based on the examples of Revelation. This book places God and the witness of Jesus Christ at the center of its claims. John proclaims a gospel of redemption consistent with the rest of the New Testament and teaches no new doctrine. Further, he makes no claim for himself and his authority other than "servant" and prophet. John's only mission is to convince hearers that the vision of triumph he has witnessed is from God. These same criteria can be usefully applied today to those persons some would call "prophets."

This calls for patient endurance and faithfulness on the part of the saints (13:10c).

7

The Woman Clothed With the Sun

Revelation 12–13

DIMENSION ONE:
WHAT DOES THE BIBLE SAY?

Answer these questions by reading Revelation 12

1. What is the first sign seen by John? (12:1)

   John first sees the "woman clothed with the sun," crowned with twelve stars and with the moon under her feet.

2. What is the woman's condition? (12:2)

   She is pregnant and very close to giving birth.

3. What is the second sign John sees? (12:3)

   John next sees a huge, red dragon with seven heads, each crowned, and ten horns.

4. What does the dragon want to do? (12:4b)

   The dragon waits for the woman to give birth so he can kill the child.

5. What happens to the child? (12:5)

   When the child is born, he is taken up to be with God.

6. What happens to the woman clothed with the sun? (12:6)

   She runs to the desert where she is cared for.

7. What does John describe next? (12:7-9)

   John describes a great battle in heaven between Satan and his angels and Michael and his angels. The outcome is that Satan and his forces are defeated and thrown out of heaven to earth.

8. What is the good news and the bad news resulting from this event? (12:10-12)

   The good news is that with Satan out of heaven, he can no longer make trouble there for Christians. The bad news is that Satan can now do great damage on earth.

9. When the story of the dragon and the woman clothed with the sun resumes, what new information are we given? (12:13-16)

   We learn how she escaped. She was given wings to fly into the desert. When the dragon tries to get her by flooding the land, the earth itself comes to her aid by absorbing all the water of the flood.

10. How does the dragon respond to his failure? (12:17)

    He is so angry that he makes war on the rest of the woman's children, "those who obey God's commandments and hold to the testimony of Jesus."

Answer these questions by reading Revelation 13

11. How is the "beast coming out of the sea" different from the dragon? (13:1)

    The beast has crowns on its horns rather than on its head as the dragon does.

12. What is the relationship between the dragon and this beast? (13:2b)

    This beast is given the "power and . . . great authority" of the dragon.

13. Which part of this new beast does John carefully describe? (13:3a)

    John carefully describes one of the beast's heads, which had been wounded but has healed.

14. How do human beings on earth respond to the beast? (13:3b-4)

They are astonished at the beast and worship it.

15. What does this beast do and for how long? (13:5-7)

The beast blasphemes God and those who dwell in heaven with God. It engages the saints of earth in war, defeats them, and rules over the entire inhabited world for forty-two months.

16. Who succeed in not being taken in by the beast? (13:8)

Those who have had their names written in the book of life are able to stand against the beast.

17. How are the hearers asked to respond? (13:9-10)

John asks the hearers to listen carefully and to exercise endurance and faith.

18. What appears next? (13:11)

Another beast appears, who looks like a lamb (with two horns) but sounds like a dragon.

19. What is this beast's relationship to the beast described earlier in this chapter? (13:12)

The second beast takes the place of the first beast, has all its authority, but seeks to make the earth's inhabitants worship the first beast, not itself.

20. What methods does the second beast use? (13:13-17)

This beast uses many methods but primarily deceit. The beast performs magical tricks with fire; it creates an image of the first beast that speaks and controls commerce by marking those who agree to worship the beast. The beast places on the hand or forehead a number that lets people buy and sell.

21. What is the number of the beast? (13:18)

The number of the beast is "666."

DIMENSION TWO:
WHAT DOES THE BIBLE MEAN?

Revelation 12:1. The woman clothed with the sun is one of the most cherished symbols of Christianity. Volumes have been written about the meaning of this vision. A large part of the Christian church believes that this woman represents the virgin Mary. While the interpretation is attractive, it does not fit well the story narrated in Revelation 12.

Our limited knowledge of the birth of Jesus and the events following do not conform well to the heavy theme of persecution here. The viewpoint of the New Testament Gospels would suggest that Mary was a continuing presence in the life of the mature Jesus. She may have been with Jesus during most of his public ministry. Nowhere is it reported that Mary went to live in the desert and was persecuted there.

The other highly favored interpretation is that the "woman clothed with the sun" represents the people of God—Israel. If the woman here is Mary, who brought forth the Messiah, then Mary could be thought of as the representative of Israel.

The concept of "sign" is of enormous importance, not only here but also in the Gospel of John. Four of the seven times this word occurs in Revelation are found in these two chapters (12:1, 3; 13:13, 14; 15:1; 16:14, 19-20). In 12:1 and 3, the two signs are the woman and the dragon. In 13:13 and 14, the lamb-dragon works signs that convince the majority that the dragon is worthy of worship. In the Gospel of John, Jesus is the great sign of God who works signs intended to reveal the salvation present in Jesus. Therefore, in Jesus sign and person are joined in a unity.

In these chapters much the same thing is taking place. The woman and her son are God's great sign of salvation. The dragon (Satan) and the two beasts of sea and earth are countersigns or imitations of the real sign. The religious thought of Revelation 12 and 13 depends on this viewpoint. God reveals the good news of salvation. Subsequently, Satan and the powers of evil at his command parody and mock this sign by presenting convincing imitations.

In John's Gospel, Jesus is presented as a prophet who works signs (John 4:19; 6:14; 7:40; 9:17). This same way of thinking is present in Revelation. Prophets—even false prophets—deal in signs. In Revelation we have both Christ and an antichrist dealing in signs. Christ and the dragon are themselves signs as well. The difficulty is that not both can be reliable signs of the truth, and mortals have to decide which sign truly reveals God's salvation. The need for such a choice makes the situation of humans in Revelation tense and hazardous.

Revelation 12:3. The word *dragon* in the New International Version is a literal translation of the Greek word *drakon.* The word will likely give modern readers a difficult time, since dragons are a standard feature of fantasy stories. In the biblical record (Job 7:12; Psalm 74:14; Isaiah 27:1; 51:9), dragons dwell in the chaos below the sea and there threaten the tranquillity of creation.

In dealing with the threat of the dragons in Revelation 12 and 13, the challenge is to find a means of releasing the dragon from its possibilities as a mythical creature. At the core, the dragon's threat is that of aborting the saving sign of Christ. This threat is serious and not to be reduced to a trivial game of dragons and damsels in distress.

Revelation 12:4. The conflict implicit in this verse may be the skeleton of a battle-in-heaven story preceding the detailed story in 12:7-9. Another, similar story is found in

9:1-6. There a star (angel) falls from heaven and is given the key to the deep tormenting locusts, which are to prey on humans.

This story continues at the conclusion of Revelation (20:1-3), where another angel seizes the dragon and locks him in the Abyss for a thousand years. (Specifically, the dragon is identified there as "that ancient serpent, who is the devil, or Satan.") This action is reversed (20:7-10) after a thousand years, and Satan is released to "deceive the nations" (20:8).

This story seems to suggest a fairly obvious, general picture of Satan's cosmic history. Satan was, from earliest time, an angel of deceit who was permitted to come and go, working evil in both heaven and earth. A crisis occurred in which Satan was exiled from heaven, taking a large company of angels with him (9:1; 12:9). From that time forward Satan and his angels were limited to earth. Satan's work came to a climax in the attempt to subvert the salvation brought by Christ (12:4b-5).

The war with Michael, described in detail in 12:7-9, would then be the attempt of Satan to follow Christ to heaven and continue his efforts to reverse the redemption of the Incarnation. This attempt fails when Satan and his angels are defeated by the champion angel, Michael, and his angelic army. Satan then realizes that the church is the continuing presence of Christ on earth and turns his full wrath on its faithful.

Revelation 12:5. The image of Christ ruling with "an iron scepter" may be an allusion to the dream and its interpretation in Daniel 2:31-45. King Nebuchadnezzar dreamed of an image made of five substances, a head of gold, chest and arms of silver, belly and thighs of bronze, legs of iron, and feet made with a mixture of iron and clay. According to Daniel's interpretation, Nebuchadnezzar was the head. The feet of clay and iron represented a future, divided kingdom (Daniel 2:41) that would be destroyed by a kingdom designed by God. This kingdom is represented by a rock "cut out, but not by human hands" (Daniel 2:34, 45) that would crush and destroy the four kingdoms to follow that of Nebuchadnezzar and the Babylonian Empire.

With this background, we can see how this simple claim (one "who will rule all the nations with an iron scepter") relies on concepts taken from Daniel. Put in this context, the full idea might be paraphrased, "In the birth of Christ, the kingdoms of this world have been smashed by the power of the Incarnation."

The Old Testament literary quality of this phrase comes through in the words the writer uses that come from Psalm 2:9: "You will rule them with an iron scepter; / you will dash them to pieces like pottery."

Revelation 12:9. Revelation 12 uses a fascinating array of names for Satan. *Satan* is the word most common to Hebrew readers. *The devil* is from the Greek term *diabolos*. The root meaning of *diabolos* is "slanderer." This root meaning is defined more completely in the next verse as "the accuser of our brothers" (12:10). Other names include "that ancient serpent" and "the great dragon."

In Revelation 12 and 13, the aspect of Satan's personality examined most closely is contained in the name "the deceiver," translated in the New International Version as the one "who leads the whole world astray" (12:9). The picture of evil in Revelation 12 and 13 is close to that in the apocalyptic passages of Matthew 24 and Mark 13. In the Gospels, Jesus says to his disciples, "Watch out that no one deceives you. Many will come in my name, claiming, 'I am he,' and will deceive many" (Mark 13:5-6; see also Matthew 24:4-5). This idea is really a good summary of most of Revelation 13, and the key idea is the same in both places. The central idea is that of subtlety. The agent who leads the faithful astray is someone who looks and sounds like an authentic prophet or even an authentic Christ. Those who claim to be another Christ usually claim that Christ has come again but remains hidden, or they talk of an alternative incarnation for the people who missed it the first time, or they claim in subtle suggestions that the person is divine. These claims, say both Jesus and John, are to be flatly disbelieved and vigorously rejected.

Revelation 12:10-12. The place of Satan's war against the saints has changed, but this is not particularly good news. A part of Satan's cosmic strategy has been defeated. The attempt to destroy the One who brings universal salvation, Jesus Christ, has failed. Satan is cast from heaven and no longer can advocate against the faith by means of his insidious whisper campaign in the company of heaven. Finally, we will learn soon that, even when limited to earth, Satan will fail to destroy the church. All this is good news. The bad news is that Satan has become more vicious and intense in the deception worked against earth's faithful. The intensity is motivated by the fact that Satan's time is just about up—and he knows it (12:12).

Revelation 12:13-17. While the story of the dragon's pursuit of the woman is provocative, it also alludes to other events. We can hear echoes of the wilderness wandering theme of the Old Testament, as well as see connections with the flight of the Holy Family to Egypt and Jesus' forty days and nights in the wilderness while tempted by Satan. Probably all these associations are intended by John.

Given the vicious persecution of Christians in the Roman Empire beginning with Nero, the message is quite clear. Just as Satan tried to divert Israel and Mary, Joseph, and Jesus in their desert sojourns, so also Satan will continue to seek and to destroy the offspring of this holy history, the faithful followers of the kingdom of God. The wilderness holds many associations for Christians. The meaning closest to the surface here is probably that of the forty years of wandering in the wilderness after Israel's disobedience. This association has a twofold theme. The people of God are sustained miraculously by God (for example, by manna), yet the wilderness represents the constant threat of separation from God. These two necessary elements of the wilderness theme struggle with each other with great creativity.

The word *offspring* as a description of spiritual descendants is found elsewhere in the New Testament (Romans 4:13; Galatians 3:29; Hebrews 2:16). Here the term refers to those who are Christ's spiritual descendants, after the fashion described in Romans 8:15-17 ("We are God's children.").

In the rescue of the woman the earth appears almost as a living, conscious being ("The earth helped the woman by opening its mouth" [12:16].). This description, together with the theme of a river of water acting as the enemy, recalls the atmosphere of Creation in Genesis 2:4-9 where humans are closely connected with the earth, almost to the extent of being partners. The threat of destruction by water recalls the Flood.

Revelation 13:1-4. The beast of the sea is conjured up by Satan as his major means of making war on the earth. This fact is not immediately obvious but becomes so at the time the beast from the earth appears (13:11-12). The connection of thoughts here is interesting. Satan's war is waged by supplying a figure who leads humans astray by convincing them to worship the beast. War is waged by means of worship. Beneath this war is an idea we see often in Revelation. The most essential human response possible is the praise of God. This response is predicted by the nature of creation. Since all things are made by God, that which best reflects the essence of creation is to praise the Creator. If this praise can be changed by evil into idolatry (that is, the creation worshiping itself rather than worshiping the One who created it), then creation has been corrupted. Satan shrewdly realizes that idolatry is the best means of deceiving the human family.

The enormous authority of the beast from the sea is based on the impulse to worship it as God. Not giving in to the praise of the beast is the heart and soul of conquering Satan.

Revelation 13:8. While these words may suggest a rigid kind of predestination, John does not intend that meaning. Such a doctrine did not exist at the time of the writing of Revelation. The verse does suggest that the redeemed are known by God even prior to Creation.

Revelation 13:9. This verse gives a stark warning. When Jesus sought to convey the mystery of the Kingdom to his disciples, he concluded his teaching with similar words (Mark 4:9): "He who has ears to hear, let him hear."

Revelation 13:10. The poetry of this statement may appear to be a direct quotation from another part of Scripture, but it is not. However, Jeremiah 15:2 is, in part, similar:

Those destined for death, to death;
  those for the sword, to the sword;
 those for starvation, to starvation;
   those for captivity, to captivity.

The poetry is haunting but can be reduced to a single idea: Sad though it may be, the time is approaching when many will suffer and die.

Rarely does John directly address those who are hearing Revelation read to them. Therefore the "call" for endurance and faith must be viewed as a shocking interruption of the narrative flow. The crisis the prophet senses approaching seems to move him to step out of character as narrator and say directly to his audience, "Watch yourselves!"

Revelation 13:11-17. The emphasis on the wounded-but-healed head of the beast (13:3, 12, 14) confirms this figure as the antichrist. Put more accurately, the beast is a counterfeit Christ. The head wounded-but-healed is a parody of Christ crucified and risen. This being the case, the second beast (13:11) is the false prophet who acts as priest of what can only be called the sea beast religion. We get more detail here on how false prophets work: Trickery and gimmicks figure high in convincing humans that the beast from the sea ought to be worshiped.

John gives us yet another keen insight based on simple economics. Whoever controls the means of trade controls all else. A false religion could become quite popular if it were the only means of obtaining food, shelter, and clothing.

Revelation 13:18. Even before the New Testament existed as a recognized collection of authoritative Scripture, discussions took place about the identity of the antichrist. The number 666 has fascinated readers virtually from the day Revelation was written. When human enemies are made to fit the number 666, this only serves to entrench us in the sin of inherited prejudices. Irenaeus, the first great theologian of the church, wrote at length about this problem as early as the second century. His advice is, if anything, more valuable today:

It is . . . more certain, and less hazardous, to await the fulfillment of the prophecy, than to be making surmises, and casting about for any names that may present themselves, inasmuch as many names can be found possessing the number mentioned; and the same question will, after all, remain unsolved.

DIMENSION THREE: WHAT DOES THE BIBLE MEAN TO ME?

Revelation 12–13

One characteristic of apocalyptic thought is a direct contrasting of good and evil, with no shades of difference. Our experience tells us, however, that often good laws, good institutions, good people, and good ideas can be used for an evil purpose. A number of the questions posed in the student book may bring simplistic, right-versus-wrong answers. The danger of answering in this way is, of course, that we may decide that good is evil. Or, we may allow serious forces of evil to prosper by calling them good.

History has taught us to be cautious about quick-and-easy decisions about people and events. Often we have to "repent at leisure" for decisions made without careful thought. An example of this kind of decision is the practice of slavery. At one time the enslavement of persons was seen as a foundation stone of civilized nations. Without slaves, some thought, economic growth would be impossible. The system of slavery was supported by religious convictions crafted out of the Bible. In other words, with hardly a murmur of protest, an economic system based on a great evil was enshrined as good in the eyes of Christians. Now we realize how terribly wrong and evil such a system was.

Revelation invites the reader to look beneath the disguise of evil. And, because the character of evil is subtle deceitfulness, we will usually find that the hidden evil lies within ourselves, those opinions we hold most dearly, and the systems we have come to think of as good.

---

[1]From "Against Heresies," in *The Ante-Nicene Fathers* (Charles Scribner's Sons, American Reprint of the Edinburgh Edition 1905); volume 1; page 559.

These were purchased from among men and offered as firstfruits to God and the Lamb (14:4c).

8
Singing a New Song
Revelation 14

DIMENSION ONE:
WHAT DOES THE BIBLE SAY?

Answer these questions by reading Revelation 14

1. What do the 144,000 have inscribed on their foreheads? (14:1)

   The Lamb's name and God's name are written there.

2. How did the voice from heaven sound? (14:2)

   The voice sounded like (1) rushing waters, (2) loud thunder, and (3) many harps being played.

3. Who is allowed to learn the new song? (14:3)

   Only the 144,000 are permitted to learn the new song.

4. How many different ways are the 144,000 described? (14:4-5)

   They (1) are chaste, (2) follow the Lamb, (3) have been "purchased from among men," (4) have been offered to God as firstfruits, (5) are without deceit, and (6) are blameless.

5. What does the first angel say to all the earth's people? (14:7)

   He tells them to fear God, give God glory, and worship God.

6. What is the second angel's message? (14:8)

   This angel announces the fall of Babylon.

7. What does the third angel announce? (14:9-11)

   The third angel announces the coming judgment of God's wrath on all those who have received the mark of the beast.

8. Who is pronounced blessed by the Spirit? (14:13)

   Those who die in the Lord are blessed "from now on."

9. Who appears on a white cloud, and how is he described? (14:14)

   The "one 'like a son of man' " comes wearing a golden crown and holding a sickle in his hand.

10. What does the "one, 'like a son of man' " do with his sickle? (14:15-16)

    Following the exhortation of yet another angel, he swings his sickle over the earth and reaps the harvest, now fully ripe.

11. Who else has a sharp sickle? (14:17)

    An angel comes out of the temple in heaven with a sharp sickle.

12. Who is the last angel described in this scene? (14:18)

    This angel comes out from the altar and is known as the one "who had charge of the fire."

13. What does this angel do? (14:18)

    The angel in charge of the fire tells the angel from the temple of heaven to harvest the "clusters of grapes from the earth's vine."

14. Where is the winepress of God located? (14:20)

    The winepress is "outside the city."

15. What does the winepress produce? (14:20)

    The winepress produces a flow of blood of immense proportions.

Revelation 14:1. The Lamb standing on Mount Zion with the band of the redeemed is a preview of the final scene of the new Jerusalem coming down from God (21:2). References to Mount Zion are rare in the New Testament, and the use here reminds us of the constant echoes between the Old Testament prophets and Revelation. The reference to Mount Zion, a place enshrined in the hearts and minds of those who know the Hebrew Scriptures well, says in effect, "God is not only in the heavenly temple; God is present also on earth."

Revelation 14:2-3. While John does not say so, this scene is like those we have witnessed earlier that take place in the presence of God's throne. (You may want to reread the descriptions in 4:1-6 and 5:6-14.) In Revelation the center of activity is the heavenly throne. The action in heaven that John sees has an impact on earth. John's vision is a visual way of saying that God is in command of the universe. The script of John's vision pivots on these throne scenes, rushing to, orbiting around, hovering in the midst of, and streaming out of the throne of God.

When the Lamb stands near this throne, the visual tapestry is complete. This tapestry portrays an all-powerful and transcendent God who is directing the destiny of our whole cosmos toward purposes held hidden from before the beginning. The Son of God, appearing frequently as the Lamb, carries out the mission of God, not in subjection or conflict with the Creator, but in perfect obedience to this eternal design.

Revelation 14:4-5. The Lamb is also a Shepherd (7:17). Therefore it is not odd that the redeemed follow the Lamb. The word *follow* is found often in the Gospels and is used as a virtual synonym for "be a disciple." Here the 144,000 have left earthly disruptions to follow the Lamb in another existence. This image ought not to be pressed too hard, but it does tantalize the imagination. Does discipleship continue after death? If the essence of discipleship is learning about salvation won in Christ, could it not be said that living with Christ involves learning even after death? This concept offers a fresh dimension; for other parts of the New Testament suggest that on being received by Christ, all knowledge is revealed.

The key idea of *redemption* depends on an exchange in which one thing is given for another. For example, in the ancient world an indentured servant was redeemed—rescued from slavery—by payment of a cash bond. While no formal doctrines of redemption are stated in the New Testament, the outcome of the Crucifixion is sometimes described as a redeeming act (1 Corinthians 6:20a; 2 Peter 2:1).

Redemption is a favorite idea of Revelation but is not fully developed. In later theology elaborate theories of atonement were constructed. At the core of these was frequently the idea that God redeemed humans from Satan at the price of Jesus' death. This idea is not even implied in Revelation and should not be assumed by readers who know about such theories of atonement. Rather, the redeemed are called "firstfruits"—that is, the first of those redeemed who remained faithful, even when tested by death. They are a premium pledge of all those who will follow. To this extent, the redeemed are held out as examples of faith.

Celibacy is probably not to be taken as a general condition for being considered faithful. In light of early Christian evidence, celibacy was not required of followers. Rather, the fact that many cults of the Roman Empire required consort with female prostitutes attached to the religion lies behind the praise for undefiled men. Christians are to abstain from such immoral sexual practices, even when supposedly justified on the basis of religious beliefs. One of the values of Revelation's place in Christian thought is to point out the impossibility of such practices being followed on a religious basis.

Revelation 14:6-7. Here again we see the universalism of John's vision. The angel's message is for all who dwell on earth. No one—good or evil—is excluded from the judgment. Fearing God is holding God in awe. The praise of God called for is the expected response to the arrival of the hour for the Last Judgment. God is also to be worshiped as the Creator, the One "who made the heavens, the earth, the sea and the springs of water" (14:7).

Revelation 14:8. Much attention will be given to Babylon in John's vision of Chapters 17 and 18. John is greatly indebted to the extensive oracles against Babylon found in Jeremiah 51 and to frequent mentions in Ezekiel, Daniel, and other Old Testament prophets.

Babylon is a commanding symbol of devastation because of Israel's tragic history with that powerful enemy. In the days of Jeremiah, Babylon destroyed Judah, the Temple, and the monarchy and took captive royalty and leaders from all levels of society and religion. Ezekiel was taken captive with this group, and much of his prophecy concerns the consequence of that captivity.

A great range of literature within the Hebrew Scriptures comes out of the period of Babylonian exile, and Jewish thinking was changed for all time by this experience. Daniel, written well after the Captivity, uses Babylon and the story of interaction with its king, Nebuchadnezzar, as a means of dealing with a more contemporary threat, Antiochus IV, who held Israel ransom by cruel occupation.

Revelation follows in Daniel's footsteps with great artistry. For John, Babylon could only be the dreaded Roman Empire. But John's thought is even more subtle. For him, a bit of Babylon threatens in every corner of life.

Verse 8 has a particular problem. Because the language here is so close to that of 17:2 and 18:3, the exact symbolic nature of the wine in Babylon's cup is unclear. From 17:2

the wine would seem to be of her own making, namely idolatry (conveyed by the metaphor of fornication or harlotry). Still, in the following paragraph (14:9-11), we will see another wine in a cup—the wine of God's wrath. If this wine is the same, and therefore the same cup of anger from God, then we would have a true irony. Babylon intoxicates the nations with the dreadful wine of God's wrath. In other words, Babylon is the unwitting servant of God. When persons drink from the cup, they are doomed.

Revelation 14:10b. Why are the worshipers of a false God tormented in the presence of Christ and the angels? The answer lies in the need for witnesses to justice. A peculiar aspect of the Old Testament prophets and of Revelation is to call witnesses to see that God's justice has been done. This witness often takes the appearance of a formal trial in which various parts of creation "stand in" as witnesses or jury. Here the Lamb and angels serve that purpose. This desire for witness in God's court is not motivated by the need to have God's righteousness attested to but simply to emphasize the truth of God's judgment.

Revelation 14:11. The "smoke of their torment" is a deliberate contrast with the "smoke of the incense" symbolizing the prayers of the faithful (8:4; 5:8).

The judgment conveyed to the beast worshipers is a preliminary glimpse. In Revelation 19:20-21, the battle between Christ and this group is described in detail.

Revelation 14:12. This verse is an excellent summary of Revelation's message. John's vision is well designed to convince the suffering saints of the Roman Empire that God is in control of the destiny of the world and its history. To serve God by keeping the law given to Moses and perfected by Jesus of Nazareth is not only worthwhile, this service is essential to life itself.

The meaning of the word translated "endurance" can also be conveyed by words such as *patience, fortitude, steadfastness,* and *perseverance.* In the Gospels, Jesus is the example of perfect perseverance. This perseverance is shown especially in his approach to the cross—his endurance of betrayal, unjust manipulation of Jewish and Roman law, beatings, and death. No wonder that this Christian response to injustice and oppression receives such a place of honor.

Revelation 14:13. This blessing (or beatitude) is an echo of 6:9-11. John shows a touching and consistent concern in Revelation for those who die under persecution. The blessing may include all Christians who die in faithfulness, whether as the result of martyrdom or not. This issue is decided on the basis of what it means to die "in the Lord." If the sense is of following the example of Jesus, then this beatitude limits its blessing to martyrs.

Does John in Revelation believe that a Christian's works play a role in salvation? Several passages mention deeds at work. In Revelation 2:2, the church of Ephesus is told,

"I know your deeds, your hard work and your perseverance." Here, it is quite clear that works are Christian virtues (such as endurance, described above). This suggests that in Revelation's view deeds or works are evidences of Christ's presence working in the saints; they are not the source of salvation. Finally, these works do not go before the faithful to obtain a place in heaven but accompany them.

Revelation 14:14-16. The title *Son of Man* as a designation of Jesus Christ is common to the New Testament, but *Son of Man* has not become a favorite name for Christ and is seldom used outside scholarly circles today. Still Jesus spoke of himself using this title on many occasions (for example, Matthew 8:20; 9:6; 10:23; 11:19; 12:8; 13:37; 16:13; 17:9; 19:28; 20:18; 24:27; 25:31; 26:64). The fact that the Gospels and Revelation agree on the importance of this title reminds us that Revelation is not from the fringes of early Christianity but close to the heart of it. (Only recently have scholars come to appreciate this fact. Recognition of this fact has caused a fresh and helpful reappraisal of this book.) This title for Jesus is used in many ways, but perhaps the most significant is reflected in this historic saying of Jesus as reported by Matthew: "The Son of Man is going to come in his Father's glory with his angels, and then he will reward each person according to what he has done" (Matthew 16:27).

Read side-by-side with this saying, the echoes of Revelation 14:14-16 are astounding. They are even more astounding because we do not know that John ever read the Gospel According to Matthew.

One of the crucial elements in Jesus' faith was that of the coming of the Son of Man in judgment. The unity between Revelation and the faith of Jesus on this point is a witness to this book's place in preserving ancient traditions that lie at the base of Christianity.

Revelation 14:17-20. The Old Testament prophets, John the Baptist, and Jesus often used the extended metaphor of vineyard and harvest as a way of speaking about God's judgment. John 15 is a classic example of an extended metaphor in which Christ is the vine and the disciples his branches.

Jesus is the wine of the Lord's Supper, as well as the bread. The connection between the wine and blood is easily made; since the blood of Christ, shed on the cross, is symbolic of his essence. Many of the specific wordings of this passage are close to, if not modeled on, pronouncements of various Old Testament prophets (for example, Joel 3:13).

The fascinating detail that this judgment scene takes place "outside the city" (14:20) raises an issue relevant to the entire chapter: We cannot reconcile groups, place, and time between this chapter and the rest of Revelation. The entire chapter is filled with references backward and forward in the book. Revelation 14 provides an excellent setting for reaffirming that the most fruitful uses of this book do not include forcing each part into a doctrinal scheme that must work for all its parts.

DIMENSION THREE:
WHAT DOES THE BIBLE MEAN TO ME?

Revelation 14

From this point forward Revelation will deal in greater and greater detail with the belief in divine judgment that leads to suffering for millions. At the same time John puts consistent emphasis on the salvation of the saints who endure in the midst of persecution. Revelation depends on a stark contrast between a small, persecuted minority and a sea of opposition, idolatry, and immorality. Revelation is, to a certain extent, a social statement concerning "we who are righteous" and "they who are evil."

At another level this statement is too simple an analysis of Revelation's perspective. John is quite clear that worship (ours and theirs) has the potential for idolatry. John may have in mind that Christian worship is constantly in danger of becoming idolatry. In other words, the enemy may be us, not them.

In discussing this chapter and the questions raised in the student book, you may wish to ask questions such as these: How do we know whether the mark on our forehead is the name of God or of the beast? How do we know whether the song of our heart is an old, sad song or the new song of the redeemed? How do we know whether the cup we drink is the life-giving sacrificial blood of the Lamb or the cup of God's anger?

— 9 —

Seven Bowls of Wrath

Revelation 15–16

DIMENSION ONE:
WHAT DOES THE BIBLE SAY?

Answer these questions by reading Revelation 15

1. What was the sign John the prophet saw in heaven? (15:1)

   He saw "seven angels with the seven last plagues."

2. Who stands beside the sea of glass? (15:2a)

   All those who have triumphed over the beast stand beside the sea of glass.

3. What are they doing? (15:2b-3)

   They are playing harps and singing "the song of Moses" and "the song of the Lamb."

4. What does the song foresee? (15:4c)

   All the nations of the world will come to worship God.

5. Where do the angels with the plagues come from? (15:5-6)

   They come from "the tabernacle of the Testimony" in heaven.

6. Who gives the angels the golden bowls full of wrath? (15:7)

   One of the four living creatures gives them the bowls.

7. What happens in the temple after this? (15:8)

   The temple is filled with smoke, and no one can enter.

Answer these questions by reading Revelation 16

8. What is the first plague poured out of the golden bowl by the angel? (16:2)

   "Ugly and painful sores" afflict the beast worshipers.

9. What is the second plague poured out? (16:3)

   The sea turns to a blood-like substance, and every living thing in the sea dies.

10. How is the third plague like the second? (16:4)

    The third plague is the same as the second but affects fresh water.

11. How are the two plagues of blood infecting water explained? (16:5-7)

    Because the saints and prophets have been murdered by those who follow the beast, God has given the beast worshipers "blood" to drink.

12. What is the fourth plague? (16:8)

    The power of the sun is increased to allow humans to be tormented by scorching heat.

13. Whom do the humans (followers of the beast) blame for the plagues? (16:9)

    They blame God, not themselves, and therefore do not repent.

14. Against what is the fifth plague directed? (16:10)

    The fifth plague is poured on the throne of the beast.

15. What is the result of this plague? (16:10-11)

    The plague darkens the kingdom of the beast, and this sends panic among his followers.

16. On what does the sixth plague fall? (16:12)

   The sixth plague falls on the river Euphrates, drying it up completely.

17. Why is the river dried up? (16:12)

   The dry riverbed is made ready for the great battle by making it easy for the armies of the East to cross the Euphrates.

18. How do the dragon, the beast, and the false prophet respond to this plague? (16:13-14)

   They send out three evil spirits whose task is to deceive the world's nations into doing battle with God.

19. Where is the final battle to be held? (16:16)

   The battle is to be at Armageddon.

20. What takes place when the seventh golden bowl is poured out? (16:18-21)

   A series of natural disasters, more devastating than ever before experienced in history, takes place. These disasters include massive earthquakes so as to dislodge islands, level mountains, and destroy cities. Also, enormous hailstones fall on people.

21. Who is particularly singled out for destruction? (16:19)

   "Babylon the Great" experiences the full force of God's wrath.

DIMENSION TWO: WHAT DOES THE BIBLE MEAN?

Revelation 15:1. The first sign was the vision of the woman clothed with the sun (Chapter 12). Now a special place of importance is given to the seven plagues, as they are the signs of the conclusion of judgment. The two chapters narrating the seven plagues (15 and 16) will be followed by two chapters (17 and 18) of oracles against the harlot of Babylon. Then John begins the narration of Christ's final victory over Satan (Revelation 19 and 20). These opening words convey a sense of finality.

Revelation 15:2-4. John often will report an aspect of his vision in comparative language and then move on to call that vision by the name of the comparison ("what looked like a sea of glass" / "the sea" [15:2]). This literary technique must be followed carefully in the text if you want to avoid confusion.

In describing the sea of his vision, John says it "looked like a sea of glass mixed with fire." We have already seen the sea of heaven with John in 4:6, but here the flickering color of fire is added. Perhaps John is trying to describe a body of water that is so smooth and clear as to reflect like glass. The dancing of flame may refer to movement or reflection of lightning flashing on the surface of the lake's transparency.

The song of Moses, recorded in Exodus 15:1-18, resembles this hymn of praise only in majesty and atmosphere. John does not use a direct quotation. Some scholars suggest that John heard this choir first sing the old song of Moses and then this new song composed by the Lamb. In any event, the remarkable part of this scene is that Moses is viewed as one of God's faithful servants, along with the martyred faithful of earth, and that Moses and Christ are characterized as heavenly choral masters.

To suggest that the ascended Jesus is a maker of music is a rich and expansive metaphor with many possibilities. At the very least, this picture suggests that some aspects of service to God and understanding of creation can only be fulfilled by the writing, playing, and singing of music. We have met this attitude previously, but here the point is made stronger.

The fourth line of the hymn presents a textual problem that scholars have debated for centuries. God is either "King of the ages" or "King of the nations." Textual evidence is equivocal, but the unmistakable wording of the next-to-last line ("All nations will come / and worship before you.") gives support to reading *nations* in 15:3, thus creating a parallelism.

Revelation 15:5. When John says, "I looked," we know that something of great significance is about to happen.

We have been used to dealing with the heavenly temple, but the building mentioned in verse 5 is a great mystery. Of course, a mobile tent of worship was used by Israel in the desert wanderings. But this Tabernacle or portable sanctuary was quite different from the temples of Solomon and Herod. The Book of Hebrews (Chapters 8 and 9) includes a sustained study on the tent-sanctuary of Israel's nomadic period. But this verse gives the only mention of the tabernacle in Revelation.

Revelation 15:7. Exactly what these bowls look like is unclear, but a difference between *bowl* and *cup* is carefully maintained by John for some reason. Some have suggested that the bowls are most appropriately thought of as basins, shallow and wide at the mouth. This shape would result in more instantaneous emptying out.

Revelation 16:2. Twice in these chapters the beast's image is singled out for special treatment (15:2; 16:2). John clearly is outraged at the image of the beast because the image is a symbol of idolatry. To conquer the beast is to conquer its image. This idea might include resistance to the power and drama of the image in ritual, beauty, symbolism, and perhaps even in music.

Revelation 16:5-7. This hymn contains several interesting and subtle details. God is just in all judgments. If God were only just and not also all-powerful, we could have no confidence in the hope for a just outcome. John has clearly established by now, however, that God is powerful beyond all powers that exist because God created all else. This affirmation is hinted at in the second line of the hymn. "Who are and who were" is a poetic way of saying that "God is eternal." Then comes the ironic twist: Human beings have poured out the blood of the prophets and saints; therefore God has poured out the bowls of wrath.

The final line is something like a response, such as might be found in a litany. The angel's song of praise ends with verse 6, but the response ("Yes, Lord God Almighty, / true and just are your judgments" [verse 8].) comes from the altar. Who are these voices? They are, we learned in 6:9-11, the martyrs of the faith who dwell under the altar of sacrifice in the heavenly temple. We heard them, with John, crying out for their blood to be avenged. Here, as a liturgical choir, we hear them again, avenged, praising God for the justice of divine judgment. In this way John deftly picks up a theme planted earlier and completes a part of a literary cycle. More importantly, he brings forward the plot in a kind of momentary climax.

Earlier Moses was called "the servant of God" (15:3), and here the prophets of the Old Testament are identified as martyrs (16:6). This adulation of the prophetic tradition recalls the mini-history of the prophets told in 11:4-13. A direct connection is established between this section of Chapter 16 and the power of prophecy in these words: "They have power to turn the waters into blood and to strike the earth with every kind of plague as often as they want" (Revelation 11:6b).

The connection reveals another level of ironic artistry on John's part. Note how many of these plagues are modeled after the plagues visited on Egypt through Moses (Exodus 7–11). The message of God in these plagues is that while humans were able to silence and kill the prophets, the time is fast approaching when judgment will come by means of prophetic acts. In this way Moses and Elijah are made present realities in the world's circumstances. This reality is, indeed, bitter irony for those who scoffed at the prophets throughout the centuries.

Revelation 16:9. John attempts to point out that repentance does not always follow divine punishment, as might be expected. This truth also links with the history of prophetic ministry. The people and their leaders refuse to learn from their experiences of God's justice. This theme is consistent in all Scripture. Revelation continues in this conviction and builds the story of final judgment around it.

Revelation 16:10-11. The results of the fifth plague are mingled with those of the first for some reason. While potentially confusing in syntax, the meaning is clear. People chewed their tongues in pain (not anguish) because of the repugnant sores of the first plague. The results of the darkness visited on the beast's kingdom are not specified.

Revelation 16:13. The dragon, the beast, and the false prophet are described collectively as three evil spirits. The third beast is identified for the first time as "the false prophet" of the second beast and its image. The mention of frogs recalls still another plague on the Egyptians (Exodus 8:1-6). This likeness does not completely explain the interesting change of images from evil spirits to frogs. However, in some Eastern religions, well known to the Roman Empire, evil gods took the form of frogs. This fact may explain the strange jump from one image to another.

Revelation 16:14. The final battle will be a "great day" for "God Almighty" simply because on that day the fullness of divine justice and power will be seen.

Revelation 16:15. This interlude is an intrusion into the narration of the vision and is given as a direct exhortation to those who hear the book read. Christ speaks directly to the hearer in the first person. The image of Christ returning as a thief is yet another firm connection with Jesus in the Gospels. In Matthew 24:42-44, Jesus compares his return with a thief coming in the night. (See also 1 Thessalonians 5:2-4.)

The interlude includes yet another beatitude (see 14:13) in which watchfulness is blessed. The exhortation to remain awake is a constant theme in the Gospels and always in connection with the return of Christ (Matthew 24:42; 25:13; 26:40; Mark 13:35, 37). This beatitude is the second firm connection in this verse with the Gospel tradition of Jesus speaking about his return.

No place in the Gospels connects conveniently with the metaphor of nakedness meaning "unprepared to meet Jesus when he returns," as is clearly the meaning here. However, we do know the fascinating story told only by Mark (14:51-52) in which an anonymous young man fled the scene of Jesus' arrest and, leaving behind his garment, went into the night naked.

Revelation 16:16. The place named *Armageddon* is given here as if it is a well-known place name in Palestine. Actually, the name appears nowhere else within Scripture or outside it.

John's narration of the final battle between Christ and Satan is modeled on the Gog-Magog battle in Ezekiel 38–39. John tells the story sketchily in Revelation 20:7-11. In Ezekiel this battle was to have taken place in the vicinity of the "mountains of Israel" (Ezekiel 39:2, 4).

Revelation 16:17. With an almost audible sigh of relief, the end of Rome is finally declared with, "It is done!" This proclamation creates a turning point in Revelation's development. The proclamation reaches back to 10:5-6 in which the mighty angel declares that "there will be no more delay." But we have already seen dramatic delay, and more delay of the same kind awaits us. The delay, however, is for dramatic effect and is not meant to convey vacillation on God's part.

Revelation 16:19. When John describes what takes place, he uses an intense phrase—"the fury of his wrath." This phrase contains two words, both of which can be translated "wrath." This sentence, then, describes a doubling up of wrath. The idea of making pronouncements more frightening by piling up terms is a technique the Old Testament prophets often used. For example, see Jeremiah 4:26 and Hosea 11:9. John uses this device again in Revelation 19:15c: "the fury of the wrath of God Almighty."

DIMENSION THREE: WHAT DOES THE BIBLE MEAN TO ME?

Several themes in Revelation 15 and 16 invite discussion: the universal dimension of God's rule, the command of God over cosmic principles of justice, the punishment inherent in idolatry, the place of worship in the language of faith, and vigilance in the faith while waiting for the fullness of Christ's kingdom.

Several passages in these two chapters affirm that the eventual outcome of God's judgment will be the ingathering of all people into the orbit of God's worship. The theology in Revelation has no place for a tribal religion that keeps to itself. The goal is that all nations on earth should confess the rightness of God's sovereign rule and praise God in joyful acclamation. John presents absolute intoler-ance for the many cults and religions of Hellenistic civilization.

What are we to make of this attitude in light of our present circumstance? More and more we are aware of the global importance of religion in conflicts of political and economic life in our world. Much of the tension that exists today is due to religious conflict and differences. Do not attitudes such as those seen in these chapters simply add to the problems? The answer, of course, lies in the goal of God's justice. God's justice does not seek the advancement of any particular nation at the expense of another but the establishment of a reign of righteousness for all persons.

Rome's destruction was seen by John as a necessary outcome of a reign of immorality, oppression, and idolatry. In other words, the failure of Rome's religious vision brought Rome's downfall. This conclusion is no different from that of the Old Testament prophets who were as quick to condemn Israel as they were to pronounce God's judgment on unrighteous pagan nations who surrounded Israel.

When John wrote Revelation, there was no Christian nation in existence to which he could speak. Christians lived in scattered bands across the Roman Empire and were still a small minority. Likely John would have found much to condemn in later Christian Rome, as indeed he could in our and other so-called Christian nations.

I will explain to you the mystery of the woman (17:7).

— 10 —

Babylon Is Fallen

Revelation 17–18

DIMENSION ONE:
WHAT DOES THE BIBLE SAY?

Answer these questions by reading Revelation 17

1. Who is the woman who sits on many waters? (17:1)

   She is described as a "great prostitute."

2. What is the charge against her? (17:2)

   She has committed adultery with kings of the earth and other earth inhabitants.

3. Where is the woman next seated? (17:3)

   She is seen seated on a scarlet beast with seven heads and ten horns.

4. What does she hold in her hand? (17:4)

   She holds a cup filled with "abominable things and the filth of her adulteries."

5. What is her name, and how do we know it? (17:5)

   Written on her forehead is the mysterious name, "BABYLON THE GREAT / THE MOTHER OF PROSTITUTES / AND OF THE ABOMINATIONS OF THE EARTH."

6. Who interprets the meaning of the mystery to John? (17:7)

   An angel interprets the mystery for John.

7. According to the angel, how are the following parts of the vision to be interpreted? (17:8-15):

   The beast with seven heads and ten horns? (17:8a)

   The beast is the same beast connected with the Abyss in 11:7.

The inhabitants of the earth? (17:8b)

They are those who do not have their names written in the book of life, or all those who worship the beast.

The seven heads on the beast? (17:9-10)

They are seven kings and "seven hills on which the woman sits."

The ten horns? (17:12)

They are ten kings who will in the future receive power for a short period.

The waters on which the prostitute sits? (17:15)

They represent a multitude of people made up of many nations and languages.

8. What does the angel say will happen to the prostitute? (17:16)

   The angel says that the beast and the ten kings will destroy her.

9. Why will this happen? (17:17)

   God will motivate the kings to give their power to the beast instead of to the prostitute to fulfill the requirements of justice.

10. Who is this woman? (17:18)

    She is "the great city that rules over the kings of the earth"— Rome.

Answer these questions by reading Revelation 18

11. What lives in Babylon, according to the angel with great authority? (18:2)

    Demons, "every evil spirit," and "every unclean and detestable bird" dwell there.

12. Who has been contaminated by Babylon? (18:3)

She has given drink of her adulteries to all nations, has committed adultery with the kings of the earth, and has fed the greed of merchants.

13. To whom does the next voice speak? (18:4)

"My people" (the people of God) are called away from Babylon.

14. Why is it important for the people to get out of Babylon? (18:4)

They must leave, or they might take part in her sins and receive her judgment.

15. On what principle will Babylon be punished? (18:6)

She will be repaid double for her sins.

16. What does Babylon think about herself? (18:7)

She deludes herself by thinking that she is as God and will never fall.

17. Who will weep for Babylon? (18:9)

All the kings of the earth with whom she has consorted will "weep and mourn" over Babylon.

18. Why do the merchants of the earth weep for her? (18:11-17a)

The merchants weep for Babylon because they no longer have buyers for their costly goods.

19. Why do those who earn their living from the sea weep for the destruction of the city? (18:17b-19)

They weep because they know that this destruction will mean a loss of the shipping trade.

20. While kings, merchants, and seafaring men weep, who is asked to rejoice? (18:20)

The company of heaven, all saints, apostles, and prophets are called to rejoice in the judgment of God.

21. In the next action of the vision, what does the angel do? (18:21)

As an illustration, the angel drops a great millstone into the sea and says that, like the millstone, so will be Babylon.

22. What will no longer be found in Babylon? (18:22-23)

The sounds of music, the work of craftsmen, the sound of grinding millstones, the shining of lamps, and the sounds of wedding parties will no longer be found there.

23. What is the final reason given for Babylon's fall? (18:24)

Babylon shed the blood of the prophets and saints and many others on earth.

DIMENSION TWO:
WHAT DOES THE BIBLE MEAN?

These two chapters of Revelation are two of the most confusing in the entire book. They both deal with only one subject—the sins of Rome and prophecies of doom that look forward to Rome's fall. The prophet John of Patmos thought a great deal like the Old Testament prophets, especially Ezekiel, Joel, Isaiah, and Jeremiah. He also had read the Book of Daniel many times. In fact, he was so familiar with these books that he often fell back on their ideas, images, symbols, and metaphors when expressing what he experienced in his vision. Nothing makes this knowledge of Old Testament prophets more evident than his choice of Babylon as a secret symbol for imperial Rome.

The Old Testament books of Jeremiah and Ezekiel are filled with prophecies about the Babylonian Empire and its evil king, Nebuchadnezzar, who defeated Jerusalem and took the people captive. The Book of Daniel was written several hundred years after the Babylonian captivity; but Daniel makes Babylon a symbol for Israel's present oppressors, the Seleucid Empire. (The Seleucids were a family of Syrian kings who ruled a portion of the Alexandrian Empire of Greece.) John follows this pattern in the Book of Revelation. John chooses the best-known enemy to God's rule, Babylon, as a thinly veiled symbol for imperial Rome.

John's dependence on the Old Testament prophets also goes beyond using this pattern, for the sayings about Babylon (Rome) in Chapter 18 are similar to those against Babylon and other nations spoken by Jeremiah and Ezekiel. Read Jeremiah 51 and Ezekiel 26–27 as you prepare to study Revelation 17–18.

Perhaps the most common Old Testament metaphor for idolatry is sexual immorality, especially harlotry or prostitution. Israel was surrounded by people who had many gods. Many of these were female deities, and often the cults surrounding these female figures required deviant sexual practices and encouraged prostitution.

In contrast with its neighbors, Israel's law did not allow prostitution in any form. This statute, along with other laws of a similar nature, did much to preserve the dignity of sexuality.

The God of Israel required absolute loyalty. Throughout its history Israel's greatest struggle was with the temptation to tolerate or even nurture the worship of other gods. Israel's devotion to one God, Yahweh, is sometimes portrayed by making Yahweh the husband and Israel his bride. Against this background we can see how infidelity might become a metaphor for idolatry. To worship other gods, was, in other words, to commit adultery against God, the bridegroom of Israel. The Old Testament prophets reflect on this imagery at length. One point they make is that Israel has behaved like a prostitute and/or committed adultery (Jeremiah 3:1, 6, 8; Ezekiel 16:15-22; Hosea 4:15).

The perspective shifts a bit in Revelation. Rome—consistently called Babylon—is a notorious provider of religious cults and gods. John does not address Israel or the church in these chapters but turns his prophetic eye for the first time directly on Rome, the source of idolatry and oppression against the church.

Revelation 17:1. John is less clear about the details of the visionary setting here than he is elsewhere. The voice doing the speaking throughout Chapter 17 is one of the seven angels introduced at 15:6. The best solution to the question "Which one?" is that the seventh angel (16:17-21) continues on from the seventh plague to take the destruction of Rome one step further. (Rome is the object of the seventh plague.)

The influence of ancient prophetic writers on John is neatly illustrated in the title "the great prostitute, who sits on many waters." The prophet Nahum called Nineveh the "harlot" (Nahum 3:4), and Isaiah called Tyre a "prostitute" (Isaiah 23:16-17). Rome's location in the Mediterranean area does make some sense of the phrase *many waters,* but the phrase applies more aptly to the original Babylon that was surrounded by the Euphrates River, canals, and natural marshes. Jeremiah addressed Babylon as "you who live by many waters" (Jeremiah 51:13). The detail concerning many waters will create some difficulty when the symbol is interpreted in Revelation 17:15 as "peoples, multitudes, nations and languages." Thus I see two strands of meaning attached to one metaphor, a fact not unusual in Revelation.

Revelation 17:2-6. The image of the inhabitants of the earth being intoxicated with the wine of the prostitute's adulteries is enforced with the powerful image of verse 4. Babylon clutches a golden cup, a beautiful vessel, filled with obscene and filthy sexual practices.

Sexual immorality in all these references must always be taken at two levels that, as we have seen so often in Revelation, are so intertwined as to be inseparable: idolatry and literal sexual immorality. The cup of Babylon's immorality will return in 18:3, 6.

Babylon not only makes others drunk but also is drunk herself. Her drunkenness is from the blood of those she has cruelly murdered. This ghastly image is established with absolute clarity. John expresses rage—passionate indignation—in Revelation over the senseless killing of people. This issue will remain important in the minds and hearts of Christians for the next hundred years or more. Eventually Christians wore down the Roman Empire by the spiritual and moral strength they demonstrated. The Christians' victory was, in part, made possible by the universal outrage over Rome's cruelty to people.

Notice the subtle word play going on throughout the latter half of Revelation. The wine of sexual immorality being hawked by the prostitute, Rome, is contrasted with the cup of God's anger, containing the wine of divine wrath (14:8; 15:1, 7; 16:1). These two cups have a close connection that borders on the dangerous. Both wines are a passion. The prostitute's passion is sexual immorality; God's passion is, to the forces of evil, the wrath and anger of punishment. Both are passions; one is impure, the other pure. John is reminding his readers that passion is part of existence. The only question is the motivation and direction that passion takes.

Revelation 17:7. John's use of the word *mystery* is rare, even though many people consider Revelation mysterious (1:20; 10:7; 17:5, 7). A more frequent term is *sign,* meaning a clarifying event or pronouncement. (In John's Gospel a sign is a miracle done by Jesus that makes understanding and faith in him possible for some persons.) In Revelation *mystery* means something of great significance that needs explanation. (The meaning of *mystery* in Matthew, Mark, and Luke is almost the opposite. The kingdom of God cannot be explained but must be received in the person of Jesus Christ, who is God's mystery. [See Matthew 13:11; Mark 4:10-12; and Luke 8:10.])

The woman and the beast on which she rides need careful explanation so the Christians to whom this vision is entrusted will better be able to know what is going to happen and how to deal with it.

Revelation 17:8-14. The interpretation of several phrases in this section has a long history of debate. The first is at the end of verse 8: "Because he once was, now is not, and yet will come." The meaning of this ambiguous phrase is, "The beast was alive, but is no longer living, and will once again appear." A similar idea is found in an equally confusing phrase in verse 10 where the mathematics of the seven kings is worked out. Out of the seven kings, five have passed from the scene, the sixth king is now reigning, and a seventh king is coming into power who will be around for only a short time. But verse 11 is by far the most potentially confusing. The translation by J. B. Phillips of this verse helps a lot: "As for the animal which once lived but now lives no longer, it is an eighth king which belongs to the seven, but it goes to utter destruction" (*The New Testament in Modern English,* Revised Edition, by J. B. Phillips, © J. B. Phillips 1958, 1960, 1972. Used by permission of Macmillan Publishing Co., Inc.). In other words, John has managed to get eight kings out of seven by suggesting that one of the kings will reign twice. Likely, John's description refers to the sea beast who has seven heads, one of which was wounded but now has been healed. This reference may be to the Roman emperor Nero, who was thought by many to have returned to rule in the person of the emperor Domitian.

John likely had it all worked out in his head who these kings were in the Roman succession. Many people have tried to reconstruct this list from general historical knowledge about the Roman Empire. They have come to no agreement about this list. One common solution would see the first five kings as (1) Augustus, (2) Tiberius, (3) Caligula, (4) Claudius, and (5) Nero. The sixth would be Vespasian and the short reign of Titus (A.D. 79–81) the seventh. (Titus led the Roman armies that destroyed Jerusalem and the Temple in A.D. 70.) In this reconstruction John and his churches are living under the cruel emperor Domitian (the eighth king), who many thought to be the reincarnation of Nero. In this scheme of things, then, an eighth king is really the fifth king returned to life.

Another solution would place John and his first readers as living under the reign of Nero. Thus Nero is the villain of the church in both cases.

The danger of specifying any such solution is that the power of the metaphor is robbed of its possibilities for all times. So we would be unwise to concentrate a great deal of attention on the historical accuracy of this list or others.

The ten kings represented by the ten horns (17:12-14) are a different matter. They almost certainly have no exact equivalents in John's mind. Rather, the portrayal is of what will take place in the final battle with Christ. These kings will be incited by the power given them by Satan. They will receive a sense of unity and purpose but only for a short, bloody encounter with Christ. This final encounter is described in Revelation 19–20 and concludes with the Final Judgment.

Revelation 17:15-18. Even though the angel invited the prophet to view the "punishment of the great prostitute" (17:1), the description of her judgment is not seen until Chapter 18. The strategy for Rome's destruction is suggested in 17:16-17. Rome will incite the nations to wrath and the ten (minor) kings, led by Satan, will rebel against Rome and destroy her. The kings will then turn on Christ and be destroyed (17:13-14).

Some persons have suggested that Revelation belongs to a kind of literature that sees two equal forces—good and evil—at war in the universe. The language of verse 17 clearly makes such a conclusion impossible. God has access to the inner motivations of both kings and demons and manipulates their actions to bring about the divine outcome. God is in charge, and God is good.

Revelation 18:1-3. Now the judgment of Babylon comes. This entire chapter is written from the future perspective looking back. Rome, in the prophet's mind, already lies in ruins. Destruction is an accomplished fact. John learned this perspective from the Old Testament prophets, but it is more than a literary device. The entire perspective reflects an attitude of total confidence in the vision entrusted to the prophet. Thus John gives us a lesson for faith implicit in what may otherwise be seen as merely a literary technique. God is so powerful and dominant that the future can be seen as the past.

Revelation 18:4-8. Anyone who has read the great Old Testament prophets will be struck by the countless echoes from the prophets as this passage is read. This echo effect reminds us that *Babylon* is a timeless and elastic image for a limitless number of places and times.

Babylon's revealing statement of self-delusion is a powerful source of reflection (18:7). All persons living in protected luxury at some time are tempted to say, "I shall live forever, and nothing bad can happen to me." Nations and groups too, in what they decide and do, proclaim, "Nothing can stop us. No adversity will deter us; nothing will stand in our way." The Book of Revelation is of great importance for the support it provides in stripping off the mask of self-deceit.

Revelation 18:9-10. The kings who have gathered to lament Babylon's destruction are all the lesser kings bound to Rome through conquest and alliance. This is not, in all probability, the group of ten kings mentioned in 17:12-14.

Revelation 18:11-19. Read Ezekiel 27:12-36, for this passage is the model for Revelation 18:11-19. As the list of import and export trade items grows, so does an atmosphere of cynicism. We are chilled to realize that these merchants only mourn the loss of trade and care nothing for Babylon. This picture is extremely powerful, for in their words of mourning the merchants and seafarers condemn themselves. Babylon has managed to create mutually degrading relationships. This situation is the certain result of greed and manipulation at work.

John concludes the list of trade items with "souls of men." The Roman Empire was built with the labor and craft of slaves, an especially cruel chapter in Roman history. Even though some Romans worked, with some success, to improve the outrageous conditions under which slaves often had to serve in the Roman Empire, slavery was the cruel, dark side of Rome's glory.

Revelation 18:20. Rejoicing over Babylon's destruction may also seem cynical and cruel. We must be clear about a distinction in this regard. Saints, apostles, and prophets are called to rejoice because God's judgment has triumphed, not because a great but cruel kingdom has fallen. Since God's judgment is always just, that judgment cannot possibly result in evil. God cannot do injustice. The careful reader will notice that not once in Revelation does anyone complain that God has acted unjustly.

Revelation 18:21-24. When Jeremiah spoke his oracle against the historic Babylon, he was asked to dramatize his message by taking what he had written; binding the scroll to a stone: and casting it into the river Euphrates, which flowed through the center of Babylon. The meaning of this prophetic act was, "So will Babylon sink" (Jeremiah 51:63-64). Something quite similar happens here.

This part of John's vision ends with a verbal walk through the ghost town that was "the great city." Remarkably enough, a quick walk through the ruins of the Forum in Rome today can recapture a great deal of the atmosphere suggested by John's description. The great irony of these two chapters is that while Rome was destroyed by marauding armies, it fell, not as a pagan empire, but as a Christian nation. Between the time of the writing of Revelation and Rome's final destruction, Rome had been converted to Christianity.

DIMENSION THREE: WHAT DOES THE BIBLE MEAN TO ME?

Revelation 17–18

Let us not oversimplify the theological perspective of these two chapters in Revelation. We have seen in other parts of this book a depth of perspective that does not encourage a quick identification of evil with *them* and of righteousness with *us*. The development of thought in these chapters is unusually dependent on vast parts of the Old Testament prophetic inheritance. A careful reflection on this fact will make it apparent that the same invectives leveled against foreign nations such as Babylon were leveled also against Israel.

We have suggested in this lesson that Babylon is an elastic, universal image for the danger of self-deception and idolatry. Because idolatry is close to the center of the biblical notion of all that is essential to human sin, Babylon can be a parable about ourselves and our institutions. We see every day in our newspapers the spinning out of contemporary examples of Babylon.

Should we ever rejoice over the defeat of another person, movement, or nation? We must be cautious in making such judgments. When the righteous are called by God to rejoice over Babylon's fall, we could easily conclude that this applies to other circumstances in which what we know to be evil is defeated. The difference is, of course, that the conclusion is drawn by God. The parable within the parable of these chapters could be that our quick judgments about who and what is evil may be examples of our own self-deception and self-idolatry.

Hallelujah! Salvation and glory and power belong to our God (19:1).

—11—

The Sword of His Mouth

Revelation 19–20

DIMENSION ONE:
WHAT DOES THE BIBLE SAY?

Answer these questions by reading Revelation 19

1. Why does the multitude praise God? (19:2)

   They praise God because "true and just are his judgments" and because "he has condemned the great prostitute" and thereby avenged the martyrs.

2. Who else praises God? (19:4-5)

   The twenty-four elders, the four living creatures, and all God's servants also praise God.

3. What is the topic of the hymn sung to God? (19:6-8)

   The hymn is about the coming marriage of the Lamb to the bride.

4. What does the angel say when John tries to worship him? (19:10)

   The angel tells John not to worship him, since the angel is "a fellow servant with you and with your brothers."

5. What are the names given to Christ? (19:11, 13, 16)

   Christ is called "Faithful and True," "The Word of God," and "KING OF KINGS AND LORD OF LORDS."

6. What does Christ come to do? (19:11, 15)

   Christ comes "with justice" to judge and make war on the nations.

7. To whom does the angel call, and what does he order them to do? (19:17-18)

   The angel calls the birds to come eat the flesh of the armies gathered to do battle with Christ.

8. Who has gathered to do battle? (19:19)

   The beast and "the kings of the earth and their armies" gather to battle "against the rider on the horse [Christ] and his army."

9. What happens to the beast and the false prophet? (19:20c)

   They are captured and "thrown alive into the fiery lake of burning sulfur."

10. What happens to the kings and their armies? (19:21)

   They are slain by "the sword that came out of the mouth of the rider on the horse."

Answer these questions by reading Revelation 20

11. What happens to Satan? (20:1-3)

   Satan is thrown into the Abyss for one thousand years.

12. During this one thousand years, what happens to those who have conquered Satan's forces? (20:4)

   They sit in authority with Christ.

13. What happens to the "rest of the dead"? (20:5)

   The "rest of the dead" do not come to life until the thousand years are ended.

14. How does John describe those who are raised? (20:6)

   They are the blessed, the "priests of God and of Christ."

15. What happens after the one thousand years? (20:7-8)

   Satan is loosed from prison, and he deceives the nations (Gog and Magog). They all gather for battle.

16. What happens to this huge army? (20:9)

    As they surround the camp of the saints, fire from heaven destroys them.

17. What happens to Satan? (20:10)

    Satan joins the beast and the false prophet in the lake of fire and sulfur forever.

18. What is the next event? (20:11)

    Next, John sees God appear on a "great white throne."

19. Why has God come? (20:12-13)

    God has come to bring to life all the dead and to judge them.

20. How is this judgment done? (20:12)

    God consults the book of life and "the books" to find out who is listed in the book of life and what they have done.

21. What happens to death and Hades? (20:14)

    Death and Hades are "thrown into the lake of fire."

22. Who else is thrown into the lake of fire? (20:15)

    Anyone whose name is not found in the book of life is thrown into the lake of fire.

DIMENSION TWO: WHAT DOES THE BIBLE MEAN?

Revelation 19:1-8. The descriptions of heavenly worship are central to the structure of Revelation. As we approach the last scene of worship in Revelation, we should reflect on this dimension in the book.

No other New Testament book includes such sustained interest in worship, poetry, music, liturgical response, and captivating visual symbols. This observation suggests to me a comparison with the Old Testament. The story there is quite different. Not only does the Old Testament present entire libraries of poetic prayers (Psalms) and other kinds of poetry (Proverbs, Ecclesiastes, much of the writings of the prophets), much of the Old Testament is devoted to describing places of worship such as the Tabernacle and the various temples in Jerusalem. In other words, both the means of worship (prayers, rituals, buildings, vessels, songs) and acts of worship occupy an enormous part of the Old Testament.

In the New Testament, Revelation is the only link with this tradition. In fact, Revelation is steeped in the Hebrew Scriptures. Revelation contains direct references to nearly all the books of the Old Testament. But John seems to have been most deeply impressed with the Torah (or Mosaic law), the books of poetry related to worship and wisdom, and the writings of the prophets.

This brief overview shows clearly that Revelation is not a book that represents the extremist margins of the Jewish-Christian tradition. The truth is that Revelation draws more evenly in its theological depth from all parts of the Old Testament than do most of the New Testament books. The impression that John knows only Ezekiel and Daniel is created by the fact that he draws on these books in a sustained, repetitive way not seen anywhere else in the New Testament.

The importance of liturgy and liturgical elements in the Book of Revelation is evident. This emphasis is the result of a circumstance. While we as free citizens of a democratic nation have difficulty understanding John's circumstance, we need to try to capture the feeling that comes from being captive, oppressed, and without options.

Imagine what it is like to be surrounded by strong enemies, ruled by foreigners, fed and housed at the whim of a despot, told precisely what to do and what not to do. In these circumstances one's view of reality can change dramatically. Jews and Christians have experienced these circumstances at various times. When they have done so, their religious ideas have changed to sustain them in their seemingly helpless situation. In these times of periodic oppression, the worship of God has surfaced as the all-important aspect of existence. Many factors can explain this increase in the importance of worship, but the most important is the need for the human to be caught up in the uniqueness of the divine.

The inner dynamic of this response of worship can be described in this way. All around us are the visible and real signs of power. This power limits us in what we do and say, where and how we live and move. This power attempts even to determine what we think. We can do nothing to change this power structure. Our freedom to flee is curtailed. To resist is possible but laughable in practical experience. We have no chance but to survive and persist in our survival.

We must see, somehow, another reality that draws us beyond the limitations that mere survival supports. In this circumstance this other, unseen reality can begin to take a form that can defeat the apparent realities of physical, political, and economic oppression. For Jews and Christians this reality has been the sovereignty of God, who controls all history as history's Creator. If God is seen as King, then this King must have a court, a ritual, and a means for his followers to pay homage. The court, ritual, and homage paying is worship and the "stuff" of worship. In the liturgy of worship we are caught up in the reality of God's sovereign role, and in this reality all else is placed in a new perspective.

This experience may be hard to comprehend in its potential power to reorder our perception of an otherwise desperate circumstance. Our difficulty in understanding it, however, does not deny the fact that millions have learned to live in this way. The hymns and liturgical responses of

Revelation are not simply pretty poetic statements that beautify the text. Rather, the worship of the Lord God Almighty invites into a new realm of existence those whose lives are tragically restrained by earthly realities of cruel oppression.

We are not describing escapism. Escape is the denial of reality, however momentary and brief the denial may be. The elements of Revelation so reminiscent of the hymns in Psalms, Isaiah, and Ezekiel describe another reality that can only be made real by means of the praise of God in worship.

Revelation 19:9-10. In verse 9, the angel is not inviting the people to the Lamb's marriage supper. The Lamb—the risen Son of God—both invites persons to and hosts this feast. This distinction creates a gateway of insight into a basic concept in John's thought. Christ is both the means and the sign of God's redemption. If, through God's intervention in history, only a great prophet had been sent to convey the message of God's love, the prophet would have been a means of salvation. However, the figure of Christ as sign also gives a particular revelation of God's love that could have been communicated in no other way. Christ, as God's definitive sign of love, is hinted at in the subject of the section, the invitation to the marriage supper.

No mention could be made of the Lamb's wedding feast without directly implying the Lord's Supper. The sacrament of the Lord's Supper is made possible by the death of Christ (as Lamb of God), and the cross gives meaning to this sacrament. At its simplest center Holy Communion represents Jesus' act of love at Calvary. We could even say that Holy Communion proclaims the cross. But the representation of Holy Communion awaits a fulfillment. The marriage supper of the Lamb is, therefore, Holy Communion made complete. Whereas in our present celebration we seek to have Christ made present by the sacrament, at the conclusion of history Christ will be really present with the faithful. The image of marriage suggests the people of God being united or joined with Christ who has been separate since his death and resurrection.

Revelation 19:11-21. John has conveniently divided this section into three parts (19:11-16, 17-18, 19), creating three small visions laid side by side to form a kind of triptych (three-hinged panels whose pictures tell a religious story). The first panel (19:11-16) describes Christ as a mighty warrior-prince whose terrible appearance convincingly conveys the certainty of victory. The next panel (19:17-18) presents an interlude cleverly disguised as a call to birds of prey in which the outcome of the battle is gruesomely described even before it begins. The third panel (19:19) shows the pitiful preparations of the beast and the false prophet. The three panels end with a surprisingly swift and clean stroke, drawing together the first two panels into one statement: "The rest of them were killed with the sword that came out of the mouth of the rider on the horse, and all the birds gorged themselves on their flesh" (19:21).

Revelation 20. This chapter is best thought of as describing three epochs and events. In 20:1-6, the thousand-year rule of Christ is described; in 20:7-10, the battle of Gog and Magog is narrated; and 20:11-15 describes the final resurrection of the dead and the Last Judgment.

All three sections contain important ideas and descriptions. For many people Revelation 20 is of sole importance, especially those people who live in a state of preoccupation with the "signs of the end." They look at Revelation 20 for clues about what may be happening in the near future. However, centuries of Christian reflection on Revelation have led to a significant and broad conclusion that you, as teacher, need to consider carefully. The accumulated wisdom is this:

1. When interpreters try to put the names of nations, individuals, and events in history on symbols, images, and scenes described in Revelation, one can be certain that the interpretation is headed in the wrong direction. Thousands of people have tried to add names to these symbols; all have failed.

2. A second element in this collective wisdom is that when elaborate and complex doctrines are extracted from brief, even sketchy, passages in Revelation, one can be sure that the doctrine is evidence of human ingenuity and not necessarily the Bible's viewpoint. When texts from Revelation are plucked from their native setting and joined together in a complex web of proof texts from completely different parts of Scripture, one should be cautious, perhaps even skeptical, of using such interpretations. The Bible does have an astounding unity in spite of its great theological diversity. But the unity is not of a sort that fits well with the finely tuned doctrinal developments that have taken place in the nearly two thousand years since Revelation was written. Those who try to make Revelation fit with a doctrinal inheritance are treading on dangerous ground.

3. Finally, those who are aware of the long and often tangled history of Revelation are better suited as guides. If you find a book or article that makes no reference to this history and does not discuss it critically, be wary. These cautions are offered to you in the event that you wish to research more fully some of the ideas in this chapter and elsewhere in Revelation.

Revelation 20:1-3. The Abyss is a favorite image in Revelation (9:1, 2, 11; 11:7; 17:8). John is well aware that hearers could easily become confused by his cast of "bad actors." Therefore he makes it clear that the evil influence being dealt with by chaining in the Abyss is none other than the archdemon, Satan. Satan is described by four names (20:2): the dragon, that ancient serpent, the devil, and Satan. John makes the power of evil in the world more believable by referring to Satan rather infrequently. Rather, Revelation demonstrates that evil has many forms and that the most dangerous are the subtle ones. All the agents and influences of evil have been removed when the beast and false prophet are cast into the fiery lake in 19:20. They will remain there forever and be joined later (20:10) by Satan. However, for the present interlude, Satan will be restrained, not destroyed. Satan will be restrained for a period of a thousand years.

Revelation 20:4-6. The thousand years is not to be taken as a literal time in history but as a period symbolic of restoration. The period of a thousand years is often called "the millennium," taken from the Latin words for "one thousand" and "year." The millennium has been discussed and argued since the first centuries following the writing of Revelation. The concept was defended by such notable scholars as Irenaeus and Justin Martyr. However, the concept of a literal millennium, together with elaborations shaped into a doctrinal position, early became associated with various movements held to be heretical. Millennialism dropped from sight for several centuries and was revived first among the churches of the "Radical Reformation," for example the Anabaptists and Moravians. Millennialism was also a center of focus for the pietists of Germany and was, therefore, a common idea in various German Brethren groups.

Actually, the description found here is quite general and sketchy. The broad picture is that Satan is chained and without influence. Therefore a period of renewal takes place on earth. The most important aspect of this period is the implied link with the Creation story in which life in Eden is without conflict, suffering, or hardship. In a sense, Eden is restored and creation is in harmony as it once was. A "new creation" of humans happens as well. This new Eden is populated by the faithful martyrs described in 7:9-10, 13-14. These are raised from the dead in a kind of limited resurrection. The faithful from this period are given a special privilege. They can enjoy the presence of Christ in a world without evil.

The broad outlines of such a restoration have firm roots in scriptural tradition found, not so much in the New Testament, as in various strands of the Old Testament, especially in the prophets of the Exile. The description found in Ezekiel 40–48 is but an example—an example John will draw on from this point of Revelation to the end of the book.

Revelation 20:7-10. Gog and Magog are taken from Ezekiel 38:1, 9, 15. For Ezekiel this unified symbol was a veiled reference to Babylon, in whose hands Israel lies captive. For John, as we have seen, Babylon is Rome. Often in Christian history "Gog and Magog" have been identified with contemporary nations or oppressors. Some people still try to identify them today.

The description of the battle and its preparations is parallel with that of 19:17-21 and ends in the same way. With the final destruction of Satan, the way is paved for the final event prior to the creation of a new existence by God.

John obviously wrote Revelation with an eye on the Genesis account of Creation. The Eden narrative concludes with the human and environmental condition of the world vastly altered by the act of human disobedience inspired by "that ancient serpent" (20:2). With Satan destroyed, a new creation is possible.

Revelation 20:11-15. With the description of the judgment before the great white throne, we are returned to the vision of God's throne in Revelation 4–5. The various visions of judgment described throughout this book began with that vision. Christ, standing before the throne, broke the seals of the scroll and set in motion God's judgment. That judgment is brought to conclusion here. Thus the circle is completed. In this cycle everything begins and ends with God's sovereign rule. God is the Creator who must follow to perfect completion that which is created. The general resurrection described here is, in effect, a second creation of humankind. In the next chapter we will see the new creation brought into existence by God. In this sense the placement of Genesis and Revelation within the Christian canon of Scripture is a profound statement.

While not all parts of Scripture witness to a belief in a general resurrection from the dead, Revelation is not alone in this faith. A more detailed description of this ancient understanding is found in 1 Thessalonians 4:13-17 and 1 Corinthians 15. The same is true of the Final Judgment. A more elaborate description is offered by Matthew 25:31-45. Both of these examples of parallel belief illustrate also the reason for not basing detailed doctrinal views on Revelation 20. In 1 Thessalonians 4:17 and 1 Corinthians 15:51-52, Paul clearly believes that many of his fellow Christians will still be alive at the time of the resurrection—a view not suggested in Revelation. Again, Matthew 25:31-45 clearly has Jesus Christ ("the Son of Man") as the primary agent in the Final Judgment. The Gospels of Mark and Luke support this idea. In Revelation 20:11-15, however, the prophet John does not mention Jesus Christ. I do not see this as a problem of contradiction. Rather, this example shows how foolish it is to base the points of doctrine on single passages of Scripture.

A particular and impressive idea in our passage is that death and the dwelling place of the dead, Hades, are conquered by this resurrection. Death surrenders its captive dead. This act is a hint that death is viewed as a separate reality that must be conquered. One could even say with Paul, who paraphrases Isaiah 25:8, "Death has been swallowed up in victory" (1 Corinthians 15:54). This suggestion is strengthened by the fact that death and Hades are cast into the fiery lake. This striking image of death being condemned to death will permit John to envision in the new heaven and earth a place where "there will be no more death" (Revelation 21:4).

DIMENSION THREE: WHAT DOES THE BIBLE MEAN TO ME?

The student book poses several questions that may cause problems for class members. Spend some extra time reflecting on these questions. Perhaps you can ask your pastor to discuss some of the questions with you or with the class members.

Christian pacifists have thought a great deal about the rather frequent use in the Bible of God and Christ as warriors who lead in the fight against evil. You may wonder how pacifists can accept such an image in light of their commitment to peace. These Christian thinkers have concluded that this biblical problem poses little, if any, incongruity. Even as a warrior, God is still God and not tainted by the injustice that almost always accompanies our decisions to act aggressively and make war.

I believe that any war in human history can find its ultimate cause in national idolatry, greed, prejudice, and misunderstanding. However, when God is portrayed as making war (as Christ and God both are in these chapters of Revelation), God is acting on behalf of pure justice. We cannot say that the battles portrayed in 19:17-21 and 20:7-10 are engaged in on the justifiable grounds of self-defense. Nor are these scenes based on a "just-war" theory in which Christ must defend the righteous from the vicious attacks perpetrated by evil forces. Rather, *war* in these passages is a metaphor for the struggle between good and evil.

The easy identification of nations with good or evil in the history of earthly wars has been a large part of the problem humans have had to live with for centuries. Do not allow this distinction to guide the discussion of these chapters in Revelation. John was thinking of historical events and nations when he wrote. As we pointed out in Lesson 10, however, the destruction of Rome did not bring about the end of the world. We are much better off to think of this evil as a metaphor for human sin.

We live in an age of terrible possibilities that would result from war, especially nuclear war. It is more important that we seek to understand the possible results of war than to speculate which are the good and evil nations of our age.

Another aspect that may raise problems in the discussion of this lesson is the interest many people have in "the millennium." I have emphasized in this lesson the fact that the millennium has been a minor part of the church's message of salvation. Some groups and individuals, however, seek to make this concept a complex and essential part of belief. The majority of Christianity has decided in another direction, all the while not seeking to deny or reject the faith of those who use the Scripture as a main tenet for their faith in the millennium.

The claim that Christ and/or God will rule over a final judgment of all who have ever lived is quite another matter. This claim is found in all parts of the New Testament and in the historic creeds. The issues involved in God's judgment that lead to the punishment of some are much the same as those issues involved when God is seen as a warrior. Notice that Revelation 20:15 is a conditional sentence: "If any one's name was not found . . ." The conditional *if* in the sentence does not assume that any particular person's name is not in the book of life. The precision with which the sentence is written deserves a similar precision in pondering its meaning. One interpretation is clearly excluded by this precision, that in some predetermined way any particular person is excluded from the book of life.

We cannot escape from the fact that judgment is an inevitable part of God's justice. However, the unifying motif of the Bible is that God's grace seeks to redeem, not to destroy.

Many persons believe that all deeds—good and bad—are kept in a kind of ledger that is somehow "totaled up" at some time in the future. This view is not encouraged by Revelation 20:11-15, even though you could easily draw that conclusion. What we do is certainly important, but inclusion in the book of life is not based on human goodness. Read Revelation 21:5-8, which is an excellent commentary on 20:11-15. There you will see that the gift of life is "without cost," freely given by God (21:6c).

— 12 —

I Make All Things New

Revelation 21

DIMENSION ONE:
WHAT DOES THE BIBLE SAY?

Answer these questions by reading Revelation 21

1. What happens to our heaven and earth in John's final vision? (21:1)

    "The first heaven and the first earth had passed away" to make room for a new heaven and a new earth.

2. What does John see "coming down out of heaven from God"? (21:2)

    He sees "the Holy City, the new Jerusalem," coming down out of heaven.

3. What image does John use to describe "the new Jerusalem"? (21:2)

    John describes the new Jerusalem "as a bride beautifully dressed for her husband."

4. Who first speaks to John in his vision? (21:3)

    John hears "a loud voice" speaking from the throne of God.

5. What is the message from the "loud voice"? (21:3-4)

    The voice announces the advent of God. God will dwell with humans as a community. God will comfort all anguish; and death, pain, and grief "will be no more."

6. Who speaks next? (21:5a)

    God speaks directly to John.

7. What does God command John to do? (21:5b)

    John is to write down the words God will speak, for they are "trustworthy and true."

8. What is the message John is to write down? (21:6-8)

    God is the cause and conclusion of all things. God freely offers the gift of "the water of life." God exhorts the readers to overcome and thereby to inherit the gift of life. God also pledges to be God and Father to those who overcome. The message concludes with a warning to avoid sin, lest their inheritance be the fiery lake.

9. Who appears next in John's vision? (21:9)

    One of the angels with the seven bowls full of plagues appears next, possibly the same one who spoke to John before in 17:1.

10. What does this angel want with John? (21:9)

    The angel wants to show John the bride of the Lamb.

11. What does John see from the "mountain great and high"? (21:10-11)

    John sees "the Holy City, Jerusalem, coming down out of heaven from God" and shining with radiance like a precious jewel.

12. How does John describe the Holy City? (21:12-14)

    The city's dimensions are symmetrical. Twelve foundations inscribed with the names of each of the twelve apostles support a great high wall that surrounds and makes up the city. This wall has three gates in each of its sides. Each of the gates is inscribed with the name of one of the twelve tribes of Israel. Posted at each of the gates is an angel.

13. What does the angel do next? (21:15)

    With a golden measuring rod, he begins to measure the city.

14. What description comes from this measurement? (21:16-17)

The city is a perfect cube, being the same dimension in height, length, and depth.

15. What is the city made of? (21:18-21)

The city and its streets are made of pure gold. The walls are made of jasper and the foundations of precious stones. The twelve gates are made of pearls.

16. Is there a temple in the city? What form does it take? (21:22)

The city has no temple, for "the Lord God Almighty and the Lamb are its temple."

17. What else is missing, and why? (21:23-24)

"The city does not need the sun or the moon" to shine, since light comes from the glory of God.

18. Who is drawn into the city by its light? (21:24, 26)

The nations of the earth and their kings come to the city and bring their splendor with them.

19. Is the city open? (21:25)

Apparently so, since the city gates are never shut in the daytime and "there will be no night there."

20. Who can and who cannot enter the city? (21:27)

"Those whose names are written in the Lamb's book of life" are permitted to enter the city. Those who do what is "shameful or deceitful" are excluded.

DIMENSION TWO:
WHAT DOES THE BIBLE MEAN?

Background. This chapter is one of the great landmarks in all Scripture. Suggesting that one or another part of Scripture is more or less important than other parts can be dangerous. Without the totality of Scripture we would not be able to guide our decisions and our faith. Still, the history of the use of Scripture by the church has clearly marked off Revelation 21 as a milepost in biblical theology. Why is this the case? We can identify several reasons.

1. Without this chapter much of the admittedly confusing parts of Revelation would not be as clear. An example of this is the extended metaphor concerning the prostitute of Babylon—as we will see in detail later.

2. Many of the historic disputes concerning Revelation's interpretation are reducible to this question: Does Revelation present a master scheme for understanding the full scope of cosmic and human history, or is Revelation a treasure house of images and insights that apply to all places and times? Revelation 21 presents the holy city as trans-historical and thus implies that one ought not to force the parts of Revelation into a rigid map for historical events.

3. The theological depth of the ideas and metaphors of Revelation 21 is so rich as to defy exhaustion by human creativity. This chapter has more treasure per square inch, so to speak, than we usually find in other short chapters of the Bible.

4. God's absolute dedication to justice is seen throughout Revelation, but often God's justice is shown in its condemning dimension rather than in its redeeming mode. In Revelation 21, the final word is one of invitation to enter the heavenly city and freely receive the grace of God. This emphasis is so clear as to be unmistakable. While present in other parts of Revelation, this aspect of God's justice must be uncovered by careful reflection. Thus Revelation 21 ends the book with a grace note that sets the rest of Revelation in a quite different light.

5. Revelation 21 not only presents a unifying vision of God's intentions for the incarnation of Jesus Christ, it also brings into union with Christ the highest visions of hope found in the Old Testament. In this way Revelation is a clarifying statement of the salvation theme seen in all Scripture. Few places in the Bible contain such a statement. The unity of redemption's proclamation is symbolized by God's self-revelation as the beginning and end (Alpha and Omega) of all things. If God is the cause and the conclusion of all existence, then unity is necessarily limited to God's intention for all things. Revelation 21 presents God as seeking the unity of all times, peoples, and circumstances by means of entering the city of God.

Revelation 21:1-4. The frankly feminine image of the bride of Christ in Revelation (19:7; 21:2, 9; 22:17) invites comparison with other female images in Revelation. The "woman clothed with the sun" (Chapter 12) is one, and the prostitute of Babylon (Chapters 17 and 18) is another. I can find no clear correspondence between the bride of the Lamb and the woman of Revelation 12. The figure in Chapter 12 is clearly a mother, not a bride. The woman's role is to give birth to a child, who in turn will create an entire people. The prostitute of Babylon, however, is a different matter. John almost certainly places the harlot and the bride side by side for purposes of deep theological significance.

In concrete terms the prostitute is Babylon, or Rome. The bride is the new Jerusalem. Neither should be limited in our minds to historical realities in time and space. Rather, both figures are extended metaphors of limitless dimensions that provide deep and rich possibilities for reflection. Babylon and Jerusalem represent the two dimensions of human possibility. The prostitute seeks to seduce with the wine of idolatry; the bride seeks to glorify the true God of light who fulfills the glory of human potential. The power of these two images is drained if they are seen as other than ourselves. As an example of John's boldness in Revelation, all cities, all institutions, all movements, at different times, can be the prostitute of Babylon or the bride of the Lamb. To claim otherwise would be an example of the idolatry John speaks against.

In 13:11-17, we came on the astounding figure of a pseudo-lamb, a creation of the beast, who became the priest of the beast's image. This religious leader functioned precisely by means of creating a beast cult that used every appearance of the true faith in a clever but ruthless way. The cult featured a dead but resurrected image in imitation of the Lamb who was slain and raised from the dead. The deceit that the pseudo-lamb works is a parable for the constant threat of self-deceit in the Christian community. How else would the most clever priest of evil work than by imitating with credible precision the elements of the true faith? To make this statement is much the same as saying that the new Jerusalem is in constant danger of playing the harlot of Babylon. This recognition may not be comfortable, but the threat is only increased if the insight is denied.

This correlation between female images is given more detail later in Chapter 21 when much is made of the kings of the earth streaming to the light of the city of God to bask in its glory (21:24). As we read this verse, we are reminded of the funeral lament of the kings of the earth at the death of the Babylonian prostitute.

When the kings of the earth who committed adultery with her and shared her luxury see the smoke of her burning, they will weep and mourn over her. Terrified at her torment, they will stand far off and cry,

> Woe! Woe! O great city,
>   O Babylon, city of power!
> In one hour your doom has come!
>   (18:10)

The artistic positioning of these two women/cities is a clear message to all the nations of the earth: To follow Babylon may, for a fleeting moment, create what kings, merchants, and artists proclaim "great"; but the attachment is false and fatal. True glory for a people is to rejoice in the light of God, the incarnate temple of the eternal city, the new Jerusalem.

As with all great images, the comparison of Babylon and Jerusalem can enlighten many human experiences. Revelation is clear that every Christian congregation can turn from spotless bride to drunken prostitute without even noticing the difference. Several of the mini-letters of Chapters 2 and 3 contain this idea. While at first we may think that suggesting the church can become Babylon's prostitute is heretical, John makes it plain that to claim anything else is the most pitiful kind of heresy. (Of course, wisdom and history teach us that we do not have a license for determining when this heresy has taken place. Quite the

reverse. When we begin to suspect other groups, we are, ourselves, in real danger of idolatry.)

The "loud voice from the throne" (21:3) also spoke in 19:5. The voice announces the outcome of the marriage of the Lamb and his bride. The point of marriage is union. This union is the completion of Christ's redemption in the formation of a community.

The clothing of the bride in 19:8 is the fine linen of righteousness, more closely defined as "the righteous acts of the saints." When paired with the negative list in 21:8, we see that the quality of the bride in Revelation 21 is that of moral righteousness. Take care not to read *moralism* into this text. John does not say that by moral righteousness the bride becomes "the wife of the Lamb." Rather, the point is that righteousness characterizes the people of God.

Revelation 21:5-8. The affirmation that God's words are "trustworthy and true" is characteristic of Revelation. Christ is described in Revelation 3:14 as "the faithful and true witness" and in 19:11 as "Faithful and True." God's ways and judgment are called "true" in 15:3 and 16:7. Why are these adjectives chosen? Revelation is, in essence, the unmasking of falsehood. John points out that daily we meet false Christs, false prophets, and false gods. In the deceit of evil, truth is the first victim. In the eyes of John the first element of victory for believers is to recognize the truth. Recognizing the truth is not presented as an easy task. Rather, seeing the truth is a struggle in itself. All else follows when the lie is unmasked and truth triumphs.

In the chaos created by evil's deceitfulness, the call to conquer evil is really the same as the call to recognize the truth. Since God is true, finding God's words in the abundance of other words becomes essential to victory. The trustworthiness of God's words relates to a different dimension of Revelation's thought world. Throughout these pages we find a description of the untrustworthy character of nations, cults, and religious and political leaders and ideas. The search for that which is trustworthy—that is, reliable and dependable throughout the test of time—is much like the search for truth. The declarations of God are as trustworthy as the words that brought the universe into being. The same One who caused all that exists, says John, is reliable as Sustainer and Perfecter of that same creation.

Using words that describe God as Creator and Sustainer should not surprise us in light of the constant claim that the words that John is commanded to write are, quite literally, the words of life (1:3; 22:7, 9, 10, 18, 19).

John refers to an unceasing source of life for the Christian as does the writer of the Gospel of John. In conversation with the Samaritan woman at the well, Jesus proclaimed, "Whoever drinks the water I give him will never thirst. Indeed, the water I give him will become in him a spring of water welling up to eternal life" (John 4:14). In Revelation 7:17, Jesus Christ is described as the Lamb-shepherd who will guide the faithful to "springs of living water." Possibly John is speaking of Christian baptism here.

However, this reference should not be thought of as the ritual of baptism. Rather, the inner meaning of baptism is at stake. In John's theology Jesus Christ is the sacrament of baptism and Holy Communion. Without Christ these sacraments would be empty forms.

Water as a symbol of life will be presented later in a beautiful passage (22:1-6) with the description of living waters flowing from the throne of God and the Lamb. The point of the images in both chapters is that God in Christ is the Source of life. This fact is a present reality and possession, not simply a future hope.

The list of moral failures in 21:8 may sound familiar, but none of these descriptions appears earlier in Revelation. (However, the similar description "those who practice magic arts, the sexually immoral, the murderers, the idolaters," and liars is repeated in 22:15.) Here persons are described by the immoralities to which they are devoted. Thus idolatry is really the fundamental sin.

Revelation 21:9-14. From this point forward Revelation is deeply influenced by Ezekiel, especially the vision of a restored, physical Temple; Jerusalem; and territory for the twelve tribes. This vision begins in Ezekiel 40 and fills the next eight chapters. When John is carried by the Spirit "to a mountain great and high" (21:10), he is reliving Ezekiel's experience (Ezekiel 40:2). (In the Bible mountains are often the sites of great revelations, as in the lives of Moses, Elijah, Ezekiel, and Jesus.)

John's emphasis on the walls and foundations of the new Jerusalem clearly has theological interest. The holy city of God is not constructed in a vacuum. Rather, the entirety of salvation history becomes the base for the city. This base reminds us that the tradition of the patriarchs and apostles contains the essential understandings for Christian reflection. A process of decision making that seeks the truth but neglects the tradition of Scripture is built on an unstable foundation. At the time of Revelation's writing, Christians did not have a New Testament. The New Testament canon was not decided until many years later. The foundation of the twelve apostles, therefore, is the apostolic confession cherished by the church even before the New Testament came into existence. Therefore John is living within the boundaries of a received tradition.

Revelation 21:15-21. Further difficulties occur with this list of precious stones. Quite frankly, no two English translations agree at every point in translating the Greek words for these stones. The problem is essentially archaeological. We cannot know in some cases what stone was called by what name in different cultures of the world.

A possible source for the list of precious stones is the description of Aaron's breastplate in Exodus 39:8-14. However, the lists do not correspond in name or in order. Precious stones are significant throughout the Bible as a means of revealing the mysteries of God.

The most important dimension of these precious stones is clear, however. Only the apostolic tradition faithfully conveyed to believers is a reliable foundation for a faith that will stand. Because this apostolic tradition concerns God, Christ, and the Holy Spirit, the faith of those who confess the Father, Son, and Holy Spirit will triumph over other, less reliable forms of revelation. If John has added an element of playfulness to his list of stones, the playfulness is intended to show the unreliability of other revelations of supposedly eternal truths.

Revelation 21:22-27. John gives us a gift in that no temple appears in the city of God. With a temple this vision would simply be a hope for the restoration or perfection of something that once was—precisely the point of Ezekiel's vision. By emphasizing that God and the Lamb are the temple, John lifts his sights beyond the banal realities of historical limitation. The point is this: If the holy city can be identified with a particular geography and nation, then all those who wish to be a part of the city must become resident aliens in that time and place. John's vision of the holy city recognizes the timeless quality of the presence of God. The temple of God is ultimately portable; it exists wherever God and the Lamb are proclaimed.

Glory best describes the presence of God in John's theology. This distinctive idea is a constant theme in Revelation. On virtually every page we find angels, martyrs, saints, and the peoples of earth engaged in praising God's glory (for example, 1:6; 4:9, 11; 5:12-13; 7:12; 11:13; 14:7; 19:1, 7). Glory is an idea with great depth in Revelation. As we have pointed out, the most appropriate human activity in Revelation's view is the praise of God's glory, or put another way, the glorification of God. This activity is appropriate because God is the Creator of all that is. Therefore, when we (the creature) glorify God, we place in the proper perspective the ordered nature of existence.

Glorification makes possible the proper perspective on all dimensions of life. For example, we tend to try to control as much of existence as possible. But what is appropriate to human control and what is not? In many situations this question becomes quite complex. The act of seeking to glorify God has the potential to clarify many of these difficult decisions. John does not suggest that the glorification of God is limited to speech. Rather, acts resulting from decision-making are a part of the glorification of God. For example, those who wear the white robes in Chapter 7 glorify God. They are identified as martyrs, those persons who by conscious decision refused to compromise in any one of a number of possible ways and were put to death for their belief. Nor does this viewpoint seek to make otherwise complex issues overly simplistic. The glorification of God is seen as a constant, dominant factor in the daily task of speaking and acting in love.

The mention of light and lamp in 21:23-24 is important. John shows a sustained interest in images of light in Revelation. In the first vision Jesus was seen standing in the midst of the "golden lampstands" (1:12-13). Then the churches are seen as "golden lampstands" (1:20). In 21:23, the Lamb is the lamp. Since complete unity exists between

God and the Lamb, however, God is also the city's light. *Lamp* and *light* are metaphors for a revelation. Jesus Christ, as the Lamb of God, brings clarity to human existence. Christ does this by revealing God's love in his act of a death freely accepted.

Why the emphasis on this dimension of Christ here? The answer reveals the profound beauty of Revelation's thought world. The goal of the Christian community, existing in all places and in all times as the city of God, is not survival but mission. The city exists to transform, to proclaim, to serve, to grace, all other cities of the world.

John also speaks of an earthly glory and honor. The kings of the nations are not belittled for the glory they possess. However, this glory and honor will never be complete until they are united to the supreme glory that belongs only to God.

The mention of nations serves several purposes. The apostolic witness gave importance to the faith of Christ as available for all peoples of the world. The struggle of the apostolic age was to present the Christian movement as a universal and frankly missionary reality. Revelation here brings this same message. The sweep of this vision is quite breathtaking. Rather than minimize the true accomplishments of nations, John presents an image that comprehends and congratulates these achievements. He also presents these achievements with a loftier reality.

Revelation 21:27 repeats a theme found often in the book. John hates all that is false and deceitful (14:5; 22:15). All that is false is not of Christ (16:13; 19:20; 20:10) because truth is found in Christ. In what is a typically circular way of thinking, Christ is truth; therefore evil can only create doubt in the minds of the faithful and others by deceiving them about the truth.

DIMENSION THREE: WHAT DOES THE BIBLE MEAN TO ME?

Revelation 21

Some of the questions in the student book are quite complex. For example, the New Testament itself struggles at length with the question of Christian morality. We learn from the Gospels that Jesus proclaimed and required a life of moral righteousness. The apostle Paul is clear that even if we were capable of living lives of moral righteousness, such activity would not earn us salvation (Romans 10:1-9). This belief has caused many persons to ask, "If we are required to be morally righteous but that righteousness does not win us salvation, why then be good, or even try to be good?" The perspective of covenant and the terms of the covenant can help us answer this question.

We could say that the history of God's dealing with humankind from the beginning of creation is characterized by the gentle and loving invitation of God to the people of God to enter into a meaningful relationship. This relationship is frequently described as a covenant.

By *covenant* we mean that pledges and faithfulness to those pledges are offered on the part of God. Furthermore, both parties in this covenant have obligations. Mutual obligations, however, do not suggest an equal relationship. God's initiative in establishing the covenant with us is based on a level of love and commitment that we can never equal. Still, all persons and communities brought into this covenant are expected to live in faithfulness to the relationship of the covenant. High on the list of these obligations is the attempt to live in a way faithful and consistent with our vision of God's righteousness.

We could say, then, that all righteousness belongs to God and our obligation is to live within that righteousness—to seek it, enable it, live by its light, and promote its concerns. This obligation is often called "the love demand." The covenant demands of us that we live in a way consistent with the love that brought the covenant into being in the beginning. Another way to put this is that we must imitate God's perfect love.

God's love is seen in its fullness in the way by which God calls people to the covenant. The premium example of God's love, of course, is the gift of the Son of God in the Incarnation, Jesus Christ. Within the incarnation of Jesus Christ, the clearest measure of God's love is seen in the Passover death of the Lamb of God. In gratitude for this gift and this display of redeeming love, Christians seek to be faithful to the vision of righteousness. This faithfulness, in essence, is the biblical understanding of the reason why we joyfully respond to Christ's call for moral righteousness.

Anyone who carefully reads the Revelation to John could never make the mistake of thinking that such moral righteousness is the basis of salvation. John is exceedingly clear that one of the fundamental flaws in the human creation since the Fall is the constant tendency to establish our own creation as our idol. This idol is quite often the product of our own creativity and inventiveness.

This premium sin of idolatry is reflected most clearly in our attempt to use righteousness as a basis for bartering with God for salvation. Since this bartering is clearly an attempt to place God under the obligation to act according to the terms we establish, it is also clear that it will never work. Not only is righteousness a free and undeserved gift from God, it is also a demonstration of the true nature of our creation as human beings.

One of the great paradoxes of human existence is that the life lived under the demands of love is also the most satisfying and happy life. This paradox is true not because acting in love is always easy. Nor does it suggest that the way of love is without suffering and misunderstanding. In fact, the way of love is a demanding way and one that frequently leads to personal and corporate suffering. However, the way of love remains the most satisfying and happy existence because it is the way that human beings were intended to live. In part, satisfaction comes from the single-mindedness and wholeness that result from this way of life. While we cannot prove this fact empirically, it has been demonstrated biographically for hundreds of years in the lives of saintly persons, both celebrated and anonymous, since the beginning of the Christian vision.

People are often disturbed by the suggestion that the church is not always identified with the city of God. The church as a gathered community of saints often permits the light of God to shine through its life of active witness and verbal proclamation. At other times the church's witness rings like a bell made of lead, and darkness seems to prevail in all its pronouncements. The church given by Christ is, of course, a heavenly reality that is clearly evident in the earthly organization of the church; at other times, this reality seems not to be present at all. John's vision of the holy city clarifies this perspective. For him the holy city of God is the dominant divine reality in all existence, without limitations of time and space. This heavenly reality can be totally earthly and human and can also at times escape the human grasp. This reality redeems John's vision from being something from another realm and time but with no bearing on the present. However, the search for the holy city of God is a never-ending search and one that must be engaged in day-by-day in each generation.

As you discuss this vision with class members, try to make your questions and issues as open and creative as possible. This vision is virtually limitless in its potential. By it we are called to a life that need not be limited by our sense of powerlessness, by the manifestations of history, and by our self-imposed limitations to see the presence of God in our midst. In many ways this vision is comparable to other visions in Scripture that lift and elevate the human spirit. The vision has its own genius because the metaphor itself is so close to the reality of daily existence. Try to help class members see these creative possibilities in your discussions.

— 13 —

The Healing Stream

Revelation 22

DIMENSION ONE:
WHAT DOES THE BIBLE SAY?

Answer these questions by reading Revelation 22

1. What is the source of the remarkable river shown to John in the vision? (22:1)

   The river comes from "the throne of God and of the Lamb."

2. What is this river's course? (22:2a)

   The river flows through the main thoroughfare of the city of God.

3. What is remarkable about the tree of life? (22:2bc)

   The tree has fruit on it perpetually, a different kind each month. Its leaves have healing properties.

4. How does John describe the city of God? (22:3)

   The city is a place for the worship of God and the Lamb. There is nothing cursed in the city of God.

5. What are the two privileges given to those who dwell in the city of God? (22:4)

   They are permitted to view God's face, and their foreheads are inscribed with God's name.

6. What has God done for his servants? (22:6b)

   God has sent an angel to show his servants what must take place soon.

7. According to the message given to the prophet John, what event is foretold? (22:7a)

   The near approach of Christ's return is foretold.

8. Who is given a special blessing? (22:7b)

   Anyone who keeps the words of the prophecy written in the Book of Revelation is blessed.

9. By what name does the author of Revelation identify himself? (22:8a)

   He gives his name simply as "John."

10. The angel warns John not to do what? (22:10)

    John is warned not to seal up the words he has written.

11. Who is to remain in the same condition in light of the nearness of time? (22:11)

    All people, evil and righteous, holy and vile, are to remain the same.

12. What will Christ and God do when this happens? (22:12)

    All will be repaid for their deeds.

13. Who is blessed, and what do they receive? (22:14)

    Those who have washed their robes are blessed, and they will have the right to enter the city and use the benefits of the tree of life.

14. Who must live outside the gates of the city of God? (22:15)

    Those who practice many kinds of unrighteous acts: magic, adultery, murder, idolatry, falsehood.

15. How does Jesus describe the book that John has written? (22:16a)

    He calls it a "testimony for the churches."

16. By what names does Jesus identify himself? (22:16b)

He calls himself the "Root and the Offspring of David" and "the bright Morning Star."

17. Why are all persons who are thirsty invited to "come"? (22:17)

They are called so that they may drink from the water of life at no cost.

18. What are the warnings given to all who might want to change the words of Revelation? (22:18-19)

Those who add to it will be plagued; those who subtract from it will be barred from the city of God and the tree of life in it.

19. Who is it that witnesses to the words of Revelation, and what does he say? (22:20a)

It is Jesus; and he says, "Yes, I am coming soon."

20. How does John respond to these words of Jesus? (22:20bc)

He affirms the pledge of Jesus to come soon and spontaneously says, "Amen. Come, Lord Jesus."

DIMENSION TWO: WHAT DOES THE BIBLE MEAN?

Revelation 22:1-2, 17. Viewed even in realistic terms, water is fundamental to life. As we have followed the visionary description of judgment in Revelation, we have seen frequently that the destruction and contamination of the earth's water supply and seas creates horrific conditions not only for humans but also for the partner creatures of earth (8:8-11; 16:4). Conversely, God is the source of life-giving water both in the real sense (14:7) and in the spiritual (7:17; 21:6). It is no surprise, then, to learn that water or springs of waters is a metaphor for God's essence. This is especially true in the poetic visions of the great prophets.

Isaiah envisions the day when "with joy you will draw water / from the wells of salvation" (Isaiah 12:3). Jeremiah weaves an extremely artful oracle from this same image. In the extended metaphor of 2:13, he rebukes the people of Judah for rejecting God, "the spring of living water," in favor of the contaminated water of "broken cisterns"—a clever reference to idols made of clay. The remarkable point in Jeremiah's words is used of an image in such a way as virtually to create a title for God; God is also known as the Fountain of Living Waters.

Throughout the Old Testament is the foundational notion of water being the source of life itself, not only by nourishing humans, beasts, and fields but also in originating creation itself. This view lies in the shadows of the Creation account of Genesis 1:2 where the action of the Spirit of God "hovering over the waters" implies that it was water that must first be dealt with as the primal matter of creation's work. Water does not have to be created; it is the stuff of life before life has form. On the other hand, Scripture makes it evident that God is in control of water. The threat that water can impose is first seen in the Flood, but this theme continues in many parts of the Hebrew Scriptures. Only because God is sovereign of all that exists do the waters of the earth and "under" the earth pose no threat.

Against this background, something of the full extent of the idea in Revelation 21 and 22 takes on full shape. Notice, for example, that the water of life flows from the throne. The student book points out that the point of origin establishes with finality that God and the Lamb are the primal sources of life. In fact, this idea is closely connected with the original Creation story. In the beginning God created life by moving over the deep. This creation is a never-ending one. God continues to create life. Thus water is only an incidental sign for the creation of life. Of course, the life spoken of here is more than physical existence. Rather, a quality is projected that is not simply "future life" but that which is given in the present and will persist into the unknown future.

The metaphor of the tree(s) of life is quite another matter. Nowhere else in Scripture is God compared to a tree—probably because of the idolatrous practices of Israel's neighbors. (Jeremiah derides those who say to a tree, "You are my father" [Jeremiah 2:27].) However, there clearly is a link with the veritable orchard in the garden of Eden and one particular tree, also called "the tree of life" (Genesis 3:22, 24). To the extent that the gates of the city of God are thrown open to give access to the tree(s) of life, Eden is again open to the human creation. Notice that this is, however, not a fully developed presentation in which the paradise of Eden is systematically reconstructed.

Finally, the careful reader will notice some minor confusion in the text. Whereas the tree of life in 22:2, 19 is consistently singular, the description of the city of God clearly envisions the river lined with many trees on both banks. This may not be confusion at all but simply evidence of the dual influence of Genesis 3, in which there is one "tree of life," and Ezekiel 47:1-12, in which there are many trees lining the banks of the river.

Revelation 22:3, 6, 9. John's understanding of himself, of the angel who guides him, and of those in the churches to whom he writes is based on the common biblical idea of servant. It is perhaps one of the most frequently repeated associations to say that the prophets are God's servants. Those who are called the servants of God in the Old Testament include Moses, David, Job, Sarah, Jacob, and countless others. In fact, the covenant nation of Israel is portrayed as the servant of God (Isaiah 44:1). Jesus is identified by Matthew as the servant of God, using the words of Isaiah 42:1-4, one of the great servant songs. "Here is my servant whom I have chosen, / the one I love, in whom I delight" (Matthew 12:18). It would not be too romantic to say that in the view of both the Old and the New Testament, the people of God consists of a company of fellow servants called and sustained by the Lord of the universe. In the eyes of the New Testament, this company is led by the example of a Master Servant (no contradiction in terms of biblical thinking) "who, being in very nature God, / did not consider equality with God something to be grasped, / but made himself nothing, / taking the very nature of a servant" (Philippians 2:6-7).

Only Revelation deals satisfyingly with a distinct problem in this common theme, how servanthood can be kept from its degrading connotations. This is accomplished by Revelation in the constant theme of worship. The throne of God is surrounded by countless creatures of God's creation. They are unified by means of their unceasing praise of the Creator. And because praise of the Creator is, in essence, the recognition of the most appropriate expression of both God's nature and that of creation's, the full divinity of personhood is made possible by means of worship itself. The point, therefore, of servanthood is not the debasing of angels and humans but the commonality of creatureliness.

This problem is also connected with a more distinct theme associated with servanthood in the Gospels. There, the point of being a servant is that of following the example of Christ, who demonstrated the inner meaning of this decision by the final act of service, his own death: "Whoever wants to become great among you must be your servant, and whoever wants to be first must be slave of all. For even the Son of Man did not come to be served, but to serve, and to give his life as a ransom for many" (Mark 10:43b-45).

Revelation agrees, also, that service is the essence of servanthood. But service is broadened in its scope in this book to redefine the core of service itself. This service is, quite simply, the worship of God. However, worship must not be limited to our idea of what constitutes worship. The worship of God means the honoring of the Creator of life in all ways—including the search more fully to complete the command to love our neighbors with all our being.

We could well ask what, precisely, the idea of worship adds to the notion of service. We find several dimensions to the answer by reading Revelation carefully. The most important of these dimensions concerns the motivation for service. Service, interpreted by worship, is not something that can be externally commanded but rather is a spontaneous expression. The many scenes portraying worship around the throne cannot be read in any other way. These narratives convey, unmistakably, that the throngs who are in the presence of God cannot refrain from their liturgical responses. Another way of saying this is to affirm that worship is love in action. The response of love is discussed in the letter to Ephesus (2:2-7). There, the church members are praised for all they do and hold dear but are warned that they have abandoned the love (agape) that they had at first. Set in the context of praise for all else, this at first appears to be a strange criticism. After all, if the Ephesians are doing everything well, what could be criticized? Perhaps the abandoned love here is that sense of immediacy, single-mindedness, and spontaneity that must characterize commitment to Christ.

Revelation makes it clear that, in times of testing, inadequately based morality will be the first to go. If worship is the most authentic human response, then worship is also the factor most likely to sustain a life of service. Service to God and neighbor is the best way to live because living a life of service is consistent with God's creation. This explanation may sound circular in reasoning, but it is necessarily so.

The classic problem in our tradition is, "Why should I love my neighbor as myself?" While we might be tempted to respond with answers that describe the structure of obligation ("Because God says you ought to love"), these will not ultimately satisfy most. The very particular answer from Revelation is quite different. It is this: You love God and neighbor because you recognize in the acts of love themselves the fullness of your own creation. Other kinds of answers occur in Scripture, but this answer from Revelation has a special kind of beauty to it that deserves greater attention. Notice that the rationale, as I have suggested it above, does not suggest that we serve others in order to be happy. This would be a distortion, if not a perversion, of Revelation's view. Rather, John suggests that service, seen in the light of worship, is the authenticating response of love that, in turn, is cohesive with and affirming of our creation.

Finally, when service is seen through the prism of worship, its joyful aspects are seen most clearly. Service done grudgingly, whether in the chapel or on the street, quickly becomes capable of doing more harm than good. Recapturing the joy of service often happens by way of joining in the spiritual worship of God. Conversely, all authentic worship will result in service to neighbor.

Revelation 22:7, 12, 20. This chapter is heavily punctuated by affirmations of the return of Christ in the very near future. What are we to make of this claim in light of the intervening centuries in which Jesus has not returned? Does this fact alone make void the entire Book of Revelation? This problem is significant and is one that the class members will almost certainly want to discuss, perhaps to the exclusion of all other topics.

The Book of Revelation stands somewhat apart from the Synoptic Gospels (Matthew, Mark, and Luke) in one aspect. In Revelation 22:20, John reports Jesus saying, in the first person, "I am coming soon." However, Jesus never said that in the Gospels. More characteristic would be this statement from Jesus in Mark 13:32-33: "No one knows about that day or hour, not even the angels in heaven, nor the Son, but only the Father. Be on guard! Be alert! You do not know when that time will come."

Therefore the emphasis in the Gospels is on diligence and watchfulness, since the precise time of the return of Christ is unknown. We can also presume from these words that Jesus meant to convey that it was unsure whether the time would be "soon" or "distant." We should also quickly add that most scholars assume that Jesus and his followers thought that this second coming would be sooner rather than later. Thus it would seem that there is an essential difference between the Jesus of the Gospels and of Revelation. However, it is quite one thing to imply the speedy return of Jesus in glory and quite another to have Jesus say, "I am coming soon."

The entire atmosphere of Revelation is replete with this sense of urgency. The very word *soon* is common in Revelation (2:16; 3:11; 11:14; 22:7, 12, 20) but never used in the Gospels in connection with apocalyptic events. The fact is, quite simply, that Revelation comes from a particular viewpoint that is credible and significant—and one without which the New Testament would not be complete. This is precisely the condition of many Christians living under vicious, sustained oppression. If we were to live under these conditions daily, we would likely also come quickly to the affirmation that Jesus is coming soon. In fact, this context is really the correct one for reading such statements as that of Revelation 22:20.

The final statement is a spontaneous cry from the prophet's heart (and notice that this verse is the first time his own prayers have been allowed to intrude in the text): "Amen. Come, Lord Jesus!" The confession that Jesus is coming soon is then a prayer caused by the real experience of a church under the heel of naked power and the threat of death.

A note of caution should be carefully reflected on at this point in our study. One of the unfortunate historical developments that grew out of this quite particular emphasis on the speedy return of Christ was the attempt of various persons to convince others that Jesus had already returned (in, perhaps, a hidden or disguised way). This development has persisted into modern times, and one can be sure that it will be tried again.

This experience is an occasion for celebrating the fact that we have, for our careful study and reflection, the whole Bible. For example, Mark's "little apocalypse" takes a very cautious approach to this question, giving a helpful and practical guideline to deal with the problem spoken of above: "If anyone says to you, 'Look, here is the Christ!' or, 'Look, there he is!' do not believe it. For false Christs and false prophets will appear" (Mark 13:21-22a). This guideline needs to be kept clearly in the class discussion; for while much the same point is made by Revelation 13, the point is not as explicit and clear there as is Mark's warning above.

Finally, this question of the speedy return of Christ must conclude, always, with the plain affirmation that Christians have from the beginning and must now live in the light of our historic faith. At a time unknown and in ways unexpected, God will act in Christ to bring an "Amen" of perfection to existence as created.

Revelation 22:7b-14. Revelation has seven beatitudes (1:3; 14:13; 16:16; 19:9; 20:6; 22:7b, 14). Two are found in this chapter. The first (1:3) and sixth (22:7b) blessings are given to those who give careful attention to the message of Revelation. A grave textual problem appears in the seventh (22:14) blessing. Some texts of the Greek New Testament say that "those who wash their robes" are blessed, while others bless those who "obey God's commandments." The New International Version text is probably correct in choosing the first translation. Revelation speaks elsewhere of keeping the commandments of God (12:17; 14:12) and also of washing robes (7:14), so both ideas are credible in the context of the book as a whole. However, it looks rather as if "obey God's commandments" has been added from 12:17 and 14:12 to create a moral mandate more fitting to the context (22:11-12).

Revelation 22:16. This description of Jesus is reminiscent of John's Gospel and the many "I am" statements made by Jesus there. While the self-description of Jesus here ("I am the Root and the Offspring of David, and the bright Morning Star") may sound familiar, it is not. Nowhere else in the New Testament is Jesus called the "Root of David," except in Revelation 5:5. The prophecy of Isaiah 11:1 is well known ("A shoot will come up from the stump of Jesse") by both Matthew and Paul. This prophecy was interpreted to mean that Jesus was the fulfillment of prophetic hopes, Jesse being the father of David and Jesus being born into the lineage of David (Matthew 1:6 and Romans 15:12). But the affirmation here (22:16) is quite different and is also typical of Revelation. To say that Jesus is both the Root of David and the Offspring of David is much the same as to say that Christ is "beginning and end" (Alpha and Omega). Rather than being a shoot from the stump of Jesse, Christ is the root of Jesse's stump.

In Revelation 2:28, those in Thyatira who keep the works of Jesus to the end will be given "the morning star." Taken with this verse (22:16), we could say that the gift in mind is a portion of Jesus Christ, who is the morning star. While stars figure highly in the images of Revelation, it is startling to have Jesus given this name. The only connection within the New Testament is in Matthew 2:2, in which the star of the East giving direction to the magi is described by them as "his star."

Revelation 22:17. The bride of Christ, we learned in 21:2, is the city of God. The picture portrayed here, then, is of the Spirit and the holy city inviting all hearers of Revelation to "come." Revelation is a book of invitation. The persuasive word *come* is used frequently (4:1; 6:1, 3, 5, 7; 11:12; 17:1; 19:17). More difficult to identify, however, is the third party who says, "come." Who is "him who hears"? This third party must be the reader. This identification is confirmed by the next sentence that is further invitation to "whoever is thirsty" and "whoever wishes . . . [to] take . . . the water of life." In this gentle and sensitive literary movement, the reader is now invited to take part in the action of the text. The city and its contents have been described. The reader is now invited to share in its potential and its bounty. These gifts are "free," that is, both priceless and without need to be purchased. This sense of salvation as the free gift of grace repeats 21:6c and is consistent with the entire New Testament witness.

Revelation 22:18-19. This warning is fascinating in light of Revelation's textual history as well as the history of its interpretation. While this teacher book has not made much of the technical details, you should know that Revelation has the most difficult and disputed text in the New Testament. The task of establishing, with even a modest degree of certainty, the original text of the Greek manuscript has exhausted the energies and talents of countless schools from the time of Jerome. We have often commented on the history of interpretation and the extent of misuse and abuse to which this book has been unfairly subjected. This problem continues to the present. Added to this problem is the early historic dispute about whether Revelation should even be included in the Christian canon. All these facts give a poignant irony to John's words of warning.

Over all, I must say at the conclusion of our study that we neglect the positive values of Revelation at our own peril. In spite of the difficult and checkered history of Revelation, its message has persisted and prevailed. Again and again Revelation has been "rediscovered" and rescued from abuse by those who find in Revelation a message that speaks to some in a way found nowhere else in Scripture and yet that agrees with the witness of all Scripture.

DIMENSION THREE: WHAT DOES THE BIBLE MEAN TO ME?

Because Revelation is a complex book, you will certainly want to help those studying with you review the major and dominant themes that have arisen in the discussion. Among these may be the notion of sin and deceit presented so profoundly in Revelation. You may also want to discuss the view of Christ as the Lamb, the only one worthy to open the sealed scroll; the glimpses of early church life provided by the seven letters in Chapters 2 and 3; the call to endurance of the saints living under the domination of Babylon (Rome), that evil city; the hope offered in John's vision of the holy city, the bride of Christ; the other beautiful poetic images and descriptions of John's vision; and the focus on worship as our ultimate service of God and the Lamb.

As a closing for your final session, you may want to offer the benediction John provides in 22:21: "The grace of the Lord Jesus be with God's people. Amen."